1 MONTH OF
FREE
READING

at
www.ForgottenBooks.com

By purchasing this book you are eligible for one month membership to ForgottenBooks.com, giving you unlimited access to our entire collection of over 1,000,000 titles via our web site and mobile apps.

To claim your free month visit:
www.forgottenbooks.com/free626842

ISBN 978-0-483-13494-2
PIBN 10626842

FOURTH INTERNATIONAL CONGRESS ON SCHOOL HYGIENE

BUFFALO, NEW YORK, U. S. A.
AUGUST 25-30, 1913

TRANSACTIONS

VOLUME V

Edited by Thomas A. Storey
with the assistance of Frederic A. Woll
and Julian Park

1914

Printed :
THE COURIER
197-199 Main

CONTENTS OF VOLUME V
Papers

SECTION IV

SESSION XXX A—SYMPOSIUM ON MOUTH HYGIENE

SESSION XXX B—SYMPOSIUM ON MOUTH HYGIENE

SESSION XXX C—SYMPOSIUM ON MOUTH HYGIENE

SESSION XLIII—CLUB WOMEN'S CONFERENCE

SECTION V

SESSION XLIV—PSYCHO-EDUCATIONAL CLINICS AND CONFERENCES

SESSION XLV—CONSULTATION BUREAU

SESSION XLVI—ROUND TABLE ON VENTILATION 718

SECTION VII

Program of Associations Meeting at the Same Time as This Congress 719

SESSION TWENTY-SEVEN

Room D.   Thursday, August 28th, 9:00 A.M.

CRIPPLED CHILDREN

ROBERT S. OSGOOD, M.D., *Chairman*

DR. PRESCOTT LEBRETON, Buffalo, N. Y., *Vice-Chairman*

Program of Session Twenty-seven

LLOYD T. BROWN, A.B., M.D., Assistant Orthopedic Surgeon to Out-Patients, Massachusetts General Hospital; Assistant Orthopedic Surgeon, Peter B. Brigham Hospital, Boston, Mass. "Occurrence of Weak Feet and Foot Strain in School Children, and Methods of Examination."

ROBERT B. OSGOOD, M.D., Assistant Visiting Orthopedic Surgeon to the Massachusetts General Hospital; Instructor Orthopedics, Harvard Medical School, Boston, Mass. "The Treatment of Foot Strain and Weak Arches Among School Children."

ROLAND O. MEISENBACH, M.D., Orthopedic Surgeon to the German Hospital and the Good Samaritan Dispensary, Buffalo, N. Y. "The Clothing and Shoeing of School Children; Their Effect on the Mental and Physical Efficiency of the Child from an Orthopedist's Point of View." (Manuscript not supplied.)

HILLS COLE, M.D., Director of Division of Publicity and Education, State Department of Health, New York City. "Weak Ankles, Flat Foot, Spinal Curvature in School Children."

EVELYN GOLDSMITH, B.S., A.M., President Seaside Home for Crippled Children at Arverne, L. I.; Honorary President and Founder of Association of Public School Teachers of Crippled Children, New York City. "The Education of Crippled Children Belongs to the Public Schools."

HILLS COLE, M.D., Director of Division of Publicity and Education, State Department of Health, New York City. "What can be Done to Diminish the Necessity for Special Provision for Crippled School Children."

THE OCCURRENCE OF WEAK FEET AND FOOT STRAIN IN SCHOOL CHILDREN AND METHODS OF EXAMINATION

BY

Lloyd T. Brown

A study of the occurrence of weak feet and foot strain in a group of school children was the object of this paper. The examinations were made possible through the kindness of Dr. W. J. Gallivan of the Boston Board of Health and they were made more easy of accomplishment through the courtesy of the principals of the schools visited and their assistants. I wish here to express my thanks to them.

A foot was considered weak when it showed variations from the normal weight bearing lines with the weight of the body upon it. Foot strain cases were judged by the presence or absence of tenderness at points of ligamentous strain.

Seven hundred children of the Boston Public Schools were examined. These were divided into primary, grammar and high school grades, both boys and girls. The method of examination can be seen from this form which was used throughout. (See Fig. I.) The age, name and nationality were recorded. The flexibility was tested in dorsal and plantar flexion and in abduction and adduction as to whether it was normal, medium or rigid. Each foot was examined for points of tenderness which would indicate foot strain. These points were at the internal lateral ligament, just below the internal malleolus, the calcaneo-scaphoid ligament, the attachment of the plantar fascia at the os calcis, the medio-tarsal or mid plantar fascia region, the anterior arch and lastly periosteal tenderness. Callouses or corns were noted as to their presence and position. The height of the arches without weight bearing was noted as high, medium or low and the condition of the anterior arch was also recorded. It was found that if the toes were curled or dorsally flexed, the anterior arch was relaxed. The arches were then examined with the weight of the body on both feet equally, for the presence of pronation or sag. If a line from the anterior superior spine of the hip bone or pelvic bone, through the patella or knee cap, to the toes included or was outside the first or great toe, the foot was considered normal as to pronation. (See Fig. 2.) If this line came inside the great toe, the pronation was considered abnormal and was a sign of faulty weight bearing. (Fig. 3, Fig. 4, Fig. 5.) If the arch of the foot with weight bearing showed more than a slight lowering from its position, without weight, this also was considered a sign of faulty weight bearing. Many investigators have tried various methods of examining the arches, hoping to find a sure way of telling what kind of feet are liable to give out under strain and what kind are not. Feiss suggested that the distance of the scaphoid tubercle below a line drawn from the internal malleolus to the internal tubercle of the first meta-tarsal, if not more than ½ inch, indicated a normal foot; if more than this, the foot was prone to become strained under stress of work. This has been used in some examinations of recruits for the navy, any case more than ½ inch not being allowed to pass.

Another test which has proved of great help in the examination of nurses is that suggested by Osgood. It is a test of the comparative strength or the balance of the adductor and abductor muscles of the foot. A muscle balance is normal when the adductor muscles, which hold up the arch of the foot, are stronger than the abductor muscles. The examination is easily made by a simple spring balance tester, and in working out the statistics, the groups considered were the adductors the stronger, the abductors the stronger, the groups equal and the groups asymmetrical.

The shoes were examined as to the shape, whether good, medium or bad. (Figs. 6, 7, 8, 9.) The question of wear of the heels was also examined as to whether it was even or the front inner corner was worn. Wear on the front inner corner is caused by the rolling inward of the foot in faulty weight bearing, while wear on the back or the outside of the heel is usually caused by scuffing and is, therefore, much less important. If the heel counters of the shoes were rolled inward, this was noted also, as a sign of faulty weight bearing. (Fig. 10.)

A rough examination without removing any clothes was made of the posture of each child. (See Fig. 11.) The position was considered good when it resembled this picture—head erect, chest high, shoulder blades flat or slightly rounded and the lower abdomen flat or only slightly relaxed or protuberant. (Fig. 12.) The posture was bad when like this—head forward, chest flat, shoulder blades rounded and lower, abdomen relaxed and protuberant. The general condition of the child was obtained from the school nurse or physical instructor, as far as possible, and, otherwise, from the general appearance and as to how many times they had been absent from school because of sickness.

There were 699 cases examined, ranging in age from 7 to 21; 162 in the primary grades; 345 in the grammar and 192 in the high schools. The primary grades ranged in age from 7 to 12—mostly 8 and 9; the grammar from 7 to 16—mostly 10 to 13, and the high school from 12 up. There were 14 different nationalities seen, but 44% were American and 36 Irish. Flexibility was normal in 98% and somewhat restricted in 2%. Only one peroneal spasm or rigid foot being found. 2% of the boys and 3% of the girls showed restricted motion.

Name   No.
Age 10   Race American   Date 6-7-13
                         R—   R   R
Flexibility   Normal L—   Medium L   Rigid L
                                 R   R   R
Tenderness o   Internal Lateral L   Cal. Scaph. L   Os Cal L
                                 R   R   R
                  Mediotarsal L   Ant Arch L   Periosteal L
                                 R   R   R
Callouses o   Ant Arch.L   Heel L   Toes L
                                 R   R—   R
Arches s wt.   High L   Medium L—   Low L
                                          R   R   R—
        c wt.   Pronation Extreme L   Moderate L   Slight L—
                  Amount of sag "   "   " R—
    "   Walking   same   L—
Scaphoid Tubercle ⅜
Right   Adduction 25   Abduction 22
Left   "   25   "   22
Shoes   Good—   Medium   Bad
                             R
                  Wear on heels L even
Posture   Good
General Condition Good
Past treatment   FIG. 1.—Form of record used.

FIG. 2.—Feet showing normal or slight amount of pronation and sag of the longitudinal arch. Note that the position of the great toe is inside a line from the anterior superior spine of the ilium through the patella.

FIG. 3.—Feet showing moderate pronation and moderate sag of the long arches.

FIG. 4.—Feet showing extreme pronation and moderate sag.

FIG. 5.—Feet showing extreme pronation and extreme sag.

FIG. 6.—Good shoes and feet. The shoes
are the proper length and are shaped
so as not to crowd the toes.

Fig. 7.—Bad shoes and bad feet. Shoes
too narrow toed. Feet show toes
crowded and curled.

FIG. 8.—Bad shoes and good shoes.

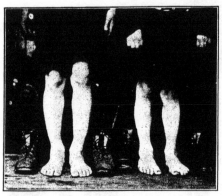

FIG. 9.—The figure on the left of the picture shows feet normal as to pronation but with more than a normal inward sag of the longitudinal arch. This boy's shoes are classed as medium shoes. The figure on the right shows feet normal as to pronation and sag. These shoes were classed as good shoes.

FIG. 10.—Shoes with marked inward roll of heel counters. The left shoe also shows wear on front inner corner of heel.

FIG. 11.—Good posture.

FIG. 12.—Bad posture.

Each foot was examined for dorsal flexibility with the knee bent and the knee straight. Although no record was made of the condition with the knee straight, the number of cases which showed limitation of this sort was so small as not to excite any especial notice. Tenderness, which has been considered an evidence of foot strain was present in 10% of the cases, the boys showing 11% and the girls 10%. The boys of the primary and grammar grades showed tenderness more commonly than the girls. In the high school it was equal in both boys and girls. It was more common in the high school than in the lower grades, thus showing that the occurrence of foot strain becomes more frequent as the child grows older. Callouses were present in 56% or a little more than one-half the total number of cases. The boys showed 49% and the girls 62%. In the primary grades callouses were present about equally in the boys and girls and in about 30% or less than one-third of each. In the grammar grades 57% or about one-half the boys and 65% or two-thirds of the girls showed callouses. In the high school the boys showed 53% or about one-half with callouses, while the girls had increased to 85% with callouses. Callouses occurred about an equal number of times in normal and pronated feet. They occurred slightly more often in feet which showed sag of the arches than in normal feet.

The height of the arches without the weight of the body upon them showed that high arches were present in both the boys and the girls in 40% of the cases. Medium arches were present in 51% of the boys and in 52% of the girls. Low arches were present in only 9% of the boys and 8% of the girls. The presence of curled toes, which was considered to be an evidence of a relaxed or weakened anterior arch or the front part of the foot, was found in 30% of the cases, 26% of the boys and 34% of the girls.

Hallux valgus, which means the bending of the great toe toward the little toes, was present in 13% of the cases. It occurred four times in the girls to once in the boys, or in 22% of the girls and in 3% of the boys. Two-thirds of the feet which had hallux valgus occurred in feet which were used incorrectly or with faulty weight bearing lines and in one-third of the cases which were used correctly.

Examinations of the arches with the weight of the body upon them showed that feet used with correct weight bearing lines were present in 67% or two-thirds of the boys and 43% or two-fifths of the girls. Faulty weight bearing was present in 33% or one-third of the boys and in 57% or one-half of the girls. The extremely bad feet were present four times in the girls to once in the boys, or 8% of the girls and 2% of the boys.

Tenderness at one or more of the five points mentioned above was taken to denote foot strain of one kind or another and was present as before mentioned in 10% of the total number of 699 cases. Tenderness was present in 4% of the high arches, in 5% of the medium arches and only in 1% of the low arches. This would seem to disprove the popular idea that because a foot had a low arch or was "flat," it was more liable to be painful than other kinds of feet.

50% or one-half the cases, 60% of the boys and 38% of the girls, that used the feet correctly showed no tenderness. The correctly used feet which showed tenderness were slightly more common in the boys than the girls. About 43% of the cases where the feet were used incorrectly were without tenderness; 55% of the girls and 35% of the boys, or three girls to every two boys used their feet incorrectly without any tenderness. The tenderness occurred most commonly in feet which showed moderately faulty weight bearing lines and least commonly in the extremely bad feet. Tenderness occurred only slightly more often in the girls than in the boys.

The distance of the scaphoid tubercle below a line from the inner ankle bone to the lower side of the great toe joint was ½ inch or less in 97% and more than this in 3% of the cases. The boys as a whole were ⅛ inch higher than the girls. The foot strain cases showed 92% of the cases with the tubercle ½ inch or less below the line. 8% were more than ½ inch. In other words this did not seem to be a test which could be relied upon if only one examination could be made.

The examination of the comparative strength of the muscle groups showed that in 38% or more than one-third of the cases, the adductor muscles or those which hold up the arch of the foot were the stronger; that in 38% the muscle groups were equal and in 15% the abductor muscles were the stronger. The statistics of Osgood and others have shown that feet with the muscle groups equal are more prone to foot strain than those with the adductor muscles the stronger. These statistics point to the same conclusion. Of the cases which showed foot strain 45% or almost one-half had stronger abductor muscles and 38% had the muscles equal and only 17% had the adductor muscles the stronger.

The examination of the shoes in connection with muscle balances showed that with good shoes the adductor muscles were the stronger in twice as many cases as with poor shoes. In contrast to this with poor shoes the abductor muscles were the stronger nearly twice as often as with good shoes. This would seem to indicate that the kind of shoe, whether good or bad, had a definite influence on the comparative strength of the muscles which support the arch of the foot. When the feet were used correctly 54% of cases showed the adductors were stronger, while only 6% showed the abductor muscles were the stronger. When the feet were used incorrectly only 31% showed stronger adductors, while 24% showed stronger abductors. From this it would seem that the testing of the muscle balance is of considerable value in that it gives an idea of how much importance should be given to the fact that a foot is used incorrectly or not.

The examination of the shoes brought out the following points: 69% or slightly more than two-thirds of the boys and 19% or less than one-fifth of the girls wore good shoes. Medium shoes were worn by 27%, a little more than one-quarter of the boys and 39% or a little more than one-third of the girls, while bad shoes appeared in only 4% of the boys and in 42% or nearly one-half the girls. 88% of the girls who wore bad shoes were either in the grammar or the high school.

The wear of the heels of the shoes was even in 82% of the cases and the per cent. in the girls and boys was about the same, the girls being a trifle better than the boys. About 18% showed wear on the front inner corner of the heels, this being slightly more common in the boys than in the girls. The heels were rolled inward in 12%, the girls slightly more than the boys.

As stated above 43% of the cases showed faulty weight bearing lines or incorrect use of the feet; also that this occurred three times in the girls to twice in the boys. Of those cases using their feet incorrectly two-thirds of the boys and one-eighth of the girls wore good shoes. About one-fourth of the boys and one-third of the girls wore medium shoes while only one-twentieth of the boys and one-half of the girls wore bad shoes. This would seem to indicate that bad shoes had a very definite influence on the occurrence of faulty weight bearing, especially in girls. It should be noted here that very commonly the boys wore shoes which though of good shape were much too large and allowed the feet a great deal of slipping around in the shoes.

As before stated curled toes or relaxed or weakened anterior arches occurred in one-fourth of the boys and one-third of the girls, or, as might be expected, more commonly in the girls than in the boys. Examination of the shoes in this condition shows that 63% or over six-tenths of the boys with the front part of the foot relaxed wore good shaped shoes, while 8% or less than one-tenth of the girls wore good shoes; 31% or three-tenths of both boys and girls wore medium shoes, while 6% of the boys and 61% or six-tenths of the girls wore bad shoes. Here again shoes seem to have a definite influence on the condition of the feet. As will be remembered hallux valgus occurred four times in the girls to once in the boys; also of all the shoes examined only 4% of the boys wore bad shoes, while 42% of the girls wore them. 65% or two-thirds of the girls with hallux valgus wore bad shoes while 31% or less than one-third wore medium shoes.

Examination of the posture of the body showed that only 25% or one-fourth of the cases stood in good posture and that 75% or three-fourths of them used their bodies in bad posture. Of these latter 18% were as bad as the picture showing faulty posture. The girls as a whole stood in poorer posture than the boys. Good posture was slightly more common than bad posture in the primary grades. It was about equally common in the grammar grades, while in the high school bad posture was nearly twice as common as good posture. Another point in regard to posture that was examined in a rough way by palpation or feeling, was the relaxation of the front abdominal wall. In general it may be said that the worse the posture, the more relaxed is the front abdominal wall, and the more is the tendency to a protuberant abdomen. 56% of the cases showed a normal condition of the abdominal wall, while 44% showed a protuberant abdomen, 14% of which were as marked as the slide of faulty posture. 36% or a little more than one-third of the boys and 54% or a little more than one-half of the girls showed relaxed abdomens. Of these 20% of the girls and 8% of the boys showed the marked type.

An examination of the statistics comparing the relation of the posture of the body to the weight bearing of the feet shows with bad postures 46% had faulty weight bearing while with good posture only 9% had faulty weight bearing. In other words, there is reason to believe that faulty use of the body has a definite relation to faulty use of the feet. This should be a very important point in the care and hygiene of our school children.

Any estimation of the general condition of the children was necessarily rough but it showed that 89% of the whole number were in good condition and 11% in fair.

Boys — Primary.............. 90 · Grammar............. 162 · High................ 97

Girls — Primary.............. 72 · Grammar............. 183 · High................ 95

Age	Boys Grades								Girls Grades						Boys and Girls
	3rd	3rd & 4th	5th	6th	7th	8th	H	Total	3rd	3rd & 4th	5th & 6th 7th	8th	H	Total	
7		1	7					8	5					5	13
8	10	4	13					27	16	9				25	52
9	20	17	12	1				50	9	16	7			32	82
10	6	17	17	3				43	2	14	30			46	89
11	6	5	13	15	1	4		44	1		31			32	76
12	2	2	11	8	3	7		33			41	4		45	78
13			4	7	4	7	8	30			24	13	7	44	74
14			2	2	3	12	21	40			12	10	29	51	91
15				1	1	4	23	29			2	7	23	32	61
16							19	19			1	1	22	24	43
17							15	15					10	10	25
18							8	8					4	4	12
19							1	1							1
20							1	1							1
21							1	1							1
	44	46	79	37	12	34	97	349	33	39	148	35	95	350	699
	Primary (44, 46)		Grammar (128)				High (97)		Primary (33, 39)		Grammar		High		

RACE	Boys Grades								Girls Grades						Total Boys and Girls
	3rd	3rd & 4th	5th	6th	7th	8th	H	Total	3rd	4th	5th 6th 7th	8th	H	Total	
American......	21	3	26	8	8	18	88	172	11	11	25	3	83	135	307
Irish.........	12	34	28	22	3	9	:	108	11	17	86	25	5	144	252
Lithuanian....	6	6	7	3	1	3	3	29	2	3	13	2	1	21	50
German........	4	:	5	2	:	3	2	16	3	3	6	3	:	15	31
Jewish........	:	1	1	:	:	:	2	4	1	1	7	2	2	13	17
French........	1	:	2	1	:	:	:	4	:	:	:	:	:	:	4
Italian.......	:	1	:	1	:	:	2	4	1	2	4	:	:	7	11
Belgian.......	:	:	2	:	:	:	:	2	2	:	3	:	:	5	7
Swedish.......	:	:	1	:	:	:	:	1	1	:	2	:	1	4	5
English.......	:	1	4	:	:	:	:	5	:	:	1	:	:	1	6
Portuguese....	:	:	:	:	:	:	:	:	1	:	1	:	1	3	3
Scotch........	:	:	1	:	:	:	:	1	:	:	:	:	:	:	1
Russian.......	:	:	2	:	:	:	:	2	:	:	:	:	2	2	4
Canadian......	:	:	:	:	:	1	:	1	:	:	:	:	:	:	1
	44	46	79	37	12	34	97	349	33	39	148	35	95	350	699

FLEXIBILITY

Total			Boys, 342		Girls, 345		
Normal present	687	98%	Present..	342	98%	Present..	345	97%
Medium "	13	2%	Present..	6	2%	Present..	7	3%.

Normal

Boys		Girls	
Primary	26%	Primary	22%
Grammar	47%	Grammar	51%
High	27%	High	27%

Medium

Primary	17%	Primary	14%
Grammar		Grammar	57%
High	83%	High	29%

Peroneal Spasm

Grammar		Grammar	1%

TENDERNESS

Total boys and girls	absent, 631	90%	present, 68	10%
" boys	" 312	89%	" 37	11%
" girls	" 319	90%	" 31	10%

	Boys		Girls	
Primary	absent, 95%	present, 5%	absent, 96%	present, 4%
Grammar	" 88%	" 12%	" 93%	" 7%
High	" 84%	" 16%	" 84%	" 16%

CALLOUSES

Total boys and girls	absent, 310	44%	present, 389	56%
" boys	" 178	51%	" 171	49%
" girls	" 132	38%	" 218	62%

	Boys		Girls	
Primary	absent, 70%	present, 30%	absent, 73%	present, 27%
Grammar	" 43%	" 57%	" 35%	" 65%
High	" 47%	" 53%	" 15%	" 85%

	Total	Boys	Girls
Inner side head of 1st metatarsal	54%	52%	55%
Inner side 1st toe	29%	14%	40%
Outer side of 5th toe	39%	35%	42%

	1st M.		1st Toe		5th Toe	
	Boys	Girls	Boys	Girls	Boys	Girls
Primary	19	11	20	7	6	3
Grammar	58	46	52	49	47	54
High	23	43	28	44	47	43

ARCHES WITHOUT WEIGHT

Total known arches.. 642

	328	323
	Boys	Girls

	Boys	Girls
.High arches...	40%	40%
Medium...	51%	52%
Low...	9%	8%

Curled Toes

	Total	Boys	Girls
Total number cases.............................. 195	30%	26%	34%

Hallux Valgus

	Total	Boys	Girls
Total number cases.............................. 87	13%	5%	22%

Boys

	High	Medium	Low	Curled Toes	Hallux Valgus
Primary.........	20%	32%	27%	11%	0%
Grammar.........	53%	37%	53%	42%	56%
High.............	27%	31%	20%	39%	44%

Girls

	High	Medium	Low	Curled Toes	Hallux Valgus
Primary.........	17%	26%	32%	7%	11%
Grammar........	49%	50%	52%	72%	60%
High.............	34%	24%	16%	21%	29%

Arches—Boys

	High	Medium	Low	Curled Toes	Hallux Valgus
Primary.........	20%	32%	27%	11%	0%
Grammar........	53%	37%	53%	42%	56%
High.............	27%	31%	20%	39%	44%

Arches—Girls

	High	Medium	Low	Curled Toes	Hallux Valgus
Primary.........	17%	26%	32%	7%	11%
Grammar........	49%	50%	52%	72%	60%
High.............	34%	24%	16%	21%	29%

ARCHES WITH WEIGHT

Total known arches—examined for pronation.............................. 684

	335	349
	Boys	Girls

	Total	Boys	Girls
Extreme pronation—total............................	4%	1%	7%
Moderate — "	42%	32%	50%
Slight — "	54%	67%	43%

	Boys			Girls		
	Extreme	Moderate	Slight	Extreme	Moderate	Slight
Primary..................	60%	19%	29%	25%	9%	34%
Grammar..............	20%	51%	50%	50%	56%	48%
High..................	20%	30%	21%	25%	35%	18%

Total known arches—examined for sag...................................... 682

	336	346

		Boys	Girls
Extreme sag—total...............................	5%	3%	9%
Moderate — "	45%	36%	52%
Slight — "	49%	60%	39%

	Boys			Girls		
	Extreme	Moderate	Slight	Extreme	Moderate	Slight
Primary............	41%	14%	32%	22%	12%	32%
Grammar..........	50%	43%	46%	52%	57%	48%
High..............	9%	43%	22%	26%	31%	20%

TOTAL CASES EXAMINED FOR PRONATION

				Without tenderness
Moderate..................	290	117 boys	173 girls	260
Extreme..................	29	5 "	24 "	21
Slight....................	363	213 "	150 "	347
	682	335	347	628

TOTAL CASES EXAMINED FOR SAG

				Without tenderness
Moderate..................	300	119 boys	181 girls	269
Extreme..................	45	14 "	31 "	36
Slight....................	338	203 "	135 "	321
	683	336	347	626

				Total	Boys	Girls
Moderate pronation without tenderness...............				38%	30%	45%
" " with "				4%	5%	5%
Extreme " without "				4%	1%	5%
" " with "				1%	0%	2%
Slight " without "				50%	61%	41%
" " with "				3%	3%	2%

				Total	Boys	Girls
Moderate sag without tenderness.....................				39%	31%	48%
" " with "				4%	4%	5%
Extreme " without "				5%	4%	7%
" " with "				1%	1%	2%
Slight " without "				48%	58%	36%
" " with "				3%	3%	2%

EXAMINATION OF ARCHES WITH AND WITHOUT TENDERNESS

Total known arches, 642   Boys, 328   Girls, 323

	Boys		Girls
	Without tenderness	With tenderness	Without tenderness
High arches..........................	40%	4%	40%
Medium "	51%	5%	52%
Low "	9%	1%	8%
	100%	10%	100%

EXAMINATION OF ARCHES FOR PRONATION WITH CALLOUSES

	Total, 396	Boys, 141	Girls, 225
Moderate pronation	46%	71%	47%
Extreme "	3%	5%	5%
Slight "	51%	24%	48%

EXAMINATION OF ARCHES FOR SAG WITH CALLOUSES

	Total, 358	Boys, 157	Girls, 198
Moderate Sag	53%	70%	60%
Extreme "	7%	9%	8%
Slight "	40%	21%	32%

CURLED TOES, WITHOUT TENDERNESS—699 cases; 162 curled toes s tenderness.

	Total	Boys	Girls
	23%	20%	26%

EXAMINATION OF ARCHES FOR PRONATION AND SAG WITH HALLUX VALGUS

Moderate pronation c H. V. ⎫	60%	55%	61%
Slight " " ⎬78 cases	32%	36%	31%
Extreme " " ⎭	8%	9%	8%
Moderate Sag c H. V. ⎫	56%	45%	57%
Slight " " ⎬76 cases	34%	35%	34%
Extreme " " ⎭	10%	20%	9%

PRONATION AND SAG

(Cases without tenderness only included in these tables)

Pronation

	Boys			Girls		
	Moderate	Extreme	Slight	Moderate	Extreme	Slight
Primary	20%	50%	29%	7%	23%	35%
Grammar	44%	25%	53%	56%	60%	47%
High	36%	25%	18%	27%	17%	18%

Sag

Primary	16%	33%	47%	12%	21%	33%
Grammar	44%	59%	33%	58%	58%	50%
High	40%	8%	20%	30%	21%	17%

Pronation with Callouses

Primary	12%	50%	21%	7%	....	6%
Grammar	48%	25%	47%	53%	61%	77%
High	40%	25%	32%	40%	39%	17%

Sag With Callouses

Primary	9%	11%	20%	8%	18%	10%
Grammar	50%	78%	54%	54%	41%	57%
High	41%	11%	26%	38%	18%	33%

Curled Toes		*Hallux Valgus*			
		Pronation		Sag	
	Boys	Girls	Boys	Girls	Boys	Girls
Primary	10%	7%		10%		11%
Grammar	46%	80%	54%	63%	54%	62%
High	44%	13%	46%	27%	46%	27%

ARCHES WITH TENDERNESS

	High Arches		Medium		Low	
	Boys	Girls	Boys	Girls	Boys	Girls
Primary	0%	7%	14%	36%	25%	28%
Grammar	55%	28%	36%	24%	25%	28%
High	45%	65%	50%	36%	50%	44%

PRONATION WITH TENDERNESS

	Moderate		Extreme		Slight	
	Boys	Girls	Boys	Girls	Boys	Girls
Primary	0%	13%	100%	42%	12%	29%
Grammar	40%	33%	0%	26%	44%	29%
High	60%	54%	0%	42%	44%	42%

SAG WITH TENDERNESS

	Moderate		Extreme		Slight	
	Boys	Girls	Boys	Girls	Boys	Girls
Primary	0%	12%	100%	28%	22%	25%
Grammar	33%	50%	0%	28%	44%	12%
High	67%	38%	0%	42%	34%	63%

CURLED TOES WITH TENDERNESS

	Boys	Girls
Primary	18%	4%
Grammar	27%	36%
High	55%	60%

THE DISTANCE OF THE SCAPHOID TUBERCLE BELOW A LINE FROM INTERNAL MALLEOLUS TO INTERNAL TUBERCLE AT HEAD OF FIRST METATARSUS

Total number of cases.. 698

Inches	Total	Boys	Girls
0-8	1%	3%	0.3%
1-8	15%	19%	10%
2-8	38%	41%	35.7%
3-8	34%	28%	40%
4-8	9%	7%	12%
5-8	2%	1%	7%
6-8	0.8%	0.5%	1%
7-8	0.2%	0.5%	0%

	Boys			Girls		
	Primary	Grammar	High	Primary	Grammar	High
0-8	....	40%	60%	100%	0	0
1-8	33%	47%	20%	36%	53%	22%
2-8	38%	42%	20%	26%	52%	22%
3-8	9%	50%	41%	16%	50%	34%
4-8	18%	39%	43%	24%	46%	30%
5-8	17%	66%	17%	14%	72%	14%
6-8	0%	100%	0%	25%	75%	....
7-8	0%	50%	50%	....	....	....

SCAPHOID TUBERCLE—IN FOOT STRAIN CASES

Total, 62	With tenderness	Boys, 30	Girls, 32
0-8..............................	2%	3%	....
1-8..............................	20%	16%	22%
2-8..............................	24%	26%	22%
3-8..............................	35%	34%	41%
4-8..............................	11%	13%	9%
5-8..............................	4%	3%	3%
6-8..............................	4%	3%	3%
7-8..............................	....	....	....

	Primary	Grammar	High	Primary	Grammar	High
0-8.............	..	..	100%	..	..	..
1-8...,........	40%	40%	20%	28%	28%	44%
2-8.............	12%	50%	38%	14%	47%	29%
3-8.............	0%	30%	70%	7%	31%	62%
4-8.............	0%	25%	75%	0%	33%	67%
5-8.............	100%	0%	0%	0%	50%	50%
6-8.............	0%	100%	0%	0%	50%	50%
7-8.............	..	..	..	..	..	..

EXAMINATION OF CASES FOR MUSCLE BALANCE

Total number of cases examined.:..	683
Total boys..	340
Total girls...	343

	Total	Boys	Girls
Adductors stronger.............................	38%	49%	27%
Abductors "	15%	10%	20%
Groups equal...................................	38%	34%	42%
Asymmetrical...................................	9%	7%	11%

Condition of Arches with Weight Bearing and Muscle Balance

	Total, 332	Boys, 133	Girls, 199
Faulty position—adductors stronger........	31%	38%	26%
" " —equal balance.............	45%	43%	46%
" " —abductors stronger........	24%	19%	28%

	Total, 265	Boys, 176	Girls, 89
Good position—adductors.................	54%	64%	34%
" " —equal.....................	40%	32%	56%
" " —abductors.................	6%	4%	10%

Foot Strain and Muscle Balance

	Total, 53	Boys, 27	Girls, 26
Tenderness—adductors.......:.............	17%	26%	7%
" —equal........................	38%	34%	43%
" —abductors..................	45%	40%	50%

Shoes and Muscle Balance

	Total, 140	Boys, 12	Girls, 128
Poor shoes—adductors..................	29%	75%	25%
" " —equal.......................	47%	17%	49%
" " —abductors..................	24%	8%	26%

	Total, 377	Boys, 250	Girls, 127
Medium shoes—adductors stronger........	43%	50%	34%
" " —equal balance..............	44%	40%	52%
" " —abductors stronger........	13%	10%	14%

	Total, 81	Boys, 46	Girls, 35
Good shoes—adductors stronger...........	57%	65%	46%
" " —equal balance...............	30%	26%	34%
" " —abductors stronger...........	13%	9%	20%

	Total, 71	Boys, 3	Girls, 68
Shoes too short—adductors stronger.......	28%	100%	26%
" " —equal balance.............	50%	...	51%
" " —abductors stronger........	22%	...	23%

	Boys				Girls			
	Add.	Abd.	Equal	Asym.	Add.	Abd.	Equal	Asym.
Primary....	31%	12%	21%	8%	24%	7%	26%	13%
Grammar...	43%	68%	44%	58%	52%	57%	51%	50%
High.......	26%	20%	35%	34%	24%	36%	23%	37%

Faulty Position

Primary....	22%	5%	25%	....	14%	8%	13%	....
Grammar...	42%	70%	31%	....	56%	60%	63%	....
High.......	36%	25%	40%	....	30%	32%	24%	....

Good Position

	Add.	Equal	Abd.	Add.	Equal	Abd.
Primary........	35%	21%	43%	40%	46%	12%
Grammar.......	44%	50%	43%	57%	34%	44%
High..........	21%	29%	14%	3%	20%	44%

Tenderness

Primary........	14%	22%	9%	0%	36%	0%
Grammar......	43%	12%	63%	50%	45%	23%
High..........	43%	66%	28%	50%	19%	77%

Poor Shoes

Primary........	33%	0%	0%	9%	14%	3%
Grammar.......	44%	50%	100%	62%	62%	54%
High..........	23%	50%	0%	29%	24%	43%

Medium Shoes

Primary........	27%	20%	8%	25%	33%	16%
Grammar......	40%	41%	65%	44%	44%	44%
High..........	34%	39%	27%	31%	23%	40%

Good Shoes

Primary........	40%	58%	80%	50%	42%	14%
Grammar......	60%	42%	20%	44%	58%	80%
High..........	....	....	....	6%	....	....

Medium to Bad Shoes—too Short

Primary........	....	....	....	6%	6%	....
Grammar......	66%	....	....	88%	82%	88%
High..........	34%	....	....	6%	12%	12%

EXAMINATION OF SHOES

Total boys and girls..	676
" boys..	340
" girls..	336

	Total	Boys	Girls
Good..	11%	15%	6%
Medium to good...........................	34%	54%	13%
Medium..	33%	27%	39%
Medium to bad..................................	8%	3%	15%
Bad..	14%	1%	27%

	Boys	Girls	Medium-Good		Medium		Medium-Bad		Bad	
	Good									
Primary........	45%	57%	22%	38%	22%	25%	20%	17%	50%	6%
Grammar......	55%	38%	41%	51%	49%	45%	50%	67%	50%	52%
High..........	0%	5%	38%	11%	29%	30%	30%	16%	0%	42%

Examination of Heels
656 Cases

	Total	Boys	Girls
Even wear (115 cases)...........................	82%	49%	51%
Front inner corner..............................	18%	54%	46%
Inward roll (79 cases)...........................	12%	49%	51%
Total shoes of cases with tenderness............	54	Boys, 30	Girls, 24
" " " " pronation.............	312	" 121	" 191
" " " " sag....................	333	" 125	" 208

Shoes	Tenderness			Pronation			Sag		
	Total	Boys	Girls	Total	Boys	Girls	Total	Boys	Girls
Good..........	22%	33%	8%	8%	16%	4%	7%	9%	5%
Medium-good...	31%	40%	8%	32%	51%	6%	27%	58%	10%
Medium........	25%	27%	33%	26%	28%	37%	34%	28%	38%
Medium-bad....	5%	....	12%	11%	4%	16%	12%	4%	16%
Bad..........	17%	....	39%	23%	1%	38%	20%	1%	31%

Shoes of Cases of Curled Toes

	Total, 185	Boys, 84	Girls, 101
Good..............................	6%	7%	.5%
Medium-good.......................	27%	56%	3%
Medium............................	31%	31%	31%
Medium-bad........................	10%	5%	14%
Bad..............................	26%	1%	47%

Shoes of Cases with Callouses

	Total, 355	Boys, 155	Girls, 200
Good................................	7%	12%	3%
Medium-good........................	30%	54%	12%
Medium.............................	33%	29%	36%
Medium-bad.........................	10%	4%	16%
Bad................................	20%	1%	33%

Shoes of Cases of Hallux Valgus

	Total, 82	Boys, 15	Girls, 67
Good................................	3%	13%	1%
Medium-good........................	9%	34%	3%
Medium.............................	35%	53%	31%
Medium-bad.........................	12%	....	14%
Bad................................	41%		51%

Tenderness

	Boys					Girls				
	Good	M.G.	Med.	M.B.	Bad	Good	M.G.	Med.	M.B.	Bad
Primary........	30%	18%	..	..	..	50%	20%	60%	33%	..
Grammar......	70%	41%	38%	..	..	50%	20%	40%	33%	44%
High..........	..	41%	62%	..	..	..	60%	..	34%	56%

Pronation

Primary........	55%	13%	18%	..	..	50%	39%	12%	6%	5%
Grammar......	45%	37%	41%	75%	100%	50%	54%	50%	74%	55%
High..........	..	50%	41%	25%	..	..	7%	38%	20%	40%

Sag

Primary........	73%	11%	11%	..	..	50%	29%	15%	9%	6%
Grammar......	27%	36%	47%	80%	100%	50%	62%	50%	73%	51%
High..........	..	53%	42%	20%	..	..	9%	35%	18%	43%

Curled Toes

Primary........	50%	8%	7%	..	..	20%	..	9%	..	..
Grammar......	50%	46%	43%	25%	100%	80%	100%	69%	100%	70%
High..........	..	46%	50%	75%	..	..	..	22%	..	30%

Callouses

Primary........	39%	13%	9%	16%	..	34%	20%	9%	13%	3%
Grammar......	56%	51%	53%	50%	100%	50%	69%	54%	71%	41%
High..........	5%	36%	38%	34%	..	16%	11%	37%	16%	56%

EXAMINATION OF CASES AS TO POSTURE

Total cases relaxed abdominal wall..............	698	Boys, 365	Girls, 333
" " " " "...............	552	" 312	" 240

Cases Examined for Round Shoulders

	Total	Boys	Girls
Absent round shoulders..	8%	6%	9%
Slight " "	16%	19%	12%
Moderate " "	58%	58%	57%
Extreme " "	18%	17%	22%

Cases with Relaxed Abdominal Wall

	Total	Boys	Girls
Slight relaxation	56%	64%	46%
Moderate "	30%	28%	34%
Extreme "	14%	8%	20%

Occurrence of Corsets or Ferris Waists

	Total girls, 85	Grammar	High
Corset	3	100%	..
Tight corset	63%	20%	80%
Ferris waist	30%	28%	72%
Tight waist	4%		100%

Round Shoulders

	Boys				Girls			
	Absent R.S.	Sl.R.S.	R.S.	R.S. +	Absent R.S.	Sl.R.S.	R.S.	R.S. +
Primary	52%	26%	22%	38%	24%	43%	25%	7%
Grammar	24%	61%	41%	46%	69%	38%	36%	75%
High	24%	13%	37%	16%	7%	19%	39%	18%

Relaxation of Abdominal Wall

	Slight	Mod.	Extrem.	Slight	Mod.	Extrem.
Primary	22%	27%	43%	30%	23%	20%
Grammar	47%	43%	50%	36%	55%	74%
High	31%	30%	8%	44%	22%	6%

Posture in Relation to Weight Bearing

	Total	Boys	Girls
Good posture and good weight bearing	11%	13%	8%
" " " bad " "	9%	8%	11%
Bad " " good " "	34%	42%	25%
" " " bad " "	46%	37%	56%

EXAMINATION OF CASES AS TO GENERAL CONDITION

		Total, 632	Boys, 339	Girls, 293
Good condition	{ good position of feet { bad position of feet	.... 89%	{ 46% { 34%	90%
Fair to good	{ good position of feet { bad position of feet	.... 3%	{ 1.4% { 1.6%	2%
Fair	{ good position of feet { bad position of feet	.... 6%	{ 3% { 3%	5%
Poor	{ good position of feet { bad position of feet	.... 1%	{ 0.3% { 0.7%	3%

ABNORMALITIES OTHER THAN STATIC CONDITIONS

	Boys	Girls	Total
Club foot	1	1	2
Contracted feet	1		1
Exostosis oscalcis	1		2
Sore throat and foot strain	2		2
Achilles tenosynovitis	1		2
Hammer toe	2	.	2
Peroneal spasm	.		1
Hip disease	1		
Hallux Rigidus	1	.	1
Ingrowing toenail	.	3	3
Scoliosis	.	1	1
Short leg	1		1
One-legged boy	1		
Store plates	.		

THE TREATMENT OF FOOT STRAIN AND WEAK ARCHES AMONG SCHOOL CHILDREN

BY

ROBERT B. OSGOOD

As a result of the careless use of descriptive terms, presumably first invented by physicians, there exists in the minds of many persons a misapprehension which we would at the outset attempt to correct. We find that most people believe that unless the arch of the foot almost completely flattens when the weight is borne, there is little likelihood that pain in the foot is due to faulty weight bearing. The converse of this is also true. People in general believe that if the arches of the feet are noticeably depressed in a standing position, the feet ought to give rise to symptoms, whether they do or not. These beliefs are not borne out by experience nor have they a proper scientific basis. Many of the weakest feet are those in which the arch is high but under strain. On the other hand we know well of the marvelous efficiency of the feet of non-shoe wearing savages, many of which show practically complete depression of the arches when standing with the muscles relaxed. This Hoffman(1) demonstrated at the St. Louis Fair.

We must seek other tests, therefore, than imprints on smoked paper or in plaster of paris if we are to rightly judge of the efficiency of feet. We must not depend upon the height or depression of its arches when the foot is at rest.

We do not wish to be understood as denying either the existence of such a thing as a painful vicious flat foot nor of the reality of broken arches, but the use of these terms should be restricted to these actual conditions and not be used to designate a class of cases better described as weak feet or strained feet. This class is far larger and far more important than the more serious and more obvious condition.

There is, in our opinion, no satisfactory standard for the height of an arch which may be considered normal. It is as if one should attempt to declare what length of nose was normal. Our feet are almost as individual as our features in respect to the height of the arch and the relationship of this height to the efficiency of the foot.

We agree with Dr. Brown in his preceding paper that the potential of foot strain may be said to exist, if in walking the inner ankle constantly seems to sag. We speak of this as pronation. If a plumb line dropped from the prominent anterior superior spine of the pelvic bone, falling

(1) Hoffman. Am. Jour. Orth. Surg., Oct., 1905.

through the middle of the knee pan, strikes the foot placed, straight ahead, farther toward the median line of the body than the cleft between the great toe and the second toe or farther outward than the cleft be_ tween the fourth and fifth toes, the weight bearing lines are not true. We believe that actual foot strain may be said to exist when in addition to this deviation from the normal weight bearing lines there is present tenderness on pressure at appropriate points of ligamentous stretching with or without symptoms of pain and discomfort in walking. We consider that the efficiency of .the feet and, therefore, of the individual may be much lessened by the presence of completely flattened or broken down arches, quite apart from the question as to whether these give rise ɩto subjective symptoms or not. We speak of these deforming conditions as valgus.

What Importance Has this Subject in Relation to School Children? There will probably at this Congress be no dissent from the opinion that the school is the place above all others to attack national problems, and this question of foot strain may be said in America and Germany at least to be almost a national problem. One manufactory of ready-made arch supporters in Cleveland admitted under oath that it sold 3,000 pairs every month to shoe stores(2) and while the sales in the shoe stores were undoubtedly stimulated by profit, we must at least suppose a receptive public, most of whom had suffered discomfort which they believed could. be attributed to the feet.

There are said ·to be some 10,000 cases annually of foot trouble in the German Army. At the 1912 joint session of the German Association for Public Hygiene and the Berlin Society for School Hygiene(3) the question of the influence of the upper school grades upon military efficiency was discussed. An investigation based on 52,650 volunteers showed that "flat foot" was one of the prevalent causes of unfitness. In a large orthopedic hospital clinic those seeking advice because of foot discomfort represent about 30% of the whole number of new cases.

An investigation of entering classes at Wellesley College under Miss Homans(4) showed 77% to have faulty weight bearing lines, and at Smith College, under Miss Rossiter, 80%.

Ewald's(5) table of 502 school children in Germany in the first to the thirteenth classes, showed nearly 60% to have pronation and 33% of these to have serious foot trouble.

Henneberg & Kirsch(6) found amongst 741 school children of the

(2) Stern. International Clinics. Vol. III, 23d series.
(3) Journ. A. M. A., Jan. 25, 1913, p. 299.
(4) Osgood. Boston Med. & Surg. Jour., Mar. 13, 1913, p. 380.
(5) Ewald. Zeit. für Orth. Surg. Vol. 25, 1910, p. 227.
(6) Henneberg & Kirsch. Zeit. für Orth. Surg. 1911, Vol. 28, p. 371.

Volkschule an increasing tendency to foot troubles and faulty weight bearing from the lower to the upper classes, until when they left the school, 25% had what they designate as "flat foot."

Brown's careful investigation of the existence of the same or worse conditions in the public schools of one of our American cities needs no further comment. We are forced to the conclusion that the subject is important not only in regard to school hygiene but in relation to the efficiency of the race.

What is the Mechanism of Foot Strain?   We must try to answer this, for only treatment which appreciates this mechanism can have a sound basis. There are two main arches in the foot formed by the bones and maintained by ligaments and muscles—(1) a longitudinal arch commonly spoken of as "the" arch, formed by the small bones of the mid-foot and the heel bone; (2) a transverse arch or anterior arch, formed by the heads of the slender long bones of the front of the foot as they join the toes. Now neither of these arches have any true keystone and unless maintained by ligaments and muscles, would fall of their own weight. The heel bone is known as the os calcis and the bone above it, which receives the weight of the body is the astragalus, while in front of it is a boat-shaped bone called from this circumstance, the scaphoid. Now the roll over, the sag, the pronation, the foot strain, takes place when the astragalus and os calcis change their relationship to each other. There is a prop on the inner side of the heel bone which, if the heel bone is properly supported, prevents the astragalus and ankle from sagging. If this little prop receives sufficient support from the muscle tendons which are beneath it, and from the strong ligament that binds it to the scaphoid bone in front and controls the position of the head of the astragalus, foot strain is very unlikely to occur. This prop and its supports are of great importance when we consider that the line of weight bearing drawn through the center of the lower leg bone, the tibia, and continued through the bone of the foot which joins it, called, as we have said, the astragalus, falls considerably to the inner side of the heel bone. Obviously there must be some active supporters of the arch of the foot else we should all pronate and sag and become flat footed. The longitudinal arch is maintained more by indirect support than by the small muscles and strong ligaments that stretch across the sole like bow strings. These latter are stretched and painful in the later stages but not as a rule early, and since our treatment should be largely preventive, we must appreciate early cases and the potential of strain. The muscles of the lower leg and of the foot, therefore, are of great importance both as active supporters of the bony arches and as protectors of the important ligaments from painful stretching.

What is the Cause of Foot Strain? We do not altogether know. Henneberg & Kirsch believe it may commonly be ascribed in Germany at least to rickets. Ewald, also in Germany, believes that rickets plays no part. We do not consider that it plays an important part in this country. All agree that faulty weight bearing lines may develop into bad foot strain, that is, flat foot, and most agree that badly shaped shoes induce to faulty weight bearing lines. Here is undoubtedly a common and remediable cause. Bad habits of walking and standing and the admonition of mothers to toe out, represent other causes. We find a small number who are born with a flat foot, just as we have an occasional club foot. We believe a faulty muscle balance, congenital or acquired, may well represent a potential strain. We are convinced that the faulty posture and general debility which a poorly nourished and poorly "set up" child so often manifests, is usually accompanied by very faulty weight bearing lines in the feet. Sometimes it is difficult to discover which is the cart and which the horse in these questions of debility and visceroptosis. There is an intimate connection without question.

There can be no doubt about the existence of foot strain and weak feet among school children. There can be no doubt about the importance of the condition in relation to the future comfort of the individual and the efficiency of the community. We have briefly discussed the mechanism, we have summarized some of the causes. What are we to recommend as treatment? It would seem at this time futile to more than touch upon the special treatment of an individual case of foot strain or to enter into any medical discussion as to the details of treatment in general. Certain suggestions we shall try to make looking to practical methods of preventive treatment.

First, there should be some simpler popular instruction given each class on the rudiments of proper weight bearing and posture. Instruction, therefore, is the primary step.

Secondly, we should recognize the existence of faulty weight bearing lines. There is a greater tendency to have more thorough physical examination of school children and we feel sure that the slightly greater time consumed in seeking out potential and actual foot strains would be economical consumption.

We urge then that the examination of the feet and the shoes be made a part of the inspection of school children. It would be difficult, probably very difficult to insist upon any standard shape of shoe for the public schools and yet we feel this would be of very great advantage. At least the cases of potential or actual strain could be advised as to shoes of normal shape and thus a prevalent cause to some extent lessened. We cannot here enter into a discussion as to the relative merits of shoes.

For feet measuring up to normal or nearly normal standard the shoe should be as flexible as possible. For all feet the shape should be nondeforming. The two most essential points are roominess for the toes and an axis so parallel that when the heels of the shoes are placed together, the inner borders of the soles touch each other from shank to toes.

Instruction in walking and in posture should be made a part of physical training in the schools and by exercises designed to increase the power of the adductors and the toe flexors, the protectors of proper weight bearing lines should be strengthened. If marked deviation from proper weight bearing lines are detected, alteration in the shape of the heel of the shoe will correct many cases. If we remember the prop on the inner side of the heel bone, which when supported preserves the integrity of the longitudinal arch, it will be seen that elevation of the heel of the shoe on the inner side beneath this prop provided the counter of the shoe is stiff and fits well, will tend to correct the inward sag and restore proper weight bearing lines.

There are feet, of course, which these simple measures will not relieve, but judging from Brown's figures, a comparatively small number in our American schools. This small number include the more severe cases of valgus, requiring the skillfully planned support of specially designed plates or shoes, and persistent, constant, sometimes operative treatment for their betterment. These should be sent to the orthopedic clinic or the orthopedic surgeon.

Finally have these suggested methods of treatment any likelihood of success? Theoretically they seem to us sound. We know of only one analogous application to these preventive measures.

For many years all probation nurses at the Massachusetts General Hospital have been carefully examined as to the condition of their feet after they began their work. Recommendations have been made on the basis of their weight bearing lines and muscle tests. The result has been the practical elimination of foot strain among the regular nurses who follow advice. If similar examination and control of school children could be had, we feel confident that one of the important problems of school hygiene could be solved and much adult discomfort could be prevented.

WEAK ANKLES, FLAT FOOT, SPINAL CURVATURE IN SCHOOL CHILDREN

BY

HILLS COLE

"One million school children in the United States of America (5 per cent. of the total school population) have spinal curvature, flat foot or some other moderate deformity serious enough to interfere to some degree with health." This is the estimate of Prof. Thomas D. Wood, M.D., of Columbia University, as reported in a paper read by him at the National Council of Education at St. Louis in February, 1912, and printed by the U. S. Bureau of Education in Bulletin 1912, No. 24, Whole Number 496.

Upon what data Prof. Wood based his estimate I do not know; so far as I am aware his figures have not been challenged--certainly not as being excessive. My personal idea is that he was too conservative, and that deviations from the normal along the lines under discussion are far more prevalent than Dr. Wood's figures would indicate.

As long ago as March, 1907, Dr. Berry of Troy said in the *N. Y. Medical Journal:* "Anyone doubting the frequent occurrence of pronated foot, should stand in front of any public school at closing time and observe the feet of the children as they come out."

To see if any data could be obtained in New York State bearing on the prevalence of foot or ankle weakness, and spinal curvature, the State Commissioner of Health of New York, at my request, recently mailed to the health officers of the cities and largest villages of the State not including New York City, the following questions:

1. Does the physical examination of school children in your community include an examination for weak ankles, flat-foot and spinal curvature?

2. If so, what proportion of the school population is found to be afflicted with Weak ankles?........ Flat-foot?........ Spinal curvature?........

One city reported that examination was made for spinal curvature, but not for weak ankles or flat foot; no statistics were given. No other city reported that examinations were made for these types of physical defects, and in the great majority of cases, it was stated that there was no medical examination of school children.

I classed spinal curvature with weak ankles and flat foot because of the evident relation between the two. When the pupil is on his feet if one ankle is weaker than the other or one foot more pronated than the other, the ankle, knee and hip on that side will be lower than on the other. This means that the pelvis will be tilted, and the spine must necessarily be twisted, as roughly shown in the accompanying sketch. And note that the shoulder on the side of the weaker foot will be higher than the other, since the head must be carried over the center of gravity.

Faulty posture at desks may be a factor in producing spinal curvature, but a weak ankle is just as important a factor.

These physical defects are not peculiar to this country for the *Medical Officer* (21 December, 1912) reported that Dr. L. A. Hawkes, during medical inspections in London schools, "noted the frequency of flat feet in 1,581 children—770 boys and 811 girls, attending three schools of the poorer class." "The feet of 65.4 per cent. of boys and 64.9 of girls were affected to a greater or less degree. In 28.8 per cent. boys and 31.7 per cent. girls, the second stage of true flat foot had been reached."

His conclusions were:

1. That children of either sex are equally affected.

2. That the condition becomes more marked during periods of sudden increase in stature and weight.

3. That where malnutrition is general, a high percentage of deformity may be expected.

4. That where the surroundings are unfavorable, a slight and curable degree of deformity tends to pass into a condition which is permanent.

Supplementary to this report on London children of the poorer classes must be cited the figures given by Dr. Dukes, the examining physician of Rugby School, to the International Congress on School Hygiene held at Southampton, England. He stated that of 1,000 boys entering that school, 325 suffered from flat feet, and gave the following list of associated defects among the same 1,000 pupils: Lateral curvature, 445 cases; bow legs, 45; knock-knees, 526; and he added that "a curiously large number of boys—437—suffered from chilblains." To one who appreciates how pronation of the foot interferes with the circulation of of the blood, these cases of chilblains have an evident relation to the large number of flat-footed boys.

These boys examined by Dr. Dukes are at the other end of the social scale from the children considered in Dr. Hawkes' report. Dukes describes them "as a special class, strong and healthy, well bred, well fed and reared mainly in the country."

What is the cause of this prevalence of ankle and foot weakness and consequent spinal curvature?

Commenting on Dr. Hawkes' observations, Dr. James Kerr says, "The effects of malnutrition are intensified by mechanical causes as excessive standing, walking or weight carrying and by the wearing of heavy, rigid, improperly shaped boots." "The great toes of many children before the age of 14 are found to be already forced outwards from the middle line as a result of wearing improperly shaped boots; practically all these children are flat-footed." "In ordinary walking the child either shuffles along the street, or with an exaggerated move_ment at the knee joint, lifts the foot off the ground and carries it forward without any flexion at the ankle joint."

From the foregoing, therefore, we must conclude that foot strain in school children is more common than eye strain, and its effects are just as serious. It is caused by the muscular effort involved in balancing the weight of the body in a shoe the bottom of which is smaller than the bottom of the foot. If the foundation of a school building did not come out as far as the side walls, the pupils would be constantly menaced by the liability of the structure to collapse. A weak ankle or flat foot is a foot that has rolled inward over the shoe bottom because the strain on the muscles whose function it is to hold up the inner arched border of the foot, has caused them to lose their grip and to let the weight of the body rotate the foot inward and downward.

Foot strain is also a matter of vital moment to the school teacher.

If the foot rolls inward under the body weight, unnatural pressure is brought on the side of the great toe joint, and a "bunion" is produced.

If the toes are cramped in shoes, the muscles of the foot cannot act freely and strain is put upon the other muscles in the effort of walking.

If the shoes are made on a twisted last, walking is more of an effort than it should be. High-heeled shoes throw undue weight on the ball of the foot, and at the same time make the foundation upon which the weight of the body has to be borne less secure; each defect involves muscle strain in the endeavor to minimize its effects.

Rolling of the foot interferes with the circulation in the foot and leads to swelling, which fills up the hollow of the arch and adds to the appearance of flatness.

In addition to these primary effects, we have secondarily a natural diminution of the general efficiency of the sufferer from foot strain. If the feet are demanding more than their share of the body's output of nerve force or vital energy, some other part, or the body as a whole, must get less than its share. If there is any foot-suffering for the mind to dwell upon, the pupil or teacher, as the case may be, must give less attention to the lessons; and the demands of the modern school cur-riculum are surely exacting enough to call for all the vital energy pupil or teacher possesses.

For the prevention of, or relief from, weak ankles or flat foot, a shoe must be worn in which the body weight is properly distributed, and with a bottom so planned that the foot has no tendency to roll over it. It is not sufficient to give plenty of room for the toes; it should be a straight shoe to conform to the natural axis of the foot; a firm sole gives stability to the foundation without necessarily interfering with muscle action; but, above all, the rear half of the shoe must be right as this is the most important part since it receives the body weight; the shank between the sole and heel should be short and wide, the heel should be of moderate height, and the heel should be long and wide and so placed on the shoe as to meet the lines of weight thrust.

Too much care cannot be given to the correct shoeing of children, not only for the sake of conserving the health and happiness of the child, but also with an eye to the future that there may be no crippling of the feet in any degree to act as a bar to progress during the later productive years of life.

As to the spinal curvatures dependent upon foot weakness, if pronation of the foot is prevented by a shoe constructed along the lines indicated, the curvature will gradually correct itself. When the foundation is scientifically constructed, the superstructure is plumb.

THE EDUCATION OF CRIPPLED CHILDREN BELONGS TO THE PUBLIC SCHOOLS

BY

Evelyn M. Goldsmith

It has become evident that America's claim of pre-eminence as the land of equal opportunity for all is less true than of old and it seems unpardonable that we should have gone so far before giving to the *crippled child* equal chance with the normal child for mental and moral training. Philanthropy has for some time turned its attention upon the crippled child for the sake of alleviating his suffering. We stand now at the threshold of his intellectual training in connection with the public school system.

In the year 1832 a Munich citizen, Mr. Kurz, made the first attempt to help cripples who until then had mostly lived a life as beggars. Orthopedics accomplished so little then that there was not much prospect of assistance from surgical operations. For this reason Mr. Kurz sought to help them in another way. He formed the plan of giving the crippled children whom he could not cure at least a specialized good education and of offering them an opportunity to learn a trade so that they could earn a livelihood. Since then we find the greatest advance in the education of crippled children in connection with the regular system of public schools in Great Britain, especially in London, Liverpool, Glasgow and Edinburgh, where many public schools of a special character have been established. In Norway, Sweden and Denmark trade schools have been organized even for adults so that crippled men and women are taught to earn their own living and thus become independent. In America the work for crippled children was begun in New York in 1861 by Dr. Knight and his daughter, in their home, and out of this small contribution of school and hospital, there grew, ten years later a new hospital for the ruptured and crippled. This was the first institution in America to employ teachers for the crippled children. There have since been many private endeavors to care for crippled children but in 1906 the Board of Education of New York City opened classes for crippled children in the regular public schools. Previous to that Chicago had established a public school for crippled children. Until within a few years ago Chicago and New York were the only two cities in America that I know of, providing for special public education for crippled children. Since then Cleveland and Detroit have been added to the list. Think of it! With our wonderful system of free education, New York State has opened special classes for crippled children in one city—the City of New York. Where are the crippled and helpless children of Buffalo, Rochester, Syracuse? In private schools? Why? There are over seven thousand crippled children in the City of New York. At present, much less than one thousand are in special classes in regular school buildings in the public school system. Children from five to fifteen are now in attendance, coming at nine, bringing a noonday lunch (unless lunch is provided) and returning at two. The expense of transportation is borne by the Board of Education for some schools and strange as it may seem, private funds are still supporting stages for other public schools, but it is expected the Board of Education will soon pay for the transportation of all her crippled children, thus relieving them of the stamp of getting a public education through private funds. Eyes have been closed to the claims of those crippled children whose parents are too poor to send them to expensive private schools and too self-respecting to send them to charitable institutions. These cannot be ignored by the educational authorities. The educational provision made for these children means much for the future of a state of country. There is a great need to educate the public more about this class. But while it is good to train them, it is still better to train them from becoming cripples and this can be done to a certain extent by medical inspection which would detect at an early stage the tuberculosis of the joints which causes most of the distorted limbs and backs, besides many slight curvatures which could be easily corrected. These unfortunates have been looked upon as harmless but the danger has been greater because they have been unnoticed. Here is a legal point: Every child is to be provided with an education. There must be a nearer approach to equality of opportunity. Philanthropy was the measure to come to the front and make provisions. For, generally speaking, the crippled child cannot cope with the vitality of the normal child, and must have special provisions. The deficient, blind, and deaf were all provided with special classes long before the education of crippled children began. It is right that we should give due credit to the philanthropic men and women who are making so determined an effort to uplift the human race—to help the crippled children, and here has been the opportunity for those who wished to be of service to humanity. It rests solely with us whether we will take advantage of these chances to help those in need of aid or turn our backs upon their necessities, and allow charity to care for these unfortunates. Dr. Virgil Gibney, speaking of cripples, says: "Certain deformities formerly looked upon with hope but little removed from despair have now come within domain of cure and restoration to perfect function of the joint." What right have we to allow a child to be incapacitated or hampered in bearing his burdens, if by any effort, any sacrifice on our part, if we can prevent it? Perhaps we are fortunate in this country that our main interest has been to cure them but now we must provide for their education and self-support. The majority of the afflicted belong to the wage-earning class with small means to secure protection and relief. Fresh air and sunlight, the great pre. ventations and curatives, are little known to them. Their life is spent behind hospital walls or in crowded tenements. Nine years ago the Driving Association was started, which gives to these helpless ones a chance for an outing in a stage once a week or so that they may get a glimpse of the outside world. Their first report starts as follows: "I visited the Hospital for Ruptured and Crippled Children for the purpose of playing with the children. It was a beautiful day and as I was leaving the hospital, one of the cripples said: 'Oh! Miss Jenny, please take me out to see the sunshine!' Upon inquiring I found that the child had not been out of the hospital since she entered there many months before, although she was up and about on her crutches and needed fresh air as much as medical treatment. I begged the superintendent to permit me to take the child driving, but he said that no exceptions could be made among the children. But he laughed and said: 'You may take the whole hospital out if you wish.' After some consulta- tion as to ways and means with financial support, I decided to take him at his word and from that day the first stage to take crippled children to parks was started. Gradually the doctors and ministers of the city noticed and heard of these stages and I was swamped with begging letters to make it a permanent thing. Mothers of poor little cripples in tenements noticing the stages, begged me to call for their little ones. On investigation I found many cases where fresh air was the crying need. I discovered cripples who had not been outside their four walls in five, six and eight years. Simply because they were too heavy to be carried any distance. I discovered little children who were resigning themselves to a life of such monotony and hopelessness as we, who do not know what it means to feel no difference between night and day, and day and night, for weeks and months and years, cannot realize. In short the need for stages to take crippled children of the tenements into the air and give them the change of *scene* and thought so necessary to their physical well being, grew so great that I could not cope alone with the question longer, and after interesting some great philanthropists, with their aid and support, the Crippled Children's Driving Fund was founded in August, 1904. Two years later these children were trans- ported to school, the brightest spot to come into their lives. A place to find employment, resources for hands and mind, a place to restore him to active life, even if unable to use the rest of his body. Strange as it may seem, in many cases when a child is helpless, affection dies and it is certainly a sad condition of affairs that often each child means to its parents only future support. The public needs more light. We need research and publicity. If these children are left alone they lose ambition, nerve, vigor, will power, for nothing paralyzes effort, saps courage, depresses and disheartens, as much as when we are held in low esteem by our fellows. It was interesting in the early days of those stage rides, to see how necessary it was to enlarge the experiences of these children. In the rides to the park I found all new children without an exception calling the big flatiron building of New York and all large buildings hospitals, later some were pointed out as schools. The maids tending door at the houses on Fifth Avenue, New York, wearing caps and aprons were recognized by the children as nurses, and later I would hear, 'Oh, there's a doctor, and there's another doctor.' This led me to see how necessary it was to enlarge the experiences of these children and replace the sad life of the hospital. There are many examples I might quote illustrating how life at school was their only pleasure, for the family quarrels added to the wretchedness of their lives. One little boy of seven, with a paralyzed side and arm, I shall never forget. When returning home he lived only for school time of the next day for his home was very desolate. After one of the fights between his parents, when he was awake all night, he came to school and said: 'My father ran away. My moder watch for him and a policeman find him. My moder cry. "You cry home?" he said. 'My moder want to go back to Europe. I don't want, I want to go to school.' That was the last I have heard from that child. They all disappeared. The school then is the 'Door of Hope.' Here, then, his environment takes on a new meaning. Life and joy are his. A specially happy frame of mind is developed. In considering the school management of crippled children it is at once apparent that one has to deal with a very mixed group, made up of those who are disabled from malformation, injury, overweighting, paralysis, bone or joint disease and other causes. The disease may be active, progressing, convalescent, latent or cured. It is clear that so varied a group must be handled carefully and individually under expert direction. These children require special consideration in the matter of transportation—fresh air, nourishment, furniture, occupation, exercise, rest, recreation, fatigue and of injury to diseased parts. A question arises, whether a crippled child should be assigned to a regular class. Every child capable of attending school and able to go to a regular class should do so, but all the others must of necessity have special provisions. It is most important that the teacher should know the nature of each child's affection and whether it is cured, convalescent or active. In the education of crippled children three problems present themselves. The first is a physical one. Here the teacher and surgeon join hands.''

The second essential is to present to the child such instruction as is especially adapted to the child's intelligence.

The third essential: Individual capacity should be noticed and developed along special fitness, with some occupation for self-support. It is necessary in selection of rooms to have them on the ground floor. They should admit sunshine, for sunshine is most important to the health of these children. They should be so constructed with many windows to allow plenty of fresh air, outdoor ventilation even in zero weather, but sufficient heat is also necessary to warm the floor and desks and iron braces worn by the children. The temperature should not be lower than sixty-six, and sixty-eight is considered very comfortable, for the circulation of the children (as a rule) is very poor and I would not encourage physical discomforture from a lower temperature than fifty-five degrees, such as is desired in some schools where cold extremities is the result and no extra clothing is worn. It is a noteworthy fact, with open windows and warm floors I can report an absence of colds. So much for fresh air. As to the equipment. The seats and desks can be secured specially constructed but most important is the need for special adjustment, with foot-stools for those who cannot touch the floor. In some cases rolling-chairs may seem desirable. Couches for resting are indispensable, for these children are easily fatigued and they ought to be free to lie down whenever they feel tired. Sand boxes invite relaxation besides furnishing an attracting method of teaching certain subjects such as geography and affording a standing position which is very restful for some cases. Rooms should be made specially attractive, decorations of plants, flowers, pictures, fish, etc., for these appeal very much to the lonely heart. An important factor in the cure of crippled children is wholesome food and plenty of it. Lack of nourishment, says a noted authority, is the cause of half these ills of crippled children, therefore it is of vital importance that we serve milk at recess and hot lunches at noon in the public schools. I can report marked improvement mentally as well as physically, from this extra nourishment. The children bring two cents in payment, but if in some cases the child is unable to pay, he is never neglected, but he helps to serve and thus earns his food in that way. I have found this past summer that with plenty of fresh air, these children have immense appetites and it is not uncommon to find a gain of from five to eight pounds in one week. Sleeping in unventilated rooms at home, the appetite is very different from what it is after a night spent under healthy conditions. We need to teach hygienic habits more and more. One boy who spent a few weeks at the seashore returned to his crowded district but he could not sleep after being accustomed to the free air of the country. The nurse of one of our well known hospitals told me recently

that this boy of ten urged his parents to allow him to sleep in the yard
and now he gets sufficient rest and fresh air. We need to inculcate
another most important habit in crippled children especially, if not in
all children. They do not get sufficient sleep. At the *Seaside Home for
Crippled Children*, where we take the crippled children during the
summer months, we have had much unhappiness in urging children of
ten, twelve and younger to retire early. From investigations following
I have found these school children even in the winter retire at midnight.
Here, it seems to me, is a chance for the teacher to enlighten parents to
the need of sufficient rest and sleep for all children. We need specially
trained teachers, for with the teacher we must depend not so much on
her intellectual training and learning, but on her tact, ingenuity, ability
to make not so much on strict rule as on insight, sympathy, point of
view. The work of crippled children must be very ungraded. There
may be an overgrown boy or girl who through illness has been unable
to attend school but he may make rapid progress, there may be a child
backward in one or two studies, another child, exceptionally bright, who
needs to be kept back from using too much vitality, still another pupil's
temperament may make it impossible for him to work in a class, because
of great nervousness. These cases and many more need individual
help adjustment and supervision, and all these pupils need special
programs, with few hours and short periods, with lessons adjusted to
the best working hours. Crippled children tire easily mentally and
physically unless they have frequent changes in activity. "Some schools
are still quite largely a place of sitting still in a seat." No child crippled
or normal should sit still longer than twenty minutes. They need
freedom of movement. The teacher should have a flexible course of
study with freedom to promote by subjects rather than by grades, and
her methods and materials should be adapted to their effect upon the
health of her pupils. Special emphasis should be on equipment for
self-support, but home work and written tests are both injurious to
health and should be considered as relics of the past. Outdoor playgrounds for recess are indispensable to the health of a crippled child.
He needs play as much from the mental and moral standpoint as from
the physical. The outlook on life of these unfortunate children is dark,
he needs a happy attitude of mind, which oftentimes is not possible
without an influence brought to bear upon him and many of these
children are rendered more unhappy and helpless than need be through
lack of exercise and free play. There should be greater opportunity
given these children for self-activity. Some of these children cannot be
very active and should play quiet games, but when left alone they create
their own games such as driver or conductor which makes him take
part in the story without being set aside and left alone to become con-

scious of his ailment. These playgrounds need supervision as morality, health, fatigue, etc., but *not* only to check spontaneous activity, only to control it. The main idea to keep in mind is to provide a natural, sane, wholesome life, so that these children who have spent so many hours in a hospital may get something of the joy of living—life, freedom, joy and hope.

"What he needs is plenty of fresh air in his lungs, not a quantity of violent exercises that leaves him weak." Formal gymnastics are not recreative in a manner commonly supposed. The only true recreation comes from entire relaxation and spontaneous play and they have no place in the public school, they belong to the doctors and the clinics. Activities out of doors must be natural, satisfying play instincts which benefits faculties and powers, arouses interest and enthusiasm. Speak. ing of the tuberculosis cripples Dr. Henry Ling Taylor says in his article on "Physical Training in Schools For Cripples": "Their activities and interests should be such as to divert and occupy their minds and stimulate their interest rather than call for any great amount of bodily activity," and he adds, "It should be remembered that formal gymnastics rank with mathematics among the most fatiguing of all forms of in. struction, that formal gymnastics in physical education correspond to drugs in medicine, both are rapidly losing their importance." And, con. tinues Dr. Taylor, in the Annual Report of 1909, the Director of Physical Training of New York Public Schools, we read these somewhat surprising statements:

"Even children with bone tuberculosis play games vigorously without harm when left to themselves. I have repeatedly seen children from one year to five years old strapped to their spinal splint and jury-mast wriggle out of their cots and disport themselves upon their backs and without harm. Neuro-muscular education by controlled and definite exercises, similar to those in our required course of study are more needed by these children with defective neuro-muscular equipment than by normal children and will be prescribed whenever necessary." In reply Dr. Taylor writes: "Such observations and ideals differ so much from standard orthopedic opinion as to justify this discussion." The Board of Education should be made acquainted with prevailing orthopedic opinion in these matters. From the standpoint of the orthopedic surgeon the following conclusions may be drawn:

1. Children should be admitted to classes for crippled children, physician's certificate to be renewed each year.

2. Formal or class gymnastics—running, jumping, long standing and rough and strenuous games should be eliminated.

3. There should be close coöperation between educator and the orthopedic authorities.

4. The physical activities of each child should be regulated by the orthopedic surgeon in charge of the case.

In June, 1911, the first class of crippled children to graduate in a public school in New York City received their diplomas. There had been individual cases of cripples who had completed the course, but not a class. Since then more classes have followed. Many of these pupils are now continuing in the High Schools of the city, others were obliged to go to work to help support themselves and their parents. As far as scholarship is concerned the children have kept in the front ranks of their classes, but the physical strain has proved too much for many of them and they are dropping by the wayside. When a child secures knowledge at the price of health, he pays more than it is worth to him. In studying conditions these conclusions have been reached. In the High Schools these children are in classes with normal children. No special provisions for transportation, seating or rest periods prevail. In the snowing weather it is dangerous for these disabled children to get about on icy sidewalks and cars. Change of classes every period some two or three flights of stairs apart,—amid this hurry and flurry up and down the stairs has played havoc with limbs and health. I have urged the necessity for special conditions in the High Schools such as exist in the elementary schools and it is hoped the Board of Education will soon feel justified in extending this work. As to their future occupations; in studying trade life in Europe, especially in Norway, and Sweden and Denmark, where they have worked out the trades with wonderful results, I have found very little to help the solution in this country, for America has her own problems. Supply and demand are the first requirements; before we consider the child, and as Professor Dewey says: "The child is the starting-point, the center, and the end." His special attitude, his individual capacity and interests must be noted all along the line. Love of one's work and happiness is the ground work for success, and should be the keynote of work for crippled children. I haven't the time to relate the unhappiness I have found among cripples who have been obliged to sit at embroidery all day, every day, year in and year out. One child was so tired of making initials that she never wanted to see another letter. Many feel this monotony after a few years at embroidery. We have classed the children like so many sheep. We have thought of basketry for the boys and embroidery for the girls (but these are weary ways to spend one's days and lead to nowhere). We are still in the experimental state, but a few trades I wish to suggest which I have found profitable as to health and finances. At the Seaside Home for Crippled Children where we have many of the High School children taking salt baths and gaining health and strength, we have started two trades: manicuring for the girls and photography for the boys. The out-of-door porches furnishes a suitable manicure parlor and last summer four graduates began their future career. At the end of the summer one girl was obliged to work and we secured a position for her in Gimbel Brothers, which she has to-day, earning fifteen dollars and more weekly. Of the others one was not strong enough for High School but the other two entered. In a few months one left and not long afterwards the other, both being obliged to leave on account of too much climbing of stairs. This summer three have resumed work, the fourth continuing with her position. In autumn we hope to open a shop especially for these girls. The boys have fitted up a photog. rapher's shop. They take pictures, but most of their business consists of developing and printing. Both are High School students; one is strong enough to continue his studies next year; the other will attend a trade school, studying mechanical drawing. In a short time it is expected these boys will have a shop in the city if it seems profitable. One boy sells papers for a few hours at the Long Island Station and another has a peanut stand, thus enabling them to pay car far to school next winter. A very noted girl student who has won many prize essays has been obliged to give up her second year in High School and is now our private secretary, doing stenography and typewriting, and we expect to secure a similar position for her next winter. Stenography and typewriting have been followed by many of these children with great success. When the education of these children nears completion in the public schools (and every child should continue as long as seems advisable) they should be carefully noted. There are many trades that might be developed such as box furniture and different varies of carpentry work. Simple sewing (specialization in aprons, kimonas, children's rompers) and plumbing may be profitable. Printing offers an excellent field and has proven of great success in Boston's private schools. Jewelry designing, various occupations of drawing and telephone operator may prove suitable.

In conclusion I would say: Every child is entitled to all the education he is capable of receiving and the state is under obligation to give it. Philanthropy may have paved the way for the education of crippled children but the state must follow it up. The future of this country is more than ever in the hands of the public schools. My plea to the members of this Congress is that they give me their influence to urge school authorities to become awakened to the need of special provision in the public schools for the education of crippled children. Every child has the right to be happy, self-respecting and self-supporting. Will you, the members of this Congress, assist him to be so?

Jacob Riis says: "It is not the things we have done here but the things we have left undone—that will give us the bitter heartaches at the setting of the sun."

WHAT CAN BE DONE TO DIMINISH THE NECESSITY FOR SPECIAL PROVISION FOR CRIPPLED CHILDREN?

BY

HILLS COLE

What proportion of the school population of this country, or of the countries represented in this Congress is made up of children wearing braces for deformities of the spines or limbs? I cannot answer this question because, so far as I am aware, there are no statistics that are any ways near inclusive. A recent attempt to get the figures for the cities and larger villages of New York State (exclusive of the Metropolis) gave a return of 102 cases—72 deformities of the limbs, 30 spinal cases—from 10 cities; but it was indicated that even in these 10 cities the accuracy of the statistics could not be vouched for, and reports received from other cities showed that no enumeration of these cases was made.

Obviously, in none of these places was any special provision made for these crippled children, either by way of free transportation by special conveyance between home and school or of special classes or schools.

In a few of the largest cities of the country, including New York, such special arrangements exist for the benefit of this unfortunate part of the school population.

The recent epidemics of poliomyelitis (the so-called infantile paralysis) make this question of crippled school children of interest at this time, since the after-effects of this malady are its most distressing feature.

It needs no second thought to acquiesce in the proposition that the carrying around of a metal brace from the foot to the knee or hip is a severe handicap to any child from the standpoint of encumbrance and weight alone; it must interfere with the child's general vitality, and what is of special consideration in this Congress, his efficiency as a pupil.

I also take it for granted that little argument will be needed to persuade the average unprejudiced person that so long as a brace is worn it acts as a substitute for muscular action so that there is no encouragement for the development of whatever power may be left in the muscles. Moreover, the bands and straps by which the brace is fastened to the limb must of necessity lead to pressure atrophy wherever applied.

The question is, can the cripple get along without a brace? Is it not a necessary evil?

I am sure I can' say that the brace can be dispensed with to the advantage of the little patient.

In the first place we must try to prevent any deformity.

Bear in mind that poliomyelitis does not cause deformity, it causes muscle weakness or paralysis. The deformity is secondary to this— the result of applying weight or pressure upon parts which no longer have the necessary amount of muscular resistance.

While the little patient is in bed, therefore, the limbs should be kept in a natural position—sand bags, etc, being used, if necessary—and the weight of the bed clothing should be kept off the affected limbs.

Passive motion should be instituted as early as possible to stimulate free circulation and to prevent the formation of adhesions between the muscles. Electrical stimulation of the muscles aids recovery of power, but is an unsafe agent except in the hands of one well acquainted with the principles of electro-physics, electro-physiology and the anatomy of the part to be treated.

Graded muscular exercises have their place in the development of muscle-power.

In the sitting posture, the seat should be of such height as to allow the feet to rest flat upon the ground, or there should be a footstool just high enough to allow the feet to rest on a level plane, so that the weight of the feet shall not fall on the weakened leg muscles.

The important point, however, upon which I wish to dwell is the prevention of deformity following paralysis after the child begins to put weight upon the limb. The affected muscles being no longer equal to the task of maintaining the equilibrium of the foot when the body weight rests upon it, there will be rotation of the foot on its long axis toward the weak side. If the muscles holding up the inner border of the foot are affected, the foot will roll to the inside; if the muscles on the outer side of the leg are affected, the foot will roll outwards. To prevent this rotation, the logical thing to do is to provide a base so constructed as to receive the weight-thrust; in other words, the bottom of the shoe, particularly the back half which receives the weight-thrust from the leg, must be widened inward or outward to such a degree as to overcome the tendency to rotation. It is the bottom of the shoe which controls the position of the foot which rests upon it, just as the foundations of a building govern its stability.

Do not thicken the sole on the weaker side. Nothing is gained if the base is wide enough; if the base is not wide enough, the foot will override the shoe-bottom in spite of the extra thickening. And on general principles the bottom of the foot should rest on a level plane to allow of the maximum of motion at the ankle joint.'

Nothing is gained by stiffening the side of the shoe, for once more it is the bottom of the shoe that controls the position of the foot; and a stiffened shoe upper interferes with ankle motion.

Provided with properly constructed shoes from the start, there is no call for braces or operations.

If deformity exists and braces are now being worn, I believe that it may be stated as a general proposition that the braces may be discarded and their place taken by suitably constructed shoes to the great advantage of the wearer, who will be relieved of the incubus of carrying around the brace, while at the same time, the muscles will be encouraged to develop the utmost of their power which is far greater than is ordinarily imagined. If we give nature a fair show, it is surprising what she can do; and I have seen many a limb which has been encased in a brace for many years converted into a very useful member when handled along the lines indicated in this paper.

I am convinced, therefore, that some of the money now being spent for special classes or transportation of crippled school children can be more usefully employed elsewhere, and the same holds true with regard to a good deal of the public and charitable funds now being used to provide braces and similar apparatus for crippled children.

SESSION TWENTY-EIGHT

Room A.   Friday, August 29th, 9:00 A.M.

THE CONSERVATION OF VISION

Organized with the Assistance of the New York Committee
for the Prevention of Blindness and the American
Association for the Conservation of Vision

MYLES STANDISH, M.D., *Chairman*

F. PARK LEWIS, M.D., Buffalo, N. Y., *Vice-Chairman*

Program of Session Twenty-Eight

F. PARK LEWIS, M.D., President of the American Association for the
Conservation of Vision, Buffalo, N. Y. "Sight Saving and
Brain Building."

FRANZ KRUSIUS, Prof. Dr., Dozent für Augenheilkunde, Berlin. "Beziehungen Zwischen Schule und Auge."

WILLIAM MARTIN RICHARDS, M.D., A.B., New York City. "Saving
the Backward School Child."

LEWIS C. WESSELS, M.D., Bureau of Health Ophthalmologist, Philadelphia, Pa. "Defective Vision in School Children from an
Economic Standpoint."

CLARKE FULKERSON, M.D., Medical Inspector of Schools, Kalamazoo,
Mich. "Preliminary Report of the Ocular Defects of School
Children Two or More Years Below Grade."

ALEXANDER RANDALL, M.D., Professor of Otology, University of Pennsylvania; Ear Surgeon to University and Children's Hospital,
Philadelphia. "The Value of Testing the Vision of School
Children and the Need of Accurate Test Cards."

ANNA W. WILLIAMS, M.D., Assistant Director Division of Laboratories,
Board of Health, New York City. "Prevalence of Trachoma
in New York City Public Schools."

ANNA I. VON SHOLLY, M.D., Board of Health, New York City. "Ophthalmia Schools for the Prevention of Trachoma and Other Infectious Eye Diseases."

GERTRUDE E. BINGHAM, Inspector of Classes for the Blind, Department of Education, New York City. "The Preservation of the Eyesight of School Children."

Papers Presented in Absentia in Session Twenty-Eight
(Read by Title)

J. HOLBROOK SHAW, M.D., School Physician, Plymouth, Mass. "Some Important Ocular Conditions Found in Backward Children, With a Report of Cases."

OTTO GRENNESS, M.D., Christiana, Norway. "Progress in School Writing in Norway."

SIGHT SAVING AND BRAIN BUILDING

BY

F. PARK LEWIS

It is an accepted fact recognized by ophthalmologists everywhere that changes occur in the eyes of children during the period of their school life, of which the most prominent symptom is a steadily progressive development of nearsight. As definitely formulated by the late Professor Dufour:

1. In all schools the number of short-sighted pupils increases from class to class.

2. The average degree of short-sightedness increased from class to class.

3. The number of short-sighted pupils increases with the increase in the school demands.

This form of myopia is not innocuous, but is dependent upon a relaxation of the tissues which give form to the eye ball resulting in a gradual stretching of the globe itself.

In its malignant form, which is fortunately rare, this ectasia, or giving away of the supporting fibres may become so extreme as to loosen the connection between the retina and its underlying tissues so that a slight shock such as a mis-step, or a fall may cause the actual detachment of the retina with consequent blindness. In its milder forms there is a constant passive congestion of the vessels at the posterior pole of the globe, predisposing to other destructive changes. It is so common that one person in four, who is of an age to graduate from the high school, has suffered from this structural alteration in the tissues of his eye.

This condition is not dependent upon constitutional weakness. It frequently appears in those who enjoy most rugged health. Neither is it due to bad sanitary conditions. It is not found more commonly among the poor than among the children of the rich, nor more frequently among the unclean and poorly nourished than among those whose every want is most abundantly supplied.

It is *not*, as has been assumed, merely an abnormal phase of development which is fortuitous in its manifestations, nor will a given proportion of all school children of necessity become near-sighted under any circumstances. It is not due in any large degree in its inception at least, to conditions external to the child, because among those living and working at the same tasks and with like environment some will acquire nearsight while others will escape.

It is, on the other hand, a logical sequence of conditions which may be recognized and controlled. Its beginnings are, primarily at least, due to congenital astigmatism and the consequent strain upon the accommodation of the eye in the effort to see. Its development is still further encouraged by the hours of constant daily application in reading and writing at that period in life when the tissues are plastic and easily moulded.

The first of the two most obvious and logical remedies is to relieve the excessive focal strain of the astigmatism or other abnormal refractive condition through its correction by suitable glasses. This, if it were done with great precision and accuracy, would probably suffice to stay the progress of the trouble, but the stretching having once begun, the tissues that hold the eye ball lose their power of resistance and they are no longer able to withstand the pressure to which a normal eye might safely be subjected.

It is of essential importance, in the second place, therefore, that with those in whom this process of giving away of the foundation fibres has begun the school curriculum should be so modified, or the studies should be so conducted, that close work on books or with the pencil or pen, should be relinquished or reduced to such limited references as would seem to be absolutely necessary. All of this almost goes without saying.

It is the purpose of this paper, therefore, furthermore, briefly to show that eye strain when continued at this period of life, not only affects the integrity of the eye structures, but it often causes such confusion and so seriously interferes with the mental processes of the child as to impede his thinking and to give an unwarranted reputation for dullness or even weak-mindedness. It is, moreover, physiologically and anatomically true that book study, or the use of the printed page, is not the most direct method of reaching the child's intelligence, and while books are necessary and must be used they have been given an unwarrantable importance in our educational system.

As the brain is developed the power of clear logical thinking is increased. Its more essential structures, the terminal neurons, are increased in size and complexity, which means increased functional activity, by the larger use of the more concrete measures in the training of the special senses.

It is further urged that it should be the imperative duty of those having to do with children during these growing years to recognize these structural changes when they begin, to correct existing defects when they are of a nature to tax the accommodative effort by rightly chosen correcting glasses, and in all initial cases to provide special training for the groups of children thus affected, and to so arrange the curriculum that the same work demanded by the course in which they find themselves can be accomplished with little or no use of books and a limited employment of the pencil or pen, or other method requiring excessive effort on the part of the eyes. That this is possible the best students of pedagogy are agreed and the achievements of the blind have proven.

In order that the thought upon which this paper is based may be made clear it is necessary to understand that there are two conditions having the common symptom of near-sight but which are essentially different. The normal eye is that in which parallel rays of light are brought to a focus on the retina without effort on the part of the muscles used in accommodation. The hypermetropic eye is one that is organically too shallow. The myopic eye is too deep. These are all congenital and the shape of the eye, as has been shown by careful measure. ments of the cranial bones, is determined by the shape of the skull, and this in turn is inherited from our ancestors. None of these eyes are because of their shape therefore diseased. The eyes of almost all infants are at first of the shallow or hypermetropic form. These pass, as Risley has aptly put it, through the turnstile of astigmatism into myopia. But this form of myopia is not a mere deformity but it is a pathological change. Alterations may be expected, not only in the posterior pole of the eye but even in the anterior pole, altering the angle and the degree of the corneal astigmatism.

The corneal astigmatism, it will be understood, is an inequality in the corneal curves so that one meridion whichever it may be, has a different radius from that to which is opposed. In order to understand how this influences the internal structures of the eye it will be necessary to bear in mind the attachments of the ciliary muscles.

The lens which it governs is directly back of the pupil. The ciliary muscles is inserted in the sclera behind and at the junction of the cornea in front. Every unsuccessful effort to adjust the focus so that sight may be more clear gives rise to a tugging at this sensative portion of the eye ball. This in time excites congestion, later a passive inflammation of the vascular coat within the eye. The scleral fibres, whose nutrition has in that way been interrupted begins to stretch and the first irreparable damage has been done. If this is continued with the added work of near study, like a rubber balloon with the pressure applied from within, it continues to give away as long as the cause of the mischief is kept up.

With a full recognition of the conditions which must inevitably develop, in such eyes as these, the provisions which are made in our schools, public and private, are precisely the same for all. The same curriculum, the same long hours of continuous study, and the same proportion of defective eyes. As the children grown more near-sighted they may be directed to get glasses which will enable them to see, or they may have their positions changed so that they are brought nearer to the blackboard, but their near work on books and in writing is not stopped as it should be. It may be urged that that would be impracticable but Rousseau, with a clear sense of pedagogic values, was recognizing a right principle when he wrote, more than a hundred years ago: "The child who reads does not think; he does nothing but read, he gets no instruction, he learns words."

Of course it will be evident that to the student the only method possible for him to get the ideas of others is in large measures, through the books which are accessible to him, but in the relation of master and pupils it is quite another matter. The letters of the alphabet are merely arbitrary smybols used to express in their combinations words and sentences. They are by no means as definitely expressive of the thing represented as would be the crudest picture of it. The rough sketch made by our aboriginal Indian of his canoe, or of his wigwam, would more immediately and promptly convey his thought than would the spelling of the words in the letters of our latin alphabet, and the grouping of these words into phrases and sentences. When those cabalistic signs have been assembled the combination has to be interpreted before the thought is understood. In order therefore to grasp the idea conveyed under the crytogram of printed words two mental efforts must be made. First that to see and to synthesize the letters and then to interpret the visualized words into the things which they represent. In doing this we are teaching the reader to get at the thought in a roundabout way. To understand what the types mean, we must first visualize that for which they stand, and this is a feeble process compared with that which comes from the direct sight of the thing itself.

The manner in which the brain cells are made to grow is by the impressions that are carried to them through the medium of our senses. We have a definite illustration of this in the arousing to activity of a dull sighted or amblyopic eye that has never been effectually used. This is found in the strabismic or squinting eye which has turned in towards the nose in the earlier years of life, and which, from non-use, has never developed the clear vision of its fellow. When both eyes are made to work together the defective nerve cells are energized and slowly sight develops in what would otherwise have always remained a defective eye. When the eyes are focally alike and work in harmony the impressions formed on the retina of each are carried through the optic nerve to the back of the brain where they merge like the picture in a stereoscope. If for any reason one eye is focally different from the other or if it be directed at a different angle the two impressions do not blend or merge but one is suppressed. The sense resulting of a blur, the one impression just failing to unite with the other into a clearly cut and definite picture gives rise to a sense of confusion which make it so difficult as to be almost impossible to follow any line of consecutive thought. The sense of mental confusion resulting, especially in those who are particularly sensitive is likely to be manifested by extreme reserve and the slowness in fixing the thought is often unwarrantably assumed to be due to stu. pidity or mental deficiency.

It is amazing how rapidly and surely the mind responds when the embarrassment of confused sight has been relieved. By using the eye, by making it see, by allowing the light to pass through the terminal rods and cones of the retina to the corresponding neurons in the brain where they are intelligently recognized the visual area of the brain is energized and in its use it becomes the more able to be efficiently used. As our consciousness of the external world is possible only through our special senses so through these media is the development of the brain and thereby its direct education the more quickly and effectually carried on. In order that my meaning may be the more freely under. stood let us consider for a moment the manner in which the brain does its work.

When all of the terminal filaments of the sensory and motor nerves are gathered together as they enter and leave the brain form a bundle of miscropic threads constituting the special cord and occupying a space no greater in diameter than the little finger. This thin cord carries fibres, which terminate in the neurons or nerve endings, and which spread out in a thin layer forming the surface of the brain. The great mass of the brain substances is made up of association fibres which are arranged in bundles and which bring into active relationship one part of this cortical surface with another. The manner in which the brain is developed may be more clearly understood by considering the way in which we become conscious of any object or of any internal sensation. Let us imagine the process which would take place in the brain of a child to whom any object, an orange for example, was presented for the first time.

Every impression comes as a new one. The eyes are open but the images which have been carried to them have been vague and indistinct. They have not been differentiated. The sound of voices comes as a murmur, a noise, possibly broken by variations in intensity, as from the crash of a falling body, or the jangling of a bell, but the nicer discriminations of sound, which may be developed with increasing refinement until the most exact harmonies or the least discordant note is at once recognized, have not yet begun. The first impression conveyed to the eyes of the child will be that of color. He will make the distinction between light and darkness. The lighted lamp will be for him, as the sunshine. When the orange is brought in his range of sight, its brilliant

salient color will attract his notice and he becomes conscious of a blotch
of color, like the sunshine or the lamp light which he has already seen,
and this, in the sight center situated at the back of his brain, will come
a flood of nervous energy, excited by the vibrations in the ether, and the
neurons of the terminal nerve endings will respond with a quickened
capacity to apprehend, to appreciate this same phenomenon when it
again occurs. It will be the beginning of those finer color distinctions
that are to come later and which are to constitute the education of his
color sense, which are to enable him to understand, to appreciate and
to feel the beauties of the color harmonies of the world in which he
lives. Then gradually this splotch of color, which is otherwise so meaningless, will take on form and he will realize that it is limited by a circle,
and in gaining this knowledge a new group of cells will be energized,·
and another essential fact in relation to his surroundings will have
been achieved. Now comes to him the realization of a new and a more
wonderful fact, *the circle has depth*, and here an enormous advance has
been made. He has been introduced into three dimensional space.
Both sides of his brain are working synchronously. He has binocular
vision. The image which has been made upon the retina of each eye
has been carried to corresponding parts of the brain, overlapping and
blending as in a stereoscope. A multitude of new impressions have
been aroused, suggestions of the outer world, indeed of the universe,
have been conveyed to him. His logical faculties have been aroused,
and without either knowing or realizing it he has done the most important
thing in the world. *He has begun to think.* The thought which he is
unable to express, has aroused his will, has excited his desire, has tempted
him to experiment. He timidly and tentatively reaches out his hand
and touches the thing that he has seen and in realizing the consciousness
of its presence he has *done* the most wonderful thing in the world. He
has established the existence of a problem, the solution of which has
been the basis of our most profound philosophies, from Plato to Kant.
He has located himself in space. He has begun to find himself. He has
commenced his education. He learns to differentiate between soft and
hard, between rough and smooth, between elevations and depressions,
between those things which oppose and those which attract. With
each new idea has come a new flood of energy, sweeping through his
brain and making the pathway easier for those which are to follow.
The skin of the orange is broken and the fragrance of the volatile oil
is carried to his nose. It brings an odor like nothing else in the world,
yet it is one of hundreds of perfumes and scents and smells that he
is to learn to recognize and to differentiate from all others, and with
sensation comes thought, with thought suggestion, and with suggestion

will, and the motor influences are aroused which are to govern this will during all of his life have been established.

The orange drops from the baby hands and falls with a dull thump to the floor. It gives a sound that to the trained ear conveys intelligence of the nature of the thing itself. It is at once evident that that which has fallen is not metallic; it has not the flat sound of a closed book nor the overtones of a hollow wooden box. It is one of a thousand possible sounds and yet it carries a descriptive story to the listening ear and the trained brain. Finally the fruit is retrieved, the skin is removed, the segments are broken apart, and everyone of these movements with the little sounds connected with them are educative. When at last a portion of the fruit is conveyed to the mouth they arouse, who can say how many groups of motor influences, the whole body is moving, the neck bends, the arms, the wrist, the fingers, each with its separate centers in the brain represented by neurons, almost without number. When the segment is placed in the mouth the muscles of the lips, the tongue, the jaws, the cheeks, all are dominated by impulses which are sent out from the brain, and finally when the juice of the fruit is tasted and this wonderful complex of sensations has been united into a conception if the entire object the whole brain has been excited into activity from front to back and from side to side giving instructions in coordination, in will, in logic, and perhaps in ethics. Each group of nerve centers has been energized in receiving impressions or in sending out commands is being educated in the only way in which it can be educated to perform the work which it is ultimately destined to do.

It is not alone while the object is within the range of our senses that these images are established. As the awakening of the brain centers, by impulses carried from the outer world to them through the special senses, has excited thought, so the suggestion of these same images when conveyed by another object which recalls them will rearouse them to activity, vividly when the relation of the impression to the original sensation is intimate as in a picture of it, and more freely when it is remote as when the symbols of printed letters and words are employed to describe it.

We know of the outer world only through our contact with it. From the facts thus learned we deduce all of our conclusions as to good and bad, of right and wrong, of cause and effect. Thus the value of such training as a moral force has been realized by all of the great teachers from Froebel to Montessori, from Rosseau to Pestalozzi. A recognition of the value of pragmatic methods is already changing the system in our schools by the wider introduction of manual and industrial training.

It is compelling our medical colleges to supplement their didactic teaching by actual hospital experience. It is the advocacy of the principle of thinking through doing. It is not urged here with the hope of changing existing pedagogic methods but in order to justify the proposition that these measures which hurt the body are not good for the mind, but that conversely through the most efficient hygiene we obtain the most moral, stable and satisfactory development of the brain and the most effective training of the mind. The fundamental laws of development cannot be in conflict. There must be harmonious and mutually supplemental. Any method which destroys an organ or an organism in the process of developing it must be based upon a fallacious principle.

We are destroying the eyes of a large number of our school children by the burden of continuous near work to which they are subjected. It is evident that on the first appearance of beginning short sight these children should be segregated from the others in special classes in which they are taught without books. It has been the intent of this paper to show that measures might be employed for such children, as indeed they have been in special instances, in which the building up of the brain, the training of the mind, in clear, accurate and quick thinking, the government of the will, and the development of all of those faculties which we regard as constituting the education of the individual, can be accomplished at least as effectually, as rapidly, and as certainly as is done to-day, but with a far less dependence than has heretofore been considered necessary upon the printed page. In other words let us have more thinking and fewer books.

BEZIEHUNGEN ZWISCHEN SCHULE UND AUGE

VON

FRANZ F. KRUSIUS

M. H., in Anbetracht der beschränkten Zeit darf ich das Ziel meines Vortrages, den ich namens des deutschen Hauptkomites heute vor Ihnen über die Beziehung zwischen Schule und Auge zu halten die Ehre habe, nicht in einem alle geschichtlichen und forschenden Entwicklungen dieser Frage aufzählenden Referate erblicken. Die gerechte Würdigung aller der ausgezeichneten Arbeiten und Forschungen in diesem Sondergebiete, die auf über ein halbes Jahrhundert zurückblicken, ist in so vornehm abwägender und ausgezeichneter Weise gerade in der jüngsten Zeit in mehrfachen sowohl streng fachwissenschaftlich wie auch allgemein verständlich gehaltenen Abhandlungen und Broschüren erfolgt, dass ich hoffe in Ihrem und des Kongresses Sinne zu handeln, wenn ich in meinem heutigen Vortrage die praktischen Ergebnisse der international vergleichenden Forschung einer historischen Betrachtung voransetze und die praktischen Gesichtspunkte den theoretischen Erwägungen.

Seit Alters haben sowohl die vermuteten wie die tatsächlich festgestellten Einwirkungen der Schule auf das Auge bald in Hochfluten von übertriebener Besorgnis bald mit Zeiten sorglosester Gleichgültigkeit abwechselnd, das Interesse der Allgemeinheit über die enger beteiligten Kreise hinaus wachgerufen. Es soll mein Bestreben sein, Ihnen eine Reihe dieser Fragen so kühl abwägend und kritisch, als ich es vermag, darzulegen, bestrebt zwischen Schwarzseherei und Sorglosigkeit in der Beurteilung der Schäden, und zwischen hygienischer Uebererwartung und hoffnungsloser Resignation in deren Bekämpfung den Massstab praktischer Tatsächlichkeit zu halten, trotz und wegen des persönlichsten Interesses und der Liebe, die ich als Mitarbeitender gerade diesen Aufgaben entgegen bringe.

Nur streifen möchte ich in dieser Betrachtung alle diejenigen Erkrankungen und Störungen des Auges, bei denen die Schule nicht durch die das Sehorgan beanspruchende Tätigkeit, sondern gewissermassen nur nebenbei durch die Massenansammlung von Menschen ursächlich in Betracht kommt. Nicht weil diese Erkrankungen etwa weniger bedeutsam wären, sonder vielmehr deshalb, weil hier sowohl für die Krankheitsentstehung und Verschleppung wie auch für die hygienischen Gegenmassnahmen so klare Gesichtspunkte und wirksame Regeln bestehen, dass wenige Worte genügen. Es fallen unter diesen Punkt der Betrachtung alle ansteckenden, epidemisch auftretenden, vorwiegend ausseren Augenerkrankungen wie das Trachom und die verschiedenen infektiösen Bindehautkatarrhe, für deren Verbreitung der nahe Verkehr und die Mengenansammlung der Schulkinder einen günstigen Boden bietet, deren praktische Bekämpfung aber durch eine rechtzeitige, am besten vorbeugende Ausschliessung und Heilbehandlung der ersten Infektionsträger wirksam und erschöpfend gekennzeichnet ist. Die schultechnisch praktischen Massnahmen werden sich eng an die allgemeinen Infektionskrankheiten gültigen anzuschliessen haben.

Eine Reihe weiterer in der Schule zu beobachtender Augenkrankheiten wären hier auch nur flüchtiger zu erwähnen. Es sind dies im besonderen die zahlreichen skrophulösen Hornhaut- und Bindehautentzündungen, die nicht seltenen und leider auch häufig unbeachteten postidphtheritischen Akkommodationslähmungen, ferner die grosse Schar der namentlich in den Entwicklungsjahren und den Examenszeiten so überaus häufigen rein funktionell nervösen Augenstörungen, das Flimmern der Lider, Asthenopien und neuropatische Akkommodationsspasmen. Allen diesen letzteren Augenstörungen ist gemeinsam, dass sie nur okkulare Manifestationen konstitutioneller und allgemeiner Erkrankungen sind, dass ihre Behandlung somit neben der lokalen eine vorwiegend allgemeinärztliche sein muss, und dass sie für die schulhygienische Betrachtung über den Rahmen des speziellen Referates hinaus in das Gebiet der allgemein schulärztlichen Fürsorge reichen.

Ausschliesslicher schon in die spezialistische Betrachtung fallen die zwar seltenen, aber doch von mir in ein zehntel bis ein pro Mille der Fälle in den verschiedensten Ländern beobachteten, Herabsetzungen der Sehschärfe durch innere Augenerkrankungen. Es handelte sich hierbei vorwiegend um grauen und auch jugendlichen grünen Star, Verwachsungen nach inneren Augenentzündungen etc. So verschieden auch hier die therapeutischen Massnahmen im einzelnen Falle sind, für die schulhygienische Betrachtung bilden sie *eine* Gruppe: In Ermanglung eines ansteckenden Charakters zeigen diese verschiedenen Leiden einheitlich den Folgezustand einer mehr oder weniger erheblichen Beeinträchtigung der Sehkraft, und diese Schüler bilden somit für Lehrer und Aerzte den Gegenstand einer besonderen Berücksichtigung, und Entscheidungen lassen sich wohl auch nur im Einzelfalle treffen, ob die noch vorhandene Sehkraft im Vereine mit der sonstigen geistigen Entwicklung der betreffenden Schüler zum gemeinsamen Unterrichte in der Normalklasse ausreicht, oder ob diese Schüler zweckmässiger einem Sonderunterrichte überwiesen werden sollen.

Den Hauptpunkt unserer heutigen Betrachtung sowie zweifelsohne auch den Hauptgegenstand des öffentlichen Interesses in der Frage „Schule und Auge" bilden aber jedenfalls die von allen Störungen zahlreichsten *Refraktionsanomalien*, und bei ihnen bitte ich etwas einge. hender verweilen zu dürfen. Die Aussenwelt ist gar zu gerne geneigt für alle Refraktionsanomalien die Schule und die dort gebotene Nahar. beit ursächlich verantwortlich zu machen, und sie findet auch für dieses Urteil insoweit eine anscheinende Begründung, als fast alle diese Re. fraktionsanomalien während der Schulzeit zwar nicht auftreten, wohl aber meist erst dann zum Bewusstsein kommen. Da ich im Rahmen des vorliegenden Referates diese ganze Frage weder historisch noch in der Begründung erschöpfend behandeln kann, so bitte ich mir zu erlauben, für die historische Darstellung auf die gute und bekannte Schrift von Professor Wingerath (Kurzsichtigkeit und Schule. Leopold Voss, Hamburg, 1910) und auf die entsprechenden Kapitel der jüngst erschienenen eingehenden Monographie von Steiger zu verweisen. Sie werden hier die volle Würdigung der grossen schulhygienischen Vorkämpfer, Kohn, Breslau und seiner Schule, der amtlichen preussischen Untersuchungen Kirchner's und Greeff's, der Anschauungen Donders, Schnabels und nicht zum mindesten der tiefgründigen und geistvollen Theorie und Untersuchungen des Strassburger Stilling's und seiner Schüler finden. Für die zusammenfassende Begründung und Darstellung des heutigen Standpunktes bitte ich aber auf eigenem Boden bauen zu dürfen und hoffe Ihnen hier durch die Berherrschung eines sehr ausgedehnten und die verschiedensten Rassen umfassenden, persönlich untersuchten Schülermateriales, einen vielleicht nicht unerwünschten Ersatz bieten zu können für eine relative Uebergehung der Literatur, da ich mich gerade vor Ihrem Forum nicht berechtigt fühlte, praktische Schlussfolgerungen aufzustellen, wenn nicht an Hand eines durchaus persönlich untersuchten Materiales und nach eigener Fragestellung und Methodik untersuchten Materiales.

Die spezialistische Darstellung meiner Untersuchungsmethoden und Ergebnisse ist eingehender in den Berichten der 38. und 39. Vers. d. ophthal. Ges. z. Heidelberg erfolgt, worin auch fast die gesamten statistischen, tabellarischen und photographischen Sammlungen niedergelegt sind. Ich darf mir somit wohl hier erlauben, nur in grossen Zügen die Methoden und Ausdehnungen der betreffenden Untersuchungen zu schildern, die im Auftrage des preussischen Kultusministeriums erfolgten: Es handelte sich vorerst um eine Ausarbeitung neuer Methoden, um den Refraktionsbefund einer Anstalt unter Berücksichtigung aller objektiven einschlägigen Faktoren (Alter, Zahl, Refraktionsart und Grad) unveränderlich und frei von aller subjektiven Wertung niederlegen zu können. Dieser Refraktionsbefund sollte dann mit einem Blicke zu erfassen sein, und es sollte somit dann auch eine objektive Vergleichung sowohl des Refraktionsbefundes zweier verschiedener Anstalten, wie auch der in verschiedenen Zeiträumen aufgenommenen

Refraktionsbefunde ein und derselben Anstalt stichhaltig möglich sein. Eine solche Methode hoffe ich in meiner "graphischen Refraktions-darstellung" gegeben zu haben, wie ich sie 1912 auf dem deutschen Kongresse für Schulhygiene zu Berlin vorführte, und nach ihr habe ich untersucht und in Tafeln niedergelegt die Refraktionsbefunde der verschiedenartigsten höheren Schulen *Preussen-Brandenburgs, Südruss-lands,* der *Türkei,* und *Indiens.* Ich hoffe, dass es möglich sein wird, nach dieser Methode untersuchend und die Befunde derart nieder-legend mit der Zeit durch die internationale Mitarbeit augenärztlicher Kollegen ein schulhygienisch und kulturell bedeutsamstes Tafelarchiv zu gewinnen. Einige derartige graphische "Refraktions-Stammbilder" erlaube ich mir Ihnen, anschliessend an meinen Vortrag, zu demon-strieren. Es liegt auf der Hand, dass auch die augenärztliche Unter-suchung der Schüler jedesmal nach demselben objektiven Verfahren zu erfolgen hatte, und zwar wählte ich hierzu die ophthalmologisch best bewertete Skiaskopie nach v. Hess, mit der auch zugleich der Astigmatismus festgestellt wurde.

In zweiter Linie handelte es sich darum, einen genaueren Einblick in die Erblichkeitsverhältnisse der verschiedenen Refraktionsanomalien zu gewinnen. Es ist für jeden mit derartigen Forschungen Vertrauten klar, dass man sich hierbei nicht nur auf die einschlägigen Befunde und Angaben bei den Eltern und Geschwistern verlassen durfte, sondern pass nur wirklich ausgedehnte Stammbäume hierin einigermassen duverlässige Aufschlüsse geben konnten. Es gelang mir bei fast 4000 zreussischen Schülern ein fast 100.000 Personen umfassendes Material zu sammeln. In den indischen Schulen Bombays konnte ich diese preussischen Stammbaumforschungen dann noch insofern sehr günstig durch Gegenprobe ergänzen, als die eigenartigen, Beruf und Stand für Jahrhunderte eisern festlegenden Kasten-Verhältnisse der Inder mir erlaubten, ein seit Generationen nah arbeitendes und ein seit ebenso langen Generationen nicht nah arbeitendes Schülermaterial unter den gleichen Schulbedingungen neben einander zu untersuchen. Eine weitere Hauptbedeutung legte ich einer neuen objektiven Untersuchung der Frage bei, ob sich ein gesetzmässiger Zusammenhang zwischen bestimmten Refraktionsanomalien und bestimmten Formen der Augen-höhle und des Schädels feststellen liess, und zwar in gleichem Sinne gesetzmässig nicht nur für unsere deutschen Schüler sondern auch für die von mir untersuchten fremdrassigen Auslandsschulen:

Sie kennen wohl alle die geistvollen Theorien von Stilling, die dieser im Anschluss an die Ideen von Beer, Phillips und Motais errichtet und soweit bis dahin möglich auch planmässig begründet hat. Sie beruht, um mit Stilling zu reden, im wesentlichen auf der Anschauung, dass die Schulmyopie als eine Deformität des Bulbus aufzufassen ist, die durch den Einfluss der Druck- und Zugwirkungen des Muskulus Obliquus Superior entstanden ist.

Erst im anthropologischen Ausbau dieser Trochlearistheorie zog er dann noch weitere Gesichtspunkte insofern hinein, als er annahm, dass die Disposition zur Entstehung der Kurzsichtigkeit, und somit auch deren Vererbung von der Vererbung des Muskelverlaufs abhänge. . Der Verlauf und damit die Wirkungsweise des Muskels aber hänge von dem ganzen Bau der Orbita und von der Lage der Trochlea in besonderem ab; der Bau der Orbita wiederum aber von dem Bau des ganzen Kopfes.

. Ohne auf die mechanischen Details der engeren Trochlearistheorie Stilling's einzugehen, kam es mir darauf an, ein objektives Urteil zu dem grosszügigen Grundgedanken der Stillings'schen Theorie zu gewinnen, ob nämlich wirklich mit bestimmten Refraktionsanomalien gesetzmässig bestimmte durchschnittliche Ausmaasse des Gesichtsschädels und der Orbita objektiv nachweislich verknüpft sind.

Ich baute hierzu eine Methode aus, die in anderer Fragestellung vor Jahren schon von amerikanischer Seite benutzt worden war, das photographische Blocksystem. Als neuer Gedanke kam von mir dazu, dass die Verschmelzung und Uebereinanderdeckung der Einzelbilder schon auf der ersten Negativplatte selbst erfolgte, dass die Methode zu einer stereoskopischen vollendet wurde, und dass durch die Negativmischung auch die Verschmelzung von Autochromaufnahmen erfolgen konnte. Bezüglich der Einzelheiten und des Verwendungsgebietes dieser vorwiegend anthropologischen Methode verweise ich auf meinen Vortrag auf der Vers. d. deut. Naturf. u. Aerzte zu Münster 1912.

Nach diesen Gesichtspunkten und neuen Methoden wurde von mir persönlich in Europa und Asien ein Schülermaterial von über 10.000 Augen untersucht. Das Ergebnis der Untersuchungen entwerfe ich Ihnen hier nur in grossen Zügen:

Unter den Refraktionsanomalien sind für die praktisch schulhygienische Betrachtung im wesentlichen zwei grosse Gruppen zu unterscheiden: Erstens die im engeren Sinne angeborenen Augenfehler, wie der Astigmatismus, die Hyperopie und die doch relativ seltene bösartige Myopie höchster Grade. Zweitens, diejenigen Abweichungen von der emmetropischen Mitte, die sich erst im Laufe der Schuljahre meist um die Pubertätszeit herum allmählig zunehmend aus der Emmetropie und geringen Hyperopie heraus entwickeln. Diese Gruppe wird fast ganz alleine von dem häufigsten Fehler, der sogenannten gutartigen Kurzsichtigkeit gebildet, die vorwiegend bei mittleren Graden Halt macht. Sehr oft kompliziert sie sich mit einem Astigmatismus der ersten Gruppe.

Die Refraktionsanomalien der ersten Gruppe sind ausgesprochen erblich. Diese starke Vererbungstendenz zeigt sich besonders auch darin, dass sie durch Inzucht sowohl dem Grade wie der Zahl nach ganz erheblich gesteigert werden. Ein ursächlicher Einfluss der Schuljahre lässt sich höchstens in einem Bruchteile der Fälle im Sinne einer komplizierenden Kurzsichtigkeit wahrnehmen. Da dieser ersten Gruppe aber eine ziemlich erhebliche Beeinträchtigung wenn nicht der Sehschärfe, so doch jedenfalls der Arbeitsfähigkeit der Augen gemeinsam ist, so ist sie schulhygienisch und volkswirtschaftlich für die Wehrfähigkeit von höchster Bedeutung.

Auch bei den Refraktionsanomalien der zweiten Gruppe spielt die Erblichkeit nachweislich eine sehr wesentliche Rolle, aber doch nicht die alleinige. Es gibt hier die Erblichkeit mehr den generell disponierenden Boden ab, auf dem dann Individualschädigungen- hier namentlich die Naharbeit- die auslösende Rolle spielen.

Ein und dieselbe Naharbeitsschädigung wirkt bei hereditär disponierten Menschen quantitiv sowie qualititiv ganz wesentlich stärker Kurzsichtigkeit erzeugend als bei einem hereditär noch nicht dazu disponiertem Materiale.

Wie man sich nun diese disponierende Wirkung der Heredität zu deuten hat, ob im Sinne einer viele Generationen hindurch gegebenen Anpassung an die immer gleichsinnig wirkende Individualschädigung der Naharbeit, also als eine realtive Vererbung erworbener Eigenschaften, oder ob man geneigt ist, hierfür in einer viele Generationen hindurch erfolgten Selektion- d. h. Ausmerzung der nicht zweckmässig Kurzsichtigen – die Erklärung zu suchen, steht erst durchaus in zweiter Linie des praktischen Erkenntniswertes. Die *Tatsachen* sind es die vorwiegend den praktischen Forscher und Hygieniker interessieren.

Mir persönlich ist der erste Erklärungsweg der wahrscheinliche und sympathischere, auch weil er für die Bekämpfungsmassnahmen der praktischen Schulhygiene der fruchtbarere ist. Es scheint nach den zoologischen Experimenten, dass die atavistische *Rück*anpassung an den ursprünglichen ·Normalzustand sehr viel leichter und schon in wenigen Generationen vor sich geht, im Gegensatz zu der Erstanpassung aus dem Normalzustand in die anormalen Bedingungen. Es stände mithin zu erwarten, dass eine vernünftige und planmässige Augenhygiene, wenn nicht in der ersten, so doch sicher in den ersten Generationen schon nachweisliche Erfolge zeitigen kann.

Was nun den von mir erforschten Zusammenhang bestimmter Refraktionsanomalien und zwar im besonderen von H, E & M mit bestimmten Ausmaassen des Gesichtsbildung betrifft, so konnte ich an dem daraufhin untersuchten deutschen und ausländischem Materiale mittels meiner Methode der stereospkoischen Mischphotographie zeigen, dass im Einklang mit den Stillings'schen Befunden sich ein gesetzmässiger Zusammenhang zwischen H, E & M im Sinne eines von H uber E zu M niedriger und breiter-Werdens des Orbitaleinganges nachweisen liess.

Wenn auch diese Feststellungen durchaus nichts daruber besagen, ob der Augapfel lang und myopisch wird wegen der Form der Augen. höhle, oder ob diese wegen der Form des Augapfels, oder ob beides Parallelerscheinungen sind, zu welch letzterer Auffassung ich persön. lich neige, so sind sie doch in einem anderen Punkte von sehr bedeut. samem praktischem Interesse: Hätte sich dieser Befund nur bei einem rassegemischtem Volke wie z. B. dem deutschen bestätigt, bei anderen oder bei solchen mit einheitlicher Grundrasse aber nicht, so wäre immer noch für die hygienisch pessimistische und unfruchtbare Auffassung Raum gewesen, dass mit einem bestimmten Schädeltypus dieses Ras. sengemisches und somit einer bestimmten Nation, Rasse oder Rassen. teil, und nur mit diesem, unabänderlich die Disposition zur Kurzsichtig. keit verknüpft sei. Diese extreme Auffassung lässt sich aber nicht halten, da ich die gleichen gesetzmässigen Beziehungen zwischen Orbital. formation und Refraktion auch bei allen untersuchten sowohl rassege. mischten wie homogenen fremdrassigen Schulen fand. Ich komme mithin für mich zu der Deutung, dass ich in der Entwicklung der Re. fraktion und der Orbita ein von der anthropologischen Grundrasse unabhängiger Parallelvorgang zu erblicken ist. Eine Auffassung, die trotz einer relativen Einschränkung dem weitblickenden Werte und den tatsächlichen Unterlagen der Stilling's'schen Theorie keinen Abbruch tut.

Gestatten Sie mir nun, meine Herren, dass ich Ihnen nach Darlegung der Forschungsergebnisse wenigstens zu dem letzten Teile meines Vor. trages, soweit er die Refraktionsanomalien betrifft, auch ein praktisch schulhygienisches Programm entwerfe: Für die erste Gruppe der im engsten Sinne des Wortes angeborenen Refraktionsanomalien kann es neben den uns hier fernliegenden rassehygienischen Maassnahmen nur ein schulhygienisches Mittel geben: Die möglichst frühzeitige und dauernde Vollkorrektion des Augenfehlers zur besten Sehschärfe. Es ist durch nichts und durch keine Tatsache noch Theorie zu begründen, warum wir diesen zahlreichen schlecht und schwach sehenden Schülern nicht zu ihrer besten und vollen Sehschärfe verhelfen sollten, vorbeugend für die komplizierende Entwicklung der Kurzsichtigkeit, und warum wir nicht den vielen Astigmatikern und stärkeren Hyperopen die ständige Ueberanstrengung ihrer Augen durch die für Fern- und Naharbeit passende Brille hinwegschaffen sollten.

Immer noch kämpfen wir hier gegen alte Vorurteile, sehr häufig auch gerade in dieser Gruppe gegen die Ahnungslosigkeit der Schüler, die den Augenfehler und den Grund der vielen Beschwerden von selbst gar nicht merken.

Auch für die zweite Gruppe der Refraktionsanomalien – diejenige der Naharbeitskurzsichtigkeit – gibt es neben der noch zu besprechenden hygienischen Prophylaxe nur *ein* wesentlichstes Mittel: Die rechtzeitige und stäudig kontrollierende Verordnung der vollkorrigierenden und eben auch für die Naharbeit zu tragenden Brille.

Diese ganze Brillenfürsorge für beide Gruppen gipfelt aber praktisch in zwei Faktoren: *Früh*zeitige augenärztliche Versorgung und best angepasste billige Brillen. Ich kann hier im wesentlichen nur auf Deutschland zurückgreifen, da mir in diesen Punkten die ausländischen Verhältnisse nicht in gleicher Weise vertraut sind. Aber doch habe ich sowohl in den deutschen wie in den ausländischen Schulen einen nach den jüngsten Klassen zu steigenden, erheblichen Prozentsatz von Schülern (zumal der Gruppe I) gefunden, die, obwohl sie Sehfehler hatten, doch noch *nicht* mit Brillen versorgt waren. Die Ursache dürfte wohl allein darin liegen, dass die Erkennung dieser astigmatischen Störungen sehr oft mit der üblichen Sehprüfung allein nicht möglich und nur durch die objektive Untersuchung seitens eines spezialistisch geübten Augenarztes möglich ist. Ich rede hier *nicht* den Schulaugen Kliniken das Wort, weil diese eine nicht zweckentsprechende und überflüssige Mehrbelastung des hygienischen Schuletats darstellen, wohl aber der ständigen Zuziehung von Schul*augen*ärzten, denen obligatorisch die genaue objektive Refraktionsbestimmung jedes neu eintretenden Schulkindes und regelmässige Kontrolluntersuchungen des Augenbefundes oblägen. Denn diese spezielle Aufgabe liegt sowohl im Interesse des Schülers wie des Arztes ausserhalb des Gebietes des allgemeinen nicht spezialistisch ophthalmogischen Schularztes, darf aber nicht vernachlässigt oder dem privaten Belieben anheimgestellt werden, sondern erfordert eben in Anbetracht der sozialen und nationalen Bedeutung der Sehfähigkeit die Verwendung ständig verpflichteter Schulaugenärzte.

Auch der *optischen* Forderung der gut angepassten, wissenschaftlich vollkommenen und doch billigen Brille kommt eine grosse Bedeutung zu, der wir ja in Deutschland dank der neuen Brillenprinzipien schon weitgehendst und vielleicht vor anderen Ländern gerecht werden können. Es spielt der Preis auch eine Rolle, denn selbst für die höheren Schulen vielmehr aber noch für die Volksschulen scheitert sonst leicht die Fürsorge an der materiellen Unzulänglichkeit der Geldmittel der Schule oder des Elternhauses für die doch oft wiederholt nötige Anschaffung der Brillen. Es richtet sich dieser Hinweis zumal an das nichteuropäische Ausland. Fiel es mir doch eben in Amerika auf, welche merklich höhern Preise dem Publikum hier für eine gute, der unseren aber keineswegs überlegene Brillenoptik abgefordert werden.

Neben diesen optisch therapeutischen Maassnahmen kommt aber

der allgemeinen hygienischen Prophylaxe für die Kurzsichtigkeits-bekämpfung eine ganz wesentliche Bedeutung zu. Hier ist der Kampf nur in zwei Richtungen möglich: Erstens durch die Schaffung der aller-günstigsten Bedingungen für die auf ein Mindestmaass einzuschränkende Naharbeit. Was hierin durch Verbesserung der Schulbänke, Beleucht-ung und Naharbeitsbeschränkung von Seiten der Schule schon getan und zugestanden ist geht schon wohl an die Grenze des kulturell Mög-lichen. Viel, sogar sehr viel, ist auf diesem Gebiete aber noch seitens des Elternhauses zu leisten, und darauf wird besser noch als der Lehrer der Schul- und der Hausarzt hinwirken können. '

Eben weil dieser bautechnisch schulhygienischen Seite und zumal auch der Frage der Beleuchtung praktisch in der Schule schon am ehe-sten entsprochen wird, jedenfalls meist weit mehr als im Elternhause, und da auch diese Frage mehr in das Gebiet anderer Abteilungen und Vorträge hinüber spielt, so will ich mich in der Frage der Beleuchtung hier nur auf die notwendigsten Leitsätze beschränken. Niemals wird bislang eine künstliche Beleuchtung die vielgestalte Wirkung des Tages- und indirekten Sonnenlichtes ersetzen können. Und bei der vitalen Bedeutung der täglichen reichlichen Einwirkung von Tages- licht für Körper und Psyche wird die Schulhygiene die Forderung natürlich tageshelle Räume stets in erster Linie vertreten müssen. Die Grade der dabei zu fordernden Mindesthelligkeit der Einzelplätze und somit die Auswertung der Plätze wird unter Verwertung des reflek-tierten, Wandlichtes am einfachsten mit dem Thornerschen Relativ-Photometer unabhängig von der jeweiligen Tageshelligkeit bestimmt. Für absolute Helligkeitsmessungen dürfte praktisch z. Z. am besten das Wingen'sche Photometer sein. Durchweg heller, nicht spiegelnder Innenanstrich der Schulräume. Nicht überängstliche Abblendung des direkten Sonnenlichtes.

Zwielicht bei genügender Gesammthelligkeit und Farbgleichheitist nicht nachweisslich schädlich, aber aus praktischen Gründen wegen der meist bestehenden Färbungsdifferenz besser zu meiden. Gerade die Bestimmung des Zeitpunktes von welcher Mindesttageshelligkeit an zu der Benutzung des künstlichen Lichtes übergegangen werden muss, dürfte einen schulhygienisch wichtigen und leider vorerst nur subjektiv zu regelnden Faktor darstellen. Solange nicht ein praktisch verwendbarer automatisch bei einer gewissen Mindesthelligkeit des ungünstigsten Klassenplatzes die künstliche Beleuchtung einschal-tender Helligkeitsmesser und Regulator konstruiert ist, wird diese Funktion dem jeweiligen Klassenlehrer zu zuteilen sein, der sich dabei nicht nach der Helligkeit seines Platzes sondern nach derjenigen des ungünstigsten Klassenplatzes zu richten hat. '

Doch ist jedenfalls bei der bautechnischen Anlage zu fordern eine so ausreichende Tageshelligkeit, dass nur eine Mindestbenutzung von künstlichem Lichte nötig ist, und dann am zweckmässigsten reflektiertes oder abgeblendetes aber genügend helles Licht. Gas wegen des erhöhten Luftverbrauches und der meist gegebenen Geruchwirkung gegenüber möglichem elektrischem Lichte zu wiederraten.

Der zweite Punkt wird nicht durch die Einschränkung von Schädlichkeiten erfüllt, sondern strebt über diese *De*fensive hinaus nach einer wirksamen *Of*fensive: Durch geeigneten Sport, Freiturnen, Zielübungen und Wanderungen sollen an den Körper und Geist die der Naharbeit gegensinnig wirkenden Anforderungen in noch erhöhtem Maasse gestellt werden. Und zwar nicht nur und erst in den oberen Schulklassen mit schon entwickelten Augenschädigungen, sondern methodisch als ständiges Gegengewicht der Stuben und Naharbeit schon von den untersten Klassen an beginnend. Dies sind Kampfespunkte, die praktisch durchaus im Bereich des Erreichbaren, ja meist schon Erreichten ,liegen. Dass eine günstige und bessernde Einwirkung der Schulhygiene für bestimmte Gruppen der Refraktionsanomalien möglich ist und somit dringend gefordert werden muss, zeigen Ihnen nicht nur meine obigen Ausführungen, sondern auch das Ergebnis der jüngsten Statistiken in Schweden. Es ist selbstverständlich dass kein denkender und die einschlägigen Bedingungen berücksichtigender Mensch von heute auf morgen eine Beseitigung der Schulkurzsichtigkeit erwarten kann nach Generationen erst, vielleicht aber schon nach wenigen Generationen, werden wir auch zahlenmässig vergleichbar den praktischen Erfolg beweisen können.

Leitsätze:

1. *Die angeborenen Refraktionanomalien, zumal Astigmatismus und Hyperopie, sind ausgesprochen erblich. Neben rassehygienischen Maassnahmen erfordern sie frühzeitig, jedenfalls zu Schulbeginn, eine entsprechende Brillenkorrektion.*

2. *Die sogenannte Schulkurzsichtigkeit ist ausser von erblich disponierenden Momenten von der auslösenden Schädlichkeit der gehäuften Naharbeit abhängig. Ihre Bekämpfung erfordert neben der frühzeitigen und ständig kontrolierten Brillenkorrektion eine geeignete hygienische Prophylaxe.*

3. *Entsprechende schulhygienische Maassnahmen sind nachweislich wirksam, die gegebene Beziehung zwischen bestimmten Refraktionsanomalien und bestimmtem orbitaltypus stehen dem in keiner Weise fatalistisch entgegen, ebenso wenig die Abhängigkeit von erblichen Bedingungent.*

4. Zu fordern ist: *Obligatorische Hinzuziehung von Schulaugenärzten zur Refraktionsuntersuchung jedes Schülers bei Schuleintritt und zur regelmässigen Kontrolle der Refraktionsbefunde. Versorgung aller dies benötigenden Schüler mit gut angepasstem und tunlichst verbilligtem Brillenmateriale. Hygienische Ueberwachung, Regelung und Einschränkung der Naharbeit, zumal aber der bislang unkontrollierten Naharbeit und Privatlektüre zu Hause. Schon von den untersten Klassen an beginnende Begünstigung und Einrichtung sportlicher und sonstiger obligatorischer Freiluftbetätigung als aktives Gegenmittel.*

SAVING THE BACKWARD SCHOOL CHILD

BY

William Martin Richards

In January, 1909, I was reading a chapter in the 5th Volume of Biographic Clinics, entitled, "Eye Strain and Crime" which Dr. Gould had presented to me. In this chapter was the report of Dr. George M. Case, Visiting Physician of the Elmira Reformatory, in which he gave his findings of 400 boys there, as illustrative of 5,000 whom he had examined.

Of the 400 boys, he discovered that 223 or 56% needed glasses in order to do near work without suffering. These tests were made without the use of medicine in the eyes so that he was unable to determine a great many cases that needed glasses.

A similar test since made in the New Jersey Reformatory revealed 83% of the boys as needing glasses. Never since that time have the ideas of this address with the results here tabulated been absent from my mind.

In the community around us we have all sorts and kinds of unpleasant conditions. Poor people and rich people, sick people and well people side by side. If it were possible to make all the poor people rich and all the sick people well, the state that we think of as the millenium would have arrived.

Just now we have many organizations working and striving for social betterment. The Health Department, the Department of Charities, Hospitals and Dispensaries, Children's Aid Societies, Charity Organization Societies, Associations for the Improvement of the Condition of the Poor, etc. These all work independently of each other; some of them duplicating the work of others, so that the whole system lacks co-ordination.

If there is a single institution in which we have a chance to help the present unfortunate conditions, it would seem wise to concentrate in this institution all the forces of social betterment. It seems to me that the school and particularly the public school, is the place where this can best be accomplished.

Under our present system we do not all get just what we deserve. Some of us get what we do not earn and some of us earn what we do not get. But if any individual under a certain environment could have his or her efficiency increased, we will better that individual's economic state even under present conditions.

You who have control of our educational institutions are, therefore, in a position to accomplish greater good in this direction than any other people in the world.

Some time ago I became impressed with the idea that the criminals I knew were also the most incompetent people I knew, and I thought there might be some relation between these two facts. Later, when I saw people in my office who were incompetent on account of some phys. ical defect, and who became competent when it was removed, I thought it likely that physical defects might be one cause of incompetence, and that incompetence might be one cause of crime.

I, therefore, made a physical examination of a good many criminals, and found that they were all of them suffering from some form of physical defects. I was not the only person who had observed this. For example, William Evers, formerly Guard on Murderers' Row, in the New York City Prison known as the "Tombs," and now Chief Guard of the Work-house on Blackwell's Island, once said to me: "I have been dealing with criminals for 29 years; perhaps I have seen more murderers than any man in the United States—possibly in the world—and I have never seen a criminal who did not have some physical defect which, in my opinion, was the cause of his being where he was."

Therefore, at the meeting of the A. P. A. in October, 1911, I persuaded a number of superintendents and wardens of reformatories to correct every physical defect whether of structure or habit, in the prisoners under their charge, at the beginning of term of sentence. The result in one of the reformatories where this method was carried out in a modified form was a reduction of 56% in the sickness rate in this institution.

In New York State, where I personally did some of this work, I noticed the criminals gave a history of defective school work, and I therefore felt that I was working at the end of the line instead of at the beginning and before the harm had been done.

About the same year I found a class of defectives in a New York City High School, consisting of 37 boys who had failed in every subject. Casual examinations of these boys, as compared with that of a room of normal boys in the same school, revealed that the class of defectives averaged not half as good vision as the normal boys did.

In February, 1912, throught the offices of Dr. A. J. Goldfarb, of the City College of New York, Mr. Angelo Patri, principal, and Mrs. Angelo Patri, assistant principal, respectively, of public schools No. 4 and No. 44, of the Borough of the Bronx, containing about 5,000 children, sent me the 40 most difficult problems in their schools. These children were of three types:

1st. The ungraded, or those who were too backward for the regular classes and formed half of the children.

2nd. Backward children who had to take more than one term to a grade.

3rd. Delinquent children, truants, and those who kicked and bit and screamed every now and then and with whom nothing could be done in a disciplinary way.

I corrected only one physical defect in these children, namely, that of vision. In other words, I fitted them with proper glasses.

Their marks in the different subjects and their records at the school were put down on a sheet of paper by the teachers. Six months after they were fitted with glasses their records were again put down on the same sheet, and comparison showed that while 8 had been lost sight of through discharge, transfer, loss or exchange of glasses, of the remaining 32, the ungraded children went up into the regular classes; the backward children were promoted and the delinquents became some of the best children in the school, one of them becoming head monitor.

Here are some of them:

Miss Eleanor Johnson of the P. E. Association thought that my results were suggestive but not conclusive, and was afraid that other people might think so. So she asked me to take a new series of 40 cases in which I corrected every physical defect, comparing them with other defective children under similar conditions whose physical defects were not corrected, *i. e.*, the faults of structure and habit which are the underlying causes of disease as well as some defects which are mental in origin.

These include correction of defective eyes, ears, noses, teeth, spines and feet. I am also introducing in the cases of these children proper regime in the matters of exercise and diet, laying particular stress upon their not being given anything containing alcohol, tea or coffee. Many of this new series reveal shocking conditions in this respect. The progress of these children we shall compare with others in whom physical defects were not corrected.

And now I come to the point of the story:

In November, 1912, at the time my first report was made public, six medical school inspectors from the New York City Health Department, with the Chief Medical School Inspector, were sent to my office to learn this work. One of them, a woman, Dr. Mary B. Hopkins, immediately began to correct the physical defects of the children in the schools under her. In the meantime I have been pretty busy in my private practice, but with considerable extension of energy and the assistance of another physician whom I called in, had managed to finish up about 40 children when Dr. Hopkins handed me in her report on public school No. 36, Borough of Manhattan, New York City, which contains about 1,700 children.

Under the direction of the principal, Miss Ellen T. O'Brien, the assistant principal, Miss Gaffney, went into the different class rooms and without the knowledge of the teachers made a list of 236 children who had received the two lowest marks, namely, "C" or "D."*

As you can see from this chart these children were all rated "C" or worse in November, 1912. By dint of continual urging, she succeeded in having corrected all physical defects in 185 out of the 236, leaving 51 uncorrected. Of these, 176 were eventually marked "B" or better by the teachers who were unaware that any experiment was in progress.

The 51 children who were not treated, and nine of those who were supposed to have been, either remained stationary or did even more defective work than before. So all of the work that I have done for the Public Education Association has turned out to be unnecessary and the proof that I have striven for has been obtained by one of my pupils. Of course I was terribly pleased in a way.

There are almost as many exciting causes of disease as there are diseases themselves, but lying underneath these are a few great causes which can be grouped under two general heads—"Faults of Habit" and "Faults of Structure." These make a favorable soil for the exciting causes of disease to act upon. Removing some of these underlying causes reduced the sickness rate in the New Jersey Reformatory 56% in one year.

Why not remove the faults of habit and structure in everybody, and reduce the general adult sickness rate 56%?

If the correction of all defects of structure and habit in criminals and defective school children is a good thing, is it not a good thing to do for normal people and for normal school children, and is not the public school the place to do this?

*In the N. Y. City Public Schools, the highest mark is "A," the next is "B," the next "B–," the next "C" and the next "D."

DEFECTIVE VISION IN SCHOOL CHILDREN FROM AN ECONOMIC 'STANDPOINT

BY

Lewis C. Wessels,

Medical inspection of school children has revealed the fact that at least 25% of the pupils have defective vision, or eye strain, sufficiently grave to require the constant use of glasses. As a cause of retardation, defective vision is the gravest condition encountered, considering the number involved, yet there is no other defect so amenable to treatment. In the majority of cases suitable glasses cause these children to take their place in class with the normal child.

In consideration of these facts, the correction of defective vision in the school child is not receiving the attention that its importance deserves. Such corrections not only increase the efficiency of pupil and teacher, but have an important economic value as well, because if a child is backward and remains in the same class for two or three years, it is costing the State two or three times as much as it should to teach that child.

In Philadelphia it costs about $35.00 per year to teach each pupil. (In 1912, $36.69.) A child is compelled to attend school between the ages of six and fourteen years inclusive, eight years in all. Under normal conditions a pupil fourteen years old reaches the eighth grade at a cost to the State of $280.00; if on account of defective vision the child only reaches the fourth grade in that time, it has cost the State $280.00 but with only $140.00 worth of result—a loss to the State of $140.00. The loss to the child is considerably more, because at the age of fourteen he is likely to be put to work, poorly equipped for the struggle for existence, his earning power is curtailed for the want of an education, so he can contribute little toward his own support, that of his family, or of the State. So again the State loses and 'all for the want of suitable glasses for the child.

While it is quite easy for the medical inspector or teacher to detect defective vision, the recommendations for glasses cannot always be carried out, on account of poverty or ignorance. These cases are treated free at the dispensaries, but poverty or indifference often prevent the purchase of glasses prescribed, and so the child continues to struggle along greatly handicapped and falls behind on account of his defective eyes.

The Department of Public Health and Charities has solved this problem in Philadelphia by establishing a Division of Ophthalmology under the Bureau of Health, where poor children can be refracted and furnished with glasses free. One clinic is established in the City Hall, in the center of the city, and one at the Southwark School, situated in one of the poorest and most congested districts. From 1908 to Jan. uary 1st, 1913, in City Hall Clinic, the writer has examined 8,167 school children and refracted under a mydriatic 7,319 and furnished 6,310 pairs of spectacles free to children whose parents were too poor to pay for them. Out of 7,319 cases refracted 5,211 or 72% were backward, representing a composite loss of 11,831 years or a money loss of $414,685.00

We now refract over 2,500 cases a year. If we save each one of these children but one year during its entire school life, we will save the city over $87,000.00 annually not counting the child's time and its increased efficiency. So the furnishing of free glasses to school children is not a charity *per se*, but is a duty and an economic problem.

In cities this work should be done by the Commonwealth, the State by reason of compulsory education is responsible for its wards and it should assume that responsibility and not depend upon the dubious generosity of charitable institutions or individuals. The character of this work requires special training and it is necessary that the results be uniformly good, but good and satisfactory work cannot always be procured from irresponsible and inexperienced attendants who do this work in some dispensaries.

This work should be done by individuals who are responsible to the Health or Educational authorities and have a heartfelt interest in the work.

Many children have come to the dispensary wearing glasses bought from some refracting optician or from a five and ten cent store. These glasses were not only unsuitable but were positively injurious to the child's eyes. Some of these opticians advertise that they do not use the "deadly drops" thus instilling a groundless fear in the minds of many people which often deters them from taking their children to competent persons for treatment. The public should be educated against this false doctrine and taught that it is impossible to refract children's eyes satisfactorily without the use of mydriatics and that such drops in the hands of competent persons are not only harmless but are often beneficial, by relieving eye strain and correcting strabismus. The writer has used mydriatics in over 15,000 children's eyes and has never seen any harmful results.

All children should have their eyes examined before entering school. If this is not possible the medical inspector or teacher in examining them should devote most of their time to the eyes of the children in the kindergarten and first grade. Thus many grave refractive errors will be discovered early and if corrected retardation will be prevented, and this will tend to relieve the congestion that usually exists in these lower grades by more frequent promotion of the visual defectives.

But it is impossible to properly refract these little ones without the use of a mydriatic or by one who is not skilled in the use of the retinoscope and ophthalmoscope.

The following table graphically shows the ages and grade of 7,319 children refracted at the City Hall Clinic, Philadelphia. These children were not selected because they were backward, but were sent to the clinic because they had defective vision and were discovered by the medical inspector in making their routine individual examination of the whole school. The tabulation was made by us from our records:

Grades	\multicolumn{11}{c}{AGE OF PUPILS—YEARS}	Total	Backward Pupils
	6	7	8	9	10	11	12	13	14	15	16		
8							1	11	20	9	6	47	15=32%
7						1	20	39	28	11	3	102	42=41%
6					1	28	94	133	58	15		334	211=63%
5				3	62	160	269	232	79	26	5	833	608=73%
4			4	70	255	336	380	288	91	19	3	1446	1117=76%
3		9	135	311	417	402	327	203	64	29	1	1898	1443=76%
2	7	107	347	406	364	205	141	84	43	11	3	1718	1257=73%
1	178	245	201	125	80	43	31	20	11	1	6	941	518=55%
Total,	185	361	687	915	1179	1175	1263	1010	394	121	29	7319	5211=72%
Backward pupils			201	531	861	986	1148	960	374	121	29	5211	
			29%	58%	73%	84%	91%	96%	95%	100%	100%	72%	

Figures on the broken line shows the number and position of the normal average school child.

Figures below the broken line shows the number and position of Backward Children.

5211 Backward Children, total loss, 11831 years = $414,685.00.

There are many interesting features connected with this table that are worthy of study.

Only 1,649 or 22% were in the normal grade and only 459 or 6% were above normal.

But few children in this class remain in school after the age of fourteen—the legal age at which children are permitted to work. This fact emphasizes the necessity of examining the eyes of children in the kindergarten and the first grades. The table shows only 483 or 6% of children above the fifth grade. Many children who left school at the working age of fourteen might have been equipped with a better education if their eyes had received attention when they were in the lower grades.

The following are the diagnoses of 9,192 refractions of school children under mydriatic at the City Hall Dispensary:

Normal	190	
Hyperopia	2,787	
Hyperopic astigmatism	91	
Compound hyperopic astigmatism	3,444	
Total hyperopic conditions	6,322	70.2%
Myopia	310	
Myopic astigmatism	27	
Compound myopic astigmatism	604	
Total myopic conditions	941	10.5%

As the blackboard and school room appear to the child with defective vision before correction with glasses.

Mixed astigmatism.. 788   8.8%
Anisometropia.. 948   10.5%
Aphakia..   3
                                                              ——————
    Total... 9,192

As 80% to 90% of these children start to improve when they procure glasses the economic advantages of a Division of this kind are obvious. The only reason all do not improve is because there were other causes of retardation besides defective vision.

In the year 1895, before the institution of school medical inspection in Philadelphia; out of 33,000 children entering the first grade, only 53% reached the fourth grade, and only 13% reached the eighth grade.

In the year 1905, when school medical inspection started in Philadelphia, out of 34,000 children entering the first grade, 64% reached the fourth grade as compared with 53%; and 22% reached the eighth grade, as compared with 13% before medical inspection.

The following is a summary with cost of work done in the Division of Ophthalmology, Bureau of Health, Philadelphia, for the six months ending June 30, 1913:

As the blackboard and school room appear to the school child with defective vision after correction with glasses.

Total number of new cases examined.................................... 3,408
Children refracted under a mydriatic.................................... 1,873
Free glasses furnished to poor pupils................................pairs, 1,532
Prescriptions for glasses verified.. 1,521
Cases examined for diagnosis... 1,381
Cases of trachoma... 14
Total visits to clinic... 7,249

Total cost of this work, including every item of expense, was $2,902.40, divided as follows:

Salaries.. $1,400.00
1,532 pairs of spectacles at 95c each................................... 1,455.40
Drugs and all other supplies... 47.00

Total.. $2,902.40
Per capita cost, 1.8 mills (city population).

1,340 children were examined in schools and institutions on account of suspected trachoma or other contagious eye diseases. The ophthalmologist in Philadelphia, is required to see all cases of trachoma and all suspicious cases reported by physicians and inspectors.

As the blackboard and school room appear to the child with astigmatism before correction.

The fact I wish to emphasize in this paper is the importance of municipalities establishing their own eye clinic for refracting and the furnishing glasses free to at least poor pupils.   That this is an economic problem rather than a charity, as it reduces the cost of education and increases the efficiency of both the pupil and teacher at the same time.

Because of compulsory education the State is responsible for its wards while in school, so the State should assume that responsibility, it furnishes the books and other things to assist a child to gain an education, but defective vision prevents many children from making the proper use of them.   It would be a matter of economy to supply glasses when they are needed to prevent the waste of this material.

From the standpoint of economy and efficiency it would pay any community to furnish glasses free to any pupil requiring them who could not or would not procure them otherwise.

The success of any large business depends upon the attention paid to details, the saving of a fraction of a cent, or the fraction of a minute, is carefully checked up in the process of the manufacture of all commodities.   The raw material is carefully selected, sorted, and treated so as to insure a uniform finished product.

As the blackboard and school room appear to the child with astigmatism after correction with glasses.

The educational system of this country is a great big institution in business of the manufacture of future citizens out of a raw material that runs anything but uniform. This raw material unselected, unsorted, and untreated, is dumped into numerous hoppers called classrooms and at the end of about eight years is dumped upon the community as prospective citizens. Some are firsts, some are seconds, and some are worthless.

It is the province of all medical inspection to detect and correct all remedial defects in this raw material, to insure a more uniform and more efficient finished product, and at a less cost to the State.

PRELIMINARY REPORT OF THE OCULAR DEFECTS OF SCHOOL CHILDREN TWO OR MORE YEARS BELOW GRADE

BY

CLARKE B. FULKERSON

My subject as first announced was, "The Importance and the Methods of the Examination of the Eyes of School Children," but as there were upon that program papers that boarded very closely upon this subject I thought that this data would be of more interest.

The data that we read about generally concerns the average population. So many have adenoids or enlarged tonsils or poor vision or the conditions are expressed in percentages. Very seldom do we see a certain class of school children studied in detail in regard to any one of these defects. I do not believe that this prevails for want of interest but for want of time and efficient clerical assistants. These are not trained in medicine, not familiar with medical terms and phrases and are subject to the call of principals, teachers and special teachers when the medical man is at work. I have not been favored with the services of a nurse as an assistant though we have one working in the grades as a school nurse. The school curriculum is so crowded and the reports so numerous that special data frequently is lost.

We all agree that the correction of any physical defect of whatever nature is indispensable to the development of a high degree of mental and physical efficiency. The more perfect the ancestry, the higher the standard of the environment, the less do these defects influence the development and the efficiency. There are examples where a moderate degree of poor vision is overcome and a high standard of school work maintained. To substantiate this, I have from my case reports the following: E. S., female, age 15, grade 10–1, vision 20–70 in both eyes. Physically normal as far as we could tell. No history of illness during childhood. She is one year in advance of grade and her work is in A and B standard. B. B., female, age 13, grade 9–1, vision 20–60 both eyes. Physically normal and ancestry good. History, negative. Nearly two years in advance of grade age but does standard work of A and B. By the ophthalmoscope, these are cases of near-sightedness and are able to do near work easily without much strain. Secondly, the good standard of ancestry and the good physique contribute greatly to their ability to compensate for the extra energy required to do a certain amount of work. These are some of the exceptions and we should not be controlled by them. To suffer throughout childhood from irritation or strain as may be caused by poor vision of the far-sighted type or marked degrees of myopic astigmatism, occasionally, is the beginning of some neurosis and once it is seated relief is remote. When we begin to study the product of poor or degenerate ancestry or a child developed in an unhealthy environment the more do we see the retro. grade influence of these defects. The symptoms are very evident. The defective child complains bitterly of the visual defect that a nearly normal child is not conscious of. The one weak point in the method of the examination of the eyes of school children is that some of the cases that read 20–20 or read normal need glasses badly. We have been instructed that we should not send recommendations to any children that read 20–30. I have spent some time in the examination of those that read 20–30. I found that some needed glasses badly and wrote out recommendations though our regulations do not permit this. Many good results followed. In the examination of these cases I depended upon the complete school, family and physical history. Too, I have attempted the systematic use of the ophthalmoscope for this class of cases but for want of time, dark room, and adequate salary I gave up in despair. With some of the cases of this group I made a desperate effort to get them to my office for examination. In this I was partly successful. Then I resorted to beneficent influence of the school nurse, who went to the home to obtain the parental consent to use drops, in part successful, and in part failed—the latter more often than the former. This mydriatic was for the purpose of diagnosis only. The people in our city are not quite ready for this step, but with the adop. tion of an educative propaganda I believe that it will come.

Occasionally we find delinquency in the normal child as a result of a refractive error but in the defective child this occurs more often. The below grade child is abnormal, but there are cases where the physical condition is normal but on account of the parents moving about often the school record is checkered, and much valuable time is lost and below grade is inevitable. Some of the parents arrange their moving propensities to suit the school year. The greater the degree of feeblemindedness or the lower the grade of efficiency the greater the struggle and thus the greater the frequency of the moving. The study of the eye conditions of the below grade child necessitates the study of the child as a whole and the many factors that may greatly influence the abuormality. The tendency is to limit one's field to the neglect of other fields. I remember very vividly when I first entered private practice I chanced to see a child that had adenoids, enlarged tonsils, and poor vision. The latter condition was judged from the fact that the child held everything small close to its face and the ophthalmoscope showed about 1 and ½ diopters of astigmatism. I gave the parents an exhaustive lecture upon the remarkable results obtained from the removal of the tonsils and the adenoids and the correction of the vision. Later, to my chagrin, I learned that the child was a mongolian imbecile and probably the correction of all these defects would have changed the child but little. This is another exception. The low grade types are changed but little by the correction of defects. Thus the question arises when we meet such cases why correct these physical defects in the feebleminded? The very low grade feebleminded child is handicapped mentally and physically and the correction of these defects do not alter hereditary stigmata, their effects may be modified; and with the high grade feeble-minded and the below grade child, these are unknown quantities. We never know what training will do for these people but we do know that to attempt to train a child with these physical defects uncorrected, particularly poor vision, is greatly disadvantageous.

This group of children was made up of 54 males and 43 females. The average grade was 4th. The highest grade attained was 7–1, the lowest, 1st. The average age was 12½ years. The oldest was 15 and the youngest 9. The average grade being four and the average age being 12½ we may consider the group 2½ years below grade. The average vision of the group was 20–30. This is high because there were 16 of the group that read normal or 20–20, yet they complained bitterly of the symptoms of eye strain such as blurred vision, frequent headaches, injection of the conjunctiva, marginal blepharitis, inability to see the blackboard without sitting in the front seats and history of styes. Some of these cases were examined by the ophthalmoscope and parents were interviewed to obtain the consent of the parents to use a mydriatic for diagnosis but we were met with opposition. The one great drawback in our work in my city is the optician. There are several and they are waxing fat off the credulity of the public. They are licensed in our state to practice but they dare not use a mydriatic. They are not licensed in medicine. This is one of the dark chapters in our statutes. Those cases in this group that obtained glasses of an optician are not improved.

Fifty-two out of the group of 97 or 53½ per cent. gave positive tests for visual defects. Some of the percentages given elsewhere range from 42, 45, and 66 per cent. for the defective child. There were but two that read below normal that did not give a history of some of the symptoms of visual disturbances. Their vision was recorded as 20–70 and 20–60 respectively. Those cases free from eye defect had the following conditions that contributed toward their inefficient work; 17 had enlarged tonsils and adenoids; one case of tuberculosis; two organic cardiac diseases, one of which resulted from repeated attacks of rheumatism, which was caused no doubt by the diseased tonsils present. No surgical relief would be adopted. 18 had some form of degenerative stigmata. A neurologist would have increased this number. Time does not permit detail in this regard. 9 out of the 18 had a visual defect, that is 50 per cent. of those with stigmata of degeneration had poor vision. When a child is under observation, the eyes should be the first point of attack. In this group, the eye defects outnumber all the others combined, with the exception of the dental defects. The mydri-atic would have increased this number to some degree, possibly 15 per cent. There were but two cases of pronounced muscular imbalance, or cross eye. This goes to show that the eye muscles are able to compensate to a remarkable degree the defect of vision. Sometimes I think that some members of the medical profession as well as the public should be better informed upon this subject of imbalance of the ocular muscles. Occasionally, a recommendation will be sent home to consult their family physician about the cross eye and permit him to employ whomever he wishes. Instead of sending the case to an ophthalmologist he says, "Let the eyes alone, the child will outgrow it." A mydriatic with the proper refraction will go a great deal toward establishing balance of the muscles. There were three cases of corneal scars, one due to injury during childhood and the other two were due to ophthalmia neonatorum. Most of these children are born under unfavorable circumstances and though preventive measures are adopted they may be infected subsequently to their birth. In Michigan there is a statute that compels all midwives and physicians to use silver nitrate in the eyes of the newborn. Some use one and some two per cent. solution. I prefer the one per cent. solution and I do not wash out the eye with any solution but allow the tears to neutralize the excess. One should be sure to instill the solution in the eye and not rub it on the outside of the lid and trust to luck that sufficient amount enters the eye. Of the 64,000 blind persons in the United States 6,000 or 7,000 were needlessly blind because this precaution had not been taken. In the schools for the blind in Pennsylvania for ten years, the average that as needlessly blind was 33.68 per cent.; and in New York the average for ten years was 28.14 per cent. There has been a great revival to stamp out this curse and a great deal has been done but there is yet much more that remains to be accomplished.

In this group there were two cases of the more rare abnormalities, traumatic cataract and hydrophthalmus respectively. In the latter case the vision in the diseased eye practically nil, in the right eye the vision was reduced to 20–60.

for the examination of the eyes of school children a
study of eye defects in children below grade. The
all other defects combined, to the exclusion of the
we enact legislation for elimination of the optician
for this work be markedly increased.

THE VALUE OF TESTING THE VISION OF SCHOOL CHILDREN AND THE NEED OF ACCURATE TEST-CARDS

BY

B. Alexander Randall

The possession of normal vision is a very important element in the equipment of the child for school work, although it is far from proving that the eyes are normal or are taking no harm from the educational process. Close, conscientious study of every eye by an ophthalmic expert, repeated at intervals during school life, may be a requisite too ideal for attainment as yet, but we should recognize how needful it is and aim ever a closer approach to its fulfillment. In the meantime examiners more or less unskilled are having opportunities in many of our schools to examine with test-cards as to the sharpness of vision and use their findings for the safeguarding of those so shown to be deficient. It is of great importance, therefore, that the tests employed should be as accurate as possible—scientific tests having a comparable value in all places if fairly lighted, not arbitrary choices of the individual exam. iner, perhaps more misleading than truly helpful. Yet an examination of the test-cards available now, as in the past, shows great discrepancies and inaccuracies and this most especially in some put forward for school work. One such published in Chicago shows error of quite 12% in the excess size of the letters used, although the faulty execution reduces variably their legibility. Such faulty cards are in widespread use, claiming generally to be based upon Snellen's, but often utter travesties of what were none too good models for imitation. While it is curious that so much poor work has been done in this direction by ophthalmic surgeons on both sides of the Atlantic, it is only fair to insist that many cards have been published for which the asserted author was not at all responsible. It should also be a source of some pride that some of the best work has been done by Americans in correcting the imperfections of the earlier tests.

More than a century ago Hooke noted that stars must have an angular separation of half a minute in order to be distinguishable. Helmholtz applied this test of separation to wires and found that rods and interspaces must subtend an angle of about 50 seconds in order to be clearly distinguished. H. Snellen then proposed that letters having their members one minute broad and interspaces about the same should be taken as the standard—hence the so-called Snellen test-type. This was a great advance and John Green, of St. Louis, soon gave us a more uniform series without awkward gaps. A few years later he gave us the perfected letter, correcting the mistake embodied in his simplified "Gothic" type. The introduction of the metric system removed much of the confusion growing out of the difference between the "Paris foot" and our English standards; and the writer corrected the error of Snellen and other constructors of test-type in making the letters subtend the tangent of 5 minutes at the desired distance and gave the true principle, which Green's type can almost perfectly exemplify—the letters should have *interspaces and members* which subtend at the desired distance *twice the tangent* of an angle of *one-half a minute* (2 tang. 0.5'). Test-letters so constructed furnish very accurate means for determining normal vision, if placed in good indoor illumination; and inability to discern at 40 feet all the details of each letter designed for that distance shows imperfect sight. Forty feet is taken as a standard because the human eye cannot recognize that light-rays coming from that distance are not strictly parallel. Commonly twenty feet (six meters) is a more convenient range; but eyes having nearsightedness of 0.6 D. should be able to see perfectly at this distance, although defective for greater ranges. Furthermore any increase of illumination, especially testing under the open sky, narrows the pupil and improves the acuity of vision for most eyes, so that double the usual standard is quite frequently attained— the normal eye can see the 20-foot letters at 40 feet or more and the eye with but half of normal sharpness might read them at more than 20 feet. Such findings have been reported as extraordinary, but are only the rule. A highly near-sighted person can see well through a pinhole without glasses if the light be adequate. Yet bright light has its drawbacks, not only for weak, over-sensitive eyes, but for all of us. Irradiation is the name given to the tendency for light surfaces to broaden apparently at the expense of darkness adjacent. Black letters on a white ground are somewhat hazy of margin, the corners rounded off and the interspaces seem increased. So there is advantage in printing on cream colored cards or in using one which has lost its freshness, if the darkening be general and nearly uniform. This is one of the reasons against the simpler forms of letters which have no adnexa to broaden the top and bottom and thus offset this irradiation—the other and more serious fault is that such letters almost never have the strokes and interspaces equal, so as to offer the *one-minute interspaces* which are the essence of our tests. Most of those who have constructed them have been content to give us letters 5 minutes high, as did Snellen, although he made some of them as much as 7 minutes broad in order to get approximately normal interspaces.

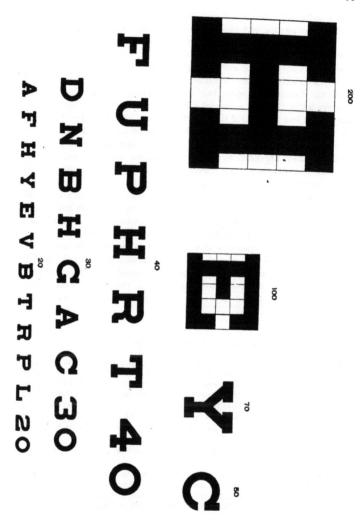

Test-card designed by the writer for the Public Education Association of Philadelphia, reduced to three-fifths of original. These letters should be legible at 120, 60, 42, 30, 24, 18 and 12 feet.

The testing of illiterates offers a difficult field. Many of them know the Arabic numerals, but these figures lend themselves very poorly, as little as the letters usually rejected, to proper construction for test objects. Figures of familiar objects may be used, but rarely offer proper proportions of line and interspace. E-shaped figures, or broken circles as to which the open side must be recognized as they are set at all angles, can furnish fair tests; but their sameness renders them rather too easy, while there is a mental effort about many such tests which makes them less automatic than is the naming of letters for a reader. This is especially true of the groups of dots offered by Burchardt as "International,Visual-tests." If few, they are easily counted: if 6 or 8 in number they are hard to decipher, although when drawn so that circle and interspace are equal they must be given more than double the interspaces which constitute our tests in the letters (2.15').

Let us hope that the study of the vision of school-children's eyes will steadily be pursued as one of the important steps towards their safe-guarding: and to such an end poor tests-cards are better than none, since they need not be taken at the face value claimed for them, but empiri-cally tested as to the distances at which their type should be discerned. A letter meant to be seen at 200 feet should have a height and breadth of 4⅜ inches (85.5 mm for 60 meters) with members and interspaces one-fifth of this—those for other distances in the same proportions. Good cards may be found if sought, although incorrect test-types are more usually offered.

INSTRUCTIONS FOR USING CARD "A."

Place the scholar 20 feet distant from this card, and ascertain the smallest letters which he can read at that distance. The card should be placed in a uniformly good light. Each eye must be tested separately, the other eye being covered but not pressed upon. If glasses are worn, vision should be tested with them. The number affixed to the smallest letter seen indicates the sharpness of sight, and this number should be recorded on the permanent record card (C), e. g., if line of letters marked 40 is seen correctly, record vision as "40" for the right or left eye; or if only the letter marked 100, then record 100.

Question the pupil regarding liability to sore or painful eyes, to headache, or blurring of the letters while reading.

If any of these be complained of, or if he fail to read the type marked (20), which ought to be legible at 20 feet with each eye, he should be sent home with a note of in-formation to the parent or guardian, Card "D." If vision be so low that none of the letters on the card are seen at 20 feet, it should be recorded as "less than 20–200."

The vision, the accommodation (see instructions, Card "B"), and the character of any complaints referable to the eyes should be entered upon the permanent record provided for the purpose.

Published by WALL & OCHS, Opticians, 1716 Chestnut St., Philadelphia

CARD B

OF THE

PUBLIC EDUCATION ASSOCIATION

OF PHILADELPHIA

As the common size of the natives is somewhat under six inches high, so there is an exact proportion in all other animals, as well as plants and trees; for instance, the tallest horses and oxen are between four and five inches in height, the sheep an inch and half, more or less; their geese about the bigness of a sparrow and so the several gradations, downward till you come to the smallest, which, to my sight, were almost invisible, but nature has adapted their eyes to all objects proper for their view they see with great exactness, but at no great distance And to show the sharpness of their sight toward objects that are near, I have been much pleased observing a cook pulling a lark, which was not so large as a common fly and a young girl threading an invisible needle with invisible silk Their tallest trees are about seven feet high, I mean some of those in the great royal park, the tops whereof I could but just reach with my fist clenched The other vegetables are in the same proportion;

INSTRUCTIONS FOR USING CARD "B"

Ascertain the nearest point with the yard stick at which the scholar can read the type on the other side of this card clearly, each eye being tested separately.

At ten years of age or under, the card should be read at three inches or less (3″).

At fifteen years of age or under, the card should be read at three and one-half inches or less (3½″).

At twenty years of age or under, the card should be read at four inches or less (4″).

If the scholar is unable to read this type approximately, at the proper age distance, he should be referred home as noted on the large test card.

Published by WALL & OCHS, Opticians

1716 Chestnut Street   Philadelphia

CARD "C"

NAME..

ADDRESS..

Date	Age	School Year	Vision		Near Point		Condition of Eyes	General Health	Remark
			Right	Left	Right	Left			
.....	....	......	......	......	......	......	......	......	......
.....	....	......	......	......	......	......	......	......	......
.....	....	......	......	......	......	......	......	......	......
.....	....	......	......	......	......	......	......	......	......
.....	....	......	......	......	......	......	......	......	......
.....	....	......	......	......	......	......	......	......	......
.....	....	......	......	......	......	......	......	......	......
.....	....	......	......	......	......	......	......	......	......
.....	....	......	......	......	......	......	......	......	......
.....	....	......	......	......	......	......	......	......	......

This card is for permanent record, and must follow the child in case of promot or transfer.

(To be placed in card index in care of principal.)

CARD "D"

....19

Dear.. The examination of the eye:

....

shows defective sight which may hinder........progress in the school work or lead permanent injury to the eyes.

It is therefore recommended that an eye physician be promptly consulted.

..............................Teacher

...............................School.

THE PREVALENCE OF TRACHOMA IN NEW YORK CITY PUBLIC SCHOOLS

BY

ANNA WESSELS WILLIAMS

Allow me to remind you that there are two theories in regard to the relationship of trachoma to follicles or granules scattered over the conjunctiva or inner surfaces of the eyelids. The one, called the mon. istic or unitarian theory, is that such granulations are always a part of trachoma, their beginning being the initial stage of this disease; the other, called the dualistic theory, is that certain granulations are benign, healing without serious consequences and having nothing to do with trachoma, and that certain others are malignant, forming a part of the lesion called trachoma.

Until recently, the New York City Health Department thought best to adopt the unitarian theory. Hence all school children who showed granulations or follicle on the conjunctiva, were diagnosed trachoma whatever the condition of the rest of the conjunctiva. Naturally, then, since follicles on the conjunctiva of school children are of common occurrence, the percentage of trachoma cases reported for New York City was very high.

For the past three years the Research Laboratory of the Health Department has been studying trachoma and allied diseases in order to determine, among other things, a practical method of diagnosing trachoma if such a disease existed, and thus to separate nondangerous cases from dangerous, and to arrive at an idea of the prevalence of true trachoma in the New York City school children.

The cases studied now number over 4,000 and were taken from the crowded lower east side district, where most of the cases of trachoma were supposed to be. An important point about this study is that many of these cases we have been able to follow closely from the beginning of the disease by the folder system of records, the value of which, in this kind of study, cannot be too highly praised. The outer folder contains the previous history of the case, the family history, notes of home visits and the original and supplementary diagnosis of the case with the result of microscopic and cultural studies; while the inner cards contain a minute description of the different phases in the course of the case. It is upon these descriptions that we chiefly rely in making up our tables, since many cases were seen by several ophthalmologists and the diagnosis given by each was often different from that given by others.

TABLE I

Groups of Cases Studied and Chief Points

	Course						Cured	
Diagnosis	Number	Follicles	Pannus	Scar Tissue	Hypertrophy	Operations	Per Cent.	Av. Time
I. Old trachoma..........	120	110.	22	120	120	80	75	4 yrs.
II. { Acute trachoma / Hypertrophic trachoma / Papillary trachoma / Papillary conjunctivitis }	320	220	1	20	320	18	98	8 mos.
III. { Follicular trachoma / Granular trachoma / Follicular conjunctivitis }	670	670	1	88	128	106	98	1 year.
IV. Folliculosis...........	1950	1950	0	6	5	6	70	9 mos.
V. Acute catarrhal conjunctivitis....	715	65	0	13	16	13	100	1 mo.
VI. Other cases...........	300	6	0	5	0	5	..	..
Total...........	4075							

Note.—Practically all cases showing scar tissue had had one or more operations (expression usually).

Now trachoma, as you know, is supposed, even with treatment, to go on to the formation of cicatricial tissue and sometimes to the production of pannus; but we have found, according to this table, that in this large series of cases treated from *the beginning or near the beginning* of the disease no pannus and no scar tissue (in cases without operation) occurred throughout the course (from the beginning to recovery) of the hypertrophic conjunctivitis cases (diagnosed at first as papillary or acute trachoma) and the cases of follicular conjunctivitis (many diagnosed at first as granular trachoma) and folliculosis.

We discovered a few other important apparently related facts during this study. We found that all of these cases diagnosed as acute trachoma show in smears made from the curetted conjunctiva the so-called trachoma inclusions in the epithelial cells, and from each of these cases we isolated in pure cultures a minute hemoglobinophilic bacillus which morphologically shows changes in its growth similar to those seen in the trachoma inclusions. (Charts.) Furthermore, we found that culturally and morphologically these bacilli cannot be differentiated from the Koch-Weeks bacillus, *i. e.*, the bacillus of acute contagious conjunctivitis or "pink eye." We thus found that all of these so-called acute and subacute trachoma cases were apparently intimately related to the cases of pink eye. Furthermore, we found clinically that most of these cases gave a history of repeated attacks of sore eyes, and that it seemed that the great majority, if not all, of our cases considered as severe papillary trachoma were simply cases of repeated infection with the bacillus of acute contagious conjunctivitis, producing finally chronic thickness of the lids.

As soon as this was determined, our efforts clinically were to devise practical means of treating acute cases of conjunctivitis until their complete recovery with absence of these hemoglobinophilic bacilli and to institute prophylactic measures both in homes and in schools. The ophthalmia school about which Dr. von Sholly will speak we consider a great aid in this work; and the importance of the home visiting by suitable nurses cannot be overestimated. For a long time we have known of the importance of this kind of work in prophylaxis, but we have not before this reached the point of doing it on any great scale.

Practically we are showing, as Table I indicates, that by this minute treatment of these cases we are getting comparatively few of the subacute and chronic cases we formerly found so frequently and we are now urging the establishment throughout the city of our system of records, of ophthalmia schools and of more thorough home visiting.

Of course the work has shown that the vast majority of the cases showing follicles are harmless cases having nothing specifically to do with the condition known as trachoma and that of these latter, there are now extremely few cases at present. We are, therefore, adopting practically the dualistic theory of follicles and our school inspectors are using the following classification in diagnosing cases of conjunctival affections.

(a) *Folliculosis, i. e.,* all cases showing follicles, however numerous, and wherever situated, on an otherwise apparently normal conjunctiva.

(b) *Conjunctivitis, i. e.,* all cases showing inflammatory symptoms, especially those cases exhibiting secretion, with or without follicles, except any included under (c).

(c) *Trachoma, i. e.,* all cases exhibiting cicatricial tissue, or pannus, or both.

(d) *Keratitis, i. e.,* all cases of inflammatory corneal affection not included under (c).

These cases are sent to the eye clinics for treatment and observation and, if necessary, more specific diagnoses are given there.

By following this method, we shall be able to bring our statistics in regard to the prevalence of trachoma more within the limits of truth and thus we shall lose our present false reputation for high percentage of trachoma cases in our public schools.

OPHTHALMIA SCHOOLS FOR THE PREVENTION OF TRACHOMA AND OTHER INFECTIOUS EYE DISEASES

BY

Anna I. von Sholly

In New York City there are more than 700,000 public school children. The 1912 Health Department report showed that 33,860 of these children had suffered from acute (contagious) conjunctivitis during that year and 15,245 from so-called trachoma. The larger part of the sufferers live in the poorest and most congested parts of the city. Their surroundings and habits are such that each one is a focus of contagion to his neighbors.

How far the school is responsible for spreading infection is a question. I doubt whether, in the classroom, the child is much of a menace to his classmates. The greater care of the person during school hours, the discipline in the classroom, the individual desks, chairs, pencils, paper, etc., are bars of prevention. It is more probable that, outside of the school during play hours, the contagium is passed from child to child through the medium of dirty hands and fingers, infected clothes, especially the coat sleeve and cloth cap soiled with eye and nasal secretion, etc. It is not at all unusual, to find a dozen or more cases of acute eye disease among the children living in the same tenement and playing together. It is less common to find more than one case at the same time or closely following in the same classroom.

The school children of New York City have been under constant and careful examination for eye diseases by the Health Department since 1902 and all children considered a source of danger to the others have been excluded from school until certified cured by a physician. As far as her authority carried her, the school nurse has forced every child diagnosed as suffering from trachoma, follicular conjunctivitis, blepharitis, acute conjunctivitis, keratitis, etc., under medical care either of the family doctor or a public dispensary. To obviate any financial hardship, Health Department eye clinics were opened in the congested districts. The children not excluded, but under treatment, have been obliged to bring to the nurse at intervals signed notes from a doctor or dispensary cards showing stamped dates of treatment to prove that they were under treatment. The excluded children have been supposed to report daily in the school nurse's office to show progress of their case. As far as possible, home visits for purpose of instruction have been made by the nurse.

The weakness of the above system of handling eye diseases among the school children—the prevailing system of all the large cities in this country and of Europe—is that neither the Health Department or the Educational Department has had full control over the children and a valuable opportunity to concentrate on education in hygiene has not been fully utilized. The exclusion of the infected child from school does not cover the situation. The feeble quarantine which it entails, does little else but call attention in a mild way to the contagiousness of the disease and the need for treatment. The necessity for a rapid cure in order to limit the period that the child is a carrier of infection and the teaching and enforcement during this period of personal and family hygiene is neglected.

The problem in New York City is not an easy one. There is a large foreign population, poor, ignorant, unclean in their habits, very suspicious of what seems like outside interference; many willing and glad to use the excuse of "sore eyes" to have the child remain at home to help in the family work. The children are self-willed and indulged and when they refused treatment are not forced by their overridden or deceived parents to submit.

The children whose eyes exhibit "follicles" on the lining conjunctiva without any acute or subacute inflammation and without abnormal discharge or "matter," yet diagnosed as trachoma by the school doctor, have been permitted, and quite rightly, to attend school regularly, provided they showed proof of being under a doctor's care. It is now agreed that these cases are not trachoma but a benign disease common to school children known as folliculosis or "schul-follikel." Experience has demonstrated that these cases do not require such frequent treatments as the child has had to submit to. The milder cases of this disease recede spontaneously under ordinary hygienic measures. Between these children and the school nurse there has been a constant conflict. The child and the child's parent cannot understand the enforced treatment where there are no subjective symptoms. The child evades the unpleasant and irksome treatment, deceives the nurse, some even going so far as to buy date stamps and stamping their own dispensary cards. Where a particularly rebellious child has refused treatment absolutely, the nurse has had to choose between allowing the child to have his will and thus undermine her and the school's authority or exerting her power to exclude the child from school until he submitted—the very object the child frequently wished.

In the case of the excluded children, with their exclusion they passed out of the jurisdiction of the school and the nurse too. Only the actively infectious cases are usually excluded. These children may roam the streets at will, carry infection to all who come in contact with them for the 14 to 16 waking hours instead of the 8 to 10 hours otherwise spent out of the school. These excluded children do not necessarily place themselves under treatment. Many are glad not to go to school. Girls take advantage of the plea "sore eyes" to remain at home to help in the housework and are even encouraged by their parents. Boys have been started, by exclusion from school, on the way to become incorrigible truants. They acquire the street habit. One little Italian girl aged 12 years, whose eyes were in bad condition with eyelashes matted together with pus was excluded from school. She was absent from her class for more than a term, coming to the clinic for treatment only when actually sent for by the nurse. Finally after repeated messages to return to the special ophthalmia class which had been started subsequent to her exclusion, she had to be brought resisting to the school by the principal's messenger, from the family washtub. Within one month after she was under daily treatment in the school, her eyes were well. Two brothers and a sister with moderately inflamed eyes who had been under irregular treatment for a long time previous to the opening of the classes were corraled at the same time and cured. No one of these has relapsed since.

There is also the financial hardship to the family when a child approaching 14 years of age is excluded and kept from getting his working papers through lack of required school attendance.

After studying the situation for several years, the New York City Health Department agreed that the exclusion principle was inadequate. It suggested to the educational authorities that experimental classes for children suffering from infectious eye diseases which ordinarily exclude them from school, be opened in one of the most infected parts of the city. In October, 1912, two classes in close connection with a Health Department eye clinic were started in the lower east side at Hester and Allen Streets. One wing of a vacated school building was fitted out. On the ground floor is the playground, one flight up two clinic rooms and a demonstration room and above these the two classrooms and a wash room. The classrooms seat from 15 to 17 children each. The washroom contains a porcelain washbasin with a gooseneck faucet worked by a foot lever so that the child touches no part with its hands. All washing is done with running water. There is a bubbling drinking fountain of porcelain also worked by a foot lever.

Three days a week a Health Department Ophthalmologist holds a clinic. All children with eye disease from some 60 adjoining public and parochial schools are either sent or brought in squads by the school nurse for treatment. The children who formerly would have been excluded are transferred without delay to the infectious eye diseases classes. The principals of their schools are notified by printed post card. The mild cases of folliculosis or "schulfollikel," are instructed to use boric acid drops and are placed under the school nurse's observation. According to her judgment, they report to the clinic. The other cases needing treatment report to the clinic as heretofore. All children are given cards with the diagnosis stamped on it for the information of the school nurse who has typed instruction as to what course to pursue.

The children retained in the special classes are given treatment, according to the prescribed directions of the clinic doctor, twice a day by the special nurse assigned to duty at the ophthalmia school. The medication formerly left to the child's discretion for use at home, is thus given in the school. We now *know* that the child receives its treatment. If the child absents himself from school, the truant officer is sent for him.

In addition to actually taking care of the eyes, the nurse in attendance teaches the children personal, family and social hygiene, by talks, demonstrations and quizzes. She also gives demonstrations on the care of the eyes to the mothers. The children are taught the value of cleanliness. They are obliged to keep their hands and nails clean and taught not to rub their eyes or wipe them with their coat sleeves or caps. Their hands and persons are inspected daily, and as a reward for cleanliness an honor button is given them. At the end of the term, the child who has had the best marks for cleanliness receives a small manicure set. At the end of the school day each child washes his own desk and chair with soap and water.

The nurse visits the homes of the children in attendance and gives instruction to the mothers in their own homes. Printed leaflets in three languages—Italian, Yiddish and English—giving instructions on the care of the eyes are distributed to every new patient in the clinic.

Two teachers are in charge of the ophthalmia school. The children range from 7 to 16 years of age and are divided into two classes of mixed grades, one of the older and one of the younger children. The children's eyes are protected from strain as far as possible. All work, as far as it can be, is oral and all reading and writing of very short duration or omitted in severe cases. The school session is shortened, the morning session begins at 9.15 a. m., and the afternoon ending at 2.15 p. m., with one hour from 12 to 1 for lunch. One-half hour in both morning and afternoon is devoted to recreation—play in the neighboring park in fair weather, story telling in bad weather. Last year's schedule was as follows:

9.15 to 9.30, assembly.
9.30 to 10.00, treatment and rest.

10.00 to 10.30, arithmetic.
10.30 to 10.45, spelling.
10.45 to 11.15, recreation.
11.15 to 11.45, English.
11.45 to 11.55, reading.
11.55 to 12.00, wash hands and dismiss.
12.00 to 1.00, lunch.
1.00 to 1.15, wash hands and rest.
1.15 to 1.45, recreation.
1.45 to 2.15, hygiene (Mondays); Geography (Tues., Wed., Thurs., Fri.)
2.15, dismissal to clinic for treatment.

Up to June 20th, 1912 (nine school months), 312 pupils had passed through the ophthalmia school. The various kinds of cases treated were as follows, namely, acute conjunctivitis, including acute catarrhal conjunctivitis or pink eye and acute phlyctenular conjunctivitis, trachoma, follicular conjunctivitis, syphilitic, tubercular, and phlyctenular keratitis and neglected protracted cases of blepharitis.

When school closed June 28th there were about 25 children in the classes, some ready for discharge. All the others who had passed through were discharged cured. Only three returned to the class after discharge with a recurrence of the disease. The shortest stay in the class was two days, the longest the entire nine months. There were eight children with trachoma among the latter.

The school principals, school nurses and teachers are all enthusiastic about the new classes. The school nurse is relieved of the unpleasant duty of hounding the children to doctors and dispensaries. She is relieved of the responsibility of the incorrigible who refuse treatment, the careless and neglected cases and the actively acute cases that carry infection, all of which are placed in the ophthalmia school.

From the point of view of the educational authorities, the child loses no school attendance, the authority of the principal is still in control since the child is not excluded, the arm of the truant officer is still powerful, school discipline is not relaxed and the child is not thrust out into the streets to become familiar with bad company and bad habits.

From the health point of view the disease is attacked early *kept under persistent treatment* so that the cure is shortened and at the same time both child and parent taught how to avoid reinfection and spreading disease to others.

The acute eye infections, especially if severe or neglected, may become chronic. There is a condition called papillary conjunctivitis sometimes called trachoma, which is caused by the same germ which causes acute catarrhal conjunctivitis. This condition, which is more or less disfiguring from the drooping of the upper eyelid, is not uncommon in New York City. In the section covered by the ophthalmia school

from January, 1910 to January, 1913, there were 320 such c
Since then no fresh cases of this disease has been seen. We f
all cases would be seen early and treated constantly we might
this disease entirely. The grouping of the early acute cas
special classes has so far not disappointed us in this hope. In
section of Manhattan and in Brooklyn, in districts similarly
where. the old system of exclusion is still in force, these
chronic papillary conjunctivitis are still seen. It seems to us
the cases of folli-cular conjunctivitis are rarer and folliculosis
the section of the city covered by the ophthalmia classes.

THE PRESERVATION OF THE EYESIGHT OF SCHOOL CHILDREN

BY

GERTRUDE E. BINGHAM

The children of to-day are the fathers and mothers of to-morrow. Their physical well-being is as important as their mental. It behooves those who have in their keeping this most sacred charge, to fulfill it in such a manner that each child may rise to his full stature.

The nation, state and city must stand back of those in whose hands the charge is placed, else in these days of great industrial and economic pressure many of these children will not rise to their full stature.

Nearly a quarter of a century ago, France made obligatory the medical and sanitary inspection of schools, both public and private. To-day the movement is national in scope in England, Belgium, Sweden, Switzerland, Bulgaria, the Argentine Republic, and "to all intents and purposes nearly equally so in Germany."

The slowness of the individual states of this country to pass laws governing medical inspection proves that a national law is necessary. While several states have permissive laws, there is but one state, Massachusetts, that makes medical inspection compulsory.*

Spasmodic examinations of the eyes of school children in this and other countries have brought to light such startling conditions that one is no alarmist when he states that if the most blessed gift of all—the gift of perfect sight—is to be preserved to our children, nation, state and city must render aid.

The following statistics show that no phase of medical inspection is performed in such a cursory manner as that of the eyes. Forty-three per cent. of American cities have established some form of medical inspection in schools. In 25% of these cities such inspection includes examination of the eyes, either by a general physician or by an ophthalmologist. In 43% vision tests are made by the teachers; in 32% no vision tests are made.

"In 415 New York villages, it was ascertained that 48.7% of school children had defects of vision, this without testing children under seven years—while 11.3% had sore eyes."†

In Manchester, New Hampshire, of 4,625 children tested, 1,106 had eye defects. (Report of School Committee, December 31, 1909.)

*Chap. 502, Acts of 1906, as amended by Chap. 257, Acts of 1910.
†William Allen Harvey in Civics and Health, pp. 72-82.

In Fall River, Massachusetts, of 14,523 children, 2,164 had eye defects. (Annual School Report, 1911.)

In St. Louis, Missouri, of 2,000 children examined, 30.6% had vision below normal in one or both eyes. Fourteen per cent. showed vision that was less than two-thirds normal in both eyes. (Interstate Medical Journal, Nov., 1909.)

In Massachusetts, omitting Boston, in 1907 19.9% had visual defects, while Boston found that 23% of its school children had such defects. (Interstate Medical Journal, November, 1909.)

There is a wide difference of opinion as to what department shall administer regulation relating to medical inspection. In my judgment this should be placed in the hands of the school authorities, as in many rural districts there are no Boards of Health, in order that the national law may be administered in a uniform manner, the administration should be vested in Boards of Education.

Divided responsibility is more often a failure than a success. The totally inadequate eye inspection of school children in New York City is an example. Where the administration of medical inspection is in the hands of Boards of Health, with their doctors and nurses, the tendency is that principals and teachers feel that the responsibility is not theirs.

Dr. S. Josephine Baker states that she feels "that the teachers are in a better position to diagnose eye-strain than the inspector or nurse, not from the fact that the child cannot read the test card but from the symptoms shown in the class-room, during the usual period of school hours."

In order that teachers may detect eye diseases and eye defects, the training school should afford instruction in the use of the Snellen test card; how to detect signs of inflammation or active pathological change, such as styes, redness or swelling of the lids; vascularity, locally or generally, in the eyeball; intolerance of light; and excessive lachrymation —all symptoms easy to detect but of such importance that when detected active steps should at once be taken to place the child under special medical care, to note symptoms of eye muscles being affected as indicated by squinting; a quivering movement of the eyeball; habitual blinking; or the holding of the head sideways or bending too closely over their work.

Boards of Education should have at their disposal a fund from which to supply eyeglasses to worthy children. The following incident is related by a parent residing in New York City:

"A child at school is told to get glasses by a nurse in school; he goes to a clinic, and after an examination, which necessitates coming with either parent four or five times at a cost of carfare and the time of the parent, he is given a card to go to the prescription department in the basement. The parent is told the glasses cost from $4.50 to $10, asked for $3 to $5 deposit (which is probably the wages of the father for half a week) and told to come in a week or two for the glasses. When he calls he gets a pair of gold-filled rims (actual cost by the dozen 30 cents each for the best manufactured), and a pair of lenses which are in stock in every wholesale supply house and are sold from $1 to $3 a dozen for the specially ground bifocal lens. After having used the glasses some time, the child, by accident, breaks one of the lenses. You have to go back to the clinic. From there they usually send you to the counter in the basement where the clerk looks at the prescription and says $1.50 or $2 for one of the lenses. He then tells you to call in three or four days, when they will be ready. At the same time he knows that he can put in the lenses in two to three minutes, as he has them in stock." The above is an exact description of the way a child who is sent to one of our city clinics is treated in getting a pair of glasses.

The Massachusetts Charitable Eye and Ear Infirmary has a special fund at its disposal. It has been found that parents who are unable to pay in full will pay on a simple installment plan.

For many years an Associate City Superintendent of New York City had the control of a private fund from which the children of deserving parents could be supplied with glasses. The principal and school nurse selected the children, who needed such aid. The parents were interviewed and were encouraged to pay a small part of the cost of glasses. The results were most gratifying. The many appeals made to me by principals and parents for help in procuring glasses and my attempts to secure them through charitable organizations have convinced me that the solution is the special fund.

Such a fund would also do away with a most serious evil, that of cheap eyeglasses, the 5, 10 and 25-cent varieties purchased from the eyeglass venders. These glasses, crudely ground and often magnifying strongly, will cause dizziness or nausea and even permanently injure the delicate structure of the eye. Parents upon receiving notice from school to procure glasses and not having sufficient money to go to an optician will resort to these cheap glasses rather than make application to a charitable organization with its attendant investigation.

The six eye clinics for school children only established by the Board of Health of New York City proves the wisdom of the special eye clinic for children. The overcrowded condition of the clinics in connection with hospitals makes the visits so long and tedious for parents that where danger is not apparent and immediate, they give up in despair after a few visits.

The appointment of the social-medical visitors in connection with such clinics is absolutely indispensable. In the Boston Dispensary

Eye Clinic for the year 1910 it is shown that one-half the refraction work was wasted. With the help of a medical social worker this was reduced to 4.5% in one and one-half years. Before the advent of the worker, 44% of the cases of iritis, phlyctenular disease, acute conjunctivitis, and blepharitis paid only one visit. Two years later the percentage of lost cases in the same clinic and with the same medical service was reduced to 24.5%. In other words the physician was saved about 20% of wasted effort. As for the effects upon the patients, the percentage of those whom the physician considered cured rose from 17%, when he worked alone, to 40.5% when he was assisted by a medical-social worker.

A girl of eight appeared at the above-named infirmary suffering from interstitial keralitis. She had been treated at twenty-eight different clinics, nose, throat, lungs, surgical, etc., as various symptoms appeared. When taken in charge by ophthalmologist, syphilologist, and social worker together this child received persistent constitutional treatment and was saved from partial if not total blindness.

In the winter of 1909 it was reported to me that a girl of nine had sore eyes, and was not receiving attention. I found the child's eyes in an alarming condition from corneal ulcers. She had a clinic card but investigation showed that she had not been to a clinic for a year. The mother had died the year before and the father wished to have this girl take charge of a younger child. The father, a drunken brute, would not allow the child to go to a clinic because if her eyes looked sore the attendance officer would not compel her to go to school. She was put into a hospital where it was found that the sight of one eye was destroyed. Partial sight was saved in the second but not sufficient to enable her to be educated as a sighted child.

The treatment of diseases of the cornea, cataract, etc., is so tedious that parents either neglect or waste medical service provided.

That early diagnosis and thorough treatment of the above-named diseases, are imperative is proven by examining the records of our schools for the blind. While neglect may not result in total blindness, the eyes are so scarred or weakened by these diseases that instruction in special schools is necessary. Not only is impaired vision a terrible handicap but the increased cost of such education is ten times greater.

While there has been a steady decline in this country during the past twenty-five years in the number of prescriptions written for myopia, due probably to the fact that more children in early life are provided with glasses, it is still a defect of such significance that the prevalence of it should be particularly noted.

An investigation conducted by Dr. Cohn in the city schools of Breslau shows that myopia progressed from 6.7% in the elementary schools to 19.7% in the academy grade and to 59.5% in the university.

Dr. Rislay found that while the elementary schools of Philadelphia showed 4.27% in the lower grades there was a steady increase to 19.33% in the academy grade, with an advance to 19.75% in the upper classes of the University of Pennsylvania, the latter fact having been determined by Drs. Posey and McKenzie.*

It is interesting to note that the maximum increase in the academy grades of the German and American schools was practically the same, while in the German University the increase was a little more than three times as great.

The Department of Special Education of the National Education Association, in 1910, appointed a committee "to study and report on the conservation of vision."

That the investigation conducted by this committee found the above statistics not exaggerated is shown by their recommendation "that where the power of vision is limited it should be conserved and developed by proper eye training, either by segregation or by the omission of certain subjects of study."

After England's Medical Inspection Act became operative in 1908 action was taken immediately to provide better eye examination. Dr. N. Bishop Harmon was made eye expert of the London County Council Schools. He found so many children seriously handicapped by eye defects that he recommended special education for such children.

The classification is as follows:

(1.) Invalid, where mischief is active.

(2.) Elementary (U. S. Grammar School), not serious for special arrangement, e. g., one eye blind from squint.

(3.) Elementary School, easy treatment, i. e., no sewing, no fine pen or close work, no geometry, Myopes 2 and 3.

(4.) Elementary School, oral teaching only, i. e., no reading, writing, or sewing of any kind. Listen and learn. Myopes 4 and 5.

(5.) Myope class, associated with elementary school. One-third oral teaching; one-third such literary work as must be known, done on blackboard in special classroom; one-third handicraft and drill.

Doctor determines play alone or with sighted on merits of each.

(6.) Blind school.

*Prevalence of Defects and Diseases, Dr. Walter Connell, pp. 582-583.

The only phase of such education requiring explanation is that of the classes of Myopes. The children for these classes are selected at the discretion of Dr. Harmon. He has no absolute standard of myopia for schools. It depends upon the age of the child and whether or not the disease is progressive. A young child would be taken in with a less high degree of myopia because the younger he is the more serious any degree of myopia. Practically there is no child in the school with less than six of myopia. In addition there are cases of cataract, corneal opacities, etc., who are not blind enough for blind school or good enough for ordinary classes in sighted school. They are what Dr. Harmon calls the "lame ducks."

The children are examined twice a year or more often if the teacher thinks necessary.

The classes are under the supervision of an inspector of children with defective sight. The maximum number of children in each class is twenty; fewer if possible. To each group is assigned a special teacher. The Board of Education pays for the transportation of all such children. There are no specially prepared books. Dr. Harmon would like charts or sheets containing printed matter set up in 4-inch letters. All written work is done on the blackboard at arm's length in letters 4 inches high. The seniors are allowed to write in two-inch letters.

A special desk has been designed by Dr. Harmon which has a square top like a table. This swings back and as it is painted black, can be used as a small blackboard. They go to classes for sighted for all lessons where reading and writing are not necessary. Much time is devoted to word lessons as the only reading that the children get in schools is what the teachers or they themselves write on blackboards. By means of oral teaching and the blackboard work above described the usual curriculum is covered as nearly as possible.

A great deal of manual work is given but no sewing is allowed as it is thought that if the girls learn how to sew the eyes would be used too much at home.

In Boston, one class for border line cases has recently been established in connection with the public school. The London plan is being followed. While there is much good in the London plan, there is one very serious objection. The pupils are given no means of reading for themselves and the result is that while they are not allowed to use their eyes for reading in school they do read at home. The solution of the problem is to have the pupils learn to read a point print system with the fingers, a simple tool which makes it possible for the handicapped child to get all his training with sighted children. There is a strong prejudice on the part of parents to have a child read with his fingers but that it is possible to overcome this prejudice is shown by the fact that there are a dozen or more of these border line cases in the public schools of New York who are following this method.

The children who receive training in special classes do not have much difficulty in getting employment after leaving school. Dr. Harmon writes as follows: "Both special schools for the blind and employees' liability legislation were designed to ameliorate the condition of those suffering a handicap; and so they do, but at the same time they intensify that handicap in other directions, e. g., the training of a blind school is a benefit to the child but it is difficult to secure work for a youth just out of a blind school."

It is the opinion of educators who have observed closely, the work- ing of such classes that they are an indispensable adjunct of the public school.

In conclusion I would summarize the following essentials for the preservation of the eyesight of school children:

(1.) A national law requiring the medical inspection of school children to be administered by Boards of Education.

(2.) The curriculum in training schools for teachers to include instruction in the diagnosis of eye diseases and defects.

(3.) A special fund under control of Boards of Education from which to supply eyeglasses to worthy children.

(4.) Establishment of special eye clinics for children only.

(5.) The appointment of the social-medical visitor in connection with such clinics.

(6.) The establishment of special classes in connection with public schools for children with defective sight.

SOME IMPORTANT OCULAR CONDITIONS FOUND IN BACKWARD CHILDREN WITH REPORT OF CASES

BY

J. HOLBROOK SHAW

In an extremely interesting and pertinent magazine article, Mr. Earl Mayo, who is a recognized authority upon questions of public health, has graphically shown that the greatest asset of any nation is its human lives. He calls attention to our agricultural products, railways and manufacturers, representing a monetary value of billions of dollars and shows that the monetary value of a human life to the community based on the conservative estimate of Professor Irving Fisher of Yale, would give a total valuation for our 90,000,000 lives far in excess of all other values combined.

The human crop then is the most valuable one which we raise and in the public schools we have opportunities for improving this valuable yield of which we have as a people, but recently begun to take advantage. With the general adoption of an adequate system of medical inspection in the schools of our country we may confidently expect, in succeeding generations, a sturdier, healthier race, whose physical and mental superiority will appreciably increase the national assets, for, in the last analysis it is the quality of human activity which really determines values.

What we put into medical inspection then for the improvement of the race is not spent, but merely invested to be returned later with interest by the increased efficiency of those who have benefitted by it. But as every child whose future efficiency we increase adds to the public wealth of the community, so every influence which hinders or prevents the normal physical and mental development of any child makes the community so much the poorer.

Millions of dollars are being spent annually in this country to care for and educate the children, but while we have a splendid system which we are constantly improving, there are certain conditions which are lessening its efficiency and increasing the expense of operation.

Dr. William H. Maxwell, Superintendent of Schools of the City of New York, in his report for 1904, called attention to the fact that a large number of pupils were shown by his tables to be above the normal age for the grades they were in. Further inquiry disclosed the fact that this condition was not confined to New York City, and it was deemed of sufficient importance to warrant an exhaustive study by Dr. Leonard P. Ayres for the Russell Sage Foundation, the results having been finally published under the title of "Laggards in Our Schools." Dr. Ayres finds, as we should expect, "that physical defectiveness has a distinct and important bearing on the progress of children," but he also shows that the child, who is normal but slow, has no chance of keeping up under our present system, is "thoroughly trained in failure" and is destined to live a life of failure. "We know them in school," he says, "as the children who are always a little behind physically, a little behind intellectually and a little behind in the power to do. Such a child is the one who is always 'It' in the competitive games of childhood."

During the past year the writer undertook an investigation of the causes of retardation of pupils under his supervision. Pupils who were unable to keep their places in the work of the schools without special attention, if at all, were adjudged "retarded" or backward for the purposes of the inquiry and were divided into groups as follows: (1) those who were mentally defective; (2) those who were normal mentally but had some physical disability like defective sight or hearing and (3) those whose mental processes were merely slow.

Those of the first group are naturally the most objectionable as they are not amenable to school discipline and often have vicious habits, thus exercising a decidedly unfortunate influence upon other and younger pupils in the lower grades where they often remain until 14 years old or more.

The second group may be still further subdivided into (a) those having remediable defects and (b) those having irremediable defects. Many of the former, as far as any prospect of improvement during their school life is concerned, most unfortunately be considered in the latter or irremediable class owing to the indifference of parents of their inability to provide suitable treatment for them. In the larger cities many of these unfortunate children get relief at the public dispensaries but in smaller communities they must at present depend upon the uncertain hope of private philanthropy, too often represented by the teacher whose sympathy leads her to contribute to this end from her hard earned salary.

In the third group are those who with special attention would do well, but who otherwise fall behind, lose interest and become mischievous and troublesome, interfering with the discipline of the school and adding to the burdens of the already over-taxed teacher.

Without going into detail, it is enough to say that investigation showed that 66% of the pupils of the second group had ocular defects. This paper aims to call attention to some of the ocular defects which are such a prolific source of retardation and cite a few illustrative cases.

It might, perhaps, seem a hopeless task to try to do anything for the mentally deficient pupils of the first group, but as a matter of fact they may frequently be greatly benefitted by the correction of existing ocular defects and should be carefully examined for them.

J. B., 7 years of age, had spent a year in school without making any progress whatever. The characters which he drew upon the paper given him for work, were utterly unintelligible. Examination showed that he was myopic, O. D. V7 / 50, O. S. V3 / 50. Correction was given him and he immediately began to improve, so that within a year he was writing complete sentences in a perfectly legible hand and taking great pride in what he could do. He has also learned to read a little though his enunciation is indistinct, but before the correction of his myopia his teachers had never been able to get him to speak.

Some children are unfortunate enough to be handicapped by physical defects which make them appear mentally deficient when they are not really so, but if these defects are not discovered and special instruction given them, they become really deficient through lack of training. There is nothing in the work more gratifying to the school physician than to discover one of these minds trying to grope its uncertain way through clouded senses and to watch its development as it is brought into intelligent relation with the outside world by means of special methods of instruction, which take into consideration the child's limitations.

Such a case was that of G. L. who, when he was found by the writer in the first grade, three years ago, had been practically abandoned as unable to learn by his long-suffering teacher, who had a large school to care for. She believed that he was mentally incompetent, and there was reason for such a belief. As there were no tasks which he could do, the child spent the long school hours practically unemployed, twisting and turning about in his seat and making strange grimaces.

An examination gave O. D. V1 / 200, O. S. V20 / 100, due to irregular astigmatism and corneal opacities. The twisting and turning were now explained. Sitting through the school session without any intelligent idea of what was going on about him, the child was simply amusing himself getting glimpses of the light which streamed into the room from the various windows.

The school physician became convinced that the child's mind was unusually keen and active. The teacher was informed of the result of the examination, and at once became interested, agreeing to do all in her power to make up for the poor eyesight of her pupil by special attention to his needs, a promise which she generously fulfilled. The parents were informed of the serious defect of vision and encouraged to aid the teacher by every means in their power. Inspired with a new hope, they took up the work with enthusiasm, and though of limited

means, even secured a tutor for a time. The results have amply justi_
fied the special care and attention devoted to the child. He now has
excellent standing in his grade, the third, sings unusually well, has a
wonderful memory and shows a remarkable aptitude for mathematics.
The following are examples of his language, spelling and number work.

"G. L.

Oak St. School   Grade III   Dec. 20, 1911.
The Fox and the Crow.

A crow had a piece of cheese. One day a Fox saw The Crow fly in a tree and th
fox said to the crow sing" but The crow wouldn't sing. And The fox said to the
crow sing." So th crow sang. As The crow sang she drope the cheese and The Fox
ran away with it."

"G. L.   Dec. 22, 1911.
Oak St. School   Grade III
Christmas   Santa Claus
santa claus   merry
Merry   candles
candles   skates
skates   secret
secret   birthday
birthday   candles
Christmas   Christmas
Santa Claus   Santa claus"

"G. L.   Dec. 21, 1911.
Oak St. School   Grade III

804	434	467	790
942	245	578	804
23	356	689	942
1769	1035	1734	2536

802	943	824	842
−497	−589	−298	−298
305	354	526	544

| 802 | 943 | 824 | 842 |

923	834	945	853
x 4	x 5	x 6	x 4
3692	4170	5670	3412

| 233 | 034 | 493 | 023 |
| 4) 932 | 3) 102 | 2) 986 | 5) 115 |

233	34	493	23
x 4	x3	x 2	x5
932	102	986	115

So much for his work in school, but one must see him at play in the sunny school yard, his face beaming with happiness and his body swaying in perfect rhythm while he sings in a sweet, clear voice with the other children at their games, in which he is unable to take a part, to understand what it has meant to him to have a chance.

This boy was saved from the neglect which threatened him as mentally incompetent and placed in the second group where with special attention he promises to become a useful member of society.

O. L., a first grade pupil, was reported to the school physician as a backward child, doing few of the simple tasks given her, and none of them well. An examination showed that she was hyperopic. Little help could be secured from the child in making the test, but the hyperopia was estimated objectively to be five dioptres in the right and one in the left eye. O. D. + 3.00 Ds and O. S. + 0.75 Ds seemed to be most acceptable and was given, when a remarkable change took place in the character of her work, shown in Figs. 1 and 2.

FIGURE 1

These are both exact reproductions of the original tracings made by the pupil over letters drawn by the teacher—Fig. 1 before correcting lenses were applied and Fig. 2 afterwards. The groping irregularity of the lines on Fig. 1 suggests the nervous energy wasted by the child in trying to drive the unwilling pencil over its blurred and uncertain course, while the easy swing of the lines in Fig. 2 indicates something of the relief she must have experienced in the removal of the accommodation strain, comparatively little though it was.

FIGURE 2

Thus pupils of the second group who have remediable defects may become physically and mentally normal.

There is one remediable defect which every school physician and nurse should thoroughly understand in order that they may impress the importance of its early correction upon parents, and that is internal strabismus. The idea is too common among the laity that children will outgrow this condition whereas as a matter of fact it will simply become confirmed. These children are hyperopic, generally highly so, and as accommodation and convergence are associated, the excessive effort which they must make in overcoming their hyperopia results in a loss of binocular vision. The eye with the higher degree of refractive error, if a difference exists, is pulled in by the strong impulse of the internal rectus muscle and the image of that eye is eventually suppressed.

The remedy is, of course, the early correction of the hyperopia by properly adjusted convex lenses. Unfortunately the test of vision made by the teachers in our Massachusetts schools does not show any but the worst cases of hyperopia, and the school physician cannot usually devote sufficient time to each pupil to discover it even if he were familiar with the usual means of testing for it, such as the ophthalmoscope, retinoscope or trial case. There is, however, a very simple procedure which will disclose any considerable degree through the associated muscular imbalance. This consists in having the pupil fix an object twenty feet or more away, the examiner alternately covering first one eye and then the other with a bit of cardboard.   If there is any considerable degree of hyperopia it will be found that the covered eye has failed to hold in line and turned in toward the nose.   This is not of course apparent until the eye is uncovered when it is seen to jump back into line and again fix the distant object.   The early application of this simple test will disclose many cases of eye-strain which if left uncorrected would eventually become strabismus.   In these uncorrected cases the eye will at first turn in toward the nose only occasionally.   If the strain is removed by glasses early, the "squint" is frequently entirely removed and binocular vision restored, while the child experiences great relief be having the accompanying eye-strain removed, but if neglected, a time will come at length when the deviation of the eye becomes confirmed and can only be corrected by surgical measures which frequently have to be repeated before a satisfactory result is obtained and even then glasses must be worn to relieve the strain.

It is not always possible to straighten an eye in this way but the chances are always better the earlier the remedy is applied and the proper glasses may afford great relief to the child by removing the eyestrain, even if they do not wholly succeed in straightening the eye.

Figure 3 shows a boy of five years found in the first grade with a very marked deviation inward of the left eye.   Notice was sent to the parents that the child was suffering from eyestrain, and they promptly took measures to have it relieved.   Figure 4 shows the same boy wearing a convex lens of three dioptres focal strength over the right eye, and one of four dioptres over the left eye, thus removing the eyestrain and enabling the eyes to work together with precision, to the great relief of the child who had been doing his school work under an immense handicap.

These facts with regard to "squint" are not new but they need to be brought to the attention of the school physician and the school nurse.

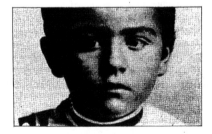

FIGURE 3

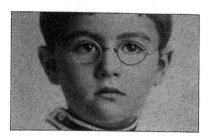

FIGURE 4

The last ocular defect to which I wish to call attention is a form of amblyopia which I have failed to find described in the literature to which I have had access. The cases which I have seen have been in young girls and were characterized by more or less irregular peripheral contraction of the visual field and imperfect vision which is not due to any refractive error or visible ocular defect or disease.

The following is a typical case:

M., a bright, vigorous, well nourished girl of seven, with none of the stigmata of hysteria was first tested in April, 1908; vision, O. D. =20 / 100, O. S. =20 / 100. The keratometer indicated no astigmatism and retinoscopy gave normal refraction. The ophthalmoscope showed normal fundi and agreed with the retinoscope as to the absence of refractive error. I could only explain the case at the time as one of malingering, but did not feel satisfied. Nearly four years later, in January, 1912, I had an opportunity to examine the child again and found O. D. V20 / 200, O. S. V20 / 100-1, practically the same as at the first test. The field of vision tried roughly with a piece of cotton on the end of a pencil suggested peripheral contraction. Two more tests were made at intervals with slightly varying results and in March, 1912, a one per cent. solution of sulphate of atropine was instilled for two days and a test made with the following result:

O. D. V12 / 200 + 1.00 Ds. = V20 / 70 +1
O. S. V12 / 200 + 1.00 Ds. = V20 / 50-2.
A trial pair of glasses was given with + 0.50 Ds. O. U. for near use.

April, 1913, one year later, another examination gave:
O. D. V20 / 70-1 + 0.50 Dc axis 180 = V20 / 70-1 (clearer).
O. S. V20 / 50-2 + 0.50 Dc axis 180 = V20 / 50-1
and these lenses were prescribed.

A careful test of the visual fields for white showed a contraction of both, Fig. 5, but more marked on the right where the defect was both nasal and temporal. On the left side the defect was chiefly temporal..

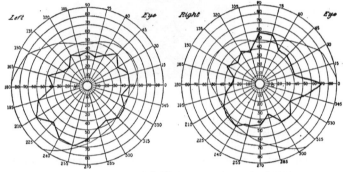

FIGURE 5

The vision in this case as in others which I have seen, shows a tendency to improve.

I believe that these are cases of imperfect development of the visual function and that the defect is central, but they need to be studied very carefully and I hope that we shall hear more about them in the future. The new-born infant with perfect visual organs is practically blind, the maximum visual acuity not being acquired much before the seventh year. Beyond that period it is possible to acquire exceptional visual powers by constant practice. To Professor Percival Lowell, whose unusual development of visual acuity enabled him to enrich the science of astronomy through his minute studies of the Martian canals, most men seemed "telescopically blind." In these children then, the development of the visual function seems to have been arrested from some as yet obscure cause, and it is important that the condition should be recognized early in order that they may not only receive whatever aid the oculist may be able to give them, but that they may also be treated with such consideration by their teachers as their limitations would suggest.

After all has been done which can be done in the way of removing physical defects, backward pupils should be placed under a special teacher whose business it should be to study the individual needs of each child and supply the particular kind of training which will be most helpful in bringing him or her up to the normal standard. To accomplish the best results such a teacher should have had experience in this special sort of work, besides being a person of intelligence and tact. With the **retarded pupils und**er such leadership the schools are relieved of those **who not only do not keep** the pace themselves but actually hinder the progress of others, while they receive a training which brings many of them up to the normal standard and saves more from a dis. couragement which would probably follow them through life.

Summary.

1.   Backward children are expensive to the community both in school and in after life.

2.   The correction of the physical defects by which many backward children are handicapped and special individual training, are the efficient means by which these children may be saved from incompetency.

3.   Investigation of backward children indicates that ocular defects are most important as a cause of "retardation."

4.   The correction of refractive errors in the mentally deficient child is beneficial.

5.   It is important to correct hypermetropia early, thus stopping a needless waste of nervous energy and in certain cases preventing or correcting squint.

6.   There is a form of amblyopia among children which is little understood.

ve seen, shows a

.::: of the visual
.: to be studied
.::. them in the
.:: is practically
:.:h before the
.:.:: exceptional
P.::::al Lowell.
.: ::m to enrich
.. :: the Martian
..:. children then.
.: :::n arrested
: : :he condition

.. ::.: they may
:: :: their limits

.:: of removing
.: :: a special
.::::.: needs of
:.: :. will be most
: .: To accom.
.:. :.::e in this

PROGRESS IN SCHOOL WRITING IN NORWAY

BY

OTTO GRENNESS

Mr. Chairman, Ladies and Gentlemen:

About 20 years ago, when the dispute over sloping and upright writing reached Norway, the Royal Church and Education Department appointed a Committee of teachers and doctors, to inquire into the question and recommend any possible improvements in our teaching of writing. The Committee came to the result that upright-writing had more advantages than sloping writing as regarded Hygiene, and recommended, moreover, a number of improvements respecting school desks and writing materials. Also new copybooks were prepared as specimens; but those did not have any wide circulation, and interest in the subject died out. In 1904 a Swedish master of writing intro-duced a method of penmanship, which was tried in the Primary Schools of Kristiania for a period of 8 years until it was forbidden by the Department of Education as not being hygienic. Had this mistaken copybook done much harm, it had, however, had the effect of causing the interest for a more up-to-date system of teaching of writing to blaze up, and it also showed how little insight into the hygiene of teaching, and especially the hygiene of writing, one was yet able to count on. In 1888 the Education Department gave their instructions for the printing and get-up of school books; these regulations still remain unchanged, and only apply to printed text books, but not to writing, arithmetic and drawing materials.

In 1908 the Parliament passed a law that all text books for the Primary Schools should be sanctioned by the Education Department. This law was first carried into effect thus: that writing, arithmetic and drawing books were not submitted for approval. On my representation of this matter in 1908, the Education Department resolved to claim approval for the above-mentioned teaching apparatus, and little by little I have had opportunity of examining almost one and all existing Norwegian copybooks. I have, unfortunately, not yet found anything which wholly satisfies all essential demands for an up-to-date hygienic copybook, but there is, however, a little progress to be traced. The most of our copybooks have one capital fault in their *all too large size.* It would appear to be *"stumbling near"* (as Ibsen has said), that the size of the copybooks would be regulated in accordance with the dimensions of the pupil; but this shows that authors and pedagogues do not pay much attention to the matter, many of the copybooks for all the 7 school years being the same size. What this means with regard to the position and sight, etc., of the pupils, will be seen from the following example. The size is 20 centimeters high and 18 cm. broad, the writing slope is 56½ degrees, and the book lies in what is known as the sloping central position in front of the pupil, so that its lowest edge forms, with the edge of the desk, an angle, opening to the right, of 33 to 34 degrees. The elbows should, according to the directions on the cover of the book, rest on the desk-edge and held a little from the sides of the body.

If one now measures the above distances the following scheme will be carried out concerning the right arm, when the right-hand page is to be written upon. The distance from the top line to the book's lowest edge is 19 cm., the distance in the lengthening of the middle line of the page to the elbow's resting place on the edge of the desk is 17 cm.; altogether 36 cm. This is, thus, for all ages in children's schools the *indicated length of arm.* My examination of 1,000 pupils in all classes in the Primary Schools, at the beginning and end of the school year, with different "litters" in a school in the poorest part of Kristiania, and in another in the best neighborhood of the town, has shown that the actual *length of arm* (from the elbow to the point of the pen) is as follows, at the beginning of the school year:

In   I school year (pupils from 6½ to 7 yrs.) from 27 to 34 cm.
In   II   "   "   "   "   7 "   8 "   " 30 " 35 "
In III   "   "   "   "   8 "   9 "   " 30 " 36 "
In   IV   "   "   · I found from a half to a third part of the pupils

with length of arm under 36 cm., and even in the V school year, up to a fourth part of the pupils. There is found besides in all the 7 school years, in all the 7 classes, a considerable number of pupils for whom it is a *physical impossibility* to reach up to the middle of the page with the point of the pen, if they are to retain a correct position, and when the book is to lie in the prescribed angle, that is to say, so that the fundamental strokes (downstrokes) are vertical with the edge of the desk, and the base line, but at an angle of 56½ degrees with the writing line. What does the pupil now do in order to be able to write? He draws the book down, so that the opening of the angle diminishes, and the distance from the edge of the desk, up the page, is shortened, and then he lays his arm over the desk, whereupon the chest is pressed against the desk-edge. As a rule, the head leans to the left, so that the left eye sinks lower than the right. I shall not go deeper into the relation of the movements of the base line, which are so well known by hygienists. We all know the abnormal writing position which arises as a consequence of too large-sized books. After my investigations of the bodily dimensions of Norwegian school children, I have found it necessary to suggest that copybooks for *the three first school years* are not of a greater length than 16 cm. and a breadth not exceeding 11 cm.; for the fourth and fifth school years 18 x 13 cm., and for the last two school years, not over 20 x 15 cm. These measurements still provide a limit for *the slope of the writing.* This ought not to be under 60 degrees, rather about 70 degrees. It is considered successful to begin, as recommended by Javal, with upright writing in the first school year, and to slope it gradually in the following classes. It is, however, my opinion that actual teaching of writing ought to be forbidden during the first school year as a process all too tiring and doubtful from a hygienic point of view for beginners. The little ones learn quite soon enough, how to write and read. In order to supply a remedy for the difficulty of the conformed slope of the writing, called forth by the great size, the authors—writers—have taken resource to the sloping lines which are so troublesome for the eyes. One has succeeded in getting such, in every form, forbidden; likewise column-lines and all kinds of dotted or indicated auxiliary lines. With printed copies with us, now and hereafter, only clear copies, without additions for help of any kind, are to be met with. The heretofore sanctioned copybooks, have all received approval on condition that such things are removed in new issue, and haste is being made to comply with the injunction. (See the enclosed specimens of new copybooks.) With regard to the *engraving* of the writing, I can state that with a micrometer I have measured the thickness of the strokes of the writing and found the condition in the whole of the copies very unsatisfactory from an ophthalmological point of view.

As well known, the space included clearly by the normal eye is limited since we can only clearly discern objects which form a visual angle of 1 minute to 4½ and 5 degrees. At a distance of 25 cm. the greatest and smallest angles include a range of vision of 0.073 mm. and 20 to 22 mm. in section. In order to facilitate the discernment of small objects, and so as not to injure it in length, the smallest visual-angle must be doubled to 2 minutes. Therefore, ought no part of the writing or white interval between to be under 0.15 mm. in thickness at a working distance of 25 cm. I reckon here with the minimum measure of working distance; this ought, of course, as a rule to be greater between 30 and 40 cm., but I dare to consider it almost impossible to employ proportionately calculated thickness of the copies. Thus for example out of regard to the *transparency* of the paper which asserts itself in proportion to the bulk of the writing. On careful measuring of the thickness of the writing in all our copybooks I have found that only a few of the newer ones have hair strokes which are thicker than 0.07 mm. Indeed some have hairstrokes which are considerably under the physiological minimum (0.073 mm.), namely, 0.06, 0.05, 0.02 mm., etc.

Under the often defective, not to say poor, conditions of lighting in our Primary Schools, both in town and country, the proportion of hairstrokes which are on, or are *under* the physiological minimum, will be a still more uncertain affair than under other more favourable conditions. In 1911 the Education Department published by subscription of Fridtjof Nansen's Fund, my work "Health Statistics of the Norwegian Primary Schools," which rendered an account of the hygienic facts and circumstances of the Primary Schools in the kingdom, at the change of the century, among others also of the conditions of lighting. (The Department has sent some examples to this Congress's exhibition.) Under directions in my work to the pleaded questionable lighting conditions, which are partly coherent with our country's northerly situation, the nature and conditions of the climate are partly caused by the faulty manner of building with too much breast-work above the windows. I have taken leave myself, in face of the authorities to present a demand for bolder strokes in the copybooks than have heretofore been used. There is, namely, no outlook that the existing defective conditions of lighting will be improved; as this would cause the corporation great expense, and the state has scarcely any effective means of compelling such rebuilding of schoolrooms; the corporation having a wide-spreading autonomy (self-government) which is of very old date. The introduction of bolder strokes in the letters in printed copybooks would, on the other hand, not cause great difficulties, but even remedy the worst defect. Effort should be made at any price to prevent the harmful *close work* which becomes consequent, when the pupil, the best to be able to see the finer strokes, bends both body and head towards the book. Even if it affects the elegance and neatness of the writing in any degree, one should pay that price in order to keep the sight of the young unimpaired; it has a far greater worth. A youth who gets his sight impaired at school, however slightly, may be cut off, on this account, from a race; or from a livelihood, which he is otherwise eminently fitted for. It is no exaggeration when I urge that this matter is of national economical importance; it is also of consequence with regard to the question of the people's *strength and fitness for military service.* I owe the explanation, however, that it is not the meaning that the pupils need write as thick as the copy. One must, before everything, strive against a *too fine* writing, but one does not therefore need to study to produce writing *too thick.*

The paper in the copybooks and exercise books has hitherto, in many cases, been of poor quality, very transparent, often shiny and loose. In this respect, hereafter, all justified claims will be carried out, which is more easily done now than before, as our paper industry has gradually become able to deliver an efficient paper for school use. No minimum price has yet been fixed for the weight of the paper per ream, but it can scarcely be under 14 kg. (28). There is, of course, no question of "extra-fine" paper, but the paper itself, at any rate, must present no hindrances for the progress and exercise of the pupils, especially of the beginners. As preparation for fine handwriting with pen and ink, I employ writing on blackboards and with red chalk on large sheets of gray paper. In all classes some cases of difficulty with the finer, co-ordinate writing movements will occur which result in an outcome of formless, bad "degenerate" writing; such cases I treat thus: by letting the pupil do his work with red chalk on large gray packing-paper; the larger the letters so much the better. After a longer or shorter time we proceed to writing books, carefully proportioned in accordance with the size of.the pupil. This mode of procedure has shown good results, even under far advanced conditions of agraphia.

The lineature in our writing books has, for the most part, double and single lines, but joined-line systems, with one or two lines of division, occur and have not been forbidden. On the other hand, I suggest improving these lines of division by making them 1.5 to 2 mm. thick, and then working them out in very pale red or blue colours. The pupil will then find it easier to pay attention that neither the dominating tall or long letters exceed the limit of measure, and children are clever in taking care that the letters do not come "out in the river" as they say.

I hold the principle that at the beginning, and the setting-off stages, lines shall not be used in writing exercises; but the opinion for this reform is not yet strong enough. It looks as though the double-measure-letter system will be carried through among us; the capital letters and the tall and long small are here double the length of the neutral small. The numbers are made either once and a half or twice the height. The neutral letters must not be over 5 mm. in height in the beginners' stage, and not under 3 in the highest class (7th school year). In the practising of copies the teacher goes through the shorter of these on the blackboard, which is provided with lineature, corresponding to that in the writing-books in every class, and which are preferably painted in a sloping direction over the blackboard, so that the fundamental strokes of the letters look perpendicular to the children's eyes—as in the copybooks. The lineature of the blackboard is boldly marked in a proportion of at least 10 times that of the books, as the lines which are to be seen at a distance of 8 meters must be at least 3 mm. thick. The writing sheets are submitted for approval, and the following claim made on the size of the writing. The fundamental strokes must not be under 66 mm. in height, their thickness not under 12, and their distance 18. Hairstrokes and smallest intervals measure 6 mm. (After Herm. Graupner.) On going through the practice of the copies the teacher is not only to reckon on the pupils' power of observation, with the help of their sense of sight, and on their attention to his more or less successful description and interpretation of forms and proportion; but he must seek also in every way to turn to account the great support which the kinesthetical sensations of movements, tactile sensations and images of writing movements can render. Since Dr. W. A. Lay's course in experimental pedagogics in 1906, which I had the pleasure of arranging, the sense for this important side of *methodic on the subject of skill and dexterity* has been awakened among the leading powers in our little pedagogical community. We hope that the time when the writing lessons were the teachers' sinecure will soon be a "matter of history merely;" and that one may be successful in awakening the sense of responsibility and also the living interest of all those concerned, for the hygiene of the teaching of writing. But it is, unfortunately, still often the case with us, that fresh progress and improvements in teaching must be first acknowledged abroad, before one dare wholly adopt them here; therefore I am glad that I can safely send the report of our tiny endeavours across the great ocean to baptism in Buffalo.

SESSION TWENTY-NINE

Room B.   Thursday, August 28th, 9:00 A.M.

SYMPOSIUM ON HEALTH SUPERVISION OF COLLEGE AND UNIVERSITY STUDENTS

Organized by MAZYCK P. RAVENEL

MAZYCK P. RAVENEL, M.D., *Chairman*

PROF. A. P. SY, Ph. D., University of Buffalo, *Vice-Chairman*

Program of Session Twenty-nine

MAZYCK P. RAVENEL, M.D., Professor of Bacteriology, Director of State Laboratory of Hygiene, University of Wisconsin. "Work of the University Committee on Hygiene at Wisconsin." (Manuscript not supplied.)

PAUL PHILLIPS, M.D., Professor of Hygiene and Physical Education, Amherst College, Massachusetts. "Care of Students' Health at Amherst College."

H. E. ROBERTSON, A.B., M.D., Associate Professor of Pathology and Bacteriology, University of Minnesota. "Problems Confronting the Organization of a University Health Service."

JOSEPH E. RAYCROFT, A.B., M.D., Professor of Hygiene and Physical Education, Princeton University, N. J. "Provisions for Safeguarding Student Health at Princeton University."

MILTON J. ROSENAU, M.D., and W. D. FROST, D.P.H., Professor of Preventive Medicine, Harvard University, Cambridge, Mass. "Sanitary Safeguards for Students and Faculty at Harvard." (Manuscript not supplied.)

ALEXANDER C. ABBOTT, M.D., Professor and Director Laboratory of Hygiene, University of Pennsylvania; Professor of Hygiene and Bacteriology, Philadelphia, Pa. "Safeguarding the Health of University Students."

WILLIAM H. McCASTLINE, M.D., University Physician, Colu
    University, New York. "Health Work at Columbia Universi

GEORGE F. REINHARDT, B.S., M.D., Professor of Hygiene and Unive
    Physician, University of California. "University of Califo
    Infirmary Student Health Protection."

CREIGHTON WELLMAN, M.D., Professor of Tropical Medicine, Tu
    University. "Sanitary Advisers for Universities." (Manus
    not supplied.)

THOMAS ANDREW STOREY, M.D., Ph.D., Professor of Hygiene, Co
    of the City of New York. "The Protection of Student He
    in the College of the City of New York." (Manuscript
    included.)

CARE OF STUDENTS' HEALTH AT AMHERST COLLEGE

BY

PAUL C. PHILLIPS

During the last quarter of a century, and particularly since the beginning of the 20th century, there has been an increasing sense of responsibility on the part of American colleges and universities for the health of their students. During the latter period this sense of responsibility has developed also in the public school system of our country, sharing in the general movement for better hygienic conditions in school life; and that in the still larger one for the improvement of national physique. The importance of proper attention to and control of these health conditions, especially among the young, has for some years impressed itself upon the civilized nations of the world.

The department of hygiene, or hygiene and physical education as it is designated, was started in Amherst College in 1860 with the definite object of improving the health of its students. President Stearns had recommended this step to the trustees for several years previously as a necessity because, in his opinion, it was becoming the rule rather than the exception for students to be obliged to give up their college course on account of ill health. It is doubtful whether at this early period, any thought of a legal responsibility on the part of the college entered his mind. Neither was the sense of a moral responsibility of public significance probably the impelling motive. The health of the students temporarily in his care educationally and morally—for this was the period when the college was considered to be in *loco parentis*—was being injured by the conditions of their college life; the authorities of the college must do something to better these conditions so that these students might be kept in health and graduate physically fit for life. As a result of his foresight and persistence the department was organized and the head of it given professorial rank. A gymnasium was built, physical exercise for all students introduced and a careful oversight of hygienic conditions instituted. These steps seem to evidence an altruistic motive practically carried out. The results on the health of the students, as indicated by statistics, accurately kept by the head of the department Dr. Edward Hitchcock, for many years, showed that whereas there had been, previous to 1860, an increasing amount of sickness from freshman to senior year under the new order of things in a few years the reverse was true, there was a marked diminution in morbidity year by year, the seniors suffering from illness least of all. The argument from statistics—others. might easily have been adduced—was sufficient to prove to the trustees the *raison d'être* of the department and it has ever since been given a dignified place in the college.

Amherst College is an institution for higher education having about 600 students and situated in a town of 6,000 inhabitants in the edge of the Berkshires. The altitude is about 300 feet above sea level and the climate is healthful, the mortality of the permanent residents approximating 16 per 1,000. Since its founders located it in this hygienically favorable environment the town has introduced the customary modern sanitary improvements, a town water supply, sewage disposal by filter beds and strict quarantine regulations.

The department of hygiene and physical education consists of one man of professorial rank, one associate, one assistant and one fellow, in addition to the trainers, coaches and rubbers employed for the varsity teams.

The work of the department in so far as it relates to hygiene may be classed as individual and general.

INDIVIDUAL

Physical Examination of Students. The individual work consists of a thorough examination of each student, made when he comes to college, to determine his physical condition. This examination made by a physician, includes the taking of his family and personal history, an examination of the vital organs, the eyes, ears, nose and mouth. The heart rate is taken before and after a prescribed exercise to determine the effect of exertion upon it. Color sense is also tested.

Some thirty measurements are taken, including principally the height, weight, girths and depths of chest and abdomen and some girths of upper and lower limbs, the capacity of the lungs is taken by a wet spirometer. Five tests of strength are also given. The whole examination lasts about thirty minutes and the student is entirely nude.

The aim of the department in this examination is to make examinations and take measurements which are of greatest importance to the individual especially those which indicate his organic vigor. General scientific value is of secondary interest.

An accurate record is made of the findings in each case and filed in the office of the professor for future reference.

Hygienic Advice. At the time of this examination advice is given to the student voluntarily, or in response to his questions, regarding his health. He is advised as to his exercise, eating, study habits, sleep, in fact anything which is of importance and necessary for him hygienically.

If he is found to having some organic defect or some defect of sight or hearing he is advised to consult a specialist at an early date. Many of these recommendations are written in a small manual which contain also the results of his measurements and strength tests, charted for comparison with others of his age and height. Much information on hy_ giene, especially that of college life is contained in this manual. The main tests of this examination are given again in sophomore and junior years.

Those students having been given special advice or referred to special_ ists are followed up personally or by letters to ensure the carrying out of the recommendations. Those who seem to the examiner unfit for violent physical work are forbidden to engage in intercollegiate or other sports which might injure them. The rules of the college require a certificate of fitness for each participant in intercollegiate sport.

Free Consultation. In addition the department is always open to and special hours are set aside for free consultation by the students on matters pertaining to their health.

The College Infirmary. For students who are actually ill or disabled the college provides an infirmary of 13 beds in charge of a matron who is a trained nurse. A contagious or isolation ward of 3 beds is included in the infirmary. Here for a moderate sum the student who is ill or tired out may rest and recover. If an operation is necessary it may take place in the operating room of the infirmary. An average of about 50 students a year are detained here for a longer or shorter period, averaging about four days.

GENERAL

Instruction in Personal Hygiene. All the members of the freshmen class are required to attend a series of 15 lectures the first half of the year on personal hygiene. These are given by the head of the department, are of a personal character and cover the topics of food, exercise, bathing, sleep, drugs, including alcohol and tobacco, the social diseases and the prevention of disease. An examination is given at the end of the course but the emphasis is put on the greater importance of applying these laws of hygiene to their own lives. A course in human physiology is given in junior year, but this is optional.

Physical Exercise. Since 1860 physical exercise has been required at Amherst for all students physically able to take it. It was introduced in the belief that physical exercise was an important hygienic measure and at that time one much neglected by college students. At first the drills were held four times a week from September to May or June, later they were reduced to three and the period shortened. The seniors were released from the requirement in 1900. The exercises consisted at first of the calisthenics and heavy gymnastics current at the time, similar to those advocated by Dio Lewis and Dr. Winthrop. Later, with new equipment a graded scheme of light gymnastics was introduced and athletics of an elementary character practiced out of doors. At present all the work of the first year is done out of doors until about November 15. From September 20th to October 15th it consists of elementary track and field athletics; October 15 to November 15, basket ball, "soccer" football and "hiking." During this period those who cannot swim are required to attend the classes in swimming in the natatorium. The results on health, as indicated statistically by increased weight and strength and by well being, seem to warrant the change for this period from indoor to outdoor work.

Inspection of Fraternity Houses. Some seven years ago the trustees of the college passed a vote requiring an annual inspection of the fraternity houses with respect to their sanitary condition and safety from fire. Forty-five per cent. of the students room in these houses. The regulation states that the inspection is to be made by a committee of three, consisting of one representative from the department of hygiene, one from the treasurer's department and one from the fraternity concerned. As a result of these inspections many improvements have been made in the sanitary conditions of these houses and their safety in case of fire has been increased. No epidemic of a serious nature has broken out in the college since the plan was introduced. The following blank is used for making the reports of the committee, through the faculty to the trustees:

....Fraternity............191
Representative of fraternity...
No. of student's rooming house...
System of heating.....................lighting..............................

ROOMS AND JANITOR

No. of student rooms.   Name of janitor....................................
Size and ventilation of rooms...
Dormitory plan..
Janitorial work...
Condition of cellar.........................attic..........................
Rubbish removal...
Remarks...

FIRE PROTECTION—constructional..........................hose..............
Pails................chem. extinguishers................fireplace..........
Screens...............................ropes................................
Ladders...
Lodge-room safeguards...
Approved by underwriters..
Remarks...

SYSTEM OF LIGHTING.........................adequacy.....................
    Condition of piping or wiring..
FUSES
    Remarks..
    ....

PLUMBING, when installed..
    Condition of bathrooms...................closets.........................
    Traps...............................vents............................
    Remarks..
HEATING SYSTEM.......................when installed......................
    Adequacy...................condition of................................

GENERAL REMARKS..
    ....
    ....
    ....
    ....

While there is no trustee rule in the matter the department has general oversight of the conditions of air, light, ventilation, heating and cleaning of the college dormitories and class rooms. As the students board largely at private houses the supervision of their food is a difficult matter and not thus far attempted.

The Daily Schedule of College. The arrangement of the daily college schedule in the interests of hygiene, while not a vexed problem as in high schools, is considered of importance by the department and although it has no power in this regard its suggestions receive serious consideration. It feels that in general breakfast should be obtainable in time to be properly eaten before chapel, which comes at 8.15 a. m.; that if possible some time be allowed between chapel and the first recitation; that at least an hour and a half should be free at noon for lunch or dinner and that an interval of one or two hours should be free in the late afternoon for exercise and play. Most of the required physical exercises come between four and six p. m.

Town Sanitation. Careful watch is kept of the town water supply at all times. This is excellent and regularly inspected by the state about once in six weeks but the chemical department of college also makes a routine examination frequently. The department of hygiene makes an inspection of the watershed annually, or oftener if deemed necessary. The sewage beds of the town are visited annually also to make sure of their continued efficiency and sanitary condition.

The relations with the health board of the town, through its medical representative, are cordial. The town has rather strict rules regarding quarantine and sanitation in general and wherever the health of the college is concerned the department finds it prompt and energetic. In cases of local epidemics for example, there is satisfactory coöperation for the safeguarding of both town and college. The importance of securing satisfactory sanitation of the natatorium was early impressed on the department. If an average of 30% of all the students use the pool daily it cannot fail to be, if untreated, a clearing house for whatever germs are current in the college community. The method of purifying the water at Amherst is by filtration through a graduated quartz-filler 7 by 12 feet, alum being used as a precipitant. The pool is very seldom emptied. The filtration alone had proven, by both chemical and bacteriological tests, quite satisfactory, the water after filtration comparing favorably with drinking waters. It was thought advisable, however, to use a powerful germicide, and for several years the routine treatment was with sulphate of copper, about 1 to 1,000,000 put in once a week. This proved efficient, when later experiments had shown hypochlorite of lime to be a more efficient germicide it was adopted in place of the sulphate of copper and six-tenths of a pound is now put in the 75,000 gallons of the pool every two or three days, or oftener if there are contagious diseases about. Tests made last winter show the water to be in a very sanitary condition, no pathogenic bacteria being found and less than one hundred per c.c. of other microorganisms.

A thorough shower bath with warm water and soap is required before a student is allowed to enter the pool, an attendant being always present to enforce the observance of the rule. Careful instructions are given to all the classes regarding this preliminary bath and its importance emphasized.

The use of swimming trunks in the pool is not allowed by the department.

The towels in use throughout the department are provided free of charge and, with the trunks, are sterilized in boiling water and then washed after each use.

Lives have been lost in some of our best swimming pools. This department has made an inviolable rule that no student may enter the pool unless the guard, who is an expert swimmer and life saver, is in attendance. For their own safety and that of others free instruction in swimming is given. Each student is required to swim at least two hundred yards unaided before the end of his sophomore year.

Believing in the hygienic as well as the educative and social and ethical values of play the department has for several years been developing intercollegiate sports. While the per cent. of students in some form of sports is now nearly 75 it is hoped still further to generalize and popularize these so-called intra-mural sports so that all shall par_ ticipate in some kind of sport during the year. The intra-mural acti_ vities have thus far been lawn tennis, baseball, basketball, ice hockey, and track work. In order that ample opportunity may be given for these intra-mural sports, a tract of 40 acres adjoining the gymnasium has recently been purchased. About one-third of this is already de_ veloped here. It will be devoted to intra-collegiate sports. While this paper has dealt thus far largely with matters of fact, it may not be inappropriate to state that the complete plans for this field include 36 tennis courts, three large areas 120 by 120 for various outdoor, ath_ letic, military or gymnastic exercise, five combination soccer and base- ball fields, a quarter-mile running track, a one-mile cross country course, hand ball courts and a section for winter sports, including tobogganing, skiing, sliding, snowshoeing, and the like. The desirability not only of furnishing an opportunity for play but of establishing the habit for its hygienic value in later life is one of the motives in the development of this phase of college life.

The organization and conduct of a department of hygiene will nat- urally differ in the college and university. The problem in the college is simpler and more personal. Here it is possible in some cases to know the physical condition of every student, to be thoroughly informed on most matters of college or town sanitation and to give personal atten- tion to each individual.

In conclusion let me emphasize once more the moral if not legal respon- sibility which each college has for providing and maintaining good hygienic conditions for its students. In matters of personal hygiene it may be said that students over 18 years of age should be given the responsibility of the care of their own bodies. It is a question, however, whether a department of hygiene would be justified in taking this attitude. These students are away from home are given unusual freedom, are under changed conditions and at an age when hygienic living is of great importance for their future. Indirectly it is of importance for many others, because, as educated men, their method of life will be taken as an example, and their words in matters of health have an added weight.

PROBLEMS CONFRONTING THE ORGANIZATION OF A UNIVERSITY PUBLIC HEALTH SERVICE

BY

H. E. ROBERTSON

Close analysis of the sociological and economic conditions which control the policies of a large university shows that essentially it is neither a commonwealth nor a corporation, although sharing in the characteristics of both.

To the corporation side belong the definite hours of labor, the contractual relations between student and administration and the otherwise almost complete absence of responsibility or authoritative interest of the student in the physical plant and equipment of the university. To the commonwealth side may be assigned the communal relations of students with each other and their faculty and the paternalism of a state which gives more than a quid pro quo to selected numbers of its citizens and which assumes certain unwritten obligations toward their mental, physical and moral welfare. The exact extent of this responsibility is a fruitful subject for discussion and it is therefore to be expected that, during growth and expansion along material lines, conceptions of the direction of what portion of the student's welfare the university should assume are constantly changing. At no one point is this fact more clearly shown than in respect to the obligations of the university toward the health and physical well-being of its population. The measures for the protection of the public health of villages, cities, states and nations, which are being used so efficiently, do not apply accurately to the special needs of a university and neither, on the other hand, can we be content with the conditions ordinarily provided by an employer for the health of his employees. Even a satisfactory solution of the problems grouped under the general heading of "School Inspection" will leave unsolved questions of major importance to the welfare of the university body—for the university cannot be likened to a public school; it is *sui generis*, and many fallacies in our entire educational system might become more readily apparent if these distinctions were given their proper recognition.

We must realize, then, that our problems, while perhaps not new or strange, are at least distinctive and, consequently, our solution, even if it does not call for fresh researches or new discoveries, certainly must assume a composite character, drawing from every possible source on the rules of procedure which govern the protection of public health.

The most important factor in this problem is the large student body. The gathering of this group of individuals from widely scattered points and their subsequent close association together are conditions common to every assemblage, for whatever purpose. From merely the assem. blage standpoint, questions of public health policy are confined to the discovery, investigation and isolation of cases of infectious diseases combined with search for, and treatment of, all possible sources for this infection, including chronic carriers. The procedure in these cases in no way differs from that commonly employed, and the wonderfully rational methods used so successfully on repeated occasions have again and again demonstrated that early, prompt and vigorous treatment of sporadic or epidemic cases of infectious disease produces adequate, satisfactory and life-saving results. Vaccination, isolation, and other prophylactic and curative measures are best carried out in a students' infirmary and under the direction of the university health officer. Board. ing and rooming places and home towns are investigated in close conjunction with the epidemiological divisions of city and state boards of health. Indeed, if this were to be the major purpose of a special health officer, his office could hardly be justified, especially in the presence of like efficient departments in city or state health bodies.

But when the university assumes responsibility in any degree for the physical welfare of its population, then questions are presented which are of larger import than the control of the spread of infectious diseases. "But why should there be any of this responsibility for the purely physical conditions?" our old-time professor argues; "the university is founded for the purpose of preparing and to a certain extent predigesting and oftentimes forcibly feeding of *mental pabulum* and this task is large enough and important enough to make other burdens, assumed toward students, undesirable and practically useless."

In our answer must lie the keynote of all modern public health activities.

Individualism must give place to communal interest and welfare. We have all in some measure become "keepers of the gate." Increase in the length of human life, lessening of the expense and suffering incident to preventable diseases, decrease in the public calamities resulting from the presence of epidemic or endemic plagues, have taken their places as public questions, and mere private rights, convictions, actions and beliefs must be superseded wherever they conflict in matters affecting the common weal.

To the university rightfully belongs a place well in the van of this general movement. The students represent an investment made by the state, surely not for individual betterment alone, but for an increase in the potential riches of the state as a whole. They are to become larger assets in the social and economical balances of the state's ledger. They are the future leaders in the constructive activities of the state, in maintaining its citizens in gradually elevating planes of mental, moral and physical excellence, as well as the closely related stages of scientific and commercial achievement.

Our university health officer becomes, then, a most important adjunct in developing the state's resources, and we must admit him at once into our plans for extension and betterment of university influence.

Having established this fact, we are in a position to consider other phases in the problems governing the organization of such an office.

For purposes of illustration we will assume that a university of three thousand population has received the proper authority for the appointment of a health officer in a specially designated sanitary district—the university grounds and buildings. He must be a large man, this health officer, a medical school graduate, with post-graduate training in public health, thus having a practical and theoretical knowledge of the principles governing preventive medicine and public health activities. Most important of all qualifications should be a broad view of public health affairs and a keen insight into the true relations between the large community embodied in the state and its expensive servant, the university.* There can be no better investment for all the people than liberality in obtaining the best equipped officer possible for this most important duty.

Once selected, a proper relation to students, faculty, special colleges (particularly that of medicine), and official boards of health must be established. If provision has been made for a school of public health, as dean of that school such an officer's relations would be well defined. Otherwise, as a special officer of the university he acquires a title as Professor of Hygiene and Public Health in the medical school and is directly responsible either to the medical faculty or to a committee appointed from the general faculty group.

His staff must consist of the men and women commonly employed in all schools as physical directors, an emergency group of medical men and women to conduct physical examinations and to act as consultants, together with such office force and service assistants as will enable his work to be accomplished with expedition and economy.

This staff having been organized, the first large problem presenting itself at the beginning of the school year is the routine, systematic physical examination of the students. The numerous objections which have been urged against this procedure seem to be founded on a misunderstanding of its purpose and the same unreasoning and, oftentimes,

*My analogies are built about the university organized and maintained under state control. However, the same fundamental principles should hold in respect to every center of so-called higher education.

purely sentimental prejudices against it which are so often encountered in public school inspections. If conducted in the proper spirit and with due regard to the student's personal welfare, such prejudices must largely disappear and the real value and importance of the work be clearly established. How thorough or extensive this examination should be is a question which depends upon the size of the student body, the number of examiners and the proportion of funds allowed for this work. That all the data should be collected within the first month, that in thorough-ness it should approach that commonly required by insurance companies, and that its value will be directly proportional to its thoroughness are all self-evident propositions.

The first result of these examinations is to place the students in proper healthful relations to their various activities. Upon their out-come should depend (1) the question of whether certain or any of the contemplated studies are advisable; (2) whether special athletics or any at all are to be permitted; (3) the instruction necessary for correcting errors of development, posture or gait; (4) advice as to care of either physical defects, such as adenoids, poorly corrected vision, bad hearing, etc., or the presence of constitutional diseases of heart, lungs, kidneys, etc. As to whether actual treatment for these conditions should be administered is a perplexing question. The economic trade status of the practicing physician probably should be protected and these cases referred for treatment to the family physician or one chosen by the student. Frequent consultations and interchange of records between the health officer and these physicians would be advantageous. The second result following the securing of this data is the important scientific interest naturally carried by such a large volume of statistics. Care-fully compiled and compared over a period of years they will unques-tionably prove to be of immense value. The weak points in our methods of physical education, the general prevalence of unrecognized defects and diseases, and the increase in mental capacities and accomplishments following the correction of physical ailments will constitute the strong-est possible arguments in favor of a continuance of this work.

For the teaching of the principles of public and personal hygiene to the general student body such a health officer with his staff would be peculiarly well fitted. Questions regarding physical training, sex hygiene, food and clothing could be discussed, but more important still, the broader general ideals which are being developed for the conservation of human life and health could be properly placed before the students and thereby within a short period of years a state and nation-wide educational cam-paign would have been inaugurated and carried on in the most rational and economical manner. Where could the question of public school inspection be better brought to the attention of future teachers, business men, and the other educated or specially trained men and women of the state? What better opportunity could be presented for assuring ourselves that in the future matters of public health would receive their proper attention and support in each local community of the state?

A still more important problem is the proper training of teachers and professional workers in public health. Such a department is rapidly becoming absolutely necessary in conjunction with every university medical school and in the organization and teaching of these courses a large portion of the responsibility might well be placed on the shoulders of the university health officer and his staff. Laboratory instruction in many practical lines would be furnished by experiences with the student body, and, working in close association with the medical school and boards of health, an ideal training might be provided.

Another essential duty of such an officer would be as official adviser to governing boards of universities in respect to sanitary regulations, care and construction of buildings and grounds. Problems of ventilation, light, etc., are not yet satisfactorily solved and architects are still looking for experienced advice on these important subjects. Such work would always be undertaken in coöperation with trained sanitary engineers, who must constitute an important part of the staff for teaching health officers.

The proper sanitary conditions surrounding student boarding and rooming houses is a fruitful subject for investigation, and much valuable advice might be offered to both students and landlords.

It would not be improper to extend to the general faculty by lectures and personal interviews the new work which is being accomplished in the lines of public health. A naturally specializing group, they are prone to get out of touch with other lines of human endeavor and, for the successful development of these plans, enthusiastic coöperation of the whole faculty would be highly desirable.

In the College of Education of the university the health officer's work is of prime importance. Discussion of the broad principles and practical application of the methods of school inspection are invaluable training for the future teacher, whose responsibility is gradually spreading over the physical and moral as well as the mental status of the pupil.

If the university is fulfilling its highest function, it is seizing every opportunity for making its resources valuable to the individual citizens of the commonwealth and to the state as a whole. One of its most important methods to this end is embodied in what is generally known as university extension work. By this movement the more interesting and practically valuable fields of university endeavor are carried directly to the people at large. In this service the public health activities of the university might have a large share. No better method could be devised for bringing home to the people not only the lessons of modern public and personal hygiene but also the work which the university is accom. plishing in this field.

And lastly, as the university has been designated a special sanitary district, its health officer becomes a member of the State Board of Health staff and a special registrar of vital statistics for this small but important division. In close and efficient coöperation with not only the State Board of Health but also the city and village boards, epidemics of con. tagious disease, unsanitary conditions in and about the campus, cases of sudden death,·etc., would receive early and expert attention without the cross purposes of mixed authority which, so often, attend these affairs.

In this plan, which has been so briefly presented, we earnestly believe that there is nothing which is impracticable or impossible of achievement. These are the days of *insistent idealism* in the conduct of public and private affairs. To the university belongs the large privilege of assuming leadership in most of the important movements for the betterment of social and economic conditions. In matters concerning public health there is a tendency to lag behind. The "problems" are really those which arise from inertia, absence of initiative. Action in any field, once instituted, affords solutions as rapidly as difficulties are presented. To the people the university owes a large debt. Useless disease, preventable suffering, unnecessary waste of resources, health and life itself abound on every hand. Knowledge of these conditions incurs due responsibility. Our faith in the broad ideals and altruistic purposes of modern universities must surely be justified.

PROVISIONS FOR SAFEGUARDING STUDENT HEALTH AT PRINCETON UNIVERSITY

BY

JOSEPH E. RAYCROFT

A consideration of the factors affecting student health in the typical college community suggests their division into two groups.   In the first group will fall those factors that may be classed as "environmental," *e. g.*:

(1) General sanitary condition of the neighborhood such as drainage, sewage disposal, breeding-places for flies and mosquitoes.

(2) Food and water supply in commons and boarding houses.

(3) Sanitary conditions of rooms in dormitories and lodging houses as regards baths, toilets, janitor service, and general surroundings.

(4) Provision for advice and treatment in dispensary or infirmary in case of sickness.

(5) Opportunities for exercise and recreation.

The second group will include the "individual factors," such as:

(1) Physical characteristics and tendencies to weakness.

(2) Knowledge and practice of the essentials of personal hygiene.

(3) Habits of exercise and recreation.

This grouping serves at Princeton University as a logical basis for the division of responsibility for the supervision of student health between two closely allied bodies: The Sanitary Committee and the Department of Hygiene and Physical Education.

The Sanitary Committee is composed of six men appointed from the Board of Trustees and the University Faculty, one of whom is a member of the Department of Hygiene and Physical Education.   It has the responsibility for the administration of those factors which I have called "environmental."   It maintains a close supervision over the administration of the Commons and the Infirmary; it employs the University Physician, and has periodical inspections made of those lodging and boarding houses used by students for whom—about 15 per cent.—there is at present no provision on the campus.   It is also advisory to the Board of Trustees on such questions as:

(1) Plans for a modern sewage disposal plant.

(2) The installation of a milk pasteurizing plant in the Commons.

(3) Plans for a new infirmary, and a study of the sanitary features of plans for new buildings.

The administration of the second group of factors, those relating to the individual himself, falls to the Department of Hygiene and Physical Education. This Department is organized and equipped to fulfill the following functions:

(1) To conduct a regular academic course in hygiene, which is required of all Freshmen one hour a week throughout the year.

(2) To make thorough medical examination of all Freshmen at the beginning and the end of the year, and of all candidates for competitive teams at the beginning of each season, or more frequently in special cases.

(3) To conduct classes in physical education, which is required of all Freshmen three periods a week throughout the year.

(4) To provide opportunities for exercise and the necessary instruction in voluntary work by upper classmen.

(5) To encourage participation in intra-mural games and competitions by those who are not candidates for the regular University teams.

(6) To stimulate the development of habits of hygienic living and of outdoor exercise and recreation among the whole student body.

Since the health interests of the University are closely bound up with those of the town, a natural and harmonious relationship has grown up between these two parts of the community for the promotion of the interests of general health. The active bodies in this work are the University Sanitary Committee and the Borough Board of Health with its Health Officer.

This Board is composed of seven men, three of whom are members of the University. The President of the Board is also Chairman of the University Sanitary Committee, thus providing an opportunity for the closest coöperation between the two bodies. The effectiveness of this relationship is shown in the measures that put in force by joint action to improve the sanitary conditions in the community at commencement time, when there are many reunion headquarters temporarily established throughout the town; and at the time of the big games when there is an influx of from 20,000 to 30,000 people with the consequent strain upon sanitary provisions. The University contributes towards the salary of the Health Officer, so his services are available, under the direction of the Sanitary Committee, for the inspection of boarding and lodging houses occupied by students; for the periodical examination of the milk supplied to the Commons and of the water in the University Swimming Pool; and for the technical supervision of the sanitary condition of grounds and buildings.

The close relationship existing among these three bodies, the Board of Health, the Sanitary Committee, and the Department of Hygiene, makes possible an effective coöperation which results in an economical and efficient administration of the health problems of the entire community.

A university in a small town like Princeton which has a population aside from the University community of about 5,000, presents a simple problem from the point of view of health protection as compared with an institution located in a large city. It may be impossible to work out such an organization as this that we have been considering in every college town; but the general principle of establishing some comprehensive and effective plan of health administration should be put into effect in every large institution.

As stated above, the supervision of the Infirmary is a function of the Sanitary Committee. The Infirmary is in charge of an infirmarian, who is assisted by the necessary nursing and housekeeping force. The building contains fifteen beds and was built nearly twenty years ago. A contagious ward of about the same size was added later. A well-equipped dispensary adds greatly to the usefulness of the Infirmary. Plans for a new infirmary are practically completed, as the present building is sometimes taxed to its utmost. The University Physician is employed by the Sanitary Committee and attends the Infirmary three hours daily, during the early morning and the late afternoon. Students are admitted upon his certificate and attended by him. A student may be attended by a physician from the town who is approved by the Sanitary Committee; and physicians and surgeons may be called in consultation if necessary.

Students are charged $7.00 a year infirmary fees. This entitles them to all the necessary care, the attendance of the University Physician, etc., except medicine for which they are charged. In contagious cases, or cases requiring special nursing the expense of the additional nurse is charged to the student. As board bills are charged to all students on their regular term bills, the Infirmary is credited with the amount of board the student would ordinarily pay during such time he may be confined to the Infirmary. During the past year there were 400 bed cases and about 4,500 dispensary calls. These figures may seem large for a student body of only 1,500, but much of the service in the dispensary, and even among the bed cases is in a measure preventive. For example, a boy with an incipient cold may be put to bed over Saturday and Sunday, and so a more serious illness and a further loss of time be prevented.

The inspection of the lodging and boarding houses is done regularly and a report is made on a form provided for the purpose. The points investigated include among others a statement as to the kind of a house, the kind of a room, the provisions for heating, lighting and ventilation, the bath room provisions, and the general character and tone of the place and people. In the case of boarding houses additional information is gained regarding the sanitary conditions of the dining room, the kitchen, the refrigerator, care in garbage disposal, and notes on the general surroundings, such as the proximity of stables, chicken yards, exposed garbage, etc. Repeated inspections are made at irregular intervals during the year. Any defects are reported to the secretary of the Sanitary Committee who serves notice upon the owners of the premises. If the recommendations are not complied with promptly, the students are ordered out of the premises. The knowledge that this will be done by the University, and the fact that the money for board and rent is paid through the University Treasurer's office, have had the effect of forcing the owners to keep the premises in proper condition.

The physical examinations are comprehensive in their nature, and lay special emphasis upon the determination of the functional condition of the eyes, ears, nose, throat and the vital organs. The information so obtained serves as a basis for advice as to special exercises if needed. Advantage is taken of the opportunity to discuss with each individual the various practices and habits that affect his mental and physical efficiency.

A follow-up scheme has been devised which makes it possible to keep in touch with special cases at regular intervals during the year and to cases referred to the home physician.

The course in personal hygiene deals with the fundamentals of health and physical efficiency; the influence of diet, exercise, bathing, etc.; the effects of personal habits, as the use of tobacco and alcohol; sex hygiene; and a study of the more common infectious diseases, their nature, cause, methods of transmission and prevention. Emphasis is laid upon the practical points of daily life, upon inducing the students to adopt a hygienic method of living, and upon the fact that health is in very large measure subject to control.

A good deal of emphasis is placed upon the effort to promote the formation of habits of outdoor exercise and recreation among the upper classmen. This is done by organizing classes for voluntary work in various branches of physical education and by encouraging the organization of teams for athletic competition. In the development of these intra-mural athletic activities, advantage is taken of every natural student division as a basis for the organization of teams, with the result that there were during the past spring 44 organized baseball teams playing regular schedules for the championships of various groups; and throughout the year there were more than 1,400 men, counting the duplications on various teams during the different seasons, and not counting those who were on the various varsity squads, who took part

in these contests. Competitions were conducted in s
polo, relay racing, rowing, basketball and baseball.

This plan of guarding and promoting student health
oped under the stimulus of the conviction that an educa
has a real responsibility for the physical welfare of it
health is an educational factor of prime importance; th
entirely well is working under a handicap and is loweri
of the institution; and that a healthy body is one of t
of clear thinking, clean living, and efficient citizenship.

SAFEGUARDING   THE   HEALTH   OF   UNIVERSITY STUDENTS

BY

ALEXANDER C. ABBOTT

The problem of the University of Pennsylvania does not differ essentially from that of other schools of similar size and surroundings. There is an annual student population of something over 5,000, for whose physical well-being we regard ourselves, within reasonable limits, as responsible.

To meet the responsibility there exists a standing committee, in the composition of which are represented the Board of Trustees and the several teaching faculties. The activities of the committee may be briefly summarized as directed to the sanitary conditions under which the student lives while under the University control. These have to do with the University Dormitories; the neighboring student boarding houses; the grounds of the University; the gymnasium, including the swimming tank and the medical care of the student in the event of illness.

The University dormitories themselves cause little or no anxiety. They are comparatively new and strictly modern in their construction. They are well lighted by electricity; heated and ventilated from the central heat and light plant of the University, and abundantly supplied with toilet and bathing facilities; the latter being throughout shower baths with hot and cold water. No tubs are provided. The general oversight of the dormitories is in the hands of an intra-mural committee consisting of University officers residing in the dormitories as proctors and of selected students resident in the several houses.

The drinking water supplied to the University throughout is from the city supply. This is now, in so far as West Philadelphia is concerned, entirely above suspicion. It is purified by filtration and since the method of purification was adopted those diseases indicative of polluted water have practically disappeared from the section of the city in which the University is located. To the best of my knowledge, nothing has ever been brought before the Hygiene Committee to indicate that life in the dormitories is under other than satisfactory sanitary surroundings.

As a safeguard for those students who reside in the neighboring boarding and lodging houses, the University prepares, at the beginning of each session, a list of such houses that have been approved by a specially appointed sub-committee. Such approval follows upon a careful personal inspection by the sub-committee of each house and this inspection comprehends not only the sanitary conditions but the moral as well. In this matter we have the full coöperation of the City Health and Safety Departments, so that defects in either particular may be easily remedied or the persons conducting the houses discouraged from offering them as places of lodging for our students. In the matter of feeding our students we are not as well off as might be desired. As yet we have no "commons," so-called, but have hopes in this direction for the future.

At present board is obtainable in the neighborhood at either boarding houses or restaurants. With regard to the latter it is proper to state that in so far as our knowledge goes, intoxicating liquors are not sold. In the latter particular we have had at least one striking experience, the relation of which may serve a purpose. Some fifteen or twenty years ago we were greatly annoyed by the near proximity of several barrooms with billiard and poolrooms attached. Their removal involved difficulties that we could not readily overcome. By a combination of circumstances, including the generosity of some of our friends, we were enabled to open a students' club and subsequently our dormitories. The Houston Club, located on the campus, and the most beautiful club house in the city, is strictly the students' club—all students are members and it is to a large extent conducted by student committees. In this club the student finds all that he needs in the way of recreation; reading rooms with almost all the periodicals; billiard and pool tables; bowling alleys; music, meeting, committee, and club rooms for the special societies and a lunch counter. It was not long before the student realized that he got more for his money and time and got it under much more agreeable surroundings at the Houston Club, than in any of the outside bar and billiard rooms. In consequence, through the simple process of competition, we have survived, while the barrooms have succumbed and disappeared.

Life in the dormitories and the responsibility of properly conducting the Students' Club have had an influence in improving the general morals of the students that I do not believe could have been accomplished in any other way.

As in all large schools, the gymnasium is an object of special concern. The intimate personal contact between the men—in the pool, on the wrestling mats, while boxing, etc., demands unremitting vigilance to prevent accidents and the dissemination of diseases.

In general the conduct of the gynmasium is similar to that we have just heard from Princeton and from Amherst. All students are subjected to careful physical examination and accurate records kept. Corrective exercises are prescribed for those suffering from remediable deformities and medical or surgical aid is recommended for those needing it. The men are under continuous observation for the purpose of detecting intercurrent diseases—especially cutaneous and venereal. To facilitate this, complete nudity is demanded of those using the swimming pool; and all users of the pool are required to take a shower bath before entering the pool. Fresh, sterilized towels are supplied by the gymnasium. In spite of reasonable precautions we have had the same annoying experiences as several of the speakers who preceded me. Two years ago there occurred a number of cases of contagious skin eruptions, the "gym itch," as some are pleased to call it. We thought it arose from the pool and the towel. Since that time the scalding of the latter has been particularly looked after and the disinfection of the former by the use (three times weekly) of calcium hypochlorite has become a routine procedure. Nevertheless we have still had an occa-sional case. Our Hygiene Committee being of the opinion that the wrestling mats might serve as a focus of dissemination, have advised special care in the cleansing and disinfection of the mats and have further recommended that a sufficient number of additional mats be purchased to enable at least two of them to be kept in a closely sealed disinfecting chest while the other one or two be in use; further that no mat be used for a period longer than a week.

Vacuum cleaning is the method adopted for the gymnasium in general. Nevertheless our committee recommends that those particular apparatus with which the nude body comes in close contact be frequently cleansed with soap and water. For some time past we have had few or no annoy-ing infections that could have been attributed to the gymnasium.

For the students who become ill we are particularly well circum-stanced. There are appointed by the University two physicians, mem-bers of the teaching body, known as "Students' Physicians," whom the students are advised to consult on the advent of any indisposition, no matter how trivial it may seem to them. For students who are suffi-ciently ill to require it or so located as to make it advisable, we have in our own hospital, located on the campus, a "student's ward." This beautiful ward, a picture of which I show, is for the exclusive use of students and the charge for its use is $7.00 per week per individual. For an average academic year the total number of occupants is about 125. In the event of dangerous contagious diseases appearing among the student body we have the new Philadelphia Hospital for Contagious Diseases, one of the most elaborate and modern hospitals of the kind in existence. For the isolation of suspicious cases or those who have been in contact with contagious diseases or those others for whom isolation for a period of observation seems desirable, we are now equipping an "isolation" or "observation" house on the University property. This we believe will be of great service in our campaign of preventive medicine at the University.

Venereal diseases, of which there are always some in large schools, can be treated and instructed at the University hospital or dispensaries. And suspicious pulmonary cases are ideally provided for at the newly completed Henry Phipps Institute for the study, treatment and care of tuberculosis. This institute is now one of the departments of the University of Pennsylvania. As in the case of other large schools we have a number of students organization that travel from time to time, viz.: the musical and debating teams, the football and baseball teams, and the crew, etc. While we cannot assume full responsibility for the health of students while away from the University, we must nevertheless stand in an advisory capacity. The person or persons in charge of such organizations are as a rule not only conversant with the usual precautions for safeguarding the health of those under their control, but are manifestly desirous that no accidents occur to interfere with the success of the trip. Between the two we have few accidents, but occasionally there is an exception. I know of no means by which such isolated exceptions may be prevented.

We at the University of Pennsylvania feel that when we invite the attendance of students, we at the same time assume responsibility for surrounding them with such safeguards as may reasonably be expected to maintain them in good physical condition. Though the various plans outlined this morning differ in certain particulars the one from the other, it is obvious from this symposium that we are all really working for the same end.

HEALTH WORK AT COLUMBIA UNIVERSITY

BY

WILLIAM H. MCCASTLINE

The departments that control the supervision of health in our schools and universities have passed the period of proof giving, when it was necessary to apologize for their existence; and have reached a point in their history when they are not only receiving recognition, but enjoy a place of importance in the general organization not below that of the standing committees on education.

The departments at Columbia having this health work in hand have as their ideal physical and mental efficiency; not so much for specialization as for a well-balanced proficiency along mental and physical lines that will give to the students, who come under the University's influence, power to meet all of the problems and pleasures of life with clear minds unhampered by the drag and strain of physical ill ease.

Columbia stands with certain other institutions in this country in believing that mental efficiency depends more upon bodily health than upon the possession of a degree. Physical energy and not the number of letters added to one's name, is the key to success through accomplishment. In our institutions of learning, we are beginning to urge upon our students a program of work that will fit their physical and mental mould rather than a schedule made upon the face of the clock and marked out in weeks, months and years, with a time limit leading to a degree that is supposed to carry with it culture and educational completeness.

Men can accomplish almost any piece of mental or physical work if the daily output of energy is in proportion to their individual reaction, and not in excess of their powers of recuperation.

At Columbia, the health interests are supervised by the interrelated departments of Health and Sanitation, and the division of Physical Education. At Teachers' College, the affiliated school of education, the health interests are under the direction of the Department of Physical Education. At the University gymnasium, the medical director assumes responsibility for the hygienic interests that naturally fall to the Department of Physical Education. At the beginning of the year, each freshman is given a thorough physical examination by competent physicians, and from the results of these tests the students are given individual advice along the lines indicated by their examinations. Throughout the year the instructors follow up the members of the class and by constant supervision and suggestion help the men to derive the most good from their required physical training. Although the sophomore courses in physical education are elective for the science men, most of these students return for credit work, so that both the science and the college men are under supervision for the first two years of their college life.

The men who have, during their early experiences at college, been thrown into intimate association with their physical education instructors usually continue to consult them during their entire four years on matters of exercise, recreation and general hygiene; hence this department has an opportunity for maintaining a high standard of hygienic instruction of a very practical nature.

At Teachers' College, the health problems are under the direct supervision of the Professor of Physical Education, who is also the college physician. In the School of Education, which is a graduate school, physical work is elective, but in the School of Practical Arts, an undergraduate school, physical training and hygiene are required subjects. In order to determine the condition of health in each individual, all students are required to report each fall to the Department of Physical Education for a health registration. Students are not permitted to complete their registrations until they have passed the requirements of this health regulation. Students who are below par have a restriction placed upon the quantity and nature of work to be undertaken during the year. The Professor of Physical Education holds office hours daily for medical consultations with Teachers' College students. There is also a physician who is responsible for the physical examination and health supervision of the pupils of the primary and secondary schools under the direction of Teachers' College. All of these children have thorough physical examinations once a year, at which the parents are encouraged to be present.

At Whittier Hall, the Teachers' College dormitory, there are two resident trained nurses, who work under the direction of the college physician.

The University dormitories for men are under the direct supervision of the University physician, as is also Brooks' Hall, the residence of the women students. There is a resident trained nurse at Brooks' Hall, who is on the staff of the University physician and acts as office nurse.

The Department of Health and Sanitation of Columbia was created a little over one year ago, with the object of developing as completely as possible resources for improving the standard of health among the students. The responsibilities of the department may be grouped into three rather distinct lines of work—curative, prophylactic and educational. There has been established upon the campus a well-equipped office for the University physician, where all but bedside cases are treated. During the past year, the University physician had over four thousand office consultations. A complete record is kept of the history, diagnosis and treatment of all these cases. Through this office, an effort is made to keep track of all cases of illness among the students, whether directly under the care of the University physician or not.

All cases of illness in the dormitories are reported to the University physician and are seen by him no matter how trivial. This prevents to a large degree the breaking out of epidemics.

The department has adopted the plan of having an Advisory Board of Specialists to whom students may be referred in case of necessity. During the past year this plan has proved very helpful and the department hopes to enlarge the board before another year. The consultations with these specialists are not gratis, unless the student cannot afford to pay. As far as possible the students who can afford to pay for these special services should do so, as it is a part of the general plan of education to make the students appreciate the value of reciprocity in social, economic and civic service. However, the first duty of our health work is to keep people well and if ill to cure them—regardless of fee or principle. Health is of prime importance and after this has been gained, principle may be emphasized. We make no distinction between the well-to-do-student and the man who is working his way through college. As an institution of learning we must recognize, as a friend of mine would say, "No aristocracy save the aristocracy of the intellect." The establishment of a Board of Advisors helps to bring about a levelling of all these troublesome factors; and the man of purpose without funds will not suffer in years to come because at a period when he most needed medical help, he could not afford it.

Columbia University, situated as it is in a thickly populated part of New York City, has a large number of practicing physicians in the neighborhood. The Department of Health and Sanitation does not hold itself responsible for bedside cases, as with over ten thousand students this would be an impossibility. And furthermore, we desire to coöperate with the physicians in the vicinity and to give the students the freedom of choosing whom they wish to attend them, or to permit the University physician to select the man who can best treat their cases. If a student is unable to meet the financial obligations of an illness the University physician is able to secure the services of a local physician gratis or for a nominal fee, or he may place such cases in one of the hospitals of the city.

Columbia University is perhaps more fortunate than the majority of educational institutions in the country in having so many first-class hospitals ready to assist the University authorities in caring for medical and surgical cases occurring among the students. During the past year there was no difficulty in securing admission and treatment for our cases.

The department hopes however to have in the near future a private pavilion in one of the hospitals of the city for the exclusive use of Columbia students. The permanent endowment of a pavilion of this kind would be a most useful and ideal memorial. I trust that health movements such as this, Congress will help to stimulate men of means to appreciate the great opportunity which such a work presents and to establish for our large educational institutions memorials of this kind as one of the most permanent and far-reaching tributes.

The department has at its command the unrivaled equipment of the Vanderbilt Clinic. Through this division of the Medical School, we may secure the advice of its department chiefs and through them may use its equipment for diagnostic and therapeutic purposes.

Every institution must determine for itself the plan whereby it may secure the best interests of its students from the standpoint of health and prophylactic measures. After a careful study of the situation at Columbia the University physician has organized a student Board of Health composed of at least one man from each of the several schools and dormitories and a man to represent the interests of the students who do not live in the dormitories. Through this student Board of Health we hope to solve many problems which an officer of the University could not handle alone unaided by the viewpoint and coöperation of the students. This board, composed of representative men from the student body, gives to the Department of Health and Sanitation a group of students who are qualified and naturally interested in the health problems of the academic community, and in the interrelated problems of the city and the institution.

It therefore constitutes a group of men for collecting facts and for studying problems of health and sanitation and the discussion of recommendations for the betterment of conditions in their own schools, in the dormitories, upon the campus, in the fraternity houses and in the neighborhood. It also constitutes a committee from the student body who are recognized by their colleague, as a group working for their benefit. Suggestions made by their Board of Health will, therefore, be received in a friendly spirit and will be given due consideration as representing the wishes of the students themselves. Each representative on this board may have his own committee to assist him in working out the unique problems of his group.

The problems before this board at present include the questions of diet, habits of life, morals and certain community matters reacting upon and vital to the University life. The board will affiliate with similar city organizations for social and civic work and thus gain knowledge and experience of the great social and health problems of a big city.

One of the most important problems that the student board can assist in solving is the question of foods and service. Most of our colleges maintain a commons, where a large number of students are served daily. These dining-rooms have in many colleges been unpopular with the students, possibly for at least two reasons. First, the fact that the spirit of destructive criticism along any line is very contagious and a few dissatisfied men can create a spirit of discontent. In the second place, these dining-rooms are frequently run as mess halls rather than as comfortable attractive dining-rooms. Psychology teaches the importance of pleasant surroundings for the development of healthy mental attitudes, and physiology proves the importance of mental enjoyment as a means to good digestion, but the college commons has not always taken into consideration these two vital points in preparing and serving food. The student board can ascertain the viewpoint of the college-men as to what would be most effective in the equipment and maintenance of the dining halls. They can measure the importance and justice of criticisms and be active in promulgating a spirit of constructive criticism that will place the commons in a position which it should maintain as an ideal dining hall and as a rendezvous for the most helpful and healthy student activities.

No matter how ideal a university commons may be as to the quality of food and service offered at a reasonable cost, a certain number of men will frequent restaurants in the neighborhood of the campus. To control this matter to a certain degree—and to offer reasonable protection to the students, the board will publish at intervals a list of eating houses that have upon their own initiative passed inspection by the board. The requirements for recommendation for this approved list include quality of food, care and preparation of food, proper kitchen and pantry facilities, enforcement of sanitary regulations compelling the help to take proper care of their persons and clothing, and the maintenance of proper toilet facilities for the help. In order to stimulate these restaurants to continue to live up to these hygienic regulations which are vital to the health of their patrons, inspections will be made at irregular intervals and without notice.

The University Commons at Columbia has been under these strict regulations and has responded to every suggestion to improve conditions.

Working under hygienic conditions does not increase in the end the running expenses of the kitchen and the scheme when once in operation benefits not only the patrons, but the employees also. Apart from the protection a supervision of this kind gives to the students it also serves as a lucrative form of advertising for the restaurants.

The neighborhood problems and the relations of the student board to similar civic institutions I will not here enlarge upon, neither can I speak of the educational aspect of the work.

To sum up then:

The health work at Columbia is carried on by the Departments of Hygiene and Physical Education and by the Department of Health and Sanitation. The curative and prophylactic work is carried on by the Department of Health and Sanitation. This department maintains on the University campus a well-equipped office for the treatment of all but bedside cases. The work of the department is supplemented by an advisory board of specialists, by the coöperation of local physicians, hospitals and clinics and by the assistance of the College of Physicians and Surgeons and by the student Board of Health.

UNIVERSITY OF CALIFORNIA INFIRMARY STUDENT HEALTH PROTECTION

BY

G. F. REINHARDT

It may be a surprising statement that the University of California Infirmary, with its large daily clinic and its hospital facilities, owes its existence less to a direct effort to improve student health than an effort to improve class attendance. Often the object nearest the observer is the thing he sees last and least clearly, and this partly accounts for the belief, still held by many faculties, that university students are a healthy crowd of young people in the full vigor of youth, and that it is no duty of the faculty to consider their aches and pains. Therefore, when in 1900 the faculty of the University of California became dissatisfied with the average attendance of students upon classes, and investigated the causes of absence, with a view to meeting out proper discipline to delinquents, the discovery was an unexpected one that sickness and not idleness or lack of interest was at the bottom of the trouble.

What was to be done? The decision was soon made to install upon the campus simple, sanitary conveniences as a sort of elemental preventive measure, and to meet the cost of this equipment by charging each student a nominal fee. The lessening of small ills was at once noticeable; and the experiment accounted more successful than had been anticipated. But it was some years before plans could be made to attempt an adequate solution of what grew to be recognized as the serious problem of student health. In proportion as the university increased in numbers, and the student population scattered more widely, just so greatly was increased the variety and the sources of infection, and the menace of uncontrolled epidemics.

It was in 1900, also, that a compulsory course in hygiene was first required of all students, and by 1907 the Infirmary was finally established. Since the opening of the Infirmary it may be said that the work done for the health protection of the student is three-fold: preventive measures of the sort begun in 1900; curative measures, supplied by the Infirmary; and educative measures, which are really a function of the Department of Hygiene.

This well-organized effort for student health in the University of California has not been made without cost to the student himself, but certainly the cost is far less than the value received. Perhaps there does not exist at the present time a better example of what can be done for the maintenance of the health of a large group of people at small cost per capita, than the Infirmary of the University of California, and its allied activities. At present each student pays a fee of five dollars a semester as a health fee, three dollars going to the Infirmary funds and two dollars to the gymnasium funds. In describing more minutely what we have chosen to call the three-fold work done for the protection of student health, we will show in detail what return the student receives for his semi-annual outlay of five dollars.

A. Preventive Measures for Protecting Student Health. It is to the gymnasium that all students go for their required physical training, where the common baths are situated, and consequently where exists the greatest danger on the campus of spreading infection, if infection exists in a single case. For that reason the first preventive measure taken was the installation in the gymnasium for men and that for women of large, grated-front, steel lockers to hold separately the clothing and possessions of each student. The grated-front lockers have the double advantage of making inspection easy, and of being conducive to orderliness. Beside this, there have been installed in the Harmon Gymnasium for men 170 shower baths, and in the Hearst Gymnasium for women 90 shower baths. The students have unrestricted use of large, full-sized bath towels and of hand towels supplied in generous number. No roller towels are found on the campus.

In all of the University buildings where there is running water, are found sanitary drinking fountains, basins, hand-towels, soap, and toilets. Waste baskets are supplied in which to deposit soiled towels. Soon after admission to the University students are told of these provisions, and the facts of their personal ownership and personal responsibility are emphasized. It is gratifying that the loss of towels is insignificantly small. In the towel supply of the University are 20,000 hand towels and 6,000 bath towels. A goodly number, sufficient for all needs. To anyone possessed of the belief that college students had nothing to learn in regard to personal neatness, the improvement in the appearance of the students consequent upon the establishment of the towel system would have been an eye-opening surprise. An astonishing difference in the atmosphere of Harmon Gymnasium made that a much more attractive place, for when students supplied their own towels, despite the fact that they were earnestly reminded of the necessity of frequent laundrying, towels were left unwashed for weeks and weeks, and became an offence to even the most casual passer-by.

As has been said, there are two gymnasia, one for men and one for women. All first-year students, of both sexes, are required to take gymnasium work, which is given in sections meeting four times a week for the first year. This work is largely corrective, its first purpose being to give students correct posture, and then by graded exercises to bring the class as a whole to that point of excellence where the body of each individual may be said to be a strong, well-poised, efficient mechan. ism. A student may elect to take a certain amount of work in the open air, but this does not excuse him from corrective work. All out-of. door games are supervised by an instructor.

The most popular out-of-door pleasure among the men is found in the swimming-pool, an ample place for aquatic sport, beautifully situated in Co-ed canyon, at a convenient distance from the campus. Two hundred and thirty-two feet long, with a breadth of seventy-six feet, and a depth varying from three and one-half feet in the shallowest part, to ten and one-half feet in the deepest part, the pool holds half a million gallons of water, which flows in from the stream locally known as Straw. berry Creek. This water is carefully sand-filtered, and is subjected to weekly bacterial tests. As additional precaution for the safety of bathers, each must take a shower bath in the bath house annex before going up for his swim. The tank is frequently treated with bleaching powder to keep down the algae. Whenever the water in the stream is insufficient for the tank, one hundred and fifty thousand gallons are pumped in daily from the city water supply. This water is afterward used for irrigating purposes and fire protection. The swimming-pool, as well as eight excellent concrete tennis courts, were built by the gymnasium fund. These courts afford a continuous place of wholesome exercise for students of both sexes, and at some not far distant day the number of courts will be increased. A swimming pool for women is in course of construction. So much for the sanitary measures taken and the physical exercises required of all students as part of the preventive measures to guard student health. We come now to a consideration of the medical phase of the preventive measures.

Most important of all is the requirement that each applicant for admission to the University must pass a satisfactory medical examination. If a student's physical condition is not satisfactory he is refused admission; under certain conditions he is permitted to take a limited amount of work. This requirement has resulted in eliminating that type of student, who knocks often very earnestly at the door of every college, who enters to work a month or two or three, grows less and less equal to his undertaking, and then disappears from his classes and the campus. Often unwittingly, but none the less unfortunately, such a student has spread his trouble among associates. But where the medical examination helps a few people, who are stricken with a disease which may be fatal if not arrested in time, it helps in far larger numbers students who have some lesser, perhaps completely curable ailment.

An eye specialist examines the eyes of all entrants, and where treatment or glasses are advisable, students are told the right means to take for their specific difficulty. A nose and throat specialist examines for cases of deafness, for infected tonsils, obstructing adenoids, and other allied difficulties, simple to deal with if taken in time, but often impossible to reach if neglected a brief year or two. In short, every effort is taken in this examination to discover and begin to correct physical defects and deformities, and to instill into the mind of the student the important fact that his future happiness, success, and usefulness depend primarily on the wholesome care of his body. The world will never be so old that each generation must not be taught, as it is taught its alphabet, the axiom that a wholesome mind is housed happily only in a wholesome body.

Another important requirement of students is satisfactory vaccination against smallpox. If an applicant comes unvaccinated, or with a scar which is unsatisfactory, he must be vaccinated. There have been no cases of smallpox since this rule was established in 1901. For a few years anti-vaccinationists raised frequent objection, carrying the matter into the California courts, but since the courts established the University's right to make and carry out such a ruling, no public objection has been uttered. Last year there were a number of cases of smallpox in the town of Berkeley, and 1,230 students voluntarily requested vaccination. The University did not think the epidemic of sufficient virulence to make re-vaccination compulsory in the University.

During the year just passed 261 students asked for vaccination against typhoid fever. The sensitized vaccine used in each instance was prepared under the direction of Dr. F. P. Gay in the Department of Pathology. Sensitized vaccine has the advantage over others that are used, in that it does not cause the frequent severe reactions that are produced by the United States Army formulae, for instance.

B. *Educative Measures Taken for Protecting Student Health.* After all, any classification made of the efforts to protect student health is more or less arbitrary. For, though sanitary precautions, physical exercises, the encouragement of out-of-door living, medical examinations, medical advice, and the rendering of students immune to the incursions of the most dreaded of diseases—may be first of all preventive in their purpose, they are all of them educative as well. Certainly, if a University did no more than this for the health education of its students, it would turn out citizens far from ignorant of the vital relation between the health of the individual citizen and the health of his family and of the community in which he lives. But the University of California does more than this. Since 1900 the attendance of all first year students of both sexes has been made compulsory in the course of general hygiene, which comprises thirty lectures given twice a week during the first semester, and certain requirements in reading. There are separate instructors for men and women, but the ground covered in all classes is much the same, the differences being chiefly in the matter of emphasis.

To comment with anything like fullness on the various courses in hygiene and its allied subjects which are open to students, might seem to transgress the bounds of a paper which has to do with the health protection of students in a given educational institution. But it is an interesting fact that the responsibility assumed by the University in regard to health conditions, the establishing of the Infirmary itself, the very existence of health regulations in regard to the individual student, have created an impulse toward the study of hygiene that has been one of the most important factors in the enlarging and perfecting of the Hygiene Department. So great grew the demand for work in special branches of hygiene, that one by one these branches have been added to the departmental equipment, which is now a singularly rich and complete one. The Department of Hygiene reaches the needs of three classes of students: first, those wishing the elementary principles of health conservation, individual and public (indeed, all students are taught this much of hygiene); second, those studying vocations not directly associated with the conservation of public health, but who will come in close contact with it; third, those wishing a professional training as bacteriologists, health visitors, sanitary inspectors, or health officers. It goes without saying that the number of students of the third class is steadily on the increase, for as the public comes to realize the importance of the conservation of public health, it demands more men professionally trained to carry on the work of conservation.

The subjects covered in the curriculum of public health are, Communicable Diseases, Child Hygiene and Eugenics, Foods, Sanitary Engineering, Vital Statistics and Social Economics, Industrial Hygiene, Applied Hygiene, Sanitary Inspection, Public Health Administration, First Aid, and Home Care of the Sick.

C. *Curative Measures.* As is apparent, the preventive and educative measures taken to protect student health are extensive in character, and touch a student's life at many points, his curriculum, recreations, mode of living, etc. As curative medicine is on the contrary intensive, so the curative measures used for restoring and preserving student health are concentrated in the Infirmary.

The Infirmary is now six years old, a well-equipped hospital capable of accommodating some forty bed-patients. The building itself is by no means a model structure. Being in the first place a residence, remodelled into a hospital, it has suffered annual additions, which have unfortunately rendered it more amorphous in appearance as they have rendered it more practicable and adequate in reality. It is hoped that in the near future the University will be provided with a modern building for Infirmary purposes.

The heavy work of the Infirmary comes in the dispensary for out patient service. This service is daily from 8–10 A.M. and 5–6 P.M. for men students and for women students from 10–12 A.M. and 3–4 P.M.

During the past year 3,501 students, 74% of the students in the University, visited the dispensary for treatment. The daily average was 91 students, the largest number was 289. The total number of treatments were 25,976. There were 9,644 cases for diagnosis. Of the class graduating in 1913, 92% of the men and 88% of the women made use of the Infirmary during their fours years' residence in college.

During the past year 433 individual students were bed patients in the Infirmary. Of these, 87 were patients more than once during the year. The largest number of patients in bed in one day was 22, the average stay was 5 days. Fifty-nine operations were performed.

The professional staff consists of five men and three women physicians; a superintendent and six nurses, extra nurses being called in when the work requires it, and one laboratory worker.

The above figures would suggest that a very large number of visits are made by students to the Infirmary each year. This is not because student health is poor, but because encouragement is given to students to report a disease in its incipiency for treatment that possible grave complications may be avoided. Indeed, the watchword of the Infirmary is "Prevention," and the first lesson the Infirmary teaches, as well as the most lasting good the Infirmary can hope to do, is to inculcate the principle of early attention to illness. In their effort at the prevention of disease all measures which the University takes for protecting student health, meet and harmonize. No case comes before the University physician where occasion is not taken to point out how such an illness might have been avoided altogether, or how its serious consequences might have been minimized.

In regard to Infirmary statistics, we have no statistics compiled elsewhere that may serve as a basis of comparison, because nowhere else does there exist a similar institution. No other universities have infirmaries of the same class, because none of them have eliminatd the participation for profit of the outside physician. Comparison might be made with the health statistics of communities or of armies and navies, but such comparison is not satisfactory as the health conditions of an army or navy apply to a selected body of men and not to a body of youths of whom less than 20% would be fit for military service.

A second lesson which the Infirmary teaches to students is the efficiency and economy of organized medical aid. Through organization a maximum of medical service is rendered for the minimum of expenditure. Our American public are sadly ignorant of the laws of health protection, but the students who pass out of the University may be the leaven that shall leaven the whole lump of citizenship. Certainly when people realize that most diseases can be prevented, they are going to organize in such a way that they may obtain the services of a physician without the repeated payment of fees. Already arguments are being raised against the possible organization of the people for medical service, because some few such organizations, made for mercenary reasons by unscrupulous laymen and physicians of questionable training, have resulted in a deserved failure. Nevertheless, coöperation is the only feasible method by which people of ordinary means can have the advice of the best physicians. That fees are high is true; that they cannot be much lower is also true. The requirement for the training of a physician in both time and money is steadily increasing. Adequate reimbursement is only just. Because these things are unavoidable, people will have to resort to some form of coöperation whereby a per capita tax will cover the main expenses, as in the University Infirmary.

A third lesson which the Infirmary teaches unconsciously but effectively, is democracy. According to an unwritten law, all students, upper or lower classmen, rich or poor, receive identical treatment. The best is done for every student; there are no special privileges to be purchased. If a student occupies a single room, it means that his case requires segregation, not, as at Harvard, Princeton, or Cornell, that he has paid for exclusive quarters. As far as those in authority can judge, this arrangement has never been criticised by the student. Indeed it seems that the Infirmary fosters among the students who report thither a sense of fellowship and mutual understanding.

For those who may be interested there is here appended a copy of the record form, which is kept on file in the Infirmary, and in which may be found the medical history of every student in the University.

"A" is the form printed on one side of the card, where is recorded the results of the medical examination taken at the time of the matriculant's entrance to the University.

"B" is the form printed on the other side, where is recorded the date, the occasion, and the description of every illness that has brought the student to the Infirmary for advice and treatment.

A

FAMILY HISTORY

(Date of exam.)

F. { Racial } .... L. aet............, Well, has ....
{ extraction } .... D. aet............, in the year............, of..............

M. { Racial } .... L. aet............, Well, has ....
{ extraction } .... D. aet............, in the year............, of..............

Wh. relatives have had Tb? .... Cancer? ....

Neurasthenia .... Epilepsy? ....

Other possibly inheritable disease? ....

PERSONAL HISTORY

a Measles
b Mumps
c Chicken-pox
d Whooping Cgh.
e Scarlet Fever
f Typhoid Fever
" Vac.,
g Diphtheria
h Malaria
i Smallpox
" Vac.
j Pneumonia
k Pleurisy
l Rheumatism
m Amygdalitis
n Chorea
o Influenza
p Otitis Media
q Gonorrhea
r Syphilis
s Constipation
t Appendicitis
u Neurasthenia
OTHERS:

Birthplace ....

Give approximate age at which student had any of the diseases listed in the square:

u. What Injuries? (*Give age*) ....

v. What Operations? (*Give age*) ....

Age of last vaccination scar: under 10 yrs.........., 10 to 20 yrs........., over 20 yrs.....

Have done ....; also ....
   (*mental work other than schooling*)   (*physical work*)

Present general health .... Appetite .... Sleep........hrs.

Tea and Cof. .... Tob. .... Alc. .... Drugs ....
[*By "mod." is understood, for tea and coffee, 1 to 2 per day of either or both; for tob.
1 to 6 cigarettes or pipes, or 1 to 3 cigars; for alc.; 1 to 3 drinks of beer, wine, or spirits daily.
Less than "mod." is marked "o." or "oc.," more than "mod." is marked "ex."*]

PHYSICAL EXAMINATION

1*Gen. Devl.*: exc., good, fair, poor. 2*N.*: thin, av., obese. 3*Wt.* .... kilos. 4*Ht.* .... cm.

5*Skin*: type ...., norm. .... 6*Acne*: ....

                            under 15 mm.
7*Joints*: .... 9*Vac.*: R.L. arm, leg, pitted, keloidal, smooth; 15–20 mm.
                            over 20 mm.

10*Vertebral col.*: norm., Lordosis ...., Kyphosis ...., Scoliosis ....

11*Teeth*: good, fair, poor, negl., false. 12*Thyreoid*: norm., ...

13*Lymph N.*: C. .... Ax. .... Ing. ....

14*Chest*: norm., ... 15*Lungs*: norm., ..., apical resonance ^R_L ...... cm.

16*Heart*: rate ...., norm., ...

17*B.P.* (max.), recumb. = ... mm.

18*Abdomen*: norm., rigid, relax. 19*Hernia* ....

20*Palpable*: Liv. ...., Spl. .... R. Kid. ...., L. Kid. ...., Other ....

21*Knee jerk*: R......., L....... 22*Penis*: norm., circum. 23*Testes*: R......., L....... 24*Varic.*: R......., L.......

25*Urine*: Col. ...., Sp. gr. ...., R. ...., Alb. ...., S: ....

26*Feet*: Long. arches: R. norm., low, flat. L. norm., low, flat. Ant. arches: R. norm., low. L. norm., low.

27*Nose*: Nor., Sep. Spur., Cr., Dev., Chr. Hyp. .... 28*Adenoids*: L., S., Chr. Pharyn. ....

29*Tonsils*: Nor., Ab., Bur., Proj., Path., ... 30*Larynx*: ....

31*Ear*: Nor., Cer., T.T., Chr. S., Wch. .... Spch. .... Whisp. ....

32*Eyes*: Lids: nor. .... Muscles: nor. .... Fundus: nor. ....; Col. vision: nor. ....
   Refraction: O.D. ....; O.S. ....

Defects	1	2	3	4	5	6	7	8	9	10	11	12	13	14	15	16	17	18	19	20	21	22	23	24	25	26	27	28	29	30	31	32
Treated (*t*)																																
Corrected (*c*)																																

Examiner ....

B

UNIVERSITY OF CALIFORNIA INFIRMARY—DISPENSARY RECORD .

Name_____Age____College_____Class_____

(Date)	(Diagnoses)	(Date)	(Diagnoses)

SECTION FOUR

SESSION THIRTY A

Room E.   Tuesday, August 26th, 9:00 A.M.

SYMPOSIUM ON MOUTH HYGIENE

ARRANGED BY THE NATIONAL MOUTH HYGIENE ASSOCIATION,

W. G. EBERSOLE, M.D., D.D.S., Cleveland, Ohio, *Secretary*

W. G. EBERSOLE, M.D., D.D.S., *Chairman*

DR. W. C. GREENFIELD, Buffalo, N. Y., *Vice-Chairman*

Program of Session Thirty A

Dr. ERNST JESSEN, Strassburg, Germany, Chairman of the Hygienic Commission of the International Dental Federation. "The Development of the School Dental Clinic." (Read by H. D. CROSS, Boston, Mass.)

ALBERT H. STEVENSON, D.D.S., Brooklyn, N. Y., Chairman Committee on Public Health and Education, Second District Dental Society; Oral Hygiene Committee New York State Dental Society. "Mouth Hygiene in the Public School Curriculum—Some Comparisons and Deductions,"

M. EVANGELINE JORDAN, D.D.S., Representing the Southern California Dental Association, Los Angeles, Cal. "What We Are Doing in Mouth Hygiene on the Pacific Coast."

SIDNEY J. RAUH, D.D.S., Chairman of the Cincinnati Oral Hygiene Committee, Cincinnati, Ohio. "The Educational and Economic Value of School Dental Inspection."

DIE FRAGE DER SCHULZAHNKLINIK IN IHRER ENTWICKELUNG

VON

ERNST JESSEN

Der I. Internationale Schulhygiene-Kongress in Nürnberg 1904 brachte in der Gruppe E „Krankheiten und ärztlicher Dienst in den Schulen" ein offizielles Inserat über das Thema „Die Errichtung städtischer Schulzahnkliniken ist eine internationale, volkshygienische Forderung unserer Zeit." In diesem Referat wurde die Notwendigkeit der Schulzahnpflege nachgewiesen. Die Möglichkeit ihrer Durchführung wurde an dem Beispiel der Strassburger Schulzahnklinik gezeigt.

Alsdann wurde von den beiden Referenten, dern damaligen Beigeordneten der Stadt Strassburg und jetzigem Oberbürgermeister von Schöneberg-Berlin, Herrn Regierungsrat Dominikus, und von mir selbst der Antrag gestellt, folgende Resolution anzunehmen:

„Eine behördlich organisierte, auch dem Unbemittelten zugängliche Zahnpflege für das Volk ist notwendig und auf dem Wege der städtischen Schulzahn Kliniken mit unentgeltlicher Behandlung, eventuell nach vorheriger Untersuchung durch den Schularzt, sowie anschliessend durch die deutschen sozialen Versicherungseinrichtungen, durchführbar."

Dieser Antrag rief eine lebhafte Diskussion hervor. Im Verlauf derselben erklärte Dr. Petruschky-Danzig: „Kariöse Zähne sind im Kindesalter eine Haupt-Eintrittspforte für den Tuberkel-Bazillus; es entstehen hierbei die sogenannten skrophulösen Halslymphdrüsen. 90% der Berliner, 85% der Danziger Gemeinde-Schulkinder sind mit solchen Drüsen behaftet gefunden. Die eminente Gefahr kariöser Zähne im frühen Kindesalter geht hieraus besonders hervor. Daher ist ein Vorgehen im Sinne der Referenten lebhaft zu befürworten. Die Untersuchung und Prophylaxis kann der Schularzt durchführen; es wird aber immer noch genug für die Zahnärzte zu tun bleiben. Den grösseren Gemeinden wird daher die Einrichtung von Zahnkliniken wohl empfohlen werden können."

Der Antrag wurde daraufhin in der Gruppe E angenommen, in der Plenarsitzung verlesen und dem II. Kongress in London 1907 zur Weiterbehandlung überwiesen. Auf dem Londoner Kongress wurde von mir ein Vortrag über „Schulzahnpflege und Schule" gehalten, der sich an meine in Nürnberg gemachten Ausführungen anschloss. Es wurde in demselben von mir über die günstigen Erfahrungen berichtet, die in der Strassburger Schulzahnklinik, Stadtverwaltung, Schulbehörde in 5 jähriger Tätigkeit gesammelt waren. Der Antrag an sich konnte jedoch infolge der Reichhaltigkeit der Tagesordnung nicht zur Verhandlung kommen. Die ganze Frage wurde aber auf dem V. Internationalen Zahnarztlichen Kongress 1909 in Berlin in der Sektion X „Hygiene" einer erneuten, eingehenden Behandlung unterworfen. Hier wurden folgende Resolutionen einstimmig zur Annahme gebracht:

1). Die Errichtung städtischer Schulzahnkliniken ist eine volkshygienisch-internationale Forderung unserer Zeit.

2), Sie ist ein wesentliches Hilfsmittel zur Verhütung und Bekämpfung der Infektionskrankheiten und besonders der Tuberkulose.

Es ist allerdings begreiflich, dass von den Teilnehmern eines internationalen „zahnärztlichen" Kongresses die Zahnhygiene als wesentlicher Bestandteil der Volkshygiene allgemein anerkannt wurde. Doch auch vonseiten der Regierung wurde von hervorragenden Vertretern mehrfach bestätigt, dass die Zahnhygiene nicht *nur* Pflege der Zähne, sondern eine Pflege der Hygiene überhaupt und ein Kampfmittel gegen die Infektionskrankheiten sei. Beispielsweise sagte der Vertreter der Königl. Preussischen Staats-Regierung, Wirkl. Geh. Ober-Medizinalrat Prof. Dr. Schmidtmann, Vortragender Rat im Kgl. Preuss. Kultusministerium: „Mit besonderer Freude begrüsse ich als Ihr ärztlicher Kollege die Bestrebungen auf dem Gebiete der Mundhygiene, durch die dem Arzte in dem Zahnarzte ein hygienischer Mithelfer und willkommener Mitstreiter in dem schweren Kampfe gegen die Volksseuchen, insbesondere die Tuberkulose, mehr und mehr erwachsen wird."

In der an den Kongress sich anschliessenden öffentlichen Versammlung im Reichstagsgebäude in Berlin hielt ich einen Vortrag über „die Organisation und den Betrieb der Städtischen Schulzahnklinik" mit Lichtbildern und stellte dazu die folgenden Leitsätze auf:

1). Das Bedürfnis nach zahnärztlicher Volks-Fürsorge ist erwiesen.

2). Es hat die Aufmerksamkeit der staatlichen und städtischen Behörden gefunden.

3). Es findet seine Verwirklichung durch die Errichtung städtischer Schul-Zahnkliniken.

4). Die Kosten derselben sind durch die Gemeindewesen aufzubringen.

5). Die Schul-Zahnklinik muss deshalb durch die Stadt-Verwaltung organisiert werden.

6). Ihr Betrieb ist von geeigneten' Zahnärzten in Verbindung mit Verwaltung, Schule und Schularzt durchzuführen.

7). Die Zahnpflege in der Schule legt die Grundlage für die weitere zahnärztliche Fürsorge durch Krankenkassen, in Krankenhäusern und in der Armee.

Diese Leitsätze dienten auf dem III. Internationalen Schulhygiene-Kongress in Paris 1910 einigen deutschen Schulärzten zum Angriffspunkt. Diese Ärzte waren der Ansicht, dass in Verbindung mit der Schule nur die Untersuchung, aber nicht die Behandlung der Kinder stattzufinden habe.

Sie sprachen damit der Schulzahnklinik jede Existenz-Berechtigung ab. Diese Auffassung wird aber widerlegt durch die nicht wegzuleugnende Tatsache, dass inzwischen in Deutschland allein 200 Schul-Zahnkliniken eröffnet worden sind, deren Entstehung durch das Bedürfnis, nicht durch äusseren Anlass hervorgerufen wurde.

Das vom Deutschen Zentralkomitee für Zahnpflege in den Schulen herausgegebene Verzeichnis gibt Auskunft über die Organisation, den Betrieb, das Personal und die Kosten dieser Einrichtungen.

(Abdruck des Verzeichnisses*)

Auch andere Länder sind dem von Deutschland ausgegangenen Beispiel gefolgt. So hat Schweden in jeder Stadt eine Schulzahnklinik eingerichtet, und der König von Schweden hat eine Kommission ernannt zur einheitlichen Durchführung dieser Bestrebungen im ganzen Land. Auch Dänemark, Norwegen, Oesterreich, Frankreich, Italien, England und die Vereinigten Staaten von Nord-Amerika haben einen vielversprechenden Anfang zur Einführung der Schul-Zahnpflege gemacht. Die grösste Schul-Zahnklinik der Welt wird im September dieses Jahres in Boston eröffnet.

Diese in allen Ländern einsetzenden Bestrebungen haben ihren Kristallisationspunkt in der Internationalen Commission für öffentliche Mundhygiene gefunden, welche in fast allen Kulturländern der Welt besondere Landes-Komitees gebildet hat und sich alljährlich zur Berichterstattung über die Fortschritte der Bewegung und zur Beratung der einzelnen neu entstehenden Fragen auf diesem Gebiet zusammenfindet.

Gesammtkommission steht unter dem Protektorat des Königs Gustaf V. von Schweden; den einzelnen Landeskomitees wenden die Landesfürsten und Regierungen durch Übernahme der Protektorate ihr Interesse zu.

Durch diese Organisation hat die Bewegung ein festes Gefüge er-

*Das Verzeichnis folgt, sobald es fertig ist.

halten, welches die Gewähr bietet, dass die einmal betretenen Pfade auch weiterhin einheitlich und zielbewusst verfolgt werden können.

Die Tatsachen sind somit dem in Nürnberg gefassten Beschluss vorausgeeilt, entsprechend den Bedürfnissen, die mit zwingender Notwendigkeit ihr Recht forderten. Es wird deshalb für den IV. Internationalen Schulhygiene-Kongress in Buffalo zur Pflicht werden, den in Nürnberg 1904 gefassten Beschluss nun mehr aufzunehmen und zu einem endgiltigen zu erheben, dadurch dass die Plenarsitzung den Beschluss bestätigt.

THE DEVELOPMENT OF THE SCHOOL
DENTAL CLINIC

BY

Ernst Jessen

The First International School Hygiene Congress held in Nürnberg, 1904, under Group E, devoted to "Diseases and Medical Service in the Schools" brought out an official statement to the effect that "the establishment of public school dental clinics is a universal, popular demand of our times." In this report was proved the necessity for the care of the teeth of school children; the possibility of providing this care was shown by the example of the Dental Clinic for school children at Strassburg.

Then the motion was made by the committee of two, namely Counsellor Dominicus, at that time delegate of the city of Strassburg and now chief mayor of Schöneberg-Berlin, and myself, to accept the following resolution:

"There is needed for the welfare of the public an official organization for the caring of teeth, which would be accessible even to the poor, and this can eventually be accomplished through public dental clinics for school children, providing for free treatment, after previous examination by the school physician, and connected with the German social insurance institutions."

This proposition called forth a lively discussion. During this discussion Dr. Petruschky-Danzig made the following statement: "Decayed teeth offer during childhood the chief passage-way for the tuberculosis bacillus; thence arise the so-called scrofulous lymph-ducts on the neck. 90% of the Berlin, 85% of the Danzig school children have been found affected by these swellings. The imminent danger of decaying teeth in early childhood is clearly seen from this. Therefore a prevention as suggested by the committee is to be highly recommended. The examination and certain preventive work can be done by the school physician; but there will still remain enough for the dentists to do. Therefore, to the greater communities the establishment of dental clinics can be well recommended."

The proposition was then accepted under Group E; it was read at the full sitting and referred to the Second Congress held in London in 1907 for further action. At the London Congress I read a paper on the "Care of the Teeth of School Children and the School," bearing on my remarks made at Nürnberg. In it I also reported on the favorable results gathered during five years activity from the Strassburg School Dental Clinic, municipal administration, and school offices. The proposition could not come up for discussion on account of the great amount of business which was to be transacted during the day.

The whole question, however, was submitted for a new, detailed consideration at the Fifth International Dental Congress held in Berlin, 1909, under Section X devoted to Hygiene. On this occasion the fol. lowing resolutions were unanimously accepted:

1. The establishment of municipal dental clinics is a universal need of our times.

2. It is an important factor in the combating and prevention of infectious diseases, especially tuberculosis.

It is entirely conceivable that dental hygiene should be generally recognized by the participants in an international congress of dentists as an important constituent part of public hygiene. But even on the part of the government it has been often asserted by prominent representatives that dental hygiene means not only the taking care of teeth, but attention to hygiene in general and that it is a weapon against infectious diseases. For instance the representative of the royal state government of Prussia, acting chief privy medical counsellor Professor Dr. Schmidtman, Counsellor of the Royal Prussian Ministry of Education, said: "As your medical colleague I greet with especial pleasure the efforts in the field of dental hygiene which will cultivate more and more in the dentist a hygienic assistant and a welcome fellow-warrior for the physician in the difficult strife against public epidemics, especially tuberculosis."

In the open meeting immediately following the Congress and held in the state-house in Berlin I read a paper illustrated with lantern slides on the "Organization and Management of the Public School Dental Clinic" and proposed the following guiding principles:

1. The need for dental care for the public has been proved.

2. It has attracted the attention of both the state and municipal authorities.

3. It can be accomplished by the establishment of municipal dental clinics for school children.

4. The expenses of the same are to' be defrayed by the communities.

5. The school dental clinic must therefore be organized by the municipal administration.

6. Its management is to be carried on by capable dentists, in conjunction with the school authorities and the school physician.

7. The care of the teeth in the school lays a foundation for further dental care through workmen's sick-funds, in hospitals and in the army.

These principles served at the Third International-School Congress in Paris 1910 as a point of attack by some German school physicians. These physicians were of the opinion that in connection with the school only the examinations and not the treatment should receive attention. They denied thereby the school dental clinic all rights of existence. This attack, however, can be met by a fact which cannot be refuted, namely, that in Germany alone there have been opened 200 school dental clinics which were called into being by actual needs and not by outward appearances. The publications of the German Central Committee in regard to the care of teeth in the schools contain information regarding the organization, the management, the personnel, and the expenses of these institutions.

Other countries, too, have followed the example set by Germany. Thus Sweden has established in every city a dental clinic for school children, and the King of Sweden has appointed a commission for the uniform carrying out of these efforts throughout the kingdom. Also Denmark, Norway, Austria, France, Italy, England, and the United States of North America have taken very promising steps in the introduction of dental hygiene for school children. The greatest school dental clinic will be opened in September of this year in Boston.

These efforts, which are gaining ground in all countries, center in the International Commission for public dental hygiene, which has created in almost all civilized countries of the world special committees, and which meets annually to report on the progress of the movement and to discuss individual and newly arising questions in this field.

The entire commission is under the patronage of King Gustav V of Sweden; the separate committees in the various countries receive attention from the princes and governments which assume a protectorate over them. Through this organization the movement has been placed on a firm basis, which gives assurance that it will be possible for this movement, once started, to be carried on uniformly and with set purpose.

Accordingly more has been accomplished than the resolution adopted in Nürnberg provided for, and this as a result of the needs which urgently demanded proper attention. It will therefore be the duty of the Fourth International Congress in Buffalo to take up again the resolution adopted in Nürnberg in 1904 and to give it an authoritative endorsement by confirming it in full sitting.

MOUTH HYGIENE IN THE PUBLIC SCHOOL CUR-
RICULUM—SOME COMPARISONS
AND DEDUCTIONS

BY

ALBERT H. STEVENSON

Have we, or have we not, been giving mouth hygiene its deserved place in the school curriculum? Decidedly, we have not, as health officers will attest and statistics will verify. The dissemination of disease can only be controlled by prevention, but how meagre is the attention given to that all important source of many diseases—the mouth. As the most common physical defect in the school child (98% being the alarming average of the school inspection reports) bad teeth and consequent filthy mouths, have aroused more than one community to action. Public dental clinics, dental school nurses, and more careful inspection have been resorted to with success, but the most effectual means to the end, a revision of the present instructive methods in the hygiene, appears to have been ignored. That much can be done toward the improvement of the child physically, mentally and morally by remedying the condition of his mouth has been proven. More will be added by unquestionable authorities at this Congress. That proper instruction in the hygiene is the most potent preventative measure is an undisputed fact. Why, then, with all our modern progress in the major and minor subjects has this received such scant consideration by our educators? Because no uniformity of rule nor systematic arrange-ment has been applied toward the establishment of a rational hygiene of the mouth. Until such a system is adopted, here and abroad, there can be no appreciable result.

An indication of the present status of mouth hygiene in the curricula of the public schools of the large cities of this country may be obtained from the following. This information was taken from the signed state-ments sent to the writer by the Superintendents of the Departments of Education of nine of the leading cities of the United States:

MOUTH HYGIENE IN THE PUBLIC SCHOOLS

CITY	*Periods per Week	Earliest Grade Taught	Dental Inspection	Tooth-brush Drill	Text and Reference Books	Public Lectures
Baltimore.....	2 2	1st	Yes	No	Conn's Elem. Phy.	Night school only
Boston........	1	1st	Yes	Yes	Conn's-Jewett's Ritchie's-Millard's	Yes
Cleveland.....	1	1st	Yes	Higher grades only	Gulick's Series	Yes
Newark.......	1	1st	Yes	Yes	Ritchie's Primer Krohn's Phy. Smith's Primer Gulick's Series	To Teachers
New York....	1	1st	Yes	Yes	Gulick's Series	Yes
New Orleans..	2	1st	Yes	No	Krohn's Phy.	Yes
Philadelphia...	2	1st	Yes	No	Many	No
Seattle.......	1	1st	Yes	No	Ritchie's Primer Gulick's Series Woods Hutchinson	No
San Francisco.	1	1st	Yes	No	Ritchie's Primer Caldwell's Primer	No

*Period—one-half hour Phy. and Hy.

It will be noted all have dental inspection and teach mouth hygiene from the first grade; however, but one-half an hour is allowed each week for the entire subject of physiology and hygiene in seven of the above cities, and but three have the toothbrush drill. Of the text and reference books cited not one contain mouth hygiene as it is understood and applied by the dental profession. The City of New York in its new syllabus in Physiology and Hygiene prepared by Dr. C. Ward Crampton, has a graded system wherein by proper correlation with other hygienics the mouth is given its deserved importance. Dr. R. Ottolingui, of New York City, together with the writer, in collaborating with Dr. Crampton, proved most conclusively the value of the toothbrush drill, and it has been incorporated in the syllabus. The city of Newark has a series of practical lectures delivered to the teachers in the various centers, and by this means the teachers are prepared directly to teach the application of mouth hygiene in the classroom.

In instruction upon the subject, two aspects, heretofore more or less ignored, should be emphasized. Firstly, the relation of the mouth as the vestibule of the body to the human habitation; secondly, the beneficial effects of a clean mouth upon the general health. Both these points, it will be noted, are of a positive nature and quite in keeping with modern pedagogics. The futile method of inspiring dread of pain as a spur to cleanliness is ineffectual, obsolete and should be discouraged. *Attention should be given* as the subject develops, 1st, to the brush, its size, and shape, its bristles with warnings; 2d, the use of the dental floss; 3rd, the dentifrice, with warnings and advice, and most of all to the method of brushing and the frequency of the operation. As to the method of brushing the most practical manner of instruction is the toothbrush drill. In this drill the teacher demonstrates to the pupils the correct use of the brush, using her own brush, dry, in pantomime and the class doing the same. The children should be notified one or more days before of the intended drill, and to be prepared with their own brushes. The use of a large demonstrating brush and model is also a good method though less effective. As to frequency, the children should be taught to cleanse their mouths after each meal and upon retiring. Physiological chemistry has proven conclusively that food retained in the mouth even an hour ferments and presents a putrefactive source of infection! Why, then, not teach the child how to keep his mouth absolutely clean?

Instruction should begin with the first grade or even in the kindergarten in simple form, advancing apace with other subjects. With the knowledge that the mouth is the gateway through which passes all food, all water, and part of the air for our sustenance, will come a wholesome respect for this cavity. In proportion to this respect depends much of the future not alone of preventative dentistry, but preventative medicine as well, for is school sanitation more important than mouth sanitation, or pure food laws than pure mouth laws?

I plead then for universal mouth hygiene, uniform, rational, life-saving. Not the hygiene of clean teeth alone only, but of clean mouths, at all hours of the day, in class or at play, and as far as possible during the sleeping hours of the child. The benefits of this condition are self-evident. With a clean and not a fertile field for bacteria; with a comfortable and not a disturbing mouth, how much more receptive will be the child for that grander knowledge which we have under difficulties been inculcating.

WHAT WE ARE DOING IN MOUTH HYGIENE ON THE PACIFIC COAST

BY

M. Evangeline Jordan

It has been said that the Pacific Coast is overflowing with surplus energy and it has been explained in this way.

The restless spirits of all ages have had the tendency to follow Greeley's advice, "Go West, young man." Americans have gone west as far as they can go, and having reached that great barrier—the Pacific —their energy must be directed into other channels.

Some of these energetic pioneers were among the first to grasp the significance of the movement now called Mouth Hygiene.

In 1889 we find Dr. John C. McCoy having realized this need, determined to bring the matter forcibly before School Boards and teachers and try to secure their coöperation. In doing this he visited many schools and with the assistance of Dr. Moore of Santa Barbara, Dr. White of Los Angeles, Dr. Hurt of Pomona, and Dr. Cave of San Diego, he got information from 7,000 school children between the ages of 10 and 18 years of age.

The fact was discovered that half of them had never owned a tooth brush and only *one-tenth* of them brushed their teeth every day.

The report of these examinations was first read before the Southern California Odontological Society and before the County School Board and teachers of Orange County.

In 1894 the same paper was read before the American Medical Association. It was published in their archives, and afterwards found its way into many European languages.

In 1892-93 we have another pioneer, Dr. Kate C. Moody, going to the Los Angeles Orphans' Home once a month to examine the mouths of the children and between these visits having the children sent to her office for the work necessary to preserve their permanent teeth. She also gave lectures before teachers, and at meetings of the foreign mothers at the College Settlement.

In 1900 Dr. Edgar Palmer, the first dean of the Dental Department of the University of Southern California felt the lack of knowledge among dentists themselves, and so added a course of lectures on Care of Children's Teeth to the curriculum of the college. To which chair the writer was appointed.

This was followed the next year by fitting up a room at the Orphans'.

Home for a clinic where the students carried on the work of caring for the teeth of the orphans under the supervision of the lecturer.

This was discontinued several years later when the college moved into its new quarters where there were better facilities for caring for the children in the infirmary of the college.

In 1901, after repeated efforts to make examinations of the mouths of school children in Los Angeles, a joint meeting of the Southern California Dental Association, the Board of Education of Los Angeles, and a committee from the State Normal School was held to consider conditions relating to the need of Mouth Hygiene in the schools.

As a result of this meeting the Southern California Dental Association published and distributed at its own expense 30,000 booklets of instruction on the care of the teeth of children. These were distributed in the nine largest towns of Southern California.

From that time dentists volunteered for lecture work before Mothers' Meetings, Woman's Clubs, and Teachers' Associations, and that work has continued until the present.

In March, 1911, the Los Angeles Parent-Teachers' Infirmary was opened. It is managed by a committee of five members with Mrs. Elizabeth McMames, to whose energy the infirmary owes its existence, as its chairman.

The Board of Education furnished the building and the members of the Southern California Dental Association furnished the equipment and paid the salaries of two dentists for half of each day.

In 1912 and since the Board of Education has paid the salaries of two women dentists and a matron for full time, and the Parent-Teachers' Association pays for an assistant and for all materials used.

The infirmary has, besides the paid members, a large number of volunteer associates who care for the eyes, ears, noses and throats of school children. Volunteer osteopaths attend to the orthopedics.

In 1913 there were 1,434 children whose teeth were cared for by the infirmary dentists. The children were sent there by the large staff of school physicians and nurses employed by the Board of Education.

The new Children's Hospital now being built by the charities of Los Angeles is having a room fitted up as a dental infirmary.

The Pasadena Board of Education has had inspection of the schools since 1910 and since 1912 has paid for one operator.

San Diego has similar conditions except that the San Diego County Dental Society has paid for the operator.

In Santa Barbara Dr. Moore has established, at his own expense, a free dental infirmary for poor children. He gives two half days a week

himself and employs a young dentist whose salary he pays.   He supplies
the poor children with tooth brushes and powders.

He has endowed this infirmary so that it shall be permanent.

In 1909-10 Dr. Suggett examined 500 school children in the San
Francisco schools.   At the present time examinations are made by the
school inspector.

In August, 1910, the San Francisco Free Dental Infirmary was
organized by the San Francisco District Dental Society and conducted
until September, 1912.   The infirmary was open five half days a week
by the volunteer services of the members of the Dental Society.

In February, 1913, the infirmary was reopened by the Associated
Charities with one paid operator serving half a day.

In 1910 the Alameda County District Dental Society established
infirmaries in Oakland and Berkeley through personal subscriptions of
the members and donations from two people of wealth.   For three years
the members contributed their services three afternoons a week in Oakland and two in Berkeley.   Each infirmary had a graduate woman
dentist in attendance when it was open.   This continued until 1913
when the Alameda County Society felt that it was time for the public
to assume the responsibility of the infirmaries.   The Society had perfectly demonstrated the necessity for, and the success of, these institutions for children.

The Oakland Infirmary is still temporarily closed but the Berkeley
School Department has taken over the equipment and employs a woman
dentist who acts as visiting nurse in the mornings and operator in the
afternoons.

In 1911 the Sacramento County Dental Society examined the mouths
of 500 school children and brought the results before the Board of Education with the result that they now have an infirmary as part of the
school department where only school children are admitted.

Two rooms in the building occupied by the Health Department,
are fully equipped.   A dentist and an assistant serve full time.   Children
are sent from the schools by a school nurse.

In the limited time at my command I got very meager reports from
the State of Oregon.

In 1910, 18,000 children were examined in the schools of Portland
and within a month the School Board appropriated $1,000 and the
dentists volunteered their services for a free infirmary, open on Saturdays
only.   In 1911 the City Council bought the equipment and continued
to operate the infirmary under the Board of Health.

I received more complete reports from the State of Washington.
In Seattle since 1911 a dental infirmary for poor school children has
been maintained by the City Council.   It has three operators working

Saturday afternoons. In the two years 555 patients have been cared for.

In Spokane for two years the local dentists cared for the orphans, the city furnishing equipment and supplies. Since January a dentist has been paid out of city funds for two half days a week to continue this work and the work for the poor school children.

In Tacoma in 1911-12 The Pierce County Dental Society examined the mouths of all the school children and the Board of Education paid for blanks and clerical work.

From the report of the Society signed by Dr. B. E. Lemley, the following is quoted to which I shall refer later. He says, "I, personally, examined the Grant School and the worst mouth I discovered belonged to a boy about twelve years of age. * * * About two weeks ago the boy came into my office * * * suffering from a toothache in one of his first molars and asked to have it extracted. I relieved the pain and told him to consult his parents with the view of having his mouth put in good condition.

"The expense would have been for the cheapest operation about twenty-five dollars. The family are not poor but have no surplus income. They live comfortably and dress well enough to go to church and in other commonly good society. Primarily, here lack of money is the chief cause of the neglect, but a contributing cause is the lack of a realization of what such a condition brings forth, or in other words, pure ignorance. There must be thousands of such cases in the schools of our coast cities. How are we going to reach them? They are above the free clinic and below the average dentist, or think they are."

Dr. Marshall, Dental Surgeon (retired) of the United States Army, tells us that when the requirement was raised from two serviceable opposing molars in each jaw—one above and one below—to two above and two below the number of eligible recruits was so reduced that the War Department was obliged to return to the original requirement.

Mouth Hygiene, to be effective in its results, *must be begun as the child enters school* and not left until the first permanent molar is breaking down.

Under modern conditions of bottle-fed babies, impure foods, and crowded city life, a large number of children begin to need dental work in the second and third year and often some of the teeth are lost by the fourth year.

For several years I have limited my work to the care of children's teeth and it has been impressed upon me, more and more, that the earlier the work is done, the more valuable it is to the child, and the less need there is for future work.

In the last four years, in my private practice, I have worked for more than five hundred children at six and younger. They have averaged at least one abscessed tooth. Just before leaving I filled the ninth pulpless tooth for a little girl on her fourth birthday.

No one who is not familiar with such cases can imagine the great strain upon the system due to the septicemia that quickly follows the death of one or more pulps in a child's mouth. I leave you to picture the condition of such a child when it reaches the age to enter the kindergarten—if it lives so long—sickly—anemic—stupid.

Every child compelled by the law to attend school has the *right* to be protected from the spread of disease through the germ-laden breaths from the filthy mouths of such children.

In working for very young children I have found that if the teeth are polished once a month and given reasonable care at home *no cavities* will form.

In studying over the most economical way in which to care for the teeth of school children I believe that the following will bring the best results because the work is begun before or about the time of the eruption of the first permanent molar which under present conditions is more often lost than any other tooth in the mouth and its loss is irreparable to the whole system of the child.

Have the teeth of all children filled before they enter the kindergarten.

Have a daily morning cleaning of the teeth as part of the exercises in the kindergarten.

The Alpha Upsilon Pi Dental Sorority has a song ready to use for such a drill which they hope to start in one of the Los Angeles kindergartens this fall. They will furnish brushes and means for sterilizing them.

Have the children marked upon their oral hygiene just as upon reading or spelling.

Give all the children in the kindergarten and first grade monthly prophylaxis. This last sounds formidable but it could easily be managed at a small expense by having an auto van fitted up as a dental office to carry five dental chairs and an office desk. The force would consist of one dentist with five dental nurses and an assistant to sterilize instruments. The van could be moved from school to school; the work in each school requiring part of a day only.

The electricity for the dental engines and sterilizer could be furnished by the engine of the van. Water could be connected at any hydrant and the waste pipe could be connected with the sewer.

The dentist in charge would oversee the work, mark the school cards, send any unusual cases to the stationary dental infirmary, and lecture at Mothers' Meetings.

The result of such work would be magical. Epidemics of colds, measles, whooping cough, etc., would be almost unknown and the amount of school work each room could accomplish would be greatly increased. This would be one of the best ways to fight tuberculosis.

The final argument in favor of such a method is that it would help the great class who fall between the two stools—the free infirmary and the paid dentist. As Dr. Lemley, of Tacoma, said, "There are thousands of such families," and the school should teach them the most valuable lesson in life—keeping the gate-way to the body clean—by repeated lessons just as it teaches them to read.

THE EDUCATIONAL AND ECONOMIC VALUE OF SCHOOL DENTAL INSPECTION

BY

SIDNEY J. RAUH

The oral hygiene movement is arbitrarily divided into three main branches—Education, Dental Inspection, Free Clinic.

Each interlocks so closely with the other that it is difficult to draw dividing lines. No one is complete without the other.

For some years propaganda work has been more or less successfully attempted in various sections. This naturally would begin by attempting to impress the community with the necessity and importance of the movement and should be started firstly—through inspection in the public schools, this in turn leading up to the establishment of free clinics. Casual effort is but of small importance so that when this propaganda is instituted it must be with the knowledge and intention of continuing for some years at least before the community could be expected to be affected. Whether the center be a large or small one is immaterial as the method would be virtually the same, the proportion of dentists in each community being more or less uniform. Organization in this as· in all other philanthropic or hygienic endeavor is most vital and coöperation with any through existing forces essential. A great deal of duplication of work almost necessarily follows the attempted establishment of new movements; therefore, the novice in this work should consult with the aforementioned institutions.

Various leaders have advocated each of the three primary divisions to the exclusion of the others, namely: one class favors lectures, demonstrations, exhibits, etc., claiming that if the public interest is aroused they would necessarily follow the instructions, thus receiving treatment. Those advocating inspection claim that through the notices received in homes and the incident educational value of this method the recipients would seek treatment which they would find. And, finally, the advocates of the Free Clinic say that the children receiving treatment in these institutions carry their instruction into the homes. However, after observing a trial of each one of the methods it appears that only through the co-ordination of all can success be obtained. Stress is laid upon this statement through fear that it might be understood that this paper advocates only the branch mentioned in its title.

It has been abundantly proven that about ninety per cent. of the people of the United States require more or less dental service in order to produce a hygienic mouth condition. It is obviously impossible to reach this large number; the logical step, therefore, is to begin with the child. To some extent he will carry the influence into the home, thus affecting the adult and, in due course of time, a better effect can be obtained by devoting the effort to the child rather than to the entire community—of course taking advantage always of any opportunity to reach the adult.

What would be an ideal dental inspection? Volunteer effort at best is not equal to professional work but in view of the fact that only periodical inspections are required better results could be obtained in dental inspection than free clinic work; therefore, organize dentists of the community into one body, whether there be two or more or a thousand. Select strong committees, turn the work over to them and they shall direct all effort. Permission must first be received to enter the schools. This might have been difficult several years back, but now statistics and material may be obtained from other centers with which to sufficiently impress the authorities so that at least an entering wedge can be made.

Forms. Considerable controversy as to forms can always be discovered. We advocate the simplest methods. An effort has been made for years to discover a form which could be duplicated and sent to the parents but as yet no better method than the one herein advocated has been devised.

July 1912-40 M.   Clinic

FORM No. 1

SCHOOL.................

.................191

Grade.................................Room Number......................

Name...Age................

Address...

RIGHT	8	7	6	5	4	3	2	1	1	2	3	4	5	6	7	8	LEFT
	8	7	6	5	4	3	2	1	1	2	3	4	5	6	7	8	

Does Child use Brush?   Yes................No..............
Condition of Mouth?   Good........Fair.........Bad......
Condition of Gums?   Good........Fair........Bad.......
Condition of Temporary Teeth?   Good........Fair........Bad.......
Family Dentist?   Yes................No..............
Teeth Filled?   Yes................No..............
Mal-Occlusion?   Yes................No..............
Remarks...
....
....
Disposal of Case...
....
        Examined by Dr...

Almost all communities have advocated the form with the tooth diagram but the lay mind does not seem to grasp it; and as we advocate strongly the employment of a volunteer force of women to assist the dentists in the examination, we have found the use of numbers more easily comprehended.

Several weeks before the holding of the inspection either a paid worker or a member of the committee should visit the school at which time he meets the principal or teachers and explains the methods to be employed. The blanks at this time are left at the school with instructions to have name, address, age, school room, etc., filled in and given to each child who, on the day of the inspection, presents it to the examiner. This will economize time.

A room should be selected with good light, preferably without school desks so as to allow easy ingress and egress. If possible running water should be at hand. At this visit all instructions should be given so that a second visit may not be necessary before inspection day. On the day of inspection all those concerned should be in their places enough time prior to the opening of school to have everything in first-class order before the children enter the room.

Each dentist should come prepared with a washable coat, a number of mouth mirrors and the various other instruments necessary for a thorough examination. An ordinary table with a chair at each end, easily obtainable in any school, is all that is required from that place. Basins for sterilizing solutions, three for each operator, are required. The first contains a one per cent. solution of carbolic acid, lysol, or some similar preparation in which the instruments are immersed for a length of time. The next, sterilized water, the instruments being immersed in this when taken from the first solution prior to being placed in the mouth. The third basin contains a one to one thousand (1-1000) solution of bi-chloride of mercury, the operator's hands being immersed in this prior to the examination of each child. An operator is stationed at each chair facing the window. An assistant facing him sits at the table, she to record all of his work as he calls off the defects. The third assistant has charge of the instruments for both operators with instructions that no instrument shall be placed in the child's mouth until it has been thoroughly sterilized, also to call the operator's attention if at any time he should neglect to immerse his hands in the bi-chloride solution between patients. If possible, boiling the instruments would be preferable. On the day of inspection, after the operators and assistants are properly placed, a group of children is allowed to enter the room. After being properly seated the inspection begins. The child hands his slip to the assistant and she records the defects and answers to the questions.

While the inspection is being carried on each operator is supposed to instruct the child in the care of his mouth and to add a word as to the necessity for treatment.

Some member of the committee' should address the teachers of the school on this day instructing them how to teach the children to take proper care of their mouths and the meaning of the inspection. The children also should be addressed, various methods being employed according to the age of the individuals, stereopticon being used if practicable.

After the inspection the blanks are taken in charge by the head volunteer who sees that the second form is filled out, which is a notice to the parents calling attention to the number of teeth that are defective whether the mouth requires special cleansing and as 'to the condition of the deciduous or temporary teeth. These forms are then either mailed to the parents of the child, or taken to the school and given to the children with instructions to carry them home.
July 1912. 40M

FORM No. II

..............................School

Room No...........

To the Parents of

Name...

Address......................................

.......................teeth *were found to need attention at the recent examination held at this school. We advise you to consult a dentist at once.*

Teeth require cleaning. Yes......No.......

Temporary teeth require attention. Yes........No........

A sound body and a sound mind are usual companions. Schools are therefore concerned with both. Neglect in the care of the teeth is the cause of so much ill health that school authorities are seeking coöperation with competent dentists. This will bring to the majority of parents first knowledge of the fact that their children's teeth need the attention of a dentist. It is our belief that all parents will be interested in having their regular dentist look after the defects pointed out by this report.

J. H. LANDIS, M.D.
Health Officer.

CARE AND USE OF THE TEETH

The chief use of the teeth is to grind and mix the food with saliva. Food which is not thoroughly chewed may cause indigestion and constipation.

They should last to the end of life.

They are lost by decay and loosening.

Bits of food sticking to and between the teeth; also poor health cause teeth to decay.

Deposits caused by uncleanliness cause teeth to become loose.

Scrubbing the teeth and gums thoroughly with a tooth brush, tooth powder and water, and by keeping up the general health, prevent decay and diseased gums.

Brush your teeth on rising and at bed-time, better after each meal, and be sure to brush the gums.

Twice a year, at least, a dentist should carefully examine the teeth.

A bad condition of the throat, the nose, and the ears is made worse by decayed teeth and diseased gums. Well-cared-for teeth and a clean mouth help prevent diseases that are due to germs.

Remember that cleanliness is the best guard against disease.

A follow-up system is essential to the success of an inspection. This must be done through the school nurse, principal, teacher, or any force at command. Even in the poorest districts a majority of children will avail themselves of private attention though free clinics are in existence. The following figures will be of interest to show results obtained through systematic follow-up in two schools in Cincinnati, Ohio.

1st Intermediate: Number examined, 664; applying to free clinic, 124; applying to private practitioner for treatment, 290; those having no defects, 74; withdrawn from school, 55; leaving 120 who require further treatment; in other words, 75% of the school were reached in this short time.

Highland School: Number examined, 326; private practitioner, 116; free clinic, 88; no defect, 22; 114 no treatment; percentage reached, nearly 70%. The children are still applying for service.

First Intermediate School Report on Dental Inspection

"Follow-up Method"

BY

Emma Meinhardt

January 21, 1913—Inspection took place.

February 10, 1913—Notice sent to parents to show the number of teeth that needed attention.

These notices were all distributed by me in the regular "Hygiene" lesson. The importance was impressed upon the pupils. They were told that a report would be taken the last week in February to see how many had consulted the dentist. "The Dental Clinic" was mentioned to each class with instructions to take advantage of it if needy. All who applied were found worthy.

"*Dental Clinic.*" Method used to keep account of appointments.

Each applicant received a "Recommendation Card" from me; after it had been properly filled out with signature of the parent, the child returned it to me; these were kept and when the Dental Clinic was ready for them I signed them and sent them to the clinic. This first visit was always made after school hours.

The child returned the "Appointment Card" to me, a copy was made and kept by means of a "Card Index." This card excused the child during school hours if the appointment was made for that time. The regular teacher had nothing to do with the sending. Very few appointments were broken; once every week I had the Dental Clinic report to me by "telephone" any such cases, and if the excuse was satisfactory to me I made a new appointment for the child.

Method Used to Follow Up the Work. The original inspection blank was returned to me by the Dental Clinic and used to keep the record.

February 24th. Each child was asked to make a written statement as viz.:

Date—Attention now—Dr..................................(Name of Dentist)
     "   soon ....
    Dental Clinic...
    No Defects...

These written statements were collected by me in the class room and the statement given copied by me on the reverse side of the original inspection blank.

March 17. This same kind of record was taken.

April 15. The original blank was given to each child in the class and the following statements written:

Date—Family Dentist. Dr...finished
  "   "   ....now
    Dental Clinic...finished
  "   "   ....now
    Nothing—Why?..

The reason for "nothing" would make very interesting reading. The "Nothing" blanks will be given out May 19, and I hope the nothing will mean zero.

Envelopes designated *Soon Now Dental Clinic O. K., etc.,* were used to simplify the work. After each record taken I read the report given by the child and on the "face" of the blank marked O. K. This made the number to be handled less each time.

Remarks. Several of the older boys attempted to use the "appointment" at the clinic as an excuse for absence (truancy). These were denied the privilege of the clinic at once. This was done to maintain discipline. No further attempts were made. The general feeling was one of entire satisfaction.

FORM No. III

SCHOOL....................

...............................1913

Grade..............................Room Number..........................

Name...Age.....................

Address...

RIGHT	8	7	6	5	4	3	2	1	1	2	3	4	5	6	7	8	LEFT
	8	7	6	5	4	3	2	1	1	2	3	4	5	6	7	8	

Does Child use Brush?   Yes.............. No...............

Condition of Mouth?   Good.........Fair.........Bad.......

Condition of Gums?   Good.........Fair.........Bad.......

Condition of Temporary Teeth?   Good.........Fair.........Bad.......

Family Dentist?   Yes............... No............

Teeth Filled?   Yes............... No............

Mal-Occlusion?   Yes............... No............

Remarks...

....

....

Disposal of Case...

....

Examined by Dr...

INSTRUCTIONS FOR EXAMINERS AT PUBLIC SCHOOL INSPECTION FOR ORAL HYGIENE.

Operators should be present promptly at the appointed hour.

Operators should either be at the appointed school on the appointed day or should send a substitute.

Equipment

A clean, washable office coat.

At least three or four mirrors.

Three or four exploring instruments.

Sterilization

Before beginning the examination hands should be thoroughly scrubbed with soap and water.

(Means are provided at the place of examination; means are also provided for sterilizing both hands and instruments.)

Hands should then be sterilized by immersing in sterilizing fluid, this process to be repeated after each examination.

After each examination instruments must be placed in sterilizing fluid. This sterilizing of hands and instruments each time is very essential.

Records

Blanks are provided for recording conditions.

A secretary is provided who records conditions reported to her by the examiners.

Report to the secretary the number of each tooth found decayed.

Report, also, the number of each tooth found missing.

Examinations

The handling of children should be gentle, since many are timid and easily frightened.

Avoid giving the slightest pain by quick or rough movements of the instruments or by inserting them into cavities or gums.

On no account should a tooth nor any part of a tooth be removed during the inspection, nor should any such suggestion be made to the children.

Do not comment on quality of work found in any child's mouth.

Make and report carefully to the secretary all examinations, since the statistics in these cases are valuable.

Deformities

Report any pronounced mal-occlusions.

Report Hutchinsonian teeth.

Unusual defects of any kind should be noted on the record blank, as shown opposite under the head of "Remarks."

Remember it is accuracy of examinations and not the number which is desired.

Where systematic inspection is to be maintained, one or more regular days per week should be selected. Each volunteer in this way reserves the same time. It has frequently been asked why a second inspection? All educators will recognize that it requires more than one impression to reach all the individuals and as the inspections are repeated they become more important in both the minds of the child and of the parents. After the first inspection it would be advisable to accept a written statement of a dentist that the mouth is in hygienic condition, thus excusing the child from public dental inspection, facilitating the work and at the same time being an incentive for the child to keep his mouth in proper shape.

The following tables show the results of Dental Inspection in Cincinnati, for the past four years:

DENTAL INSPECTION—CINCINNATI SCHOOLS

SCHOOL 1909	No. Exam.	Cavity 1st Mlr.	Other Defects	Total Defects	No Defects	Use Brush		Teeth Filled		Mal-Occlus.	Per. Missing
						Yes	No	Yes	No		
6th Dist..........	920	2036	670	2036	85	414	590	....	....	77	113
1910 5th Dist..........	356	615	434	1049	64	109	232	34	315	63	7
15th Dist..........	690	1282	780	2062	116	323	355	48	604	152	34
27th Dist..........	583	1349	357	1706	90	343	230	24	550	134	....
1st Int..........	905	1866	2054	3920	71	476	419	167	688	214	58
Avondale..........	263	386	282	668	62	124	72	36	142	45	21
Guilford..........	402	780	294	1074	86	143	258	55	338	50	64
Morgan..........	646	1473	450	1923	131	231	413	46	598	157	9
Sherman..........	749	1119	278	1397	172	357	388	58	687	160	14
	4594	8870	4929	13799	792	2106	2367	468	3922	975	207

DENTAL INSPECTION—CINCINNATI SCHOOLS
1911

SCHOOL	Dly. Att'd.	No. Exam.	Cavity 1st Mlr.	Other Defects	Total Defects	No Defects	Use Brush		Teeth Filled		Mal-Occlus.	Per. Missing
							Yes	No	Yes	No		
1st Dist.	773	590	1199	426	1725	102	232	326	50	547	84	119
10th Dist.	835	630	1151	479	1630	146	313	317	82	550	111	...
11th Dist.	1287	974	2113	750	2863	181	294	655	69	698	79	88
12th Dist.	865	574	1141	280	1521	252	266	400	16	513	69	28
14th Dist.	726	565	1035	212	1247	75	188	325	29	410	60	26
20th Dist.	790	604	1334	273	1607	208	253	449	29	520	93	15
23rd Dist.	750	677	1731	1044	2775	164	481	352	227	561	85	35
28th Dist.	678	502	1254	268	1522	130	319	269	21	435	70	39
3rd Int.	410	267	423	420	843	46	184	84	86	180	51	...
4th Int.	...	547	1055	1115	2170	43	298	236	117	422	167	...
6th Dist.	925	862	1271	246	1517	137	288	502	47	738	77	50
Blind.	...	15	23	10	33	3	7	8	2	13	1	...
Boy Special.	...	60	123	83	206	7	16	45	3	58	5	8
Cent. Fmt.	420	371	572	198	770	36	221	150	37	334	57	157

DENTAL INSPECTION—CINCINNATI SCHOOLS—*Continued*
1911

SCHOOL	Dly. Att'd.	No. Exam.	Cavity 1st Mlr.	Other Defects	Total Defects	No Defects	Use Brush		Teeth Filled		Mal-Occlus.	Per. Missing
							Yes	No	Yes	No		
Fulton........	...	241	689	239	928	35	71	201	18	236	59	2
Guilford......	450	434	733	390	1123	125	126	308	68	364	84	...
Highland......	375	340	601	254	855	37	99	241	40	300	82	37
Jackson.......	891	650	1275	523	1798	155	13	419	13	419	119	...
Lincoln.......	650	594	805	258	1063	79	269	325	63	531	60	31
Linwood.......	330	312	512	163	675	81	168	144	46	266	56	9
McKinley......	450	411	607	271	878	82	185	221	39	372	52	3
N. Fmt.......	400	353	453	219	672	52	260	89	25	314	60	356
Oral.........	...	36	67	24	91	9	16	17	4	29	9	...
Oyler........	625	521	1104	499	1603	84	212	293	47	394	116	59
Special No. 3..	...	59	113	69	592	10	14	45	7	46	4	19
Vine St.......	...	360	774	224	998	33	210	151	27	336	49	...
Webster.......	...	560	1284	301	1585	99	322	230	35	509	61	...
Totals........	12630	12109	23442	9238	33290	2411	5325	6836	1247	10122	1820	1081

DENTAL INSPECTION—CINCINNATI SCHOOLS
1912

SCHOOL	Dly. Att'd.	No. Exam.	Cavity 1st Mlr.	Other Defects	Total Defects	No Defects	Use Brush		Teeth Filled		Mal-Occlus.	Per. Missing
							Yes	No	Yes	No		
5th Dist..........	360	265	404	221	625	54	68	197	37	228	46	55
16th Dist..........	800	655	990	327	1317	115	473	182	217	442	138	52
22nd Dist..........	550	498	915	584	1499	77	322	176	165	333	44	39
25th Dist..........	507	447	937	396	1333	42	217	231	35	408	144	72
30th Dist..........	790	727	1470	792	2262	67	466	238	151	378	113	...
3rd Int..........	425	328	578	610	1188	25	201	181	132	250	79	156
Chase..........	633	528	772	216	988	119	444	84	94	434	79	29
Columbian..........	600	525	930	377	1307	76	448	104	114	438	126	98
Evanston..........	500	426	804	657	1461	57	328	102	108	317	54	61
Garfield..........	650	561	1014	383	1397	50	223	338	34	527	72	87
Harrison..........	350	312	590	25	815	54	132	180	28	284	45	48
H. Mann..........	260	231	322	116	438	36	164	67	57	175	24	15

DENTAL INSPECTION—CINCINNATI SCHOOLS—*Continued*

1912

School	Dly. Att'd.	No. Exam.	Cavity 1st Mlr.	Other Defects	Total Defects	No Defects	Use Brush		Teeth Filled		Mal-Occlus.	Per. Missing
							Yes	No	Yes	No		
Hoffman	604	504	857	527	1384	79	412	92	220	284	117	73
Kirby Rd	670	615	1123	825	1948	87	429	186	190	424	93	68
Morgan-Mt.Adams	700	551	1006	396	1402	65	202	349	80	471	71	41
Riverside	400	338	742	498	1240	38	171	167	23	315	34	50
Sherman	900	747	1403	262	1665	95	321	426	70	677	76	56
St. Xaviers	950	805	1468	924	2410	127	345	455	131	674	118	184
St. Frances	750	657	1270	448	1718	66	276	381	63	594	69	99
St. Augne	650	611	1237	385	1622	44	351	260	45	566	113	116
St. Patrick	170	118	215	55	270	14	40	78	6	112	2	15
Washington	976	829	1139	929	2668	44	396	403	81	495	186	…
1 Ⓐ	580	430	573	214	787	101	300	130	99	331	61	25
Totals	13775	11735	20777	10167	31744	1532	6729	5007	2180	9157	1886	1439

DENTAL INSPECTION—CINCINNATI SCHOOLS

1913

School	Dly. Att'd.	No. Exam.	Cavity 1st Mlr.	Other Defects	Total Defects	No Defects	Use Brush		Teeth Filled		Mal-Occlus.	Per. Missing
							Yes	No	Yes	No		
1st Dist..........	875	825	1502	476	1978	124	470	345	91	744	105	121
11th Dist.........	1200	1125	2174	635	2809	92	465	677	120	1023	45	167
12th Dist.........	625	564	1115	252	1367	86	283	281	39	525	50	29
27th Dist.........	680	565	1189	375	1564	31	278	287	45	521	128	91
1st Int...........	919	667	889	1035	1924	73	409	256	203	464	121	223
Retarded 1st Int....	...	171	292	293	585	14	66	104	15	156	29	55
Boy Special........	75	66	139	81	220	5	9	57	9	57	11	9
Highland..........	375	326	743	354	1097	22	172	154	51	275	28	31
Jacksen...........	695	599	937	313	1250	73	234	366	47	552	90	79
Oral..............	40	31	63	27	90	4	17	14	3	28	4	4
Sands.............	850	764	1396	666	2062	81	438	326	107	657	56	186

DENTAL INSPECTION—CINCINNATI SCHOOLS—*Continued*
1913

SCHOOL.	Dly. Att'd	No. Exam.	Cavity 1st Mlr.	Other Defects	Total Defects	No Defects	Use Brush		Teeth Filled		Mal- Occlus.	Per Missing
							Yes	No	Yes	No		
St. Paul.........	75	62	104	26	130	6	27	35	8	54	2	10
St. Paul.........	650	624	1278	367	1645	83	229	396	53	570	69	...
St. John.........	650	574	1078	348	1426	18	89	485	66	508	85	164
Vine St.........	500	379	834	261	1095	30	162	212	51	319	50	20
Westwood.........	690	566	979	685	1664	98	368	204	119	453	80	81
Webster.........	800	709	1390	393	1783	34	310	293	64	645	129	108
Woodward.........	1100	1041	1060	1678	2738	315	753	288	762	279	89	568
Warsaw.........	350	267	564	276	840	20	114	153	53	214	55	43
Whittier.........	600	502	798	277	1075	74	314	188	124	378	34	72
Totals.........	11749	10454	18514	8818	27342	1283	5207	5121	2030	8422	1260	2061

If the figures of dental inspection are to be of scientific value, they must be carefully compiled and care rather than speed must be insisted upon. Only persistent effort will have an educational value and those sections, which believe an impression can be made through casual inspection are doomed, to disappointment. The work must be started with the intention of persisting, for there are few communities that are financially capable to-day of taking over complete oral hygiene movements. Cincinnati, with a school population of about 55,000 children, would require an annual expenditure of at least $25,000 to do the work without volunteer effort. In view of the fact that the health budget is a trifle over $105,000 it is manifestly impossible to expect so large a sum; but we do believe that each year the sum will be increased for this purpose until the work will be efficiently done through the municipality. The educational value of persistent effort can be no better demonstrated than through the study of the so-called Experimental Class which has been maintained in one of the schools through two entire school terms. The class average in the Experimental Class was somewhat over 85%, while in the Control Class the average was 69%. These children were constantly under supervision and it will be interesting to note what permanent value the instruction will have upon them.

In the exhibit held, in connection with this meeting, all branches of the Cincinnati effort are shown. For this reason we will not go into detail as to the various activities.

In conclusion we advocate: First the regular persistent examination of all children of school age at least once per year.

Second: A follow-up system which will impress both the parents and the child as to the necessity for the work.

Third: Regular instruction, either by the teacher or dental lecturer, as to the care of the mouth.

Fourth: Thorough coöperation with every existing force that works for the general betterment of the hygienic conditions in the school or for the betterment of the physical being of the child.

SESSION THIRTY B

SYMPOSIUM ON MOUTH HYGIENE

Arranged by the National Mouth Hygiene Association

W. G. EBERSOLE, M.D., D.D.S., Cleveland, Ohio, *Secretary*

W. G. EBERSOLE, M.D., D.D.S., *Chairman*

DR. D. H. SQUIRE, Dean of the Dental Department, University of Buffalo, *Vice-Chairman*

Program of Session Thirty B

THADDEUS P. HYATT, D.D.S., Dental Consultant and Lecturer N. Y. State Department of Health, and Lecturer N. Y. City Department of Education. "Mouth Hygiene; Its Relation to the School Child Mentally and Physically." (Manuscript not supplied.)

MISS CORDELIA L. O'NEILL, Principal of Marion School; Member of Board of Governors of the National Mouth Hygiene Association, and President of the Cleveland Auxiliary of the National Mouth Hygiene Association. "Mouth Hygiene, What It Has Done For Us, and What It Can Do For You." (Illustrated in part by members of the Marion School "Experiment Class.")

MISS LILIAN T. MURNEY, Principal of Murray Hill School, Cleveland, Ohio. "What Mouth Hygiene Did For One Little Girl: A Remarkable Case."

ALFRED C. FONES, D.D.S., Chairman of the Oral Hygiene Committee of the National Dental Association. "A Plan That Solves the Fundamental Problem in School Hygiene."

EDWIN N. KENT, D.D.S., President, Dental Hygiene Council of Massachusetts. "Illustrated Lectures on Oral Hygiene: A Plan for Extension of the Field."

MOUTH HYGIENE

What It Has Done For Us—What It Can Do For You

BY

CORDELIA L. O'NEILL

Recently a prominent physician in an address at the Royal Dental Hospital of London said:

"Oral hygiene—the hygiene of the mouth—there is not a single thing in the whole range of hygiene more important to the public than that."

He does not stand alone in his contention. But unfortunately the static approval rather than the dynamic refutation of this idea has nullified the results obtainable. School, as we understand it, is the training camp for life. School hygiene, intelligently practiced, will produce healthy and efficient life. Hence the wisdom of utilizing every phase of hygiene during this important period.

My message to you this evening is to present a report of an experiment made to test the value or relation of oral hygiene to mental ability and growth. The narrative must of necessity have a decided local coloring.

As you no doubt have observed the educational world is more conservative in making innovations to fit the exigence of the times than any other working force. Before the first city in the United States adopted school medical inspection pioneer work had to be done by the few to demonstrate to the public its value. The same experience came to the second city and so on down the ranks. Cleveland was no exception. Conclusive proof in one community seemed to carry no weight in the neighboring communities.

In 1905, because of the personnel of our Board of Health, the opportunity presented itself of doing some work in medical inspection in our own school building. Since we had always greatly respected the thought of "A healthy mind in a healthy body," and also had executive authority we seized the opportunity and had the work established. A few other buildings in the city did likewise. At the end of four years the physical moral and mental improvement due to the eradication of disease and the prophylactic effect of cleanliness was most marked. We were all proud of the results.

In June of that year, 1909, the Cleveland Dental Society secured the permission of the Board of Education to make an examination of the pupils in four buildings of the city: Doan School, in one of the beautiful resident sections of the East End; Lawn School, in a middle class, well-to-do section in the extreme West End; Murray Hill School, in an Italian settlement, and Marion School, in a down-town congested, cosmopolitan and ghetto section.

The results of the examination in the four schools representing different types of children showed that 97% of the mouths were in faulty condition. Among the 846 children examined in Marion School only three were found whose mouths were in perfect condition. Many had teeth covered with green stain; some had two or three abscesses. Disease and neglect was very evident. That revelation was somewhat startling. While it did not shatter our faith in medical inspection it proved rather conclusively that medical inspection is very good. Yet, though, to get the best results mouth hygiene cannot be ignored.

We were, therefore, quite ready to coöperate in experimental work when our assistance was asked by the Chairman of the Oral Hygiene Committee of the National Dental Association.

The proposition made by the dentist was that if the pupils practiced oral hygiene, and if their teeth were put and kept in a clean healthy condition, their mental ability would be increased at least 15%.

We knew that medical inspection for the four preceding years had increased the efficiency of our pupils, but we had no way of knowing how much improvement had been made. We were not disposed to encourage the Oral Hygiene Committee to gather any laurels from our medical inspection work; but we were most willing to lend every effort to discover any means of furthering the interests and improving the opportunities of our pupils.

We believe the educator should coöperate with any and every profession that can give aid to our work. We, as educators, should be the vanguard in the army of reform and improvement, not only to the pupils in the class room but to humanity at large. It is not for us to use tallow candle methods in this age of electric light; or stage-coach theories in the day of the aëroplane. True mental processes are the same as in the time of Plato and Aristotle; but present day environment and requirements demand the greatest conservation of human energy. If the large manufacturing plants feel the necessity of maintaining at great expense experimental and chemical laboratories; if our government supports experimental stations to obtain the maximum result from the soil and farm products, is it not reasonable to believe that education can be much benefitted by laboratory experiment and investigation? Reasoning along those lines you can see a justification for a teacher assuming the responsibilities of an experiment suggested and planned by the committee of the National Dental Association.

We have no interest in the success of dentistry, and the work was undertaken in a critical frame of mind, somewhat skeptical of the claims made, but willing to bear the chagrin of lost time and energy if the experiment was a failure; or receive sharp criticism of results and motives if it were a success.

Therefore we agreed to begin the work that would prove whether oral or mouth hygiene, practiced faithfully, would increase mental power.

We had all the pupils in the building carefully examined by a competent dentist. His assistant recorded on duplicate charts the condition of the mouths and teeth. From the charts of the pupils in the 4th, 5th, 6th and 7th grades we selected the 40 charts showing the worst oral conditions. We selected from those particular grades because pupils below the 4th grade could not sufficiently understand the requirements of the mental tests, nor of themselves carry out the practical care of the mouth. The pupils of the 8th grade would be promoted into high school before we had finished our experiment and we would have too much difficulty in getting the children together for group meetings. Having selected only according to the condition of the mouth and teeth, we found that the group of forty represented a variety of types of children. It was typical of the school. Some were bright, well-meaning; some had strong leanings toward incorrigibility and the others varying between those two extremes. Many were behind grade. Of those who completed the tests 8 were up to grade; 9 one year behind; 5 two years; 3 three years and 2 four years.

The services of a psychological expert were secured, who planned six sets of tests. They were tests in memory, spontaneous association and differentiation, perception and calculation.

A nurse was engaged to have supervision over the children and instruct them in the necessary practices.

The Chairman of the Oral Hygiene Committee of the National Dental Association had made all plans and was present when each and every test was made.

The assistant principal of our building, a special German teacher, and one room teacher assisted at the test meetings. With this corps of workers our first meeting was held May, 1910, at Marion School, Room 15.

The children were told the purposes of the experiment. They were asked to assist us in making it and were informed of what would be expected of them if they decided to coöperate.

1. They were to attend each and every meeting called.

2. They were to brush their teeth three times a day during the entire time of the experiment.

3. They were to masticate thoroughly their food and were not to interfere with its proper insalivation by combining solid food with liquids during mastication.

4. They were to keep the passages of the oral cavity clear by correct inhalation.

Each child was to be given, free of charge, a tooth brush, tooth powder, drinking glass and any dental work necessary to put his teeth in good condition. Because of the very bad condition of the mouths this pro_ fessional work in most cases took considerable time.

Since we were dealing with children it was necessary to make our appeal fit the comprehension of our subjects. Pupils from the fourth to the seventh grade could hardly be expected to appreciate the value of dental prophylaxis and undergo much extra inconvenience to prove its worth to the doubting public. For that reason a reward of a five dollar gold piece was promised to each child at Christmas if he faith. fully did his work. This reward was feared by some to be the main incentive. But, inasmuch as the children were just as faithful and responsive for the remaining seven months after the gold pieces were awarded as they were before, we looked upon the award as somewhat similar to the helpful little tug guiding the ship out of the harbor into the open sea where it is able to direct its own course. The thought of a tangible reward started the children in their practice. When they began to feel the benefit of the work they needed no further incentive.

When the children understood what was required of them, five of the number immediately withdrew. They were unwilling to undertake the work.

The remaining thirty-five took the first psychological tests. These were, as before stated, prepared by a psychological expert. Minute directions were given as to the time allotted to each test; the manner of conducting each, and the credits in marking. Each of the tests were given by me. The psychological expert was present at the first and directed the manner of procedure. Each succeeding test was conducted exactly as the first. The tests were all taken at the same time of day; in the same room; and each child occupying the same seat first assigned him. The chairman of the Oral Hygiene Committee of the National Dental Association timed the exercises with a stop watch always, however, assisted by one other time-keeper. The nurse, with the three, teachers mentioned before, assisted in the distribution and collection of manuscripts and papers. The conditions and atmosphere surrounding the children during each test were as nearly uniform as it was possible to make them. The nurse marked all the papers, following minutely each direction laid down by the psychological expert, thus assuring uniformity of judgment.

Two tests were given before the children began to take care of their teeth; two were given while the teeth were being treated, and two some little time after all work was finished.

After the first psychological tests were given the children were shown by the dentist how to brush their teeth. The nurse followed up the work in their homes and it was some time before several of them had mastered the process.

They were then taught how to properly masticate their food. Puffed wheat and cream was given them; the process of mastication and insalivation explained by the nurse; they all chewed until the wheat was reduced to the proper consistency, then, when permission was given, they swallowed. This was done to give them a correct idea of the proper consistency of food before it should be swallowed.

All the demonstration work was given in the school building. All the dental work, except extractions and some work in orthodontia, was also done in a dental room fitted up in the building. The nurse then visited in the homes at irregular intervals to see that each individual member understood and was properly carrying out directions. Every effort was made to preserve a perfectly normal atmosphere in the class room and in the home of each child. No special attention in any way was attracted to these children in the dental squad. The meetings were held after all other children had been dismissed; notice of meetings were given individually and not by public announcement. In fact, so quite and commonplace had been our work that some teachers as late as December did not know who, if any, of their pupils were in the Dental Class. The above-named precautions were taken to reduce to a minimum any effect that might be produced by undue attention being attracted to the children. Anyone who has dealt with children knows that phenomenal results may be obtained from certain types by singling them out and bestowing on them unusual attentions. We strove to avoid any such condition.

Experiments with human beings are manifestly more difficult to conduct than with any other forms of nature. So many influences enter in to disturb the findings; so difficult is it to control conditions. An effort was made to anticipate every possible interference with a clear, just and candid result. We could see nothing to be gained by forcing conclusions and we stood ready at every stage to censor any movement that would favor the point sought. As we mentioned before, we had absolutely no interest in or desire for proving the correctness of the theory advanced by the dentist.

So much for the preparation and conduct of the work. Now for results.

During the time it was found necessary to drop eight from the class. If the pupils failed to attend meetings, showed evidence of neglecting to brush their teeth, or in any way violated directions, they were dropped. Only uniformly correct work could be considered. Twenty-seven pupils fulfilled every requirement for fourteen months to the complete satisfaction of those conducting the experiment. Their continuity of effort was most commendable.

Demonstrations of the home practice of the children were made during September and October in the school building. Each child showed the way in which he had been brushing his teeth. Results of daily application were very evident. A dinner consisting of meat, vegetables, fruit, bread stuffs, etc., was served. The children ate under close observation and each child showed that he mastered what had been taught him; that he was forming correct habits of mastication and insalivation.

The psychological tests given before, during and after the correction of oral imperfections showed an increase in mental power of 99.8% for a class average. That is, those children, the majority of them repeaters had almost doubled their mental power. Nor was that all. There was a very marked improvement in the health, complexion and conduct of the children. It was a revelation to those who were dealing with them. The self-respect engendered in the pupils by the conscious. ness of clean, healthy mouths was not the least important gain, though it could not be measured by per cents. Making every allowance for natural growth, we believe (as we knew those children), the great improvement mentally, physically and morally was due to the practice of mouth hygiene.

We have met the following criticisms since finishing our work: "The number of pupils was too small to furnish a basis for conclusion."

When the United States Government was making its industrial investigation, conducted by the Department of Commerce and Labor, 10% of any class of people was considered a sufficient number to investigate in order to determine the conditions of the class. We selected a little more than 10% of the class of children on whom we reported.

Then again we were criticized for not making a record of weight, height, respiration, etc., before and after the tests. Since the growth of children during the adolescent period is abnormal, and many of our squad were at that age, we decided to attempt no testing along those lines. We confined our efforts to just the one point—*Growth in Mental Power*. But with growth in mental power came also a remarkable improvement in physical and moral power.

Another objection was made that a "control class" had not been carried at the same time. That is, a class of the same ability taking the psychological tests but not the mouth hygiene work. Such a class would enable us to measure exactly how much gain was due to mouth hygiene alone. While we know that such a class would enable us to gather more detailed information as to the exact amount of gain due to mouth hygiene, we were first concerned to find out if there would really be a gain. We undertook to investigate just one thing: Would there be a gain? Now we are ready to go further and by carrying two classes measure the exact gain. We have tried to clear up in the preceding pages of this paper the other points that were raised.

Dr. William Hunt, physician to the London Fever Hospital, and Lecturer on Pathology to the Charing Cross Hospital, London, in an article on Oral Sepsis, and again in an address before the faculty of the McGill University, Montreal, calls attention to serious results that follow from neglecting to guard against diseased conditions in the mouth. After ten years of special investigation he has concluded that oral sepsis produces diseases of the tonsils, pharynx, stomach, liver and kidneys. He cites several instances where correcting the mouth condition has cured the above-named ailments. He has put himself on record as believing that if all danger of infection from oral sepsis could be eliminated from the system we might easily ignore all danger from the other sources of sepsis in the body since, as he says:

"It (oral sepsis) is more important as a potential disease factor than any other source of sepsis in the body."

In *every* published report that we could secure by school medical inspectors of the cities of the United States, the diseases of the mouth and teeth are found to be more numerous than any other recorded. Dr. Hunt claims that the only reason serious results of disease from septic mouths is not more prevalent is because of the great resisting power possessed by the mucosa of the mouth and gums. Why force the system to resist poison when the source of poison might be eliminated?

Dr. Charles Mayo, of Rochester, Minn., said:

"It is evident that the next step in medical progress in the line of preventive medicine should be made by the dentists. The question is, 'Will they do it?'"

The schools cannot afford to wait to see if they will do it. Medical inspection points out to us that the most universal physical defect is oral disease. The leading physicians and surgeons here and abroad warn us of the serious results of oral sepsis. A sore on the surface of the body discharges its poisons without additional harm to the system. But the decayed tooth and diseased gum send their poison directly into the parts of the human system that will distribute it throughout the entire body. More disastrous results are prevented because nature prepares the anti-toxins in the system to counteract the poison.

In our experiment with the children we found that when we relieved nature of the responsibility of counteracting disease, by cleaning the mouth, she turned her attention to clearing the complexion, invigorating the body, and stimulating the mind, producing thereby a much better quality of boys and girls. That is the aim of the school—the purpose of education. If our twenty-seven children were improved so greatly in one year by practicing mouth hygiene, the same thing can benefit yours. Not a child received medical attention of any kind during the entire time, except one little girl whose adenoids were removed four weeks before the last test—too late to affect the results.

In this day of crowded factories and keen competition our children will be better prepared to assume the duties of citizenship if they have formed the habits of intelligent personal cleanliness and health. To accomplish this, we would repeat what Dr. Osler has said, "That in the whole range of hygiene there is none more important than oral hygiene."

WHAT MOUTH HYGIENE DID FOR ONE LITTLE GIRL—A REMARKABLE CASE

BY

Lilian T. Murney

Following the general dental examination of Cleveland school children in the spring of 1909, Dr. Ebersole, Chairman of the National Committee, appointed Dr. Varney E. Barnes special examiner of the children of the Murray Hill building. This second examination was made in the autumn of 1910.

At that time, Carrie Mangino, a thirteen-year-old girl, was a member of a special class for backward pupils in Murray Hill School.

The examining dentist found that her mouth and gums were in bad condition and that there were evidently two impacted teeth.

On hearing the doctor's report, Carrie's teacher offered to give any assistance in her power. She had felt for a long time that the child was under some strain and she longed to help remove the physical handicap under which the child struggled.

The parents' consent was obtained, and teacher and pupil made the necessary visit to the office of Dr. Barnes, who had generously arranged to have the corrective work done.

An X-ray negative was taken, confirming Dr. Barnes' diagnosis and locating the missing teeth; a couple of fillings were made; and finally two teeth were extracted. This last operation occurred on Saturday morning and the following Monday, the teacher, who had been present, came to tell me all about it and to report that Carrie was not in school that day because of a little soreness in the gums.

I was extremely interested in the case and requested the teacher to send Carrie to me as soon as she returned to school.

The next morning the child walked into my office with a happy smile upon her face and I noticed that the eye-glasses that she had been wearing for months had been left off. Upon closer inspection, I saw that her beautiful brown eyes, that had been badly crossed, were now perfectly straight—straight as any eyes I had ever looked at.

Astonished at the sudden change and wishing to hear the child's unprompted account of it, I remarked that she was not wearing her glasses and asked if there was any difference in the way she saw things. Without the slightest hesitation she answered, "Yes, I used to see everything there," indicating a point to the side, "and now I see them straight in front of me."

Carrie was in the backward class because she could not get along satisfactorily in a regular grade. She was nervous and irritable, she tired quickly, was easily discouraged and made little progress. (About three and one-half grades in seven years.)

After her dental work was done the teacher watched her carefully and noted with great pleasure that improvement in the child's mental and physical condition set in immediately. The expression of her face changed at once—it became placid and her manner showed greater repose.

Within six months the impacted teeth came through. By that time Carrie's progress was such that her teacher recommended that she be promoted to a regular class and allowed to do regular school work. The promotion was made.

Last February, Carrie passed into the sixth grade and because of the financial condition of the home, she was taken from school to go to work, much to her own and her teacher's regret, for Carrie had become a most satisfactory pupil—cheerful, willing, confident and untiring.

I met her on the street the other day and stopped to talk with her. Her big, brown eyes are still perfectly straight and she is as bright and attractive a sixteen-year-old girl as you would be likely to meet.

A PLAN THAT SOLVES THE FUNDAMENTAL PROBLEM IN SCHOOL HYGIENE

BY

ALFRED C. FONES

To analyze the subject of hygiene for the uplift and betterment of the children in our public schools, we must first determine what are the main factors existing at present that act as a detriment to proper development and also as the chief cause of illness in child life.

The large number of papers presented at this Congress, covering so many phases of the subject, merely proves that we must reach a conclusion, first as to where we should concentrate our energy, and then one step at a time eliminate the most conspicuous evils that beset the school children of our country.

If our large steel plants and rolling mills were obliged to reroll from fifteen to twenty-five per cent. of their stock, it would not take them very long to find out what was the matter. No business nowadays could withstand such a high percentage of loss in doing its work over again.

In our public schools throughout the country it is a fair estimate to say that the percentage of children in the first five grades who are reviewing their grade will range between fifteen and twenty-five per cent. In a majority of the cities the average would be nearer the latter figure. What is the matter? Is it our system of teaching, crowded schools, poorly lighted or ill ventilated buildings, or is the chief cause to be found in the material itself—the child?

Let us examine the average boy of ten years of age and see what we find. Face, ears and nose unclean, hair unkempt, hands grimy and dirty finger nails. Shoes splashed with dry or wet mud, clothes soiled, and an odor percolating through the atmosphere to excite suspicion that his little body has not been washed for some time. His eyesight may be good and yet it may be defective. If his face is washed it may disclose a color that is lacking in the bloom that a boy of ten should have and we might say, anaemic.

If otherwise his body appears normal we ask him to open his mouth. If his external appearance troubles us, his internal appearance would shock us. Here we find teeth covered with green stain, temporary and permanent teeth badly decayed, possibly fistulas on the gum surface showing the outlet for pus from an abscessed tooth or teeth and decomposing food around and between the teeth. Why examine this child any further? Here at the gateway of the system is a source of infection and poison that would contaminate every mouthful of food taken into his body. With decomposition instead of digestion taking place in the alimentary tract, it is no wonder that the child suffers from an auto-intoxication which produces eyestrain, anaemia, malaise, constipation, headaches, fevers and many other ailments.

Such a mouth is an ideal feeding ground for germ life and a child with such a mouth is far more susceptible to infectious diseases than those whose teeth are sound and kept free from food debris. Suppose at the entrance to our cities such a rank condition existed. How long would it be before disease and sickness would be swept in among the inhabitants? This boy described is but duplicated in the girl of ten. Decayed teeth constitute the most prevalent disease known. It is difficult to find two children out of one hundred with perfectly sound sets of teeth. In a thorough dental examination of five hundred and fifty school children in the town of Stratford, Connecticut, but one child was found to have a set of teeth free from decay.

Look over the reports of the medical inspectors in the public schools who have made but a glancing examination and you will find that decayed teeth outrank all other physical defects combined.

Therefore we must deduce from our analysis for school hygiene that the most conspicuous defect of the child is the unsanitary condition of its mouth. Like a pigpen or garbage drain slowly seeping its poison into the brook, which flowing into the reservoir contaminates the water supply to a city, so do the products of abscesses and decayed teeth with decomposing food slowly but surely poison the human system. Such mouths breed disease. Such children laugh and sneeze millions of germs made virulent and active in an ideal feeding ground. And then again the teeth as a crushing and masticating machine are frequently ruined by the time the child has reached twelve or fourteen years of age. It is true that they can limp through life with this dreadful handicap, the same as an automobile can climb a steep hill on three cylinders, but you can rest assured that the child with a wrecked mouth at fourteen is traveling on his second speed until he reaches thirty-five and from there he drops into his low gear to finish the journey in a slow and uncertain state. It is true that many have lived to a ripe age with unclean mouths and wrecked teeth, not on account of such conditions but in spite of them.

If it be conceded that the most unhygienic feature of child life is its mouth we then come to the problem: How can we establish clean mouths, sound teeth and the tooth brush habit? To try and fill the teeth of the children in our public schools is a noble charity but an endless chain. Like an immense flood decayed teeth have spread over the civilized world to such an extent that hardly one-tenth of the population of a country such as ours could find a sufficient number of dentists to fill their teeth. I believe it to be a conservative estimate to say that the children found in the first five grades in our public schools would average not less than six good-sized cavities in their teeth. If you will but figure out how many children there are in your city in the first five grades you can roughly estimate the immense amount of work there would be for a corps of dentists to cope with such a task as filling their teeth. This would not mean merely plugging a hole in a piece of ivory, it means the painstaking work of a dental operation on live tissue as well as the tedious and slow work of treating and saving teeth which have dead pulps and possibly abscessed roots.

But let us assume that it is possible to fill these teeth and save them for the time being, how are we to prevent a reoccurrence of decay as well as to check the flood with the children coming into the schools in the primary grades each year? Surely every dentist knows that the tooth brush alone will not stop it and every dentist also knows as well as the parents how difficult it is to induce children to properly brush their teeth and take care of their mouths as they should. Would it not be better to evolve a system for the prevention of dental decay and the establishment of clean mouths than to try to cope with the hopeless task of filling the thousands of decayed teeth? I am heartily in sympathy with the scheme that every city should have a dental clinic for the school children for the relief of pain, and I believe it is inhuman in this twentieth century to allow the poorer class of children to suffer as they do from toothache. But let us draw a line on the conditions as they exist to-day and I would present this plan, partly suggested by Dr. Ottolengui of New York, for your consideration.

It is a clinical fact that fully eighty per cent. of dental decay can be prevented if monthly or even bi-monthly surface polishing of the teeth with orange wood sticks and fine pumice can be systematically followed. These treatments of course to be augmented by the faithful and correct use of the tooth brush, floss silk and lime water as a mouth wash.

Suppose it were possible to start a year from this September and place in our schools trained women who would confine their efforts the first year to the children in the first grade. These women to be trained and educated as hygienists who would be competent to give each child a surface treatment of the teeth once a month. Each woman to have the supervision, to start with, of two hundred children. These children in the first grade to be taught the proper use of the tooth brush, mouths inspected daily for cleanliness and no child permitted to enter the class room who had not brushed his teeth. Hands and face to be clean and hair combed. Bodily cleanliness also insisted upon and efforts made to secure the coöperation of the parents. Several teachers in the primary grades have told me that even on the coldest days in winter it is impos. sible to close the windows for five minutes on account of the odor from the children's bodies. Such a condition of affairs should not be per. mitted and is unnecessary in a country where water is so plentiful. Talks in the class room as well as the use of the stereopticon in the assembly room would greatly aid in securing the desired results. These nurses could also be of great aid to the medical inspectors. At the end of the year they would follow the children into the second grade and a new corps of nurses would enter the first grade with the new pupils. This to be repeated for five years until the first corps of women were caring for their class in the fifth grade. It is doubtful if it would be necessary to carry this work beyond the fifth grade as the child would be cared for through the most susceptible period for dental decay.

Now what would such a system mean to the children? It would mean that from the first day the child entered school it would be taught cleanliness. That when the first permanent tooth entered the mouth it would be under the supervision of the nurse who would teach the child how to keep it clean and who would also aid with the monthly polishing. It would mean that during the first five years of school life habits of cleanliness would be established that would mould the boys and girls into new types of men and women. Fully three-quarters of the diseases incident to child life would be eliminated. With an additional knowledge of food values and how to properly masticate their food instead of bolting it, the main factors for hygiene would be covered.

Booker Washington once said, "If I can teach a colored man the gospel of the tooth brush I fell that I can make a man of him." Those of you who see but little of children can hardly realize what an uplift and different point of view there comes with a clean mouth and polished teeth. It is interesting to see a child whose teeth have been polished and a washbowl instruction given in the use of the tooth brush, gradually change in general appearance regarding cleanliness. I have known them in a few weeks to choose a new set of companions because the old friends no longer looked attractive to them. No one ever saw a rowdy with a clean mouth, for cleanliness breeds refinement. The proper food supply to the body and cleanliness are the two main foundation pillars for health and these must be taught and practiced before we can hope to obtain satisfying results in the betterment of child life.

There is much in life worth while besides teeth but I know of no one factor that is more conducive to health than sound teeth and a clean mouth.

The question may be asked: How are we going to educate these women to be hygienists and dental nurses? In every large city there are men in both the medical and dental professions who are competent

in the prophylactic treatment of the teeth would of course be
by the dentists. Both of these professions are anxious to aid in
cause so worthy and I believe they would willingly give their tim
knowledge to start such a movement.

It is impossible in this paper to give the details concerning the e
tion of these women and their full duties in the schools, but enoug
been stated to permit those in charge of our public school syste
consider the proposition in a general way and determine if this
is a solution of the main problem regarding school hygiene.

ILLUSTRATED LECTURES ON ORAL HYGIENE—A PLAN FOR EXTENSION OF THE FIELD

BY

Edwin N. Kent

Educational work in the line of oral hygiene is accomplished prin_cipally in three ways, or by the use of three mediums, viz, the public lecture, the public exhibit and the press, and whatever special importance may be attached to either of these methods of preaching the gospel of mouth cleanliness it cannot be questioned that each has its place and in that place is indispensable.

Our organization in Massachusetts has, during the past six years, been active in all three departments of the field.

We are a little proud of the fact that we were responsible for the first exhibit, devoted exclusively to Oral Hygiene, which was placed before the public, and this element in our educational work has perhaps received more of our attention than any other since its introduction.

It is loaned freely wherever there is a demand for it and we are firmly convinced of its educational value.

We also fully appreciate the "power of the press" and the presentation of our subject in the public prints has had its share of attention.

Almost all classes of periodicals open their pages freely to matter of an educational nature coming from an authoritative source, and when we consider the enormous field covered by some publications (one chain of papers in this country claiming six million daily readers) we cannot ignore the importance of the printed article.

No one can long be interested in oral hygiene educational work, however, without finding himself, sooner or later, drawn to the conclusion that the medium through which to reach the public most effectively is the illustrated lecture.

The reasons for this conclusion are many:

First, perhaps, is the fact that the illustrated lecture combines, in a way, the advantages of the exhibit and the printed article, presenting them in such connective form that the comprehensiveness of both is increased.

Second, and possibly of greater importance, an educational article is monotonous, dry reading to the class of mind it is most important for us to reach; an illustrated lecture, on the contrary, setting forth the same general ideas, may be made so interesting as to hold the attention of that mind from beginning to end.

No one who is in the habit of facing audiences in this work can fail to realize that very few of the eyes that are riveted upon him with every evidence of earnest attention would ever travel the pages of a printed article setting forth the same thoughts in cold type.

Our prime object in this special branch of educational work is to convince as many individuals as possible of the importance of Oral Hygiene; not merely to place before them facts and figures, but to *convince* them of their significance.

The facts and figures necessary to convince an earnest student of the logic of our proposition would occupy but very little space.

We are not, however, as a rule dealing with earnest students; we are called upon to enter a field in which we find men, women and children who need reform, and before we can expect any class of people to change their habits of life we must first show them in terms they understand good reasons for so doing; we must excite their interest; we must awaken them from a condition of indifference and, then, with their minds in proper condition for the reception of the new idea, we may tell our story with some expectancy that the main points will be understood and retained.

This can all be accomplished with the well planned, graphically illustrated lecture as in no other way.

But when we reach this conclusion we open up a large problem, for while we make our strongest and most effective appeal from the lecture platform, the small number of people reached on each occasion, and the scarcity of available speakers, under present conditions restricts the field to such an extent that the sum total of good accomplished is hardly worth the cost.

This paper is intended to offer a logical solution for this problem; to present a plan by which the author believes that the field covered by this most important educational medium may be extended, practically and economically.

Our experience with the lecture problem in Massachusetts which has led up to the present plan is probably not materially different from that of organizations which have operated in other sections.

We first established a board of lecturers, consisting of ten selected speakers, and school authorities and others interested were informed of the service we were prepared to render.

We were at first encouraged but later somewhat embarrassed by the result.

Applications for speakers to appear before school classes, mothers' clubs, hospital nurses, and every other conceivable species of audience came to us in every day's mail and we soon discovered that the demand would quickly exhaust the supply.

In an attempt to eliminate these difficulties we next formulated a lecture outline (which has since been published in the Journal of the Allied Societies) and, at the same time, systematically catalogued prints of our lantern slides, our object being to extend the assistance of the council to any dentist who might be able and willing to give talks in his own district—First, by aiding him in framing a lecture, second, by furnishing him with our lantern and an equipment of slides of his own selection, at a nominal fee.

This plan promises good results and we believe is a move in the right direction.

It gives the dentist who is willing to do his part in the campaign, but who is hampered by lack of time and facilities very valuable and necessary assistance in producing a creditable and interesting lecture easily and economically.

After a somewhat extended investigation of the subject, however, including many conferences with those who, it seemed to me, should meet the lecture needs in their localities, and prompted to a great extent by their logical reasons for declining or neglecting to do so, I have reached the personal conclusion that a further step is necessary before the problem will be completely or satisfactorily solved.

Let me for a moment detail some of the points in my conception of the problem which form the basis of my reasoning in offering a plan for its solution.

Generally speaking no one district needs Oral Hygiene education more than another.

Any lecture scheme, then, whether it be fostered by an international, a national or a state body, to be consistent, must eventually contemplate the covering of no less a field than every inch of ground within its special jurisdiction where human beings reside.

Considering this as our proper end and aim, place beside it in comparison the work possible of accomplishment by a dozen, thirty or even fifty appointed lecturers (more I believe than are at present organized to cover any state in this country) and the inconsistency of such a system and its utter inadequateness seem apparent.

Dissected into its component parts I believe we find three requisites in connection with the practical and effective presentation of our subject before a public audience.

First, and of greatest importance, is a well planned lecture; not a mere collection of statistics, rules and facts presented in disconnected form, which could only be absorbed by an intellectual student, but a graphically illustrated, entertaining talk, so put together and produced that it will stimulate interest in a sluggish, indifferent mind and hold that interest until its educational points have been driven home to be retained; opening with an introduction that will convince the most skeptical or disinterested auditor of the vital value of the subject to him; containing in the body of its text each point in the great lesson of Oral Hygiene so consecutively and connectedly arranged that the mind is easily carried from one step to another, gradually unfolding the details of the theme in such a manner that each idea suggests and anticipates the next; closing with a résumé which will leave important points stamped on the memory.

Such a lecture is best prepared by a selected essayist with the help of able editors; it may be prepared by the man of average ability after sufficient study which, in the case of most of us would mean several months of available spare hours; such a lecture is *never* delivered offhand by anyone but a finished orator of an exceptional type.

An average man who practices a branch of medicine as a profession and essays oratory as a side line should not attempt it.

Consider for a moment how much easier a task it is to prepare such a paper as the one I am now reading, the purpose of which is simply to present a few theories to an audience already interested in the subject, than to prepare a lecture for a more or less disinterested company of individuals, the purpose of which is to inspire, educate and reform them.

A carefully prepared lecture, then, based on extended study and properly compiled statistics is the first and most important item.

Second among the requisites is a well selected collection of lantern slides and other accessories necessary to the proper illustration of the lecture.

The importance of the lantern slide in connection with lectures on educational topics cannot be overestimated.

Even rules and statistics become interesting when projected on the screen and the opportunities in our subject to effectively emphasize its lessons with pictures and drawings force us to accept the lantern as an indispensable element in our work.

The slides should be made for the lecture and not the lecture built around the slides as we too often see it.

They should be designed with care and with due consideration for the lack of scientific knowledge of the average auditor; from thirty to sixty being necessary to properly illustrate a lecture.

The third of our requisites I would tabulate as of the least importance —the speaker.

These are the requisites for the production of a good lecture; who can supply them?

A dentist of average professional knowledge and ability, who is a good writer; who has sufficient interest in the work and spare time at his disposal to study up statistics and prepare the lectures and illustrations specified, and who may be able and willing to spend the several dollars necessary for lantern slides, could, in most cases, produce an ideal lecture alone and unaided.

It cannot be denied, however, that there are few men to fulfill these requirements.

Summing the matter up, the problem as it stands, seems to me to present the following conditions:

First. Lectures on oral hygiene are needed in every inhabitated section of the country.

Second. Such lectures as are delivered for public education should be of a standard type; all instruction as to the care of the mouth, etc., being in accordance with the *concensus* of opinion among men who have given the matter special study rather than expressions of *individual* opinion; all quoted statistics in accordance with authentic records.

Third. A board or organization of volunteer lecturers, though they may be selected men who are able and willing to devote the time necessary to prepare lectures of a standard type, cannot begin to cover the necessary field without an unreasonable sacrifice on their part which should be divided among men in each district.

Fourth. The average practicing dentist, though he may realize the need of lectures in his section, has neither the time nor facilities necessary for the production, without assistance, of a standard type lecture.

My plan for the solution of the problem is as follows:

I would propose, first, that the National Mouth Hygiene Association, and such other organizations as may be engaged in Oral Hygiene educational work, prepare a series of lectures with an equipment of lantern slides for each lecture arranged to meet the requirements of all types of audiences, *i. e.*, a lecture for young children, one for older children, one for mothers, one for hospital nurses, one for the mixed audience, etc.

I would propose that these lectures in printed form together with the lantern slides for same be loaned to any dentist, physician, nurse, school teacher or other person properly fitted to present the matter to the public, who may make application for them, at a stipulated fee, such fee being sufficient to make the plan self-supporting. The principal expense being the renewal of lantern slides, I would suggest that a rental fee of about five cents per week be charged for each slide, the lecture reading to be furnished gratis.

Any person desiring to take advantage of the service would make application by filling out a printed form giving details as to the date of lecture, the type of audience he or she was to meet, length of lecture desired, etc., and possibly signing an agreement to pay for any breakage of slides at a stipulated rate.

On receiving the application the association would mail to the applicant at once a printed copy of the lecture that seemed best to meet the needs of the occasion.

The lectures should be printed on typewriter paper in typewriter type, with conspicuous markings for slide signalling to facilitate easy reading.

This lecture reading, so-called, should be mailed several weeks before the date of the lecture to give the applicant time to become familiar with the text.

The slides should then, in due time, be shipped in a specially constructed container, proof, as far as possible, against breakage, and easily repacked by the applicant for return shipment.

The details necessary to the easy and practical handling of the service would only be a question of proper systemization, which would offer no special difficulties.

Such a plan would, I believe, accomplish two objects:

First. It would ensure a standard type of Oral Hygiene lecture, not only with reference to authenticity, but with the rhetorical construction needed to present the subject in interesting and instructive form.

Second. It would enable any person of average oratorical ability to present a comprehensive talk on "Oral Hygiene" at very slight expense and without the necessity of spending hours of valuable time in studying up statistics and other necessary preparation.

I believe that there are members of the dental and medical professions, nurses, school teachers or other hygiene workers in every community where man resides who could be interested in this work and who would gladly take advantage of an opportunity to give talks on Oral Hygiene were it made so easy for them to so do, who otherwise would not or could not meet the expense of time or money necessary for its accomplishment.

And, finally, I believe that such a scheme, properly organized and managed, would extend the lecture field so widely as to bring about results in the education of the public on the subject of Oral Hygiene possible in no other way.

SESSION THIRTY C

SYMPOSIUM ON MOUTH HYGIENE

Arranged by the National Mouth Hygiene Association,

W. G. EBERSOLE, M.D., D.D.S., Cleveland, Ohio, *Secretary*

W. G. EBERSOLE, M.D., D.D.S., *Chairman*

DR. J. O. MCCALL, University of
Buffalo, *Vice-Chairman*

Program of Session Thirty C

DR. ALBIN LENHARDTSON, Secretary of the H. C. F. D. I.; Secretary
of the Swedish N. M. H. A.; President of the Hygiene Commission
of the Swedish Dental Association; Director of the School Clinics
in Stockholm. "A Few Important Points Relating to Public
Mouth Hygiene."

DR. ALBIN LENHARDTSON, Secretary of the H. C. F. D. I.; Secretary
of the Swedish N. M. H. A.; President of the Hygiene Commission
of the Swedish Dental Association; Director of the School Clinics
in Stockholm. "The Chief Points of the Present Mouth Hygiene
Work in Europe."

GEORGE F. BURKE, D.D.S., Secretary-Treasurer Detroit Auxiliary
of the National Mouth Hygiene Association, Detroit, Mich.
"The Ideal Method of Spreading the Oral Hygiene Propaganda
in Communities."

DR. HUMBERTO FERNANDEZ DAVILA, Lima, Peru, Representing the
Dental Association of Peru. "Dental Hygiene in the Schools
of Peru."

HOMER C. BROWN, D.D.S., President of the National Dental Association;
Member Ohio State Board of Health, Columbus Ohio. "The
Dental Phase of School Hygiene and of Public Health Problems."

on Ways and Means, National Mouth Hy
"The Tooth Toilet Article in its Relation t
Education."

W. G. EBERSOLE, M.D., D.D.S., Secretary-Treasure
Hygiene Association, Cleveland, Ohio. "Pu
Clinics a Possibility in Each Community; A
Securing and Maintaining Them."

A FEW IMPORTANT POINTS RELATING TO PUBLIC MOUTH HYGIENE

BY

ALBIN LENHARDTSON

The development of school dental clinics has now progressed to a stage where we must make every effort to sift the evidence and lay down certain rules for the continued activity of these clinics—such rules to be founded on past experience—or I am very much afraid that the whole question of dental clinics in the schools will drift into questionable channels. Certain tendencies point to that view. When we have succeeded in convincing the authorities of the need of dental clinics in their schools, we must face the inevitable question: "How do you propose to arrange the work; have you any definite plan for carrying on the public dental hygiene work in the cities as well as the country?" I believe that in the majority of cases we should be compelled to reply in a negative sense, and therein lies, in my opinion, a great danger. We must assume responsibility. In arousing the civic authorities we give them the right to demand the very best efforts of our intelligence in bringing this important public matter to a satisfactory completion. I am confident that all who are interested in mouth hygiene agree with me in respect of the foregoing, and now beg leave to submit some points of actual importance for discussion.

I. In what manner shall the treatment of the teeth of public school children in the rural districts be carried on most effectually?

This problem does not admit of an easy solution which at the same time is a satisfactory one. It appears necessary to devise some kind of ambulating dental clinics. The promoter of a bill in the Upper House of the Swedish Riksdag of this year concerning a scheme for the regulation of public mouth hygiene, particularly in the country districts, proposes that the country be divided into districts with a dentist in charge of each district, on analogous footing with the present district physicians. In that case the dentist in charge should, of course, be paid by the State for a daily attendance of, say, six hours. It should be settled once for all that only children 7 years of age receive conserving treatment, followed by an annual examination. In this way it is possible to keep the mouths of the children of a school in a healthy state for the smallest cost.

II.   Should all treatment be free of charge or should children with means pay a stipulated low fee?

There is something to be said on both sides of the question. In some Swedish cities such parents of the children whom the teachers consider to be in a position to pay are charged one krona a year; in other cities, the treatment is free. The authorities of Stockholm, where I am Director of the public school dental clinics, take the view, that if a septic mouth is a danger, not only to its owner but also to his surroundings, it cannot be left to the judgment of more or less ignorant parents whether the mouths of their children should be attended to. Very little is gained by applying hygienic measures to the mouths of only a certain percentage of the children in a class—we must give treatment to all. This argument strikes me, too, as being the most logical. Another not unimportant point in favour of the view outlined above is the support it might command where there are many Socialists on the Town Councils. It is easier to force through a scheme that includes free treatment to all, as it falls in with their communistic ideals. It can, on the other hand, scarcely be denied that people value a thing they have paid for more than something they receive for nothing. Personally I incline to a middle course. The first complete treatment of the children's mouths ought to be free. Work which may be done at subsequent annual examinations ought to be at the expense of the parents, as, in the majority of cases, it is caused by neglect of hygienic precautions on the part of the children, and it is the duty of the parents to instruct and admonish the children in that respect. It seems rather too much to ask of the community that it should pay for the neglect of children and their parents. The city authorities, however, overruled my modification as unsuitable.

III.   Is the wholesale extraction method supported by English dentists to be recommended?

Messrs. Colyer, Lloyd-Williams and Wallis have lately propounded a radical theory; viz: that all teeth in a child's mouth that cannot easily be filled, and teeth which lack antagonists, should be extracted. Judging by discussions which have taken place, it appears that this theory has met with pretty general acceptance in England. Their opinion, based on weighing of the children before and after such a radical cleansing of the mouth, is that the organism suffers less from the inability to masticate the food than from the septic condition of the mouth. That such a method of treatment tends greatly to simplify the work of school dental clinics cannot be denied. I confess, however, to being rather sceptic until further proof can be adduced. Furthermore, I do not think that these gentlemen have produced sufficient evidence to show that the occlusion of the subsequent permanent teeth will not be wrong. At the Stockholm school clinics we try as much as possible to save the milk fives and the permanent sixes, even if they are considerably damaged. Other milk teeth are extracted if they are much damaged. Flat cavities are subject to caustic treatment, particularly if the dentine is fairly hard.

It would be particularly interesting, however, to have the opinion of English school dentists present on this subject.

IV. Should whole-day or part-day dentists be employed in the school dental clinics?

This is also a controversial matter.

For my part the employment of part-day dentists appears to be the more suitable plan and that for several reasons. Primarily, it is indispensable that school dentists be persons of experience. They must know how to work rapidly and yet well. They must have a suitable manner towards children, parents and the teachers. They must have aptitude for statistics and be able to make observations.

If whole-day dentists who are not allowed to practise privately are employed, the authorities must pay them very well in order to get first-rate, experienced dentists. That throws too great an expense on the community, but by offering comparatively small salaries none but rather inexperienced dentists could be got. And it is not to be expected that such young dentists from social or altruistic motives will remain in their places after such time as they consider sufficient to gather experience to start a practice of their own. Frequent changes of dentists at these school clinics is, however, a serious disadvantage as children are sensitive and suspicious towards strangers. The pay of two half-day dentists, certainly, is somewhat higher than what a whole-day dentist would demand for the same time, but in the long run the community would gain financially by employing part-day dentists. It must also be kept in mind that work in a school dental clinic, day in and day out, is extremely hard and trying, and it is unthinkable that any one could, in the long run, keep his interest alert for more than 3 hours daily. Seen in that light the community will find it better economy to pay more for the energetic work of two half-day dentists than less to the whole-day dentist who jogs along at a leisurely gait. Looking at the question from a professional point of view, I believe that dentists would prefer half-day employment with opportunity to practise privately. The difficulty is that the educational authorities, at any rate in Sweden, do not willingly include persons in the civil service list that do not give up their whole time to the work in the schools. But that obstacle does not appear insurmountable.

THE CHIEF POINTS OF THE PRESENT MOUTH HYGIENE WORK IN EUROPE

BY

ALBIN LENHARDTSON

Race hygiene, as yet only in its infancy, is no doubt destined to occupy a dominant position in the sphere of hygiene. A more altruistic view is spreading, if somewhat slowly. The understanding that we are all parts of one whole organism is gaining acceptance more and more. If one organ is hurt the whole system will suffer from it. Of what consequence is the accidental power of a nation if the people are degenerated? The conflicting views of the day—political, social, economic—appear rather small in comparison with the race hygiene efforts which, with all obtainable means; try to better both physical and mental development of the future generation.

Amongst the nations, as with individuals, the Darwinian theory, "the survival of the fittest," applies with equal force. In the fight against race degeneration hygiene of the mouth is an important element. Of course, some people do not regard caries of the teeth as a sign of degeneration, but I can't understand that point of view. Degeneration itself means deterioration—a falling off; thus, in the case of the human body, a change for the worse in the cells of which the organism is composed. Nobody can very well deny that degeneration has taken place with regard to the cells of the teeth. Somebody might reply that this is true enough, but does negligence of mouth hygiene contribute to the decline of the race? The answer to this ought to be easy. As soon as certain cells in an organism degenerate the entire system will suffer from it. The indirect effects of a neglected mouth hygiene I shall not dwell upon; they have been shown in a conclusive way by several eminent investigators, not only upon the ground of odontology, but even more upon the field of general medicine.

I have deemed these preliminary remarks necessary to make clear the importance of dental hygiene from an hygienic, pedagogic and social-economic point of view. Few if any authorities, however, have investigated the subject sufficiently to be able to view the question in its entirety. And this is not to be wondered at seeing that the researches concerning mouth hygiene are of relatively recent date. It is only through the works of Fletcher, Bramsen, Ebersole, Jessen, Marshall, Pickerill, Ritter, Röse, Wallace, Walkoff and others, that a new light has been thrown on these problems. It is not my intention to give a detailed account of the works of those gentlemen, as I take for granted that they are well known, at any rate to the delegates to the Dental Hygiene Section of the Fourth International Congress of School Hygiene.

Jessen was the first in Europe to demonstrate, at all events, practically, the importance of dental hygiene to the community by setting up the first dental clinic for school children in Strassburg,. Germany. Through his own enthusiasm he succeeded, in spite of many hardships, in inspiring the city authorities with some of his own ardour.

City after city has followed the example of Strassburg and at the present time there exist in Germany about two hundred school dental clinics. The English nation is more conservative and has a great respect for tradition. A further reason for the slow progress of the school dental -clinic movement in England may be found in the fact that nearly all charitable work in that country is depending on philanthropy. The slow development of the movement in France must be sought in the disinclination of the authorities to pay the cost. And that in one of the richest countries of the world.

Owing to the efforts of the recently constituted Association for the Promotion of Dental Hygiene in the schools of Austria, the authorities of Vienna and a few other places have set up school dental clinics in their respective communities.

We have in Sweden, with a population of less than one-tenth of Germany, about 40 dental clinics in schools and children's homes. Complete arrangements, however, for the care of the teeth of all children in the common schools have been effected only in the cities of Stockholm and Gothenburg. We have been fortunate enough to find, not only the former and the present cabinets, but also the Parliament in full accordance with our views as to the importance to the nation of mouth hygiene. Permit me to give a brief account illustrating this.

The Swedish Dentists' Association and the Swedish National Association for the Promotion of Dental Hygiene petitioned the government to appoint a Royal Commission to confer and report on the question of a system of dental hygiene in Sweden. Our petition in due course went before the Royal Medical Board which reported unfavorably upon it for reasons that seem rather weak. The government, too, favoured the appointment of such a commission, but in the meantime the Parliament went into session. Bills for the regulation of dental hygiene work were introduced in both Houses although, of course, it was known that the government had the matter under consideration and also that the Royal Medical Board had reported adversely on our petition. The explanation of this by-play is that it was deemed desirable to impress the government with the importance of the matter in hand.

Both Houses directed that the government be asked to investigate the question and submit plans for a system of effective care of the teeth, taking particular consideration for the rural districts. The government has now decided that the commission asked for shall commence its labours already in September. And, further, the Secretary of the Interior has assured me that he has found the time ripe for the appointment of a dentist on the Royal Medical Board. That appears to me to be the proper arrangement.

We are now in possession of arguments, strong enough to prove to those concerned that there are no insurmountable obstacles to the state undertaking the promotion of dental hygiene in other countries also. I hope that the investigations which are now being constituted in Sweden will prove of particular value in the promotion of this important movement in all parts of the world. In Sweden, at any rate, it has been found that the seed sown has ripened quickly.

In Europe the mouth hygiene movement has, as I have stated before, rapidly come to the fore in some countries. That is well and good in itself. But we approach a critical period in its development if, indeed, we have not already reached that point.

The authorities are now demanding that we, practising dentists, submit thoroughly worked out plans for the proper organisation of the mouth hygiene work as it affects both the state and the local authorities. I believe that in many respects we are compelled to admit that no thoroughgoing system is in existence as yet. That is, of course, a weakness which I consider it our duty to remove as soon as possible by means of united effort. We have no thoroughly sifted and accepted system in respect to any of the important questions. It may be objected that the organisations of dental practitioners in the different countries are the proper bodies to carry out such work in their respective countries. That is no doubt, true as regards some questions, but a great many others are of such nature that the conditions are not materially different in the various countries. I wish to point out some such matters, with no intention, however, of subjecting them to a close scrutiny. How best organise dental hygiene in the cities? Some urge a central dental clinic, even in large cities, while others consider a dental clinic for each school or at any rate one for each district more suitable. The former system is employed, for instance, in Gothenburg, while in Stockholm, where I am director of the school dental clinics, the latter plan is adhered to. Further, how arrange for effective dental treatment of the school children in the rural districts? Are ambulating clinics to be recommended? Which methods are most suitable for a school dental clinic? Is wholesale extraction, recommended by many English dentists, to be adopted? Should whole-day or part-day dentists be employed? Should children whose parents are able to pay, contribute an annual, though small, fee? Or should all treatment be free of cost? The former plan is adopted in Gothenburg, the latter in Stockholm. The salaries of the school dentists, on the other hand, is a question that can hardly be settled internationally. Cost of living, etc., varies considerably, for different places. How many times are the children to be examined annually? To what extent are statistics to be kept? Is the condition laid down by Sir George Newman, Chief Medical Officer of the English Government Board of Education, "that all arrangements for each area should be under the supervision of the School Medical Officer," to be recommended? Has the State a right to order conscript dentists to work at military dental clinics during the greater part of the time they are to serve in the army? What degree of importance is to be attached to the published theories of Pickerill and Wallace concerning the diet as prophylaxis? There are no doubt, many more questions of importance which do not for the moment occur to me. But I merely wish to ask, with reference to the foregoing, if there is any country possessing a settled plan that contains definite answers to these queries? I think not, at any rate in Europe. It lies near at hand to conceive the wrong path into which the movement may be deflected. Signs to that effect have not been wanting. Unsuitable methods are employed at certain school clinics. In others the dentists are underpaid. No statistical records are kept at some clinics, while too comprehensive ones at some others. The dentists in certain German cities are already on the civil service list with right to pension, which seems the proper position. The majority of school dentists, however, are not in such a fortunate position. Fédérations Dentaires Internationales, Hygiene Commission, as a central office for the entire mouth hygiene movement, has unquestionably a great mission in this field. Nothing can be done by the commission, however, if the dentists of the different countries fail to take an interest in its work, or, at least, maintain contact with the delegates by submitting reports, suggestions, etc., etc.

Now, when the authorities have become interested and aroused to a consciousness of the importance of mouth hygiene to the nation at large, here in America no less than elsewhere, it behooves us dentists to come forward with the most practical plans for the carrying out of the great work.

THE IDEAL METHOD OF SPREADING THE ORAL HYGIENE PROPAGANDA IN COMMUNITIES

BY

George F. Burke

I am going to quote to you, from one who is generally regarded as an impressive authority, a statement which may incur the displeasure of the valiant cohorts who are banded together against the devastations of the Demon Rum, but I would make it clear that it is not because I love their cause less, but my own more, that I refer to Dr. Osler, who said: "If I were to say whether more physical deterioration was produced by alcohol or by defective teeth I would unhesitatingly say defective teeth."

There are few who have not been, either directly or indirectly, confronted with the havoc wrought by excessive indulgence in alcoholic stimulants, but the havoc of defective teeth is far less spectacular and more insidious and so more dangerous to the health and happiness of a humanity unwary and therefore unprepared to meet the foe that menaces it. It is because of these facts, obvious to anyone who has given them the most superficial thought that I consider Dr. Osler's opinion so valuable and illuminating.

Few of us even who regard ourselves as deeply initiated have a right appreciation of the hidden horrors that lurk in the neglected and diseased mouth; I believe we shall soon awaken to a somewhat startled realization of the overwhelming importance to human welfare of clean wholesome mouths.

But this isn't exactly a comfortable idea to dwell upon when we consider how rare, how very rare are the clean, well-cared for mouth and sound teeth.

But I need not plead before this gathering the cause of oral hygiene. My part consists rather in telling you the story of how the first steps toward a better order of things have been taken in Detroit, how this was made possible and what forces were brought to bear. It is not a spectacular or dramatic story, in any sense but is chiefly significant because Detroit was one of the first cities in the United States to provide for the care of the teeth of its school children. My story will be valuable only insofar as I shall be enabled out of our experience in Detroit to point the way to some extent at least, to others who are anxious to do a similar service to the future citizens of their community.

Merely to be imbued with the spirit of altruism, or to be ready to

sacrifice ever so valiantly will, I believe, avail little unless the propa-
gandists are as shrewd as they are unselfish, as diplomatic as they
are valiant.   Especially is this true, if your cause is, or seems, a
new one.

Those who plead for universal oral hygiene are practically preaching
a new doctrine.   The great mass of human beings—that great mass
whom it is most necessary to reach—have never heard of it.   *Nor are
they keen for the news.*   To tell the bald truth, they are bored to death
with all the new preachments that have been thrust upon them during
the past few years.   The great humanitarian wave that has been rolling
larger and larger, has touched them again and again, not only to bring
them relief but to urge new efforts and impose new obligations upon
them.   The visiting nurse with her pleas for open windows, ventilation,
cleanliness and the rest; the babies' milk fund associations with their
detailed instructions for keeping the infant's milk clean and cool, and
himself sweet and happy during the torrid summer days; the health
and hygiene committees, with new ideas for the care of garbage; the civic
improvement bodies showing how to convert a filthy alley into a shining
vine-bordered lane; the juvenile courts auxiliaries, eloquently pleading
for greater vigilance over the boy and girl—and a dozen others.

And nearly all of these things are put up to the mother.   If her
family be large, she is already over-burdened with innumerable harass-
ing drudgeries and now she is asked to learn new lessons by the score,
to take in countless new ideas, bewildering often, and nearly always
difficult.   But right here let me offer my humble tribute to this mother
of the masses.   I believe that most workers in the field of social service
will agree with me that she is far more receptive of new ideas, far more
open-minded and responsive than the man of the same class whose
almost invariable objection to any innovation is that he was brought
up on the old methods and that what was good enough for him is good
enough for his children.

The mother's more intelligent and less egotistic attitude is embraced
is a desire to give to her children something better than she ever knew.
I have wondered if this is not a rather forceful argument in favor of the
feminist movement—but, as Kipling would say, "That's another story."

But far more discouraging and inexcusable than the inertia of the
poor, is the smug indifference of the provincial-minded, who being
themselves protected against the devastations of defective, decaying
teeth, absolve their consciences by refusing to credit the reports of those
who have made a thorough and intimate study of conditions.   Not
that I mean to imply that the well-to-do, nor even the rich need not
have the doctrine of preventive dentistry preached to them.   The truth
is that the use of tooth brush, the diseased mouth and a general ignorance

regarding the meaning and importance of oral hygiene are only less common among the prosperous than the poor.

How, then, with the ignorance and apathy of the great mass of the people to reckon with could you expect ardent espousal of this long-neglected cause on the part of their public servants in the boards of health and education, or a lively response from the aldermen and estimators for appropriations for this work from out of the public funds?

Clearly it is a matter or education among the high and the low, the wise and the foolish. But education, even of the most superficial kind, is a slow process. We wanted to do it as well and as quickly as might be. How to send out the news into the highways and byways. How to let the fathers and mothers know that often their children were frail and sickly because they were ill-nourished in spite of plenty of food. How to show them that malnutrition was directly due to the wrecked teeth—the black ugly stumps, foul and diseased that might have been white and sound, supplying the means that nature provided for the proper mastication of food and the resultant well nourished body. How to make them see that the neglect of their children's teeth was the perpetration of a cruel injustice upon those they loved—that it all meant a future of suffering and humiliation, of almost inevitable disease and retarded physical and mental development. How to reach the growing girl, to warn her that unbrushed teeth meant a future full of humiliations and hurt vanity as well as physical deterioration that would damage her good looks irrevocably. How to bring home to those who are entrusted with so large a share of the public welfare that in Detroit, as elsewhere, fully 96% of the school children have defective teeth. To make our voices heard where so many others are clamoring was a problem. The question was how to reach the greatest number of people with a minimum waste of effort and in the shortest possible time.

There is much criticism in our day of the press, just as there is of the pulpit. How much or how little deserved I do not know; but this I do know that there is no power so overwhelming, so far-reaching, so swift and penetrating as this power of the press. The papers reach all the people, all the time. *Despite pooh poohing to the contrary, print is impressive.* This, too, I have discovered out of my experience: If the mother in the home is indifferent because over-burdened; if the father is indifferent because naturally reactionary; if the well-to-do are indifferent because untouched by the needs of those lower in the social scale, and if the political boards are indifferent because of the indifference of all these others, there is one who by the very nature of his profession cannot afford to be indifferent. He is the newspaper man. To the newspapers I cannot give too large a share of the credit for the success of our movement in Detroit and Michigan. Intelligent and sympathetic reports of the efforts being made by some of the dentists to save the children in this regard were given in the news columns, interviews on the need and the best methods of meeting it were used, editorials setting forth the meaning of this special phase of the big humanitarian impulse were printed in all the papers, and what perhaps reached the greatest num_ bers were the Sunday feature stories with their striking headlines running across the entire page and illustrated to show graphically how terrible a thing the neglected mouth may become.

No other means of education, of spreading the news, goes so far or so swiftly as this. No influence for conquering indifference, especially on the part of politicians is half so powerful. Those among them who had preferred to regard as a "fad" the effort to save children's mouths from wreck, changed their view-point with gracious alacrity. There is no ally so powerful as the newspaper and for the encouragement of those who have been disheartened by the slow progress of this great work of saving the future generations from the results of their neglected mouths I wish to point to the increasing numbers of newspaper articles appearing in the various metropolitan dailies. Only a couple of weeks ago a New York paper with a tremendous circulation printed a striking article in its Sunday feature section, popularly treated and copiously illustrated and setting forth the facts in trenchant style. That article entered the homes of tens of thousands on a day when people have leisure to read.

I have been asked to speak to you on the ideal method of spreading the propaganda of mouth hygiene in communities; I do not know whether we adopted the ideal method in Detroit, but we endeavored to act as wisely as possible, not to be precipitate, although it was our earnest desire to get results as quickly as possible.

Briefly, our course has been this:

It was about five years ago that the First District Dental Society of Michigan passed a resolution providing for the appointment of a local hygiene committee. The committee, with Dr. W. A. Giffen as chairman immediately set to work to find a suitable place to begin operations. Grace Hospital, one of the largest in Detroit, furnished us a room and we, with funds raised from among our own members, equipped it. Several of the younger dentists offered their services on Saturdays and so for three years this little philanthropy continued while we kept our enthusiasm alive with the thought that this was the nucleus, the first impulse toward the larger movement in oral hygiene which would ultimately include all the school children in our fast growing city. The clinic was a success; hundreds came, so at the end of three years another was established in the health board building. It was still up to us to provide funds for the equipment and this we did by asking the aid of the local dealers and dentists. The health board paid the salary of one regular operator. Hundreds of children were treated and the favorable attention of the hospital authorities, the Board of Health and the newspapers was thus attracted to the need of this work. It was then a fortunate event occurred for the progress of our aim. Hon. Chase S. Osborn, then Governor of Michigan, appointed to membership on the Board of Health Dr. Charles H. Oakman, a prominent dentist and oral surgeon. He is a man of breadth and sympathy and he spared no efforts to secure an appropriation for dental clinics and inspection in the schools. ·It was chiefly through his efforts that $5,000 was included in the health board budget. The local oral hygiene committee still possessed a fund of several hundred dollars, enough to do the thing it needed most to do—to inaugurate a campaign for the spreading of sentiment in favor of this work—a sentiment whose existence was already being felt. We still had to make sure that the city authorities would allow for the oral hygiene work included in the health board budget. We approached the newspapers and of their great aid I have told you. Immediately following upon their editorials we sent out five hundred petitions calling attention to the suffering caused to helpless children from neglect of their teeth and to irremediable results upon their general health if allowed to continue. These were sent to dentists, to the women's clubs who are active in behalf of progressive measures in our city and circulated through the stores and factories. In a month we had secured some twenty thousand signatures. I shall not bore you with the details of our efforts for bringing to bear upon the alderman and estimators every possible pressure so that they would not refuse the $5,000. They did not refuse but allowed the entire sum.

Now we begin to direct our energies to ascertaining just how this money could be used with the greatest possible good to the children of our city. We referred to well known authorities on mouth hygiene and found from such men as Ebersole, Evans and Warthin that there should be at least one general dental inspection each year and the balance applied to clinics.

This year with a precedent and a record of service to point to, we felt safe in asking for an appropriation of eight instead of five thousand dollars. It was granted. We are in this way enabled to employ two additional inspectors and establish two new clinics and the young men employed in this capacity look upon their work as more than a mere "job." I believe that without an exception it is to them an opportunity for service in a field where it is woefully needed. No account of the progress of oral hygiene in Detroit would be half adequate without reference to Dr. Charles E. Chadsey, Superintendent of Schools in

Detroit. A man of broad outlook, who realizes that education is far more than a mere academic process, who knows that it must follow the child into the innermost sanctum of his home life and help him to conserve and nourish his physical forces and show the way to a right mode of living, Dr. Chadsey more than once raised his voice in behalf of the tooth brush and systematic inspection and care of the teeth of the school children.

I should say that no scheme for spreading the doctrine and extending the practice of oral hygiene was ideal without lectures. Well-delivered popularly-treated, illustrated lectures will carry the message to hundreds who otherwise would be unreached. In Detroit the Federation of Women's Clubs has for years maintained a series of winter lectures given evenings in the school houses, in the social centers and settlements and in the various clubs organized among the men and women of the working classes. There is such a strong penchant for organization of every sort and kind in our day that it is an easy matter to find groups of people gathered for an evening's diversion. If you can teach them a new lesson pleasurably they will listen. The story of what ruin a neglected mouth may work deftly handled is not without its dramatic possibilities.

Lectures, inspection of the teeth of school children by dentists, clinics as many and as well advertised as possible, with always the backing of the press and their coöperation in printing stories—these are the media through which the child may be helped and saved from the tragedy of a wrecked diseased and disease-producing mouth.

It isn't always an easy thing to start the ball rolling—to overcome the prejudice and apathy inherent in so large a proportion of people of all classes. But the fight is tremendously worth while and if professional jealousies and petty, befogging issues can be forgotten and coöperation among the dentists achieved, the struggle is not half so hard, the results far quicker and more splendid.

ADDRESS IN BEHALF OF THE DENTAL ASSOCIATION OF PERU

BY

HUMBERTO FERNÁNDEZ DÁVILA

Gentlemen, Colleagues of the International Congress of Hygiene, and Friends:
It is a pleasure to extend to you of the Congress, representing all the leading nations of the world, and yourselves individually, the greeting and good will of the Dental Association of Peru. Many of those in our profession will be apt to think of it as a development of science in the United States; but it is with a feeling of national pride and of personal satisfaction that I must dispute this claim and create a different impression, not only of our advance in professional skill, but in general knowledge and education. I am told that the oldest institution of learning in the United States, Harvard University, was founded in 1636, while the University of Pennsylvania in Philadelphia dates from 1741. The University of Lima in Peru is actually the oldest institution of learning in the new world and was founded in 1576. It is therefore sixty years older than Harvard and one hundred and sixty-five years older than Pennsylvania. This will be no surprise to those who recall that when the Cavaliers were landing at Jamestown and the Puritans on the shores of Massachusetts Bay, the viceroys of the kings of Spain represented in the new world a power immeasurably the greatest of its time and then in its third and fourth generation of prosperous and even wonderful expansion in the new world. The Dental Department of the University is the oldest in South America, and dates from 1854, being now, therefore, in its sixtieth year of operation. This, I am sure, compares in point of age very favorably with any Dental school in the world. It is, therefore, with a feeling of entire security and satisfaction that I extend to you the welcome of the oldest University in the new world, and of one of the oldest established Dental colleges; and I am pleased to report that in my country, Peru, not alone is the question of age reserved as a matter of local satisfaction, but that the governing body of the University has at all times kept abreast of progress in the science of the profession and has instituted many movements for enhancing its dignity and extending its practical benefits throughout the educational system of the Republic.

DENTAL HYGIENE IN THE SCHOOLS OF PERU

BY

HUMBERTO FERNÁNDEZ DÁVILA

It is worthy of notice that in this modern era of scientific progress, when all branches of hygiene have been encouraged and have been greatly advanced, that on the other hand one of the most important and primary of these branches has been sorrily neglected, ignored and allowed to remain in a dormant state. I refer to dental hygiene.

At present, the importance and necessity of dental hygiene among school children is being recognized as it never was before, although it is only recently that its chief place in relation to bodily health has been acknowledged.

In nearly all the European countries, chiefly Germany, France and England, and also in America, in this great nation, a vigorous campaign has been pursued along this line, enlightening the public as to the importance of dental hygiene, showing them the indispensable function that the oral cavity plays in the health of the individual, and at the same time this commission has been entrusted to public officials who have at last become aware of its purposes, it being the first duty of a state to look after the public's education; the next in importance should be to care for its citizens' health as well as for the future of the nation, for these things together assure the country of the strength which is necessary to insure its intellectual development, and also its forward strides to progress.

In South America dental hygiene in the schools is in a progressive state, and in the Argentine Republic during the last Pan-American Medical Congress, which was held in Buenos Aires, in the section on Odontology the following vote was unanimously approved:

WHEREAS dental caries being an organic disease, it is resolved to permit the making of hygiene laws applicable to the teeth of the school children.

In Peru relatively very little has been accomplished in this respect, recognizing that it would be wise and desirable that our profession should endeavor to profit by the great and extensive experience accumulated by other countries, which have for the last 50 years been engaged in this same struggle, and which through their improved methods have attained the most gratifying success in their campaign in behalf of dental hygiene in the schools. With this end in view, we have been observing and studying the methods and the form suitable to our country. The Executive Government of my country, following a well marked national sentiment, has commenced in this campaign by entrusting me with the study of the improvements in this our great sister Republic, relating to dental hygiene in the schools in order to the adoption of the necessary measure to carry out similar improvements among ourselves and in this manner to provide for one of our great present necessities.

In the city of Lima, the lack of dental hygiene among the school children is considerable, and upon this neglect rests the responsibility for the excess of caries of the teeth among the school children.

During an examination of buccal inspection which I made in the early part of last year, at one public school, I found that out of 200 children examined, ranging in ages between 9 and 14 years, only 6 of their number had their teeth in a satisfactory condition, thus leaving an average of 97% of decayed teeth among these school children.

This maximum average shows at the same time a coëfficient of 4 decayed teeth for each school child, while there were as many as 6 decayed teeth in a deplorable state.

I was also able to observe from the examined children the frequency of caries affecting the 4 first molars, between the ages of 6 and 7 years; that is to say, during the critical period. In almost every case I noticed the total lack of dental hygiene.

In one of the reports which I presented on this subject to the faculty of medicine of Lima, last year, I emphasized the fact that the situation was the source of great injury to the physical and intellectual development of the children, because of the influence that the dental apparatus in a poor condition exerts upon the health in general, chiefly on account of the neuralgia, abscesses and periostitis that decayed teeth frequently give rise to, as well as for the digestive disorders that necessarily follow the incomplete mastication of food.

If we take into consideration the amount of suffering and disease that could be prevented by means of opportune treatment, and above all the increase in value—from the standpoint of health—of the condition of the physical and intellectual strength accomplished for the lifetime of each child that has been treated, then it is evident that the social value of these children would be increased in such proportions as to surpass any sums that may be employed in the promotion of dental hygiene in the public schools.

We all know that from the physiological point of view, the teeth exert, because of their masticating function, a useful and necessary action over that of nutrition in general. The lessening or abolition of mastication we already know provokes at a nearer or later date gastrointestinal disorders, these in turn being a fruitful source of diverse ills.

Viewed from the pathological standpoint dental caries visibly reduce the vital resistance of the human organism, in the constant struggle that it has to wage in order to preserve its existence. At the same time dental caries imparts a permanent pathological condition to certain particular tissues, destroys the functions of our most essential orders, and predisposes to all sorts of infections in general, and particularly tuberculosis, it having been proved that this latter disease has a close relation to all oral infections.

In Lima, our capital city, and in Callao, the principal port of Peru, there is to be established in the near future a service of dental inspection, among the public schools, which will be under the direction of two dental surgeons, to one of whom will fall the duty of dental inspection of the children, while the other will have charge of the required treatment of these children.

During the inspection, the dentist is to give consultations, he shall examine each pupil at least twice a year; he shall set the date for the oral inspection according to the model set by the dental school of Paris, which presents the advantages of calling in due time the school children's attention, as well as the families to hygiene and the proper care of the dental apparatus. These dental inspections will be compulsory throughout the public schools, and it would be highly desirable to also extend it to the private schools as well.

I am of the opinion that the state should direct the placing in all schools, colleges and institutions of learning, descriptive pictures, some representing the oral anatomy, and still others the pathology of the teeth, and maxillary bones. The regular inspection being aided by these pictures would simplify the task of explaining the dental hygiene and the necessity of observing it daily, in order to benefit the health. At the same time there should be introduced in the program of examinations questions on the subject of this branch of hygiene. It rests upon the teachers of the schools and colleges to enforce these principles by their personal examples. Besides the teachers themselves should be recommended to attend to the matter of oral hygiene in their own persons, and they should periodically remind their pupils as to the care of their mouths, and in their teaching when an occasion should present itself, should encourage among their pupils the habits of buccal hygiene. For instance, in the grammar exercises, they could dictate to their pupils sentences bearing maxims of hygiene. It is also advisable that in the boarding schools the use of the tooth-brush be made compulsory.

The services of treatment are to be given at a special clinic. The dentist will treat only those children who are appointed on that particular date. This clinic is not to operate more than once a week in order not to interfere with the children's studies. The dentist commissioned with this service is to give only those treatments designed by the inspecting dentist at the day of each appointment.

These treatments are confined to obdurations and oral prophylaxis, and are to be free of charge.

But in many instances the school discipline, however excellent it may be, does not give the expected results. This is due to influence that predominates at the home, and being the case, it is earnestly hoped that the parents will carry out this reform in the privacy of the home.

Being aware of the influence that the press possesses over all social classes of the country, and the great assistance that it can and should lend in behalf of all good propaganda, the Odontologic Association of Peru is making request of the editors of the daily and periodical press to use their recognized power in favor of dental hygiene.

With this purpose in view, it is asked of all editors not to miss any occasion of publishing brief editorials, such as articles having an educating tendency on this subject, and in a general way to make known to our people the advances that are taking place in other countries.

The Odontological Association will periodically hold, through some of its members, conferences on buccal hygiene in all the public schools of the Capital, with the object of illustrating for the public and spreading the sentiment of the good attained through dental hygiene in respect to general health.

In countries worthy of imitating, because of their culture, such as Germany, England, France and the United States, these teachings are improving from generation to generation the moral spirit of the people to such a degree as to train them to a spontaneously applied and practical hygienic ideal.

In an essay I shall present this year to the Pan-American Medical Congress, to be held in Lima in next November, I shall state a certain number of means, especially suitable to our country in relation to scholastic dental hygiene, which, though they may not give immediate results, will no doubt do so in the near future.

The Government of my country, with a clear understanding of the subject upon which a group of our professional men are bent, as I have stated the propaganda of buccal hygiene, will certainly not hesitate to offer a solid encouragement in favor of the innovation we have already proposed, and which has arisen out of a desire for the welfare and healthfulness of the people, and which should not be subjected to unreasonable delay. The Government is called upon to give vigorous support in this already initiated reform.

The labor, the undismayed perseverance, the lively interest displayed by our profession in this direction, should be recognized by prompt action and not be nullified through any needless and wearying postponement.

Fortunately the destinies of Peru are controlled by a man of solid talent and preparation, Mr. Guillermo Billinghurst, and the Department of Education has as head Mr. Justo Perez Figuerola, of clear intelligence and strong will, whose name is well known in this country. Both names are the best of guarantees for the success of our beneficent campaign.

THE DENTAL PHASE OF SCHOOL HYGIENE AND OF PUBLIC HEALTH PROBLEMS

BY

HOMER C. BROWN

It is a distinct privilege to contribute in any way to the success of the Fourth International Congress on School Hygiene and especially so in the dual capacity as the representative of the National Dental Association and the Ohio State Board of Health. In my opinion this should be the most important Congress ever held in this or any other country, as it should mark the beginning of a new era in our educational system whereby the body and mind may be developed in unison.

For centuries the development of the mind has naturally received first consideration, but as civilization has advanced the child's opportunities for physical development have been very greatly reduced. To-day the necessity for intellectual development is better appreciated than ever before and likewise the conserving and developing of the physical child is receiving such attention that many recognize it to be quite as important to develop the body as to educate the mind.

Nothing is so stimulating in the progress, standing and happiness of a nation as a healthy and educated people and their status in civilization and society is thus largely determined. Therefore, our most important responsibility should be to bring about better health and educational conditions for the present which will automatically create greatly improved conditions for the future. In classifying the factors responsible for this progress, we would head the list with health and immediately follow with education.

We must assume that the individual is the unit of society, and each community should endeavor to establish and maintain the highest possible percentage of effective and productive units. It should not require any very strong argument to establish the fact that nothing so completely disturbs the equilibrium of the individual, or so wholly disarranges all plans, as sickness. Sickness and happiness are incompatible terms, and the chances for progress, except under extraordinary circumstances, are very greatly reduced. Education without health avails little, but education fortified by a rugged constitution means much in the upbuilding of the home, the municipality, the state and the nation. Thus, the emphazing of every possible precaution to prevent disease, rather than to cure it, is strictly in accord with all humanitarian principles and economic policies and this becomes more essential in thickly populated centers. Guilt is personal, but preventable diseases are social problems and are due to social offenses.

The physician may successfully treat a child through some serious illness and finally restore it to as nearly a healthy condition as is possible, and this service and skill is worthy of unlimited praise. The dentist may restore lost tooth structure to as nearly a normal and useful state as his skill will permit, and this too is worthy of commendation. But who will deny that the greatest service that could have been rendered in either case, would have been to have so surrounded both with conditions which would have prevented such diseases, since through them efficiency has been perceptibly lessened. "An ounce of prevention is worth a pound of cure," is an appropriate expression and of general application, but the writer is strongly in favor of revising this to meet present day requirements and is in sympathy with increasing the ratio, in favor of prevention, one hundred fold. Therefore, the supreme effort of the physician, the dentist, the school and health authorities and all others interested in progress, should be to prevent rather than to cure and until this principle is a recognized part of our educational system, we will not have discharged our full responsibility to our fellowman in developing an intellectual and physical race.

Assuming that education is compulsory in all countries, and that the age of entrance to the public school is at six years, I am impressed with the fact that the child enters upon school life at an age when it is a very easy matter to establish certain principles and to create a system of self-preservation and development that will not only aid in its educational advancement, but will go far in better equipping it for its life work. In many instances children enter school from homes where unfavorable environment has played a conspicuous part. Through force of circumstances it is often seemingly necessary for parents to neglect many things that would be advantageous to their children, and they like others more favorably situated, follow the line of least resistance. Therefore, when such a child reaches the school age and receives initial instruction in hygienic questions, which has been wholly disregarded in its home life, it is not only quite susceptible to such teaching, but if this is explained in a thoroughly practical and interesting manner the child becomes enthused and takes home these new ideas and much good may be accomplished therefrom.

The teacher has a grave responsibility and wields a very potent influence, and in view of this, we are prompted to say that the teaching profession is generally underpaid and not at all times fully appreciated. The teacher may emphasize the same instruction that has been given at home and the child is much more favorably impressed and takes an entirely different view of the question from that time on. For instance, a child may give little attention to a parent's direction as to the care of its face, teeth and hair, but if the teacher should in some sympathetic way make like suggestions, the child is far more responsive. We frequently hear a mother tell of her troubles in having Robert or Mary brush their teeth before going to school, but suppose a primary teacher should ask the question: how many present brushed their teeth before coming to school this morning? Do you not suppose those who had neglected this part of their toilet, and had tooth brushes, would give this more attention the following morning?

School hygiene, systematically and effectively applied, will do much towards instilling in the youth of to-day, the men and women of to-morrow, the benefits to be derived by observing at least ordinary hygienic precautions. Further, I am fully convinced that by intelligent use and care of the teeth, there is no single phase of hygiene which is so readily under individual control and where personal effort will produce such substantial results. Dr. William Osler is credited with saying: "There is not one single thing more important to the public in the whole range of hygiene than oral hygiene."

In this connection, I will quote from a paper entitled, "Dental Inspection in Public Schools," which I wrote some three years ago, as follows: "Two factors are largely responsible for the unhygienic conditions existing in the mouths of so many school children. First, ignorance on the part of the parents of the true existing conditions, as well as ignorance of the importance of observing hygienic precaution in this particular. Second, fear of pain in having many of these diseased conditions corrected. Both of these can very largely be eliminated by regular examination of the teeth of the school children, of from six to fifteen years of age and the necessary treatment of the unhealthy conditions thus found, together with an outlined course of instruction in oral hygiene in the public schools. In my opinion, the item of expense plays little or no part, except with indigent families and provision should be made for these, as I am fully convinced that parents would make any reasonable sacrifice, if necessary, to correct such unhealthy conditions if they fully appreciated what such neglect meant to the child and realized by so doing that they would save it from unnecessary future suffering."

From data collected in New York by the Russell Sage Foundation, under the head of Physical Defects and School Progress, one-half of the school children examined are credited with having seriously defective teeth and it states that on an average it requires one-half year of additional school work, of such individuals, to complete the eight grades. These data were compiled some five years ago when dental diseases were not receiving such careful consideration as to-day, and were largely the deduction of medical and school authorities.

Therefore, the Dental Phase of School Hygiene and of Public Health Problems is certainly worthy of the most careful consideration in formu_ lating any policies better to safeguard the health interest of our people. This has only recently been receiving anything like the consideration that its importance justifies, but if only of brief history, the opening chapter has been written, and the relation of oral hygiene to health and disease is so definitely established that all who run may read and benefit thereby.

The individual with sound teeth and healthy gums is particularly well fortified to resist many of the infectious diseases which may be responsible, directly or indirectly, for a long list of systemic disturbances which tend greatly to reduce the power of resistance and makes for inefficiency instead of efficiency. It matters not whether this inefficiency is in a pupil in the public schools, who is unable to do the regular school work, or whether it be in an adult in the discharge of some specific duty, which provides sustenance for one or more. The result is the same; failure, or at least partial failure. With the school child, the inability to make a passing grade and merit advancement means another year or two of school work. With the adult, no advancement and some_ times loss of position, since there is always a disposition to replace an inefficient employee with an efficient one.

Dental caries is the most prevalent of all diseases, but it is generally recognized that if a normal tooth can be kept scrupulously clean that it will not decay. We are very conservative in stating that three-fourths of the oral diseases can be eliminated if an absolutely hygienic condition of the mouth can be established and maintained, but we appreciate that it will require a great deal of personal and professional care to accomplish this. However, the nearer we approach this condition with both the temporary and permanent teeth, the better have we discharged our duty to ourselves and the nearer have we approached immunity in this particular. Dental diseases occur largely through neglect. An unclean mouth is a diseased one, even though there are modifications of such disease. "Cleanliness is next to godliness," and no exception should be made of the mouth.

It is quite important that the tooth brush be used in a manner to cleanse the teeth rather than as a means of packing particles of food between them, as is so frequently done by the ordinary process of brushing. All surfaces should be carefully cleansed and the final brushing should be in the direction of the long axis of the teeth, with a rotary movement from the gums to the incisal and occlusal surfaces, or in plainer terms, the exposed or free ends. Particular care should be taken not to brush the reverse of this, since more or less recession of the gums can be attributed to brushing too vigorously against the gum margins. The careful use of dental floss is beneficial in removing remaining particles of food from between the teeth and detecting rough margins of fillings or approaching caries. Quill tooth picks are also useful in removing such food particles, especially when impinging upon the gum tissue, but the use of the ordinary blunt wood tooth pick frequently does more harm than good and metal picks have but few advocates. The habit of some in trimming a match for a tooth pick, or chewing matches, is a practice which should be strongly condemned, since the liability to phosphorus necrosis, in this manner, is not to be wholly disregarded.

Carrying out the details of the dental toilet in the manner described, better insures the removal of any debris which may have lodged in the interproximal spaces, either from being forced there by the process of mastication or by a careless procedure in brushing the teeth. The ideal standard in establishing and maintaining hygienic oral conditions would be to cleanse the mouth and teeth after each meal, as well as just before retiring and the first thing in the morning. This may seem too idealistic and exacting, but results will be in proportion to our approach to such a standard. This should be done for the same reason that you would insist upon having clean table service for each meal. The tongue should receive attention in many instances, especially in the morning, and this can be accomplished by the use of a tongue scraper or the tooth brush may be utilized as a substitute with some benefit. The use of a good tooth powder or paste in connection with the foregoing will be advantageous and if the tissues of the mouth are much inflamed a mouth wash should be used as per direction of the dentist.

Civilization brings us many blessings and opportunities, yet statistics are in evidence to show that health deteriorates as the race becomes more civilized. This deterioration is especially conspicuous in the teeth. According to Dr. Karl Rose, only about two per cent. of Eskimos have carious teeth, ten to twenty per cent. of American Indians and Malays, about forty per cent. of Chinese, and eighty to ninety-six per cent. of Europeans and Americans. From these statistics, which are supported by other forceful evidence, we are led to believe that habit and mode of living have a distinct bearing upon the individual physically. The fact that it is necessary for those less civilized to use their teeth more vigorously accounts for a much smaller percentage of defective teeth, as vigorous use in mastication is the normal method of cleansing. As civilization advances the arrangement and structure of the teeth more or less deviate from the original types and food is so differently prepared that it does not bring them into such vigorous use; this very largely accounts for the marked increase in dental diseases.

Development depends upon proper nutrition and systematic exercise;

this forcibly applies to the teeth, the alveolar process and all contiguous tissues, which is brought about naturally by thorough mastication. This thorough mastication also excites the necessary secretion of saliva which performs its function in the process of digestion and nutrition, and therefore, mastication is the first and most important step in nutri. tion. Indigestion and malnutrition can very definitely be traced to imperfect mastication which may result from a number of causes, namely: Carious and abscessed teeth, loss of teeth, impacted teeth, malocclusion and pyorrhea aveolaris. Any of these conditions may very materially interfere with thorough mastication and insalivation and tend to lower the general resistance, which opens the way for many infectious and general systematic diseases, the direct origin of which may never be suspected by the patient, the physician or the dentist. The presence of any of these conditions, which in any way interferes with mastication, likewise interferes with development of the parts referred to and makes "bolters" of those thus handicapped. This naturally calls for additional work from other organs.

The mouth is the natural port of entry for everything that sustains life, except the air we breathe and there is, unfortunately, a disposition by some to use it instead of the nose for this purpose. Proper use of the mouth and teeth develops the face and plays an important part in the development of the system generally. The chewing of gum is not an aesthetic pastime, but it gives exercise to the muscles of mastication and the tissues of the mouth and acts as a cleansing agent to the surfaces of the teeth, and in this way serves a purpose. We all understand that if an arm be bandaged to the side and kept there for a sufficient length of time the muscles will become so atrophied that its use will be practically lost.

The Ohio State Board of Health is preparing to take systematically up a plan of public health education, and in this the dental phase will receive due consideration. At the last session of the Legislature, $40,000 was appropriated to be expended under the direction of the State Board of Health in this educational health work, covering a period of two years. The principal object in view is to combat the ravages of tuberculosis and other communicable diseases, but several other features will be incorporated with a view to educating our citizens in better safe-guarding themselves against preventable diseases. This campaign will be conducted by persons well qualified for the work with lectures, moving picture films, stereopticon, models, charts, etc.

From a dental phase we will endeavor to show the close relation of the oral cavity to health and disease and to impress upon all that the proper use and care of the teeth and mouth will do much towards fortifying the individual against disease. We hope to impress upon parents the ill effects of thumb and tongue sucking, adenoids, enlarged tonsils and associated mouth breathing, and in this manner educate and encourage them to take every precaution in controlling such habits and correcting such deformities.

We feel fortunate in Ohio in having a chief executive who is capable, progressive, industrious and courageous and one who recognizes the child as an asset and wants its interests conserved on the same basis that protection is given to property rights.   Just prior to his inauguration a health conference was called, at his instigation, to outline progressive health legislation and the results of this conference had his full approval and loyal support.   We also have a School Survey Commission actively engaged in investigating existing conditions to the end that our school system may be improved.   In a recent address Governor James M. Cox said: "The expense to the nation from deaths that need not occur has been calculated at eight times the loss from flood and fire.   Should the prevention of that be in politics?"   He further said, "We are coming to realize that this is a new era, when humanity stands before property.   The political wall is growing lower and regard for human rights is growing higher."

The benefit of such executive influence and of this Congress will increase just in proportion to the earnestness and thoroughness with which these general policies are received and advocated by school and health authorities and supported by the laity.   It has very appropriately been said, *"The health of the people is the supreme law."*

THE TOOTH TOILET ARTICLE IN ITS RELATION TO MOUTH HYGIENE EDUCATION

BY

T. W. McFADDEN

To teach, two minds must work simultaneously. If the child's mind is not in a receptive mood the child is not being taught and the teacher is not teaching. So the all-important thing is to get the child's mind in a receptive mood.

We might compare this to the cranking of an automobile. You might crank your head off if you did not have the spark plug in place, even if the carburetor and batteries were all right and you had a supply of gasoline; but put your spark plug in place and your engine will respond. The dental toilet articles in the above instance is the spark plug.

If you simply hand the tooth paste to the child without any obligation attached to it or without the child having to make any effort to obtain it you have done as much harm as good. You have failed to make the spark.

Through the whole mouth hygiene movement the dental toilet articles, when intelligently used, are the spark plugs and they, in a marked degree, make the difference between teaching and talking mouth hygiene to or at children.

You will agree with me that through the whole educational movement the efforts of the teacher are a success or a failure just in proportion as the child's mind is in a receptive or non-receptive mood, and the expense of educating the child is reduced just in proportion as we are able to remove or supply the thing that prevents the child's mind from becoming in a non-receptive mood. Toothache, for instance, and the train of troubles caused by neglected teeth and undeveloped dental arches, are very potent in increasing the expense of educating the child.

I believe that the dental toilet articles rightly used are very potent factors in mouth hygiene education, and if handled intelligently, will make the difference between the success and failure of the mouth hygiene movement.

The demand for dental toilet articles is or *should be* largely created by the dental profession, and it would only seem just that the dental profession should utilize the dental toilet articles to further the mouth hygiene movement for the benefit of humanity.

a tooth brush or dentifrice. If this could be increased to 50% or
it would mean a big increase in the sale of dental toilet articles.
ever increase is made along these lines depends greatly upon the
of persons interested in mouth hygiene and it would seem onl
that these efforts were turned into dollars for the benefit of the s
child.

With this thought in mind experimental work has been cond
in my home town with very gratifying results.

If mouth hygiene—clean mouths—is what we are after I thin
plan we have been using with some modifications to suit a na
movement will accomplish what we are after.

PUBLIC SCHOOL DENTAL CLINICS A POSSIBILITY IN EACH COMMUNITY

A Practical Plan of Securing and Maintaining Them

BY

W. G. EBERSOLE

I have the honor upon this occasion of representing the National Mouth Hygiene Association, an organization which was formed for the purpose of spreading the mouth hygiene propaganda so that the American people might be led to know and understand the importance that mouth hygiene bears to the general hygiene of the body.

This organization was formed for the purpose of permitting all people who are interested in this important subject to coöperate in the interest of humanity.

While it is the purpose of the organization to deal with the problem as a whole, we have found it necessary to divide the work into a number of divisions, placing each under a department of its own.

One of the most important divisions of the work is that which deals with the establishment of dental clinics, hospitals or dentariums, where proper care and treatment may be afforded those who are unable to care for themselves; providing not only dental service but furnishing tooth toilet articles which will enable the poor to take care of the "gateway" to the human system in a manner which will permit of the highest development from a physical standpoint.

It is my mission upon this occasion to state that after years of experimentation and investigation we are able to come before this body with the statement that we have evolved a practical plan for the establishment and maintenance of school dental clinics in the various communities throughout the United States.

It is the purpose of the National Mouth Hygiene Association to not only establish dental clinics for the care and treatment of the worthy poor, but to raise an endowment fund sufficient to guarantee the successful operation of these clinics indefinitely.

It is impossible in the length of time allotted for papers to be presented in connection with this Congress to enter into a full and complete explanation of the methods to be employed by the National Mouth Hygiene Association in establishing these clinics.

In a nut shell, we will state that the National Mouth Hygiene Association's campaign embraces all that is good in the great campaigns which have dotted this country with beautiful Y. M. C. A. buildings, and also all that is good in the great money raising campaigns that have made it possible to build hospitals, establish dispensaries and erect many of the great philanthropic institutions that flourish in every part of the universe.

Our campaign embraces all that has meant success in these or other money raising campaigns and in addition it embraces a feature which if employed alone would result in the successful raising of funds to meet the work we are undertaking.

Our campaigns are waged in the interest of the school child and therefore the school child is the hub of the campaign.

The Young Men's Christian Associations are established for the purpose of saving the souls of young men.

Hospitals and philanthropic institutions are for the healing of the sick, the relieving of the wounded, or the care of those who are physically unable to care for themselves.

Worthy institutions these, and I would that we had more of them; but great as is the cause in which these institutions have been erected, greater still is that for which the National Mouth Hygiene Association has been formed.

The National Mouth Hygiene Association stands for the removal of the shackles that are binding the school children down to sin, sickness and death by forcing them into schools where they are surrounded by conditions which, if we accept the statement of the Michigan State Board of Health, is destroying 27.6% of the public school teachers, who preside over these children, from tuberculosis, which is only one of the many diseases that are destroying thousands of lives annually.

The Association is not interested alone in the school child but in the teaching profession as well, and it does not stop there. It is interested in the health, strength, and working efficiency of every individual in the universe.

But for the present we must deal with the school child and those interested in its welfare.

The work of the Association is educational, and it employs the four greatest educational institutions: The Public School, the Public Press, the Public Platform and the Motion Picture. The greatest of these is the public school, and it is through the school child that we hope to accomplish most.

It is for this purpose that the Association has undertaken to establish dental clinics in the schools of the country.

The national body is not interested in the dental clinic except as an educational feature. The local auxiliary on the other hand is inter-es̈ted in both the educational feature and in the benefit that it will do the community.

The clinic cares for the indigent, dealing with the few. The National Mouth Hygiene movement must deal with all the people, the rich, the poor, and those of the middle class. All walks of life need mouth hygiene instruction.

Therefore, in the employment of the campaign for raising funds, the plan embraces a method and system which will bring to every indi-vidual in the community an invitation to become a part of and contribute to this great movement in the interest of the health, strength, and working efficiency of humanity.

Working in the interest of the school child we work through the school children and a message is carried to every individual in the city and through them an invitation is extended to the individual to become a part of the great movement which has for its purpose the production of healthier and stronger American citizens.

The first move necessary to secure the coöperation of the National Mouth Hygiene Association in your local work is the formation of a local auxiliary to that body in your community.

In accomplishing this end the interested party will find in the early stages that the people most willing to coöperate will be the dentists, physicians and school teachers, and it is from these professions that the foundations must be secured for a successful local auxiliary.

Following the organization of the local auxiliary an application must be filed with the Secretary-Treasurer of the National body, request-ing the installation of a publicity campaign in the community in which such auxiliary was formed. Applications will be filed and acted upon in the order received.

When the Association is ready to operate in any given community the preliminary publicity work will be directed by one of the officers of the National Mouth Hygiene Association, who will visit the city where the campaign is to be conducted in advance of the field secretary, and it will be his purpose to arouse public interest through the news-papers, from the public platform, and in other educational ways.

That some definite idea may be had as to the manner in which the public interest may be aroused will say that these officials will cause bacterial tests to be made in public places, such as school buildings, street cars, theatres, etc.

He will also make tests in the mouths of the school children, steril-izing mouths and then employing gauze masks, transferring the children and then exposing them in the various public places for the purpose of showing how quickly the sterile mouth may become infected and the various kinds of bacteria that will be found in these mouths after a few minutes exposure in public places.

Following this will be a period in which the Association employs newspaper advertising.

At this time the Association will send into the field a professional organizer, whose business it will be to raise the money to secure a clinic and endow it for an indefinite period of time.

The preliminary work that this organizer must do is to secure the support and coöperation of the health and educational authorities in the community. The coöperation and support of all municipal and civic organizations must be secured.

Following this the teaching profession of the community must be organized and their support and coöperation obtained.

When this has been done we are ready to start with the financial campaign. This will cover a period of a week of active work.

It is utterly impossible for me to go into full details relative to the organizing and conducting of such a campaign. Let me say, however, that in addition to the solicitation of large contributions the local auxiliary, which has the work in charge, will endeavor to raise a large percentage of this money by waging the strongest kind of a campaign for membership; the dues to be turned into the general fund.

The membership in the local auxiliary is composed of two classes: "contributing members" and "working members." The first class is composed of those members who make contributions of $1.00 or more. The second class is composed of those who are not able to make financial contribution but are willing to devote a definite amount of time to the work of the Association in carrying out its plans and policies in the community.

To the latter class belongs the school child in whose interest the campaign is conducted.

Working in the interest of the school child of the community the plan embraces, insofar as practical, the employment of the school children as workers in the field.

The younger children will be used in the distribution of a booklet and other educational matter, making a strong appeal for support of the movement.

The booklet used will be entitled the "Cry of the Shackled Child— A Plea to Aid Mentally Crippled School Children, Whose Proper Development is Held Back by Bad Teeth and Unhealthy Mouths."

This booklet will contain a strong appeal that cannot fail to reach the heart and create a deep interest in the success of the work undertaken.

For the purpose of giving you some idea of the contents of a booklet of this kind I beg to quote the following extract, which is taken from the inside of the front cover:

"THIS booklet has been placed in your hands by a school child. In justice to your juvenile friends and relatives, the least you can do is to read it.

"Educators, clergymen, civic workers, city officials and all other public.spirited citizens have approved the movement it promotes.

"At any rate, it will present some facts to you that will surprise you and take only a few minutes of your time in reading it.

"In a few days you will be called upon to aid this great work by becoming a mem. ber of the National Mouth Hygiene Association's local auxiliary. You can help ma. terially by giving the young solicitor courteous attention. If you cannot see your way clear to join the children, at least do not dishearten the child who calls upon you by an abrupt or harsh rebuff. He is working for humanity and certainly deserves encouragement."

This booklet explains fully the purpose of the campaign and the need of coöperation.

A day or two following the distribution of these booklets an older child calls soliciting membership in the local auxiliary, collecting the fee of $1.00, and issuing a membership card which, in addition to calling for educational literature contains a coupon which, when presented at any drug store in the city, entitles the bearer to a full "dollar's worth of tooth toilet articles."

The booklet which has been distributed explains to the individual, whom the child solicits, that the National Mouth Hygiene Association has placed in operation a plan which makes it possible for its local auxiliaries, that are conducting campaigns, to buy and place in the hands of their members packages of the highest grade of tooth toilet articles, which ordinarily retail for $1.00, and by the transaction be able to set aside 50% of the membership fees for the endowment and maintenance of dental clinics.

These membership packages contain four large tubes or boxes of tooth paste or powder, such as ordinarily retail at 25 cents per tube or box.

These "four-tube" or "four-box" packages are supplied to local auxiliaries in a manner which enables them to place same in the hands of the druggist at a cost of about 40 cents per package. The druggist is allowed 10 cents per package for reclaiming the membership coupons. This makes the "$1.00 membership package," delivered to the member cost the local auxiliary 50 cents.

The new member, for the $1.00 paid, receives a full membership in the local auxiliary and a "$1.00's worth of tooth toilet articles," and by the transaction places in the hands of the local auxiliary the profit which otherwise goes to the manufacturer of tooth toilet articles. In this case the profit amounts to 50 cents on the $1.00 and is retained in the community and devoted to endowing and maintaining school clinics.

The National Association has also arranged a plan whereby the same tooth toilet articles may be supplied through the regular commercial channels on a basis which will enable the community to reap the benefit of the profit from such sales.

This is done by the placing in the carton of each 25-cent package a metal disc, which when collected by the local auxiliary, entitles that organization to collect 5 cents for each disc, to be used in its local work or in maintaining dental clinics.

The difference between the profit accruing to the auxiliary from the "$1.00 membership package" and the four 25-cent packages sold through regular trade represents the difference between supplying large quantities to the local auxiliaries at cost and the commercial and overhead charges in handling these goods through the regular commercial channels.

This is a coöperative method which permits the people in a community to turn the profit that now goes to the tooth toilet manufacturers of the country into a local fund for the purpose of not only establishing school dental clinics and other clinics, but supplying tooth toilet articles to the poor of the community. Such a plan would enable these individuals to have at their command methods and means to care for themselves in a manner which would permit them to reap the benefits of healthy mouth conditions and thus remove the possibility of their becoming a public menace through neglect or inability to care for the mouth properly.

In order to give some idea of the tremendous profit that accrues from the manufacture and sale of these articles, I wish to say that some of the leading manufacturers have been and are paying as much as from five to seven thousand dollars an issue for the back cover page of some of the most popular magazines.

I can readily understand that immediately within the mind of the skeptic or doubter there arises the question of graft or the attempt to advertise some tooth toilet article; but I wish to announce to the world at large that the plan has been drawn and safeguarded in such a manner as to make it absolutely impossible for anyone associated with the National Mouth Hygiene Association or any of its auxiliaries to receive one penny of profit or graft from the transaction.

I wish also to state in the most emphatic terms that no manufacturer of tooth toilet articles is directly or indirectly interested in the promotion of this plan.

There are four things which have led to the adoption of the plan herein suggested.

First. The need of funds to carry on the work of the Association in the various communities.

Second. The success attained in raising funds for Y. M. C. A. buildings, hospitals, dispensaries, etc.

Third. The popularity and success attained in raising funds through the sale of Red Cross stamps.

Fourth. The fact that the National Mouth Hygiene Association's Campaign is unique in that every effort put forth to educate the public as to the importance of mouth hygiene creates a demand for tooth toilet articles.

In adopting the plan for supplying tooth toilet articles as herein outlined, the Association has combined the raising of funds and the supplying of a need; and it is believed that this feature will become as popular and more effective than the Red Cross stamp feature of the Anti-Tuberculosis League.

In conclusion let me say that the whole success of the plans and policies mentioned herein depends both upon the employment of thoroughly competent experts in the different lines of work and upon the presentation of the matter in a way which will convince the public that this is absolutely a philanthropic and economic proposition.

The National Mouth Hygiene Association has undertaken to do this work in the interest of humanity and it guarantees that every step taken and every act committed will bear the most rigid inspection and investigation; for upon the honesty of purpose and purity of action must rest not only the success of the scheme but the good name of the Association and those associated with it.

SESSION THIRTY-ONE

Room D.   Friday, August 29th, 9 A.M.

SYMPOSIUM ON SCHOOL FEEDING (Part One)

Arranged by School Lunch Committee of the American Home
Economics Association,

MRS. LOUISE STEVENS BRYANT, *Secretary*

CAROLINE C. HUNT, *Chairman*

MRS. LUCIEN HOWE, Buffalo, N. Y., *Vice-Chairman*

Program on Nutrition and Malnutrition in Childhood and Youth

IRA S. WILE, M.D., Member of the Board of Education, New York
City. "Medical Inspection and the Nutrition of School
Children."

HELEN MACMURCHY, M.D., Toronto, Canada. "Malnutrition and
Mental Defectives." (Manuscript not supplied.)

JOHN AULDE, M.D., Philadelphia, Pa. "Special Studies in Correlation
of Malnutrition and Disease."

MRS. LOUISE STEVENS BRYANT, In Charge of the Social Service Department, Psychological Clinic, University of Pennsylvania, Philadelphia, Pa. "History and Present Status of the School Feeding
Movement."

EDWIN A. LOCKE, M.D., Boston, Mass. "The Nutrition of Anemic
and Tuberculous Children."

MARGARET MCMILLAN, London, England. "National Conservation
and Nutrition During Childhood."

MEDICAL INSPECTION AND THE NUTRITION OF SCHOOL CHILDREN

BY

IRA S. WILE

If we approach the problem of school lunches and medical inspection with a consciousness that they are interdependent and coöperating to secure the same end, we shall better appreciate their educational importance. Both are designed to act in a preventive and curative way in all phases of physical and mental health. Medical inspection seeks in part to eliminate contagious diseases from the public schools, while school lunches aim to increase the resistance of children to contagious diseases. Medical inspection seeks out physical and mental defects; school lunches aim to prevent or relieve physical or mental defects. The common ground of school lunches and medical inspection might well be said to be the prevention, determination, and relief of malnutrition.

Medical inspection as related to the public school system makes note of many symptoms which are apparent among the children, but all too frequently fails to get down to the factors responsible for them. Preventive medicine demands a knowledge of causes in order to assure efficient prophylaxis. The personal equations of the medical examiners and their lack of judgment in differentiating the significant defects render most of the available statistics of little analytical value.

There is a noteworthy ratio between physical defects and school progress; in brief, the more defects, the slower the advance in school. The relation between physical defects and malnutrition has not been fully established—nor indeed has adequate study been given to. the question of school progress and nutrition. Some educators are beginning to appreciate the importance of good nutrition among school children as a prerequisite to securing attendance, attention and apperception. As Bacon states, "The brain is in some sort in the custody of the stomach."

During the early years of school life nutrition may suffer owing to incorrect adjustments to school life. A late and hurried breakfast, or after oversleeping a rush to school without any food followed later by a bolted lunch may be manifested in loss of weight and supervening pallor.

During the years 8 to 10 metabolic activity is decreased. This resting period requires especial care as physical resistance may decline while susceptibility to infectious diseases increases.

The metamorphosing years before puberty tax nutrition, and the malnourished child requires a longer period of time for this most im-portant development. Consequently there may be evidence of asthenia and enfeeblement to the watchful medical inspector.

Physical training takes cognizance of the general development of the children, and even goes so far as to give marks for posture, chinning, and other exercises. Motor training, however, is not merely muscular, but involve stimuli for whose prompt action good nutrition is essential. Endurance is not independent of food, and the physical training of children of the elementary schools requires for the successful development of the children an abundant, varied, and sufficient food supply.

It is most striking that lunches are now being supplied for curative purposes to cripples, anemic, tuberculous, and other subnormal children after the medical inspector has called attention to the physical deterioration of the children. These efforts to better nutrition have been accompanied by a reduction in physical and mental defects together with a marked advancement in mental and moral progress. It is all well and good to supply abnormal children with food and fresh air, as well as the mental pabulum, but it seems more rational to give the same opportunity for the preservation of health to the normal children instead of placing a premium upon ill health. In every community there are many poorly fed children, the inadequacy of whose diet is shown in part as anemia, underweight, enlarged glands, and similar symptoms. Malnutrition is a factor, though to be sure not the only one, in the etiology of tuberculosis, adenitis (enlarged glands), anemia, defects in vision, mental defects, chorea (St. Vitus Dance), protracted convalescence from diseases, and impaired resistance to infections.

The immense proportion of dental defects has been given attention without appreciating the fact that the permanent teeth develop during the school period. The importance of proper food calling for mastication for the development of dental structure has been lost sight of in contemplating the enormous number of cavities. Poor food, deficient in lime and other salts, means poor teeth and consequent decay. As the result of decay, infection and toothache, proper mastication becomes impossible, appetite decreases, malnutrition supervenes. There then results a lessened supply of food for dental growth and more decay ensues and a vicious circle is formed. General nutrition depends in part upon a good set of teeth—proper teeth demand proper food.

A second factor in malnutrition to which insufficient attention has been given, is the effect of under-nourishment before a child's entrance upon school. The relative starvation in protein, lime, iron, calcium, and magnesium during the first five years of life helps to produce the child suffering from malnutrition upon entrance to the public school. The report of the medical inspector, however, will probably class such a child as belonging to the group with such physical defects as enlarged tonsils, anemia, or enlarged glands.

Chronically underfed children are far more vulnerable to contagious diseases and more susceptible to protracted colds and bronchitis. Their poor musculature and sluggish circulation make them more likely to fall victims to the various diseases to which they are exposed through the intimacy of school life, and as a result their absences are more numerous. For the same reason their convalescence is retarded, their complications are more numerous, and their loss of education and training through absence is far greater than that of other children of the same age in a a better state of nutrition. One of the underlying factors in chorea is a disturbance of nutrition. The New York Committee on the Physical Welfare of School Children found 26.2% of chorea among children suffering from malnutrition as opposed to only 3.6 per cent. for 1,400 children examined by them.

The purpose of school lunches is not to relieve acute hunger, but to relieve chronic underfeeding. Hogarth has defined malnutrition as "an abnormal or disordered growth in the development of the tissues and organs of a child's body not necessarily synonymous with underfeeding," and he wisely states: "Malnutrition is at once the most common, and until recently, the least observed of all the unrecognized diseases and affections among children attending elementary schools." The problem of malnutrition is not concerned merely with the breakfastless children or those without any particular single meal, but with all the children who for long periods of time are receiving at home a dietary that is not adapted to their needs, and in consequence of which there is marked physical deterioration.

Dr. McMillan of Chicago found 15.9% kindergarten children physically below par and estimated that underfeeding was the cause of 11% in kindergartens and 7.8% in other grades. Dr. MacKenzie regards one-third of all the school children in Edinburgh as poorly nourished. Dr. Maxwell is reported as saying to the National Educational Association in 1904 that there are hundreds of thousands of children unable to learn because of hunger. Dr. Francis Warner and Hack Tuke found 28.5% of London school children suffering from deficient feeding. The New York Committee on the Physical Welfare of School Children in 1907 declared 13% of 990 children examined to be suffering from malnutrition, and Dr. Sill in 1909 estimated that 40% of the children in the elementary schools of New York City were illy nourished. The New York School Lunch Committee in 1910 in an examination of 2,150 children adjudged 13% to be marked cases of malnutrition. In Chicago in 1908, of over 10,000 children examined, 12% were reported as suffering from malnutrition. In Boston, in 1909 underfeeding was found in

16% of over 5,000 children. In Philadelphia, 24% of 500 children examined were found to be suffering from underfeeding. In St. Paul in 1910, 20% of 3,200 children in schools in the poorer districts were reported as manifesting the evidences of marked underfeeding.

What does all this underfeeding mean? It means that the problem of nutrition has been neglected. I admit that the causes of under-nourishment are numerous and closely connected with faulty housing, overcrowding, low wages, under-employment, alcoholism, poor hygiene, and ignorance of food values. The first step in the problem is the determination of malnutrition. The potentialities of educational measures may be regarded as dependent upon the state of nutrition. Lord Dufferin has remarked that "our mental functions, our memories, our attention, our power of continuous application are even more dependent for vigor and vitality on the general condition of our health than is the play of our muscles."

The symptoms of malnutrition which have been overlooked are noted as anemia, pallor, muscular weakness, squints, diseases of the external eye, lassitude, inattention, backwardness, and mental dullness. Among the results are stunted growth, delayed physical and mental development, weaknesses of the spine, increased susceptibility to infectious diseases, and marked liability to tuberculosis. Twenty-five per cent. of our public school children fail to attend school 75% of the time. Preventable disease is a large factor in this unfortunate number of absences, and malnutrition plays no small part in preparing the soil for such preventable diseases.

Medical inspection of children under twelve years is of the utmost importance in order to safeguard physical development at puberty. To neglect the state of nutrition during the early years of school life is to cast aside an opportunity of protecting the growing child from the strains and stresses of puberty against which the nervous system should be well fortified.

Puberty is a period of general acceleration of growth. There is an increase of height, of weight, of strength; there is a modification of the nervous system with the development of the emotional side of the child's nature, and a susceptibility to impressions such as occurs at no other period of life. In addition to this, puberty forms the period of the development of the sexual characteristics which bring to bear upon educational problems all the variations that may come from the dominance of sexual emotions and the manifestations of sexual development. Physical education must embrace more than a question of muscles; it involves brains, sex life, and general stability. It is not a question as to whether a muscle is hard or soft, or short or long, or thin or broad, but it is a question as to the general physical efficiency of the child, and this involves its mental as well as the ordinarily termed physical attributes. The opportunity to affect the pubertal development of the children is given only during the pubertal period, and this represent the period of greatest activity of the schools.

Gershel has demonstrated that dependent Jewish boys grow 14.86 inches from their fifth to their fifteenth year, while Bowditch shows that the Boston boys grow during the same period 20.8 inches, while according to Porter, St. Louis boys grow 18.1 inches, and the English Anthropological Committee find 21 inches to represent the boy's growth during this period of life. At five years of age the average Jewish dependent boy is 1.6 inch shorter than Boas's average; at ten and a half years he is 1.68 inch behind; at eleven and a half years 3.40 inches; at fourteen and a half years 5.58 inches, and at fifteen and a half years 7.9 inches behind the average for boys of the same age, according to Boas.

Gershel accounts for this by stating that during "the important age of puberty he had undergone many sufferings and privations at an age when freedom and proper nourishment are absolute essentials." If the home is unable to supply adequate nourishment, it is wise to extend the institution of making a food supply available in the elementary schools for the purpose of preventing the physical, mental, and often moral breakdown of the children during the period of elementary school life.

The paramount activity of the medical inspectors should be among the children entering schools for the first time. To be of maximum value medical inspection must virtually become medical supervision. The medical inspector has the marvelous opportunity of becoming an established prophylactic advisor for six, seven, or eight years to the most important part of the community, the race determiners of the next generation.

Frequent inspection is indicated because the new school environment with poor air, overstrain, excitement and worry may spend itself upon the appetite and digestion with a resultant deterioration in nutrition. The early recognition of lassitude, anemia, and irritability may be the means of preventing a marked decline in nutrition and vitality. To quote from the Report of the Poor Law Commission, 1909: "I am satisfied," writes Dr. Newman, "that much illness is prolonged quite unnecessarily, and that there is a lamentable and disastrous amount of failure to deal with the beginnings of disease. Neglect of this leads to mortality more than any other factors."

The reports of medical inspections are not uniform, as may be judged by the single fact that in 1906 malnutrition was reported in New York City as 6.3 %, while Minneapolis in 1908 reported 23.3%. It is obvious that such disproportion does not exist. This fact is accentuated by a comparison of the diseases and defects in the two cities, which are closely related to the problem of malnutrition. For example:

RELATIVE PREVALENCE OF DISEASES IN SCHOOL CHILDREN

KIND OF DISEASE	New York, 1906	Minneapolis, 1908
	Per Cent.	Per Cent.
Anterior cervical glands enlarged..............	37.3	53.0
Posterior cervical glands enlarged...............	11.0	....
Chorea..................................	1.7	0.2
Defective vision...........................	22.8	23.9
Defective teeth............................	55.0	43.5
Hypertrophied tonsils.......................	23.3	31.1
Adenoids.................................	12.0	12.8

Obviously these figures relating to the symptoms of malnutrition show that the New York figures of 1906 are too low. Statistics of medical inspection make another extremely misleading error where they are calculated in terms of the number of children examined. It is, therefore, impossible to know the exact number of defects in any one child or the relative number of children in the school population suffering from any single pathological condition.

The relation between defects of vision and malnutrition is suggested by the examinations in Cleveland in 1907 when the defects of eyesight in well-to-do districts were stated to be 32.4%, while among the children in congested districts, they were 71.7%.

Among the 20,000,000 school children of this country, Dr. T. D. Wood has estimated that 5% have spinal curvature, flatfoot, or some other moderate deformity. Even the question of flatfoot or scoliosis is not always a question of muscle, as much as it is a question of relaxation from under-nourishment. Five per cent. are said to suffer from defects of hearing, 25% from defects in vision, 30% from enlarged tonsils, adenoids or enlarged cervical glands, 50% from defective teeth, and 25% are regarded by him as suffering from malnutrition, in many cases due in part at least to one or more of the defects noted.

The relation between cause and effect may not be clear where so many varying factors are concerned; but malnutrition is not regularly considered in its causative relation. Whenever another defect is noted, malnutrition is not regarded as worthy of notation unless starvation be apparent.

In some systems of medical inspection, no attention is given to malnutrition, as where the State of Massachusetts in 1906 and 1907 reported the examination of 343,000 children having 27,342 defects, but malnutrition was not numbered among the conditions reported.

Regardless of the primary factor in malnutrition, whether it be due to a deteriorative reaction against an oppressive physical environment, or to unhygienic home conditions or to lack of adequate or sufficient food, no inspection card should be regarded as complete without some notation regarding the state of nutrition. This position is strengthened by the comment of the Chief Medical Officer of London (1910): "It is certain that malnutrition and physical defects are closely associated and react upon each other, but it is difficult to determine their exact relation to each child or to say in what degree malnutrition causes the other physical evils. Merely to increase the supply of food would in many cases not solve the complex problem of the individual child, although in many cases lack of food lies at the root of the mischief."

The relation between nutrition and medical inspection is patent. Medical inspection should be so thorough as to indicate not merely the names of various symptoms and conditions, but should suggest whether or not malnutrition could possibly be an underlying factor. Under such conditions school lunches could serve in a remedial way by raising the standard of nutrition. Frequently medical inspections reveal some children not possessing marked defects, but who are very close to the health poverty line, and for them school lunches could be instituted for prophylactic purposes. Most civilized countries have already installed school lunches as a natural and normal part of an educational movement without laying unnecessary stress upon its value as a health measure. As medical inspections are regarded as advantageous to the school system through the lessening of disease and the improvement of the mental calibre of the children, careful attention to nutrition may supply a valuable means of increasing mental activity and building up the physical health of our school children.

SPECIAL STUDIES IN THE CORRELATION OF MAL-NUTRITION AND DISEASE

BY

JOHN AULDE

Introduction. The value of the science of dietetics to the health of school children need not be emphasized. It is not my purpose to thresh over old straw, but to direct attention to certain defects in the studies which have hitherto been overlooked. While much has been accomplished through municipal and philanthropic activities, there still remain important questions relating to metabolism which have not been studied. It is not enough to inspect the milk supply, to establish dispensing stations, to conduct baby clinics, to employ visiting nurses, to instruct mothers, and give directions regarding the dangers incident to the presence of flies and other insects, because these are extrinsic questions. We are concerned to-day with questions relating to physiology and chemistry, and it is an important fact that for the most part all activities in this direction have been conducted upon traditional lines rather than with a view to determine the scientific aspect.

Incompletion of Modern Dietetics. One reason why modern dietetics is incomplete is that the toal caloric or fuel value of the various food stuffs, protein, fats and carbohydrates, is assumed to be the final stage of investigation. To estimate properly the real food needs of a child requires experimental investigation of the approximate capacity for each of these different foods, so that there will be a certain percentage of proteins, fats and carbohydrates, bringing the toal caloric value of the diet up to a certain number of food units (calories).

These principles are seldom applied in actual practice. Children are allowed to take those foods which they like, and a balanced ration in respect to mineral salts is rare. Thus, some children dislike fats; other children seem to subsist principally upon proteins, and suffer the deleterious effects arising from such a dietary. However, most children take readily to carbohydrates, and as a consequence, they lack the necessary proteins and fats, and besides, the carbohydrates alone lead to fermentation and decomposition in the intestinal tract. Along with this comes headache, sleeplessness, together with various forms of indisposition so that they must be withdrawn from school.

Usually in such cases, the child has no appetite for breakfast, because of the intestinal decomposition. The poisons formed in the intestinal tract during the night are "sucked" up by the lacteals, carried to the thoracic duct, and find their way, in solution, directly to the general circulation. Hence, the child wakes up dull, morose, inattentive, and depressed. The mother says, "Tommy can't go to school to-day, he feels too bad, and I think we'll keep him home or send him to the country." Unfortunately, this treatment is attended with dire results; Tommy goes out to play with other boys, eats candy and nuts and drinks soda water and ginger-pop, so that when night comes he has a complete chemical laboratory in his bowels in active operation.

Demand For Mineral Salts. I shall be adding nothing new to scientific literature by directing attention to the demand for mineral salts in the dietary, but it will be safe to prophesy that this question will serve in the future as a scientific searchlight on the subject of dietetics. For instance, we know or believe that phosphorus is an important mineral, and this is usually taken into account in studying disease. Because little attention has been given to the study of function and structure in connection with the presence in the dietary of magnesium and calcium (lime), I propose to devote my attention largely to this. For example, the human brain contains ten times as much magnesium as lime, while muscle structure contains three times as much magnesium as lime. However, when we come to study bone formation, we have a notable excess of calcium. Suppose for instance that we have a child suffering from intestinal indigestion and showing the symptoms previously outlined; and then suppose again that the effect of this indigestion is to deplete the lime content of the brain as well as of the muscle. Would it not follow that we should have a derangement of mentality and a physical debility characterized by loss of muscular stability? Add to this the loss of lime from the bones which would naturally follow, and we have a substantial basis to account for "softening" of the bones, bow-legs, rickets, hydrocephalus, failure in nutrition, and necessarily intestinal indigestion, with a tendency or susceptibility to acute infections, such as diphtheria, typhoid fever, influenza, and the like.

Nitrogen Equilibrium. In consequence of intestinal decomposition with the formation of indican, which has an acid reaction, along with putrefactive toxins, also acid, there is a derangement of the nitrogen equilibrium, a condition which leads to symptoms of anemia and invites tubercular infection. Because of the fermentation and decomposition, we have to contend with an excessive acidity, and this excessive acidity, carried directly to the circulation, diminishes the alkalinity of the blood and lessens its oxygen-carrying capacity. Nature provides for the temporary deficiency by drawing off nitrogen from the body fluids and tissues in the form of ammonia, evidence of this being found in the excretion of ammonia through the kidneys. We have an interest_ing and instructive demonstration of this complementary action in the case of diabetic coma, where the output of nitrogen in the form of ammonia in the urine is often six times the normal amount, while that going to form urea is twenty-five per cent less.

In addition, however, we must bear in mind that the presence of ammonia in the blood also gives rise to the presence of nitrites in the secretions, so that in every instance of intestinal decomposition with the formation of indican, bacterial toxins and nitrites, the effect upon the normal activities is apparent. And further, the condition as well as the symptomatic deviations can be demonstrated with scientific precision. In a former article,* I have quoted the experimental investigations of Sherman, Mettler and Sinclair, of Columbia University, covering their observations with an exclusive cracker diet. The subject was an adult and subsisted entirely upon crackers and water for a period of three days, during which time he lost two pounds in weight, and devel_oped the usual symptoms attending intestinal indigestion—"lack of appetite, with a feeling of fullness and thirst after meals." The most notable feature of this experiment relates to the absolute loss of mineral salts, namely, over 17 grains of lime above the intake, 2 grains of mag_nesium above the intake, while the loss of phosphorus was nearly double the amount supplied by the cracker diet. In addition should be men_tioned the excessive output of nitrogen in the form of ammonia through the kidneys, over 61 grains daily. We have, then, a demonstration showing that an unsuitable dietary, even when it furnishes the necessary amount of proteins, fats and carbohydrates, may be the means of setting up intestinal indigestion with derangement of the nitrogen equilibrium.

As a result of an unsuitable dietary, school children as well as adults, suffer constantly from intestinal fermentation and decomposition, and I have seen numerous cases of this class where treatment for anemia had been conducted for months without apparent benefit. Still, they responded immediately to the administration of suitable lime salts, carbonate, phosphate and sulphate.

In the experiments with the cracker diet, there was an unusual loss of lime, while the loss of magnesium was comparatively trifling, showing that the intestinal indigestion with the attending acid excess had caused lime depletion, and as a matter of fact, in such cases, there was replace_ment by magnesium. In other words, there was an infiltration of the magnesium which involved the tissues including nerve tissue, and thus interfered with the uninterrupted transmission of nerve impulses. The clinical fact is readily perceptible, because lime being the stronger base combines with the acid, leading to elimination, while magnesium

*The Acid Test in Therapeutics, Medical Record, June 7, 1913.

is substituted. In the case of the brain structures, for instance, we can readily understand how important is the small percentage of lime, and we can also make a rough estimate of the effects arising from its complete displacement.

In all cases where the nitrogen equilibrium is upset there are certain objective symptoms. Thus, the salivary reaction is changed in character, showing that the blood has lost its normal alkalinity; the cutaneous reaction is also notably affected; both conditions are fully confirmed by the abnormal reflexes, the knee-jerk for example. The most striking and easily demonstrable results of this unfortunate combination are first, impairment of the digestive capacity; second, acid excess, and third, magnesium infiltration.

Calcium Depletion. When we come to study the effects, somatic (physical, corporeal) and cellular, of calcium depletion, we have very little difficulty in systematizing the investigation. In the first place, we may have impairment in the development of structure; that is, the skeletal structure of the body shows deformity or failure in nutrition. In the second place, we have derangement of motility, that is, there is impaired muscular development, so that we find evidences of arrested growth or lack of vitality. Perhaps the most notable symptom arising from calcium depletion relates to impairment of function. There is very imperfect mental co-ordination or inability to maintin nerve tension. That is to say, these children seem to be alert, active, and receptive, but they fail to make any perceptible advance, because they lack the ability to remember things.

It would not be profitable in this connection to discuss the influence exerted upon the nerves by the ductless glands, for the simple reason that in all such cases where we have to deal with acid excess, the ductless glands themselves are involved. For example, in the case of goitre, we can readily trace its development to calcium depletion, and prove the assumption by administering calcium in excess. That is to say, the working hypothesis of magnesium infiltration, with involvement of the thyroid gland, is due to a chemic deviation, an excess of acid in the system; that this acid excess produces or creates depletion with the coincident or consecutive substitution of magnesium. To overcome disordered function then in a case of this character, we must employ calcium for the purpose of promoting magnesium dissociation, according to the law of mass action. Chorea is another disorder occurring in school children which is readily amenable to precisely the same treatment, and fortunately, it does not require great skill or learning to make a demonstration. Within a few days, we can note the definite changes which have taken place, by the usual methods available to all physicians, the acid test.

The Acid Test. The acid test shows the chemic deviation; the mag_nesium infiltration is the effect, and as I have shown, this may involve structure, motility and function, from its influence upon the transmission of nerve impulses.

To simplify the problem of making the acid test, let me suggest the employment of blue litmus paper to show the chemic reaction of the saliva, as well as the cutaneous reaction. The saliva is derived from the parotid, submaxillary and sublingual glands, and of course it comes from the blood, and should be alkaline or neutral in reaction. If we could test the lymph, we should find that also alkaline or neutral, and the same is true of the pancreatic secretion and the bile. Neces_sarily, the products of the ductless glands, whatever they may be, should be alkaline or neutral, because they are also derived from the blood. In other words, with the exception of the gastric fluid, all secretions incident to the upbuilding process are alkaline, while the retrograde or waste products are characterized by acid reaction, acid perspiration, acid urine and acid mucus. The exception of the acid gastric fluid seems to be a wise provision, since it tends to maintain the physiologic equilibrium by utilizing the acid. This is well illustrated in the employ_ment of the lactic acid ferment for intestinal indigestion; in suitable cases the effects are truly marvelous. Finally, the chemic deviation is further shown by the condition of the reflexes, the knee-jerk for example. In well-marked cases of magnesium infiltration, there is always derange_ment of the reflexes, showing that the effects, that is, the magnesium deposits in the nerve structures, interfere with the uninterrupted trans_mission of nerve impulses, and it will be found that the application of these principles makes for simplicity and efficiency.

Sanitary Aspect. From what has been said, it must be apparent to the most casual observer that the sanitary or applied aspect of this problem hinges entirely upon the digestive apparatus, and it is not diffi_cult to outline a method or methods by which we can adapt these prin_ciples to the ordinary dietary. Intestinal indigestion gives rise to the production of acid products, indican and bacterial toxins, together with nitrites, so that practically intestinal indigestion means the "leaching" by the body of acids and nitrites, on the same principle that we have leaching of poisons from cesspools and cemeteries. Such remedial measures as washing out the stomach, flushing the colon, hypodermo_clysis, administering digestive ferments and sedatives, the employment of antiseptics, etc., must be regarded as superserviceable, when it can be shown that the excess of acid which has given rise to the calcium depletion is the pivot, the line of demarcation between health and sickness. Besides the value of lime salts to recoup the nervous system, it is admitted by chemists and physiologists that they also possess important catalytic properties, making lime essential to the maintenance of function and structure. To regulate the dietary in accordance with these principles, certain practical rules must be followed.

In the first place, it should not be "sloppy." A sloppy dietary permits or affords solution of the food stuffs, but we lose almost entirely the effects of ptyalin upon the starchy foods, so that these substances act as an irritant to the stomach for at least two hours. With a dry diet, which requires thorough mastication, the starchy foods would enter the stomach at least partially, if not completely, digested. We must learn to make a distinction between solution and digestion.

In the second place, the ingestion of nitrogenous foods (meats), leads more quickly to acid production, and hence is more liable to produce an acid condition of the system, as in the case of diabetic coma. While it is not denied that children should have nitrogenous foods, the proportion should be regulated according to their age as well as their environment and status, and this is a matter which requires skill as well as discretion on the part of the medical attendant, because indigestion is liable and likely to produce or create an unnatural craving for unsuitable foods. As an evidence of this may be mentioned the popularity of the soda fountain, due to the persistent intestinal indigestion, and the demand for liquids, preferably those charged with carbonic acid gas. And it should be remarked that this carbonic acid gas is a valuable adjuvant to digestion, owing to its destructive action upon microorganisms in the stomach—and its functions in the production of carbonates.

In the third place, we have to contend with foods containing an excess of magnesium. I say, contend with such foods, because the magnesium excess will itself set up indigestion, in consequence of its obtunding effect upon the nervous system. Under certain conditions, magnesium oxide combines with the colloids of the nerve structures, and impedes, hinders or destroys their capacity for the uninterrupted transmission of impulses. Here again we have to deal with the water-drinking craze. Even physicians advise patients to drink all the water they can—an utterly useless procedure when it can be shown that we have to deal with a chemical union upon which water has no influence whatever. In the case of children and adolescents, we must administer lime in sufficient quantities to promote magnesium dissociation.

To make practical use of these principles, it is necessary to be familiar.

with the variations in the proportion of calcium oxide to magnesium oxide in different foods.*

For example, in eighteen kinds of common breakfast foods, includiug eggs, milk and milk products, cereals, bread and syrups, the variations are as follows:

In eggs there is nearly seven times as much calcium as magnesium. In milk and milk products, the ratio of calcium to magnesium varies from 9½ to 1 in the case of milk, to 25.3 to 1 in the case of cheese.

Cereals and cereal derivatives on the other hand, show in general an excess proportion of magnesium over calcium, showing from 3 to 1 in the case of oatmeal, to nearly 15 to 1 in the case of corn meal. Molasses and maple syrup show a slight excess of calcium. Honey shows an excess of magnesium with a ratio of 6 to 1.

These differences enable us to account for the peculiar dietary demands of children suffering from calcium depletion and the consecutive nervous manifestations. They dislike oatmeal, hominy, cornmeal, rice, graham bread and flaked wheat breakfast-food and honey, but crave eggs, butter, milk and syrup, because of the excess of lime. Indeed, the salvation of the child depends upon the lime content of the milk supply, a clinical and scientific fact, susceptible of demonstration under the most forbidding circumstances, such as mental deficiency and backwardness, chorea, epilepsy, mucous catarrh and skin diseases and bedwetting. Especially valuable is lime in the treatment of all acute intestinal disorders, cholera morbus, cholera infantum, diarrhœa and dysentery, etc., and thus we begin to grasp the essentials in the sanitary aspect of dietetics in the health of school children.

*See *Calcium, Magnesium and Phosphorus in Food and Nutrition* (1910), prepared by Sherman, Mettler, and Sinclair, Department of Chemistry, Columbia University (New York).

HISTORY AND PRESENT STATUS OF THE SCHOOL FEEDING MOVEMENT

BY

LOUISE STEVENS BRYANT

The school feeding movement is a part of the larger provision for the child's physical needs, which has grown out of the realization of the dependence of mental progress on bodily condition. It includes first the study of the child's nutritional condition, and then the practical question of providing food at school. As a rule, the term is narrowed to include the provision of warm meals, either breakfast or lunch, at a small sum covering the cost of the food, and its preparation and service.

The problem has not been considered by an international body of educators as a distinct problem until this session. At the Second International Congress on School Hygiene, held in London, there were several scattered papers referring to nutrition, but there was no treatment of the school feeding movement as such, although this Congress met just after the close of the four-year campaign for the provision of meals to elementary school children in Great Britain.

Considered externally, the movement is quite old, as its beginning antedated compulsory education in Germany, and was associated with the first constructive attempt on the part of municipalities to meet the social needs growing out of the industrial revolutiom at the end of the eighteenth century. Through the efforts of Count Rumford, municipal soup kitchens were built to accommodate workingmen out of employment and migrating in search of work. From the first, these kitchens were designed not alone as relief for the few, but as public conveniences to all the people, and the schools were invited to send children to them at noon, who otherwise would go without lunch or fare badly. Although not organized, this work was never discontinued, and in 1876 a municipal ordinance required that all Munich school buildings should have kitchens and dining rooms attached. With pedagogical and hygienic progress, the provision of meals in German municipalities has spread, until now it is a national movement, with agitation for compulsory national control.

In France, the Cantines Scolaires had a quaint origin. One of the Sections of the National Guard, located in the Nineteenth District, found at the close of the year 1849 that they had a small surplus in the their treasury. The men wished to use it for some good purpose, and looked about them to see what the neighborhood needed. At that time, public schools were being provided for such as wished to attend. Many of the people could not afford to clothe and feed their children properly enough for school, far less pay for the expensive books. The money was therefore turned over to form the nucleus of a school fund which should help all children to go to school. This school fund grew, and other sections adopted the plan. In 1867 the school law provided that funds might be set-aside in any commune in France for this special purpose, and in 1882 the school funds were made obligatory, though the exact use was left to the local authorities to decide. One of the main uses has always been the furnishing of meals. The school restaurant is now universal in France.

Victor Hugo gave the first impetus to the provision of school meals in England when in 1862 he invited a group of children from a neighboring school to a daily dinner at his summer home in Guernsey. In 1866, the Destitute Children's Dinner Society was founded in London, the first of many similar charitable ventures, which by 1905 numbered 360 in England. These societies were in the main conducted by teachers or private individuals with little other effort than to relieve acute distress during a few weeks in winter. There was no attempt at central organization, and little grasp of the educational possibilities. For the most part, the meals were designed to discourage any but the absolutely necessitous children, and from all accounts, they achieved this end.

Toward the close of the Boer War, the country received a shock from the publication of a statement by the Surgeon-General that three out of five of the men applying for admission to the army were rejected for physical unfitness. This was the beginning of the rumor that England was deteriorating as a nation. Four Royal Commissions in successive years considered the physical make-up of the country. They found there was no reason to expect progressive racial degeneration—that is, each new generation seemed to start life on the same plane as the preceding; but the conditions of life for the vast majority were such as to more than counterbalance the good start at birth. The condition most repeatedly noticed was malnutrition, which was found to exist at all ages. It was with the idea of helping to prevent this that the "Provision of Meals Bill" was finally passed in 1906, which gave the local educational authorities permission to install school restaurants as part of the regular school equipment.

It is significant that the Provision of Meals Act was the first piece of legislation growing out of the fear of national deterioration. It preceded the Compulsory Medical Inspection Act, the codification and revision of all legislation dealing with children known as the Children's Act, the foundation of the National Anthropometric Survey, old age pensions, the minimum wage board and the National Society of Eugenics —all steps toward national conservation in England.

In Italy, the work has grown up with the system of public schools, and from one-third to three-quarters of all school children in all the large cities attend the Refezione Scolastica, for the most part as paying patrons.

In the United States the lunches in various forms began with High School lunches in 1892, extending later to special classes—such as classes for mental defectives, open air classes for physical defectives, and finally to the regular elementary schools. The movement here has been almost entirely prompted by considerations of hygiene, and the same striving toward the socialization of the school that is found in medical inspection, playgrounds and social centers.

In the main, the workers in the School Lunch movement in America are convinced that if the school is to assume responsibility for the feeding of the children, it must be because of the conviction that warm nourishing meals, served at cost, are a benefit to 100 per cent. and are not merely temporary remedies for acute distress among the 10 per cent.

Five years ago there were four cities with school lunch experiments under way. There are now something over 90 cities with lunches in the regular elementary schools. In nearly all of these, the School Board assumes at least part responsibility. In an increasing number, it assumes entire responsibility. Lunches are provided as a regular part of the equipment in nearly all the open air schools, which are now opened in over 100 cities, while the High School lunch is provided as a matter of course.

Legislation in regard to the provision of school meals is national and provisional in Holland, England, Denmark and Bavaria. Is national and compulsory in Switzerland, France and Scotland. It is the subject of extensive municipal legislation in Germany, Italy, Sweden, Norway, Finland, Austria, Belgium and the United States.

In 1913 an Act providing for the use of school funds towards the support of school restaurants was passed in the Massachusetts Legislature. The provision of warm lunches in public schools is a part of the political platform of the National Socialist Party and has been inserted in the New York Municipal platform of the Progressive Party.

Internal Development. In most places, the work of feeding children has grown out of the need of the few for food. A considerable number of children were found who were failing to profit by the school work for the reason that they were underfed. As the work of meeting their physical needs began, it was found that the children who were actually starved were only a small part of a far larger group who were being fed the wrong things and suffered indirectly, not from hunger, but because they failed to reach the best level of vitality and resistance to disease and fatigue. As the needs of this larger group became apparent, it forced the consideration of the education of the people at large in the principles of nutrition and feeding. It was a simple enough matter to appease the hunger of a few starved children, but to do more than this —to get at the root of the problem, the universal ignorance of elementary physiology and hygiene combined with low and sometimes perverted food habits, required scientific investigation.

Dr. Tonsig, in Padua, was the first to attempt to make the school meals meet the standard of a scientifically planned dietary. The meals had begun there, as in most places, with little regard for exact measure of food values. Wholesome food was provided as a matter of course. By analysis and study Dr. Tonsig found that he could give nearly double the amount of actual food for the same cost as formerly, and was able to make special provision to meet the deficiencies he found in the children's home meals.

One of the most notable phases of the scientific work was the development in the city of Bradford of a set of menus, which provided all of the essentials of successful feeding, that is, properly proportioned food, yielding energy and tissue building material for the growing body, variety in food stuffs, and an attractive service. To meet all the real needs of thousands of children each day, and to keep the cost down to three cents including all items, was a task in efficiency. In Bradford, these menus adapted to the needs of a family of seven, are supplied to parents, which enormously enhance their general educational value.

In 1908 Dr. Gastpar in Stuttgart demonstrated the fact already empirically noted that bad nutrition leads also to non-resistance to disease. From an examination of more than 8,000 children, who were grouped according to several classes of nutrition, and according to diseases and physical defects present, he was able to show that the vulnerability to disease is in regular and direct proportion to the lowering of the nutritional standard. The children showing the best nutrition were found to have 18 defects among each 100, as opposed to 79 defects out of each 100 of the most poorly nourished. The proportion of defects increased steadily with the malnutrition. Dr. Gastpar continued his examinations for four years and has now the data from over 65,000 cases. The original results are confirmed and emphasized by the larger study.

Other investigators have concerned themselves with the measurements of growth of children attending and not attending school meals. One of the striking results of scientific experiment in this field has been the increasing tendency to base the estimate of the child's physical condition on his general nutrition rather than on isolated physical defects or diseases. This has meant the development of standards of measurements and methods of determining nutritional conditions.

By the compulsory medical inspection code passed in England in 1907, an estimate of the nutrition of each child is required. In Scotland, with a separate medical act, this requirement was extended to include the provision of meals to all children found to be suffering from malnutrition by the medical inspector.

To summarize: Wherever the school feeding movement develops, two things happen:

First: In all countries, school feeding begun by private philanthropy as a relief measure, or by semi-official attempt to encourage school attendance, becomes gradually recognized first by municipalities and then by states as a legitimate extension of the principle of compulsory education.

Second: As soon as the state begins to take part in the provision of food for its children, the meals lose the character of relief measures and become factors in education, with the double result that the suitability of the dietaries is considered with fare more care than before, and the hygienic and aesthetic aspects of the service receive attention.

The greatest need of the School Lunch movement is not propaganda —it is going forward with its own momentum. What is needed is the development of technique in medical examinations and in dietetic plans, the application of the principles of efficiency to the administrative system; and finally the constant extension of scientific experimentation in this field, which because of the large numbers involved and the normal character of the cases, affords an unrivalled opportunity for the development of the science of nutrition.

THE NUTRITION OF ANAEMIC AND TUBERCULOUS CHILDREN

BY

Edwin A. Locke

Peculiar impórtance attaches itself to our knowledge of the nutritive needs of children in the case of those affected with tuberculosis in early years, for at this period even more than in adults, nutrition of the indi‑vidual is of paramount importance. In the case of tuberculous and anaemic children we have to deal not alone with an impoverished con‑dition but must also furnish material for a growing organism. More‑over the nutritive needs vary to a far greater degree than in adult life in accordance with many factors. The first essential then is the selec‑tion of a diet appropriate to the age and diseased condition. In order to exercise precise control over the diet in such cases it is obviously neces‑sary to have a very definite idea of the requirements of the normal child.

Normal Requirements in Childhood. Unfortunately there is no accepted dietary standard for this period either with respect to the total twenty‑four hour needs or the proportion of individual constituents. Medical literature contains surprisingly few reports of exact investigations in this field and practical experience has given extremely variable results.

Among the available figures giving the total food values and grams of the several nutrients according to the age period Camerer's (Camerer: Der Stoffwechsel des Kindes. Tübingen, 1894. s. 60) classical table is probably the most reliable as it is based on most careful observations made on his own children for a long period. It is arranged to show the total grams of each type of food in twenty-four hours according to age periods.

TABLE I

GIRLS

Ages	2–4	5–7	8–10	11–14	15–18	21–24
Average weight in kilos	12.7	16.6	22.3	31.9	41.0	44.5
Total grams food	1183	1402	1638	1723	1612	1990
Grams protein	46	50	60	68	60	67
Grams fat	39	30	30	44	35	71
Grams carbohydrate	117	182	221	270	219	242
Grams water	957	1120	1315	1322	1273	1586

BOYS

Ages	....	5–6	7–10	11–14	15–16	17–18
Average weight in kilos	....	18.0	24.0	34.0	52.8	59.4
Total grams food	....	1517	1699	1909	2314	2378
Grams protein	....	64	67	86	102	100
Grams fat	....	46	32	34	73	83
Grams carbohydrate	....:	197	251	262	287	302
Grams water	....	1200	1333	1510	1810	1850

Observations by Hasse (Sophie Hasse: Untersuchungen über die Ernährung von Kindern im Alter von 2 bis 11 Jahren. Zeitschr. f. Biologie. B. 18, '1882' s. 553) show:

TABLE II

AGES	Protein Grams	Fat Grams	Carbohy-drate Grams	Total Calories
2 yrs. 6 mos.– 3 yrs. 3 mos	56.45	46.13	134.44	1211.7
3 yrs. 6 mos.	50.76	37.52	204.96	1397.4
4 yrs. 9 mos.– 5 yrs. 6 mos	64.64	58.61	171.88	1514.8
8 yrs. 9 mos.– 9 yrs. 4 mos	81.77	86.07	218.82	2037.9
10 yrs. 6 mos.–11 yrs. 3 mos	87.75	108.72	255.96	2420.3

Uffelman (Uffelman: quoted by Hasse, loc. cit.) combined his own figures with those of Camerer and gives the following as normal requirements:

TABLE III

AGES	Protein Grams	Fat Grams	Carbohy-drate Grams	Total Calories
1 year, 6 mos	42.5	35.0	100.0	909.8
2 years	45.5	36.0	110.0	972.4
3 years	50.0	38.0	120.0	1050.4
4 years	53.0	41.5	135.0	1156.8
5 years	56.0	43.0	145.0	1224.0
8–9 years	60.0	44.0	150.0	1270.2
12–13 years	72.0	47.0	245.0	1736.8
14–15 years	79.0	48.0	270.0	1877.3

Herbst (Herbst: Beiträge zur Kenntniss normaler Nahrungsmengen bei Kindern. Jahrb. f. Kinderheilkund., N. F. 46, 1898, s. 245) publishes the following averages as the results of a study of six children between the ages of two and fourteen years:

TABLE IV

AGES	Body Weight in Kilograms	Protein Grams	Fat Grams	Carbohy-drate Grams	Total Calories
Boys					
2 yrs. 3½ mos.....	15.0	54.4	62.2	134.2	1352
4 yrs. 4 mos.....	15.5	58.1	58.1	138.8	1347
9 yrs. 10 mos.....	27.5	62.2	68.7	227.0	1860
Girls					
10 yrs. 9 mos.....	43.15	61.4	70.4	250.9	1973
12 yrs. 6½ mos.....	47.5	69.3	85.8	211.8	1951
14 yrs. 6 mos.....	49.87	70.7	71.4	225.5	1878

Steffin (Steffin: Ueber Ernährung in kindlichen Alter jenseits der Saüglingsperiode. Jahrb. f. Kinderheilkunde., N. F. 46 1898, s. 332) gives a child of from four to seven years a diet containing an average of 95.49 grams protein, 92.55 grams fat and 197.99 grams carbohydrate, representing a total of 2,061 calories. Baginsky's (Baginsky: Lehrbuch der Kinderkrankheiten. 1902. s. 53) figures for afebrile children between the ages of four and nine are 102.81 grams protein, 75.59 grams fat, and 363.46 grams carbohydrates, or 2,615 calories; for those from nine to fourteen, 122.43 grams protein, 88.45 grams fat and 451.74 grams carbohydrates, or 3,176.68 calories.

The averages given in the above tables on the whole show fairly constant and uniform results, that is a gradually increasing number of calories as well as grams of protein, carbohydrate and fat, proportional to the age. Individual cases, however, present striking deviations from the average. All authors agree that these variations are largely due to the difference in body weight and it has been conclusively shown that the physiological requirements very according to the body weight and not necessarily in accordance with the age. Children of different ages but of the same body weight require approximately the same quantity of nutriment while children of the same age but of varying size necessitate different standards. Figures then for the nutritive needs according to age are of value only when taken in relation to the body weight. Values are usually expressed as so many grams or calories per kilogram of body weight at different ages.

For convenience in comparison I have combined in a single table such averages obtained by some of the best observers on children of nearly uniform age.

TABLE V

Author	Age	Protein	Fats	Carbohy-drates	Calories
		Grams per Kilo.	Grams per Kilo.	Grams per Kilo.	per Kilo.
Camerer....	1½ yrs.– 2¼ yrs...	4.4	4.0	8.9	91.7
	3 yrs.– 4 yrs...	3.4	3.1	7.7	74.3
	5 yrs.– 5¾ yrs...	3.5	2.5	11.0	82.7
	8½ yrs.– 9¼ yrs...	2.7	2.1	9.2	68.3
	10½ yrs.–11¼ yrs...	2.9	2.0	11.5	77.6
Hasse......	2¼ yrs...........	3.9	2.8	15.5	105.6
	2½ yrs.– 3¼ yrs...	3.6	2.9	8.5	76.6
	3½ yrs....:......	2.9	2.2	11.8	80.7
	4¾ yrs.– 5½ yrs...	3.8	3.5	10.2	90.0
	8¾ yrs.– 9⅛ yrs...	2.6	2.8	7.0	65.4
	10½ yrs.–11¼ yrs...	2.2	2.7	6.5	60.8
Herbst.....	2¼ yrs...........	3.6	4.2	9.0	90.7
	4⅓ yrs...........	3.8	3.8	9.0	87.8
	9¾ yrs...........	2.3	2.5	8.3	66.7
	10¾ yrs...........	1.4	1.6	5.8	44.4
	12½ yrs...........	1.5	1.8	4.5	41.3
	14½ yrs...........	1.4	1.4	4.5	37.2
Steffin	1 yr..............	6.6	6.0	5.9	107.1
	2 yrs..............	5.6	5.5	6.5	100.8
	3 yrs..............	5.6	5.3	8.8	108.3
	4 yrs.–7 yrs........	5.3	5.1	11.0	114.3
Uffelman...	2¼ yrs...........	4.1	3.0	8.8	80.8
	4¼ yrs...........	3.6	2.9	8.9	78.2
	10½ yrs..........	2.6	1.8	8.2	61.0
	14¾ yrs...........	2.0	1.2	7.1	48.5

A comparison of Table V, with Tables I to IV demonstrates at once the fallacy of expressing the nutritive needs according to age without reference to the weight. Whereas the absolute number of calories, as well as the quantity of protein, fats and carbohydrates increases rapidly from the younger to the older, as shown in Tables I to IV, reference to Table V shows a nearly constant relative decrease in all. This relative decrease in each case will be discussed in detail later.

In attempting to establish a dietary standard whether for the child or the adult, it should always be emphasized particularly that we can only determine rather wide limits between which there is a considerable margin of safety. This applies to the total fuel value of the diet as well as to the relative amounts of the various kinds of food. Individual factors, such as the amount of body activity, state of nutrition, demands for heat, sex, age, and others, necessitate a wide latitude in the choice of an appropriate diet for the individual. Experience proves that, especially in children, there is a high degree of adaptability on the part of the organism to variations in the quantity and kind of food. Our concern is largely by the application of the standard diets or averages, as it were, to make sure that the individual is not under nourished, and on the other hand, that a burden is not put on the organism by a diet of too high value or one improperly balanced as to the proportion of the several constituents. More care is often necessary in the selection in disease than in health.

With the exception of Steffin, all the authors quoted in Table V, present figures for the calories per kilogram of body weight which decrease steadily from infancy on. This is in accordance with the law of Rubner that animal metabolism is directly proportional to the size of the body surface. In other words, the caloric needs expressed in accordance with the unit of weight are proportional to the body surface. Smaller children have a surface area, which in proportion to the weight is greater than that of larger ones. Rubner proved that increased requirements in those with relatively large surface area is due to the increased loss of heat on the surface. His results are based on careful metabolism experiments on two boys of approximately the same age and height but one thin and the other fat. Because of the relatively greater body surface the thin boy require 52 calories per kilo, the fat boy only 43.6 calories to maintain normal nutrition. The apparent deviations from Rubner's law sometimes seen are due to conditions of general nutrition, amount of work and so forth, which independently influence the needs for nutriment.

No absolute standard of calories per kilo for the different ages can be established but probably the combined averages for approximately the same ages given in Table V are a safe general standard.

Age	Calories per Kilo
2 years	94
4 years	82
8 years	67
10 years	61
14 years	43

The question of the percentages of protein, fats and carbohydrates constituting a normal diet for the child, according to age and weight, is much more difficult to settle than the total calories, and is unquestionably subject to far greater variations which may be considered as within normal limits. Equally good results may be observed in the dietary of children from the use of widely different combinations of the three types of nutrients. Such variations as are shown in Table V may be partially explained by the difference in the places where the observations were made, the social condition of the families studied, and the general development of the children.

Nearly all authors find that the ratio of animal to vegetable food decreases from the younger to older children (see Table V), that is, with the development of the child, the diet becomes richer in vegetable food and poorer in total protein. Camerer's ratio of 1 : 2.2 for younger children is generally accepted. Because of the relatively greater body surface, children oxidize proportionately more protein and fat to furnish body heat.

Since the functioning body tissues are nitrogenous, it is obvious that during the period of growth the protein foods are the most essential because the protein of the blood must not only repair tissue waste, as in adults, but in addition, answer the demands for tissue growth also. Protein is of both animal and vegetable origin and can be supplied to the body from either source, though in childhood, not with good results if derived solely or largely from the latter. Meat contains roughly 15 to 25 per cent. protein; fish 17 to 20 per cent.; milk, 3.3 per cent.; eggs, 13 per cent.; cheese, 20 to 30 per cent.; bread of various kinds from 5 to 10 per cent.; crackers, 9 to 12 per cent.; beans, 7 to 22 per cent.; peas and lentils, 25 per cent.; nuts, 6 to 30 per cent., and chocolate, 13 per cent.

Under ordinary conditions, at least one-half of the protein of the child's diet, and in adults one-third, should be of animal origin. It is doubtful if it will ever be possible to determine exactly the amount of protein necessary to the growing child. If an amount of fats and carbohydrates necessary to meet all the needs for heat and energy is supplied, the growing organism can maintain nitrogen equilibrium on a surprisingly small amount of nitrogenous food. The protein is, however, very readily oxidized in the young (estimated as 90-92 per cent. absorbed) and probably a considerable per cent. of the energy developed should be from this source. On the other hand an excessive quantity of protein food, not only may upset the digestion but puts an unreasonable tax on metabolism, especially as a result of the increased work of excretion of the end products of nitrogen metabolism. The figures for protein of Steffin (Table V) are probably too large.

In children of the school age the protein furnished by milk, meat and eggs is to a considerable degree supplemented by vegetable protein. Sommerfeld (Pfanndler and Schlossmann: The Diseases of Children, 1908, Vol. I, p. 427) has compiled the following table giving in per-centages the sources from which protein should be derived at different ages:

TABLE VI

From	2-4 yrs.	5-7 yrs.	8-10 yrs.	11-14 yrs.
Milk, per cent	42	28	18	9
Meats and eggs, per cent	36	39	42	45
Vegetables and leguminous plants, per cent.	22	33	40	46

The various standards differ, widely in the amount of fat given. In general, fats are well metabolized by children (unless excessive, 92 to 94 per cent. being absorbed) and the relative amount, to a consider-able extent, seems to be a matter of indifference. Table V shows for all authorities a constantly diminishing number of grams per kilo with increasing years, although the amounts vary within rather wide limits. Fats are less essential to the diet than either of the other food constitu-ents and may be largely or even entirely replaced by an isodynamic amount of carbohydrate (100 grams fat equal 232 grams starch or 234 grams cane sugar) or *vice versa*.   Fat is more essential, however, when the diet is deficient in protein (Rubner) and when a considerable amount of fat is given the protein need is materially lessened.

The ability of the individual to metabolize fats is subject to greater variations than in the case of protein and carbohydrates.   This is espe-cially true of children and many can digest and absorb but a small amount.   Fortunately the degree to which the fats are digested can readily be determined by examination of the stools.   Those forms easiest of digestion are the fluid or those with a low melting point, and the forms best adapted to children from five to fifteen years are butter, milk fat, cheese, meat fat and olive oil.

Few evils as a rule attend even extreme reduction of the fats and they may be classed together as moderate disturbances of general nutrition. The commonest ill effects of an excessive quantity of fats are various disturbances of the gastro-intestinal tract.   These more usually occur in delicate individuals or those debilitated by disease, especially in children when, in an effort to improve nutrition, the fats are largely increased.

As a rule, then, the fats may be given healthy children in accordance with very flexible standards depending on circumstances, usually not under one or two grams and seldom over four per kilo. It should always be kept in mind that a gram of fat has more than twice the heat value of either protein or carbohydrates when metabolized, and therefore fat is of immense value when it is desired to increase the total calories.

Tables I to IV all show an almost constant increase in the total grams of carbohydrates with succeeding ages and with few exceptions proportionately greater than in the case of the protein and fats. Table V, likewise, as in the case of the other two nutrients, shows on the whole a relative decrease though more irregular and less marked. In the early years (Table V) one quarter to one third of the total calories are furnished by the carbohydrates, while in the oldest children at least one half are derived from this source. The carbohydrates are then a most important element in the diet of children but like the fats are subject to great variations. They may to a very large extent be replaced by fats and protein but if reduced too low there is always grave danger of acid intoxication with its attendant serious results. In children it is usually safe to regard 50 to 80 grams per diem as the miminum carbohydrate requirement. Much less commonly in children than in adults are evil effects observed as a result of a too great increase in the proportion of carbohydrate foods, but if they are present they take the form of gastric disturbances due to the great amount of cellulose ingested or to acid fermentation. For the ages under discussion the best forms are the various kinds of bread, crackers, well-cooked cereals, rice, macaroni, thoroughly cooked vegetables and selected fruits.

Requirements of Anaemic and Tuberculous Children. I shall consider these two conditions as one in discussing the diet indicated since the condition in each is in many respects essentially identical. The tuberculous children usually suffer from more or less anaemia and the anaemic are frequently tuberculous, though not recognized as such; in both the most important condition is one of impoverished health.

The difficulties in defining strict standards of diet for the normal child mentioned above, become much greater when the attempt is made to lay down rules governing the nutrition of the sick child. We have to consider in such a task not only the physiologic standard but also the individual factors and the nature of the disease. The tuberculous child is, on the whole, less active than the well child, and in so far metabolizes somewhat less food in the form of energy, but other factors combine to far outweigh this slight decrease. The tuberculous child, because of the greater or lesser degree of emaciation, has a surface area proportionately greater than the well-nourished and thus, at a given age, requires a relatively larger diet. He has more tissue to build besides providing resistance to an exhausting disease. If treated properly he is living in the open air both night and day, and during the winter months especially, thus increasing the expenditure of energy in the form of heat. To further complicate the last, we have to deal in many cases with definite gastro-intestinal disorders or general lowered vitality which limit the powers of digestion and absorption.

In the afebrile, ambulatory cases, who are under a regime of open air treatment, a judicious selection of the food with supervision in eating, makes it possible, without serious difficulty, to give a very satisfactory diet.

So great is the variation in weight and development in this class that the age is of hardly any significance in many instances, and in my own work I have arranged the diets almost entirely with respect to size. The body weight of the tuberculous child of ten years is frequently the same as that of a well child of six.

A very important guide in regulating the diet is the weight curve which should follow a steady upward course. In favorable cases the curve shows a much more rapid rise than in health, gains of from one to even three pounds in one week sometimes being observed.

Any gastro-intestinal symptoms should always be carefully looked for as they are apt to be the earliest signs indicating over-feeding. Whenever possible the stools should be examined as a routine at regular intervals, for in this procedure we have a very reliable and exact means of measuring how completely the system is utilizing the diet prescribed.

The experience on which the diet given below is based was gained at the Boston Hospital School at Franklin Park (Locke: A Report of Dietary Studies Made at the Franklin Park Hospital School for Tuberculous Children. Proceedings of the Sixth Congress of the American School Hygiene Association, 1912). The general physical condition of the children was under the constant observation of a trained nurse and the diets under the strict supervision of an expert dietition. Careful attention was given to every detail regarding the diet and in all cases figures are based on actual weighings of the individual dietaries. Although close attention was given to providing an adequate diet, in every case the amount eaten was left almost entirely to the appetite of the child, no forced feeding in any sense being undertaken.

The children were to a considerable extent divided into groups to facilitate the study of the effects of various types of diet on the weight and general nutrition. The most exhaustive observations were made on a group of children daily for five months (October to February), thirty-five in all completing the full time with a record of regular attendance. These results have been selected as most fairly representing the average type of diet used in the Hospital School. The children in this group ranged from seven to fifteen years in age and comprised twenty-five girls and ten boys. All were definitely tuberculous but afebrile.

An especial effort was made to furnish food such as can be provided in the homes of the poor and at the lowest possible cost. The dietary was made up chiefly of milk, cocoa, sugar, selected sweets, syrups, dried fruits, bread, crackers, cereals, dried beans, rice, macaroni, spaghetti, simple nutritious puddings, butter, nutritious soups, fish (with simple sauces, chowder, etc.), meats (mainly the most inexpensive kinds), vegetables and fruits (usually cooked).

A sample day is:

Breakfast

Cocoa,	2 cups.
Bread,	3 slices (3x4x½ inch).
Butter,	2 balls.
Stewed prunes,	3 with juice.

Dinner

Creamed codfish,	3 heaping tablespoonsful.
Mashed potatoes,	2 heaping tablespoonsful.
Milk,	1 glass.
Banana,	1 average size.
Bread,	1½ slices.

Supper

Milk,	2 glasses.
Graham crackers,	5 crackers.
Cream cheese,	1 cubic inch.

This represents, roughly, 100 grams protein, 100 grams fats, 266 grams carbohydrates or a total of 2,400 calories.

The average results in the group of thirty-five cases mentioned above, arranged according to age, are given in the following table:

TABLE VII

Age	Sex	Body Weight in Kilograms		Calories			Grams Protein per Kilo		Grams Carbohydrate per Kilo		Grams Fat per Kilo	
				Total	per Kilo	Average per Kilo						
			Average					Average		Average		Average
7	M	19.1		2933	153.5		5.5		19.0		5.7	
7	F	19.6	21.0	2888	147.3	140.0	5.2	5.1	18.4	17.4	5.4	5.1
7	F	20.9		2830	135.4		4.9		17.4		4.7	
7	M	24.5		3039	124.0		4.7		14.9		4.7	

TABLE VII—*Continued*

Age	Sex	Body Weight in Kilograms	Average	Calories Total	per Kilo	Average per Kilo	Grams Protein per Kilo	Average	Grams Carbohydrate per Kilo	Average	Grams Fat per Kilo	Average
8	M	19.1		2962	155.1		5.8		18.9		5.8	
8	F	23.6		2921	123.7		4.4		15.6		4.5	
8	F	26.4	24.5	3212	121.6	125.9	5.0	4.7	14.6	15.5	4.4	4.6
8	F	29.1		3007	103.3		3.6		12.8		3.9	
9	F	25.0		3080	123.2		4.2		15.6		4.5	
9	F	23.6	26.6	2870	121.6	113.5	4.2	4.0	15.4	14.3	4.4	4.1
9	F	29.1		3066	105.3		3.7		13.6		3.7	
9	F	28.6		2976	104.1		3.9		12.6		3.9	
10	F	23.2		3132	135.0		4.6		17.8		4.7	
10	M	27.3		3441	126.0		4.5		15.6		4.7	
10	F	24.1		2934	121.7		5.0		15.0		4.3	
10	F	27.7	27.5	3291	119.1	118.1	4.7	4.4	15.0	14.9	4.1	4.2
10	M	29.6		3487	117.8		4.0		15.4		4.1	
10	F	28.6		3058	106.9		4.2		13.1		3.9	
10	F	31.8		3190	100.3		3.6		12.6		3.6	
11	F	18.6		3086	165.9		6.3		20.6		6.0	
11	F	26.4	27.5	2919	110.5	118.5	4.0	4.4	13.7	14.8	4.1	4.2
11	M	31.8		3193	100.3		3.6		13.0		3.5	
11	M	33.2		3230	97.2		3.7		11.8		3.4	
12	F	17.3		2698	156.0		5.7		19.1		5.7	
12	F	28.6	31.4	2982	104.2	105.1	3.6	3.7	13.7	13.2	3.5	3.8
12	F	38.2		3238	84.6		3.0		10.3		3.0	
12	F	41.4		3126	75.5		2.6		9.2		2.9	
13	M	28.6		3874	135.4		4.5		17.3		4.9	
13	F	24.1		3107	128.9		4.6		16.7		4.4	
13	M	30.9	33.8	3295	106.6	105.3	4.0	3.7	12.6	13.4	4.1	3.7
13	F	36.8		3511	95.4		3.3		12.3		3.4	
13	F	40.0		3450	86.2		3.1		11.1		3.0	
13	F	42.3		3355	79.3		2.9		10.3		2.6	
14	F	40.0	40.0	2983	74.5	74.5	2.6	2.6	9.3	9.3	2.7	2.7
15	M	55.5	55.5	3263	58.8	58.8	2.1	2.1	7.3	7.3	2.2	2.2

The table at first glance indicates a rather constant decrease in the total number of calories and calories per kilo of body weight, but closer examination shows many exceptions and on the whole a considerable variation. The grams of protein, fats and carbohydrates fall almost equally with the increasing ages.

TABLE VIII

Body Weight in Kilograms	Group	Age	Average	Sex	Calories per Kilo	Average	Grams Protein per Kilo	Average	Grams Carbohydrate per Kilo	Average	Grams Fat per Kilo	Average
17.3		12		F	156.		.7		19.1		.7	
18.6		11		F	165.		.3		20.6		.0	
19.1	17–19	8	9	M	155.9	155.5	.8	5.7	18.9	19.2	.8	5.7
19.1		7		M	153.		.5		19.0		.7	
19.6		7		F	147.5		5.2		18.4		5.4	
20.9		7		F	135.4		4.9		17.4		4.7	
23.2		10		F	135.0		4.6		17.8		4.7	
23.6		8		F	123.7		4.4		15.6		4.5	
23.6	20–24	9	9.1	F	121.6	127.2	4.2	4.6	15.4	16.1	4.4	4.5
24.1		10		F	121.7		5.0		15.0		4.3	
24.1		13		F	128.9		4.6		16.7		4.4	
24.5		7		M	124.0		4.7		14.9		4.7	
25.0		9		F	123.2		4.2		15.6		4.5	
26.4		11		F	110.5		4.0		13.7		4.1	
26.4		8		F	121.6		5.0		14.6		4.4	
27.3		10		M	126.0		4.5		15.6		4.7	
27.7		10		F	119.1		4.7		15.0		4.1	
28.6	25–29	13	9.9	M	135.4	114.8	4.5	4.2	17.3	14.4	4.9	4.1
28.6		10		F	106.9		4.2		13.1		3.9	
28.6		9		F	104.1		3.9		12.6		3.9	
28.6		12		F	104.2		3.6		13.7		3.5	
29.1		9		F	105.3		3.7		13.6		3.7	
29.1		8		F	103.3		3.6		12.8		3.9	
29.6		10		M	117.8		4.0		15.4		4.1	
30.9		13		M	106.		4.0		12.		4.1	
31.8	30–34	10	11.25	F	100.	101.1	3.6	3.7	12.	12.5	3.6	3.7
31.8		11		M	100.		3.6		13.		3.5	
33.2		11		M	97.8		3.7		11.8		3.4	
36.8		13		F	95.		3.3		12.3		3.4	
38.2	35–39	12	12.5	F	84.6	90.0	3.0	3.2	10.8	11.5	3.0	3.2
40.0		13			86.		3.1		11.1		3.0	
40.0	40–44	14	13.0		74.	'78.9	2.6	2.8	9.3	9.9	2.7	2.8
41.4		12			75.		2.6		9.2		2.9	
42.3		13		F	79.3		2.9		10.3		2.6	
55.5	55.5	15	15.0	M	58.8	58.8	2.1	2.1	7.3	7.3	2.2	2.2

The above table, in which the same results are grouped according to the body weight in kilograms, presents a much more regular picture and emphasizes the importance of the principle laid down earlier in this paper, namely that the diet of the child should be chosen with reference to the body weight rather than to the age. The average number of calories per kilo of body weight falls with extraordinary regu‐ larity from 155.5 for the child of seventeen to nineteen kilos, to 58.8 at 55.5 kilos. These figures are so much larger than those for the normal child that they appear to need justification. In the first place a diet of this strength was found necessary to bring about the desired improve‐ ment in general nutrition and increase in body weight, and the children ate only as much as their appetites prompted. Furthermore it must be remembered that the group was made up of tuberculous children, suffering from marked general debility in most instances, many much under weight, and all were living constantly in the open air with several periods daily of active exercise. We saw no reason to consider the diet too large. There were no gastro-intestinal or other symptoms suggest‐ ing over-feeding. Neither did we see any ill effects from the rather high protein content of the diet. The ratio of the nitrogenous to the non‐ nitrogenous food was almost the same in all groups, ranging from a minimum of $1 : 4.37$ in the first to a maximum of $1 : 4.59$ in the fifth. This high ratio for the ages five to fifteen was found to give better results than a diet with a lower one.

The grams of carbohydrate per kilo of body weight, especially for the younger children, although considerably above the figures usually given, diminish in about the same uniform manner. Exactly the same may be said of the fats.

To many the diet prescribed at the Hospital School will seem of unreasonably high value but our experience with the class of cases treated was very definitely that such a maximum gave the most satis‐ factory results.

It would easily be possible to discuss many variations of diet given above and adapted to special conditions but in this brief paper it does not seem necessary to do more than to lay down general principles of feeding, leaving the choice of the particular type and caloric value to be determined in accordance with the needs of the individual case.

NATIONAL CONSERVATION AND NUTRITION DURING CHILDHOOD

BY

Margaret McMillan

"Thanks be to God we eat plentifully, and be not gone crokyed and hungry as others are!"—*Old Chancellor of the Exchequer.*

It has often been noted that very great reforms are nearly always brought about by very small and weak creatures. The little child under five years has somehow managed to show that the methods of schools for much older children are mostly wrong. The defective or backward have forced on the study of brain function and physiological method. It is now the turn of the poor little starveling to enter the arena, and it looks as if it were going to be the mover in the greatest reforms of all. Dr. Burney, in the last Report of the Deptford Health Centre says that 90 per cent. of all children are very well born. But only ten per cent. are at all well bred, or rather well fed. And if the helpless multitude of little creatures could speak and knew what to say there is no doubt that they would cry out in chorus: "Please give us real milk, mother's milk, for nine months if possible, and then go on giving us plenty of good milk fat for years." Alas! the good milk that will make good brains is yet far to seek in many parts of even the great capitals of the world. Thousands of London babies are fed on skimmed milk. Not only ricketts, adenoids, anæmia, also backwardness; but also every kind of mental shortcoming are associated with this "skimmed," lean, starchy, and faulty diet. The brain is a very great and wonderful organ. But so far as we know it is composed mainly *of fat.*

This is probably why a child under ten does not need anything like so much proteid and carbohydrates as a grown-up person, but does require at least half as much fat as the adult in his prime. And as he is going to do such wonderful things with it surely it should be his just as freely as air to breathe, or water to drink, "fat to make a great mind." We say, Yes. In the natural order of things the means are always simple. It is the end that is sublime. "Out of these stones God can raise children unto Abraham." Yes indeed, for out of dust arose the soul. But in human affairs, alas, and more especially in politics (as Balzac pointed out) this order is quite reversed. After years of talk, and the appointment of ministers and officials at high salaries, after upheavals, leaders in all the papers, discussion, we get, say, a Milk Bill that does not provide Milk. It provides inspection, but no one can live on inspection, except, perhaps the inspector. The inspector regulates, prohibits, and often it may be keeps poison out of the home.

That is very well. But that is not Milk. The business of providing good milk, and bringing that good, pure milk into every home where there is a child or children is not the work of an inspector. Even the latest Milk Bill excludes the *problem of supply*. The rich and well-to-do can have good milk. Their milk supply can be made safer. Every kind of precaution is taken. Yes, but the birth rate is falling in Mayfair. It is *not* falling in Shoreditch or Deptford where guaranteed milk will not come. In legislation one has to think of the children of mean streets, because there are the roots of the nation. For good or ill these are to carry on the life of the race, and everything depends, therefore, on good milk getting into the Deptford or Shoreditch home. It seems reasonable to hope that the great county councils and city councils who engage in so many business enterprises and who supply milk already to hospitals, infirmaries and workhouses, should at last start farms and dairies outside of the cities for supplying milk to the children of the people. In any case the problems of education can not be solved till the milk question is settled.

For the semi-starved, the under-fed, and ill-fed never get any real hold of the past, or even of the present. They forget their parents like small children. "Where is your mother?" I said one day to a tall girl in a train. She looked amazed for an instant, and then said in a dull voice, and without feeling, "She drowned herself in the dam." That may have been an extreme case, and for that reason it may serve to show the real nature of forgetfulness in many other less striking cases. In the special drill classrooms, and school camps where teachers stand for the first time before elementary school children the process of teaching is complicated at first by the brain dullness of even well-endowed children. "Please shut the door, Emily!" Emily takes no notice. "The door is open; shut it." A light glimmers in Emily's eyes. "Shut the door." At last she hears and obeys gladly. She is not deaf through the ear. She is not disobedient. She is deaf through the brain, and this kind of deafness is the result of want of food and want of stimuli. In that state of dullness millions pass their lives. They are diagnosed as naturally dull, unfit for secondary education. But why should we jump to such a wild conclusion? It would be better to try the effect of good feeding in early childhood. To come now to the child of school age. What kind and quantity of food does he or she require? Dr. Clement Dukes has worked out an answer in the interest of the preparatory school-boy. A child under fourteen (and over nine) requires, he declares, daily:

> Starches............13   ounces
> Carbohydrates........34.4   "
> Proteids.............11.1   "

He allows ¾ lb. of meat per day so as to get the full amount of protein (which, however, can be got from some other foods). Chemistry is not yet developed so far that the man in the street can do without that "prepared" grass or vegetable that we call beef, mutton, game. Two facts indicate, however, that a non-meat diet is the goal towards which the race is progressing. The first is that human milk resembles more nearly the milk of the herb-eating animals than that of the carniverous. And the second is that civilized beings no longer eat it raw, and dilute it moreover (with vegetables, fruits and cereals) so that they reduce it in effect so that it is, so far as its elements are concerned, no longer meat at all. Highland oatmeal consists of: Water, 15.00; Albumen, 12.60; starch, 58.40; sugar, 5.40; fat, 5.60; salts, 3.00. Compared with beef plus potatoes (the ordinary English dinner) it is superior in every item excepting water.

During the past year I have given two meals daily to over forty children in a very poor district of London. These were all anæmic cases, unfit to attend the ordinary schools, and excluded by the doctors of the Health Centre. They slept in an open shed throughout the winter and lived entirely out-of-doors. Breakfast consisted of fine Highland oatmeal porridge with milk. (Every child had a pint of milk daily.) For supper there is boiled pudding, rich in fats, with sweet syrup, or vegetable stews with hard protein biscuits, milk and sometimes hard fruit such as apples.

During the months between October and March the boys put on weight rapidly. The average increase was 6 ounces per week. Formerly, at home, they were probably gaining 1 ounce per week. A few boys remained stationary. One, who made a notable cure from chorea gained nothing in weight. During the summer months the increase is less. The boys gained on an average four to five ounces per week.

The girl campers did not stay to supper. They merely slept out and had oatmeal and milk breakfast at their own camp. Within two months three-fourths per cent. of all the girls gained substantially in weight. Two girls gained over 3½ pounds in a month. One child gained 2¼ pounds in three weeks. Another gained one pound in three weeks. Three out of seventeen lost weight—one very slightly. There was in the case of boys and girls a great increase as a rule in weight on the first week after entrance, as usually happens in all such experiments. In the Xmas holidays, at home the boys lost weight rapidly, the average loss being 8 ounces per week.

The children were greatly improved in appearance. Sallow and pale, they became blooming, fair-skinned, rosy-cheeked and bright-eyed. The tonic effect of pure air, by day and by night, was doubtless one great cause of the change, but I think that the breakfast also had a great effect, even though some of the children were under-fed. One object in leaving the home to provide the dinner is that in this way the parents may be drawn in to take part in the experiment.

It is perhaps unnecessary to speak to an American audience of the cheap menus that had to be worked out in the older countries. For more than a hundred years chemists have labored to put a really good diet within the reach of all. Count Rumford's experiments at Munich never became popular in England except among the learned (even among the rich his dinner of pease and barley pudding and purees were never popular because cooks had not the patience to let things boil slowly). And later efforts to feed the poor and the children of the poor were not carried out on any scientific basis. Moreover, to make things worse, the under-fed and the very poor have not always a healthy appetite, but quite the contrary. "Give them anything," says the man in a hurry, "they'll be glad of it." "Give them what they like, buns and prunes," cries the young philanthropist. "Biscuits and ice cream" may vary this menu in America. Only very slowly do the great masses of the people even begin to see that the problem of nutrition is the gravest of all, that it involves all the others, even the loftiest.

The ideal dining hall should be outside, or rather in the pavilion, or open building of a camp-school. It is impossible to make the surroundings too bright and too lovely. The shed walls should be tempered in light colour, and the floor polished and dustless. The smaller tables, with tiny chairs should be set in the middle, and here a monitor should sit. The table should be covered with a snowy cloth, and gay with flowers. Every day children should be appointed to arrange the flowers, to keep the dishes and dining utensils bright and to arrange the pavilion for dinner. Paper table napkins should be used, and the standard of cleanliness cannot be too high. Every child will take a pride in the cleanliness of his hair, nails, hands, clothes, etc., if encouraged to do so by example, and *by having the things he needs for washing.*

The supper or meal hour should be for children the happiest of the day. Joy helps digestion. And yet it takes a good deal of time and thought to prepare children of the poorest class for this new happiness. They are used to bolting any food they have, and have no joy at all in eating but the joy of stilling hunger. I have tried at Deptford to have guests to supper at least once every week, usually on Friday. To that day the children now look forward. Some of them sit at the guest's table, which is a great privilege. They talk a little at times and they listen to conversation, which is a new and glad experience for them. Sometimes they will fix their eyes wonderingly on the stranger who comes from far-off lands, the gentle Brahman, the bronzed Canadian or American, the German or Frenchman or the Swede from the far North lands.

On the floor of the pavilion there is a huge map of the world, and after supper they are often eager to see where Denmark is, or the Bahamas, and to look at the great Indian Ocean or the Pacific, over which their guests have passed. The children at the other table talk freely though no shouting is allowed, and sometimes, if something very interesting or amusing is said at the guest's table they are called on to share it. All troubles, and hardship, and failures of the day are forgotten.

This eating with the children and making every meal a sacrament of joy and human fellowship must follow the mere selection of foods, else were the enterprise not worthy of a true democracy. It is the thing that is missed at all mere charitable functions, and it degrades these to the level of mere foddering—the satisfaction of animal feelings. At the public dining table, spread by the public spirited, a new order of civilization may be founded.

SESSION THIRTY-TWO

Room D.   Friday, August 29th, 2:00 P.M.

SYMPOSIUM ON SCHOOL FEEDING (Part Two)

Arranged by School Lunch Committee of the American Home Economics Association,

MRS. LOUISE STEVENS BRYANT, *Secretary*

CAROLINE L. HUNT, *Chairman*

MISS EUGENIA DIEM, Buffalo, N. Y., *Vice-Chairman*

Program on Systems of Public School Feeding

ALICE C. BOUGHTON, Superintendent of School Lunches, Philadelphia, Pa. "The Administration of School Lunches in Cities."

MABEL HYDE KITTREDGE, Chairman New York School Lunch Committee, Washington Square, N. Y. "Relation of Menus to Standard Dietaries."

MARY E. L. SMALL, Director of Domestic Science, Department of Public Instruction, Buffalo, N. Y. "Educational and Social Possibilities of School Lunches."

MARY L. BULL, Department of Agriculture, University of Minnesota, St. Paul, Minn. "Hot Lunches in Rural Schools."

JULIA PULSIFER, Superintendent of School Lunches, Women's Educational and Industrial Union, Boston, Mass. "History and Development of Lunches in High Schools, With a Discussion of the Elements of Cost in School Lunch Expense."

EMMA SMEDLEY, Superintendent of School Lunches, Board of Public Education, Philadelphia, Pa. "High School Lunches Under School Board Control."

CAROLINE L. HUNT, Office of Experiment Stations, Washington, D. C. "The Training of the School Dietitian."

LEON MEYER, M.D., Medical Inspector Schools of Paris. "Cantines Scolaires."

THE ADMINISTRATION OF SCHOOL LUNCHES IN CITIES

BY

ALICE C. BOUGHTON

Ten years ago school lunches were being served in two elementary schools in Philadelphia. To-day they are being served in more than seventy cities from Pennsylvania to California and from the Great Lakes to the Gulf.

The movement has passed the experimental stage and become a recognized part of the modern school system.

It is the purpose of this paper to deal with some of the questions, in the order of their relative importance, which must be considered by any community about to organize school lunches. These problems are such as must be taken into account regardless of the extent of the service to be organized.

The relative merits of the central kitchen and the individual school kitchen is one of the first problems to be considered. In the central kitchen it is possible to have a trained person in charge of the actual work, so that a more uniform standard can be maintained. This is especially true where women's clubs or other volunteer agencies are responsible for supervision. Competent, responsible assistants are essential.

For the central kitchen, food can be bought and stored in large quantities. This spells economy. Our experience in serving school lunches is not yet sufficient to warrant the statement that the central kitchen plan results in actual money saving. The cost of food distribution is considerable, but there seems to be little doubt that a better standard of cooking and of serving as well as greater variety may be obtained for the same money if the food is prepared in a central kitchen or, in a large city, in a chain of kitchens each of which serves one or more school districts. So far the possibilities of combining the work in the high and elementary schools have not been given a trial. There would seem to be no real difficulties, other than those of administration, in taking advantage of the high school plants for the preparation of food for the elementary schools. In most high schools it is possible to have steam cooking utensils, dish washing machines, potato peelers and other labor-saving devices; which because of expenses, cannot be installed in the small elementary school kitchen. This coöperation between high and elementary schools would permit of greater variety and lower food and service cost for both.

On the other hand, with such a system as that in Philadelphia, where the cooking is done in each school, the children come into close contact with the working assistants, observe the preparation of food, and unconsciously acquire higher standards. Many of them show great interest in what goes on in the kitchen, ask questions, and learn the names and uses of the various utensils. However, it is probable that the advantages of the individual kitchen could be incorporated with the central plant.

No matter what system adopted, too much stress cannot be laid on the necessity for a good cost accounting system. Whether the lunches pay in full or in part only the cost of maintenance, those in charge should know exactly the expense of running the plant in terms of rent, heat, light, deterioration, renewal of equipment, distribution, preparation, service and supervision, as well as the cost of the food. They should also know whether the gain through buying food in large quantities is sufficient to cover the running expenses of the plant, and whether, if the selling price covers service cost as well as food cost, the child gets as much for his penny as he does when he buys at the corner grocery. The collection of this information does not pledge us to the adoption of any given system of administration. It does, however, give us a scientific basis for the measurement of results and a means for accurately comparing the work of one city with that of another.

A system of records carefully worked out to meet special needs is almost indispensable. This should include weekly menu cards for the saleswomen at each school, with spaces for daily receipts and weekly totals; a record for each school showing total receipts and expenditures for the month and sufficient space for an itemized expenditure account. A time sheet is needed for registering the working time of employees. This time sheet furnishes a basis of comparison between the various schools where employees are paid by the hour, and shows the gain in time through convenient kitchen arrangement and equipment. There should be petty cash sheets so that the saleswoman will have no difficulty in keeping an account of her emergency fund. There should be order sheets of uniform size which fit into the director's note book, and loose sheets of the same size for miscellaneous memoranda. Care and thought in these details insure efficiency with a minimum of effort.

In any city having more than two or three schools, there should be a central office where the assistants can get into daily touch with the director, bring their record cards each week for criticism, and confer with her regarding the difficulties they encounter in their work. Once a month it is well to have a general experience meeting with the whole force. This will help to keep all interested and develop a spirit of team work. Very often the director gets valuable suggestions from her assistants, who through daily contact with the children acquire first hand knowledge of their needs and tastes.

The efficient administration of funds available for school lunches depends largely upon the intelligence exercised in the purchase of raw materials. The director must be governed in her selection of food stuffs, not by guess work but by scientific measurement. Each food sample should be tested for the per cent. of protein, fat, and carbohydrate, and for its caloric value. The school director should make her purchases on the basis of food values, although this does not mean that she must make the chemical analysis herself. In every city arrangement can be made to have foods tested in the university or municipal laboratories, and the school lunch director will generally find the municipal authorities glad to coöperate.

Another important problem is the equipment of kitchen and lunch rooms. The school children are not obliged to buy the lunch prepared for them. They will not buy it unless they can get as much for their money in just as attractive a form as the street vendor offers them. In selling cheap food careful attention must be given to service, and no matter how simple, the equipment should be pleasing in appearance. When possible the serving dishes should be white. They appeal to the children as being clean and attractive, and what is no less important, the director can tell at a glance whether or not they are properly cared for. In Philadelphia white enamel has proved most satisfactory for this purpose.

The lunch hour may become one of the social features of the school if due attention is given to making the lunch room attractive. This is especially true in high schools. In elementary schools the lunchroom should be easy of access to playground or playroom so that as soon as the children have finished their meal or while they are waiting for their turn to be served, they may be playing out-doors.

If the director or her assistants have had normal training in domestic science, they may give lessons in the physiology of digestion, using the school lunch as a working basis.

The whole system of lunch room expenditures should be the common property of the children. They should understand just what their money goes for, what proportion for rent, what proportion for service, and what proportion for food.

In the past, correlation between school room and lunch room has not been close, yet it seems evident that the school lunch offers a laboratory where valuable instruction to school children can and should be given. Such correlation, however, is not practical unless the director of the department possesses certain important qualifications. In order to fully develop the educational possibilities of the school lunch, she must be not only a business manager, an accountant, a skilled housekeeper and a trained dietitian, but also an intelligent and well equipped teacher.

A question which will undoubtedly arise in the future, as it has already in connection with medical inspection, is whether the administrating of school lunches should be under the direction of the educational or health authorities. Most of us who are engaged in this work feel strongly that the responsibility must rest upon the public school system. The health authorities, through the Department of Medical Inspection, deal primarily with the child who is ill, and pay little attention to the healthy child. The School Lunch Department places emphasis not upon the sick but upon the well; its primary aim is to serve best the abnormal, not the normal child. The School Lunch Department might very properly coöperate with the Department of Medical Inspec-tion in the preparing and serving of special diets to the under-nourished, or other requisition of the Department of Charities in serving food free of charge to children of indigent parents. In other words, the school lunch might serve as a food clinic to children suffering from malnutrition.

Coöperation between school and health authorities should be close and constant, but for purposes of effective administration it seems evi-dent that the provision of food for normal children to be served in the school buildings should be under the direction of the school authorities.

The control of the School Lunch System should be in the hands of a central committee composed of representatives from the Depart-ment of Superintendents, Departments of Health, Recreation, and Domestic Economy, and other interested persons or associations. If public funds are spent, the members of this central committee would properly be appointed by the Board of Education. This committee should meet several times during the year to settle questions which arise, but there should be a smaller executive committee meeting monthly to work with the director and aid her in keeping the system running smoothly. Whether or not the director of a luncheon is a paid employee of the Board of Education or of an outside organization, she should have full authority over the details of the work for which she is responsible, subject, of course, to the approval of the executive committee. She should be responsible, in part at least, for the purchasing of food, and wholly responsible for preparing and serving it. She should make all menus and know the food values of whatever articles are sold. She should be consulted in the buying of all equipment.

School feeding is a big business. In Philadelphia alone the 170,000 children in the elementary schools are spending approximately $200,000 each school year. As only about 6,000 of these elementary school

largely to the street vendor. During the past year 10,
in the high schools spent $92,000. Their money was spe
nutritious, and palatable food, prepared and served in a sani
in a clean and attractive room under expert supervisio
overwhelming proportion of elementary children for who
school lunches have been provided, spent their pennies o
getting in return for their money dirty, adulterated food
is in the schools. He wants food, and has the money with
it. The practical question for us to settle is, How shall he ge
worth?

RELATION OF MENUS TO STANDARD DIETARIES

BY

MABEL H. KITTREDGE

In starting school luncheons in New York in 1908, two experiments were tried by the School Lunch Committee before the present plan was adopted, both of them consisting of different fashions of so-called table d'hote meals, rather than the present and more successful à la carte plan. At first we arranged economic and well-balanced daily menus at the cost price of three, four and five cents, the three-cent meal con_ sisting of soup and bread, the nutritive value never under six hundred calories; the four and five cent meals including cocoa, or cocoa and des_ sert, having a nutritive value of at least 880 calories, thus making the noon meal at school the real dinner of the day, one-half the total daily ration required. But the three-cent children were ashamed before and jealous of the five-cent children, and the five-cent customers were proud, and even refused to buy at all if they had but three or four cents. Therefore, these different priced menus were given up after one winter, and the three-cent light meal, or lunch, with an additional penny table for sweets, was introduced in six of our public schools, and tried for three years. We fed, on an average, 1,135 a day, and for three cents each child received not less than ½ pint of soup and 2½ ounces of bread, the two yielding from 600 to 700 calories. The menu was made out each day by a person with thorough training in foods, who was held responsible that no child left the lunch table underfed. After the soup and bread had been purchased, the desire for sweets which every child has could be gratified at the table where there was always cocoa, which gave the child, for one cent, 137 more calories; fruit, cooked and raw; salads; one kind of sandwiches, either egg, butter, lettuce, or jam; one or two varieties of crackers; one pudding, rice, bread or apple; peanuts; such vegetables as corn or sweet potatoes, and often apple pie or small cakes. Every child who bought the three-cent meal was well fed, and we reckoned rightly in thinking that our customers would manage to have at least one penny over to spend at the penny table. In reality, at least 50% of the children had more than one penny extra, as will be seen from the fact that in one year, 1911–12, we received from sales at the penny table, over and above the regular three-cent lunch, an average of a thousand pennies a day.

We found, however, that instead of feeding the indigent children in the schools, we were catering to the wide-awake, better class, and we were getting too small a proportion, even, of this class. In one Italian school where it had been estimated that 13% of the children of the four lower grades were suffering from malnutrition, we were reaching but few of these children. Many boys and girls who had more than three pennies would deliberately walk past our luncheons (often with longing glances at the penny table) and go out and spend all of their money at the nearby push carts. They would not be dictated to as to the expenditure of that first three cents. And children with only one or two cents in their pockets would try to deceive those in charge of the lunch; a boy who had bought the three-cent meal would rent his tray out again and again, and let it be taken to the penny table, its used condition a proof that the boy now holding it and wishing to spend his one cent must have previously bought the three-cent meal, or a sister would buy a three-cent lunch and then share it with a smaller member of the family, neither in this way getting enough to eat. Many children were given the three cents in the morning to buy the lunch check, but passing a tempting push cart on the way to school and not calculating on the noon hunger, one cent would be spent, and at noon the two remaining pennies were not sufficient to let the then hungry boy purchase anything at all unless he resorted to cheating. Some mothers with large families could not afford to give each child three cents.

In 1912, having learned our lesson the New York street child is used to buying each article for one penny and making his own choice, we gave up the three-cent meal, only requiring now that every child shall spend one cent for soup before availing himself of the miscellaneous penny table. Even the purchase of bread is not compulsory. The argument which won the day for penny lunches is that it is better to give one cent's worth of hot soup than not to reach the children at all. Nevertheless we must endeavor by education to raise the standard until a penny lunch will seem impossible to the mother of the tenements as it does to us at present.

The difficulty of finding education for the eradication of malnutrition is realized by everyone. In 1910 the Chief Medical Officer for the Board of Education in London, stated that "While defective nutrition stands in the forefront as the most important of all physical defects from which school children suffer, there is no condition harder to grapple with than such complex and interwoven causes."

Not underestimating the complexity of this problem, I still believe that we will have taken one step forward when we realize clearly that the penny lunch, if taken alone without the perfectly possible accompanying education in foods, food values and education in buying, does but little toward lessening the evil of malnutrition among school children.

As Phyllis D. Winder says in her late book on the "Public Feeding of Elementary School Children," "The greatest danger, perhaps, of a provision of meals is that they act as a salve to the conscience of the community who, seeing the children being fed and thinking all is well, look no further."

I believe the school luncheon will lessen the causes of underfeeding just so far as it gives to those children who buy the full knowledge of the kind of food they are buying, knowledge of its preparation and its value over impure, unwholesome food.

In a list of causes of malnutrition, I notice that in England poverty is put first, but it seems to me in this country ignorance comes first, and this ignorance cannot be conquered by ladling out a penny's worth of soup and tempting children to buy graham crackers and rice pudding and fruit from a penny table. The general raising of standards will, of necessity, be slow, but are we doing all we can to change the habits of the families of the children who buy luncheons from us? Take, for example, the habit of setting no table at home, and having no regular time for meals. This habit among many of our immigrants comes from the confusion of living. The school hour at noon does not fit into the husband's hour off, little children demand food more frequently than their elders, the rooms are small and overcrowded, and after a time it seems too much trouble to set the table.

Thus the habit of "eating off the stove" grows into the habit of eating at any time, and even into always munching something. I know many children who, whether hungry or not, are seldom seen without food or gum in their mouths. Such children soon reach the malnutrition class.

Every child in our schools should be taught that health is only possible with regular meals; not taught it once, but repeatedly. Every mother, through mothers' meetings, or by circulars printed in her own language, should be made to understand that the school lunch is simply one way to make possible regular hot meals for her children, that we are not feeding her children because of poverty but because we realize the confusion of conditions that she is obliged to meet; and incidentally that if she does not give her child at least three cents a day for his lunch she has not done her part.

Last year there were in our New York schools 388,000 girls, 43,500 of whom had some education in cooking, and 344,500 had nothing to suggest even that food was a matter of importance. Think of the added efficiency of those 344,500 girls if they had had the privilege of buying good cooked food at the noon hour and had at least one lesson a week on food preparation, food value, and what each article purchased from the school lunch table gave to the buyer in food and tissue-making material. As it is now, almost all children, and the large proportion of mothers at home whom we hold responsible for the physical defects in the child, do not know how to do any better.

One million immigrants a year come to us, and the children of these immigrants go to our schools. It is there, if anywhere, that the education of these children in the matter of health in its relation to food must begin. And it should not be difficult, for the girl of school age shows as natural an eagerness to learn to cook as the boy is eager to use a hammer and saw.

But even before we get a universally ideal educational system, I believe we who are serving luncheons can do a great deal more than we are doing. For example, in New York next year we are to serve a noon meal in seventeen elementary schools. We estimate that we shall feed 5,000 children a day. If these 5,000 know each day the name of the soup they have eaten and go home and tell their mothers about it, something will have been done. Cannot we have on the class room blackboard the ingredients used in the soup and, possibly, a short explanation of their food value, showing, for example, the food value of a bean soup over a candied apple, both being the same price, and the latter very popular? It would make the lunch much more interesting, and children do care whether they are strong and big or not. The boy would like to get his money's worth from the penny table. When he saw on the blackboard that the penny he spent to-day for rice pudding gave him four times as much good, growing, running, fighting stuff as the penny he spent yesterday for a sweet cake, it would arouse something in him that would be one step toward better health for that boy.

The children in my housekeeping centers in New York can plan out a dinner with protein, carbohydrate and fat proportions perfectly, and yet they never use these words, but they know the substitute for meat, and they plan their dinner as unconsciously and as well as you do. Only by constant reiteration and habit has this knowledge come.

A few facts comparing the menus of the three nationalities may be interesting. We have served luncheons this past year in eight schools. Next fall, with seventeen schools, we will cook, as we do now, in five kitchens, but we will increase the number of schools to be served from each central kitchen. Two centers are Italian, one Jewish, and two mixed (Irish, colored, and just poor American). It has to be remembered always that each child is an independent purchaser, out for himself. He has his choice between spending his penny with us, doubling or losing it at craps, or buying hokey pokey from the push cart. At present, without the necessary education, it is not of any interest to him whether he is getting the requisite food value or not. If he likes our soup he will buy it, and if he doesn't he won't. Or if he likes what is on the penny table he will buy the soup to get it.

In the Italian districts we have only Italian cooks, who know how to cook macaroni with oil and garlic, as the children like it. One day when I cooked the soup a small girl said to me: "You Americans take all the nerve out of our macaroni;" and so with the rice, menestra, peas and beans, only an Italian can season to suit the Italian child. Our love of salt is distasteful to a child who knows only Italian cooking. Each Italian child receives for one penny one-half pint of a thick soup. The average cost of each is ¾ cents per child per day for the raw material, and the average energy giving value of this one-half pint of soup is 158.40 calories. These Italian children, to a great extent, bring bread from home. If not, and if they have the second penny, they are apt to spend it for bread, raising the nutritive value to 339.66 calories for the two cents. If it is ever decided that the children shall pay only for the raw food material, the Italians in the New York schools can buy for two cents soup and bread amounting to 425 calories. The Italians prefer their own soups and Italian bread to anything the penny table can offer. This is shown by the number of children buying two bowls of soup. The supervisor kept account every day for a week in one of the schools, and at least 25% of the children took double quantity of soup, most of them bringing bread from home. This menu worked out by the child himself gave him one-third of the total daily ration as exactly as we arranged it when we dictated the three-cent meal. But, unfortunately, this inborn wish to eat the right thing is not universal.

The soups of the Jewish schools average even more nutritive value than the Italian. The cook is Jewish, and only kosher cooking is allowed, as we are periodically inspected by the rabbi. The soups are potato and barley, peas with noodles, lima beans, rice and milk, noodles and milk, and a few others. Milk is used in almost all of the soups, and it brings up the food value to an average of 189.61 calories a day per one-half pint, over the Italian 158.41 calories. The average cost per child is the same, ¾ cent for the extra cost of milk is balanced by the use of crisco instead of oil or butter. The Jewish children, as well as the Italians, do not like variety. They have about six favorite soups, and are disappointed when a new one is tried. Meat is never used in the Jewish schools; beans, peas, milk and noodles, egg sandwiches, being the most important substitutes. Some of the Jewish children bring bread from home; others sandwiches, but there are some who spend only one penny for soup and eat no bread, which is seldom true of the Italians. In all of these foreign schools the mothers come in large numbers at first and watch to see what is being sold to their children, but after a week or two they learn to trust us and disappear.

The American-Irish schools are less satisfactory than the foreign, for here the average caloric value of ½ pint of soup per day per child is only 119. The American likes thin soup and not much of it, and won't buy it at all if, as he puts it, "it feels thick in his mouth." He wants things highly seasoned, and he wants the taste of meat, and feels cheated if the meat substitutes are used. But while the Italian children get on an average 5¾ grams protein per day, and the Jewish child 5½ grams, the American got 8½ grams for his expenditure of one cent, losing in carbohydrates against the Jew and in fat against the Italian, and in calories at least fifty a day under both Jew and Italian. But, as is always the case, this protein gain had to be paid for, and while we made over and above raw material ¼ cent per child per day in the foreign neighborhoods, we lost nearly ½ cent per child per day in the American meat-eating schools, and this entirely on the soup. If each child paid only for food material, the comparison of the food values of the soup and bread paid for with two cents by the three nationalities would be as follows:

> Italian, 15 grams protein, 425 calories in all.
> Jewish, 14.94 grams protein, 463 calories in all.
> American, 14.86 grams protein, and only 300 calories in all.

Children who use the penny tables differ greatly in their tastes. The American child buys soup just to get to the penny table, only about half of them stopping to buy bread, and never bringing bread from home. He wants sweets; will buy sweet crackers, sweet chocolate, cake, and when he buys cocoa he wants it "thin like tea." He averaged last year 3½ pennies a day, while the Italian and Jewish child spent but two cents a day; but while the foreign child nearly always supplements his school lunch with food brought from home, the American customer depends entirely on the school for his noon meal. The Jewish children seem to care little for the extras and at the penny table demand as little variety as in soups. "Bubs," or their large peas which look like beans, they would like every day; they want lock or sardella, their kind of fish, sandwiches; only a few of our American sandwiches tempt them. Fortunately, these are the nourishing kind such as cheese and egg. Peanuts they would like every day, but they won't touch peanut butter or salads, and very few of our sweets can be sold. The cakes made in both Jewish and Italian schools are made with oil and very little sugar. The Jewish child cannot be tempted to buy cooked fruit, while the Italian child would like baked apples every day. Our sweets appeal to the Italian child no more than to the Jew; salads and fruit seem to be his idea of dessert. Cocoa, rice and bread pudding, which are very popular with the American child are not liked by the foreigner. We are able to substitute for these nourishing dishes on the tables of the foreign schools graham and oatmeal crackers. The Italian child will never buy sweet crackers, as he wishes to break crackers into his soup, and he always explains that the sweet kinds spoil it.

Since substituting the penny lunch for the three-cent meal, our average attendance has increased, but under the old three-cent lunch system each child averaged four cents a day, and now under the penny system we take in but 2.6 cents per child per day. The deficit per lunch is the same, as for two cents a child in our New York schools now gets more than two-thirds of what he used to receive for three cents. In other words, we are gradually dropping the idea that school luncheons can pay for themselves, excepting as far as the raw material is concerned. We believe that the profit made in the high schools should pay the deficit on the elementary schools, and this may eventually be brought about.

One very interesting thing about school luncheons is the similarity of its unsolved problems the world over. Each country has faced the same question, and many of them are still unanswered. For example if the menu, carefully arranged by the scientific director, is not carefully supervised at the noon hour there is no guarantee that the supposed caloric value has been fairly given to each child, neither is the object lesson of neatness, order and an attractive table and refining atmosphere possible without the intelligent hostess who each day must be present in each school.

In New York there are 660 elementary schools. Five dollars a week is the least that paid supervision costs. That would mean $126,000 a year for this one duty of hostess, when elementary school luncheons become universal. Even with the seventeen schools in New York where we are to serve luncheons this year, it would cost the School Lunch Committee $3,780 if they put this paid supervisor in each school each day. Most countries, according to reports, have turned to the school teacher, begging for her help at this noon hour. So oppressive has this demand become in England that in the early part of 1906 a clause was inserted in the bill making provision for meals for school children that "No teacher seeking employment or employed in a public elementary school shall be required as part of his duties to supervise or assist, or abstain from supervising or assisting in the supervision of meals, or in the collection of the cost thereof." Germany, Norway, Sweden, Italy, all have worked over this problem, as I am sure have the fifty-two cities in America where school lunches are attempted.

Voluntary and irresponsible help at the luncheon hour we all know is not reliable. Just because it is easy to arouse sympathy for the under-fed child, it is too easy to get promises for this noon time supervision, but the hold is not strong, the social problem does not seem large enough. Next winter in New York we are going to draw these supervisors from our domestic science colleges, the pupils of these colleges to be on duty for a month at a time, one week in being trained by the former pupil, the last week in training the new pupil, and the two intervening weeks alone. It seems certain that the month of practical field work will be as valuable to the domestic science student in its way as hospital service is to the young doctor.

In most foreign countries many children are served free. The law which Holland passed in 1900 is not unusual. That law provided school meals and clothes for all children who were unable, because of the lack of food and clothing to go regularly to school. In Switzerland, provision is made that all children who, on account of poverty, do not receive a sufficiently nourishing breakfast shall be given milk and bread before lesssons and a full meal at noon consisting of 816 calories, or one-half of the day's total rations—what we gave to New York children in our first experiment. But we did not find this half pay and half free feeding successful. The children who could pay often sought in every way to get a free check; the children who received free checks sold them for two cents and went without food. The poor but honest parent was hard to find and often unwilling to have his children fed when found. The self-respecting children drifted away with the excuse that they were not going to belong to any free soup kitchen. Every principal was against it, experience having shown him that all public school children should be treated alike.

With our present system, for two cents, if two ounces of bread are brought from home, a child can receive a full meal, one-third the total daily rations. If this is beyond a mother to give, the case is too serious to be settled by any such simple method as the School Lunch Committee's handing out daily to one member of this family one meal. When such poverty is found, the home must be investigated, not the surface scratched by giving one meal to one member of this family. The problem of school lunches is a great one, and it will need the aid of all who are interested in domestic science to solve it.

EDUCATIONAL AND SOCIAL POSSIBILITIES OF SCHOOL LUNCHEONS

BY

MARY E. L. SMALL

The basic principle underlying the establishment of school lunches is the conservation of the child's physical strength. In the initial stages of the school feeding movement this physical value was the only one considered. A great hue and cry was raised about the "malnu_ trition of school children" and the statement was sweepingly made that a large percentage of our public school children was underfed. As you all know, after careful investigation, the "malnutrition" was found to be the result of other conditions than starvation, *i. e.*, lack of fresh air, over feeding, indigestible food, and inherited tendencies. Many of these conditions are the result of the ignorance of over-indulgent or negligent mothers.

To supply the immediate need of food, private philanthropy estab_ lished in some places the "penny lunch" and while it filled a need, there were many criticisms—pauperizing, relieving maternal responsibility, creating wrong values and in many instances promoting wastefulness and disorder.

Under these conditions the system did not commend itself to many educators, and after a trial, in some cases the plan was abolished; the chief reasons being that the person employed to prepare the food was disinterested in the children, lacked the power to promote habits of courtesy or order, and moreover she was often an indifferent or poor cook, so that even the first element of good was deficient.

At this point the city was asked to assume control, which it did, turning the management over to the domestic science branch of the Department of Education, and wherever this has been done, the manage- ment given to trained domestic science teachers of culture, the status of the school lunch has improved.

The domestic science teacher finds just as many, sometimes more, opportunities for exercising all the powers of her training, both personal and professional, in the school lunch room, as in the domestic science laboratory.

To begin with the very practical side, the food content of the meal. Times without number, an article of food new to the children, is served; they like it, tell about it at home. The pupils all know that they are getting full value, no more nor less, for their money, and the parent is taught a much needed lesson in the economic and nutritive value. Some-

times when there is adequate equipment, the pupils assist in the preparation of the luncheon, thus acquiring knowledge to be applied in the home.
Often the mothers visit the school and learn for themselves, first hand.

To take away the stigma of "pauperizing," the city ordinance commands "food to be sold at cost of material," the fund appropriated
being available only for maintenance. Under these conditions, parents
in the very best districts have petitioned for the warm lunch for their
children, when the distance of the school has precluded the possibility
of going home at noon. The children of the well-to-do parents and the
children of the poor have learned to sit quietly as one family, to talk
pleasantly with each other, to eat their food properly, and many acts
of courtesy and generosity have been encouraged.

These lunch rooms reflect the personality of the teacher in charge,
and I have seen rooms with a north or west exposure which appear to
be full of sunshine in the noon hour; the gentle, smiling teacher (of whom
the children said: "Oh, we love our pretty cooking teacher!") the
happy children, a flower or two or some growing green things on the
white tables, an uplifting quotation on the blackboard, with perhaps
a picture or two on the walls. A favorite picture for the lunch room is
"Thanksgiving" (Jessie Wilcox Smith) and its silent example is much
more potent than many words on the subject of thankfulness.

There is much illustrative material ordinarily used in domestic science
laboratories, which is readily adapted to the lunch room, and which
adds interest as well as educational value.

The Perry Picture Co. has many beautiful copies of fruit, vegetables,
nuts, fish. Dr. Langworthy's Food Charts are invaluable. The Baker
and Huyler Cocoa Charts are excellent. These pictures form the subject
of many informal lessons in the nature of talks, the children acquiring
much valuable information almost unconsciously.

Habits of neatness are inculcated, running water, liquid soap and
paper toweling provided, and the children required to wash their hands
before the meal.

The physiology of digestion is taught in simple talks on *what* to eat,
and *when*, and *how*, and *why*. One principal testifies that since the
"Cocoa Treatment" was instituted in her school, she has ceased to
doctor children in the afternoon for head and stomach aches.

The nutritive value of the school lunch is undisputed; the social
and ethical sides are not so universally recognized except by those in
close touch with the work. To those actively engaged this is the most
important part of the movement. Perhaps nothing will more clearly
express what can be accomplished along these lines than in giving two
personal observations.

As a nation we are somewhat lacking in chivalry; in no case more strongly marked than in the half grown youth, who is apt to be brusque and self-conscious. In one of our schools here, at the end of the luncheon, one can see daily the fifteen or sixteen year old boys, passing through the aisles collecting the trays in an orderly courteous manner with never a question of the girls sharing in this arduous work, and never a giggle nor nonsensical remark, as the boys perform this voluntary task. Altogether a remarkable example of a rarely seen chivalry.

In one of our poor districts—poor as regards money, but rich in school spirit and loyalty to ideals—the pupils, for various reasons brought their luncheon to school. The girls ate their cold meal in a class room, but the boys in a miserable basement. Upon the installation of equipment to provide hot cocoa to supplement the cold food, permission was granted the boys to share the privileges of the class room, which privilege those nice boys never lost. In a few months all the "newspaper wrapped" lunches had disappeared, and in their places paraffin paper and wrapping paper contained appetizing, well balanced lunches. The spirit of interest and coöperation between principal, teachers, pupils and parents was wonderful. At the end of the first year when the teacher in charge, herself a gentle woman, proposed a birthday party, every child responded with enthusiasm to the suggestion, and boys and girls alike vied with each other in anticipation and effort to make it a gala day; they begged that the members of the Commission be invited to share in their party. No brighter, more genial, more truly illuminating scene can be imagined than that of those happy faces, when the birthday cake with its one candle was cut and shared by guests and children. There could be no doubt that more than a penny's worth of food had passed into their hearts.

In another East Side school where love and generosity reign supreme the serving of soup or cocoa is presided over by the principal herself— a woman full of the joy of consecration to service. The lunch room is called the "Coöperative Cafeteria" for everyone delights to help.

To produce such results the teacher must be imbued not only with knowledge, but enthused by the ideal that she is feeding not only bodies, but minds and souls.

The influence of her personality can create a harmony of mind, contentment of body, and a cheer which will remain with the child and go with him into the home, instead of the irritability from poor food, combined with the restraints of school.

We find in those schools where the proper and warm lunch is presided over by a woman of force, ideality and love for her work, children running home at the day's end, happy and cheerful, showing many little acts of kindness for each other, not so commonly seen in schools where this opportunity for personal teaching has not been offered.

HOT LUNCHES IN RURAL SCHOOLS

BY

Mary L. Bull

The doctrine that food and dietetic habits are most important factors in health and disease is not new; but the problem of *human* feeding has only recently begun to receive the consideration which a subject of such vital importance deserves.

Food and its relation to the physical, mental and moral development of children is a subject of national importance and is recognized by all progressive people as such.

School feeding in cities and towns has, in the last few years, received the attention of many of the best educators and more progressive people of the day. Through the untiring efforts of enthusiastic advocates, the problem has been developed sufficiently to satisfy even the more skeptical.

Results show an increase in the efficiency of the children and a decrease in the expenditure of money in many cases.

Warm lunches in rural schools is a very different, as well as a more difficult problem than warm lunches in city and town schools, (1) because of their being so widely separated; (2) and because of the conservatism or lack of real interest felt by the average country school board in matters pertaining to the betterment of school conditions. "Children in the country have always eaten cold lunches and gotten along all right, why try new fangled ideas?"

At first thought it might seem that there was little need of the warm lunch in a rural school. That there would be no lack of nutritious, wholesome food for children coming from farm homes, where such staples as milk, eggs and vegetables may be procured first hand.

Investigation shows that there is not a lack of food, but rather a lack of thought or knowledge as to the use of food. That in many cases more scientific thought is given to the feeding of farm animals than to the feeding of farm children. Children on farms, as well as children in cities (in a large majority of cases eat little or no breakfast) often walk long distances from one-half to two or three miles to school which makes it necessary for them to carry a cold lunch. Thus the child has no warm food until supper and not always then. All of which seems to indicate that something warm at the noon hour is advisable.

Just how to prepare and serve a warm dish to twenty-five or thirty children in a one-room rural school, with no conveniences, is a question hard to answer. But "where there's a will there's a way" has been demonstrated in Minnesota.

The first step in carrying out any project is to "interest the people." In this case the *parents*, teachers and pupils must be interested. Parents and teachers must be made to appreciate the very close relation of food to health, the relation of health to efficiency, and the relation of efficiency to success, in every walk of life. They must come to realize that home making is a profession, and that to be successful in this most important profession a better knowledge of the subjects underlying the home is necessary.

The coöperation of some progressive, wide awake County Superintendents made it possible to visit a large number of schools in their counties. Parents were invited to visit the school and meet the County Superintendent and extension workers. The subject of foods, their use in the body, preparation, etc., was discussed in a general way, special emphasis being given to the value of common food materials as milk, eggs, cereals and vegetables. The "Langworthy Food and Nutrition Charts" were found most helpful in interesting parents and children (even the primaries) in the nutrients found in the foods spoken of. The knowledge that these common foods had some special purpose to fulfill made these everyday things seem of importance.

Wherever advisable a simple demonstration was given showing desirable and pleasing combinations, trying always to use only such materials as were easily obtainable in the vicinity in which the school was located.

The value of a warm dish as an accompaniment to the cold lunch was mentioned and a possible dish suggested. How materials for such a dish might be procured and the work of preparing and serving done with little trouble to anyone was spoken of, care being taken to suggest only some dish which might be cooked on the stove which furnished heat for the building.

This work was followed by leaflets with printed recipes of two or three simple soups in which cereals or vegetables were combined with milk and a chowder, the ingredients of which were potatoes, salt pork, crackers and milk. Directions for preparation and time required for cooking were also given. Later a bulletin on Domestic Science in Rural Schools was published and sent to County Superintendents for distribution among the teachers.

In this bulletin the recipes were followed by short articles dealing with material used in the recipe. Milk, nutritive content, care of milk, cooking of milk, use in body, care of utensils, etc. Following each article were questions which might be used in bringing out the essential points in the preparation, food value and proper use of the food.

This work was done in the spring of 1911. The next fall a larger number of teachers tried to carry out the suggested work than was expected, and last fall one county put two-burner kerosene stoves and simple equipment for the work into some twenty schools. In order to ascertain how the idea was received by parents, children and teachers, a list of questions was sent to the County Superintendents, with a request that they be sent to such teachers as they thought best. In answer to the question of amount of time consumed in preparation of dish, the almost universal reply was from "ten to fifteen minutes of school time" or less; much of the work being done before school, at recess or at home. The work in most cases being performed by pupils with suggestions from the teacher, different teachers using different methods.

The equipment was procured in various ways, purchased by the board, given by individuals, or purchased by the school with proceeds from entertainments, socials, etc., given by the children and teacher for that purpose. One teacher with her pupils held a little reception at the school house and at the bottom of their written invitations wrote "Domestic Science Shower." The guests responded very liberally with spoons, kettles and staple supplies, as rice, cereals, salt, etc.

Many teachers made an effort to develop the educational side of the idea, using the questions given in the bulletin and correlating the work with other studies, as physiology, reading and others. Language by writing the manner of preparing a dish used at lunch; writing a paper on rice and how to cook it to make it most palatable and digestible. Arithmetic—dividing large recipes or taking a small recipe sufficient for one and ascertaining the amount necessary for the entire school or the family at home; estimating the cost of the dish served to the school, also cost per pupil—a lesson not only in arithmetic but market prices, etc.

Some of the replies to how the heater might be successfully used were very interesting. One teacher had one of the boys make a stout wire frame to fit over the top of the stove which was round and would not hold a kettle without something of the kind. But by the use of this simple device it was possible to serve a soup, cereal or chowder every day during the entire winter term.

In almost all cases the parents gladly coöperated with the teacher, furnishing material when called upon and in many other ways. A furnishing this week or day and B next week, as the case might be.

To the question of "what benefit do you consider the work," the replies in nearly all cases spoke of the (1) aids to discipline, especially at the noon hour; (2) of the possibility of training in manners, neatness, consideration of others; (3) absence of lunching between meals. Mothers spoke of lessened desire on part of children for candies, etc. Some thought that children did better work and that the attendance was more regular, especially with children who were not strong.

Many spoke of this social homelike meal hour as helping to solve social problems which every rural teacher has to deal with. All agreed that parents took greater interest in the school and felt that the time spent in the discussion of home making problems was well spent. The manner in which different teachers developed the plan is of great interest to me, but time will not permit of detail.

I believe "warm lunches in rural schools" is a subject of importance, *not a passing fad*, and that through it may be reached a large number of people not otherwise reached who should be interested in a better understanding of human feeding and its relation to life, a life of health, happiness and success.

HISTORY AND DEVELOPMENT OF LUNCHES IN HIGH SCHOOLS

With a Discussion of the Elements of Cost in School Lunch Expenses

BY

JULIA PULSIFER

"The story of the beginning of lunches in the High Schools of Boston is the story of the beginning of the school lunch movement in America." In 1894 the Boston School Committee passed an order to the effect ".that only such food as was approved" by them "should be sold in the city school houses." The order was the result of an agitation begun under the leadership of Mrs. Ellen H. Richards, whose interest had been aroused by a realization of the educational value that lay in placing properly prepared food before young people. She was also keen to see the menace to health that lay in the "goodies" the children were purchasing at recess from the corner stores, and in some cases from the lunch counters installed by janitors in the school buildings. After the passage of the above-mentioned order, the New England Kitchen, then in the early days of its food experiments, was asked to provide the food for the school luncheons. The original menus were carefully worked out under the supervision of Mrs. Richards, and the whole scheme was not only excellently planned from the point of view of scientific nutrition, and of social service, but it was also on a good business basis. All the food was manufactured at the Central Kitchen and distributed to the serving centers at the schools. Here the city provided the space for serving, the stationary equipment, and the fuel for reheating. This is practically the organization that exists to-day, nearly 20 years after, except that the work is under the management of the Women's Educational and Industrial Union, and the general supervision is in the hands of an advisory committee composed of three representatives from the Union and three High School Head Masters, elected annually by the Association of Head Masters of the Boston High and Latin Schools. The business has doubled in the past seven years, and luncheons are now being served to upwards of 5,000 children at 16 different High Schools. The deficit in the smaller schools is made up by the profit in the larger ones, so that all get the same service. During the past winter the management of the Women's Educational and Industrial Union, realizing that the next point in progress must be along educational lines, and feeling that to accomplish this the School Committee itself must be responsible for the lunch work, has endeavored to turn over its stewardship to that body. This change has not yet been accomplished, but we hope for it soon as the next point in the development of the High School Lunch System of Boston.

In the meanwhile the development of luncheons in High Schools all over the country has been rapid and noteworthy. From tables in dark basements where janitors dispensed candy and stale cake we have advanced to huge light airy lunch rooms on the top floors of new buildings with all that is modern and up-to-date in equipment, and with a menu varied and tempting. This is especially true of the newer High School buildings of the West. Back in the East we are still struggling with the dark, congested lunch room in the basements of old outgrown buildings.

An investigation during the winter of 1910-11 in the State of Massachusetts showed that in 67 cities and towns lunch was served in High Schools. Ten of these lunch rooms were under the direct control of the school authorities, forty-three were money making enterprises, six were managed by women's clubs, one by a church society, five by the students themselves, and two by the Domestic Science Department of the school. In schools where the lunch rooms are run for the profit of the managers little or no attention is paid to the laws of hygiene and nutrition. The young people are provided with the food which they are most likely to buy—sweets and pastry. In lunch rooms run as social service enterprises by women's clubs, definite effort is made to provide nourishing food at a low price, and usually high food standards are maintained. This is true also of lunch rooms under school control, and in addition in these schools some connection is occasionally made with the school curriculum.

Another investigation during the past winter has shown that in sixteen of the larger cities of this country the lunch work has been placed under the control of school authorities after various experiences with outside management. This investigation also revealed the fact that there is a general tendency toward centralization—the management of the several lunch rooms of a city by one director, the natural and most frequent method of organization being under the Domestic Science Department. The benefits resulting from school control are obvious. So far very little advantage has been taken of the educational opportunities latent in lunch work. Yet there is a growing feeling everywhere that the lunch room plants may be used in connection with the courses in chemistry, hygiene, domestic science, decorative art, social training, business methods, etc. To come to a full utilization of these educational possibilities of course teachers and school boards must have full responsibility for the lunch work.

The financial status of school lunch rooms has been the object of much attention with us, and we have been requested to devote a considerable portion of our discussion to this phase of the subject. We have found in our investigations that almost never are two school lunch rooms on the same financial basis. The term "covering all expenses" requires careful definition, and for the purposes of this paper I shall take the phrase in its literal meaning. To cover all expenses means to pay not only for food and service but for superintendence, equipment, fuel, heat, rent, light, water rates—in brief *all* the expenses which a commercial lunch room must meet. It is obvious that if a school restaurant had to meet all these charges the prices would be prohibitive—especially in small schools where the overhead charge per capita would be very high. Since the School Board requires the attendance of the child at an hour when he is in need of food, that Board should make it possible for him to buy that food cheaply by providing a comfortable room in which he is to eat it, free of rent, and at least simple equipment for preparing it. Some school boards go much further. It is in this matter of subsidy from the Board that school lunch rooms vary so greatly. In our investigation of last winter we found no High School lunch could properly be said to be "paying all expenses." The centralized lunch system of Boston comes nearest to this status of any, because the School Board there provides no place for the cooking of the food. The rent, heat, light, fuel, etc., at the central kitchen are paid for out of the receipts from the luncheons. These overhead charges in Boston during the winter of 1911 and 1912 amounted to upwards of $4,000. That the system can carry such large additional costs, and still maintain prices as low as other High School lunch rooms not so burdened is undoubtedly due to the saving in food costs and supervision that accrue under a centralized system of cooking. It is also somewhat due to the use of the less expensive forms of food, which affect not the wholesomeness and nutritive value of the lunches, but possibly to some extent their variety and attractiveness. At the other extreme as regards subsidy from the School Board was a school restaurant where the receipts were required to cover only the cost of the raw material. All other expenses were met by school funds. The majority of school lunch rooms, however, were in a class between these two extremes—almost no two being exactly alike. Some pay for their own fuel, more do not. Some pay superintendent's salary, others do not, and so it goes. In many there is practically no book-keeping at all, and it is impossible to discover their actual financial status. As a general rule, the lunch rooms in small schools where the patronage is small, receive the most help in the way of subsidy from the Board. In a city where there are both large and small High Schools and a centralized management, the profits of the large schools pay the deficit in the small ones, and all get equal service. In cities, however, where there is no centralized system, the large schools are very apt to be exploited by business firms who draw considerable profit from the enterprise, while the small schools suffer from high prices and poor food.

A study of the elements of cost in our own system, and a comparison with these same elements in other systems has been very suggestive to us. First we compared the Boston financial statement with that of Bradford, England—the only other school lunch system having a central kitchen like ours which we have personally investigated. We found that the food in both Boston and Bradford amounted to 54% of the total expense. The delivery in Boston was 4% of the total, in Bradford 17%; the wide difference being due to the fact that in Boston there are only 16 serving centers, in Bradford 25; also, in Bradford the dishes are carried back and forth each day, the cleansing of them being done at the central plant. The labor item, however, is much higher in Boston, being 32%, while in Bradford it is 18%. This is partly due to the higher wages paid generally in this country. It is also much more economical of labor to concentrate all the heavy work of dish washing at one point and to do it with up-to-date apparatus. However, it is significant that the labor and delivery together in each city amount to 36% of the total expense, showing that there would be apparently nothing to be gained in Boston if we adopted Bradford's method of sending the dishes to the central plant each day, the extra delivery costing as much as the saving in labor. We have grouped all other expenses under the head of "general;" in Boston they amount to 9% of the total, in Bradford 9½%. The similarity of all these costs made us feel in Boston that we had a system *equal* at least in economy of administration to that of Bradford which had been held up to us as a model. Our next comparison was with the High School lunch system of St. Louis. We found that food costs there were 67% of receipts, and during the same time 53% with us. After studying the situation in the two cities we realized the reason for this divergence. In St. Louis most of the bread stuffs are purchased as well as the ice cream, so that the cost price includes the labor and the manufacturer's profit. In Boston all the bread and rolls are manufactured at the central kitchen, and there the cost price represents only the value of the raw material, the cost of the labor on these goods showing up in our labor item which is 3% more than in St. Louis, no manufacturer's profit being included at all because we do our own baking. Another reason for the higher labor cost in Boston, it being 32% there and only 29% in St. Louis, is the division of the business into 16 centers where $5,000 less was received than in the six centers of St. Louis. Of course a system where the sales amounted to $57,000 at six centers would be more economical of labor than one where the sales amounted to $52,000 at 16 centers. This comparison is interesting because it is of two systems receiving very different amounts of subsidy from their respective school boards. Boston could not afford to bring its food costs up to 67%, because it has $4,000 of overhead charges to meet, items of expense which do not appear at all in the St. Louis budget, being borne indirectly by the Board itself. (There the Board provides kitchen space in the schools free of rent, heat, light and fuel charges, thus relieving the school lunch system of the expense of a central plant.)

Another comparison of value to us in Boston is that of our own annual statements year by year. We have found, as would naturally be expected, the food costs steadily rising from 49% in 1907 to 54% in 1912—a difference which would have necessitated the raising of prices if it had not been for the fact that along with this increase came a corresponding increase in the volume of business, almost doubling in six years. This lowered our service cost per capita and made it possible to maintain our old prices for food which was costing us much more.

These points which I have tried to make merely go to show that as regards the business side of the High School lunch room problem, it is like any other business—centralization goes for economy of administration, and the higher the costs the more must be received for the product unless sales increase in proportion.

In conclusion I want to point out again that it is with the School Board itself that the responsibility for the school lunch work must ultimately rest; in many cities the Boards have shouldered this responsibility, in others they are planning to do so, and I wish to lay before this meeting the discussion of the question which we have found settled so variously in the different cities of this country. Should the school lunch restaurant pay all expenses, including charges for rent, heat, light, etc., or is it legitimate that the School Board should lower the price to the students by taking upon itself some of the financial burden? In the latter case to what extent should the school lunch be subsidized? Is it possible to set a standard?

HIGH SCHOOL LUNCHES UNDER SCHOOL BOARD CONTROL

BY

Emma Smedley

The school lunch has become a recognized department in every well appointed high school. It is a natural and normal part of the child's education, because it increases the mental activity, builds up the physical health, and incidentally teaches valuable lessons in food values and creates a normal taste for wholesome foods, which are frequently not provided in the home.

The School Board that is alert to its responsibilities will require that an educated dietitian, with a corps of qualified assistants, be placed in charge of the school lunch, just as school medical inspection is under the care of qualified physicians.

It has been impossible at this time for me to obtain information regarding the methods employed by school boards in other cities, and my remarks are therefore confined to the work in Philadelphia, Pa.

In this city, some members of the Board of Public Education have for several years been dissatisfied with the lunch system which existed in the schools—where the janitor was allowed to sell to the children such food as he could conveniently handle with the help of his assistants or where a caterer paid the school board for the privilege of conducting a cheap restaurant in the school building. In both cases the chief object of janitor or caterer was to make money regardless of quantity, quality or wholesomeness of the food.

As a result of this dissatisfaction, in September, 1909, the committee having charge of the high schools decided to make a practical experiment for a year in one school, to ascertain if it were possible to conduct a first-class lunch room for pupils and teachers which would be self-supporting and at the same time supply wholesome, attractive food.

From this experiment has developed the coöperative system now employed in nearly all of our high schools.

The word coöperative is used because we are indebted to the Board of Education for its generous support in providing rooms, fuel, heat and light, and furnishing the equipment required for starting a lunch room; to the principal and teachers in each school for their sympathy and encouragement, and to the pupils for their hearty approval and help in maintaining the system.

Our experience has shown that this coöperative system has developed a splendid spirit in the school, and the problem of discipline at the lunch hour has been solved in many schools since its establishment.

The Superintendent of the Department of High School Lunches is appointed by the Board of Public Education, and consults with one of its committees. She is authorized to act as general purchasing agent and to have the administrative care of all the schools; to pay all salaries together with the current expenses, including the auditing of the accounts, from the receipts from the sales of food in the schools.

It will be noted that in Philadelphia the School Board wisely holds the Superintendent responsible for administration and purchasing of supplies. She is, therefore, free to consult with the architect when plans are being prepared for a new kitchen, and to arrange specifications for its equipment, including china, silver, linen and cooking utensils. She is at liberty to purchase all food in the open market at the 'lowest price for the best quality, and to reject anything that does not conform to the high standard which has been established.

The size of the portions served, and the selling prices are arranged to meet the financial requirements. Food is not sold at a profit but it is necessary to have a working balance to offset a possible deficit due to unforeseen emergencies.

The Superintendent brings the general working plan of the system to the notice of the teachers and pupils by speaking in the morning assembly in the schools. The idea of wholesome food, attractively served, at a net cost, appeals to all. Thus the pupils appreciate that the luncheon is for their benefit, and that the size of their sandwich, the quantity served in their soup bowl, and other portions, will be increased as the service expense is reduced. With this thought impressed upon the mind of the pupil, it is an easy matter to train them to understand that each one must be his own and her own waiter or waitress, carrying the food from the counter to the tables, and returning soiled dishes to the counter as they leave the dining-room.

In each of the High Schools, there is an adequately equipped kitchen and dining-room. Each is presided over by a trained dietitian who is responsible to the Superintendent of Luncheons for the fulfillment of all plans made by her and for the details of food preparation and serving.

The dietitian is recognized in each school as the official representative of the Department of High School Lunches. She consults with a member of the faculty to secure the names of desirable pupils to assist in serving at the counter during the lunch hour, and attends to other details connected with her school. Her presence in the kitchen and lunch rooms has a wonderful influence in creating an atmosphere of refinement and wholesome dignity, which makes it possible to secure an efficient corps of untrained assistants.

The Superintendent holds monthly meetings at a central office, with the dietitians, where all important matters, size of portions, menu, etc., are freely discussed, so that the conditions in the various schools will be as nearly uniform as possible. The Superintendent is in communication with each school daily, either visiting it in person or by telephone.

With this general supervision, each dietitian prepares the menu and market order for her school, and sends it to the Superintendent for approval or correction. All supplies are ordered by the Superintendent from the central office, and deliveries are made by the dealers to the individual schools.

An accurate record of the daily receipts in each school is kept by the dietitian in charge, or by the cashier, who signs this record at the end of the week and sends it to the central office with other weekly reports of supplies on hand, menu, market orders, etc. The money is deposited each day in a conveniently located bank.

The salary of the dietitian is one of the expenses of administration, and is met by the receipts from the sale of lunches. The amount paid corresponds to the scale of salaries paid the teachers of domestic science in the public schools.

The number of assistants required, varies with the number of pupils in the school. With an enrollment of 500 pupils and 25 teachers, the dietitian has two helpers during the whole day from eight until four o'clock, and at the serving hour five pupils assist during the first half of the period. These pupils who esteem it a privilege to don white coat or apron and assist with the serving, are paid two 5-cent luncheon checks for their voluntary services. In a school having 2,000 pupils and 100 teachers, where lunch is served in two half hour periods, one man is employed to do the heavy work and operate the dish washer, and six women from 8 until 4 o'clock, and three women for three hours during the busiest time of day. In addition to these regular helpers ten pupils serve at the counter during each period.

With our system of serving it is difficult to ascertain the number of pupils who avail themselves of the lunches, many of whom bring from home sandwiches, fruit and cake and supplement this box luncheon with a bowl of soup, a cup of cocoa, milk or a dessert. Others depend entirely upon the school lunch because their parents realize that it is cheaper and more convenient than to put up the cold lunch at home. The average daily sale is one and a half portions for each pupil in attendance, or about 4½ cents per day per pupil.

The patrons of our lunch counters are allowed the opportunity of choosing their lunch from the menu which is posted near the cashier's booth and above the serving counter. The food is paid for as it is taken from the counter, with aluminum checks which are previously purchased from the cashier.

The items on the menu are changed each day, but it always consists of soup and a roll for 5 cents, one substantial hot dish and a roll for 5 cents, such as macaroni, baked beans, creamed beef on toast, scalloped fish, etc., cocoa with whipped cream 3 cents; two or three varieties of sandwiches at 5 cents each, one pint of milk for 5 cents or one-half pint milk 3 cents (served with a straw), a home-made dessert 3 cents, such as cup custard, tapioca custard, fruit jelly, etc., ice cream 5 cents, fresh fruit, figs, dates, sweet chocolate and cookies of various kinds from 1 cent to 5 cents, according to the season and the size of the portion.

For ten cents one can purchase a luncheon which yields 700 calories, for example:

Baked beans and roll..............................	$0.05
½ pint milk.......................................	.03
Fruit...	.01
Sweet chocolate...................................	.01
	$0.10

or:

Cocoa and whipped cream...........................	$0.03
Egg sandwich......................................	.05
Fruit...	.01
3 cookies...	.01
	$0.10

It will be noticed from the above menu that coffee, cinnamon buns, cream puffs, pies, crullers, cakes and candies are not included in the list. These have been omitted from the menu because they do not furnish the essentials of a wholesome midday luncheon for an active, growing person, whose mind and body should be properly nourished without imposing unnecessary effort upon the digestive organs. When the Philadelphia High School lunches were started along these lines four years ago, it was predicted by many persons that the pupils would not patronize the system; that it would be a failure because children would eat *only* pie and coffee, or cream puffs and pickles. But these High School pupils enjoy the substantial lunches that are served, and there is a constant increase in the sale of soup, macaroni, home-made desserts and cocoa, and a corresponding decrease in the sale of ice cream. There is a noticeable improvement in the health and scholarship of the pupils since it is not possible to purchase unwholesome food during school hours. The High School lunch rooms of Philadelphia are utilized by the Domestic Science Department of Drexel Institute, as practise fields for the pupil dietitians. These students spend one morning each week for two months in one or another of the sixteen schools, assisting the dietitian in her varied duties, planning the menu, preparing and serving lunch, etc. This practise has proved very helpful to many of the Drexel students who have later secured positions as dietitians in this or other cities.

A system of bookkeeping has been established under the direction of a certified public accountant, which makes it possible to ascertain at a moment's notice the financial standing of each school, and other details which are of interest from a business standpoint.

The annual report for the year ending June 30, 1913, shows the receipts to have been $92,000 or an average expenditure of 4½ cents for each child in attendance at the schools. The cost of administration and service $26,000, upkeep of the plants about $2,000, and food $64,000.

In conducting the High School luncheon, or restaurant, as many prefer to call it, where it is not under the control of the School Board, there is a temptation to use it as a means of revenue for some student activity in the school, or for the benefit of the person who is in charge of the work, but the experience in the Philadelphia High Schools has clearly shown that if the best quality of materials is used, the cooking done by domestic science graduates, fair size portions given and good wages and salaries paid, there will be no balance in dollars and cents at the end of the year. But the grateful parents and healthy, happy pupils will represent a far greater surplus than can be estimated.

THE TRAINING OF THE SCHOOL DIETITIAN

BY

CAROLINE L. HUNT

In entering upon a discussion of the training of the school dietitian, it is safe to begin with the statement that if terms are to be strictly defined, the school dietitian has hardly an existence to-day. It is safe to say, also, however, that so rapidly is public opinion growing in favor of expert supervision of school feeding that the time cannot be far distant when the school dietitian will have a position in the educational system as well recognized as that of the teacher. Since, therefore, the dietitian is imminent, the time has arrived when those who are looking forward to her coming may profitably form ideals for her qualifications and for the training which should be expected of her. Since, on the other hand, she is still but the creature of our hopes, these ideals will of necessity be as varied as the imaginations of those who form them. Any statement, therefore, like that which I have been asked to give to-day, of that which should constitute the training of the school dietitian is likely to be colored by personal opinion and can at best serve only as a subject for debate.

The statement that the dietitian has not as yet come into being should not be taken to mean that there are not to-day in connection with school lunch rooms many positions, that of manager, for example, quite as honorable and important as the place which the dietitian will fill. There is no question here of comparative importance but rather of difference in function. In truth those who have gone before the dietitian have, by their recognition of new educational needs and by intelligent devotion to the welfare of the children, given us the very building stones out of which our ideals are being formed. Even Miss Matty, benignly presiding over her little shop in Cranford and selling almond comfits to children at a financial loss to herself "because the little things liked them so much," and substituting ginger and peppermint lozenges at an equal financial loss when persuaded that almond comfits were unwholesome, gave us an important foundation stone for our ideal—sympathy with and understanding of children. A willingness to take the preferences of children into consideration, or, better still, an appreciation of the importance of so doing; of occasionally providing "almond comfits" and of coating with sugar, if need be, the "ginger and peppermint" of the diet, is one of the first requisites of the successful dietitian. As Dr. Clement Dukes, Consulting Physician to

Rugby, said in a recent address:(a) "The natural 'likes and dislikes' of the young in the matter of food are very powerful, and while they should not be encouraged, allowance should be wisely made for their satisfaction. They form a physical function of the age and constitu. tion, and vary according to the stages of life—a craving at one time becoming a loathing at another."

Miss Matty, beloved prototype of the school dietitian, went bankrupt, of course, or would have done so if her brother had not returned from India and paid her debts. She was followed by a long succession of small shop keepers, more or less amiable and well disposed towards children, but usually either ignorant or willfully unmindful of their physical needs. Yet with all their shortcomings, those among them who achieved material success contributed another stone for the upbuilding of our ideal, for they were able to count costs and to make financial ends meet. However lofty our standards for the dietitian, we must not lose sight of the fact that she will be expected to deal with material things, to buy in the markets of the world and to sell at a profit. She, like the small shop keeper, must be able to strike a good bargain but the profit which she will be called upon to make will be the future health and physical well-being of the children who come under her care. Upon her business ability will depend to a large extent the quality of the food she will be able to serve, the degree of cleanliness she will be able to maintain, and the amount of beauty in furnishings which she will be able to place before her patrons. The school caterer who is above the task of careful buying, often finds herself obliged to economize in places where saving is dangerous; in the matter of the persons employed to wash dishes, for example. Upon the foundation stone of our ideal, the one which stands for understanding of and sympathy with children, we must, therefore, place another upon which we will write "*business ability*."

After the small shop keeper came the lunch room manager, granted space in which to sell food within the school itself and more or less directly responsible to the school authorities for the character of the food offered and for the manner of serving it. A connection once established between the person selling food and the educational system, there came a demand often poorly defined, to be sure, for a knowledge of food values on the part of the caterer, and for ability to serve balanced rations and scientifically prepared foods. This demand, when relieved of its indefiniteness, stands forth as a reasonable insistence upon the part of the more intelligent school patron that if science has anything to teach about the relation of foods to the upbuilding of the bodies of children, such

a. "Our Children's Health at Home and at School," Report of a Conference on Diet and Hygiene in Public Secondary and Private Schools. London, May 13, 1912. Published by National Food Reform Association, Westminster, 1912, p. 34.

knowledge must find practical application in the school lunch room. An understanding of foods, particularly in their relation to the needs of growing children and a familiarity with the literature of nutrition are now expected of the lunch room manager and must form a third stone in the ideal which we are building for the school dietitian.

The coming expert will be expected to have at her command a knowledge of those facts about food and those principles of nutrition that are generally recognized among scientists as established. This will always be necessary to a wise selection of food materials, good methods of cooking and of preparation in general, rational combinations of foods to form dishes or meals and adequate precautions against impurity and uncleanness. All this is obvious and needs no elaboration here. But in addition to this argument (which we may describe as positive) for familiarity with the literature of nutrition and for ability to follow the work of investigators, there is another argument, equally potent, though negative in form. This has a bearing not so much upon the benefits to be brought to the children directly as upon errors which, for their sakes, the dietitian should avoid. It relates to the danger of confusing with facts the theories which are constantly forced upon the attention of those who cater for others as the result of the enthusiasm of faddists, of personal preferences in the matter of flavor and of family traditions about the digestibility or wholesomeness of various foods.

The theories which the dietitian will be in danger of accepting as facts without adequate reason for the faith which is in her will differ with the years. Perhaps the most continuous snag which she will encounter will be her own preferences and her own family traditions about that which is wholesome or digestible. There are few people in the world who are not obliged to avoid some one or more articles of food, even when in health. Such idiosyncracies are probably more wide-spread than we suspect, for the reason that it is not considered good form to make them a subject of conversation. The person who has no thorough knowledge of dietetics is likely to generalize upon these personal peculiarities and to exclude from the meals which she prepares for others many wholesome and desirable food materials and dishes. The objections to such a proceeding on the part of the school lunch room manager or dietitian are many. Among others, we may name the fact that it tends to perpetuate error, which is unfortunate from an educational point of view. Again, if children are to be educated to be agreeable table companions, they must be trained to be catholic in their tastes with reference to food, and should not be encouraged to reject this or that article of diet without due cause. The school dietitian has something to do besides influencing children to avoid unwholesome foods. She is under obligations to society to do her part toward preventing them from growing finical, and toward training them to enjoy the great variety of foods which Nature provides.

The pressure of faddists upon those who cater for others takes one form to-day and another tomorrow. At present, its influence is being exerted in the direction of making certain food materials seem exceptionally valuable because they contain elements indispensable to the proper nourishment of the body. These faddists often leave out of account entirely the fact that if a person takes a mixed diet, it is almost impossible for him to avoid these much-vaunted elements. Tomorrow the faddist will take a different turn, and only those who know what has been proved and also what has not been proved in connection with the subject of dietetics will take his teaching at its true value.

The faithful, conscientious labors of those who have charge of school lunch rooms have contributed yet another qualification for our ideal dietitian, for these women have realized that they were not only feeding the children of to-day but training the parents of tomorrow. They have sought to teach by their daily practices correct methods of preparation, the art of bill of fare making and good taste in furniture and table furnishings. They have acted upon the principle that children must acquire so much by laborious, painstaking methods, that it is only fair that they should be given a chance to learn by their almost unlimited power of imitation the essentials of good taste and good breeding.

The lessons which the school dietitian will find most important to teach by example, like the snags in dietetics which she will need to avoid, will change as the years pass. She will always find some practical reform ripe for her coöperation and just in the stage to profit by her assistance. What it will be tomorrow we cannot say, but to-day it is doubtless the clean food reform. There is probably no greater menace to health from a single cause at present than from the uncleanly methods by which food is handled in public places and from the stale food which is served. The public is awake, aroused, horrified, and educational demonstrations of cleanly methods of handling food on a large scale would probably accomplish one hundred times as much to-day as they would have accomplished ten years ago. Every school lunch room, therefore, and all places where food is kept or handled, should be not only thoroughly but also conspicuously clean. They should be thoroughly clean for the sake of the immediate safety of those served and they should proclaim their cleanliness in order to establish higher standards in public places.

In a certain group of lunch rooms in Boston, owned and conducted by a scientifically trained woman, the work of disposing of food which is left unused at the end of the day and of deciding what shall be rejected and what shall be saved is entrusted only to the highest priced and most thoroughly trained employees. Similar attention is given to the washing of dishes, to the preparation of fresh vegetables, and to the care of all cloths used in cleaning the tables on which food is prepared or served. If the kitchens in these restaurants could be opened to public gaze by means of glass partitions or otherwise, they would be of more value than much formal teaching of bacteriology.

To take an example of a different sort: In a certain renowned state university, a water cooler with a common drinking cup attached, stood in the registrar's office just outside of the president's room for months after the bacteriological department of the university had been engaged in preaching publicly against such practices. Who can tell how much the campaign against the common drinking cup was retarded by the failure of this university to live up to its own teaching? Universities, however, influence directly a very small number of people in comparison with elementary schools. The trained food expert in the lower schools has therefore a weapon against filthy practices in the handling of foods, whose possible effectiveness almost passes the bounds of imagination. Lunch room managers have fortunately often recognized and embraced their opportunities to teach and have by this means raised the standard for the training of their successors.

Up to this point we have spoken only of qualifications which school managers and dietitians should have in common, but in large school districts a separation is sure to come in time between these two trained officials. Then the manager will assume charge of the details of every-day administration, leaving the dietitian to make the lunch room a laboratory for the solution of problems bearing on the general subject of the feeding of children.

The opportunities for research offered wherever food is served in large amounts under intelligent supervision have been recognized and demonstrated by the United States Department of Agriculture, and also by private organizations, physicians and health officers. The investigations of the Department of Agriculture have been mainly dietary studies(a) conducted for the purpose of determining the amount of food actually provided in well-conducted institutions where the children appeared to be well fed and in good bodily condition. These investigations have resulted in the establishment of certain dietary standards for children which are to be found recorded in the publications of the Department.(b) The Department, by coöperating with individuals and institutions, has not only shown the invaluable opportunities for research offered by institutional dining-rooms but has also given training in methods of investigation.

a. U. S. Dept. Agr., Office of Experiment Stations, Bulletin 223.
b. U. S. Dept. Agr., Office of Experiment Stations, Circular 110.

The studies made by private organizations, physicians and school health officers have, up to this time, been chiefly in connection with conspicuous cases of malnutrition. Their purpose has been to determine the relation of malnutrition to underfeeding, bad housing, and other untoward conditions of living. These two lines of work, studies of normal and abnormal children, suggest that in connection with the school system there should be an expert who is not only in touch with investigators but also trained to take for herself advantage of the enlarging opportunities for investigation offered by the growing custom of serving meals in the schools. We look, therefore, for the coming of the school dietitian who, relieved of the details of administration, will have only the final decision as to what food shall be served and will be able by her own studies to contribute to our knowledge of food in its relation to growth and development.

Understanding of child nature and some familiarity with the principles of pedagogy; business ability; knowledge of the literature of nutrition; an acquaintance with methods of investigation and research—these are qualifications which we may reasonably expect of the school dietitian.

Since it is obviously out of the question to outline here courses of training and study we must be content to let the qualifications suggest the character of the preparation. The recognized need of thorough courses in chemistry, physics and the biological sciences as foundation for a working knowledge of dietetics and sanitation puts out of the question the possibility of any short cut to the profession. The widening opportunities for adding to knowledge which, if neglected will entail serious loss to the public, tend to lengthen the path and to extend it into the graduate school. The need for close contact with children on the other hand, and the demand for business experience suggest pleasant side trips into apprenticeship. The larger universities offer the long broad path of scientific preparation and also through their normal departments and lunch rooms, the enticing by-paths where practical experience is to be gained.

Formal courses of training, however, no matter what their length or their breadth, can never create those kindly impulses in which the successful work of the school dietitian must have its origin. The best they can do is to make recognition of the value to the coming generation of the desire to substitute peppermint lozenges for almond comfits and to direct it toward a scientific system of school feeding, for after all the Miss Mattys of the world are from the Lord; they may be moulded but they can never be made by educational institutions.

CANTINES SCOLAIRES

PAR

Leon Meyer

Dans les écoles primaires de la ville de Paris beaucoup d'enfants ne peuvent prendre dans leur famille le repas de midi, le père et la mère étant occupés au dehors.

Il est donc indispensable que les enfants puissent prendre ce repas à l'école.

Beaucoup d'enfants appartenant à des familles pauvres font souvent leur meilleur repas à la cantine scolaire.   A Paris les cantines scolaires furent créés en 1881.

Avant cette création les enfants *apportaient* en venant à l'école, un panier renfermant les aliments necessaires à leur repas de midi.   Le but de la cantine est surtout de donner à l'enfant des *aliments chauds*. A Paris les cantines scolaires sont organisées par les *Caisses des Ecoles* qui fonctionnent dans chaque arrondissement.   Chaque caisse des Ecoles nomme *une commission dite des Cantines* (chargée de tout ce qui concerne la cantine,—achats d'aliments,—cuisson des aliments—surveillance du personnel) les caisses des Ecoles étant des *établissements publics* dont les ressources sont exclusivement constituées par des cotisations, dons, legs ou subventions, certains arrondissements renfermant parfois une population peu aisée et très dense, beaucoup de caisses des Ecoles ne posséderaient pas les fonds suffisans pour faire fonctionner les cantines.   La ville de Paris accorde une subvention totale d'environ 800 mille francs par an.   Par l'attribution de cette subvention on tient compte

1°   de l'effectif scolaire.

2°   du coefficient de nécessité (pourcentage des administrés secourus).

Fonctionnement.   Chaque école ou groupe d'écoles a sa *cantinière*, chargée, sous la surveillance de la commission des cantines, de préparer, de distribuer les aliments, de nettoyer soigneusement la vaisselle.

Les denrées alimentaires sont livrées directement par des fournisseurs attitrés, désignés par la caisse des Ecoles.   La cantine est surveillée d'une façon constante par les Directeurs ou Directrices d'Ecoles sous le contrôle d'administrateurs délégués par la caisse des Ecoles.

Le rôle du médecin-inspecteur doit consister à surveiller avec soin *l'établissement des menus*, la qualité et la préparation saine des aliments.

L'enfant doit apporter son pain et sa boisson.

Quelques caisses des Ecoles riches fournissent le pain et quelquefois un dessert. Quelques-unes distribuent même des médicaments avant le repas à des enfants désignés par le médecin. Le Directeur ou le maitre chargé de la surveillance journalière de la cantine doit verifier avec soin le contenu du panier, surtout en ce qui concerne la nature et la quantité de boisson apportée.

Matériel. Bancs et tables très simples, faciles à nettoyer et à laver. Les ustensiles (assiettes, gamelles, gobelets) sont en fer battu, étamés fréquemment. Les enfants déjà grands recoivent un couvert complet, les plus jeunes ont une fourchette et une cuiller. La cantinière coupe elle-même la viande. Les écoles maternelles possèdent un hachoir mécanique d'un nettoyage facile. Chaque enfant doit apporter la serviette et l'instituteur doit s'assurer qu'elle est propre; le change doit être fait au moins une fois par semaine.

Aliments. Menus. La question des aliments a une très grande importance; l'établissement des menus pour les cantines scolaires con_ stitue un problème complexe; les menus doivent d'une part répondre aux exigences *scientifiques* et d'autre part aux nécessités *économiques* et *pratiques*. En effet, ces menus doivent comprendre tous les aliments nécessaires à l'alimentation de l'enfant, ne pécher ni par excès, ni par défaut, le prix de revient doit être minime et en dernier lieu la cuisson des aliments ne doit pas obliger à des préparations culinaires trop compliquées. Il y a lieu de faire remarquer que la ration alimentaire de l'enfant doit être supérieure à celle de l'adulte, car l'enfant a droit en dehors de sa ration *d'entretien* et de *travail*, à une ration *d'accroisse- ment* dont il faut tenir compte.

Viande. Les auteurs sont très partagés en ce qui concerne la viande. Quelques uns (Nobécourt) autorisent la viande dès le 19ième mois, d'au- tres ne permettent pas la viande avant la 5ième ou même la 7ième année (Maurel). Nous pensons qu'il faut donner de la viande deux fois par semaine aux enfants audessous de 4 ans et tous les jours aux enfants plus agés. La quantité de viande donnée à l'enfant varie suivant l'age de 40 à 60 gr. La charcuterie, saucisses, petit sale; lard est proscrite. La préparation des viandes est aussi simple que possible, rôties le plus généralement—ragôut au minimum.

Les oeufs. L'oeuf, aliment excellent, figure dans les menus de nos cantines maternelles.

Le lait. Sous forme de soupe au lait, de riz au lait, d'œufs au lait fait partie des menus de nos écoles maternelles.

Les légumes. Les pommes de terre, les légumes secs.

Les pâtes alimentaires tiennent une place importante dans les menus de tous les repas.

Nous donnons ci-après un exemple de menus pris dans nos écoles:

Menu d'une école maternelle.

Lundi. Soupe au bouillon vermicelle, bœuf aux pommes de terre.

Mardi. Soupe aux lentilles, purée de lentilles.

Mercredi. Soupe au lait vermicelle, riz au lait et aux œufs.

Jeudi. Soupe aux légumes, sardines, pommes de terre en purée.

Vendredi. Soupe aux haricots, bœuf rôti, purée de haricots.

Samedi. Soupe au lait, œufs, nouilles.

Menu d'une école primaire.

Lundi. Pot au feu; bœuf; macaroni.

Mardi. Soupe aux poireaux; veau aux carottes.

Mercredi. Soupe au lait; bœuf rôti; purée de pommes.

Jeudi. Soupe aux lentilles; veau aux lentilles.

Vendredi. Soupe aux fèves; épaule de mouton aux fèves.

Samedi. Soupe aux légumes; porc frais; purée de pommes.

Boisson. En ce qui concerne la boisson la cantine scolaire doit fournir à l'enfant de *l'eau pure.* Le rôle du médecin-inspecteur doit s'appliquer à *la surveillance des boissons apportées par les enfants dans leur panier.* Nous prohibons *les boissons alcoolisées,* le café fort.

La repas du matin. Dans certains arrondissements on donne une soupe chaude aux enfants dés leur arrivée à l'école. C'est une pratique a encourager. Cette distribution de soupe le matin existe à l'etranger. En Suède la cantine scolaire sert à l'enseignement ménager (in Hygiéne Scolaire,-Dufestel).

Prix des repas. Le prix des repas oscille entre 0, 15 et 0, 25 ou même un peu plus suivant la gestion plus ou moins sévère des caisses des Ecoles. Les cantines arrivent à récupérer, très faiblement d'ailleurs, une partie de leurs dépenses en faisant payer les enfants dont les parents ne sont pas indigents. Beaucoup d'enfants appartenant à des familles nombreuses peuvent obtenir *la demi gratuité* ou la *gratuité complète,* après enquête des administrateurs délégués par la caisse des Ecoles.

Le conseil municipal de Paris, toujours soucieux des intérêts des humbles de notre grande cité, a depuis quelques mois, sur l'initiative de Monsieur Frederic Brunet, installé auprès de la caisse des Ecoles du 17ième arrondissement, *des cantines scolaires du soir,* qui permettent aux écoliers dont les parents rentrent très tard au foyer familial de prendre à l'école *le repas du soir.*

Les médecins-inspecteurs chargés de la survèillance de ces écoles ont été priés d'établir des fiches spéciales pour ces enfants afin de suivre attentivement leur developpement et de leur fournir une alimentation appropriée.

Nous savons qu'il y a encore beaucoup d'améliorations à réaliser, mais nous pensons que grâce à la collaboration des hygiénistes, nous arriverons peu à peu à faire de nos cantines, des cantines modèles.

SESSION THIRTY-THREE

Room A.   Friday, August 29th, 2:00 P.M.

SYMPOSIUM ON SCHOOL ILLUMINATION
(Part One)

Arranged by the Illuminating Engineering Society

HERBERT IVES, *Chairman*

W. R. HUNTLEY, Buffalo, N. Y., *Vice-Chairman*

Program of Session Thirty-three

E. L. ELLIOTT, Consulting Illuminating Engineer, New York. "The Illumination Primer of the Illuminating Engineering Society." (Manuscript not supplied.)

ELLICE M. ALGER, M.D., Professor of Diseases of the Eye, New York Post Graduate Medical School. "The Relation of Illumination to Ocular Hygiene."

C. E. FERREE, Professor of Psychology, Bryn Mawr College, Pa. "The Efficiency of the Eye Under Different Systems of Lighting."

M. LUCKIESH, Physicist, National Electric Lamp Association, Physical Laboratory, Cleveland, Ohio. "Glare from Paper."

MATHILDE GSTETTNER, M.D., Assistant Oculist Vienna Policlinic High School, Secretary Austrian School Hygiene Association, Vienna, Austria. "The Lighting of Schoolrooms and the Influence of the Position of the Blackboard on the Illumination of Desks."

THE RELATION OF ILLUMINATION TO OCULAR HYGIENE

BY

Ellice M. Alger

As we know more and more of the psychological processes by which the child absorbs knowledge we are forced to admit that if he is to make the greatest use of his powers he must see both clearly and easily. For this reason the last decade has seen a great deal of study of the practical school conditions which affect the child's visual comfort and endurance as well as his acuity of vision. To a very great extent these studies have been directed to the dioptric and focusing apparatus of the eyes, the literature on eyestrain from refractive and muscular anomalies with its relationship to various nervous and physical phenomena being very voluminous.

The dependence of sharp vision on lighting has been so obvious that till recently very little critical attention has been paid to the subject. But modern investigation has shown that bad lighting not only reduces visual acuity but may also be a very important factor in ocular comfort and endurance. Furthermore we are coming to see that good lighting means far more than superabundant lighting; and that over lighting or improper lighting may easily be more harmful than insufficient lighting. One could write almost without limit on the manifold reactions between the light on the one hand and the eye and brain on the other, but I shall limit myself to a very brief consideration of a few of the chief bearings of light on ocular hygiene, with the idea of providing a framework for discussion.

Brightness. Light is the sensation caused by the impact of certain vibrations or waves on the retina, which produce photo-chemical changes in proportion to the intensity of the stimulus and the length of exposure. The brightness of light is therefore a matter of very great importance. If we look directly at a very bright light that portion of the retina on which the light is focused becomes temporarily exhausted and blind and is incapable of seeing anything till the photo-chemical substances have been regenerated. Looking at the midday sun directly might easily produce a permanent blind spot. In fact this very thing has happened many times in the incautious observation of eclipses. To a lesser degree a retinal exhaustion occurs when we gaze long at objects which reflect too much light. But within limits the

0

retina adapts itself to too much light and one accustomed to it can work comfortably in light which would have dazzled him badly at first. The eye can also become accustomed to very dim light and after a time see surprisingly well. But the change from bright light to dim and *vice versa* is always uncomfortable if suddenly made, and causes a tremendous failure in visual efficiency for the time being; as we all know from our personal experience. People very often insist on having very bright lights because they have become so accustomed to them, and have so blunted their retinal sensitiveness that they cannot see without them. In others the retina becomes hypersensitive instead of blunted, and they finally become almost incapable of bearing any light at all. This condition is seen at its worst in hysterics, when it is not, of course, the result of overlighting, but it is common enough among school children.

So far as the *actual* brightness is concerned we can measure it quite accurately with any one of the ingenious photometers which you will see demonstrated at this meeting but its *relative* brightness is just as important. So far as its effect on the retina is concerned the intensity of a light depends very largely on the luminosity of its surroundings. A very bright electric light may be positively painful to look at in a room otherwise dark, while in daylight it would hardly attract notice. A bright light near the line of sight not only keeps distracting the attention but causes dazzling and discomfort out of all proportion to its actual brightness if its surroundings be relatively dark. For this reason the arrangement of the schoolroom so that the scholar need not face the window may be an important factor in his efficiency. The effects of light are essentially the same whether it falls directly on the eyes or is reflected into them. If the reflection is from a polished surface practically the whole amount of light reaches the eye. If the surface is rough or mat the reflected light is broken up and reflected in all directions while at the same time the surface itself becomes visible. If one looks at a reflection of the sun in a mirror he might almost as well look directly at the sun, while if he substitutes for the mirror a printed paper the glare is in proportion to the polish of the paper while the visibility of the print depends on the mat surface.

The human eye is exposed to so many variations of intensity and dimness that it has developed a very beautiful mechanism of its own for regulating the amount of light so that the retina may not have to adapt itself to such extremes of illumination. When the light is dim the pupil dilates and when it becomes bright it automatically contracts. Constant exposure to bright light necessitates constant contraction of the pupillary muscle, which causes in many people fatigue and pain.

Steadiness. A flickering light is very much more tiresome and painful than a steady one because it results in a very rapid dilation and contraction of the pupils. Even if the light be not very bright in itself its variation is so much faster than the retinal adaptation that it seems alternately very bright and very dim and the pupillary reaction is correspondingly sharp and tiresome.

Shadow Formation. Another very important factor in lighting, whether natural or artificial, is its shadow formation. An intense light from a small source gives a very bright illumination but also a very marked shadow, while the same amount of light from several sources or from one very large source would cause a relatively slight shadow. Now shadows are very necessary. We learn as the result of experience to form visual judgments from what we see that become so rapid and automatic that it is sometimes difficult to tell just where the ocular element ceases and the mental part begins. Many of our ideas of height and depth and relief are visual judgments based on shadows and our judgments are likely to be more constant if not more correct when the shadows are also constant. This is, of course, the reason that the artist, the photographer and the draughtsman prefer the north light which is by common consent taken as the standard of illumination.

Color Sense. The light in which they are seen affects not only our judgment of the form of objects but of their color as well. Our retinal sensations depend to a great extent on the character or length of the light waves. The longer ones give us the sensation of red. As they get shorter and shorter one sees in succession all the colors of the rainbow while the mixture of all these waves together produces the sensation of white light. None of our artificial lights contains exactly the same mixture of waves as daylight and this affects the color of objects. Every woman knows that her costumes, if not her complexion, must be calculated for the light in which they are to be displayed.

Actinic Effects. The photo-chemical changes in the retina which result in vision are most pronounced under exposure to the yellows and greens of the mid spectrum. The long red rays are not stimulating enough to be very useful for purposes of illumination while the short violet ones may be said to be irritating rather than stimulating. But there are other waves besides those of the visible spectrum—longer ones than the red, which can be felt as heat and shorter ones than the violet which, though invisible to the eye, have a very active chemical action. As the demonstrable result of this chemical activity we have the familiar phenomena of tan and sunburn, which may be considered as the *acute* manifestations, while it is quite possible that the *chronic* results are still more serious. The ultra violet rays, which are absorbed by ordinary glass, and in the eye by the cornea and lens, may in the opinion of many observers produce the degenerative change we call cataract, and, perhaps, other diseases of the deeper structures of the eye. It must be remembered, too, that the violet end of the visible spectrum approaches the ultra violet in its chemical activity. Most of our recent artificial lights contain a very high proportion of violet rays as compared to daylight and some of them contain many ultra violet rays as well. Nearly every one has experienced the discomfort, if not the actual damage that may come from reading by unshaded incandescent light and many physicians are making extensive use of amber glasses and shades, which soften the light and exclude the actinic end of the spectrum.

Acuity and Efficiency. So far as mere visual acuity is concerned it may reach its maximum, not only with natural light but with artificial light of several types. Indeed it has been found that acuity is actually greater with monochromatic light than with the mixture of colors that constitutes white. But when it comes to comfort and endurance there is a tremendous falling off under artificial light as compared to daylight. A very interesting series of experiments seemed to show this conclusively under incandescent electric lighting, though the momentary sharpness of vision might be even better than with natural light. Whether this will prove true of all artificial lights, only a long series of careful experiment can determine and I believe we are to have in a subsequent paper a report on such an investigation.

The Ideal Light. So far as we have got daylight is by far the best method of lighting. In the first place it is the natural illumination, to which our eyes by generations of use have become adapted, and it is a universal standard. A good north light is the pleasantest to the eyes, it is the best diffused, it causes a minimum of shadow, it is the steadiest and most constant, and affects color values least. It is least harmful to the eyes and allows a maximum of sharpness with a minimum of fatigue. But it is not always possible to have this ideal light because of the situation of the room or the height of surroundings or the season of the year or the hour of the day. Furthermore the use of natural light in the school or factory necessitates to a great extent the subordination of the work to the light instead of that of light to work.

Illuminating engineers have, therefore, long been engaged on the fascinating problem of constructing an artificial light which should have the same composition or spectrum as sunlight and at the same time be more manageable. We can pass light through a prism and break it up into its component parts for comparison with other lights and we can measure its *brightness* and *illuminating power* by various photometers.

It is possible to control the *composition* of light by the interposition of shades or screens or reflectors, which may exclude the rays that are not wanted and to regulate its *volume* and *intensity* by increasing the number or the power of the units employed, or by diffusion through frosted shades or by reflection from rough surfaces. But so far the solution of the problem has eluded us. When such a light is found it will by reason of its capacity for being regulated and arranged to suit the needs of the individual rather than the group largely displace daylight in our schools and factories. Till that day comes we must, in our schools at least, depend so far as possible on daylight and teach both pupils and teachers to restrict as much as may be the work which must be done under artificial light.

THE EFFICIENCY OF THE EYE UNDER DIFFERENT SYSTEMS OF LIGHTING

BY

C. E. FERREE

Up to the present time the work on the problem of lighting has been confined almost entirely to the source of light. The goal of the lighting engineer has been to get the maximum output of light for a given expen-diture of energy. Until recent years little attention has been given to the problem in its relation to the eye. It is the purpose of the paper to outline in a general way some of the more important features of this phase of the subject, and to give some of the results of work that is now being done on the problems they present.

Confronting the problem of the effect of lighting systems on the eye, it is obvious that the first step towards systematic work is to obtain some means of making a definite estimate of this effect. The prominent effects of bad lighting systems are loss of efficiency, temporary and progressive, and eye discomfort. Three classes of effect may, however, be investigated: (1) the effect on the general level or scale of efficiency for the fresh eye; (2) loss of efficiency, as the result of a period of work; and (3) the tendency to produce discomfort. Of these three classes of effect the last two are obviously the more important, for the best lighting system is not the one that gives us the maximum acuity of vision for the momentary judgment or the highest level of efficiency for the fresh eye. It is rather the one that gives us the least loss of efficiency for a period of work, and the maximum of comfort.

In 1911 The American Medical Association appointed a committee to study the effect of different lighting systems on the eye. The writer was asked to share in the work of this committee. The problem pre-sented to him was to furnish tests that would show the effect of different lighting systems on the eye, and more especially to devise, if possible, a test that would show loss of efficiency as a result of three or four hours of work under an unfavorable lighting system. In his work directed along these lines he has succeeded in getting methods of estimating effect which, after eighteen months of trial seem sufficiently sensitive to differentiate between good and bad lighting systems on all these points. Aided by the other members of the committee, and by the Illuminating Engineering Society, he has undertaken, therefore, to determine: (1) the lighting conditions that give in general the highest level or scale of visual efficiency; (2) the conditions that give the least loss of efficiency for continued work, and (3) the conditions that cause the least discomfort. This plan of work, it is scarcely needful to remark, will involve a wide range of experimentation. The crux of the problem is, however, to secure reliable methods of estimating effect. Having these methods, the factors, whatever they may be, distribution, intensity, quality, position of the light relative to the eye, etc., can be varied one at a time and the effects be determined. From these effects it should not be difficult to ascertain what lighting conditions are best for the eye, and what is the relative importance of the factors that go to make up these conditions. Further, it should be possible on the practical side to test out and perfect a lighting system, before it is put on the market; also to determine the best conditions of installation for a given lighting system, to investigate the effect of different kinds of type and paper on the eye, to study the effect of different kinds of desk lighting, etc. In short it is obvious that the usefulness of such tests is limited along these lines only by their sensitivity.

A detailed description of the tests we are using has already appeared in print. Time cannot be given to them here. A brief report only of some of the results of the work in which they have been employed is possible in the time placed at my disposal.

In the study of the problems presented to us in this field it has been thought best to conduct the investigation at first along broad lines in order to determine, in a general way, the conditions that affect the efficiency and comfort of the eye. Later a more detailed examination can be made, if desired, of the ways in which these conditions have been worked out in the various types of lighting systems in use at the present time. There are, in general, three aspects of lighting that sustain an important relation to the efficiency and the comfort of the eye, namely, the distribution of light* and surface brightness in the field of vision, the intensity, and the quality. Each of these aspects will here, in turn, be briefly discussed. The ideal condition with regard to the distribution of light and surface brightness is to have the field of vision uniformly illuminated and no extremes of surface brightness. When this condition is attained, the illumination of the retina will shade off gradually from center to periphery, which gradation affords the most favorable condition for accurate and comfortable fixation and accommodation.

The factor of distribution can be most conveniently discussed perhaps with reference to four types of lighting in common use to-day—illumination by daylight, direct lighting systems, indirect lighting systems, and semi-indirect systems. In the proper illumination of a room by

*Distribution of light is used here to include both the type of delivery of light to the working plane and the diffuseness of light.

daylight, we have been able, thus far, to get the best conditions of distribution. Before it reaches our windows or skylights daylight has been rendered widely diffuse by innumerable reflections and the windows and skylights themselves, acting as sources, have a broad area and low intrinsic brilliancy, all of which features contribute towards giving the ideal condition of distribution stated above, namely, that the field of vision shall be uniformly illuminated and that there shall be no extremes of surface brightness. Of the systems of artificial lighting the best distribution is gotten by the indirect systems. In this type of system the source is concealed from the eye and the light is thrown against the ceiling, or some other diffusely reflecting surface, in such a way that it suffers one or more reflections before it reaches the eye. It gives the best approximation of the distribution characteristic of daylight of any that has yet been devised. The direct lighting systems are designed to send the light directly to the plane of work. There is in general in the use of these systems a tendency to concentrate rather than to diffuse the light, and, therefore, a tendency to emphasize brightness extremes rather than to level them down. Too often, too, the eye if not properly shielded from the light source and frequently no attempt at all is made to do this. The semi-indirect systems represent a compromise between the direct and indirect systems. A part of the light is transmitted directly to the eye through the translucent reflector placed beneath, and a part is reflected to the ceiling. Thus, depending upon the density of the reflector, this type of system may vary between the totally direct and the totally indirect as extremes and share in the relative merits and demerits of each in proportion to its place in the scale. By giving better distribution this system is supposed also to be a concession to the welfare of the eye, but our tests show that the concession is not so great as it is supposed to be. In fact, installed at the intensity of illumination ordinarily used, or at an intensity great enough for all kinds of work, little advantage is gained for the eye in this type of lighting with reflectors of low or medium densities; for with these intensities of light and densities of reflector, the brightness of the source has not been sufficiently reduced to give much relief to the suffering eye. Until this much at least is done in home, office and public lighting we cannot hope to get rid of eye strain with its complex train of physical and mental disturbances.

It is not our purpose, however, at this time to attempt a final rating of the merits of lighting systems. For that our work is still too young. Moreover, there are relatively good and bad systems of each type, and good and bad installations may be made of any system. What we hope to do is by making an appropriate selection and variation of conditions to find out what the factors are that are of importance to the eye, and from this knowledge as a starting point to work towards reconstruction.

With regard to the effect of the distribution of light and surface brightness on the eye a brief statement will be given here only of its effect on efficiency, and in the consideration of efficiency, loss of efficiency will receive the major part of our attention. No attempt will be made, for example, to present the results of the study of the factors producing discomfort. The study of these factors have constituted for us an entirely separate and independent piece of work, investigated by separate and independent methods.

Our tests for loss of efficiency show that when the intensity and quality of the light are equalized at the point of work, the eye loses practically nothing in efficiency as the result of three to four hours of work under daylight. It loses enormously for the same period of work under the system of direct lighting* selected for our work and almost as much under the system of semi-indirect lighting. Under the system of indirect lighting, however, the eye loses but little more than it loses in daylight. The results of these tests show also that acuity of vision, as determined by the momentary judgment, is higher for the same foot-candles of illumination for the daylight system than for the artificial systems, and that for the artificial systems it is the highest for the indirect system, next highest for the semi-indirect system, and lowest for the direct. It will thus be seen that for all the purposes of clear seeing, whether the criterion be maximum acuity or the ability of the eye to hold its efficiency for a period of work, the best results are given in order by the systems that give the best distribution of light and surface brightness. The effect of this factor is not so great, however, on the ability of the fresh eye to see clearly as it is on its power to hold its efficiency.

A set of charts has been constructed to show the eye's loss of efficiency for a period of work under each of these four systems of lighting. These charts are typical of the results obtained from all of our observers. In constructing these charts units of efficiency are plotted along the ordinate and time of work along the abscissa. Each one of the large squares along the abscissa represents an hour of work, and along the ordinate an integer of the ratio representing efficiency. Chart I is con-

*Space can not be taken here for an engineering specification of the installations used and the lighting effects produced. A full report of the work including brightness and illumination measurements and photographs showing the illumination effects, details of installation, etc., will be published in the Transactions of the Illuminating Engineering Society. The systems of lighting employed are in common use and were selected for this work to show the influence of differences in distribution effects on the power of the eye to hold its efficiency for a period of work. As rapidly as possible the tests will be applied to other examples of each of these systems of lighting.

structed to show the comparative loss of efficiency of the eye for Observer R for three hours of work under the four systems, and Chart II for Observer B for two hours of work under these systems. Column 1 of the data for the charts gives the system of lighting employed; Column 2, the total wattage of the lamps used; Column 3, the voltage at which these lamps were operated, and Columns 4, 5 and 6, the foot-candles at the point of work, measured respectively in the horizontal, the 45°, and the vertical planes. As stated earlier in the paper, care was taken to have the intensity of illumination for all the systems equal at the point of work. Since this equalization could not be made exact in all of the three planes in which our photometric readings were taken, it was made approximately exact in the vertical plane and as nearly as possible exact in the other two. The vertical plane was selected as of primary importance in making this equalization because in making the test this plane was occupied by the test card.

An inspection of these charts will show how widely different in amount is the loss of efficiency for the direct and semi-indirect system, as com-pared with the indirect system and daylight, and how closely the amount of loss corresponds for the direct and semi-indirect systems and for the indirect system and daylight.

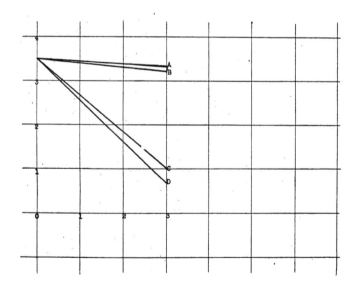

CHART I
DISTRIBUTION SERIES (OBSERVER R)

Lighting System	Watts	Volts	Foot-candles		
			Horizontal	45°	Vertical
A–Daylight..............			3.12	2.15	.841
B–Indirect..............	680	107	2.94	1.995	.864
C–Semi-indirect.........	760	107	3.24	2.1	.865
D–Direct...............	880	107	2.845	2.0	.867

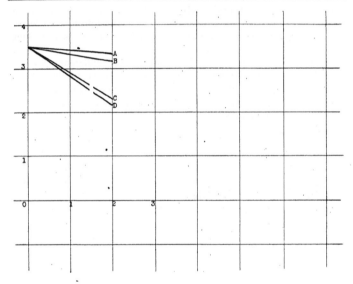

CHART II
DISTRIBUTION SERIES (OBSERVER G)

Lighting System	Watts	Volts	Foot-candles		
			Horizontal	45°	Vertical
A–Daylight.............			3.12	2.15	.841
B–Indirect..............	680	107	2.94	1.995	.864
C–Semi-indirect.........	760	107	3.24	2.1	.865
D–Direct...............	880	107	2.845	2.0	.867

The loss of efficiency found in the above work seems to be predominently, if not entirely muscular, for the tests for the sensitivity of the retina show practically no loss of sensitivity as the result of work under any of the lighting systems employed. The following reasons are suggested why the muscles of the eye giving both fixation and accommodation should be subjected to a greater strain by the systems of direct lighting, and semi-indirect lighting, than by the system of indirect lighting and daylight. (1) The bright images of the sources falling on the peripheral retina which is in a perpetual state of darkness adaptation, as compared with the central retina, and is, therefore, extremely sensitive in its reaction to such intensive stimuli, set up a reflex tendency for the eye to fixate them instead of, for example, the letters which the observer is required to read. (2) Likewise, a strong reflex tendency to accommodate for these brilliant sources of light, all at different distances from each other and the lettered page, is set up. (3) These brilliant images falling on a part of the retina that is not adapted to them, causing as they do acute discomfort in a very short period of time, doubtless induce spasmodic contractions of the muscles which both disturb the clearness of vision and greatly accentuate the fatiguing of the muscles. The net result of all these causes is excessive strain which shows itself in a loss of power to do work. In the illumination of a room by daylight, however, with a proper distribution of windows, the situation is quite different. The field of vision contains no bright sources of light to disturb fixation and accommodation and to cause spasmodic muscular disturbances due to the action of the intensive light sources on the dark adapted and sensitive peripheral retina. As has already been pointed out the light waves have suffered innumerable reflections and the light has become diffuse. The field of vision is uniformly illuminated and there are no extremes of surface brightness. The illumination of the retina, therefore, falls off more or less gradually from center to periphery, as it should to permit of fixation and accommodation for a given object with a minimum amount of strain.

It is not our purpose, however, to contend that distribution of light and surface brightness is the only factor of importance in the illumination of a room. We have chosen to begin our work with types based on distribution, only because it has seemed to us, both from our own work and from a survey of the work done by others, that this is the most important factor we have yet to deal with in our search for the conditions that give minimum loss of efficiency and maximum comfort in seeing. The quality of light and its intensity at the source are already pretty well taken care of, apparently better taken care of, at least in general practice relative to their importance to the eye, than is distribution. A systematic study of factors, however, cannot stop with an investigation of the effect of this one alone. The intensity and quality of light must also be taken into account. For example, one of the most persistent questions asked by the illuminating engineer is, "How much light should be used with a given lighting system to give the best results for seeing?" We have undertaken, therefore, to determine the most favorable range of intensity for the four types of installation mentioned above. Charts have been made showing the effect on the efficiency of the eye of three or four hours of work under different intensities of light, for the direct and semi-indirect systems; and rough comparisons have been made for the indirect system and for daylight. Detailed tests will be made for these latter two systems early next year. Our tests show, in general, the following results: A very wide range of intensity is permissible for daylight and the indirect type of system. For the semi-indirect system the eye falls off heavily in efficiency for all intensities with the exception of a narrow range on either side of 1.7 foot-candles, measured at the level of the eye at the point of work with the receiving surface of the photometer in the horizontal plane. For the direct system no intensity can be found for which the eye does not lose a very great deal in efficiency as the result of work. Thus it seems that distribution is fundamental. That is, if the light is well distributed and there are no extremes of surface brightness as is the case for daylight and the indirect systems of artificial lighting, the ability of the eye to hold its efficiency is, within limits, independent of intensity. In short, the retina is itself highly accommodative or adaptive to intensity, and if the proper distribution effects are secured, the conditions are not present which cause strain and consequent loss of efficiency in the adjustment of the eye.

Details of the conditions of installation and of the methods of working cannot be given here. It will be sufficient to state that the work was done in the same room, with the same fixtures, and in general with the same conditions of installation and methods of working as were used in the tests for the effect of distribution. Nor can a full statement of results be made. Time will be taken, however, for a more detailed examination of the results obtained for the direct and semi-indirect systems. For the semi-indirect system, our test showed that the intensity most favorable to the eye was secured when the photometric reading with the receiving surface in the horizontal plane showed 1.696 foot-candles of light at the point of work, 1.123 foot-candles in the 45° position, and .404 foot-candles in the vertical position. At this intensity of illumination, the semi-indirect system, so far as its effect on the eye's loss of efficiency is concerned, compares very well with the indirect system at such ranges of intensity as we have employed. At intensities appreciably higher than the most favorable value, or lower, the loss of efficiency is very great. At the intensity commonly recommended in lighting practice, the semi-indirect system is almost, if not quite, as damaging to the eye as the direct system. The intensity recommended by the Illuminating Engineering Society, for example, in its primer, issued in 1912, ranges 2–3 to 7–10 foot-candles, depending upon the kind of work. Five foot-candles is taken as a medium value. This medium value, it will be noted, is approximately three times the amount we have found to give the least loss of efficiency for the type and installation of semi-indirect system we have used. The intensity we have found to give the least loss of efficiency for this type of lighting, does not, however, give maximum acuity of vision as determined by the momentary judgment. At an intensity that does give maximal acuity for the momentary judgment the eye runs down rapidly in efficiency. That is, in this type of lighting, one or the other of these features must be sacrificed. High acuity and little loss of efficiency cannot be had at the same intensity. This can be had only under the indirect system or under daylight. However, the amount of light we find to give the least loss of efficiency seems to be sufficient, for much of the work ordinarily done in the home or office. It is not enough, though, for drafting or work requiring great clearness of detail.

In case of the direct system, we were able to improve the conditions, so far as loss of efficiency is concerned, by reducing the intensity; but the system never proved so favorable in this regard as even the semi-indirect system. In the tests made under the direct system care was taken to have the fixtures exactly in the same position in the room in every case as they were for the semi-indirect system. The most favorable intensity is secured by an installation that gave 1.003 foot-candles in the horizontal, .789 in the 45° position and .337 in the vertical.

The effect of variations of intensity for these two systems of lighting will be shown also by means of a set of charts representing the loss of efficiency as a result of a period of work. Three hours was selected as the period of work in each of these cases. Very briefly stated, the procedure was as follows: The most favorable intensity was determined and variations were made on either side of this intensity until it was certain that the characteristic effect of increase and decrease of illumination was obtained. In all cases clear tungsten lamps were used. Chart III shows the loss typical for the semi-indirect system. Seven variations of intensity were used. Charts IV and V show the results for the direct system. The fixtures for our direct system were constructed to hold two lamps each, or sixteen in all. By using sixteen lamps, however, we could not get as great a reduction of intensity as was desired. Two series of experiments were run, therefore, one for a total of eight lamps, the other for sixteen. Chart IV shows the results of the sixteen

lamp system, and Chart V for the eight lamp system. The
able intensity it will be noted was secured with the eight la
with a total wattage of 200, 40 less than the smallest total
that could have been secured with the sixteen lamp system.

B

A

E

F

CHART III

INTENSITY SERIES

Lighting System: Semi-indirect (8 lamps)

	Watts	Volts	Foot-candles	
			Horizontal	45°
A.............	200	107	1.285	.951
B.............	200	110	1.398	1.048
C.............	320	107	1.696	1.123
D.............	320	110	1.789	1.2
E.............	480	107	3.01	2.066
F.............	800	107	4.42	3.025
X.............	760	107	3.24	2.1

At this intensity, however, the loss in the efficiency of the eye for three hours of work was almost four and one-half times as great as for the most favorable intensity for the semi-indirect system; and more than four and one-half times as great as for a wide range of intensities for either the indirect system or daylight.

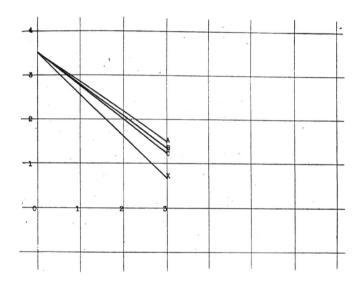

CHART IV

INTENSITY SERIES

Lighting System: Direct (16 lamps)

	Watts	Volts	Foot-candles		
			Horizontal	45°	Vertical
A.............	240	107	.799	.561	.193
B.............	.365	.107	1.359	1.099	.395
C.............	400	107	1.517	1.245	.557
X.............	880	107	2.845	2.0	.867

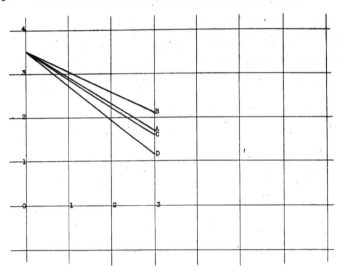

CHART V

INTENSITY SERIES

Lighting System: Direct (8 lamps)

	Watts	Volts	Foot-candles		
			Horizontal	45°	Vertical
A.............	120	107	.409	.313	.145
B.............	200	107	1.003	.789	.337
C.............	320	107	1.245	.868	.386
D.............	480	107	2.06	1.424	.682

In concluding this section of his report the writer wishes to emphasize two points: (1) Of the lighting factors that influence the welfare
of the eye, what we have called the distribution of light and surface
brightness apparently is fundamental.   It seems to be the most important
factor we have yet to deal with in our search for the conditions that give
us the minimum loss of efficiency and the maximum comfort in seeing.
If, for example, the light is well distributed in the field of vision, and there
are no extremes of surface brightness, our tests seem to indicate that
the eye, so far as the problem of lighting is concerned, is practically
independent of intensity.   That is, when the proper distribution effects
are obtained, intensities high enough to give maximum discrimination

of detail may be employed without causing appreciable damage or discomfort to the eye. (2) For the kind of distribution effects given by the majority of lighting systems in use at the present time, our results show that unquestionably too much light is being used for the welfare and comfort of the eye.

The effect of quality of light on the eye has been the subject of much discussion and much misunderstanding. There seems to be a feeling even among lighting engineers and ophthalmologists that colored light gives better results for seeing than white light. Some, for example, hold that the kerosene flame furnishes the ideal source of light and that its virtues are due largely to the yellow quality of the light it gives off. While the writer has not as yet begun a systematic study of the effect of quality of light, and while he is, therefore, not as yet willing to commit himself on this point, he will say that when intensity and distribution are equalized, an installation of clear carbon lamps, which gives a light comparatively rich in yellow and red, causes the eye to fall off more in efficiency as the result of 3–4 hours of work than an installation of clear tungsten lamps, the light from which is more nearly white. In short, the question whether or not white or colored light is better for the eye cannot be answered until definite tests are made of this point alone under conditions in which all other factors are rendered constant. The effects of the kerosene flame, for example, as compared with other sources of illumination, must be tested under a system of installation that gives the same intensity at the source, and, as nearly as possible, the same distribution effects in the field of vision as is given by other illuminants. This has not been done at all. Our judgment of the comparative merits of the color quality of the light given by it have been based on the roughest kinds of impression, obtained under conditions of installation in which there has been no attempt at control of the other factors that influence the effect of light on the eye. The work that has been done up to this time on the relation of quality of light to seeing has been confined to visual acuity as determined by the momentary judgment, and even this work which alone can give no safe grounds at all for drawing general conclusions as to the effect of light on the welfare of the eye, shows, whenever the comparison has been made, that clear white light gives a greater acuity of seeing than lights of any of the colors. If, as has been maintained by some on the grounds of their working experience, the kerosene flame is easier on the eye than the more modern sources of illumination, the writer would be inclined, more especially in view of his results on the effect of differences in intensity on the efficiency of the eye, to ascribe the benefit, whatever there may be, to the low intrinsic brilliancy of the kerosene flame. For it may be safely said that for the kind of distribution effects we are getting from the large majority of our lighting systems, unquestionably too much light is being used for the welfare and comfort of the eye. Added to this is the effect of the position of the light in the field of vision. The kerosene lamp may be placed at the back or side of the person using it, and, if in the field of vision, it is usually at or near the level of the eye. In the two former cases the effect of concealed lighting is given, and in the latter case the lamp occupies the most favorable position possible for an exposed source. That is, if the source of light is to be in the field of vision at all, it should be as nearly as possible at the level of the eye. This is because of the greater tendency of a light source to produce discomfort and loss of efficiency when its image falls on the upper and lower halves of the retina than when it falls in the horizontal meridian. These facts have been clearly brought out in our work on the effect of position of the light in the field of vision.

In addition to studying the conditions that give us maximum efficiency, it is important to determine the lighting conditions and eye factors that cause discomfort. In fact, it might well be said that our problem in lighting at present is not so much how to see better as it is how to see with more comfort and with less damage to the general health on account of eye strain. Any comparative study of the conditions producing discomfort necessitates a method of estimating discomfort. As stated earlier in the paper, our method of estimating discomfort is entirely distinct and separate from our method of studying efficiency. Time cannot be taken here to go into details of either the method or of the results of this study. It will be sufficient to say that the effect of distribution of light and surface brightness in the field of vision, intensity, and quality are also being studied in their relation to the comfort as well as to the efficiency of the eye.

In conclusion, the writer wishes to point out that no one of the factors he has mentioned can be safely omitted in the search for the most favorable conditions of lighting. Nor can one be investigated and a correlation between it and the others be taken for granted. We have been content, heretofore, to base our conclusions with regard to the relation of a lighting system to seeing on the conventional visual acuity test. While this test may tell us something about the general level or scale of efficiency of the fresh eye, it can tell us nothing of loss of efficiency, because the muscles of the eye, although they may have fallen off enormously in efficiency, can, under the spur of the will, be whipped up to their normal power long enough to make the judgment required by the test. Moreover, it tells us nothing of the conditions that produce discomfort. In short, the general level or scale of efficiency of the fresh eye, loss of efficiency as the result of work, and the tendency to produce discomfort constitute three separably determinable moments, no one of which should be neglected in installing a lighting system.

GLARE FROM PAPER

BY

M. LUCKIESH

On first thought this subject may appear to be somewhat outside the scope of the Illuminating Engineering Society, however, interest in it is the natural outgrowth of the fight against glare. Early in the days of scientific lighting glare from light sources in the field of view was recognized as a serious cause of eyestrain and impairment of vision. The natural remedy was found in placing the units out of the field of view or equipping the sources with diffusing shades or screening them with opaque reflectors. But it was found that these precautions did not afford complete protection from the ever annoying glare. Obviously a person sitting in a normal position could by means of a mirror see the images of the lighting units about him. This is practically what obtains when one finds it necessary to read from glazed paper.

Those who are interested in the hygienic aspects of lighting naturally recognize other causes of eyestrain than glaring or misplaced light sources and as a result prominent illuminating engineers have long been advocating the elimination of polished surfaces from general use. Obviously this must be done in order that the full benefit of a well designed lighting system may be enjoyed. Though such surfaces as glazed walls, smooth blackboards, glass and polished desk-tops, and glossy ink are active in producing ocular discomfort, glossy paper is no doubt the most serious offender.

Glare from glossy paper has also received attention in other quarters but as yet no concerted movement has been inaugurated for its elimination from general use. Among the "remediable causes of eyestrain in present school conditions" embodied in a report of the Association of Women Principals of New York City glazed paper receives the first consideration, with the recommendation "That hereafter no calendered or coated paper be permitted in the text books given to the children as the dazzle of such paper is injurious to the eyes."

At the Dundee meeting of the British Association for the Advancement of Science in 1912, the Committee on the Influence of School Books upon Eyesight presented a very valuable report, in which the quality of the paper used is seriously considered with the final recommendation that "The paper should be without gloss." Further recommendations regarding the paper involved its texture, weight and color. A white paper or one slightly toned towards cream color was recommended for average conditions of class-room illumination. Here it might be stated that there is much difference of opinion regarding the color of the paper to be used. Many lean toward a yellowish tint, but no authentic data are known to the writer which settle this ·question. Several valuable papers, giving attention to glare from polished surfaces, have been presented before various medical societies and a number of publishers, having recognized the ease of reading from unglazed paper, have adopted it. But all these activities have been separate undertakings and insufficient to bring about a general demand for the use of non-glazed paper. There is a need for a concerted movement in this direction.

In order to clearly appreciate the desirability of unglazed or diffusely reflecting paper and ink, it is interesting to analyze a particular case. Glossy paper reflects light somewhat like an imperfect mirror. Besides the brightness of the paper, due to diffusely reflected light, there is an imperfect image of the lighting unit regularly reflected from the paper. When the paper is held in a certain position this imperfect regularly reflected image of a certain brightness is seen superimposed on the bright background. It will be further noted that the brightness of the reflected image remains constant, while the brightness due to diffuse reflection varies inversely as the square of the distance of the paper from the light source. This is readily verified for it will be seen that glare from glossy paper, while very annoying when the paper is at some distance from the source, quite disappears when the paper is brought very close to it. The conditions are readily understood by constructing a model by placing a pane of clear glass over a sheet of white blotting paper. In attempting to distinguish the printed matter the reader is constantly annoyed by glare from the reflected image of the light source. Hence in spite of the precautions taken in properly placing the lighting units outside the normal field of view, glare from their reflected images results from the direct reflection from polished or glazed surfaces.

The process of obliteration of the printed matter is somewhat complex yet a simple example will serve to illustrate the general principles. Black characters on white paper are visible owing to the contrast. Any condition tending to greatly diminish this contrast is objectionable, although it may ultimately be proven that slight decreases in contrast, such as obtains with black on yellow paper instead of on white, are beneficial. Assume that the ratio of the brightness of the black characters, due to diffusely reflected light to that of the white background is 4–100. This might be called the contrast ratio due to diffusely reflected light. If the paper and ink are somewhat glossy they will also reflect light regularly as a mirror does. Assume that each directly reflects the image of the light source with a degree of brightness which results in a contrast ratio, due to reflection alone, of 200 in the units of brightness

as the first ratio. These brightnesses, due to regular and diffuse reflec.
tion, are of course superimposed with the resultant contrast ratio of
$\frac{4+200}{100+200} = \frac{204}{300}$. In fact, due to the pressure of the type during printing,
the contrast ratio as expressed above is often reversed with the result
that at certain positions of the paper the black characters are actually
brighter than the paper. Of course the regularly reflected image is not
accurately focused upon the retina because the eye is focused for the
printed matter. Therefore the image of the light source is spread out
over the retina forming a veil which reduces the contrast. There is
also the distracting effect due to the tendency of the eye to turn toward
the glare-spot. Thus it is seen that the contrast can even be reduced
to zero with an additional annoyance from the glare-spot which no
doubt effects the size of the pupil and brings about other disturbances
of vision.

There are important considerations in the conservation of eyesight
in school children. It must be remembered that the eye of the child
is a growing eye, immature in structure and in function. Of course,
the natural stimulus of proper use is essential to its development, but
unnatural efforts are certainly injurious. It is claimed by some that
tests show a gradual impairment of vision in school children with increasing age. It is certain that an appreciable percentage of school children
are found to have defective vision. Of course there are many cases of
eyestrain, besides glare from polished surfaces and what has been stated
regarding glare from glazed paper, applies as well to polished desk tops
and smooth blackboards all of which should be eliminated as far as
possible in order to safeguard vision. It has been seen that the obliteration of the printed matter is more or less dependent upon the intrinsic
brightness of the lighting unit as a whole, hence this discomforting glare
can be diminished by diffusing the light. This fact can be verified by
simple experiments with direct and indirect lighting. But glare results
even with natural lighting, which is usually considered quite diffuse.
As an additional safeguard the child should be taught to hold the paper
properly but these are only make-shift remedies and the most practical
method will be found in abandoning the use of glossy paper and other
shiny surfaces.

The Illuminating Engineering Society has appointed a Committee
on Glare from Reflecting Surfaces which is devoting most of its attention
to glossy paper. This committee has communicated with many publishers of school books and school officials in large cities of this country.
The responses from school officials have been few and in general disappointing, while on the other hand publishers of school books generally
seem to have given considerable attention to the subject of "non-glare"
paper. In most cases they have expressed a desire to coöperate, but

usually claim it is impossible to obtain an unglazed paper which will reproduce halftones commercially and yet fulfill the requisites of cheapness and durability. It is obvious that this movement requires the hearty coöperation of those officials who control the selection of school books.

It was evident that the next step to be taken by the committee was to inquire into the status of paper manufacture. Here is was found that the large demand for highly glazed paper is, in part, due to the peculiar development of printing processes. Previous to the advent of the halftone process glossy papers were rare. This process, however, required a smooth non-absorbent paper, which was produced at first by coating machine-finished paper with a solution of clay and calendering between hot rolls. Thus the ideal smoothness was obtained but the paper was shiny. The printer, being able to get results with this smooth finish, continually sought paper of higher glaze, under the mistaken impression that this shine was absolutely necessary. But the time came when it began to be realized that not only the ability to read from such paper decreased but also that eyestrain was a common result. The demand then began to come from some quarters for paper with less gloss until now unglazed paper, when used with more refined printing processes, is satisfactory for halftone printing. This demand has stimulated some paper manufacturers to experiment with the hope of producing highly practicable unglazed paper. Publishers' needs differ but it appears possible to find a suitable paper for most cases and yet be free from this source of eyestrain.

Glossy paper is now being used in many cases where there is no excuse for it. The greatest progress toward the ultimate elimination of glossy paper from general use will arise from a concerted demand for the use of *non-glare* paper. Let us hope that the Congress will lend its hearty coöperation and support this movement for the conservation of the eyesight of school children.

THE LIGHTING OF SCHOOL ROOMS AND THE INFLUENCE OF THE POSITION OF THE BLACK-BOARD ON THE ILLUMINATION OF DESKS

BY

MATHILDE GSTETTNER

Mr. Chairman, Ladies and Gentlemen:

One of the many, and in different ways, questionable points on school hygiene is the quantity of illumination necessary for school rooms. Some may agree that the school room cannot get too much daylight. This opinion will be held especially from the point of view of bacteriology, whereas the oculists will be satisfied if suitable shades (1) are used in case of too much daylight or if a good artificial light is introduced where the natural light is insufficient.

It seems to me advisable to make a few introductory remarks on school room illumination, to show the importance of a proper location of blackboards. It is to the credit of the first and the most celebrated writer of Austria on school hygiene, Dr. Leo Burgerstein, to have called attention in his "Handbuch," the richest and most up-to-date of all manuals of such kind, as in other matters of school hygiene, to the question which will be treated now.

It is proved by the papers of Angelucci, van Genderen Storts and Engelmann that the lighting is of influence on the eyes, as the retina of animals having been kept in dark before death differs remarkably from the retina of those who were exposed to light. If one kills such a "dark-frog" and exposes its eyes under sodium-light, in a liquid which conserves the elements of the tissues in the state in which they were before death and examines cross sections of the retina, one sees that the external part of the rods and cones are surrounded by a stratum of brown pigment, which is situated in special cells of pigment epithelium. Those cells send out prolongations between the rods and cones and those prolongations contain no pigment, whereas the retina of a frog having lived in daylight before death shows that the pigment has entered into those prolongations and covered the rods and cones. We see certain forms in the "light-frog" which seems to be on the edge of that stratum, whereas the "dark-frog" has them on long processes between the rods and cones, so that we must conclude that those processes shorten

1) Burgerstein u. Netolitzky, Handbuch der Schulhygiene, 1912, Barth Leipzig, third Edition.

themselves under the influence of light. The secretion of visual purple in an eye in kept dark proves again that the eye works differently in light than in dark. Similar conditions to those I spoke about are to be found with birds and fishes. No doubt analogous changes are going on with the human retina, too. Therefore we can say that the retina not only receives the impressions of light and is not only the receiving station for conducting those impressions to the brain, but there are movements and chemical and perhaps other changes going on, and we can understand that the intensity and quality of light entering the eye may produce changes in the retina able to put it in a morbid state. A. v. Reuss (1), my venerated chief at the Allgemeinen Poliklinik of Vienna, discusses consequences of protracted work in too strong light, which can be followed by a hyperæsthesia or hypæsthesia of the retina. In the first category he counts snow-blindness in consequence of looking a long time on large white or glaring planes especially on planes of snow. Further he explains partly from the above facts, the nightfog which is observed mostly in badly nourished individuals, if they must work too long a time, in presence of large surfaces reflecting glaring light, as is the case with masons and sailors and others. I add here the cases which the chief of the Greifswald University Eye Clinic, Dr. Paul Roemer, showed me last year as disturbances of vision in consequence of observations lasting some minutes with unprotected eyes, of a partial eclipse of the sun. Those disturbances lasted several weeks with some patients; in one case one could see a persistent destruction in the region of macula lutea by the ophthalmoscope.

Every one can observe for himself by looking for a moment at the sun, the bad influence it has on his vision.

Other observations one can make daily are twitching, epiphora, hyperaemia of conjunctiva, and of the lid margins in persons who continually and repeatedly work in too strong a light, and also in those who use their eyes persistently in insufficient light, examining small objects, which is a proof that poor light has also a bad influence on the eye. There are many authors who show that poor illumination also is not good for the eyes. The accommodating apparatus of the eye is too much strained in that way and more so if the eye must be approached to the

1) A. v. Reuss: Beiträge sur Kenntnis des jugendlichen Auges. Graefes Archiv. XXII—1.

A. v. Reuss, Die Augen der Schüler des Leopoldstädter Real—u. Obergymnasiums, in Wien.

A. v. Reuss: Augenuntersuchungen an Wiener Volksschulen, Wiener medizin Presse 1881.

A. v. Reuss über den Einfluss d. Schule auf Entstehung u. Wachstum der Kurzsichtigkeit.

object to get a clear picture on the retina. The fewer rays single points reflect from the surface of objects the nearer the eye must be to see sharply. In addition, the axes of the eyes must be converged properly and for that work other muscles must be put in action; that is, new work must be performed.

Professor A. v. Reuss has especially made several investigations along these lines. He shows in his works the dangerous influence close work has on the eyes of the pupils in Vienna.

As early as 1865, Hermann Cohn (2) proved by his investigations of pupils of Magdalena Latin School in Breslau that insufficient lighting of school rooms is one of the causes of myopia and has asked energetically for well-lighted school rooms.

The late Professor Schnabel of Vienna, to whom I feel very much indebted as a pupil, has investigated also the vision of school children and has stated emphatically the rapid increase of myopia in the age of development in pupils with a hereditary disposition. He proved also that the school should not be made alone responsible for near-sightedness.

Taval of Paris also has occupied himself assiduously with the question of illumination in schools and has stated that school rooms will have sufficient daylight only if they are at a distance from the opposite houses equal to at least twice the height of these houses. M. v. Gruber in Munich has given new formulæ, but in big cities, space is too expensive to satisfy completely such demands and as one cannot give up every old schoolhouse, Taval introduced in Europe the first American luxfer-prismas to augment the lighting in old schoolhouses.

It is true that the eye is capable of self-adaption. It is to be supposed, in consequence of Angelucci's observations on frogs' eyes quoted above, and from the fact that one can distinguish objects only some seconds after passing from a brilliantly to a poorly lighted room, that the conjecture of several authorities that the human retina has a similar apparatus for adaption to differences of light is right. Furthermore, we as well as most animals have another regulator for light in the iris.

It is not at all easy to state the limits for the hygienic maximum and minimum of light, starting from the object looked at. This limit is individually different and there are also amblyopic pupils to be kept in mind of whom there are more or less in every grade.

It was Professor Leonhard Weber in Germany who first, by means of the photometer invented by him, called attention to the enormous differences he detected to which the eyes are actually exposed daily, and Cohn says the eye does not imagine the difference shown by the

2) H. Cohn: Wie soll der gewissenhafte Schularzt die Tagesbeleuchtung in den Klassensimmern prüfen? Allgem. mediz. Central—Zeitung 1901—39—43.

photometer ("Das Auge ahnt nicht die Differenzen, welches das Photometer aufdeckt.")

A unit for measuring light has been introduced. This is the illumination which a normal candle produces at one meter distance on white paper, that is, 1 metercandle (Meterkerse M.K.). Even on winterdays H. Cohn saw by the help of the photometer differences of 579 to 9863 metercandles on a horizontal rough glassplate and in summer time the differences were from 4519 to 76,560 metercandles. It is astonishing how quickly the eye is able to adapt itself to such enormous differences. I, myself, observed in the lapse of a few seconds differences up to 250 metercandles on a desk in the middle of a school room at noon.

To see if the right quantity of light is provided for a given desk, one must first of all know how much is necessary from the hygienic point of view. It is again Prof. Cohn, whom I have quoted before, who demands in a very categoric manner that every place showing less than ten metercandles in red light should be no more used ("Alle Plätze, die weniger als 10 Meterkerzen in Rot geben sind unbedingt zu kassieren.") He regards fifty metercandles as desirable. Therefore, architects should take care in planning school rooms that requisite provisions for daylight are supplied and that all obstacles to good illumination should be avoided. Further, a good artificial illumination is very difficult in school rooms in consequence of the losses produced just where the light is especially necessary because a great many places are shadowed (1) by the body and hand of the pupils when working and especially when writing.

In H. Cohn's paper quoted above, we find also the remark that naturally the color of the walls, and the height and color of the wainscotings, are important for the reflected daylight. I must add also for the reflected light, if artificial one is used and also the color of the desks, the doors, the ceiling, etc. The reflections of the wall opposite to windows are, as Pleyer states (2), especially important for the desks up to -3 meter distance from that wall. It is the part of wall from about 25 cm. above the desk to about 225 cm. above the floor from which the illumination

1) Ostroglaseff in F. Erimann: Zur Frage der Schattenbildung bei direkter und indirekter Beleuchtung der Schulzimmer, Report VII Inter. Congress on Hygiene and Demography, Budapest Vol. 3, page 376, 1897.

Erismann: Künstliche Beleuchtung der Schulzimmer, Zeitschr f. Schulgesundheitspflege vol 10, page 529, 1897.

M. Oker Plom: Vergleichende Messungen der Licht,—u. Schattenverteilung. Internat. Magazine on School Hygiene, vol 7, 93—1911, page 93, 1911.

2) F. Pleier: Der Wandreflex. Zeitschrift: Schulgesundheitspflege, Vol. 22, 1909.

of those places gains reflected light. The percentage of light which will be reflected from the wall is with clear blue 30, with yellow 40, with green, 48, with white 92 per cent. Though white would be the most favor_ able color in that sense, it would be, on the other hand, too glaring if just opposite to eyes, and Burgerstein (1) says: "It is doubtful whether one would wish to make the one wall in question greenish and the other walls white. But in every case, we must decide that expect in exceedingly well-lighted rooms, pictures and much more the large blackboards common in the United States, cannot be at all favorable to good illumination.

I have followed with pleasure this author's suggestion to investigate this matter further.

Prof. Sigmund Exner, the great physiologist of Vienna, had the kind_ ness to introduce me to Prof. Sahulka in the Electro-Technical Institute of Vienna, who placed at my disposal a photometer, and by help of a member of the executive committee of the Austrian School Hygiene Association, Consular Schaufler and by help of Dr. Kart, the Vienna City Council permitted me the use of light and school rooms for my investigations.

I used Marten's photometers. If one looks into one of these photom_ eters, one sees two semicircular fields which he compares as to illu_ mination. By turning a screw two small mirrors, placed at an acute angle in the box, can be moved horizontally along a scale to bring the two fields to the same illumination. To get more exact results one searches the red and green portions and finds in this way the number of metercandles for white light of any kind for which the instrument is rated. This can be done by means of suitable conversion tables. If one works with another kind of light one must find the number of comparison.

Through the kindness of the inventor, Director Prof. Dr. Anton Kauer, my honored professor, I was able to use a second photometer (2) manufac_ tured by Rohrbeck in Vienna. Unfortunately I got this photometer too late. I could use it only for checking. The instrument works exactly and is easy to handle for every kind of light, and the inventor has published very exact extensive tables and lent to me supplements of those tables not yet published.

To get my results as exact as possible, I observed each time first, the portion for red then that for green and calculated in the usual way, as I have described by means of the constants for the quotient of green and red, the number of metercandles of the quality of light which I inves_ tigated.

1) Burgerstein "Handbuch f. Schulhygiene."

2) Dr. Anton Kauer's Photometer: Schilling Journal für Gasbeleuchtung u. Wasserversorgung 1904. Directed by Bunte in Karlsruhe.

The measurements in daylight are very tiresome It is necessary to get exactly the same intensity of light as far as possible, but the oscillations are not at all insignificant, even if the sky seems to be quite clear.

The measurements give always the value at the moment, therefore one must have a great many measurements for use. Approximately correct absolute values could be secured if one could find in a short time a very great number of maxima and minima, or if one could have a light of a tolerable constant intensity.

The weather at the time of my investigations was very changeable. I first of all used artificial light; once only was I able to get some results fit for use with daylight. I used school rooms where the windows are on the left of the pupils, as is usual in Austria. We have never had other than left sides daylight in school rooms, since it is preferable from the hygienic point of view. Generally these rooms have three large windows.

Also with artificial light the constancy is not as great as one might suppose. With incandescent gaslight (Welsbach lamps) the burning of more or less light which is supplied from the same mains, as well as other circumstances, cause change in the pressure and with that in the quantity of light sent out by the individual lamps.

It is similar with the electric light, especially in consequence of the changes in electrical tension. According to Seidener (1) 4% change in the voltage of metallic filament lamps is followed by 32% difference in the change of light intensity and for carbon filament lamps 6% difference in voltage causes 48% change of intensity of light. I found in an empirical way the time when the intensity of light is tolerably constant, and naturally preferred just that time for my measurements.

One needs much practice for such work but one acquires this quickly enough if one is endowed with good natural ability to distinguish fine shades. On the whole I made nearly 3,000 measurements. I restrict myself to report only in general. The photometer was put in the middle of the desk in question and the number of metercandles seen on the scale, as well as the name of the color in which it was seen, was noted only after I had observed that the field had been through some time equally clear or dark and after every movement of the screw showed a difference in the illumination of both. The measurement was then repeated exactly on the same place, while raising and lowering the blackboard, and was then repeated with the blackboard on the wall opposite windows, as is customary in America. The measurements in artificial light were made with direct and indirect lighting as well as with incandescent (Welsbach mantle) gas lamps and metallic filament and carbon filament lamps and arc lamps in different schools. The number of metercandles for the different desks (as well as for the

1) Seidener, Taschenbuch für Starkstronitechnik, 1913.

different places between the desks) are shown in the following tables I must remark that I generally could not make the investigation with full light because in the holidays it was generally impossible to get it.

In Austria in primary and in high schools there are on the walls opposite the pupils almost generally two blackboards at a distance of two meters from one another, whereas in grammar schools, colleges, and universities there is mostly one big blackboard on the same wall. The results are almost without any value in consequence of the oscillations mentioned before, if the quantity of light was measured on several places continuously with the sidewall blackboard and then in absence of such. Therefore, I felt obliged to limit my measurements to a few places only in order to get the results with as much equality of intensity of light as possible and to be able to make as correct a comparison as possible. The difference between the results with and without side blackboards, grew much higher when I used white sidewall boards instead of black ones. In the first case illumination was diminished, in the second increased. I generally used sidewall boards from four meters in length and 1.2 meters wide.

I was the less satisfied with the results I got in that way, as I had no numerical values at that time of the variations in oscillations of the intensity of light. Therefore I took care afterwards to get light of a constant intensity. Professor Sahulka was so kind as to interpose two resistances and two ammeters in the two circuits I used so that I had at last equal currents.

The loss of light produced by the black sidewall boards are, if measured in white light, in consequence of one of my tables, for instance:

In maximum metercandles.	....	5.48	about 18%
In minimum "	....	0.13	" 12%
In average "	....	2.30	" 15%

of light.

If measured in red light:

In maximum metercandles	....	6.1
In minimum "	....	0.1
In average "	....	1.59

of all light only for a blackboard on one side.

If after subtracting the loss of light due to the interposition of the pupil's body, we further subtract the loss due to a single blackboard on the wall, the measure of the illumination of the desk will be less than Cohn's minimum of 10 M.K. in red. This measure of illumination will be still less if the maximum of loss due to other interferences be deducted.

If a school room with sufficient illuminations is given a sidewall blackboard or even a blackboard at the back of the room, the loss may be so great that the desk lighting is far below Cohn's minimum.

It should be remembered that we are nowadays accustomed to work in an artificial light which is much nearer to daylight than in former times. In consequence of all we know we are entitled, to say that the sidewall blackboards, though recommendable from a pedagogical and practical point of view, are surely objectionable from the point of view of hygiene if they are boards with black surfaces. On the other hand, from the standpoint of the oculist, boards with a white surface or better with a surface of a light color are to be recommended. They could be objectionable only if the reflected light causes shadows of the right hand on the desk.

Sidewall boards with a black surface may be used only if the desks are supplied with an extremely bright daylight or an adequate artificial light, the latter having economic disadvantage. The price of a sidewall board with light surface will certainly be less the cost of artificial light. On the other hand, parts of rooms that have been useless because of poor illumination may be saved for regular class room purposes through light colored sidewall boards.

May I give my best thanks to all those who enabled me to carry on my investigations especially the council of Vienna and Dr. Burgenstein, and all those who were so kind as to listen to me.

. Part of a Schoolroom in Vienna with Direct Illumination. First Curtain (Black) from the Three Windows is Down. (Investigation Has Been Made with Artificial Light for Photographing the Room. The Photo was Taken at Daytime.)

Lighting of desks in one of the schoolrooms 2 Big Arc-lamps. (Indirect Illumination.) in metercandles. Vienna, Austria. The 3 windows have been closed with black jalousies.

INDIRECT ILLUM.

First cyphers signify the results only with the usual 2 blackboards before the children.
b—with sidewall blackboard.
w—with sidewall board with white surface.

Red	Green	Red	Green	Red	Green	Red	Green	Red	Green	Red	Green	Red	Green	Red	Green
6.2	11.8 9.2		20.1	12	28 12.3	27 12	30	10.7	16.8 7.6		17.6
								6.8 7,	13.8 6.8, 13.8	8.5, 14.8	10.0
7.0	15.8 9.2		15.1	12.3	28 12.2	27 12	30	7.8	21.6 7.0		21.5
				11.2	23 11	23 11.5	25	6.5	7.6, 13.8 10.5	6.4, 12.6	12.2
6.8	13.7 7.5		16	10.3	23.5 10.3	24 11	26.2	7.0	21.6 6.8		15
				11.2	22.3 10.5	23.6 11	23	7.6, 17	7.5, 15.3	15.3	
7	13.9 7.3		16.2	10	20 9.5	22.1 11	25	7.5	13.7 7.4		13
				11	29 12	27 12.1	26	8.0	8.2, 15	8.0, 19.5	15
6.1	10 7.4		16.8	10.9	29 12	26.8 11.2	27	9.6	20.5 8.2		16
				13	29.5 13	30 13	30	9.2	9.7, 21.2	9.2, 20	16
6.8	14 9		19.1	12.8	28 13.2	29 12.2	29.5	9.8	22.8 8.6		16
				15	34.5 14.6	33.5 14	32.1	11.8, 23	9.5, 20.3	15.3	
8	16.9 10		20.1	14.5	32.5 14.2	30.5 13.5	30.5	9.5	21.8 8.2		15
				15.4	34.5 15.4	33.5 15.1	32.8	10	22.8 .		21
7.2	14.3 8.5		16.8	15	34.2 15.4	32.5 14.7	30.7	11.3, 26	9.8, 21.5	19
				14	31 14.5	31 14.5	31	9.6	21.5 7.5		17.5
6.5	12.7 7.9		16.3	13.5	29.5 14	30.3 13	30.5	10.2	7.9	9.5, 20	
				12	26.5 13.2	27.5 12	26	11.0, 22.2	217.2	16	
								9.4	9.5, 20		17.5
				12	22.5 11.2	23.5 10.8	25.5	8.4	16.8 7.8		16
								9.5, 21	9.5, 21	16.3	
								8.0	14.6 6.8		13.2
								9.5, 21	8.0, 19.5	19.3 12.2	

Left 50 cm · 50 cm · 50 cm · 50 cm · 50 cm · 50 cm · 50 cm · 110 cm · Right 60 cm

STOVE · BIG · SIDEWALL BOARD · WALL · WALL

DIRECT ILLUM.

Lighting of desks in one of the schoolrooms, Vienna, Austria. The windows have been closed with black blinds.   7 New Welsbach Mantel Gas Lamps. All was burning. Direct illumination.

First cyphers signify the results only with the usual 2 blackboards before the children. b—with sidewall blackboard 120 centimeter by 400 centimeter.

Sidewall blackboard

Red	Green	Red	Green	Red	Green	Red	Green	Red	Green	Red	Green	Red	Green	Red	Green
21.5	43	17	47			25	58	29.5	69.4			27.5	64	18.2	42 [b]
b15	36	12.8	31.5			25	57	29	67			26.5	60	16.2	38 [b]
22	57	32	85			22	54	25.5	55			25.5	59.9	17	39.5
b20	54	33	85			21.5	46	25.5	55			24	53	15	37 [b]
21.9	54	25.9	55			27	62	25	60			23	50	20	45
b19	50	22	51			28.6	61	25.2	57			22	48	18.1	43 [b]
33.5	70	36	85			36	82	29	72			26.5	67	21	49
b30.5	65	33	70.2			35	80	32.5	79			25.5	65	20	40 [b]
33.5	73	51	112			26.5	64	28.5	66			22.8	56	15.3	41
b30.0	68	49	94			30.5	70	31	72			21.5	52	15.3	36 [b]
25.5	65	28.5	63			26.5	60	24	55			25	50	23.1	49
b22.6	55	27	62.5			26.5	54	24	48			26	49	21	43.7 [b]
33.5	70	31	67			34	78	36	85			33	85	24.5	57
b27.5	59	26	61			33	75	37.5	85			33	80	22.5	50 [b]
32	65	52	120			32	70	31	72						
b31.5	69	46	95			30	66	33	70						
22.5	51	34	75												
Left 25	53	31	66												

Right

SIDEWALL BLACKBOARD   LIGHT WALL

DIRECT ILLUM.
AUERLICHT—WELSBACH MANTEL GAS LAMPS

Red	White	Green	Red	White	Green	Red	White	Green	Red	White	Green	Red	White	Green	Red	White	Green	Red	White	Green	Red	White	Green
22.8	41.95	58	24	44.9	62	32	58.88	80	24	40.3	52	24	40.3	52	52	86.32	110	36	61.6	80	21	36.96	49 b
16	30.08	42	21	37.6	50	33	54.45	70	27	50.3	70	30	5.1	66	27	47.79	63	22	40.5	55	16	28.48	38 b
22.6	42.48	58	32	58.9	80	29	54.23	75	18.7	36.1	52	26.5	43.7	55	37	64.38	85	30	51.9	68	20	38.19	54
18.5	34	45	26	41.3	51.5	29.5	59	87	22	37.6	49	27.5	45.5	57	28	50.12	67	21.8	36.2	46	15	24.45	31 b
20	38.4	55	19	34.2	48	18.8	35.81	54	31.5	50.4	79	36.5	62.3	82	25	45.75	62	35	52.5	62	23	41.17	55
22	33	40	17.5	31.5	42	17	32.64	46	28	46.2	59	35	56	70	22	41.14	57	27.5	44	55	20	36.8	50 b
27	49.68	68	31	53.9	71	40	69.2	90	27	50.5	70	32	53.1	68	64	10.56	135	37	56.24	68	26	48.88	68
26	41.6	51	31	53.9	71	35.2	60.89	80	36	56.5	70	34	60.2	80	50	87	114	32	46.96	60	24	41.76	55 b
22	37.4	49	33	49.7	80	36.5	63.87	84	24.5	46.6	65	25	43.5	57	40.5	63.58	79	25	46.5	64	17	33.66	49
22	37.4	49	30.5	53.1	70	35	73.5	79	21	40.9	58	26	44.5	58	30	54	72	22.6	40	53	15.8	28.12	37.6 b
16.5	33.3	50	20	35	46	23	40.71	54	31.5	54.8	72	31.5	55.4	73	23	43.94	60	23.5	46.5	68	25	43.0	56
15.5	27.9	37	20	36	50	22	38.06	50	28	48.4	63	27.5	49.5	66	21	37.59	50	23.5	38.5	59	18	32.4	43.5 b
25.5	48.9	69.3	29	52.2	70	44.5	74.3	95	25	44.0	58	32	54.1	70	50	87.5	115	25	46.5	64	20	31	38
25	45	60	28	51.8	70.5	74.3	74.98	95	27	45.9	60	27	45.9	60	45	75.15	96	24	41.76	55	17	30.6	41 b
25	44.5	59	37	62.3	80	33	55.77	72	22.5	41.9	58	26	55.5	60									
23.5	39.9	52	37	61.1	78	35	59.5	77	23	40.3	53	22	38.1	50									
20.5	36.3	48	25	60.6	62																		
21	37.6	50	24	41.8	55																		

METALLIC FILAMENT LAMPS.

A Little schoolroom in the Electrotechnical Institut of Vienna.

b sign—blackboard.
w sign— with light surface in the front of the pupils.

Color of light	Red	White	Green	Red	White	Green	Red	White	Green	Red	White	Green	Red	White	Green	Red	White	Green	Red	White	Green
w.	12.3	15	16	12.6	15.75	17	12.2	18.17	21.9	15.6	21.84	25.1	15.5	21.54	24.5	14.2	20.73	24	14.1	18.04	20.5
b.	8.5	11.05	12.3	10.5	10.92	11	12	11.64	11.5	13	15.86	17	12.5	16	17.5	13	16.12	17.5	13.5	14.17	15.4
w.	11.7	15.62	14.7	12.6	15.42	16.3	14.6	18.98	21	15	19.8	22.1	14.9	19.81	22.3	14.5	17.98	20.3	12.9	16.77	18.5
b.	9.5	11.59	12.5	10.3	12.26	13	11.2	12.99	13.6	12.5	14.12	14.7	12.5	15.5	16.7	11.5	14.95	16.6	10.5	13.02	13.8
w.	11.1	12.87	13.5	12	14.40	15.2	13.6	14.55	14.8	14	17.08	18.2	14	17.5	19	13	15.21	16.2	11.9	14.16	15
b.	10	12	12.8	10.4	11.85	12.4	11.2	13.1	13.9	11.6	13.45	14.1	11.1	13.2	13.9	11	12.54	13	9.6	11.42	12.1

B

Little schoolroom
in the Electrotechnical Institut of Vienna

b = With sides all blackboard

Blackboard in the front and

Sidewall board (black)

11	14.08	15.4	13.3	16.22	18	15.5	19.84	22	16.2	21.7	24.5	15.2	20.36	23	14.9	19.96	23	14	18.2	20.3
11	13.66	14.7	12	14.16	15	12.4	15.6	17.2	13.9	15.98	16.8	13.9	17.37	19	13.3	17.82	20	11.6	13.69	14.5 b
15.7	14.75	15.3	13	14.95	16.7	13.3	16.22	18.4	13.5	17.09	20.5	14.4	17.5	19.6	14	17.7	18	11.6	15.08	17
Ma 10.8	12.42	14	12.2	13.42	14.0 Mi 13.2	16.1	17.1	13.5	674	18	11.9	15.47	17	11.9	14.04	14.8	10.3	12.26	13 b
13	14.95	16	12	14.64	16	13.5	14.8	16	13	16.25	20.3	13.5	17.55	97	12.5	16.5	18.5	12	15	16.2
10.6	12.29	13	11.5	12.65	13.1	12.5	35	17.1	13	16.25	17.5	12	15.12	16.5	11.1	13.32	14.2	9.8	176	12.5 b
12	14.6	15.5	11.8	14.49	15.3	11.9	14.87	62	11.6	13.45	14	12.8	13.5	14	10.4	13.5	15	11.8	14.74	15.8
10.3	11.9	12.6	11.2	13.89	14.9	12.1	59	17.	13	16.25	17.5	12.4	14.38	15.2	10.9	125	13.4	9.8	11.37	12 b
α2 Mi	12.75	13.9	114	13.79	14.8	11.1	13.87	15	11.8	14.04	15	11	14.3	15.9	10.8	14.25	15.9	12	13.4	15.1
10.1	11.61	12.3	10.3	12.98	14	12.6	14.49	52	13	15.73	16.8	12.1	14.76	16.0	11.2	14.56	16	9.6	11.23	11.9 b
10	12.2	13	10.8	13.39	14.4	10.9	13.51	14.6				10.9	12.64		10.5	12.49	13.3	9.8	13.13	14.8
9.8	11.81	12.9	10.3	12.56	13.5	11.6	13.84	15				10.9	12.32		12.9	11.1	12.87	13.5	9.8	10.78	11.2 b

C   Little schoolroom in the Electrotechnical Institut of Vienna.   Blackboard.

Metallic Filament Lamps—10 over the space over the desks the other 14 for illuminating the only blackboard (5 meter +1.2 meter) before the desks *a*—up, *d*—down so that it was covered by the sideboard of the table (5 meter + 1m)

A meter show 4 220 volt direct illum. +—not to use.

The doors, desks, table are in light brown wood, the walls in light colors, the blinds in the same color.

Light Color	Red	White	Green	Red	White	Green	Red	White	Green	Red	White	Green	Red	White	Green	Red	White	Green	Red	White	Green	
a	11	14.08	15.4	13.3	16.22	18	15.5	19.84 Ma	22	16.2	21.7	24.5	15.2	20.36	23	14.9	19.96	23 Ma	14	18.2	20.3	a ⎫ 75
d	10.6 12	18	13	11	12.87	14	13.3	14.36	15.2	13	17.42	17.4	20	13.6	17.4	19	12.5	15	16	12.3	14.6 16.2	d ⎭
a	13	14.95	14.64	16	13.5	14.8	16	13	16.25	20.3	13.5	17.55	19.7	12.5	6.5	18.5	12	15	16.2			a ⎫ 75
d	9.6	11.27	12.2	10.8	12.4	12.9	14.6	14.04	15.2	11.9	13.8	14.5	11	13.9	14.5	10	12.2	12.9				d ⎭
a	12	14.6	15.5	11.8	14.49	5.3	11.9	14.83	14.36	16.2	11.6	13.45	14.2	12.8	13.5	14	10.4	13.5	15	10.8	14.14 15.8	a ⎫ 75
d	10.3 11	53	12	11	12.65	12.3	14.3	13.3	12.1	13.75	13.67	14.3	12.1	13.67	14.3	12.6	10.6	12.5	13.2			d ⎭
a	10.2 12	75	13.9	11.4	13.79	14.8	11.1	13.87	15	11.8	14.04	15	11	14.3	3.9	10.8	14.25	15.9	10	13.4	15.1	a ⎫ 75
d	9.7 11	93	13	10.2	12.39	13.9	11.5	14.37	14.4	12.4	14.2	14.8	11.8	13.3	14.1	10.9	12.17	11.8	10.2	11.7	12.3	d ⎭
a	10	12.2	13	10.8	13.39	14.4	10.9	13.51	14.6	Skiopticon	10.9	12.64 Mi Mi	13.5	10.5	12.49	13.5	10.5	12.49	13.73	14.8		a ⎫ 75
d	9	9.99	10.4	9.9	11.48	12	10.5	12.18	13		10.8	12.5	13.2	10.4	12.58	13.9	13.2	10.4	12.58	11.27	11.6	d ⎭
	50 cm	½ m	1 m	1 m	1 m	1 m	1 m	1 m	1 m	1 m	1 m											1 meter Right

Distance of the desks behind another 75 cm. The measurements have been made in every 1 meter distance from the right sidewall.

SESSION THIRTY-FOUR

Room A.   Saturday, August 30th, 9:00 A.M.

SYMPOSIUM ON SCHOOL ILLUMINATION (Part Two)

Arranged by the Illuminating Engineering Society

HERBERT IVES, *Chairman*

W. R. HUNTLEY, Buffalo, N. Y., *Vice-Chairman*

Program of Session Thirty-four

DANIEL W. WEAVER, M.D., County Health Commissioner, Greensburg, Ind. "Overhead Illumination for School Houses."

JAMES KERR, M.D., Department of Education, London County Council, England. "Classroom Illumination."

B. B. HATCH, Electrical Engineer, Boston, Mass. "School House Lighting in General from the Standpoints of an Engineer." (Manuscript not supplied.)

GEORGE W. FITZ, M.D., Formerly Assistant Professor of Physiology and Hygiene and Medical Visitor, Harvard University. "Practical Methods for Testing Natural Illumination, With Demonstration of a New Apparatus."

W. L. COFFEY, B. Pd., School Commissioner, Sheboygan, Mich. "Rural School Illumination." (Manuscript not included.)

OVERHEAD ILLUMINATION FOR SCHOOL HOUSES

BY

D. W. WEAVER

The light, to be comfortable to the eyes, must be free from reflections and shadows, must be steady, of sufficient quantity, diffused and with a minimum of actinic (heat, violet and ultra-violet) rays. The diffused daylight is the best for school purposes.

The question of supplying a light to all the pupils, in all parts of the school room, equally, must be considered. It is not justice to the pupils that some few pupils, alone, should have the light ideally and the larger number have an objectionable light.

Therefore, considering daylight, or for that matter artificial light, the one provision that would serve as a means of providing all pupils with the best light obtainable should be adopted in school house lighting. When one considers the various directions from which light can be secured as from the right, left, front, rear or over-head, singly or combined, there are all open to objections. Let us make analysis granting first that all have the same source of light—daylight—which would dispose of the question of quality.

First, light from the right side. This is objectionable because it will throw shadows upon the desk of all right handed pupils sitting in the fore part of the room, and reflections in the eyes of those in the back part. The pupils on the right side will have an abundance of light while those on the opposite side of the room will have an insufficient amount.

The light from the back is objectionable, from the pupil's point of view, as also the teacher's. The teacher will have a glaring light in the face, which is very objectionable. The pupils all will have shadows upon their desk work and very probably an insufficient amount of light.

The light from the left is objectionable for the same reason as light from the right, except that it does not throw shadows upon the desk for as many pupils as light from the right does, because few pupils are left handed. The reflections in the face of the pupils in the back part of the school room are the same as when the light comes from the right. As school houses are usually constructed, the foremost windows are about on a line with the front row of seats. One can easily see that even the pupils upon the front row get a glare of light from these front windows, in their eyes; this means reflections. One can also see that with the average width of school rooms of 40 feet that the pupils upon the front row upon the opposite side of which the windows are located, whether right or left, get a reduced amount of light. Either the ones next to the window receive too strong a light for comfort or the ones upon the opposite side receive an insufficient amount. Again, when the light is from the left, and the pupils upon the front row to the right, have any blackboard work to look at, they receive a glaring reflection of light from the blackboard in their eyes. The pupils in the back seats upon the side of windows get reflection in their eye from the windows in front of them. The pupils on the rear seats upon the opposite side of the room get no light at all over their left shoulders as intended by a left-sided light, but get all of it from various angles from in front of themselves making reflections in their eyes. The amount is also insufficient.

Light from in front is objectionable because of the glaring reflections in the eyes of the pupils.

Light from right, left and rear is objectionable on account of the reflections and shadows produced upon the desk work, yet the amount would be more equally distributed to all pupils.

Another objection to one-sided lighting, whether right or left, is that the light cannot be properly controlled for the various periods of the day any season. It is true if the light is upon the north side this objection would be eliminated but in buildings of three or more rooms the light cannot reach all rooms from the north.

If the windows face the west, the light can be controlled in the forenoon but in the afternoon the shades can be swung in any position and yet the glare is not overcome, and if the shades are entirely drawn the light will be insufficient. Another objection that is serious is the shutting out of the light by adjacent buildings, also certain times during the day a glare from the reflections from the windows of the adjacent buildings become very annoying.

Light from overhead is the least objectionable. It can be distributed to every corner of the school room equally, and in sufficient quantity. It can be diffused and in this way overcome glare and reflection. It is free from shadows upon the work; it falls upon the desk at, or near, right angle. It does not vary, being the same at all meridians of the sun. Adjacent buildings will affect the light but slightly. It is equally appropriate for left and right handed pupils. From an anatomical point of view the light comes from the ideal direction. Eyes are provided with prominent eyebrows that protect the eyes from light from above, as also the forward position of the head, as is usually indulged in while at desk work will do.

The plan of construction of the overhead light is as follows (This is only applicable to one-story school houses): Cut four skylights, equal to one-eighth of total floor space of the room to be provided with light. These skylights are distributed over the room so as to make the light as nearly uniform as possible and so as to receive the light equally well during different hours of the day. Below the skylights

Note the reflections from the left side of the blackboard from left side illumination. Twenty-four cases of conjunctivitis out of thirty pupils.

in the ceiling of the room are placed diffusing, prismatic glasses to cut out all the direct, glaring rays of light.

For rooms that have a floor above so skylight cannot be used, the light can be received from both sides and back through high prismatic windows which will throw the light to the ceiling or over the head of the pupils; this will give a diffused overhead light that will be comfortable to the pupils and will be practically free from shadows and reflections.

When artificial light is used the lights should be placed high and reflectors below the lights to divert all light rays against the ceiling, this will give the room a somewhat diffused light and practically free from shadows and reflections. In all cases whether the light is taken through skylights, through high prismatic side windows, from artificial sources, the rays must be diffused, evenly distributed to all pupils, free from shadows and reflections, and the overhead lighting methods will provide such light. Many industrial plants have provided skylight illumination for their establishments. Many offices are illuminated

by the overhead indirect method successfully.   Allow me to again state
it matters not whether a direct or indirect system is used, providing
the illumination is from such a position that no unbroken or undiffused
rays of light fall upon the eye.

Cleveland Hardwood Co.'s Office.   Overhead Lighting.

Fig. 2.

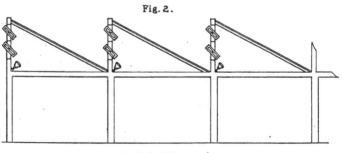

Method of Construction.

CLASSROOM ILLUMINATION

BY

JAMES KERR

Although in steady daylight the eye takes little account of differences of five to five hundred foot candles, the only final test of illumination is the continuous satisfactory performance of visual work.

Cohn's test of the capacity of a normal eye to read diamond type with facility at the distance of half a meter is one of the most reasonable tests of sufficiency. Objects can, however, be seen in light which is not good enough for continuous work, and the test may therefore be used as suggested by Kaz of St. Petersburg, who states that light is sufficient for continuous work if type is visible in it when looked at through a smoked glass which stops 96 per cent. of the light.

Physiological Considerations. Like other organs the eye possesses a considerable working reserve and under natural circumstances performs well within its capacities. Strain is only noticed under artificial conditions of continuous work in defective light. Strain is due to fatigue from overwork, to glare, or to both causes combined.

The overfatigue of maintained muscular effort is felt especially in the hypermetropic eyes of children. Anyone may notice it in illumination so poor that extra effort has to be made to maintain a steady accommodation and the fixation necessary for a sharp image, or in flickering light where rapid enough changes in the eye cannot be accomplished.

Certain protective mechanisms come into play to protect against glare. There is almost instantaneously some pupillary reaction which persists while by pigmentary changes the eye becomes slowly adapted to the intensity of the illumination. An eye is relatively insensitive in full brightness, but ten minutes in a dark room makes it about twenty-five times as sensitive, and in half an hour or more it attains to over thirty times its sensitiveness when in bright light. This range of sensitiveness varies much in individuals. In extreme cases the variation may be ten times as much in one person as in another. The capacity of the eye is, however, so great that an electric bulb which causes intense glare by night may burn almost unnoticed by the eye adapted for daylight.

In glare the protective mechanisms fail to give sufficiently rapid protection and distress results. The altering eye slowly integrates the illumination around but is usually adapted for the average brightness mainly corresponding to the most sensitive part of the retina which receives the images of objects looked at.

Glare can be roughly divided into two varieties. A primary glare, where there is actual physical change beyond the normal physiological range, and often of a persisting, lasting, or even permanent nature. A kind of burning out effect is produced in the retina. The cases of permanent scotoma seen after solar eclipses are extreme instances of this kind. Persistent after images seen on looking at bright lights or incandescent surfaces, and which may sometimes last partially for weeks, are due to less intense but similar changes. Sir Isaac Newton was reported to suffer for a long time from an image of the sun, and the philosopher Fechner is said to have lost his vision through too intense study of after images. Under ordinary circumstances of health and use an after image should quite disappear in a few minutes and should not cause subjective trouble for more than a few seconds. Primary glare as thus described fortunately scarcely comes into consideration in schools.

Secondary glare is apparently not due to the same cause as the burning out effects, but is due to a peripheral image which is relatively brighter than the image at the macula for which the eye is adapted. This secondary glare from peripheral images may be due also to bright lights or incandescent surfaces of relatively small area, but is most frequently caused by large areas with but slight excess of regular reflection, from the comparatively smooth surfaces of walls, books, furniture and so on. It seems more easily set up the nearer the object is to the visual axis, and especially if in the lower half of the visual field.

These physiological conditions of glare are often aggravated by debilitated conditions of the tissues due to anæmia or fatigue and with persistent after images are commonly complained of in migraine or neurasthenia.

In addition to the small proportion with defective light sense is a large percentage of elementary school children in English towns with diminished visual acuity. The acuity is below ($V = \frac{6}{18}$) one-third normal in ten per cent. and materially reduced in another twenty per cent., so that one-third of school children require better illumination than would be necessary with normal eyes.

The points of ocular interest to be continuously borne in mind in all questions of illumination are (1) that muscular and nervous strains are enormously increased in the exact efforts made to maintain clear visual perception in faint light.

(2.) The eye varies in its sensitiveness from twenty-five to thirty-five times according to the general illumination for which it is slowly adapted.

(3.) Individual differences exist varying from one to ten times in the capacity for seeing in poor light, and in addition one third of school children in towns have defective visual acuity, which in ten per cent. is a serious handicap even in light sufficient for normal working.

Natural Illumination. Illumination can now be precisely defined. Measurements may be made in foot candles by means of photometers. The main lines of the subject were settled with costly and scarcely portable instruments. At first Weber's and during the past ten years Wingen's photometers have been used. Recently electric lamps have rendered handy and accurate instruments possible. The lumeter of Messrs. Dow and McKinney can be recommended on this account for school work. These instruments measure the brightness on or from surfaces. They are of general use for working out scientific data, and for the investigation of artificial lighting.

For daylight where the variations are rapid and great any measurements in terms of an unvarying standard are not likely to be satisfactory without controls, and the daylight must be used as a standard. A relative photometry is wanted which will express the illumination at school places in terms of the outside light. Thorner's little light tester which measures the illumination at any place against the brightness of an image of the sky is most useful. The image of the sky is thrown by a mirror and lens and its brightness varied by the aperture of the lens. The brightness should be greater than that of the sky image with F-6 stop. Fitted with a graduated iris this is a most useful instrument. The co-efficient of local lighting to daylight can then be rapidly determined for any place.

Tested by these instruments the variation in lighting in most rooms is very great. For instance, a school hall 45 x 25 feet, one end surrounded by class rooms, the other by windows, gave readings along the centre line varying from 30 to 800 foot candles, and in one corner where sunlight fell it exceeded 2,000 foot candles. On the other hand, a classroom remote from the sun gave readings from 13 to 70 foot candles. With varying weather, however, readings in foot candles may vary tenfold in as many minutes. A place may be suitable with 4 to 5 foot candles, or too dark with 6 to 7 foot candles. Everything depends on the general daylight and condition of adaptation of the eye.

Cohn, who originally formulated the demand "mehr Licht" for the schools, wanted at least 10 meter candles (measured with red light) for any lighting of a school place. This corresponds roughly to one foot candle in the international (English) measure. For daylight this is indeed a minimum, making no allowance for other than normal eyes, and cannot be taken to satisfy present requirements. It is a poorly lighted place which has not ten times this amount. In his scheme for school inspection, the first question regarding lighting is "How many places have less than 50 meter candles?" The measurement of 10 meter candles has been accepted in the past as a standard and not, as Cohn intended, as an absolute minimum in bad weather. Double this amount must now be asked for, not as a standard daylight illumination but as a minimum below which no school place is to be permitted as usable.

It is not enough to determine the brightness of illumination of an existing place. The lighting in planning buildings has to be estimated at any spot. Javal related the brightness of any place to the area of sky visible. Cohn formulated this by saying that 50 reduced solid degrees of sky should be seen. In measuring solid or square degrees by the stereogoniometer the measurements are reduced by a calculation to the equivalent area of zenith illumination. Pleier has simplified this determination by using a pinhole camera. He calculates a reduced square degree gauge and photographs the window or sky through this gauge, thus getting at once a measurement and record. This method can be much simplified and the cost of photographing each place eliminated. The areas of reduced degrees as projected on a wall from a certain point are calculated, then making a chart on the wall, and photographing the chart from the fixed point a gauge is obtained always true for that lens. A lens of 9 Dioptres is practically convenient. It is convenient to do this with a lens tilted to 30°. The lens is then used tilted at 30° in a camera obscura. Thin paper, on which the gauge has been printed being centered on the glass screen of the camera obscura, a pencil is run round the image of the window and thus permanent records of the reduced square degrees subtended by sky at various places in a room can be made in a few minutes. I find, however, the measurement of the sky of little value to the school doctor and have not gone beyond using a rough model of this solid angle gauge, which cost about a shilling to construct. This 50 reduced square degrees of Cohn corresponds to the 10 meter candle minimum and will be insufficient unless full and intelligent use is made of wall and roof reflection.

Others have stated that the angle of the line drawn from the upper edge of the window to a school place must not be less than 27° with the horizon and that there must be a vertical opening of sky of at least 5°. These estimates are also erring on the low side.

As regards windows when a school is of many stories and situated on a street or in proximity to other buildings something may be done by making the top floor rooms a little lower, and increasing the height of the bottom floor rooms, but this is a particular architectural problem not to be dealt with by the doctor.

Whilst lighting interests demand windows as large as possible the interest of heating and ventilation restrict their size. In any case it is the upper parts of the windows which are of most importance. They should be carried to the ceiling whilst the lower sill need not come lower than four and a half feet from the floor. A room height above 13 to 14 feet is lost space so far as ventilation is concerned, and a window to this height will give light from the top at an angle of not less than 27° to the horizontal to a desk about 21 feet off. This limits the useful width of a classroom to 22.5 feet. The class limit is likely to remain at 40 pupils for the next generation in Great Britain. A room 25 feet long would give 14 square feet and nearly 200 cubic space for each scholar, with seven changes of air an hour, which is the maximum possible without propulsion, there would be about 1,200 cubic feet of air per head per hour. The British Association Committe on school ventilation estimated for 3,000 cubic feet per head per hour as the physiological requirement. A smaller room would be unhygienic for 40 children. If the allowance of one-fifth of the floor space be taken for window area it is usually suitable for a room of this width. For wider rooms a larger ratio of window area is required. This would mean a floor area of 562.5 square feet in the typical classroom, and a corresponding 112 square feet of window area. With windows eight and a half feet vertically, allowing for mullions the windows would have to extend horizontally to about 15 feet of the 25 foot wall.

Illumination falls off rapidly with distance from the window successive rows of desks in a typical room gave 100%, 75%, 42%, 28% and 23% lighting. Annually many hours increase in artificial lighting is required and at other times much light is lost on walls and by absorption from darkly painted surfaces. The ceiling and walls above the level of the children's heads should be merely faintly tinted and as nearly white as possible, being matt enough in texture to prevent glare. Woodwork should not be stained or varnished but lightly painted nearly white. This not only saves light, but money in gas or electricity bills. It is the wall on the scholars right hand which is most effective in reflection and in decreasing intensity of shadows. Pleier has attempted to work out the effects of wall reflections mathematically but in practice even with the photometer they defy this analysis as their effect on adaptation of the eye might make continuous work difficult in a poor light. This effect is more likely to be marked with artificial light than with daylight, where it would be entirely masked by the greater effect of the windows or sky on adaptation of the eye.

In recent efforts to obtain effective cross ventilation some English schools have been built with right and left cross lighting. So long as the left lighting is most prevalent some lighting from the right would seem rather an advantage in mitigating shadows and increasing general illumination, but with right-handed people there is danger of glare from writing paper unless the windows throw the right-handed light from behind also. From experience I can only condemn right hand lighting in any degree. Although not officially recognised in England top lighting has immense advantages in single storied schools. Lighting from the scholars backs on account of shadows, and glare in the teacher's eyes, and worse still windows *en face* with the children should lead to condemnation of a classroom and its withdrawal from use for reading or writing.

Poorly lighted rooms may have some improvement by use of external mirrors or reflectors, or with prism, ornamental or fluted glass. Great care has to be taken with these devices. Irritating glare can be caused by badly set prisms, or by fluted glass where small bright rays or beams cross the room nearly horizontally or on a level with the children's eyes. Similar results occur in western rooms during the afternoon towards sunset.

Artificial Lighting. Artificial lighting of schoolrooms is generally unsatisfactory, it is however subsidiary in importance for elementary schools.

As a result of much experimenting during the past eighteen months by a committee of the London Illuminating Engineering Society the minimum artificial illumination for a school place has been fixed at 2 foot candles, although several members of the committee pressed for a higher value of 2.5 foot candles. For assembly halls and places where no reading or writing is done one foot candle suffices. For special work, art classes, drawing offices, and so on, 4 foot candles will be necessary. Special lighting of blackboards by lamps screened from the pupils was deemed necessary to the amount of 60 per cent. over that on the school desks. Blackboards require much attention to keep them in condition, and chalks especially when coloured have to be selected with a view to visibility in artificial light.

The shadows cast from points of light can be greatly modified by increasing the area of apparent source of light by suitable reflectors, by opal shades, or by prism cut glass covers, holophane glass, and by lightly tinted walls. The use of indirect lighting from roof and wall reflection aids removal of deep shadows although the softer and more restful effect on the adaptation of the eye probably means that greater actual illumination is necessary for fine work. The best general effects seem to be obtained by semi-direct units where the opal transmitter tones down the direct rays to nearly the same order of brilliancy as those reflected from the neighbouring surface of ceiling. The opal shades then are free from after image production, and shadows are not deep.

The greatest contrasts and also greatest effect of illumination at place is got by local lighting, and for fine work this is probably the economical. In relation to general school cost economy in arti lighting is a very poor policy. With local lighting the colour of the need not be considered and in any case they are more likely to be li coloured for daylight than tinted to suit artificial lighting. Inca cent gas probably gives the greatest amount of light for the mone electricity has hygienic advantages in cleanliness, absence of deter tion of the atmosphere through heat and moisture and readiness o tribution. The selection of one or the other will probably be on other than hygienic grounds. The most important things for ficial lighting are the elimination of glare, and the maintenance brightness in every school place of not less than 2 foot candles.

PRACTICAL METHODS FOR TESTING NATURAL ILLUMINATION, WITH DEMONSTRATION OF A NEW APPARATUS

BY

G. W. FITZ

At the present time, we may consider that there are four principal procedures for the practical determination of the minimal natural illumination of school rooms. As a basis for this determination it has been conclusively established that the natural illumination of a room in which much use of the eyes in reading is required, must not fall, even on the darkest day of the year, below a minimum equivalent to ten metre candles (one-foot candle).

To determine the minimal illuminating efficiency of a school room, one may measure the minimum directly by testing the illumination on a dark day, at a remote desk, toward the close of the school session, by means of a photometer or an illuminometer. This method gives absolute results, but its difficulty lies in the fact that it involves an expensive apparatus, an expert observer, and very probably a protracted delay, since the apparatus and the trained observer may not be available when the dark day finally arrives. This procedure is, therefore, not available for ordinary practical use.

Secondly, he may determine the illumination at the most remote desk, by means of the same instrument, upon any convenient day. In this instance he must allow for the various factors which raise the illumination above the minimal, such as the brighter condition of the sky; the increases in reflecting efficiency of walls of buildings, foliage, roadbed and ground; the presence of snow, and the seasonal changes in the sun's altitude. The variations in the excess lighting, thus present at the time of measurement, are most difficult of evaluation by even a highly trained observer. Any estimate of them may fairly be considered to be subject to a probable error of fully fifty per cent. As it would not be unusual on clear days for the excess illumination to be three or four times the minimal itself, any photometric measurement not made under minimal conditions, is obviously of little practical value in determining minimal illumination.

Thirdly, the observer may use fine test types to determine on a dark day the visual acuity at the remote desk in question, or he may use as a test the ease with which fine type is read. This procedure, although much recommended because of its simplicity, is open to the objection involved in all similar subjective tests of illumination. Their chief inaccuracy lies in the fact that the eye adapts itself to the decreased light, by an increase of retinal sensibility and by an enlargement of pupil, so that the deficiency of light intensity may be subjectively almost counterbalanced by the greater amount of a light admitted to the retina and by its increased sensitiveness. Hence the fair visual acuity or ease of reading which comes after the first moment of adjustment is an exceeding deceptive and unsafe test of proper illumination, since the enlarged pupil uncovers the optical defects of cornea and lens and introduces thereby serious eye strain, even for apparently normal eyes. All procedures, therefore, which involve subjective tests for minimal lighting, are to be absolutely condemned.

Fortunately, through the studies of L. Weber, confirmed by Cohn and others, a fourth method is available, which is at once simple, reliable and practical. This consists of determining at the remote desk the amount of visible sky surface.

L. Weber, after extensive photometric studies of school rooms under all conditions of weather and season, found that the efficiency of the minimal lighting was in direct ratio to the amount of sky which, on a dark, wet day when external reflecting surfaces were dulled, sent its light directly into the school room. He found that at least fifty square degrees of sky surface must be visible from each desk, if the minimal illumination was to be equal to the standard minimal requirement of ten metre candles. The only instance in which any allowance has to be made in the test is when the sky is partially obscured by the foliage of trees. It is then easily possible to make a sufficiently accurate estimate of the part thus covered and, by subtracting it from the total area, to determine the actual amount of clear sky available.

To measure the sky surface Weber invented an apparatus which he called a "space angle measure" ("Raumwinkelmesser") consisting of a lens which focuses an image of the window upon a plate, divided by lines into square millimetres or degrees. This instrument and the procedure have found little use here in spite of expert endorsement, possibly because the apparatus is somewhat clumsy and expensive and because most observers have felt that they must measure the light itself, in spite of the fact that such measurements are difficult to make, require expensive apparatus, expert observers, and, if subject to reduction for excess lighting, involve large indeterminate errors.

Since Weber's results have been tested out by trained observers using photometric measurements taken on dark days, and have been proved adequate in determining a safe minimum of light, I have experimented to devise an apparatus for measuring the sky space, which should be sufficiently accurate and simple for use by the untrained observer, and yet so inexpensive as to be within reach of all who wish to make tests of illumination.

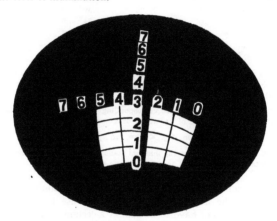

Space Protractor (Fitz) showing use in measuring sky area outlined by a window 28° wide by 47° high (1,316 sq. degrees). Principle of use (according to L. Weber), 50 square degrees of unobstructed sky space showing from the most remote part of a school room insure on a dark day an illumination equivalent to ten metre candles (1 foot candle), the minimal for safe use of eyes in reading.

My space protractor consists of a uniformly curved watch crystal, cut from a sphere of two inch radius and blackened upon the inside. Its convex surface gives a reduced image of objects, and is graduated empirically into ten degree spaces. The dimensions of any object can be measured when the protractor is held in the hand at the surface of the desk. It requires about fifteen seconds to measure and record the sky space contributed by each window.

Since fifty square degrees furnish a minimal illumination of ten or more meter candles, the estimate of how much the minimal light will fall above or below the standard requirement can be instantly made without complicated computation.

The chief source of inaccuracy in this method lies in the fact that the efficiency of the sky light in relation to the desk top varies as the sine of the angle of its inclination above the desk level. In case, therefore, greater accuracy is required, allowance must be made for this variation by using as a factor the natural sine of the angle of incidence to the desk top. This angle can be measured directly by the protractor.

The factors corresponding to the angular altitude are given in the following table:

Altitude		Factor		Altitude		Factor
90°	=	1.0		30°	=	.5
64°	=	.9		24°	=	.4
53°	=	.8		17°	=	.3
44°	=	.7		12°	=	.2
37°	=	.6		6°	=	.1

To reduce the observed sky space to the vertical sky space giving an equivalent light, multiply the observed sky space by the factor corresponding to the angular altitude of the center of the observed sky space.

Problem: Find reduced sky space corresponding to an observed sky space 30° wide by 10° high at an altitude of 24° above desk horizon.

$$30° \times 10° = 300 \text{ sq. deg.} \times .4 = 120 \text{ sq. deg.}$$

Since 120 sq. deg. is 2.4 times the minimal standard of 50 sq. deg., the illumination in this instance is seen to give an ample margin of safety.

This protractor combines fair accuracy with such simplicity that it can be used by the untrained observer. Such use is facilitated by the fact that it does not have to be held at a certain distance from the eye, but gives equally accurate results at all convenient distances. It has the further advantage of portability and cheapness, since it is no larger nor more expensive than the ordinary dollar watch.

SESSION THIRTY-FIVE

Room D.   Wednesday, August 27th, 2:00 P.M.

SYMPOSIUM ON SEX HYGIENE

Arranged by the American Federation for Sex Hygiene

President CHARLES W. ELIOT, *Chairman*

J. H. FOSTER, *Secretary*

HUGH CABOT, M.D., *Vice-Chairman*

LUCIEN HOWE, M.D., Buffalo, N. Y., *Vice-Chairman*

Program of Session Thirty-five

CHARLES W. ELIOT, President-Emeritus, Harvard University. "Public Opinion and Sex Hygiene."

THOMAS M. BALLIET, Ph.D., Dean of School of Pedagogy, New York University. "Points of Attack in Sex Education."

HUGH CABOT, M.D., President American Association of Genito-Urinary Surgeons; Assistant Professor Genito-Urinary Surgery, Harvard Medical School; Chief Genito-Urinary Department, Massachusetts General Hospital, Boston, Mass. "Education Versus Punishment as a Remedy for Social Evils."

MISS LAURA B. GARRETT, New York City. "Some Methods of Teaching Sex Hygiene."

REV. RICHARD H. TIERNEY, S.J., Professor of Philosophy, Woodstock College, Md. "The Catholic Church and the Sex Problem."

WILLIAM TRUFANT FOSTER, Ph.D., LL.D., President Reed College, Portland, Oregon. "The Social Emergency." (Manuscript not included.)

WINFIELD SCOTT HALL, M.D., Northwestern University Medical School, Chicago, Ill. "The Psychology of Youth and Its Relation to Instruction in Sex Hygiene." (Manuscript not included.)

WINFIELD SCOTT HALL, M.D., Northwestern University Medical School, Chicago, Ill. "The Teaching of Social Ethics and Its Relation to the Conservation of the Child." (Manuscript not included.)

PUBLIC OPINION AND SEX HYGIENE

BY

CHARLES W. ELIOT

During my somewhat long active life I have never seen such a change of public opinion among thoughtful people as has taken place among them within the last ten years on the subject of sex hygiene, using that term in its broadest sense.

The policy of silence on all the functions and relations of sex, whether normal or morbid, was almost universally accepted for centuries by physicians and clergymen, and in family life. In the Protestant denominations of the Christian church the normal processes of procreation and birth were associated with the supposed fall of man and his total depravity. In the Catholic church the offices of a priest were necessary for the mother and the new-born infant by way of purification; and the perversions of the sexual passion were to be dealt with only by the priest in the confessional. The miserable victims of the venereal diseases were excluded from all hospitals and dispensaries, or were treated by compassionate physicians only by stealth. Venereal diseases were regarded exclusively as diseases of sin and shame, until their frequent communication to wholly innocent persons had been demonstrated within recent years.

Certain rather recent medical discoveries have contributed to the extraordinary change in public opinion. When blindness in the newborn was traced to gonorrhea in the mother, a potent cause of the crowding of blind asylums was thus brought to light. Insanity and general paresis were in many cases traced back to syphilis, and an explanation was thus given of the increase of insanity in civilized communities. It became known to the medical profession, and later to many unprofessional persons, that the consequences of gonorrhea were almost as bad as those of syphilis, in regard to the infection of innocent persons and the destruction of family happiness. Quite recently a treatment for syphilis has been discovered which has proved satisfactory in many thousands of cases, although the permanence of the cure cannot yet be confidently affirmed. It has been proved that by persistent treatment gonorrhea can apparently be permanently cured in a large proportion of cases. In obscure disorders the Wasserman test for syphilis gives the physician, who is trying to make the diagnosis, on the one hand a strong indication of the presence of a serious complication, or on the other of its absence. As a guide to treatment either determination is invalu-

able. The same test can supply evidence that a cure has been effected.
It will also probably furnish in time trustworthy statistics concerning
the prevalence of syphilis in the community at large, statistics greatly
needed, because the previous guesses and estimates on that subject
and the results of some recent applications of the test to considerable
numbers of public hospital patients are disquieting. To refuse to treat
venereal diseases in hospitals and dispensaries, now that we know they can
be effectively treated, does not seem tolerable or possible in any humane
and instructed community. The treatment of other contagious diseases is adequately provided for. Shall these most destructive of all
contagious diseases be exempted from registration, isolation during
activity, and treatment at either public or private expense adequate
to the protection of the community? If the community is to be protected, however, the policy of silence and the concealment of venereal
cases must be abandoned by the medical profession and by boards of
health. The duty of the medical profession to the family as the best
of human institutions, and to the public health as the foundation of the
common efficiency and happiness, must qualify the duty of the physician as the recipient of his patient's confidence.

The recent medical discoveries to which I have referred raise important
ethical questions. Will the fact that syphilis can apparently be cured
in many instances increase sexual immorality? Will the fact that a
few dissolute men and women escape venereal diseases, and the further
fact that there are antiseptic precautions which diminish somewhat
the dangers of licentiousness, make young men readier to encounter
the dangers of sin? These are questions which only experience can fully
answer. The Navy Department reports publicly that the crews of the
sixteen battleships that went round the world returned with a better
record in respect to venereal diseases than those of any earlier American
expedition. It is clearly better for the community as a whole that the
diseases consequent on vice should be reduced to the lowest possible
terms, both by cure and by prevention. The sum of human misery
from licentiousness, when followed without restriction or repair by the
diseases consequent upon vice, is greater than it would be if the consequent diseases were effectively contended against with all the means
now available for mitigation and cure, and the hope that the race can
maintain itself against the evils of artificial living, unhealthy herding,
and commercialized vice will be strengthened by active and incessant
war on venereal disease.

Public opinion has been moved strongly toward the subject of sex
hygiene, because of the many signs of physical deterioration among
the civilized nations which suffer from the eager rush out of the country
into the city, from the factory system, and from alcoholism and the

sexual vices. Many thoughtful persons are anxious about the diminishing size of young men at the age of admission to the national armies, the rapid reduction within fifty years of the size of the average family, the common inability of women to nurse their babies, the terrible infant mortality in cities, the alleged increasing number of physically or mentally defective children, and the increasing proportion in civilized communities of persons, young, mature, or old, who are practically unable to earn their livelihood. The humanitarian policies in regard to the treatment of the defective, the incompetent, and the criminal classes seem to tend to increase the burdens carried by the normal and industrious portion of the population; and these burdens react on the vigor and happiness of the normal people. The increase of liberty for all classes of the community seems to promote the rapid breeding of the defective, irresponsible, and vicious.

The new interest in sex hygiene is not due, however, only to speculations on the durability of modern civilization, or on that of the white race. Political philosophers and biologists naturally take a strong interest in those large problems; but the individual young man or woman has a narrower sentiment on this subject, though one quite as intense. The young people have lately heard for the first time what the risks of marriage are; what the physical enemies of happy family life are; how the different standard of chastity for men and women has worked during the slow development of the society now called civilized. With these young people the problem becomes an intensely personal one. "How can I best regulate my own conduct, in order to win the moral satisfactions of family life? How can I be protected from the ignorance or sinfulness of associates? In short, how can I steer a safe course through the swirls and tumults of the sexual passion, which seems to be a principal source not only of the normal satisfactions and delights of human life, but also of its worst anxieties and afflictions?" Intelligent fathers and mothers feel a new sort of duty towards their children—the duty of protecting them from vicious allurements and giving them in due time knowledge of good and evil in sex relations. Teachers in public schools see before them a deplorable proportion of children who have bad inheritances both physical and mental, and who live in bad environments; and sharing the new freedom in the discussion of social problems they are eager to be told how they can contribute to the arrest and prevention of these miserable tendencies. Churches are taking a new interest in the questions which arise out of unhappy marriage and easy divorce. Many persons who get a smattering on eugenics are eager for legislation to make marriage conditional on bodily and mental health, and to keep in confinement the feeble-minded, the alcoholic, and the insane not only till they are of age, but till they are incapable of breeding their like. Some knowledge of social hygiene and eugenics has led many persons to advocate hastily prepared legislation as a pan. acea for evils which terribly afflict modern communities, and yet are very ancient. Such is the genesis and such the immediate outcome of the new and widespread interest in sex hygiene.

The most important question before this American Federation for Sex Hygiene is the question: What forces can now be put in play against the formidable evils which gravely threaten family life, human happiness, civilization in general, and the very life of the race? Some. thing must be done. Christianity, democracy, and humanitarianism have all failed thus far to cope with these evils which are sapping the vitality of civilized society. What can be done? It is clear that no one force or agency is to be exclusively relied on. All the uplifting forces of society must be simultaneously enlisted in this cause—state, church, school, college, industrial and charitable corporations, all productive industries, and both preventive and remedial medicine. The attack must be directed against the three principal causes of the present evil condi. tions—first, against lust in men; secondly, against the weakness, depend. ence, mental deficiency, and lack of moral principle of the women who supply the demands of men; thirdly, against the greed and depravity of the wretches who maintain a profitable commerce out of this licen. tious demand and supply.

The struggle against lust in men must bring into play a variety of defensive agencies, such as full occupation for body and mind, manly sports, ambition and energy in the earning of the livelihood, timely knowledge of the good and the evil in sex relations, temperance in both food and drink, and deliverance from mischievous transmitted beliefs, such as belief in the harmlessness of gonorrhea or in the necessity of sexual indulgence for the maintenance of health and vigor in men. For the giving of the information which all young men need a variety of agencies must be utilized. The best source of the information which the young man needs is the parent—the mother in childhood, the father later; but inasmuch as many parents are too ignorant to give this infor. mation, it is indispensable that schools, churches, Christian Associa. tions, and the various kinds of clubs maintained for good social purposes should all be utilized. The public press, too, or that part of it which has moral purposes and a sense of responsibility, must lend its aid; and the policy of silence must be abandoned in favor of a policy of high. minded and reserved exposition. It must be made impossible for either young men or young women to plead ignorance as their excuse when they fall into moral and physical degradation. The general policy in thus employing all available defensive agencies will be the exclusion of evil thoughts and acts by the incessant suggestion and practice of pure and useful thinking and acting.   Does anyone say that these are slow-acting forces which will be long in bringing about hygienic sex relations? True; but must it not be a long labor to modify towards purity and chival-rous gentleness the strongest of the animal instincts of man?   It is not likely that any short and easy road can be found to the redemption of society from centuries-old licentiousness in males.   All the more reason for entering at once on the best roads to be found that lead in the desired direction.   It is obvious that most of the forces to be employed are educational, to be applied as widely as possible not only in childhood but throughout life.

The second attack must be directed against the lack of moral and mental stamina in girls and young women whose inheritances have been low, and whose environment has been dull and miserable.   Pros-titution is voluntarily resorted to by some responsible women whose propensities are naturally bad; but the great majority of prostitutes are physical, mental, or moral defectives in the strict sense of that word. It is the interest of all such defectives and of society at large that they be first discovered in their families, or at school, or in the churches or social settlements, or in hospitals and infirmaries, and then segregated and confined under wholesome conditions, where they cannot be seduced. to a vile life, or be abandoned even for an hour to their own imperfect self-control.   Here is a great service that the public schools can render to society, and here lies a strong argument in favor of the extension of attendance at school beyond the age of thirteen or fourteen, which is now the limit of school life for a great majority of American children. Family, school, church, and all good social organizations should steadily contend against indolence, love of excitement, self-indulgence, and luxurious tendencies in girls; should prevent the depression or joyless-ness of extreme poverty, and should provide and cultivate systematically both helpful work and healthful play for all sorts of girls and young women. Orphaned and unprotected girls should be always the special care of benevolent organizations or friendly societies.   Courts and police authorities should reinforce and assist parents and school authorities to control, before it is too late, girls that manifest vicious propensities. The best control for such girls is of course that of a loving home; but in the absence of that best control the community itself should exercise the next best, in its own defense.   Again, we see that the forces which must be brought into play in attacking the second cause, or source, of licentiousness are mostly educational, and therefore slow-working.

The third assault which society should make against licentiousness may be undertaken with prompt decision and with expectation of effecting rapid improvement.   This is the assault on commercialized vice.   There need be no hesitation in attacking with all the powers of the law the men and women who pander to men by seducing or compelling young women to the horrible existence of the prostitute owned or leased by a dealer in the gratification of lust, and provide shelter and facilities for the worst of human vices. In that shameful business much intelligence and shrewdness, and much capital are employed, and much money is made. Some of the money made is freely used to secure immunity, or periods of immunity, from prosecution in the courts. This iniquitous commerce should be put an end to by vigorous action under existing laws. No third party should be allowed to make any profit out of licentiousness. No brokers or commission merchants in vice should be allowed to exist in a civilized community; and no real estate owner should be allowed to use it himself, or lease it to others, for immoral purposes. But one may say, "The segregation and regulation of brothels are policies which have come down through unnumbered centuries in many nations and under all the great religions of the world. Are we to attempt the uprooting of such ancient policies of toleration and license?" I answer, "Yes, we are;" because those ancient policies have everywhere failed to protect the human race from evils which in the long run, will work its destruction. Former generations were not sure of that failure. This generation knows it. Former generations had no adequate means of contending against the diseases which in the human race accompany the perversions and excesses of the sex instincts. We possess those means. Earlier generations had not appropriated the idea of government "of the people, for the people, and by the people." For us the interests of the mass override the interests of the individual, particularly when the alleged interests of the individual are corrupting and degrading.

The policy of segregation in defined quarters has not been carried out successfully in any place in the world, not even in Japan, where the policy is traditional and has come down through many centuries, and where the conditions of prostitution are in some respects less horrible than in any Christian country. In all the cities which have long practised the policy of segregation scattered vice exists in great amount outside the recognized quarters. The regulation of prostitutes through medical inspection and certification is a recognized failure in every country where it has been long carried on. The inspection is perfunctory and quite incapable of supplying evidence that no disease exists in the person inspected. The certificate issued by the inspector is founded on no good evidence when it is issued, and may be made absolutely false within a few minutes of its issue. In other words, segregation is never even approximately complete, and it would not diminish licentiousness if it were complete. On the contrary, it supplies facilities for vice. Regulation has no significant effect to reduce venereal disease, although it accomplishes in some rather small proportion the temporary segregation of active cases; and it increases licentiousness, because young men are deluded into thinking that the worthless certificates mean diminished risk of contracting disease.

It is said, in opposition to the suppression of brothels, and in favor of the toleration of vice in special quarters of a town or city, that it is better to permit vice, public and regulated, in certain parts of a city than to drive vice into secrecy, and spread it all through the residential quarters. The reply to this argument is, that there is a large gain to the community as a whole whenever any vice or wrong practice is driven into secrecy, and its gratification made difficult or inconvenient instead of easy. It is one of the lessons of the long struggle against alcoholism that great gain comes from making the use of alcoholic liquors private instead of public, even if the total consumption of liquor in the community be not much reduced. It has been demonstrated that the policy of no license for saloons diminishes drunkenness in the community which adopts it. The same is true of gambling houses and the gaming habit. Public toleration and ease of access to the means of gratifying any vicious habit increase the number of victims. It is also said against the proposal to suppress brothels that criminal assaults on girls and women will increase to a formidable extent in any community which adopts such a policy. Fortunately the social resistance to assaults on women is now strong enough to enforce against all such criminals any penalties likely to be deterrent. Asexualization, or castration of the criminal, in addition to whatever other penalty the nature of the assault may indicate, will be demanded by public opinion, if either shall prove to be effective to prevent the crime. Here and there, and from time to time, police authorities in large cities have proved that it is possible to suppress brothels. It remains for public opinion to demand the execution of existing laws, and of any new laws which experience may show to be needed for the suppression of commercialized vice. One common practice of the police and the courts will need to be changed. These authorities now attack prostitution chiefly by arresting and punishing the women concerned; they should also punish the men concerned, for they are the primary offenders. It should be one of the chief functions of this Federation and of all kindred bodies to educate public opinion on this subject of suppression in place of toleration. Much progress has already been made in this direction, and the advance of medical science, and especially of preventive medicine, is contributing every year new weapons for this warfare.

The interest of many thinking people in the subject of eugenics is closely allied to interest in sex hygiene; but zeal for wise breeding is apparently leading to some hasty or ill-considered legislation. The existing legislation to limit selection in marriage is evidence of a wise recognition of the dangers in continuing stocks burdened with inherit. able weaknesses, and is so far welcome; but not all the proposed prohibitions can be justified by biological science at its present stage. The educated public have much to learn with regard to the proper mating of persons who have some nervous defect. Such persons should mate with those whose ancestry has no such defect. Although it is undesirable that feeble-minded, epileptic, or insane persons should have children, yet if such a person mates wisely, and the children of such a union again mate wisely, the progeny of the third generation will probably be quite as free from nervous defect as the general population is. Again, the reproduction of the feeble-minded will not necessarily be diminished by laws which prevent them from marrying. Such persons ordinarily have very little self-control, and if left free will have children whether married or not. The laws against undesirable marriages need to be revised in most of the American states; and the public needs to be convinced that no such law can eradicate the evil. Nothing but the compulsory seclusion of all defectives under humane housing, training, and labor conditions will accomplish the eugenic object of the community. Laws which provide that candidates for marriage must be free from syphilis or gonorrhea do good, provided that proper provision be made for the certificate to that effect from a trustworthy physician appointed by the state. The appointment for this duty of an adequate number of physicians by the state boards of health would give a new and important function to these boards. The maintenance of such a staff, furnished with all the means of applying adequate tests in doubtful cases, would be somewhat expensive, but this expense might perhaps be covered in part by a moderate addition to the fee for a marriage license. Each physician would probably require the aid of a man and a woman competent to inquire into the family histories of the applicants for a marriage license.

It is probable that much public instruction will have to be given through newspapers, magazines, lectures, and discussions in men's clubs and women's clubs before sound and effective eugenic legislation can be placed on the statute books. Again we find that public progress in relation to sex hygiene and eugenics is to be procured chiefly through educational methods. It is therefore of the utmost importance that the processes adopted for diffusing sound knowledge about the normal and the morbid sex relations, the dangers of licentiousness, safe mating with a view to healthy progeny, the prevention of the reproduction of defectives, the destruction of commerce in vice, and the prevention of venereal contagions should all be carried on plainly but delicately, without exaggeration or morbid suggestion, without interference with parental by voluntary associations, as is usual in social reforms; be the constant aim of these private organizations to enl the public authorities in this vast undertaking, and to tr public treasury as fast as possible the support of all those work which experience proves to be of sure and perm advantage. The pioneering in regard to both research measures will probably continue for many years to be the untary associations.

POINTS OF ATTACK IN SEX EDUCATION

BY

THOMAS M. BALLIET

The necessity of sex education in some form in case 'of the young as well as in case of adults has become, within the last half dozen years, very generally recognized. The knowledge, formerly confined to the medical profession, of the havoc which the social diseases make among the innocent and their consequent. dangers to the family; the dangers of the social evil as the source of infection; and the revelations which recent investigations have made of the extent of the white slave traffic, have convinced many thinking men and women that the only effective way of coping with this evil of the ages is public intelligence. Light is our best disinfectant.

While it is needless, therefore, to discuss the necessity of such instruction, it is extremely important that we determine its matter and method and the order in which it should be undertaken. To do the right thing in the wrong way, or at the wrong time, is in such a matter in its effects practically equivalent to doing the wrong thing. It is one of those instances in life where, as it has been said, a blunder may be more serious than a crime.

Young children need such instruction; adolescent youth needs it; young men and women need it; parents need it. Where shall we begin? What shall be the first points of attack? Shall we begin where it is probably most needed, or at all events where it is needed on the largest scale—in our public schools with their nineteen millions of young people? It seems to me it is eminently timely to consider this question lest enthusiastic friends may take steps and urge measures in their various communities which may be entirely premature, if not ill considered. We must first of all bear in mind that we are here dealing not only with a scientific and an educational question but also with an administrative one. We must take into consideration not merely the need of such instruction, but also the conditions necessary for giving it effectively. The two main conditions are the preparation of the teachers and the public sentiment of the community.

It is needless to say that the teachers in our public schools are not at present qualified to give such instruction; they have not received the necessary training either in the matter or the method of such instruction; and to introduce it at present into the elementary schools, beyond certain forms of it to be discussed later, would lead to much blundering of a serious kind which would be likely to create in the community a revulsion of sentiment against it that would defer the day when it can be given effectively.

While popular sentiment is rapidly growing in favor of public enlightenment on this subject, there are still many thoughtful men and women who question the wisdom of giving such instruction to children in schools, and among the uneducated there exists a quite strong prejudice against it. Popular education needs the support of public sentiment, and it is unwise to incorporate any important new feature into our public school system until it will receive this support. A reaction means a setback and ultimate delay.

As a matter of wise public policy and as a means of accomplishing ultimately the greatest good, sex education should begin where its necessity and its practicability are universally recognized, and where mistakes during its experimental stage will be much less serious than in the case of such instruction to young children in school.

Accordingly, the first point of attack should be the parent. No one questions the possibility of doing a vast deal of good by enlightening fathers and mothers on this vital subject. Public sentiment is ripe everywhere for this step and competent persons can be found, usually among the medical profession, to give this instruction. Furthermore, the proper instruction of parents will be the most effective means of creating public sentiment in favor of giving such teaching in proper form to children in the schools. When the parents of the children will call for such instruction in school, there will be no practical difficulty, so far as public sentiment is concerned, in the way of its introduction.

Such instruction of parents, as it is for the common good of the community, should be provided at public expense and should be in charge of the Board of Education. There is no reason why private individuals should charge themselves with the expense of what is so clearly for the common interest.

Such instruction of parents might well include: Sex hygiene and sex morality in general; the simple facts of heredity in their bearing on the life of offspring; how to care for the child's sex life before it enters school, and consequently before it can receive such care from anyone else; how to answer their little ones' questions as to the origin of human life; how to instruct their older children as to sex hygiene; the dangers to their daughters from public dance halls, the street, public parks, from certain conditions existing in factories and mercantile employments, and especially the dangers from the white slave traffic; the danger to their sons in certain employments like that of messenger boy in telegraph offices, and the serious danger from social diseases in "sowing wild oats," a phase of boy life which many fathers still regard lightly and which even many mothers are too ready to condone. Such parents' meetings can be held expressly for this purpose, or as a part of a series for the discussion of larger social, ethical, or religious subjects. It is customary in all cities to hold mothers' meetings in schoolhouses after school hours. At such meetings some of the topics above indicated can be discussed, if not all.

Another point of attack for which we are ready is the army and navy. There is no place where such instruction is more needed, and its necessity and practical value are not seriously questioned by anyone. It should be given entirely at the Government's expense, and usually by men who have had medical training; and it should not be given merely spasmodically, as is now done, but systematically and thoroughly and on a scale large enough to reach every enlisted man. If the facts which emphasize the need for such instruction were known to the people as they are to medical men and to army and navy officers, there would be a strong popular demand that it be provided without delay. Such instruction should not be confined to the nature and dangers of social diseases, but should include a general discussion of the nature and function of sex, sex hygiene and sex morality, and the simple facts of heredity in relation to sex hygiene.

A third point of attack for which we are ready and which has already been quite vigorously begun is sex instruction in the colleges, both for men and women. With this class of students, the entire field of such instruction should be covered in connection with the usual courses in hygiene, biology, sociology, and ethics. Such instruction will not merely meet the personal needs of students, but will equip those who are to become teachers in elementary and secondary schools to give it to pupils in these schools.

A fourth class of persons to whom sex instruction can now be effectively given are groups of young men in Young Men's Christian Associations, and young women in Young Women's Christian Associations, in social settlements and similar organizations. Much has already been done in some communities with these and like groups of young people; but for want of sufficient number of competent persons to give the instruction, the work has been spasmodic and but partially effective.

Much can be and, in fact, is being accomplished by the publication of books, pamphlets, and leaflets for adolescents and adults. The good which well-written publications of this kind unquestionably do altogether outweighs any possible harm which may in some instances result and which is in any case largely theoretical. Unfortunately, the deep popular interest aroused in the subject within the last few years has created such a market for books treating of it that their production has become so profitable that many are written by persons poorly qualified and published mainly for profit. To meet this situation all the various societies for sex hygiene, organized in most of the states under various names, and united in this Federation, should, as many of them do, publish under virtually non-commercial conditions, literature written by competent persons, which would go out with the imprimatur of the societies as authoritative on the subject.

Each society ought also to issue a list of books, published by regular publishing houses or by their authors, which is approved by the society. It is needless to suggest that the committees charged with the duty of making out such lists should be appointed with the greatest care. Several societies have already published lists of this character, and this Federation proposes soon to publish one. In this way the flooding of the market with inferior literature for the sake of profit merely can be to some degree checked and a menacing harm to the cause be averted.

In every state an effort should be made by the friends of this movement to secure legislation forbidding the publication in the public press of the advertisements of the quack doctor whose baleful influence upon young men, as careful investigations have shown, has been enormous.

These are all points of attack for which we are ready and which public sentiment will strongly sustain.

We may now consider briefly what can wisely be attempted in public schools in the way of sex education and what cannot. The necessity of such instruction of the young in itself is no sufficient reason for introducing it at the present stage of the movement, if the conditions do not exist which are essential to its success. As already stated, the two chief conditions are the preparation of the teachers and the support of public sentiment. Only in exceptional cases are teachers in the elementary schools qualified to assume this type of instruction. Most of them are unfamiliar with both the matter and the method, and if they should attempt it, they would run the risk not merely of doing harm by teaching what is not true, or teaching the truth in the wrong way, but their blundering would create a prejudice against such instruction in school which would seriously delay the introduction of it on a large scale later. Nor is it public sentiment ready to support such instruction, in elementary schools, at this time.

Then, too, there are a number of important questions as to such instruction in elementary schools upon which experts are not in entire agreement. To what extent should it be given privately, and to what extent in class? If given in class, what material can be given to co-educational classes and what should be given to each sex in separate classes? Should the instruction be given in the elementary schools by the regular class-room teacher in connection with the courses in nature study, hygiene, and morals, or should a specialist give it? What specific knowledge of sex should be imparted to pupils at a given age? Under what conditions should the instruction be given by a teacher of the same sex as the class? These are illustrations of the many questions of detail upon which there exist differences of opinion among special students of this problem and which can be determined only by careful experiment by competent teachers. Such experiments should be made under especially favorable conditions and on a small scale, so that mistakes may neither do serious harm nor excite public prejudice.

So far as the high schools are concerned, the problem is a far less difficult one. Many, if not most, pupils at this age have already acquired extensive information in regard to sex, much of which has been obtained from impure sources and has connected with it in their minds impure associations. The chances of doing harm by giving such instruction prematurely, which some people fear in case of elementary pupils, are therefore reduced to a minimum in the high school. Furthermore, the need of such instruction in case of adolescents, both in the interests of their health and their morals, is very generally recognized by parents, and in most communities public sentiment will support it if wisely conducted. There is no good reason why such instruction should not be given in high schools as an integral part of the courses in biology, hygiene, sociology, and ethics. Some of it, at least in special cases, should be given privately; and it is obvious that for certain vital topics the sexes should be separated, but such separation can be easily carried to extremes and thus fail to impress the pupil with its seriousness and its sacredness. It should never be given as a course by itself detached from these other courses, nor should it be given by "sex specialists" who teach no other subject. Nor does it seem wise for the Board of Education to make public announcement beforehand in the local newspapers, as has been done in some cities, that such instruction has been introduced, and thus arouse discussion of it in the presence of pupils among classes of persons who are neither intelligent nor high minded, and whose attitude towards questions of sex is wholly wrong. Superintendents of schools ought to be willing, in the interests of the public good, to forego this one opportunity of advertising the progressive character of their schools.

But, in spite of obvious difficulties, is it not possible to do something even now in sex education in the elementary schools? It seems to me it is.

1. In connection with the course in nature study, the subject of reproduction should be taught, and in the upper grades should receive much emphasis. Beginning with reproduction in plants, the cycle of life from seed to seed should be traced, the necessity of fertilization should

be made clear, and many illustrations should be given of the wonderful ways in which it is effected by nature and her marvelous methods by which she provides for the perpetuation of plant life. It is not difficult to impress upon even young pupils, where there is a school garden, the necessity of selecting the best seeds for planting and thus inculcate in a practical way a fundamental fact in heredity which may later be given its moral implications in a higher sphere. Reproduction in the lower forms of animal life can be taught in a similar way. All this need not be called "sex instruction;" it is plain nature study, requires no special permission of the Board of Education, and has the support of public sentiment, except in very backward communities where nature study is still spoken of as a "fad."

2. In connection with lessons on morals, such as ought to be given in elementary schools, topics related to sex morality, like purity of speech, respect for woman, avoidance of bad companions, etc., can be effectively discussed in class.

In the upper classes, where children have reached the age of adolescence, the best literature dealing with romantic love should be read. This is one of the most effective means of spiritualizing the sex instinct and of inspiring the pupil with lofty ideals as to the sex relation.

3. Specific instruction in sex hygiene and sex morality in the human sphere, where such instruction seems especially needed, should in all cases, for the present, be given privately in elementary schools, usually by the principal, or, if not, by a teacher authorized beforehand by the principal. In cases where the precaution seems necessary, the previous consent of the father or mother should be secured. The instruction should aim solely to protect the child from harm to health and morals, and should be carefully guarded against arousing prurient curiosity. Such instruction should not be attempted by classroom teachers generally. The large majority are not qualified by training, maturity, or personality to give it effectively. The responsibility for it should rest upon the principal, whether he gives it himself or designates someone else to give it.

4. Class instruction in sex morality other than that which is implied in (1) and (2) should not be attempted in elementary schools at the present time. The teachers are not qualified and public sentiment is not ready to support it. Some special students of the subject question even the possibility of it at any time. Under these conditions, it would be extremely unwise to attempt it, except in an experimental way, on a very limited scale, under conditions exceptionally favorable. As in so many other educational experiments, actual experience may

ultimately prove that many theoretical difficulties do not exist in actual fact. The question must be finally decided by experiment and by experience which invokes common sense as an aid in interpreting experiment.

The situation as to sex instruction in elementary schools, as above stated, emphasizes among others two things:

1. It emphasizes the need of making adequate provision for the training of teachers to give such instruction. All normal schools should provide it; and all colleges and universities should organize courses in their department of education in which the subject may be thoroughly treated in the light of a broad background of knowledge of biology, physiology, sociology, and ethics.

2. It emphasizes the necessity of providing instruction, at public expense, in this subject, as already pointed out, for parents. This is the most effective way to create a public sentiment which will support any form of such instruction which experience may prove to be effective in elementary schools.

These two are among the most important points of attack of this whole subject for which the time is ripe.

In conclusion, I may add briefly the suggestion that one of the most important results of sex education, in the case of adults as well as of children, is the giving them a decent vocabulary in which to discuss the subject of sex and sex hygiene. The terminology picked up in the street is the only terminology which all but educated adults are familiar with, and it is the only vocabulary which children hear who get their knowledge of sex from impure sources. The terminology of science is the only terminology that is free from indelicate associations, and the very first condition of success in sex discussion, either with young people or with adults, is to give them a vocabulary free from these associations.

EDUCATION VERSUS PUNISHMENT AS A REMEDY FOR SOCIAL EVILS

BY

Hugh Cabot

The problems which we have set ourselves to discuss this afternoon, arising as they do from misdirected or undirected play of the sex instinct, are as old as the world. They have been attacked by the best minds and it may well be that nothing we can suggest or try has not been said and done before. Yet the conditions of our civilization have changed and it is at least arguable that even though we find nothing new, the old may have new application. To remedy a condition we must comprehend it, and though there are still those who believe that the problems of sex are not fit to be discussed out loud, the sound majority is against them and whether they like it or not they must now listen.

Since it is chiefly by the study of our failures that we rectify error let us see what our methods have been in the past and why they have failed. It is not necessary to inquire into the methods used in the long distant past, partly because such methods can scarcely be regarded as applicable to present conditions, and partly because we have no reliable knowledge as to what these methods were. If we consider the general plan of attack during the last half of the nineteenth century we shall probably uncover most of our sources of error.

Methods of the Last Half Century. In order to face the question squarely we must look at it from two sides and consider first what equipment was given our younger citizens with which to face their problems, and second, how we have dealt with their failures, which, be it remembered, were our failures.

The Equipment. As a general proposition boys have been given no systematic training or instruction in the nature of their sexual make-up. In isolated instances an unusually enlightened parent has instructed his son, but even then the instruction has been haphazard, fragmentary, given in too large quantities, at the wrong time, and often without sound knowledge of the facts. Such instruction, though insufficient and rare, has of course been better than none, yet the number of cases in which it was supplied was so small as to be a negligible minority. But if the boy's equipment was not cared for by education it was not neglected by nature. He was supplied with a natural and intense curiosity, provided with sexual cravings always active and not infrequently oppressive.

In this connection we shall do well to remember that in the male the intensity of the manifestations of sex is by no means equally distributed and is particularly serious at two general periods. The first difficulties come with the advent of sexual maturity, when the manifestations of this change come as new and often rather terrifying phenomena to the uninformed. Boys know not what to make of conditions and sensations wholly new and quite inexplicable. If they fall into error at this period it is only what might naturally be expected of ignorance facing the unknown. If a boy weathers the early squalls—and most do—he may get along without overwhelming difficulties until his period of active growth is over, a time which may be postponed until twenty-five or even thirty. Then not infrequently he will again be driven by his sexual self to an extent almost incompatible with efficient living—this of course assuming that he has not married. We should not omit to mention the religious teaching which boys have received, which as a rule included lectures on the desirability of chastity—generally confused with asceticism—the desirability of early marriage and the sanctity of the marriage bond. This teaching, though edifying and beautiful, was somewhat vague. Thus we see that he has had but little direct instruction, yet we cannot deny that he acquired a fund of alleged information from his supposedly ignorant contemporaries in the form of misstated fact or even the direct lie, to the general effect that sexual capacity, manliness and vigor were substantially one and the same thing.

The girl was given even less information. Many, perhaps most, had literally no knowledge of their sexual life, not even of their relation to the function of child bearing. Our attitude has been "Don't ask." If they persisted in asking we lied to them, which of course constituted a beautiful basis for the teaching of truth. In one direction, and in one only, were most girls given information by their parents and this was in regard to the double standard. Very frequently they were definitely told that the standard of chastity, up to which they were expected to live, was not to be required of their brothers and upon this has depended in large measure their brothers' standard. Of religious teaching the girl as a rule had more than the boy. Stress was laid upon the beauty and sanctity of marriage, but this failed somewhat of being instructive since she did not know what the marriage relation was. To this equipment we should add, as in the case of the boy, a certain amount of misinformation picked up from gossip, always incorrect; often actually misleading. According to the extent to which she lived a protected life, this information was much or little, enlightening or beclouding.

Such was the equipment with which we expected the rising generation to face the demands of their sexual being and lead a life passably free from error. Briefly, it taught asceticism—not chastity—before marriage, and after marriage a licentious sexual life, limited only by its compatibility with human existence. This standard we proposed to enforce by punishment.

The Backsliders and Their Treatment. The boy, ignorant and deceived, followed his instinct, which, in all the muddle of his growing mind, was at least clear and direct. This course frequently resulted in infection with what we have been pleased to call venereal disease. When this occurred he must face his problem alone. He had the best reasons for believing that he could not go to his parents for advice. No help could be expected in that quarter. Frequently he had neither money nor knowledge with which to seek competent advice and an unvoiced feeling that all the respectable part of the community was against him. Many boys have I seen who came to me and frankly said that they supposed I would not look after them because they had done wrong. In this quandary many sought the kindly quack, half brother of the genial barkeep, both of whom have at least the saving grace of being kind to those in error. As a consequence of the inefficient treatment thus obtained came the legacy of complications, chronic disease and failure to achieve cure. These boys we have taught secrecy and this part of the lesson at least they have learned. They keep their secret, their uncured disease. They marry and infect their wives. Look at another view of the same picture: The boy of strong character, largely due to heredity but in part perhaps to sound moral teaching, adopted asceticism and man-fashion faced its consequences. There came to him storms of the nature of which he was ignorant, nervous strain and tension which he had no equipment to handle. He not only had no machinery within himself but no knowledge of where to turn. Again, he turned to the gentleman who offered his services, the quack, who led him to believe that harmless physiological processes were vitally affecting his life, was drained of his money, his health, at times almost of his reason. If this picture looks to you overdrawn study some of the facts.

What has been the career of the girl who failed to live up to the standard? She started her life with no knowledge of her sexual make-up. She was ignorant of the very nature of the feelings aroused in her by the opposite sex and of the pains and aches of unrecognized sexual stimulation. Her natural defense, that of comprehension, was denied her and she had none except the almost physical protection of a guarded life. Where this was lax or absent she yielded to she knew not what. If pregnancy resulted she was at once disgraced, outcast or must contract an ill-considered and probably unhappy marriage. Brought up on concealment, she tried to avoid either of the alternatives and resorted to criminal abortion with resulting infection, sterility, occasionally death. If she avoided these she was at least hardened, confirmed in her suspicion that mankind was against her and that her salvation lay in her ability to beat the world at its own game, deception. Some prostitutes are made in this way. Should she have received sufficient instruction from her sadder but wiser sisters to avoid pregnancy she then stood about the same chance as her brother of acquiring disease and in this contingency she was worse off than he. Her anatomical structure made the condition more difficult of management and her psychology and fear of disgrace made her more prone to concealment. She had before her the alternative of concealment or disgrace and she adopted the less obviously serious and either neglected herself entirely or had totally inefficient care. The results were, if possible, more serious than in her brother—chronic infection, sterility, invalidism.

Punishment and Its Effect. Perhaps we can no better exemplify the failure of punishment as a remedy than in its effect upon prostitution. The prostitute is a result, not a cause. A demand has created a supply. Can it be that this demand is a result of our lack of teaching? We have not troubled ourselves to inquire upon this point. In practice we object officially to soliciting by the female but it is not recorded that we object seriously or actively to soliciting by the male. The women we arrest, fine, imprison. We make them hard, reckless, cruel, as the result of treatment hard, reckless and cruel. The fines are not paid by the women but by the men. Their imprisonment costs them nothing, society pays the bill. By means of prisons and so-called reformatories they spread their mental and physical disabilities. The only certain effect of these procedures is to convince these women that they must protect themselves at any cost against a pitiless world. Let us at least be logical in this business. If we arrest and fine these women for soliciting it is our clear duty to arrest, fine or imprison her male companion for soliciting or employing her. Does anyone in his senses believe that an attempt to enforce such a regulation would end in anything but riot?

We have been discussing certain concrete examples of the effect of punishment but it may not be unwise to consider for a moment the theory of punishment. Though I have been at some pains, I am unable to construct any intellectual process which will bring me to the conclusion that punishment can deter from acts, the nature of which is unknown. We have told our boys that they mustn't do it. When they ask what "it" is we reply "don't ask" and upon this lucid explanation we proceed to punish them. The effect of punishment thus dealt out is concealment, lying. We have been dubbed a nation of liars, and it is by no means clear that we have not laid the foundations of untruthfulness in precisely this way. Concealment and lying undermine character, and the wonder is not that character is less firm and robust than we desire but that any firmness or vigor exists.

Such, roughly, has been the method of the last half century and it has not, as I think, met with large measure of success, but if this success has been less than we anticipated we may as well face the fact now as later that the continuance of this method will meet with even less success in the future. We have employed it in the face of a changing civilization, with increasing factors stimulating sex, with a tendency, too obvious to be mistaken, to softening of national fibre and a very marked delay of the time at which marriage takes place. This half century has seen the achievement of the economic independence of women and has been marked by a general relaxation of conventional restraints. The effect of these changes is so clear that he who runs may read. The dangers arising from the mismanagement of the sex instinct are increasing. Control by punishment which has failed in the past is necessarily doomed to more tragic failure in the future. If we are to stand any chance of success it will be upon a basis of intellectual comprehension and by the deliberate strengthening of the personal defenses of the individual which enable him to guide successfully his own life. Dependence upon an abiding faith, based upon accepted dogma, is not suited to the spirit of the times. Faith has waned. Can it be because we have been faithless? We have lied and the failure of faith is the dividend paid for our untruthfulness.

Education. It would be unseemly were I to attempt to instruct this eminent body of educators in the technique of education but I may perhaps venture what seem to me certain truths in regard to the general principles of instruction. The sex instinct should be a potent force in the determination of character but our system of sexual ignorance and denial has tended to break down rather than to build up. If we are to depend upon this instinct to do its share of the molding process it must come through comprehension of that instinct and not through ignorance. It is an old and trite saying, but one singularly applicable to present conditions, that the beneficial effects of punishment come from within. We have meted out punishment senseless, cruel, terrible, without the slightest evidence of benefit. Would it not be wise to try whether on a basis of comprehension of this pervasive instinct we could not make effective punishment of the individual emanate from himself and not from the unsteady arm of the law? To secure comprehension, a thing far more fundamental than knowledge, instruction must be given early, must be continuous and progressive. It must teach clearly and honestly the true nature and effects of the sex instinct. Instruction leading to comprehension will require men and women of unusual breadth and strength of character but I believe that no other form of education is more likely to produce profound and lasting influence upon national character. This teaching must not be in isolated form.

We must guard against the ever present danger of bringing people, old as well as young, to regard sexual morality as different and removed from other forms of morality. We must so plan our instruction as to clearly relate this form of morality to truth, honor, courage, virility.

I cannot leave this absorbing question without calling attention to what seems to me a serious and fundamental failure of our whole educational system. By this I mean not strictly that part of education which is imparted in the school but the whole process by which we teach our boys and girls the art of living and equip them for the battle of civilization. I believe it to be true that in the last half century the education of our women has improved, but at the same time, and in greater measure, the education of our men has declined. In earlier times the requirements of environment brought out the best qualities of male virility but as this environment has changed, as the world has in many respects become a softer place to live in, we have failed to correct this by education. Our boys are to-day distinctly less tough in fibre, both physically and morally, than they were a century ago and this cannot be answered by saying that in those days the weaker did not survive. We have ordered that the weak shall survive and having done so we must assume the responsibility for seeing that their weakness does not pull down the general average. Not a little of the failing virility of our boys must be attributed to the feminization of our schools. Much as I admire and respect our women, they are not equipped to teach our boys the rougher virtues of strength, toughness and courage which make for virility and we must face this fact or feminize our population.

But to return to that branch of education leading to a comprehension of the sex instinct. Sooner or later we shall come to realize that this teaching is the function of the public school, though we are very far from such a realization to-day. We still cling to the idea that this instruction can be given in the home, forgetting that a large proportion of parents are not equipped, and never will be equipped, either by nature or by art to give this instruction. If we depend upon the home as the source of teaching that teaching will not be given. We have just seen in a neighboring city an example of the depth of this prejudice against such teaching in the public schools. A sound attempt to introduce it has been blocked by opposition which cannot properly be regarded as intelligent. It is clearly our duty to see to it that those who oppose progress bear the responsibility. Let each of these persons who oppose teaching in the schools, not because they object to method but because they object to theory, be held directly and personally responsible for the failures from the mismanagement of the sex instinct. Let them shoulder, if they can bear the burden, the blame for the countless thousands of lives wrecked through ignorance.

SOME METHODS OF TEACHING SEX HYGIENE

BY

LAURA B. GARRETT

There is much talk nowadays about teaching sex hygiene to young people as though it were a separate subject and something children had never heard about. We must remember most children have always been taught about sex, generally by the wrong teachers and in the wrong way, at least by untrained teachers and by unscientific methods. Some say, "Children are too curious about this subject"—let us be thankful they are not feeble-minded, as all normal children are curious about everything, and we stimulate this curiosity by old-fashioned secrecy concerning sex subjects. Others say, "We are putting ideas into their heads"—that is just what we wish to do, give them correct ideas and ideals. Some say, "They will talk too much if we tell them." Most children always have talked, to each other or to unwise older folk, only those who are capable of correcting their mistakes did not hear them. After they have been trained correctly, they will be less curious and do less talking than ever before. They will take no more interest in sex subjects than they have in all life problems around them. Anyhow, we don't intend to teach sex to children; what we wish to do is tell them stories of the reproduction of life, never over-emphasizing and always correlating this knowledge with other vital interests.

We sometimes think the drawings and remarks made by them show there is filth in their minds. Let us remember that many times the filth we think is in their minds is in our own, and we have only to give them plainly and honestly the facts they are ready to understand. Any adult who is not ashamed of the creative power in his own body can talk to the children about it and give them better ideas and ideals than they get in any other way. There is an old teaching that we have been "created in sin." It is true that many children have been and are continuing to be created in sin; but we must get this idea into the mind of the present generation and teach the eugenists that all children must be well conceived and then well bred.

We must give the children from the first a good vocabulary. One reason for the dense ignorance is that our young people have no words they are willing to use when seeking knowledge of this subject. Correct language dignifies their ideas and gives them freedom to seek information from those worthy of respect.

Numbers of children are curious about the appearance of the opposite sex, and while seeking to gratify this curiosity sometimes are led into mistakes. To prevent this, they should be taught to respect the whole body, that every organ is good and is a gift to be cared for and used rightly. They should see the whole body of a little brother or sister or of any baby; then they would learn to know its form in connection with a person whom they loved and the reproductive part would not be emphasized. The correct use of the best pictures or statues of the nude in connection with literature or art is good.

The National Committee for Mental Hygiene places sex ignorance as one of the causes of disordered minds. I have met with numbers of young people, mostly girls, who were worried about some mistake of childhood or of youth. Afraid and ashamed to speak of this to anyone, they have been carrying a secret dread of consequences of their former ignorance. Intense relief was felt then the lessons suggested that no harm had resulted and would not, that they had been fortunate, that they now had a chance to drop this burden and having correct knowledge to live according to highest ideals.

Groups should be arranged according to the maturity and mentality of the children. Boys and girls can be taught together in the elementary work. If the group is small enough, nor over 15 in number, the teacher can watch each individual and give him privately what he may need beyond the class instruction. Much of the concrete knowledge of sex organs and their functions should be given the child before adolescence. He is then unconscious of sex or largely so. If he has misinformation, it must be eliminated as soon as possible before he begins wrongly to use the incorrect knowledge. If trained properly, he has preparation for the great changes that are coming to him later.

This training should begin in the home while the child is under the direct influence of the parents. In fact, it does begin here in three ways:

In some homes, the only training he gets is to be told to run away and not talk about such things. He runs away fast enough and talks to anyone he finds. In the meantime, while at play, he overhears, or half hears which is worse, the whisperings of his elders, of birth, of the marriage relations, of vital subjects.

In some homes he hears with brutal frankness much he should know, but all the beauty, the higher ethics, and social values are omitted.

It is from these homes we hear the parents brag that their children are innocent. They mean ignorant. About no other subject do they brag of innocence or ignorance. We know first that nature's truth are good for the children, and second that this knowledge, by allaying their curiosity, prevents them from hearing the incorrect or the filthy language of the street.

In some homes where parents themselves have had biological and social training, the children are being taught in the best of ways. Plainly, honestly, beautifully, they are told what they are ready for as they develop. Let us hasten the day when all parents of the coming generations may be so trained that they will tell their children of these truths of life, that they may enjoy these intimate confidences, that each child may have someone who can meet these at just the time, in just the way, that will be best for his later development.

Mistakes will be made, but they are now being made. Mistakes of omission and of active teaching. Careful intelligent study may help us to a wider knowledge of the great needs of our young people, and above all we may learn the value of this training, and the relation it bears to other training and other influences which affect our development of our youth. Complete knowledge of sex organs and their functions, and of reproduction should be given each individual as mentality and maturity develop. Tell the young people clearly, plainly, completely what they need to know, and then stop. A group of boys said, "Tell mother not to rub it in."

Who shall do the teaching? Shall we have special teachers, or shall we have all teachers trained? The present method is to allow the boys and girls to teach each other, or we allow older, vilely ignorant folks, to teach them. Let us not forget that every teacher does something with this subject, either positively or negatively; either by ignoring the suppressed giggle, the nudge of the shoulder, the filthy note, or by actively dealing with the common happenings in the school-room. Surely every teacher must be trained, first given the information, not just biological or physiological facts, she herself needs, but the ethical significance of this knowledge. Then she should have some instruction in methods of training the children. Then for older children, specially trained teachers should give the information, always correlated with biology or physiology or gymnasium work or in connection with ethics or history.

In connection with regular gardening, nature work, or outdoor tramps with parents or teachers, the following ideas can be given the little folks, under the following topics:

Cradles, or Preparation for Parenthood. That most plants and animals prepare some protection for their young before they bring them into the world; that plants produce cradles (seed-pods), all rough on the outside and smooth within, to keep off wind and weather and enemies that would eat the seeds; that many fishes and birds have the nest ready for the young before the eggs are laid; that rabbits dig holes in the ground or prepare nest for their young—the mother lines the nest with fur from her body and then carefully guards her young while they need her protection; that the human mother has, after long months of loving care, prepared the cradle or the basket for the little one that is to be welcomed into the home.

The story of the cow-bird can be given as an example of the parent who takes no thought for the little ones. The father bird mates with the mother bird and then flies away, giving no thought for the mother or the young ones. The mother cow-bird places her eggs in the nest of another bird and then she flies away and leaves her young to the care of the foster mother. A big, square-backed boy from the rear of a tene-ment-house district, hearing the story of the cow-bird, kicked a stone and announced, "Say, I call that cow-bird father a mean skunk." Perhaps, if we teach our boys before adolescence, we may safeguard them from becoming irresponsible fathers and from bringing children into the world until they are ready to protect them.

Motherhood. Children can be taught that hidden within the blossom of each plant are ovaries, the organs where seeds are found; that these seeds have hidden within a tiny "spot of life" which grows into the same kind of plant as that from which it came; that hidden within the body of each animal are ovaries, the organs where eggs are found; that these eggs have hidden within a "spot of life" which always grows into the same kind of animal as that from which it came; that some animals deposit these eggs into the cradles or nests, and then give them all the care needed until the young are hatched and able to care for them-selves; that some animals keep these eggs in their bodies a long time until they are better developed, and then bring them forth alive. In this way, the young are safeguarded a longer time and are better able to care for themselves when born.

After children have been trained to care for their pets during the time they are with the young, they are then ready to be taught the facts of life with regard to human motherhood. But again we must remember that until the teacher herself has the correct ideas with regard to the reproduction, she cannot influence young people under her care, nor can she eliminate the old filthy notions unless she earnestly and honestly respects the creative power in her own body.

Fatherhood. The beauty of motherhood and reverence for mother-hood has been taught by poet and artist for many generations, but the dignity and beauty of fatherhood generally has been omitted. As we visit our schools we see pictures of the mother hen with her chickens, of the cow with her calf, of the lioness with her cubs, of the mother with her child. This is absolutely unscientific and unethical. Our picture must include the whole family—the rooster, hen and chickens;

the bull, cow and calf; the lion, lioness and cubs; the father, mother and child.

For a long time the fertilization of plants has been freely talked about; but we have foolishly hesitated to talk about the father's part in animal life. Little Jim, a street urchin, after many weeks of teaching, said, "It takes two 'spots of life' to make anything grow, don't it, huh?" and then added, "and they'd better both be pretty good spots, too, hadn't they, huh?" If we could get this well understood by our young people, and the real message from Jim instilled into their minds, the need of further teaching would be eliminated.

In the gardens children should have a pair of birds, pigeons or chickens, and a pair of mammals, possibly rabbits; and if the parents are distinctly different in some trait, and the young watched for three generations, they can get this information: That it makes a difference what kind of father and grandfather chickens have. For example, a bantam rooster and a Plymouth-Rock hen were watched by some of my little folks, and when the chickens came out, "they were the craziest lot of little chickens you ever saw." This same lesson can be taught by having a difference between the father and mother rabbit. Thus, over and over again, by plant and by animal, they get the lesson that the young show the kind of family they came from; that the traits of the father and mother may crop out in the coming generations.

We teach the children that the stock-breeder is very careful to have the best of animals from which to raise young, and instead of keeping quiet about the male in the foolish old-fashioned way, we teach them that the bull is a very valuable animal, that he was selected with great care, and that is the reason the calves are so good. We teach them that the pedigree of the stallion is kept for generations, and that the age, the size, disposition, and family of the father is of great importance if we are to have good colts.

In the same way, we must teach that great care be used in the selection of the human father, that he be fit, mentally, physically, and morally to reproduce his kind. Every boy should be taught that he has within his body "spots of life" which do not belong to himself alone, but to the coming generations; that he must run no risk of bringing little folks into the world until he is ready to protect and care for them; that he dare not introduce into his system any of the great racial poisons, and thus risk marring the strength of his descendants.

Those who have not had a biological training and who wish to teach the facts of life, can read "Sonny" by Ruth McEnery Stuart to the children. In connection with this story, children ask questions, which, if answered carefully, will explain all the little folks need to know. Sonny's father says, "Poor leetle, eenchy, weenchy bit of a thing! Ef he ain't the *very* littlest! Lordy, Lordy, Lord*y!* But I s'pose all that's needed in a baby is a startin' p'int big enough to hol' the fam'ly ch'racter-istics. I s'pose maybe he is, but the po' little thing mus' feel sort o' scrouged with 'em, if he's got 'em all—the Joneses' an' the Simses'. Seems to me he favors her a little thess aroun' the mouth."

In this way, again, we get the story of inheritance and the message of the importance of parenthood. If children are not properly trained, they may make mistakes which will cause intense suffering to themselves and to others. The country is now suffering from a great scourge, a physical, mental, and moral unfitness, much of which might be prevented by careful scientific training, first in the normal facts of life, and then in the use of the reproductive organs and their functions in connection with the racial instinct. With this training, the boy may be taught to understand the message of the poet about Sir Galahad, that his "strength was as the strength of ten because his heart was pure." And later we may have a nation whose strength is as "the strength of ten"—if we learn that all sex life is good, that we should be thankful for it. Not shame of racial instinct and abuse of it, but pride in re-creative power and proper use may be the new message to our people.

Away with the secrecy, the shame, the darkness; away with the old church doctrine "conceived in sin" both within and without the marriage tie. Let in the new light, the newer thought of honor, respect, joy, in the recreative power. Instead of the old teaching to control, to suppress this racial instinct, let us teach expression. Suppression often means more intense feeling later or feelings localized around the sex organs, or an intense nervous break, or even worse, misuse of this function which may harm the individual and others. Beauty and love and home life are due to this great power. The vital energy or recreative power must be used to create, to express in life work or in children, joy and beauty and blessings to the individual and to others.

THE CATHOLIC CHURCH AND THE SEX PROBLEM

BY

REV. RICHARD H. TIERNEY

The opportunity of addressing this Federation is a source of great pleasure to me. As a Catholic priest and a teacher whose life is consecrated to the education of boys and young men, I rejoice at the chance of paying tribute to the lofty purpose and unselfish zeal of the members of this Society. Your purpose, gentlemen, is sublime; your zeal inspiring. And it is good that such is the case. For there is need of both in view of the delicate problem which is calling for solution.

This question of sex hygiene is not merely pedagogical, nor yet one that affects temporal interests only, such as the health of the individual and the present welfare of the family and state. Though it does not neglect these, still it reaches beyond them and has its chiefest concern with the eternal destiny of man, the fate of his immortal soul. Man's temporal and eternal interests are involved in the problem. Hence its unique importance.

In the last analysis the question concerns the abolition of sexual sin. Many suggestions have been made for the accomplishment of this. That which is most in favor at present, advocates the public teaching of detailed sex hygiene to our school children.

A careful study of the proposed courses reveals therein two elements, one intellectual, the other ethical. The former is detailed; the latter vague and purely naturalistic. The course adopted, therefore, will appeal primarily to the intellect. Its main effect will be knowledge, information; not will-power, not virtue, either natural or supernatural. The course is incapable of arousing strong moral forces. The appeal is made to the wrong faculty. The emphasis is put in the wrong place. Hence motives for right conduct will be weak and ineffective. Information, ay, even love of learning, cannot keep a man upright before God, cannot cleanse a heart or keep it clean. Knowledge is not moral power. There is a deep psychological truth in the horrid sneer of Mephistopheles that man used reason to be more bestial than the beast. Does not Coleridge insinuate a similar idea by saying that it is principally by the will that we are raised over the estate of an animal? Both men read history and knew something of psychology. They were not theorizing. Knowledge of itself saves nobody from delinquency.

Almost all our sinful men and youths realize that some dread disease follows sexual sin. The result is not virtue, but precaution to avoid the disease. Better sanitation, not more morality is the outcome.

A race of hygienists, not a galaxy of saints is the result. An apostle of this movement sums up my contention in this pith sentence: "I confess that I am not moral, but I am hygienic."

Gentlemen, hygiene is a barrier of straw before the onrush of the primal passion in man. Christ, not hygiene, saved the world. Christ, not hygiene, will clean the world and keep it clean. Hygiene will but give point to Sophocles' burning words:

> " Καλλος κακῶν ὕπουλον ἐξεθρέψατε."

Some ten or twelve years ago the physical dangers of this sin were brought to the attention of our college boys. The horrors of venereal disease were laid bare in lecture and pamphlet. Nothing was hid. A marked improvement in morals has not been noted. Your Society is discussing a play called "Damaged Goods," whose lesson is my lesson, to wit, knowledge is not a protection against evils which arise from unrestrained passions. The keen psychologist William James approaches the same truth when he insists that sensuous images must be combatted by ideals which lie beyond the intellect.

Why, ladies and gentlemen, if belief in a personal God and an eternal hell is at times scarce sufficient to keep men clear of impurity, is it too much to say that insistence on hygiene will be altogether ineffective for the preservation of chastity? Solomon, who was wise beyond measure answers: "As I knew that I could not otherwise be continent except God gave it, * * * * I went to the Lord and besought Him." As it appears to me, not only will the detailed teaching of sex hygiene prove ineffective of the very noble purpose in view, but it will even thwart that purpose.

This phase of the question must be examined critically and dispassionately. Such an examination necessitates the consideration of some facts concerning children of ten or twelve or fifteen years and youths of eighteen and nineteen years. At these ages the faculties are untrained and to a large extent undisciplined. The imagination is flighty and irresponsible and extremely susceptible to sensuous images. These images impress themselves on the phantasy and notably influence the actions and often the whole life of the youth. Moreover the will of the child and youth is weak and vacillating, and subject to the allurement of pleasure in whatsoever form it may appear. Now the sex passion is for the most part aroused through the imagination. As a rule the first impulse is not physiological. It is psychological. It almost invariably begins in the phantasy. A vivid sensuous image occupies the phantasy. Sensible pleasure is then experienced, and there is no force to combat it effectively. The will is weak, untrained. It appreciates a good, and either fails to it forthwith or delays its poor resistance till the soul is aflame with the fire of concupiscence. The detailed teaching of sex hygiene—especially if it be done through book and chart—will make a strong impression on the young imagination. Sensuous images will crowd the faculty as bats crowd a deserted house. The conditions already described will follow, viz, sinful thoughts, sinful desires, sinful conversations, preludes to other crimes which we prefer to pass over in silence.

Nor is this all. For obvious reasons, this instruction is apt to put forward by some years the time of suggestion and temptation. Temptations which normally belong to the age of eighteen will be experienced at the age of twelve or fourteen. Experience and psychology tell the result. A month ago a medical doctor told me that the pastor of some boys who had attended lectures on sex hygiene, complained that he found his boys joking and laughing unseemingly over the pictures drawn by the lecturer on the board. There is scarcely need of pointing the lesson; but I will say that we cannot afford to concentrate the attention of our children on sex details. Safety lies in diverting their attention from them. In truth, the safety of most adults, trained though they are, depends on the same process. A moment's reflection will convince the thoughtful that even physiology supports this contention.

But to continue: Two of the great natural protections of our children are modesty (reserve, if you will) and shame; not prudery, mark you, but healthy and healthful shame. Both are sniffed at as an outgrowth and upgrowth of dogma and superstition. They are neither one nor the other. They are an instinct of nature. This is true, especially of the latter, which is seen in children before they reach the age of reason. Modesty and shame, then, are natural protectors of chastity. But the public and frequent discussion of sex details will destroy both. Familiarity will breed carelessness. The lesson of the class will become the topic of conversation. Reserve will go. Shame will disappear. Sin will follow. Thus your good intentions will be frustrated. Not long since a careful periodical announced that discriminating critics attribute the deplorable condition of morals in one of our high schools to the very cause just now discussed.

The more I ponder the means advocated to combat the social evil, the stronger grows my conviction that this whole movement will eventually fail of its high purpose. Successful house building does not begin high in the air at the steeple top. It begins in the ground. Therein are laid firm and fast foundations which ultimately support the tower. Chastity is the tower. Deep down in the soul must be placed foundations for its support. Such foundations are self-control, self-sacrifice, obedience to conscience and external authority, modesty, love of purity, respect for self and others, high reverence for motherhood, and all the traits which combine to make a sweet, noble, strong character. Ele_mental character training is the first important step towards purity. Sex instruction will not give character—if for no other reason, because it is not deep and comprehensive enough. Without character sex instruc_tion is as chaff before the wind. And, sad to say, our children lack character. Their ideals are low. Their wills are slack of purpose. At home the youths are absorbed in luxury or frivolity, or both. And for reasons which we need not discuss here, our schools do not open the eyes of their souls to the higher and finer realities of life. For only too many life is but food and raiment and pleasure. In their estimation, meat is more than life; raiment more than modesty; pleasure more than virtue.

If your movement would be successful, it must first concern itself with this state of affairs. It must reach down to the very elements of character. It must acquaint the child with the things of the spirit, and then teach him to love the things of the spirit. A child is naturally moral. Even the new experiences of the age of puberty are accompanied by strong moral impulses. As a consequence the task of forming his soul is not supremely difficult. Failure in this matter does not come from the difficulty of the task, but from neglect of the task. A boy properly managed is as willing to care for the soul as the body. His delight over his growing muscle is often exceeded by joy over his growing strength of character. Athleticism of the spirit can be made as congenial to him as athleticism of the body. But, alas, his instructors are often more concerned with the latter than the former. *Mutatis mutandis*, all this is also true of the girl.

But do not misunderstand me. Though I insist that such formation is both the first necessary step towards your final aim, and an excellent, though perhaps indirect, training for purity, yet it is sadly inadequate. Life on the highest plane is impossible without God and religion. And chastity belongs to life on the highest plane. The conclusion is Solomon's: "Chastity is a gift of God." And if you dislike Solomon, the conviction is Plato's and the converted Carlyle's, and others who have fought the battle of life. This is not mere rhetoric. Experience as a priest has taught me that the children of religious schools are vastly more moral than the children of non-religious schools. The difference between the two classes is striking to a degree little appreciated by most people. There is a certain fiery nation, a Niobe amongst nations, distinguished for its faithfulness to religion. The result is a purity which is the admiration of the unprejudiced.

A month ago, a doctor who has given lectures on sex hygiene in one of our Western states spoke to me of her work. No one could have been more earnest in your cause. Yet she insisted on two points: the difficulty of getting suitable instructors,—an item worthy of your consideration,—and the futility of sex instruction which is not supported by an appeal to God and prayer. As far. as she could see, the boys and girls got profit through that alone, if not entirely from that. Unfortunately her appeal to the religious sentiment raised so strong a protest that it had to be discontinued. Will the same not happen if this saving element is introduced into the lectures by this Federation? And if such an element is not introduced, will your lectures be fruitful of good or evil?

Be convinced, ladies and gentlemen, that religion alone will be of lasting benefit in this campaign. God, not hygiene, is the supreme need of the hour. Our children must have brought home to them the idea of a personal, omnipresent, omniscient God, who rewards virtue and punishes vice. Nothing can replace God in their souls. The human heart is made for God. It is a-hungered for Him, a-thirst for Him. Without Him there is a void in the soul, a craving for something that should be and is not, a haunting sense of lack, which, in St. Paul's judgment, causes the ungodly to make unto themselves gods of the things of earth. The need of this Federation bears eloquent testimony to the nature of the thing of earth, which is the god of many.

On the other hand, if God is put into the life of the child, all is different. The child is consecrated to something holy, and has no strong attraction for sin. God is present in his thoughts, God is present in his words, God is present in his actions. The child and all that is his—thoughts, words and actions—are wrapped round with divinity. He stands with God and for God, not with vice and for vice. Herein is the lasting hope of your movement. Herein is profit, herein protection, herein eternal life.

These, then, are my convictions. They are not favorable to your movement in all its details. Neither are they altogether adverse to it. Eliminate from your lectures the details of sex hygiene; cast aside text book and chart. Train your children's character. Teach them that purity is noble and possible; that vice is vile, and carries with it punishment; that marriage is inviolable; that the family is sacred. Your boys— teach them that their bodies are vessels of honor, the habitation of an immortal soul made in the image and likeness of God, redeemed in the blood of Christ; train them from their early years to reverence womankind, to fall down in veneration before motherhood, God's sweet gift to women. Your girls—teach them reserve, modesty in manner and dress; tell, oh, tell them that in them, in their purity and self-sacrifice lies the hope of our beloved nation. This done, carry your campaign further. Purge the press, cleanse the novel, elevate the theatre, abolish animal dances, frown on co-education after the age of puberty. In the words of St. Paul: "Insta, opportune, importune; argue, obsecra," so that all men may realize the great obligation of life, which is to know God and to do His behests.

SESSION THIRTY-SIX

SYMPOSIUM ON TUBERCULOSIS AMONG SCHOOL CHILDREN

Arranged by the Society for the Study and Prevention of Tuberculosis,

LIVINGSTON FARRAND, M.D., *Secretary*

JOHN H. LOWMAN, *Chairman*

DR. GEORGE J. ECKEL, Buffalo, N. Y., *Vice-Chairman*

Program of Session Thirty-six

EDWARD C. BRENNER, M.D., Visiting Surgeon Home Hospital, New York City. "The Tendency of Tuberculosis in Children of Tuberculous Heritage, With Unique Means of Caring for Such Children."

S. ADOLPHUS KNOPF, M.D., Professor of Medicine, Department of Phthisiotheropy, Post Graduate Medical School, New York. "Rest and Exercise for the Tuberculous and the Predisposed Child at School, with Practical Demonstrations of Breathing Exercises and a Device Combining Open-Air Study and Window Tent."

MARY E. LAPHAM, MD., Highlands, N. C. "The Prevention of Tuberculosis by the Medical Inspection of Schools."

CHARLES BOLDUAN, M.D., Visiting Physician Tuberculosis Preventorium for Children, Farmingdale, N. J. "The Tuberculosis Preventorium."

JOHN B. TODD, M.D., Syracuse, New York. "Fresh Air School Rooms, The Problem Solved."

TENDENCY OF TUBERCULOSIS IN CHILDREN OF TUBERCULOUS HERITAGE, WITH UNIQUE MEANS OF CARING FOR SUCH CHILDREN

BY

E. C. BRENNER

In the past decade numerous reports have been published relating the incidence of tuberculosis in children under fourteen years of age who have been reared in homes where one or both parents have phthisis. The percentage of tuberculosis among such children has varied so greatly according to different observers that it seems expedient to report a series of observations obtained under rather unique circumstances.

In March, 1912, the Association for Improving the Condition of the Poor of New York City founded the Home Hospital, the purpose of which is to demonstrate the practicability of treating tuberculosis in the home and especially the feasibility of protecting the children from infection.

This institution, ideally situated at 78th Street and the East River, occupies an entire staircase of the East River Homes. An open staircase leads to the 24 apartments, consisting of from two to four rooms each, including one or more bed chambers with open air sleeping balconies. No expense has been spared to give a maximum amount of sunlight and ventilation to each apartment, even the windows extending from ceiling to floor, are arranged in three sashes so that when open two-thirds of the space is unobstructed. On the roof is a spacious solarium with hedges of privet and geraniums. A part of this solarium is reserved for the adult patients. Here in reclining chairs they take the cure. Another part of the roof is a children's playground where there is no premium on fresh air and sunshine. Another part is occupied by a fresh air school.

Three of the apartments are used for administrative purposes. One comprises the office and clinic; another is equipped as a store in which is sold all the food stuffs used by the families; a third has been equipped as a general kitchen and dining room. The Diet Kitchen is also used for a class room where cooking lessons are given.

The selection of families for the hospital has been made from the indigent tubercular class of the city dispensaries. In several instances both parents have the disease.

During the past year we have cared for 27 families in which there have been 65 children and 16 infants. In the 27 families 36 adults had definite sign of pulmonary tuberculosis on admission, 13 of them having open lesions with bacilli in their sputum.

The children claim our greatest attention and a diagnosis of thoracic tuberculosis is made only after repeated examinations and careful observations. Realizing the great difficulty of diagnosticating pulmonary tuberculosis in children and also the difference of opinions of pediatricians as to what syndroms constitutes active pulmonary tuberculosis, we have adopted the expedient of classifying our suspected children under two groups.

Group A: Those under 12 years of age and presenting the following:

1. Under weight for age.

2. Constant or frequent cough.

3. Occasional or constant temperature of undiscoverable origin.

4. Rales near one or both nipples (constant or inconstant) interscapular dullness.

5. Positive Von Pirquet Reaction (under four years).

Group B: Those who are delicate and present some of the above symptoms and physical signs.

For purposes of description, we term those in Group A, cases of probable active tuberculosis (pulmonary or bronchial glands), and classify them as patients. Those in Group B are termed suspects.

According to this classification, of 65 children under care, we find 15 patients and 18 suspects. In other words, 24% of the children who have tubercular parentage already have thoracic tuberculosis, and another 27% are excellent candidates for the disease. No doubt a similar appalling percentage holds true of the thousands of unrescued tenement children. Think what a vast army of tubercular children there must be in a great city like New York where there are over 30,000 reported cases of adult tuberculosis and an estimated number of 50,000 adult cases. You may say that our families are a selected series for experimental purposes, that such a percentage of tuberculosis in children is an exaggeration of the true existing condition of tenement life. But our families have not been carefully selected ones—we have admitted them because they seemed worthy and possible of rehabilitation physically and economically and moreover the children's condition entered in no way into deciding the fitness of a family. We have adult cases in all stages of the disease and in most cases only the adult members have been examined prior to admission. To be sure the number of children under observation has been small and yet in all probability the percentage is a fair index of the incidence of thoracic tuberculosis in childhood of this class of society.

Most of the children presented pathological conditions which contributed to their poor health and lack of development. Eighty-six .% had enlarged glands, 70% hypertrophied tonsils, 66% adenoids, 53% dental caries, 11% errors of refraction, and 8% phimosis. Tonsillectomy and adenoidectomy have been performed respectively in 36 and 38 cases. Following these operations there has been a distinct subsidence of the enlarged cervical glands, and a marked diminution in otitis media. Many of these cases before operation gave histories of repeated colds. Not one has developed a coryza or bronchitis since operation. Much dentistry has been done. Glasses have been provided in all suitable cases.

The children who are old enough attend an open-air school on an adjoining roof. The schedule of this is similar to that of the best open-air schools. The sessions begin at 9 A.M. At 10 A.M hot milk, broth or gruel is given. At 12 o'clock the children eat a hot lunch and then have a recess until 1 P.M. Following this is a thirty-minute rest, during which they recline on cots in the open air. Before dismissal at 3 P.M. nourishment is again provided.

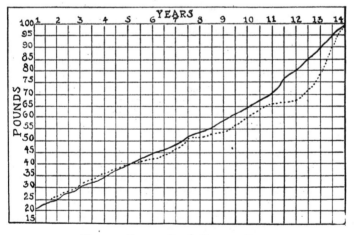

WEIGHT OF CHILDREN ONE TO FOURTEEN YEARS

The upper line indicates the average for normal children; the lower (dotted) line that for children at the Home Hospital at the time of admission.

GAINS IN WEIGHT

On admission practically all the children were under weight for their age. In the chart on this page the black line represents the average normal weights for children according to age, and the dotted line the average weights of the children at the Home Hospital on admission.

The next chart is a comparative study of the gains in weight according to age of healthy normal children and of those at the Home Hospital for a period of six months. The white columns represent the average gains in weight for a normal healthy child, and the black columns those of the children under our care. It will be noted that our underdeveloped children have made a gain not only comparable to that of healthy children, but considerably in excess, so that at the end of six months many have reached a weight normal for their age. (Without exception every child has gained in weight.)

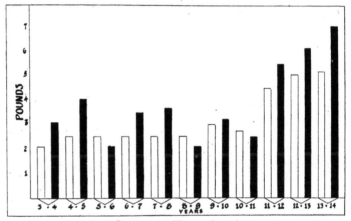

COMPARATIVE WEIGHT CHART*

White columns represent the average gain in weight in six months of a healthy normal child, ages three to fourteen (Holt).

Black columns represent the gains of the children at the Home Hospital.

*The chart (black columns) is based on the following number of children according to respective ages:

AGES	No. CHILDREN	AGES	No. CHILDREN
3 to 4 years	2	9 to 10 years	5
4 to 5	5	10 to 11	2
5 to 6	6	11 to 12	3
6 to 7	4	12 to 13	3
7 to 8	1	13 to 14	2
8 to 9	4		

These generous gains in weight are but a mild index of th general improvement in the children's appearance. The p type with sunken eyes and forlorn expressions have changed some, bright-eyed, happy boys and girls.

These excellent results are conclusive testimony of the influence of tenement life and demonstrate in striking compa great value of hygienic living. After all, the keynote to the g bat against tuberculosis is prophylaxis. The ideal treatme disease is its prevention. And if we can develop robust chil adolescents there need be little fear of tuberculosis later in life.

REST AND EXERCISE FOR THE TUBERCULOUS AND THE PREDISPOSED CHILD AT SCHOOL, WITH PRACTICAL DEMONSTRATIONS OF BREATHING EXERCISES AND A DEVICE COMBINING OPEN-AIR STUDY AND WINDOW-TENT

BY

S. Adolphus Knopf

There exist such a great variety of opinions among phthisictherapeutists as to the amount of exercise and rest the individual tuberculous adult should take, that it is obvious that to regulate the matter of exercise and rest in children must be still more difficult. It is not an easy problem to solve. No tuberculous individuals are constituted alike, be they adults or children, yet in order to manage or supervise a class of tuberculous children, or even those predisposed to the disease, it must be necessary to have some general conception of what is good and bad for such a pupil.

It goes without saying that I cannot here consider the child afflicted with tuberculous joint disease where the surgeon feels that the particular member must be kept absolutely at rest. We must also leave out of consideration that class of cases which have pulmonary lesions and a temperature approaching or exceeding 100° F. In all such cases individualizing is of prime importance and no general rule is applicable. Thus, for example, a child who is surgically treated for hip-joint disease may not be allowed to walk but may be permitted to take regular breathing exercises. Another child with pulmonary lesions and febrile in the afternoon may be allowed to take a short walk in the forenoon during the afebrile state but cautioned to breathe quietly.

But to come to general rules which should be the guidance of the teacher managing an open air class composed of afebrile children, not actively tuberculous, or only predisposed, as first maxims let us put down the following: Never overwork the tuberculous child. Never start the child to work when it is evident that it is tired. Every tuberculous child or child predisposed to the disease tires less easily in the open air than indoors. This class of children should be allowed to rest 10 to 15 minutes before and at least half an hour after meals. This rest they should preferably take on portable cots provided with a pillow. During rest time it is good to enforce silence in order to assure complete rest and quiet for those desiring it. In cold weather it is essential that the children be warmly covered during rest time.

It must likewise be borne in mind that during hot weather the children need more rest than in winter. In summer they should always rest in the shade, while in cooler weather they may be allowed to rest in the sunshine, providing their heads are protected from the direct rays of the sun. All these children must have the privilege of reporting to the teacher whenever they feel that they are not sufficiently rested or that the work assigned to them tires them too much. In such a case their temperature should be taken and the child referred to the physician for individual advice or care.

And now as to exercise. Let us first consider those which can be taken in conjunction with studies. All outdoor recitations and singing constitute healthful exercise for the lungs. Singing particularly has a beneficial effect on lungs and heart, on the pulmonary circulation, on the blood, the vocal apparatus, the upper air passages, the general health, on metabolism, and on the activity of the digestive organs. Season and weather permitting, short botanical and geological excursions should form a part of the regular curriculum of the tuberculous, the anaemic, or otherwise predisposed child. These promenades in the open constitute the very best exercise, providing, of course, they are not overdone.

What other kind of exercise may we add to recitation, singing, and walking in the open air? While all kinds of calisthenics may be productive of good, I have found in my experience that when we can combine the movements of upper and lower extremities and trunk with deep breathing such exercises are doubly efficacious.

Before demonstrating to you a series of exercises whereby every member of the body, including the head, neck, trunk, and the lower and upper extremities, comes into motion, may I be permitted to defend my enthusiasm for respiratory exercises judiciously taught and judiciously practiced, which I consider one of the most valuable means to prevent pulmonary tuberculosis, particularly in children. I confess that I am an adherent to the Freund(1)-Hart(2) theory, that the phthisical thorax arises very often from arthritic or rhachitic changes in the first rib or the adjoining vertebra—thus producing a stenosis in that region preventing expansion of the apex and its bony covering. The sooner we anticipate these changes in the upper portion of the thorax by constitutional treatment aided by proper respiratory exercises, the more

1. Freund; "Der heutige Zustand der Frage von dem Zusammenhang primärer Thoraxanomalien mit gewissen Lungenkrankheiten." Berliner klin. Wochenschrift, 1912, No. 36.

2. Hart; "Der Thorax phthisicus und die tuberkulose Disposition." Berl. klin. Wochenschrift; 1912, Heft 43.

certain are we to combat successfully the development of pulmonary tuberculosis.

And now let me in brief demonstrate to you these exercises.. To begin with, the pupil has to learn to stand straight, assuming the position of the military attention, heels together, body erect, and hands on the sides. With the mouth closed, he takes a deep inhalation (that is, breathes in all the air possible), and while doing so raises the arms to a horizontal position remains thus, holding the air inhaled for four or five seconds, and while exhaling (breathing out) brings the arms down to the original position. The act of exhalation, or the expiration, should be a little more rapid than the act of inspiration.

The act of inhalation occupies about four, the act of exhalation about three seconds, and as has already been said, the act of retention of the air about five seconds. The child should be taught to count mentally during these three acts so as to be systematic about holding the air. One can move the hands up and down twice, counting four, and on the fifth second begin to lower the arms and exhale.

When the first exercise (A) is thoroughly mastered, one may commence with the second exercise (B). The pupil places the hands one above the other, in front of the chest, with the fingers bent. The arms and shoulders make a backward movement, the hands moving apart with a motion as though wanting to tear open the chest (the fingers remaining bent), while he takes a deep inhalation, holds the breath, counting four by tapping the chest four times with both hands, and at the fifth second he starts to exhale, bringing the hands and forearms into the position from which they started. This exercise has the advantage that it can be taken in the sitting position, or even when lying on the back.

The third exercise (C) consists in raising the arms from the sides to the horizontal and then above the head, taking a deep inhalation during this act; then bending back as far as one can and remaining in that position four seconds while retaining the air, counting the seconds by moving the hands alternately, forward and backward, and on the fifth second one exhales gradually while resuming the original position. During this exercise it should be borne in mind that when the arms are raised until the hands join, one should not bring the arms close to the head, but rather form a circle above the head by bending the arms outward enough so that the meeting of the index fingers and thumbs form a triangle.

The fourth exercise (D) is for the purpose of bringing the abdominal muscles also into play, or, in other words, combining abdominal and chest breathing. To this end one assumes an erect position, like the beginning of all the exercises, the hands meeting in front, with the little fingers and the edge of the palms touching the abdominal muscles. While taking a deep inspiration, raise the diaphragm, concentrating all attention on this act, and while doing so move the joined hands upward, sliding them along the thorax up to the chin, then turn them and continue to raise them until they are above the head, as in exercise C. Remain bent backward during the four seconds while retaining the air, and then exhale, lowering the arms gradually to the horizontal and to the original position of "attention."

The fifth breathing or respiratory exercise (E), which may also be called a dry swim, requires more strength and endurance. It should not be undertaken until the others have been practiced regularly several times a day for a few weeks, and until an evident improvement in breathing and general well being has been observed. One takes the usual military position of "attention" and then stretches the arms out as if in the act of swimming, the backs of the hands touching each other. During the inspiration one moves the arms outward until they finally meet behind the back, remains in this position for the usual four seconds, counting by moving the hands while retaining the air, and on the fifth second exhales, bringing the arms forward again ready to start for another swim; or if this is the end of the dry swim, the arms return to the original position of "attention." This somewhat difficult exercise can be facilitated and be made more effective by rising on the toes during the act of inspiration, and descending during the act of expiration.

It will be seen that with the aid of these five respiratory exercises every muscle of the body, from the nostrils down to the toes, is put into play. The face alone is at rest and can serve as an indicator that the exercises are properly done; for it must be borne in mind that they should be taken with the muscles not actually in use, relaxed, and all unnecessary contraction of muscles or tremorlike movements must be avoided.

Of course, when out of doors, one cannot always take these exercises with the movements of the arms without attracting attention. Under such conditions one assumes a position similar to "attention," raises the shoulders, making a rotary backward movement during the act of inhaling; remains in this position, holding the breath for four seconds, and then exhales while moving the shoulders forward and downward, assuming again the normal position. This exercise (F) can be easily taken while walking, sitting, or riding in the open air.

Young girls and boys, especially those who are predisposed to consumption, often acquire a habit of stooping. To overcome this, the following exercise (G) is to be recommended: The child makes his best effort to stand straight, places his hands on his hips with the thumbs in front, and then bends slowly backward as far as he can during the act of inhaling. He remains in this position from four to five seconds while holding the breath, and then rises again somewhat more rapidly during the act of exhalation, assuming the original position with hands on hips.

The strikingly beneficial results obtained by the regular practice of breathing exercises in schools is shown by the effect on height and chest expansion, and chest capacity. This has been recently beautifully demonstrated in one of the common schools of Paris by Professor Meunier and his co-workers. It was observed that the children learned the exercises easily and performed them with pleasure. There were fewer absences from school during the six months of experiments than during the other part of the year. The results were universally good, especially in sickly children.

The following is a table showing the gain of height, chest capacity, and vital capacity:

Age	Height in Centimeters		Chest Girth in Centimeters			Vital Capacity in Liters and Centimeters			Number of Pupils
	Beginning	Sixth Month	Beginning	First Month	Sixth Month	Beginning	First Month	Sixth Month	
6...............	115	118	51	53	57	0.54	0.78	0.85	19
7...............	125	125	52	55	59	0.66	0.80	0.93	14
8...............	124	126	53	56	60	0.79	0.86	1.13	27
9...............	130	132	55	59	63	0.89	1.00	1.17	29
10...............	141	143	59	62	64	1.20	1.36	1.51	28
11...............	138	142	58	62	66	1.05	1.31	1.70	18
12...............	145	149	59	63	67	1.47	1.67	1.95	22
13...............	148	151	70	74	77	1.93	2.26	2.26	16
14...............	147	153	62	66	74	1.83	1.92	2.15	7

How much this increased lung capacity must mean to a child in danger of developing pulmonary tuberculosis must be evident to you when you recall that careful physiological experiments on the process of respiration in the adult have shown how much more oxygen can be inhaled into the lungs by deep inspiration and expiration, in spite of the fact that in the adult the bony frame of the thorax has become ossified and yields but very little. In the child the relative softness of bone and cartilages allow them to yield considerably to the pressure from within.

For the purpose of demonstrating to you the value of an additional

respiratory exercise, indicated for the individual with a non-active
tuberculosis or one with a strong predisposition and a badly developed
chest, let me recall to you the following figures: The amount of tidal
air, that is to say, the volume which is inspired and expired in quiet
respiration—is only 500 c.c., the complemental air—the volume which
can be inspired after an ordinary respiration—1500 c.c., and the supplemental or reserve air—the amount which can be voluntarily expelled
after a deep inspiration, is about 1240 c.c. There remains of course
a good deal of residual air even after such an increased respiratory
act as would be accomplished by any of the exercises above described.
Now, if it is desirable to increase the process of hematosis, a second
expiratory movement can be accomplished and as much as 500 to 600
c.c. of supplemental and residual air expelled. To do this effectually,
the individual should inhale and exhale as deeply as he can accompanying
this action with movement of the arms or not, and then immediately
after the act of expiration make an additional effort to exhale, without of course any preceding inspiratory movement whatsoever. This
second expiration can be greatly facilitated by supinating the arms
and pressing the thorax with them. This exercise is somewhat difficult
to teach, and at the beginning it may be well to have the pupil pronounce the German word "eins" or the English word "inch," prolong-
ing the sound during the secondary expiratory effort. The accompanying figure shows the attitude the pupil should assume during
this forced expiratory effort.

Leaving aside the above-mentioned frequent phthisical thorax due
to bony deformation, it is a well known fact that even in a seemingly
normal thoracic frame the tuberculous process begins very often in
the apices. The frequency of an apiceal beginning had been explained
by an inherent bad inspiratory function of that part of the lung. This
supposition is, I believe, erroneous. I agree with Hanau(3) who demonstrated as far back as 1887 that the apices inspire excellently well,
almost too well, for dust and all sorts of micro-organisms enter and
lodge there most easily. Careful post-morten examinations have
demonstrated this fact too often for it to need any further proof. What
is faulty is the expiratory function of the apices. A thorough expiration followed by a forced expiratory effort, as described above, is, to
my mind, the only possible way to improve this defect and prevent
stagnation and congestion, which, as is well known, produce excellent
media for the development of bacilli.

It must be self-evident that in a school for tuberculous and predisposed children individualizing in prescribing breathing exercises is as

3. Hanau, A., Zürich; "Beiträge zur Pathologie der Lungenkrankheiten," Zeitschrift f. klin. Medizin, XII, 1887.

essential as with all other exercises. As a general rule I can only state the following: Commence with the easier exercises (A), and do not go on to the more difficult ones until the former are completely mastered. Take from four to six respiratory exercises (one of A, one of B, one of C, one of D, or one of E), or when outdoors simply exercise F, four to six times every half hour or hour, or at least four to six times a day, and on rising in the morning and retiring at night. Continue this practice until deep breathing has become a natural habit.

When judiciously regulated, I believe these breathing exercises to be of incalculable benefit as a means to help a tuberculous child to combat its affliction and to aid the predisposed child to increase its resistance to the development of the disease. I recommend to your kind consideration the careful practice and study of these exercises.

In conclusion, let me call your attention to one more point. Judiciously supervised rest and exercises in the open air is not only essential for the tuberculous or predisposed child while attending school, but should also be carried on at home. If we really wish to cure the child of its affliction or its inclination to become tuberculous, we must provide for it exercise, rest, and sleep in fresh, pure air during the entire 24 hours of the day. To facilitate the open air regimé—rest and exercise at home as well as at school, I beg leave to present to you a device showing a combination of an open air study and window tent.

To give a pupil attending public school or college, particularly when he is tuberculous or strongly predisposed, an opportunity to attend an open air class is, of course, most laudable. But if we wish to be in earnest to thoroughly strengthen this child we must give it a well-nigh constant outdoor life. We must not be contented with giving this boy or girl lessons in the open air for a few hours during school lessons.

My experience with the little device which I brought before the medical profession some eight years ago under the name of the window-tent, intended for the consumptive tenement house dweller, has given me the inspiration to devise a scheme which will give to the pupil not only outdoor life during sleep but also while doing his lessons at home and while resting or reading for his amusement.

I am indebted to the Kny-Scheerer Company for their great courtesy in carrying out my ideas on this subject and enabling me to present to this Congress a model which will give a splendid idea of the workings of the device.

I take pleasure in presenting you to-day this combination of an open air study and window tent. As you will see it resembles in the main my original window-tent, only it is larger, extending out from the window 4½ feet instead of 2½, so as to allow room for desk and chair for the pupil when at work. This device consists of an awning which instead of being placed outside of the window, it is attached to the window pane inside of the room. It is constructed so that the air from the room will not enter or mix to any extent with the air in the tent.

It is composed of four frames of Bessemer steel rods, suitably formed and furnished with hinged terminals operating on a stout hinge pin at each end, with circular washers interposed to insure independent and easy action in folding the frame.

This frame is covered with an extra thick yacht-sail-twill, attached to the metal frames by tapes on the inside to admit of its removal for the purpose of being laundried or disinfected. The tent is attached to the frame of the window a few inches below the upper sash, so that when the lower part of the window is pushed up there will be a space to allow the hot air from the room to pass out. By lowering the window the space can be reduced according to need. The cold outdoor air enters from without at the bottom of the open window, describes a half circle and makes its exit at the top carrying with it the exhaled carbon dioxide.

My friend, Professor Sherman G. Bonney, of the University of Colorado, has verified this action by the use of a delicate instrument, known as the air-meter which showed the current to be perceptibly inward at the bottom and outward at the top. In cold weather it is apparent that the outward direction of the air current at the top is facilitated by the passage of the heated air from the room through the aperture above the window-tent.

While in the typical window-tent the flaps of the awning need to be only long enough to allow them to be tucked under the mattress, in the combination device the awning is long enough to touch the floor. When used for a study, a screen composed of three pieces of wainscoting, 34 inches high, hinged together, surrounds the entire tent. The lower portion of the canvas is attached to the interior of the screen. The screen and canvas protect the pupil sitting in his study from drafts from beneath and help to keep his feet warm.

In winter the pupil must, of course, be warmly dressed, and I believe there is nothing better for the purpose in the market than the ingenious sitting-out bag devised by Mr. Frank H. Mann, the Secretary of the Tuberculosis Committee of the City of New York. This garment provides adequate warmth for the upper part of the body without having the more or less cumbersome bag portion extend up any further than those usually manufactured. Freedom of movement of the hands and arms is of course a necessity for work in the tent and is fully provided for by the cape idea, without sacrificing the needed warmth about the shoulders.

The garment is made of heavy brown felt. The bottom is square in shape and reinforced with extra heavy material about one inch in thickness to protect the feet from the cold. In addition, the bottom is covered with a special detachable piece of canvas to insure against wear and tear. The system of fastening was specially devised to facilitate convenience in getting in and out of the bag. A series of snap catches all the way from head to foot make the means of access far more practical than the old way of stepping in and out from the top. Hooks around the garment at the center enable the wearer to buckle it snugly about his waist. Another interesting new feature is the pocket at the side provided for handkerchief and mittens.

In the middle upper portion of the tent is inserted a transparent celluloid window 8 x 10 inches, which however can be made larger. Through it the pupil can be observed during his lessons or he can look into the room and converse without raising the flaps.

We also have the study transformed for the night into a comfortable window-tent. With the aid of a pulley the frame and canvas can be raised so as to be entirely out of the way while arranging for day study or preparing to retire for the night. On extremely cold nights the pupil can close the window before retiring so that he can dress in a warm room and then open the window from his tent-bed. He can of course also close the window in the same way in the morning and have the room get warm before rising to dress.

The entire tent is attached to the window frame simply by two hook-clamps so that, if necessary, the entire device can be lifted off with ease.

It is of course desirable to have outside shutters on the window, but if that is impracticable a Venetian blind may be attached on the inside. These shutters or blinds may often be needed in stormy, rainy, or snowy weather. In very cold or windy weather an ordinary wire screen can be placed in the window or a light frame made and covered with cheesecloth. Dr. J. B. Todd of Syracuse has recently devised a ventilating screen made of such material which will serve the purpose admirably.

THE PREVENTION OF TUBERCULOSIS BY THE MEDICAL INSPECTION OF SCHOOLS

BY

Mary E. Lapham

The old doctrine of predestination almost seems to be the only explanation of the confusing mass of contradictions surrounding this disease. We see the terrible effects of bad housing, overcrowding, overworking and underfeeding upon the spread of the disease but we do not see why all are not equally affected thereby. Here are men and women and children enduring the greatest hardships with no danger whatever from tuberculosis and here are others living under the best possible conditions and nothing can save them from it. We know that by the time our children reach maturity that practically all of them are infected by tubercle bacilli and that two per cent. must die, but we do not know just what influences the selection of this particular two per cent. out of all our children nor why one child should be taken and the other left. Nor have we been able thus far to foresee the future of our children or to have any idea as to whether or not there was any danger from tuberculosis. Thus far we have not been able to infer from the child the future of the man.

That death from tuberculosis may possibly be due to individual idiosyncrasies is suggested by the death rate of infants. When an infant manifests tuberculosis during the first year of life it rarely recovers. We have considered this inevitable death as due to exposure and infection and the helplessness of infancy. It is possible that there is another explanation. With improved methods of research we are learning that there is a much higher percentage of intrauterine infections than we had believed and because of this increasing knowledge we have come to ask whether the high death rate during the first year of life may not be the manifestation of an inability to establish a toleration to the presence of tubercle bacilli. If so death is not due to exposure but to a fundamental flaw in the newly made organism which existed at the start and was merely manifested at the end. If we eventually find that there is a very considerable number of these intrauterine infections then the question of individual characteristics will assume greater importance because so much depends upon this factor. The importance of individual characteristics increases with the frequency of infections because protection becomes more impossible against infection and resistance more necessary. If we admit that the infection is universal, then the degree of resistance to this inevitable infection is all we have to save us.

After the first year of life the manifestation of tuberculosis is not necessarily fatal and the chances for recovery increase with each year so that at maturity the death rate is only two per cent. This reduction is obtained during years when the per cent. of infections is steadily rising until at maturity it is over ninety. We explain the rise in the number of infections and the fall in the death rate as being due to the same cause; the development of biological characteristics enabling us to detect the presence of the infection and the bearer to resist it.

If the intrauterine existence has developed a certain amount of resistance the manifestation of the disease is correspondingly delayed. The adjustment of the organism to the new conditions of existence will accelerate the disclosure if it is not normally accomplished and the final result remains uncertain in many cases and the conflict is prolonged on through childhood and even into adult life. Over ninety per cent. of our children settle the question favorably and there is no more trouble but when this equilibrium is not established the future is uncertain. With all of our children infected how shall we know which are in danger and which are not. The ninety and nine are safe but in order to save the hundredth one, we must first of all know that such a danger exists and then we must determine which one out of all the hundred is in danger. It may be that our suspicions are aroused by evident signs of abnormalities: The pale, anemic, weak, listless child readily attracts our attention but a robust child may be equally threatened without once arousing suspicion. A tuberculous process so small as to be detected only with difficulty by the unaided eye may affect the nutrition of every part of the child's body and impede its development mentally, morally and physically. Or the process may slowly weave its threads throughout the lungs until it is ready to strangle its victim, while the general health remains good. Because of this lack of manifestations we are not safe in inferring the absence of danger, and therefore our children should be regularly examined to see if this flaw exists for the future depends upon its detection as soon as possible. There are surgical conditions that are harmless to-day and malignant tomorrow and at the first suggestions of danger their removal is imperatively demanded. In tuberculosis the change to malignancy gives no sign. From one microscopic nodule to another the disease insidiously advances and gives no hint of its presence until it can no longer be concealed and then only too often we say that it is too late. When a man of thirty or forty or fifty comes crashing down with tuberculosis we do not always realize that the beginning was far back in childhood and that we had unlimited opportunities for its detection and correction that were persistently neglected. Surrounded by medical skill and with every opportunity for safety, one man after another loses his life because the lungs were not carefully examined at regular intervals to discover the first indications of an inherent weakness. It is impossible to avoid an infection by tubercle bacilli but we can detect their pathological influence and overcome it.

If a man or child is well and strong it does not occur to us to question appearances. When the business of life is being carried on by a man in the very heyday of his strength and ability we no more think of his having tuberculosis than of his having a rattlesnake. The robust, ruddy child playing with his fellows, eating and sleeping with all the zest of health, gives no intimation whatever of the dark road he has to travel in adult life when tuberculosis claims its own.

The presence of tubercle bacilli does not necessarily mean tuberculosis but it does mean that there is a possible source of danger which may develop at any moment and which must be carefully watched throughout life, from the cradle to the grave.

Our public schools offer unrivalled opportunities for the study and detection of what von Adelung has so well called pathological tuberculosis meaning thereby these early beginnings of danger. Our diagnosis is chiefly made to-day upon the effects produced. To detect this flaw as early as possible our medical inspectors of schools must require a far higher ability than is generally found to-day. Physical signs in the lungs will be superseded by the X-ray, tuberculin, the examination of the blood and biologic tests upon animals. To say whether or not there is any danger from tuberculosis is not only difficult, but even impossible and time alone can decide in some cases. When the flaw is detected the knowledge is worth everything to the future of the child for thenceforth its future is seen to be different because of the necessity for safeguarding it.

The constant training in the detection of these difficult cases will give us an insight into the beginnings of the disease and the data accumulated in the records will furnish a comprehension as to the best methods to combat it that could be obtained in no other way. Our public schools will offer vast opportunities for tracing these hidden stories from the beginning to the end, and we shall learn that death is more often due to delayed diagnoses than any other cause.

I have recently had under my care five young women who were all apparently well until the beginning of the end came. Think of those years in school when systematic examinations would have revealed the danger and turned death into victory.

Our people are dying from careless, ignorant neglect, from blunders and mistakes and incompetency; and from delayed diagnoses far more than from an infection by tubercle bacilli. Delayed diagnoses mean death and to wait for physical signs in the lungs or for manifestations of ill health may be very dangerous. Have our teachers report for examination all children below par for any cause but do not rest content with this. Each child should be regularly examined and the report entered upon his school records. Then in after years the efficiency of our system can be tested by the number of cases escaping detection, for the attending physician can look up the records of a case coming to him in later life and if the methods employed prove to be inadequate they will have to be improved. The status of the whole nation as regards tuberculosis will be on record and the responsibility of the inspectors be exposed to the most searching tests. Published reports of the year's work will bring the work up to a high standard for the public will soon be sufficiently educated to judge the value of the work. Tuberculosis must be studied where it starts in the public school so that we may overcome it in our children and thus cut off our future supply of consumptives. The child is father to the man and to prevent the death of the father we must begin with the child.

THE TUBERCULOSIS PREVENTORIUM

BY

Charles F. Bolduan

There is a large group of children coming from homes in which there is tuberculosis, whose needs are not met by the open air schools, or by the day camps, or by the fresh air summer homes, or yet by the tuberculosis sanatoria. The children I refer to are anaemic, undernourished, flabby and without resistance. They are what von Behring calls "consumption candidates," and show by positive tuberculin reactions that they already harbor tuberculous infection. What they really need is sanatorium care, but the sanatoria do not admit them because they do not show signs of manifest tuberculosis. Some years ago, through the initiative of Mr. Nathan Strauss, a special institution was established for these children, an institution modelled on the lines of modern tuberculosis sanatoria. This is the Tuberculosis Preventorium for Children, and is located on the pine belt of New Jersey not far from Lakewood. Estimates of the number of poorly nourished, physically handicapped children in the City of New York may vary greatly, and are difficult to compile, but all estimates agree in placing these figures far in the thousands. It is clear that at present the community can not look after such a large number of children. However, we have endeavored to select the most needy of this large group—the children who are not only poorly nourished, but in addition are exposed to the infection in their homes. Dr. Herman M. Biggs has estimated that New York City has 40,000 of these young unfortunates. If any group can be chosen as marked to fall by the wayside, it is this sad group, the children of the tuberculous poor—children not only predisposed but exposed to tuberculosis.

At the Preventorium at Farmingdale, N. J., we accommodate somewhat over 150 children, and as we keep them for an average period of about three months, we are enabled to provide for about 600 children a year. I shall not take the time to give a detailed description of the institution; suffice it to say that in addition to a reception pavilion, where all children are quarantined for three weeks in order to prevent infection of the larger group, we have four open-air shacks, each accommodating 32 children. We have a small infirmary, school-rooms for boys and girls, a large administration building, with a dining-room which can seat all the children, and last, but not least, 170 acres of land in the sandy pine belt, over which the children can roam.

The plan of treatment is simple. It consists of plenty of good food, a twenty-four-hour day in the open air, an intimate acquaintanceship with the fields and the woods, and a practical lesson in cleanliness and hygiene. The children, as you can imagine, gain in weight, improve in physical condition, in their bearing, mentality and spirits. Indeed, in some cases such a change takes place that it is difficult to realize that we have before us the same child for discharge which we examined some few months previously upon admission. The average gain in weight has been about seven pounds, but some have gained as much as 25 pounds.

A preventorium, to do its full amount of good, should be closely associated with the other anti-tuberculosis activities of the community. Tuberculosis institutions have become so numerous, and the problem of caring for the sick and needy so complex, that any organization which attempts to stand alone is apt rather to block, than to favor the wheels of progress. Our work is intimately inter-locked with that of the many tuberculosis clinics scattered throughout the boroughs of New York. These clinics, under the direction of Dr. James Alexander Miller, constitute our admitting stations, and their chiefs kindly act as our admitting physicians. They recommend children for admission to the institution, selecting the children of the tuberculous adults who come to them for treatment, and in this way offering help to the young as well as to the old. All the children are examined before they are finally accepted for admission, at the Hospital Admission Bureau, the central office of New York for all the activities concerned with tuberculosis.

During the three to six months' stay of the children at the preventorium conditions in their homes are investigated. Here lies one of our most difficult problems, as those of you who come face to face with the tuberculosis problem of the city realize. There are some homes which it is impossible for us to improve. There are others, however, which we can better by sending the tuberculosis member of the family to a sanatorium, by giving instruction as regards cleanliness and hygiene and the proper disposal of the sputum, or by considering their needs with relief organizations, and obtaining aid or additional assistance. Every six months our children are revisited in the home, and their physical condition and surroundings are ascertained. In a large metropolis with a heterogeneous population such as New York, follow-up work is enmeshed in difficulties; the people move so frequently that they get lost in the swarm. At first this important work was greatly handicapped by the failure to locate the families, but more recently, since upon admission we have obtained not only the home address of the child but, in addition, two other addresses of friends or relatives to whom we can refer for information, our records show fewer lacunæ in this respect. If a child is found not to be doing well, a second or even a third visit to the preventorium is recommended. We have had many children who have been to Farmingdale more than once, and we welcome the admission of children for a second time if their condition shows retrogression. It is premature to attempt to present our results in statistical form. However, I think it may safely be said that these children maintain their improvement in weight and strength surprisingly well; that they are taught a lesson in hygiene, and that a method of living is demonstrated to them which never can be blotted from their memory; that not only the advantages, but the pleasure of life in fresh air has been instilled into their very natures.

There is one more subject which I desire to mention in connection with the work of the preventorium, and that is the schooling of these children. Since the children accepted at the institution are between the ages of four and fourteen years, it is obvious that the large majority will be children of school age. It is therefore important to provide instruction for them, so that they do not fall behind in their studies when they return to school in the city. We have three licensed teachers for this purpose, and provide a two-hour school period. This amount of instruction, that is to say, ten hours a week, has been found sufficient to keep the children up to grade, so that they do not lose in their school standing by their stay at the preventorium. In fact, if we cared to increase the period of instruction, we could readily enable many of these children to advance a class. This mental invigoration may be attributed partly to the improvement of the physical condition of the pupils, but mainly, I believe, to the stimulating effect of the open-air school. Dr. Knopf has already told you of the effect of fresh air in combating fatigue. In this connection, we would add that our records show that our children are one grade in scholarship below the standing they should have for their age. Many of them are still more backward, thus exemplifying how physical and mental vigor go hand in hand.

In addition to the regular schooling, which is conducted along the lines of the public school, the girls are given sewing lessons. In the summer the boys are stimulated to care for their individual gardens, and almost all children do chores in the shacks or in the dining-room.

FRESH AIR SCHOOL ROOMS—THE PROBLEM SOLVED

BY

JOHN B. TODD

> Give me truths;
> For I am weary of the surfaces,
> And die of inanition.
>
> The south-winds are quick-witted,
> The schools are sad and slow,
> The masters quite omitted
> The lore we care to know.—
>
> *Emerson.*

The need of open air school for children who are subnormal is becoming recognized and many municipalities in Europe and America have provided means to care for this class of children. Knopf (1), speaking of the value of open air schools in anti-tuberculosis warfare, says, "Those of us who know the invaluable benefits which can be derived therefrom must wonder why open air instruction is limited to a few classes in primary schools." In Rochester, N. Y., (2) the children remain in the open air school for an average of one year, and a follow-up system is in use to prevent relapse. This work entails an extraordinary burden of expense, and is really locking the barn after the horse is stolen.

While this work is doing much good, it is becoming generally recognized that the ordinary school room is inadequately supplied with fresh air and tends to produce the subnormal child. "The time has arrived when the value of attempting to ventilate school buildings and hospitals at all is seriously questioned by many hygienists and physicians. The fact that existing conventional ventilating system does not always satisfactorily perform its functions when carefully designed has caused this dissatisfaction"(3). The children all lack the stimulus of fresh air while those of low vitality developed adenoids, tonsils, or become infected with tuberculosis. "A very common explanation of ill-health in school children is over work." The fact that the school houses are poorly ventilated, and that the air is bad, is very seldom considered. As a matter of fact there is overwork, but it is the overworking of the defenses of the body in keeping off infection" (4).

It is in accord with the physiological law that increased use of an organ causes it to increase in size. Thus the breathing of germ-laden air in the closed school room causes increased work in the lymphatic structures of the nose and throat—the tonsils, adenoids and other lymphatic glands—and they soon become enlarged. Fully recognizing the underlying causes of enlarged glands, Danziger (5) states, "The cause of hypertrophy of these lymphatic structures is therefore to be found in the physiological attempt to overcome a pathological condition of the mucous membrane of the nose and buccal cavities."

The ordinary school room provides the conditions to develop a sub-normal child, then when his physical condition becomes bad enough, he, in some favored cities, is sent to an open air school, when he generally rapidly improves, and is then sent back into his old environment to deteriorate again. "It is a serious matter," says Kingsley (6), "when a school into which a child is forced, actually contributes to his decline. The dull and backward pupil who cannot get his lessons is often kept after school. He has sat for hours at a rigid desk in an unnatural posture, in an over-heated room, the over-dry thirsty air sapping his already wilted system, the windows of the school room never opened, because the janitor, the ventilating engineer, and perhaps the teacher, who likes to have the room at 75 or higher, says 'No.' "

The results of closed school rooms without fresh air is first to produce mental and physical fatigue. The mental fatigue results in lowered efficiency. Lea (7) states, "Fatigue is a physical phenomenon, a lessened power of work, which has as its basis certain metabolic phenomena." There is a lack of interest, and lagging in work—their minds are slow to respond and their progress in their work is retarded; the physical results of fatigue is first lowered resistance, which, with the increase of dust and bacteria, favors infection; the lymphatic gl nds, tonsils, and adenoids become enlarged, cases of tuberculosis do occur. According to the Michigan Department of Health (8), fifty-two per cent. of the deaths among school teachers between the ages of twenty-five and thirty-four were due to tuberculosis. In relation to the prevention of tuberculosis infection children Putnam (9) says, "We cannot destroy all tuberculosis germs, nor any large part of them. The one sure way of most nearly eliminating it is by increasing the powers of resistance of every individual up to at least that of the millions who now conquer it, although always exposed to it." These conditions require the child to be cared for in special open air schools at a greater cost to the community, or may even require severe surgical operations and hospital care. What would one think of a manufacturer whose process allowed all of his stock to become exposed to damage and some of it ruined?

"The great point to be achieved," says Kingsley (10) "in all this work is that the whole 19,000,000 should get their share of fresh air which the good Lord has made plenty for all. If they are educated to the right feeling for fresh air and for health needs and health rights the problems of smoke nuisance, bad air in theaters, churches, street cars and trains will be on the high road to solution. It only needs the right attitude on the part of the public to obtain its rights in this respect, for fresh air is present everywhere, only waiting to be let in, and certainly the intelligence of the American people will find a way."

. The public have to be educated to the use of fresh air in schools and rooms. We are all more or less governed by custom and inborn prejudice, so it will take time for the public to learn that fresh air and comfort are not antagonistic terms, but there are many who are easier persuaded to submit to a major surgical operation than to appreciate the value of fresh air sleeping rooms. The real valuable test for ventilation is the physiological test. The room should be free from the well-known "institutional" odor always so perceptible in crowded places. If there are no odors in the room and the children are free from headaches, with no hacking or coughing, and are alert, we may conclude the room is properly ventilated.

"Do not be dismayed," writes Kingsley (6), "if the new significance of ventilation and fresh air discredits the system of which you have been so proud. You have one great known quantity. There is an abundance of fresh air outside of every door. * * * The friends of the open air school movement are interested in all of the children and will be content with nothing short of the right conditions for the whole one hundred per cent."

The problem of school efficiency is a very complex affair, and really cannot go beyond public opinion. It is a matter of real economy and efficiency to furnish fresh air for all the school children, provided it can be done to the satisfaction of the teachers, school officials and the public. As truly stated by Rice (11), "It is absurd, inefficient, and poor economy to give it freely to a selected few at a large per capita expense, and to refuse it to the remainder." Any change that is not endorsed by public opinion cannot stand, but the public is ready to try out everything that promises to be of benefit, and real efficiency is sure to be endorsed. The cordial coöperation of the school officials, teachers and medical inspectors is needed, and, further, the employment of a qualified superintendent of hygiene is absolutely required by every municipality that desires to advance efficiency.

During the winter of 1912-13, the writer worked out an experiment in school ventilation that received the unqualified endorsement of the teachers, pupils, janitor and the public. It was as simple as it was efficient. The problem was to introduce a sufficient quantity of fresh air into a warm room to make it livable and at the same time to avoid drafts. Drafts in a room are currents of air with velocity enough to be perceived, and if such air is cold, they are uncomfortable. So the problem was to introduce cold air but of a very low velocity, but if of very low velocity there must be a large inlet to get sufficient volume.

The experiment was tried out in Sumner School in Syracuse. It is a modern 16-room building, with a registration of over 600. It is equipped with a fan which forces hot air into the room; there are also steam-heated pipes along the outside walls under the windows. During school hours the windows and doors are closed to keep the ventilating system in working order. The rooms are stuffy and close, and the well-known school room odor is present. Many of the pupils suffer from headaches, and sometimes one will faint. One day last fall a sturdy boy of ten fainted and lay for an hour. The air in the room was very close.

The speaker had a plan to relieve this condition and had been waiting for an occasion like this to get permission to try it out. One of the teachers was willing to adopt it, and permission was given by the principal and janitor to try it out although they both expressed the opinion that it would not work. The speaker had been using a sleeping porch for two years. In the winter the only protection is afforded by screens, covered with the cheapest unbleached cotton cloth. This proved to be a comfortable sleeping place through the severe winter weather, the inside temperature being from 15 degrees to 36 degrees warmer than the outside, depending principally upon the direction and velocity of the wind. The light cloth allowed the fresh air to slowly come in but did not radiate or conduct the heat outside. From these observations it seemed that cloth screens might be useful in securing better school ventilation.

The school room in which the experiment was made had five windows facing the east. The lower sash opening was 40″ x 36″. Wooden screens were made and covered with the lightest grade of unbleached cotton cloth. After they were put in place the windows were kept open during school hours. The stuffiness and odor entirely disappeared, as did all snuffling and coughing in the pupils. No more cases of fainting occurred, complaints of headaches ceased and the pupils have done better work.

Before school opens in the morning the janitor closed the windows and warms the room to 70 degrees by hot air from the fan. This is humidified by a steam jet in the mixing room; when school opens the windows are raised and the hot air inlet closed.* The windows have been open through all the days of winter although the children sit within five feet of the open windows. There are no cold draughts, the velocity of the warm air rising from the radiator is greater than that of the cold

*Every class room, coat room, and hall is now (April, 1914) screened; six hundred and forty-five square feet of opening, and the fan is not used at any time. Registration 760 and every one exulting over the improved air conditions.

air, which is being slowly diffused through the screens, so that resulting direction of the air current is upward.   February 10th was the coldest day of the year.   At 10 A. M. it was at zero outside and 70 degrees in this room with every window open, fifty square feet of opening.

5-1 Grade Sumner School

February 10th was the coldest day of the year.   At 10 A. M. it was at zero outside and 70° in this room with every window open, fifty square feet of opening.

The screens furnish fresh air of very low velocity from a large surface (about 50 square feet in this room) with no heat loss from conduction, whereas, with the windows closed, we have a large area of glass cooling the bad air; glass transmits twenty times more heat than cotton (12). The slow diffusion of fresh air does not seem to cool the air in the room any more than it would be cooled by the glass if the windows were down. The janitor says that the room has been warmed as easily as it was before the screens were used.

The educational value of this fresh air experiment has been of much benefit to the community.   The teachers and pupils have learned the benefit and comfort of fresh air; the school was visited by representatives of the Associated Women's Club of Syracuse, and they gave the screens their endorsement, and by resolution asked the Board of Education to place them in every school.

The following letters are from fresh air teachers of Sumner School:

The principal, Alice S. Town, of Sumner School, writes:

"When you first suggested screening one room for an experiment, while I agreed to try it, I was doubtful of its success. After weeks' trial I was completely convinced of the success of the experiment. Since then eight rooms have been equipped with the screens at the request of the teachers in those rooms, and I hope before another year we shall have them in every room in the building."

Miss Whalen writes:

"The open air room was enjoyed from November to May. The class entering the room at midwinter made no objection to change of temperature. Twice only were the windows lowered because of strong wind. Attendance was unusually good. There were no colds until April. One case of measles and one of scarlet fever occurred. The children are quiet and attentive, showing little, if any, fatigue to the end of the day. Upon entering the room the fresh clean air was always noticeable; winter seemed forgotten here."

Miss Hinsdale, head of the Kindergarten, writes:

"Your fresh-air window screens have certainly been most satisfactory in our kindergarten. Our attendance of little folks during the winter months was unusually good, reason for this, the children seemed to be free from colds, thanks to plenty of fresh air. Children more wide-awake, less restless and not tired when session closed. As teachers, we both found our voices stronger and throats less sensitive."

Miss Reisig, of the 2-2 grade, writes:

"Since having the open air windows I find the children less restless. It is very much easier to keep their attention. They do not seem tired even at the close of the school. The attendance has been good. The children themselves like the fresh air and do not complain of feeling the cold. Personally, I have felt benefitted by the fresh air."

Miss Marie Keefe, of the 5-1 grade, writes:

"After using the screen windows for the past term, I feel as if I should never want to teach in a school room without them. There are five windows in our room and I can recommend and praise them most highly as they are a wonderful help. The discipline is easier as the children do not become so uneasy and restless. I have also noticed that there has been less coughing in school during the past winter than ever before. It is my opinion that the screen windows would prove a great help in every class room."

Miss Amelia A. Morris, of 8-1 grade, writes:

"In four of the eight windows in my school room I had cloth screens placed in last December. They were there until May, and I was greatly pleased with the results. The air was much fresher all the time than by the old method of ventilation. The windows were open during all kinds of weather, only a strong wind making it necessary to close them partly or entirely. I had no cold during these months and very few pupils were absent because of colds. I am heartily in favor of the cloth screens as I think it the only safe way to keep the air fresh and pure in a room occupied by so many people."

Miss Kinsella, of the 5-2 grade, writes:

"We have enjoyed our open air room very much this term. The air has always been pure and fresh and the room did not at any time seem close as it often does with closed windows. When we moved during the middle of the term from an open air room to a closed room, both the children and I were greatly disappointed. The prin. cipal said we might take the screen windows with us but as it was impossible to have them transferred for a few weeks the children and teacher who were then in our former room had enjoyed the open air room so much that they did not want to give up the windows. The principal then very kindly had some made for our room and we were happy again. I have found the discipline of the room to be much better since we have had the screens. The children do not get so restless or tired as formerly. During the winter the children had fewer colds than usual, which I believe due to being in the fresh air all the time. I also found this to be true in my own case. We are all very glad that you tried the experiment in Sumner School."

From Madison School Annex—an old furnace-heated building—Miss Frances T. Daley writes:

"We tried your cloth screen method of ventilation, as an experiment in our school this year and were highly pleased with the results. The temperature of the room was not lowered, and there was absolutely no draft. The air, being sifted, entered gradually, yet was changing constantly. Only in case of severe rain or snowstorm was it necessary to lower windows. I think it surpassed artificial ventilation, for in the latter air usually comes in over the heads of the children, increasing danger of colds from drafts. A naturally dark room might be made too dark, yet, in our rooms we all liked the subdued light. To a certain extent screens might be receptacles for germs. I think they should be occasionally sterilized. I will be pleased to discuss the method with other teachers, and recommend their use in other schools."

It would seem from the success of this experiment that we have found the way to provide fresh air rooms for all of the children. It is a supplemental system and not antagonistic to heating the rooms with air driven by a fan, or indirect radiation from steam pipes. In cold weather a fan is needed to warm the rooms before school opens, when the screened windows should be opened and the air kept fresh and pure throughout the day. The windows that are opened to strong winds should have the screens covered with heavier cloth than of less exposed positions, the object being to keep the incurrent of air at low velocity. All screened windows should have steam radiators between the window and floor. The cloth screens prevent much of the outside dust from entering the rooms; after they have been used for a time the cloth becomes very much discolored and dirty, when they should be cleaned and new cloth put on.

The screen frames were made from $\frac{7}{8}''$ x $1\frac{3}{4}''$ pine, with a little batten $\frac{1}{4}''$ x $1''$ projecting enough to cover the crack between the screen and blind stop and were fastened in place with a sash bolt. They cost from 75 cents to $1 each, painted two coats to match window frame

and fitted in place. The making and fitting of these fresh air sc
would be valuable training for the Sloyd pupils; it would give
practical demonstration of the simplicity and efficiency of fres
living that would be reflected in their own homes and lives to the pe
nent benefit of the community, as Kingsley (10), truly states, '
lesson in right living successfully taught in the school immedi
reacts upon the home."

References:

1. Knopf, C. A., M.D.   American Journal, Public Health, v. 3, No. 4.

2. Whipple, E. C., M.D.   Discussion on Tuberculosis in Children, N. Y.
     Soc., 1913.

3. Bass, Frederick.   American Journal, Public Health, May, 1913.

4. Hessler, Robt., M.D.   Dusty Air and Ill Health.

5. Danziger, Dr. Ernest.   N. Y. Med. Journal, April 19, 1913.

6. Kingsley, Sherman B.   Open Air Crusaders.

7. Lea, Frederick S.   American Journal, Public Health, v. 2. No. 2.

8. Public Health, Dept. of Health, Michigan, Dec., 1911.

9. Putnam, Helen C., M.D.   Child Welfare Magazine, v. 7, No. 4.

10. Kingsley, Sherman B.   Report National Ed. Assoc., 1911.

11. Rice, Allen G., M.D.   Boston Med. and Sur. Journal, May 29, 1913.

12. Snow, Wm. G.   Furnace Heating Manual, 1909.

SESSION THIRTY-EIGHT

Room E.   Monday, August 25th, 2:00 P.M.

SYMPOSIUM ON CHILD LABOR

Arranged by the National Child Labor Committee

Owen R. Lovejoy, General Secretary

E. N. Clopper, Ph.D., *Chairman*

Dr. Edwin A. Bowerman, Buffalo, N. Y., *Vice-Chairman*

Program of Session Thirty-eight

Ira S. Wile, M.D., Member of the Board of Education, New York City. "The Relation of School Hygiene to Industrial Hygiene."

George A. Hall, Secretary New York Child Labor Committee. "The New York Law and Physical Examination for Working Papers."

E. N. Clopper, Ph.D., Superintendent of Children's House of Refuge, Cincinnati, Ohio. "Effects of Street Trading on the Health of School Children."

Leonard P. Ayres, Ph.D., Director of Division of Education, Russell Sage Foundation, New York City. "Medical Inspection in School, a Factor in Improving the Health of Working Children."

THE RELATION OF SCHOOL HYGIENE TO INDUSTRIAL HYGIENE

BY

IRA S. WILE

The constructive value of instruction in hygiene is rapidly permeating our school systems. The hygienic facts accumulated during the past 15 years are fraught with greater significance for the welfare of the world than the accumulation of knowledge during any other similar period of our history. While some progress has been made in disseminating hygienic information to adults, the importance of prophylactic education for the coming generation has not impressed itself sufficiently upon curriculum makers. The stress of present day methods has been placed upon securing a hygienic environment for abnormal children.

The rational processes of education suggest that the hygienic training of normal children should be the paramount issue in hygienic education to promote future communal welfare. Recognizing school hygiene, as at present constituted, to be inadequate in example and instruction, it becomes important to consider how hygiene may be related to the life of activity for which elementary school education is the preparatory institution.

Bulletin No. 4, 1911, of the United States Bureau of Education, states: "There is an increasing feeling that this subject should be closely allied to the demands of modern life; particularly is this true in courses of study for city children who live in congested districts." Assuming the position that the teaching in hygiene should be related to the occupations into which school children enter, it becomes important to know the early industrial activities of boys and girls upon leaving school.

The New York City Bureau of School Census in 1911 reported the nature of the work begun by boys and girls after leaving school. While this study involved only 25,000 children, it is fairly indicative of the early industrial activities of New York school children. This report showed the following to be some of the main industries to receive more than one hundred workers, totalling 22,781: Errand boys, house work, clerks, machine operators, feathers and feather dusters, bookkeepers, tailors and tailoresses, dressmakers, seamstresses, stenographers and typewriters, hair dressers and hair goods, paper box makers, neckwear, artificial flowers, drivers, printers, confectioners, newsboys and newsgirls, leather workers, cleaners and sweepers, and fur workers.

The principal industries, which received less than one hundred workers, totaling to 1692, were paper hangers, plasterers and plumbers, elec. tricians, machinists, tobacco and cigar makers, pressmen and lithog. raphers, dyers and cleaners, masons, painters and decorators, brass workers, mechanics, carpenters, bakers, laundress and laundry workers. The main occupations receiving less than twenty workers, totaling 292, were engravers, iron workers, wood polishers, compositors, upholsterers, hostlers, stonecutters, coppersmiths, photographers, and sorters.

The relation of occupation to mortality does not require elaborate discussion at this time. It is suggestive to learn from the census report of 1908 that for the decade 25 to 34 years, carpenters and joiners, bakers and confectioners, machinists, bookkeepers, clerks and copyists suffer a mortality from typhoid fever that is above the normal rate for all occupations. For a similar decade, pneumonia possesses an unusually high mortality for laborers, draymen, hackmen, brick and stone masons, iron and steel workers, dressmakers and seamstresses and servants.

The mortality from accidents falls with particular force upon steam railroad employees, miners and quarrymen, iron and steel workers, engineers and firemen, carpenters and joiners, farmers, planters and farm laborers, and teachers in school.

Pulmonary tuberculosis, the dread white plague, attacks with greatest oppression compositors, printers and pressers, farmers, gas and steam fitters, tailors, servants, clerical workers, barbers, laundresses, mill and textile factory operatives, machinists, painters, glaziers and varnishers, draymen, hackmen and teamsters, dressmakers and seam. stresses.

Bright's disease of the kidneys is particularly noted in the mortality of blacksmiths, machinists, plumbers, tailors, clerical workers, hack. men, boot and shoe makers, barbers and hair dressers, laborers, masons and laundresses. I have selected these particular diseases as indicative of the general groups of infectious diseases, diseases of exposure, acci- dents, diseases of environment, and general diseases.

The striking fact immediately presents itself that the occupations with unusually high mortality are included as the principal occupations into which boys and girls go in large numbers. This to be sure, is based merely upon a single investigation in New York City, though the study of the general occupations considered may be regarded as fairly representative of urban conditions throughout the country.

The relation of school hygiene to industrial hygiene is equally patent from a study of the occupations or from a study of the mortality or morbidity figures.

Accidents themselves are frequently due to youth as has been shown in the statistical reports available. In Minnesota the general accident rate was 27.56 per thousand workers while under 16 years the accident rate was 70 per thousand. The factory inspectors in Michigan, 1906, evidenced an accident rate of 2.3 per thousand for workers 16 years and over, with a rate of 4.5 for workers under 16 years. Similarly, in Pennsylvania, among fatalities to slate pickers the accident rate was found to be 300% more for boys under 16 years than for pickers over the age of 16 years. The enthusiasm of youth, the thoughtlessness, the carelessness, the bravado, the playfulness, the restlessness and the immaturity, make the employment of children at band saws, planers and power presses dangerous. Similarly youthful workers are subjected to unusual liability to accident from gears, belts, set screws, and moving machinery.

Industrial diseases from the use of alcohol, the handling of lead in many industries, as mining, pottery, and painting, the glare of light and the power of heat in the glass industry, the irritations from dust and dirt in upholstery and sorting, represent the results of occupations wherein the morbidity of children is preventable. Industrial diseases may be generally grouped as due to the following causes.: 1. Metal poisons; 2. Toxic gases, vapors and fumes; 3. Toxic fluids (acids, alkalies, etc.); 4. Toxic or irritant dusts; 5. Organic germs. Not alone are these specific forms of industrial irritants harmful, but there are an environmental hazards due to variations in air pressure, temperature, humidity, and light. As far as industrial poisons are concerned there are three modes of entry into the human body: 1. The mouth and digestive system; 2. The respiratory system; 3. The skin.

In recent discussions relating to employers' liability and workingmen's compensation insufficient force has been laid upon the legislative measures necessary to secure the installation of protective devices by employers. Almost all figures relating to industrial accidents and diseases indicate that there is a wide range of education essential in order to secure the coöperation of employees in protecting themselves from the hazards of industry. Scarcely any employment may be said to be wholly free from danger. The education in industrial hygiene should not be left entirely to the employer nor should the community shift the burden of hygienic instruction upon commercial institutions which supply the means of living alike to employer and employee. The responsibility of the community for the existence and continuance of industrial accidents and diseases makes it necessary to attempt the educational processes through established educational institutions at public expense.

The danger of wood alcohol poisoning from the handling of varnishes, polish and dyeing materials may be lessened by attention to ventilation on the one hand and personal cleanliness on the other.   \

The arsenic poisonings in the mines and foundries, the glass industry, printing, dyeing, wall paper manufacture, taxidermy, tanning, making of artificial flowers may be lessened through the removal of gases and dust on the one hand and by scrupulous personal cleanliness on the other.

The harmful effects of chromium from dyeing and printing, match manufacture, photographic work and the handling of aniline colors may be abated through frequent bathing and the protection of the nose.

Lead poisoning with all its unpleasant manifestations from the handling of lead pipes, lead colors and paints, and lead alloys may be prevented largely by washing the hands and the face, cleansing the mouth, and brushing the teeth, attention to the bowels, abstinence from alcohol and the cessation of eating, drinking and smoking in the work room.

From this enumeration of the methods of prevention of a few industrial diseases, it is obvious that hygienic measures form the bulwark to withstand the attack of industrial poisoning. It points out strikingly the relation between hygiene that should be taught in the schools to the practical hygiene of industrial life.

The wide extent of defective teeth suggests the importance of giving instruction in dental and oral hygiene, impressing the need of careful mastication, the use of the tooth brush, the value of the correction of dental deformities and the relation of the teeth to malnutrition and metallic poisonings.

Many sedentary occupations result in poor posture and weak chests such as are conducive to pulmonary disease. It is necessary to inculcate good postural habits during school life so that they may offset the disadvantages of the sedentary indoor occupations of cigar makers, weavers, bookkeepers, engravers, cobblers and tailors. The habit of deep breathing through the nose, the assumption of proper attitudes when sitting and standing can be firmly fixed through school hygiene so as to constitute a valuable asset during industrial life.

The pulmonary diseases are frequently induced by the dust and the extremes of temperatures and humidity in foundries, glass works, laundries, grinding establishments, masonry and the sorting of rags and hides. The preventive measures involve the necessity of school discussion of the correct methods of breathing, the care of the sputum, the danger of infections by direct contact, the dangers of dust and the importance of skin ventilation. Obviously children predisposed to irritations of the throat or lungs should be discouraged from entering upon such vocations until their physical condition renders them safe. The enlarged glands so frequently found during childhood are often indicative of tuberculous infection or predisposition. Taking advantage of this theme, the school may advantageously devote attention to the general hygiene of environment, the value of fresh air, the nature and methods of ventilation, the danger of overcrowding, the germ theory of disease, the value of open windows and abundant food. These are practical measures which will tend to lessen pulmonary mortality in irritant industrial pursuits.

Various industrial callings require severe strains or sudden stresses for which the body is unprepared and as a result the heart dilates and the usefulness of a worker is impaired. In order to lessen the baneful influences of the stressful occupations the hygienic problems of the school period must consider the vascular system, the relation of exercise to heart action, the dangers of overstrain, the advantages of physical education and the importance of economy in muscular activity, the relation of fatigue to endurance. All these themes are designed to protect handicapped workers so as to prolong their activity in the industrial world. It is readily understood that sufferers from cardiac disease should not be placed in a position carrying with it a responsibility for the lives of others.

Defects of vision or the loss of one eye demand careful attention to the occupation for which the worker is fitted. Eyestrain under such conditions should be avoided lest eyesight be further impaired or the remaining eye suffer from sympathetic irritation or inflammation with blindness as a possible result. All the defects of vision show the necessity for further teaching the importance of adequate illumination, the dangers from contagious eye diseases, the relation of optical defects to general health and the damages that occur to vision as a result of industrial accidents and diseases.

The skin is subject to many irritations, particularly among bakers, laundresses, and hide handlers. By inference, the topic exacts instruction as to the hygienic value of bathing, the nature and effects of various types of baths, the use and abuse of soaps and the importance and value of individual towels. The place of the skin in absorption of industrial poisons and the relation of the free action of the skin to freedom from industrial disease, constitutes this topic as of more importance than many of the themes now dwelt upon in schools.

Furthermore the problem of shoes for the prevention of flat feet; the necessity of well-fitting and proper clothes to lessen the danger from belts and gears; and the influence of alcohol and tobacco upon the susceptibility of the worker to industrial disease and accident, challenge the thought of careful instructors of school hygiene

That there is need of the type of instruction which I have thus far indicated, it is only necessary to call your attention to the fact that during 1911 the medical inspection in New York City of 282,463 children revealed only 75,369 children free from the physical defects sought by the medical inspectors. There were 7,913 children with malnutrition,

1,167 with tuberculous lymph nodes, 2,227 with heart disease, 798 with pulmonary diseases, 3,800 with skin diseases, 1,514 with orthopedic defects, 28,884 with defects of vision, 2,854 with defects of hearing, and 162,962 children with defective teeth. This marked evidence of the nature of the defects that exist in our school population indicates the type of remedial hygienic instruction which is essential for the correction of such physical defects.

During the period of life from 10 to 19 years, which covers the period of early industrial activity, we find an immediate gain in mortality from tuberculosis, epilepsy, acute endocarditis, organic heart disease, the pneumonias and the diseases of the kidney. This is partially due to a lack of knowledge of the prophylactic hygienic measures which serve to prevent the diseases.

It is unfair to allow a child to enter industrial life without any knowledge of its inherent hazards. It is a thoughtless policy to omit teaching the best methods of safeguarding health and welfare during the years to be devoted to self-support. Industrial hygiene involves information regarding the dusty trades or the beast or burden trades. It unfolds the dangers from metals, dusts, gases, and fumes, the importance of protective devices and guarded machinery, the horrors of belts, gears, and saws. The adjustment of a boy to his labor is of immense hygienic importance. The impression upon the child mind of self-control, caution and the spirit of coöperation should be part of the training of every child. Furthermore, in considering the accidents, it might be well to institute instruction in first aid to the injured.

From the standpoint of the protection of employees, it is well to teach the hygiene of hours of labor and the hygiene of rest, to give knowledge regarding sanitary regulations as far as they pertain to air, light, cleanliness, washrooms, toilets, cuspidors, drinking water and seats for women. The question of food is not to be overlooked; and the importance of pure milk, pure water and the best types of food with their variation according to the seasons and the severity of occupation might easily be taught. Naturally there arise the questions revolving about individual glasses, cups, and towels. Saito's experiment has shown that the bulk of soluble dust poisons enter the system through the alimentary tract. The importance of nasal breathing becomes evident, likewise, the necessity of abstention from eating and drinking in the workroom.

In the manufacturing and the mechanical trades Hoffman has shown that 18.8% of the total mortality arises from tuberculosis. This disease also expresses itself in the ill health of some workers in the open air trades, particularly the street industries. Bootblacks and newsboys suffer from irregular habits of eating and sleeping and the bootblacks particularly develop serious chronic difficulties which predispose them to pulmonary diseases.

Industrial hygiene is obviously linked to home hygiene. The problems of city and house congestion, the problems of ventilation and unsanitary homes, immorality, intemperance, ignorance of home economics are related to industrial life. A lack of ability to apply the hygienic precepts to home life is reflected in the environment of the factory, the shop, or the workroom. Practical hygiene as applied to the various affairs of every day life should be taught. The course in school hygiene should make children conscious of their civic duties and develop a spirit of social hygienic responsibility. Thus industrial hygiene is related to civic hygiene. Industrial hygiene should tend to keep minors out of injurious trades. The least that can be done is to open the eyes of school children to the variations in the degree of healthfulness of various occupations and industries.

Dr. Ludwig Teleky has already indicated that physical development goes on rapidly until the 17th and 19th year. The statistical investigations of tuberculosis and industrial accidents show that children of 14 to 15 years of age are unequal to the demands of industrial labor. Except for rare exceptions, industrial labor should be prohibited for children under 16 years of age. These physiological facts should be given to the children that they may appreciate that the protection of their health is the fundamental basis for legislation of this character.

A closer relation between school hygiene and industrial hygiene would be possible through the correlation of the medical inspection of school children to their adaptibility for industrial life. In the upper grades of the school, physicians should be available to advise children with regard to their adaptability to specific vocations, in order that they may not rush into employment for which physically they are unfitted.

The school system affords abundant opportunity of correlating theoretical hygiene to practical hygiene. Every child upon entering school should be supplied with a card of health. It should go through school with him. When he is sick the card should be checked, when defects are noted, they should be stated on the card, when corrections of defects are made or when unwillingness to correct exists, the card should indicate it. In addition, there should be stated thereon the yearly record of height and weight. Upon leaving school each child should receive a copy of this health record to serve as his medical certificate for securing working papers. The general types of industry for which he is unfitted might be indicated [upon his working papers so that a employer would be able to protect himself by carefully questioning the applicant to ascertain his real adaptability for the specific employment. Furthermore, the child himself would be protected in entering upon industrial life, prejudicially to his health, providing of course, that the health suggestions were carried out.

The relation of school hygiene to industrial hygiene should be exceedingly close. Teaching of school hygiene should be based upon the practical use that is to be made of it. A large portion of life is spent in occupation, wherefore, the importance of the industrial hygiene cannot be gainsaid. If public schools are to prepare for citizenship, it should aim to prepare citizens conscious of their hygienic duties and sanitary responsibilities. An intelligent, trained, industrial citizen is an asset worth possessing. He protects himself and he protects the community. The cost of teaching industrial hygiene is a negligible amount compared with defraying the expense due to failure to prevent the **avoidable industrial** accidents and diseases.

THE NEW YORK LAW AND PHYSICAL EXAMINATION
FOR WORKING PAPERS

BY

GEORGE A. HALL

Child labor legislation in the United States may properly be said to have had its beginning in the school attendance laws of certain of the New England States enacted during the period 1836-1847.

It was not, however, until after a lapse of three decades that provisions as to age of employment, hours of work, or educational qualifications began to appear in the laws of more than half a dozen states. Since 1879 such enactments in various states have increased yearly, and the number of states showing gains since 1894 has more than doubled. Dr. William F. Ogburn* has given us a most illuminating discussion of the development of these statutes during this period—1879-1909. His data (brought up to date by the writer) is based upon a careful study of more than 500 enactments and furnishes us exceedingly significant facts regarding what might be termed the drift of child labor legislation in this country.

Prior to 1879 the chief emphasis seems to have been placed upon the length of the working day or week—twelve states having regulations on this subject. Provisions as to age of employment and educational or school attendance qualifications appear to have received less attention—only seven states showing enactments in each of these groups, while but five states at that time required working papers for children. In 1913 we find (including the District of Columbia as a State) that 49 have age requirements, 46 have hour provisions, 44 prescribe educational standards, and a like number demand working papers. But not until in the half decade ending 1884 does one find any state (and then but one) requiring a health certificate as a prerequisite for work. After 34 years, furthermore, only half of our states have passed any law upon this subject.

It may be enlightening to note in passing that among the states on the black list of those entirely neglecting in their laws the physical fitness of its children for work are such industrially important states as Illinois, Pennsylvania, North Carolina, and Virginia.

The character of the legislation in the states which seek to see that

*Monograph. "Progress and Uniformity in Child Labor Legislation." Submitted 1912 in partial fulfillment of requirements for the degree of Doctor of Philosophy, Columbia University.

only those physically fit go to work differs considerably. In most states applicants for working papers must merely satisfy the issuing officer that they have reached the normal development of children of their ages, and that they are in sound health and physically able to perform the work they intend to do. The inadequacy of such legislation ob_viously lies in two directions—first, the lack of uniform standards as to what is the *normal development* of a child of its age, and second, the difficulty with a majority of applicants in being able to state the nature of the job they hope to find. That such a provision, however, is not necessarily valueless is testified to by the work of certain health officers.

A conspicuous example of this is found in the manner in which Dr. George W. Goler, Health Officer of Rochester, New York, has been giving thorough physical examinations for working paper applicants during the past eight years. In 1909 an excellent card was put in use to record the results of these examinations. Special consideration was given to the child's diseases and age at which contracted, and the condition of the teeth and throat. Diagrams on the reverse side of the card enabled the medical examiner to indicate readily the actual conditions observed. Under this system more than 10% of the 1,600 applications during 1909 were temporarily refused.

Unfortunately, however, experience has shown that the enforcement of such a provision in too many instances is a mere form. In one of the larger cities in New York State a glance at one of the old reports—covering 1906 and 1907 shows that in that city where more than 20,000 children during each of those years were granted working papers, the refusals for physical incapacity numbered four for one year and five for the other. The writer has witnessed physical examinations of a kind which might be described in the following conversation: Doctor: "Well, Sissy, you're a good looking girl. How much do you weigh?" Girl: "95 pounds." Doctor: "That's about what I thought. Now, how tall are you?" Girl: "I don't know." Doctor: "Well, I guess I can hit it pretty close. You stand up there against that door. Now, I should say you are about five feet tall; anyway, that's near enough." A cursory looking the child over completes this farcical examination.

Other states provide that the officer issuing the working paper *may* demand a physician's certificate of physical fitness before issuing the employment certificate. Such a plan is open to the first mentioned objection and adds another evil—that of imposing upon the issuing officer discretionary authority in a matter of vital concern to the applicant. When the child's future usefulness to himself and to society is at stake should such an officer or the state be the deciding authority as to whether a child's physical fitness for work should or should not be considered? Experience moreover has demonstrated that the most effective labor laws are those containing clear cut definite provisions. Or, as Mrs. Florence Kelley has most aptly phrased it, "the less the discretion the more the enforcement."

The provision in effect in a few states of requiring the presentation of a certificate of physical fitness from the Board of Health or from a physician designated by such Board has more in it to commend itself. Under this law at least all children receive some sort of physical examination, which in a majority of cases may be expected to be fairly thorough. All of these provisions, however, even if conscientiously carried out have in them an inherent weakness—the lack of any uniform method in making a physical examination. Such laws inevitably result in as many standards or methods of examination within the same state as there are physicians who make these examinations.

New York State until 1912 had only the generally indefinite provision that children not of a normal appearance might be given a physical examination. The weakness in such a statute was brought to light in the testimony taken by the New York State Factory Investigating Commission during the winter of 1911. Along with others the writer called the attention of the Commission to the perfunctory manner in which these physical examinations were being conducted in some places, and urged the importance of writing into the statute some definite standards to aid in determining more satisfactorily the physical fitness of children for work. In this Commission's report we find the following recommendation: "The Commission recommends the amendment of the Labor Law to provide for a thorough physical examination of the child by a medical officer of the Department or Board of Health before a certificate is issued, and for the transmission of duplicate records of the result of such physical examination to the Department of Labor."*

These recommendations were enacted into law without opposition, the new amendment taking effect October 1st, 1912.

In compliance with this duty the then Commissioner of Labor, Hon. John Williams, prepared a form for this purpose. In this form obviously lies the kernel of this law's usefulness. The Labor Commissioner was given practically unlimited powers regarding what should go into the blank. It was recognized, however, that the form to be generally workable throughout the State must not be too complicated or detailed. Furthermore, only such equipment as would be as readily available in a hamlet as in a city could be properly required. With these considerations in mind, and after seeking suggestions from prominent physicians, specialists in children's diseases, health officers and social workers, the form now in use was devised and distributed throughout the state.

*Report of New York State Factory Investigating Commission to the Legislature of 1912. Vol. I. Page 107.

The blank was planned to require a minimum amount of work upon the part of the health officer who is directed in the law to file the original record in his office and the duplicate with the Labor Commissioner. These ends were readily accomplished by using ordinary carbon paper and a book in which the forms are printed in duplicate, the original or top sheet being of thin paper, especially suitable for use with carbon paper. Another important advantage of this plan is the elimination of a certain percentage of error which invariably occurs in transcribing records. As an economy in time and effort the principle was followed as far as possible of indicating the desired information by check marks. Only a minimum amount of writing is therefore required. As a result, with the assistance of clerical help to enter the answers upon the blank—the practice in New York City—it has been found that a child can be completely examined in five or six minutes. This includes the time occupied in loosening the dress or blouse for the heart and lungs examinations. Reports from health officers in other places indicate that working without assistance an examination consumes from 10 to 30 minutes. A study of a filled out blank given below shows that the main physical features of the working paper applicant are covered. Much other interesting data might have been called for but it was thought best, however, to ask a report on only a minimum number of essentials. The form, therefore, calls for data on the following points: Child's name, address, and date of birth; eye-sight, eye diseases and hearing; height, weight and pulse rate; condition of teeth, heart, lungs, and pharynx; manner of breathing; neck glands, anaemia and hernia; condition of speech; spine and joints; skin diseases and goiter; vaccination and father's nativity.

Each eye is tested separately, using the Snellen Test Card. Hearing is tested with an acumeter. The Labor Commissioner warned Health Officers of efforts of some children to increase their weight by heavy substances in pockets or elsewhere about the person. In the New York City working paper office an accumulation may be seen of many pounds of lead, shot, and other heavy articles taken from the pockets of applicants. No attempt is made to go thoroughly into the condition of the teeth other than to indicate whether good or bad, the latter meaning marked decay. Heart sounds are observed with a stethoscope over the bared skin excluding hemic murmurs. The pulse rate is taken at the wrist with the child seated. Record as to hernia is based on answers to inquiries merely—not an actual examination. In order that the reports filed might be of the fullest possible value, particular care was taken by the Labor Commissioner to send to each health officer (the authority in New York State who issues working papers) detailed instructions with a filled out blank explaining exactly how the form was to be used.

But even the most careful work of the medical examiner may be

NAME _Ladislawa Bennwka_ ADDRESS _77 Butler St_ DATE OF BIRTH _5/31/99_

BOY ____ GIRL ✓

RIGHT							/LEFT					
20	20	20	20	20	20	20	20	20	20	20	20	20
20	18	16	14	12	10		18	16	14	12	10	

(FOLLOW TEST PRESCRIBED BY SNELLEN)
EYE SIGHT (SIZE OF PRINT READABLE AT 20 FEET)

_5_ FT. _1_ IN.
HEIGHT IN SHOES

ANY ACUTE EYE DISEASE — NO ✓ — YES (KIND)

RIGHT / LEFT

14	14	14	14	14	14	14
14	12	10	8	6	4	
14	14	14	14	14	14	14
14	12	10	8	6	4	

TESTED ✓ STOP-WATCH AND ACOUMETER AT 14 FEET
HEARING

WEIGHT _96_ POUNDS
TEETH (CONDITION) GOOD ✓ BAD

HEART SOUNDS (TAKEN WITH STETHOSCOPE ON BARED SKIN EXCLUDING HEMIC MURMURS) NORMAL ✓ ABNORMAL

CONDITION OF PHARYNX—PALATE

PULSE (RATE) _64_
LUNGS (ABNORMALITY IN EITHER SHOWN BY AUSCULTATION AND PERCUSSION OF CHEST) RIGHT—YES — NO ✓ LEFT—YES — NO ✓

MOUTH
BREATHING NONE

CONDITION OF PHARYNX—PALATE

GLANDS (NECK) YES — NO ✓
ANAEMIC YES — NO ✓
HERNIA YES — NO ✓ (REDUCIBLE) (TRUSS WORN) YES — NO

SPEECH NORMAL ✓ STUTTERS

VACCINATED (HOW LONG AGO) YES ✓ — NO
SKIN DISEASES (SCABIES) YES — NO ✓ (RINGWORM) YES — NO ✓ (IMPETIGO)

GOITER YES — NO ✓

SPINE YES — NO ✓ (SCOLIOSIS) YES — NO ✓ (KYPHOSIS)

CONDITION OF	SHOULDER	ELBOW	WRIST	HIP	KNEE	ANKLE	HAND	FOOT
NORMAL	✓	✓	✓	✓	✓	✓	✓	✓
LIMITED								
ANKYLOSIS								

BIRTHPLACE OF FATHER _Poland_

ABNORMALITIES NOT ELSEWHERE MENTIONED _Defective Vision_

Disapproved

Approved Defect Corrected June 2 1913

Dr. V. McClure (SIGNATURE)

DATE OF EXAMINATION _May 31 1913_

FOR DEPARTMENT OF HEALTH OF _Buffalo_ (CITY, VILLAGE OR TOWN)

Buffalo EXAMINING PHYSICIAN

RECORD OF PHYSICAL EXAMINATION—FORM 118. 12-4-12 50 000 (30-196)

DUPLICATE OF THIS RECORD TO BE SENT TO COMMISSIONER OF LABOR IN EVERY CASE materially impaired or nullified by improper surroundings. For example, the difficulties are obvious of trying to test the hearing accurately when the examination room windows open upon a city street where heavy trucks constantly rumble by over cobblestones. A primary requisite to the best work is a separate examination room. As a means of securing quietness, privacy, and freedom from excitement and other distracting influences common to the usual crowded city working paper office, a special room devoted to the work is most essential. This has already been recognized in the larger cities in New York State, and it is to be hoped that the others will soon make similar provisions.

Some persons predicted serious opposition when the law first went into operation. Health officers, however, report but few instances where objection has been raised either by the child or the parents. Undoubt. edly school medical inspections in our larger cities account in a large degree for this attitude, while the anxiety to have the children secure their working papers will cause them to go to almost any length of trouble or inconvenience. In New York possible objection on the ground of having girls examined by male physicians has been overcome in a com. mendable manner by assigning a woman nurse (usually in uniform) to assist the physician.

It is interesting to learn that in the city which acts as our host to-day excellent work with respect to the physical examination of working paper children is being carried on. A splendid equipment, with a separate examination room well located, point to the desire of the local authorities to care for the health of its children who must go to work. Buffalo also is to be congratulated in the manner in which it gives to the public regular information on this subject. Its monthly bulletin contains a very interesting summary of the work of the Division of Child Labor, the statistics including the number of physical examinations, the number refused, with the nature of physical disability, and the physical conditions of all children examined. This plan of reporting physical examinations might well be emulated in other cities.

A few of our health authorities are realizing that their responsibility does not cease with the physical examinations. The children rejected because physically unfit, they point out, should receive special attention so that their defects may be remedied. This has been recognized in Rochester since 1906. Children excluded because of defective dentition, tonsils or adenoids are given free treatment if the parent is unable to pay for it at a dispensary of the Public Health Association. Recently in New York City an arrangement has been made to have referred to school nurses for after care treatment, certain of the children rejected because physically unfit, particularly those suffering from malnutrition or anaemia. Through public and private agencies many of them have thus been materially aided to improved health by a few weeks or months' stay in the country, or by providing eye glasses for them. It is to be hoped that all our large cities will soon make some systematic provision for the after care of physical refusals.

Duplicate physical examination blanks have been coming in monthly to the Labor Commissioner's office from all parts of the State. After the close of the first year of their use, the Bureau of Statistics of the Department plans to make a tabulation of this data, with a view to publishing a report on the subject. On October 1st, 1913, when the year ends, there will be probably over 50,000 of these blanks filed. One city alone—New York—will undoubtedly file at least 40,000.

Pending this tabulation, through the courtesy of the Department of Labor, the writer has been permitted to examine and tabulate 1,800 of these blanks. The object of this study was two-fold—to find out how the law was actually working, the defects in the blank or its use, and secondly, what the physical characteristics were of the children examined.

An examination of these 1,821 filled out blanks reveals a general compliance with the instructions as to the manner of entering the data. The percentage of evident error or irregular method in filling out the records is encouragingly small. Moreover, the statistics viewed from the light of medical experience seem to show that the method of examination was uniform, as was intended. Slight variations show up in different communities, probably due to the difference in character of children examined, to difference in degree of thoroughness of the examination, or to the special interest of some medical examiners in particular subjects, such as hearing, vision, or dentition.

The statistical study discloses, however, the folly of asking for certain information or requiring certain methods of examinations. For example, when the figures show 42% of the 1,821 children had bad teeth, i. e., showed marked decay, such a fact is undoubtedly correct, but that the other 58% had good teeth, is open to serious question, especially in the light of other statistics. The fault lies in the instructions leaving it to the discretion of the examiner that when teeth showed "marked decay," they were to be recorded as "bad." Again the figures as to spinal trouble are of little practical value because of the difficulty of discovering real conditions without removing the clothing. Similarly, answers to the question as to the prevalence of anaemia undoubtedly greatly understate real conditions which could only have been accurately found out by taking a blood test. Less than 1% of anaemia (as shown by the statistics) among these children, many of whom live under impoverished conditions in our large cities, clearly does not tell the whole story.

Discussing only a few of the items recorded (as time will not permit a full summary) it is interesting to note that the percentage of children with normal or next to normal vision and hearing was high—75% for the former and 87% for the latter. In the case of vision the test presumably represents corrected conditions in many instances (as nothing was said in the directions about removing glasses). The height or weight statistics also show that a majority of the children had the development usually found in a 14-year-old child. 71½% of boys and 66% of girls were over 95 and 98 pounds weight respectively—Burk's figures for children 14½ years old. As to stature our statistics show that 76% of the boys and 81% of the girls were five feet or over. While the percentage of children showing heart abnormality or lung trouble is small, two-fifths of 1% having heart irregularities, and 1% abnormal lungs, the discovery of even 25 children with such defects seems to us well worth while. Only 53 or 3% of the children are reported as mouth breathers. This small number probably does not represent all such, as when under examination many children would unconsciously shut the mouth when usually mouth breathers. Enlarged tonsils were found in 6% and glands in neck in 3% of the total. The figures as to tonsils are probably also an understatement. Approximately 2% of the children had goiters.

In spite of local regulations in most of our larger cities, it is surprising to find that 9% had never been vaccinated.

A high degree of normality as to pulse rate was found as well as a general absence of eye or skin diseases or joint abnormality. But 15 stutterers and 5 children with hernia appear in these records.

Taken altogether, the first nine months' operation of this law seems to indicate a fair degree of thoroughness in the examination, as reflected in the recorded data. With closer supervision—possibly next year under a new law giving the Labor Department supervisory power over the issuance of working papers—even more may be accomplished.

What are the results thus far of the operation of New York Law? In the first place practically all children granted certificates for factory work during the past nine months received a physical examination. Heretofore but a small percentage were given what might properly be called by such a name. Moreover, the examination, which covered more ground than ever before, was practically uniform in character and in method. Furthermore, careful records of all the examinations filed in a central place are available for study. Previously records of examinations were rarely made and never filed with one State authority.

These results alone (while important in themselves) would have been disappointing to the framers of the law unless attended by another improvement. The main question is: Did the law prevent a larger number of physically unfit children from going to work? The statute itself contains no new provision specifying under what conditions a child should be refused for physical incapacity. It was believed, however, that the new law's emphasis upon the physical condition of working paper applicants would automatically react in favor of withholding more certificates from those physically weak. It is therefore gratifying to find that the results seemed to bear out this forecast. In New York City—six months' operation of this law shows that 324 as against 206 for the corresponding period the year previous, were refused for this reason. Thus 118, or 57% more children were saved from going into factory work because physically unfit.

Such, briefly stated, are the main features of the New York Law and its results. It is recognized that nine months is too short a period to judge accurately of the effect of any new statute. It is interesting, however, and not without significance to review the accomplishments for even so short a period. But what of the future of this work? Is it to stop with the present law and procedure in making and reporting physical examinations? The *first* forward step has been taken in the providing of machinery whereby *all* children may be assured of a uniform examination. But this alone is clearly not enough. Replying to a query as to whether there had been an increase in refusals because of physical disability, one health officer says: "We have no regulations regarding causes of rejection of child because of defect," and he recommends a "limit of defect or regulation permitting refusal because of certain defects." In other words, he would like to have some minimum standard adopted by the Department of Labor or by the Legislature to guide him in his decisions. This raises the question: Is is possible to establish a minimum physical standard which all children must reach as a prerequisite for working papers? In New York City, where immigration makes for a large variety of nationalities, physical variations, particularly in stature, constantly show themselves in the children applying for employment certificates. The local Health Department has adopted as a tentative standard a minimum weight of 80 pounds and a height of 58 inches. Failure to measure up to this standard is not sufficient cause alone for rejection. It serves, however, as a useful danger signal, showing that the child's physical condition demands further attention. This is accomplished in part through another examination by a second physician. Many children not up to this standard have been issued working papers if the double examination failed to disclose evidence of malnutrition, anaemia, or other serious physical defects.

As a layman the writer does not presume to say whether or not any minimum standards can be drawn up for placing in the law. Some more definite guide, however, than the 1912 law, as an aid to deciding when a child should be rejected as unable physically to go into industry, seems eminently desirable. It is possible that criteria other than height and weight will be found more serviceable as an index of the child's physical fitness for work.

It is most important to remember that rejection for physical troubles is in no sense final. If, for example, the child's teeth are in a serious condition, withholding working papers on that score would be a matter of but a few days' delay while being attended to. The underlying basis of all child labor legislation lies in the protection of the health and welfare of children, because they are wards of the State. Yet the State is constantly failing to fulfill this obligation when it allows children to go to work handicapped, perhaps for life, by some serious physical defect.

At all events, it is earnestly hoped that the Labor Department's tabulation of these physical examination blanks, together with the interest in this subject of health officers, physicians and social workers, will ultimately result in the securing of some workable standards which may be enacted into law.

Until then, the New York Law may be rightly called a good first step toward real protection of the health of our children who go to work. May it not also, in conjunction with our age and schooling requirements, result in helping to bring about the entire elimination of child labor at least under the age of sixteen years.

EFFECTS OF STREET TRADING ON THE HEALTH OF SCHOOL CHILDREN

BY

EDWARD N. CLOPPER

The term "street trading" as applied to the economic activities of children in our public thoroughfares, is unfortunate. It implies widespread commercial freedom and fosters the common impression that all children who engage in such work are "merchants" who have invested their tiny capital and are earning money on their own account, subject to the despairing fluctuations of profit and loss, and are therefore entitled to the moral support that honest, independent effort should always command. This is not the fact. The newsboy or peddler who is employed by an older person and sells his wares on commission or for fixed wages, is quite as common as the lad who sells for himself alone; the itinerant bootblack who goes about with his own equipment slung over his back, has almost disappeared and in his place we have ill-paid Greek boys stationed at a "stand" whose earnings and even tips form the proceeds of the padrone who conducts the establishment; and the child who tends a market-stand from morning until late at night, is the hireling of adults. Hence, this child labor in the highways and byways of our cities would better be known as *street work*, which is a far more comprehensive term than *street trading*.

Among all the many and varied gainful activities of children, street work occupies a distinctly inferior position with regard to desirability, yet in the progress of child labor reform it is one of the last to meet with consideration. The figures of the last federal census relative to the occupations of children are not yet available, but anyone endowed with ordinary powers of observation knows there are thousands of diminutive workers in the streets of every large city, and the few who have given the subject careful thought realize that the physical, mental, moral and material effects of prolonged labor of this kind, under conditions necessarily hard, and in an environment inevitably sinister, are markedly bad. Social workers have testified before official boards of inquiry that newsboys and other juvenile street laborers often suffer from physical exhaustion, chest troubles, permanent hoarseness and loss of voice, although not necessarily of weak constitution for a mass of evidence has been submitted showing that strong, healthy children were injured in this way by sheer excess of fatigue. If street work could be kept within moderate bounds and the child were well-fed and clothed, the physical effects of such labor, if performed for only one or two hours daily in addition to attendance at school, would not be harmful but long hours, undue exposure and over-exertion are sure to result in serious injury. It would seem that work in the open air would invigorate and strengthen the children, but the irregularity of their habits combined with malnutrition and the bad conditions under which they live and work, counteract this benefit, causing deterioration of physique. Indeed, under the present methods of conducting these street activities the children are not afforded much of an opportunity to enjoy the beneficial effects of out-door exercise because, as a rule, they do not run about and consequently are deprived of the exhilaration that follows free movement in the open air. This is true of the newsboy who stands hour after hour on the corner or on the spot he controls in the middle of the square; it is true of the bootblack who cannot leave his chair; it is true also of the child behind the market-stand who is on his feet in one position for weary periods. Such stationary employment is not exercise, and the constant standing on hard city pavements tends to break down the arches of the feet and result in the painful lesion known as "flat-foot."

Witnesses testifying before the British Departmental Committee of 1910 relative to the injurious effects of the exposure to inclement weather endured by juvenile street workers, declared that pulmonary disease was manifest in many such children who had been physically sound before they subjected themselves to the rigors of the street. Others who had had the opportunity to contrast street workers with children in inside employment, testified that the two classes could be easily distinguished because of the inferior physique and nervous tension exhibited by the former. The head resident of a settlement which devoted special attention to newsboys said, "We had a football club but the boys, while active enough for a short period, had no stamina and were too light in weight to stand against boys of like age from a working-class community. Several cases have come under my notice of newsboys being rejected by the army recruiting officer owing to their physical unfitness."

The studies of Dr. Thomas of the London County Council's Education Department, have shown that with respect to newsboys who attend school, the physical effects of their work become intensified as the period of time devoted to it increases. For the purposes of his research several hundred typical London newsboys were thoroughly examined while stripped to the waist. The time given to their work out of school by these boys was divided into three groups and progressive deterioration was found under the following headings:

Time Per Week	Fatigue	Anaemia	Heart Strain	Nerve Strain Nervous Complaints	Deformities Chiefly Flat-foot
Under 20 hrs.	60%	19%	none	16%	none
20 to 30 hrs.	70%	30%	5%	35%	10%
Over 30 hrs.	90%	73%	27%	37%	10%

The fatigue was found to produce an effect on the muscles and in loss of voice and in facial expression.

The irregularity of newsboys' meals and the doubtful value of their food constitute one of the worst features of street work and are a real menace to health. Most newsboys are in the habit of eating hurriedly at lunch counters at intervals during the day and night, while others snatch free lunches in bar-rooms. The use of mild stimulants is common and the demand for them is to be expected because of the nervous strain consequent upon the work. Liquor is not consumed to any appreciable extent by these children, but coffee is a favorite beverage; in large cities where "night gangs" are found, from four to six bowls of coffee are usually taken by each boy in an evening. Tobacco is used in great quantities and in all its forms; many boys even appease their hunger for a time by smoking cigarettes and the smallest "newsies" are addicted to the habit.

Work at unseasonable hours is most disastrous in its effects upon growing children, and the occupations of peddling, newspaper-selling and market-tending engage the labor of boys in our larger cities at all hours of the night. Newsboys are in some instances up all night so as to assure prompt service to patrons. In the absence of public opinion in the matter this abuse flourishes unrestricted and the children's health is sacrified to meet the insistent demand for news and vegetables. The very early rising of young newsboys to deliver the morning editions also contributes to the impairment of their health. The old adage is a mockery in their case. The early morning delivery of newspapers and milk has been declared by medical inspectors to be quite prejudicial to the well-being of boys because of the fatigue it occasions.

John Spargo states that the proportion of newsboys who suffer from venereal disease is alarmingly great and that those who are committed to reformatories are, on the average, one-third below the ordinary standard of physical development—a condition which will be readily appreciated by those who know the ways of these lads, their irregular habits, scant feeding, secret vices and unwholesome manner of living. With such a low physical standard, the ravages of venereal disease are tremendously increased.

The testimony of Sir Lauder Brunton, M.D., given on the occasion of the inquiry into physical deterioration in Great Britain, is to the point in his statement that "one of the very worst causes is that children in actual attendance at school, work before and after school time."

The records of 230 newsboys attending school in this city of Buffalo showed 18% truants, 23% ranking very low in attendance and deportment, and 28% below the minimum requirements for promotion as against only 15% among the other children. The percentage of retardation in school among the street working children of other cities has been found to vary from 15% to 20% in excess of that of the other pupils. There are, of course, other factors which contribute to bring about this condition, such as malnutrition and ill-health, but there can be no doubt that the evil effects of this work are in large measure responsible for the poor showing made in the schools by the children who follow such occupations. Their business experience sharpens their wits in a way, but associated with this advantage there is developed a distaste for application to school work, an inattention and restiveness which robs the child of his power to concentrate his mind upon school tasks and consequently he loses interest in them. The independence of street life renders the discipline of the school irksome and this distaste is intensified by the toxin of fatigue. The combination of these factors often brings about the failure of the child in his studies and so serves to augment the retardation of pupils in our schools. But this vaunted sharpening of the wits, which is the great desideratum in the opinion of those who favor street work for children, is merely another term for the development of commercial cunning. It is not a quickening of the intellect, but rather a training in the tricks of the trade and a not altogether desirable asset. In fact, the earnings and other alleged advantages of street work are not commensurate with the sufferings of the child, for deterioration of one kind or another is strikingly apparent in most boys and girls who have pursued street careers and been exposed to such bad environment for any length of time.

What is to be done?

There is no reason why newsboys—by far the most numerous of street workers—should not be displaced as the medium for the sale and delivery of newspapers by old men, cripples, the tuberculous and those otherwise incapacitated for regular work. It has been demonstrated in other countries that children are not essential to this industry; in fact, it has been shown that selling at stands or kiosks and the use of men instead of boys are both feasible and satisfactory. There is no reason why such practices could not be introduced into the United States. In addressing the convention of the International Circulation Managers' Association held at Cincinnati last June, Mr. Charles Scholz, circulation manager of *The Milwaukee Sentinel*, declared that in the sale of newspapers much better results could be secured from the use of recognized news-stands on the principal street corners of a city than from newsboys, and that in New York and Chicago, where special exception had been made in favor of news-stands to the exclusion of all other stands, the circulation managers of newspapers were greatly in favor of the elimination of the shouting "newsie." There can be no doubt as to the advisability of this step, but the change will certainly not be effected to the extent required by either the children or the newspapers. The law must force the issue by prohibiting street work under a certain age, which should at least correspond with the minimum age for employment in factories, shops and errand service.

Because legislation is an ever-ready agency it is the most generally used remedy for social maladies. Our passion for quick action and our demand for instant results make legislation our most effective specific. But too often our quick action is based upon a fragmentary conception of conditions. We do not wait until we gain a comprehensive knowledge. We see a certain state of affairs that should not exist and a law is promptly enacted to abolish it. The common drinking cup suddenly came under the ban, but evil methods of supplying the drinking water, which is quite as easily contaminated, remain undisturbed. The need of some kind of help for poverty-stricken families is observed and at once a mothers' pension bill is passed without any consideration of other means of relief already provided. The spirit of opportunism governs social reform.

Social legislation as applied to industry has sought primarily to control the relation between employer and employee. It has been concerned largely with prohibiting the exploitation of the latter by the former. "Thou Shalt Not," stands between these two factors of production to protect the one from the encroachment of the other. This is true of our laws on child labor; they prohibit merely the *employment* of children by others within certain limits. The child may not sell or give away his labor to another person but he may use his own labor for his own purposes in any independent pursuit as he sees fit, no matter what his age. There is really no child *labor* law—there is only a child *employment* law, for there is practically no restriction upon the work of a child on his own account. He shall not be exploited by another, but he is free to exploit himself. In order to enjoy the state's protection he must abandon independent work and seek only the hire of an employer. This curious circumstance is due simply to the persistence of an old idea—the arrogance of custom. The freedom of our child street merchants is a remnant of the long and jealously guarded independence of capital; great scope has been allowed the capitalist in the past to encourage the establishment of new enterprises, and despite recent attacks and agitation much of this freedom of action is still uncurtailed. But the new theory of restraint has not yet been applied to the child capitalist except in a few isolated cases and there only to a very limited extent.

This singular neglect of the child trader as compared with the relative wealth of protection bestowed upon the child employee is due, in other words, to the old economic distinction between profits and wages. We have held that the wage-earner was at the mercy of his profit-seeking employer and that for the good of society the weaker must be shielded from possible abuse of the stronger. At the same time the entrepreneur enjoyed the utmost latitude for the investment of his capital and the creation of new industries, for this was held necessary for the development of our great natural resources and the promotion of national prosperity. It has never occurred to us in our snug satisfaction with the established order of things, that any but a wage-earner needed protection nor that there could be any element of the capitalistic class that might be injured by this very essential feature of freedom. Thousands upon thousands of tiny capitalists and employees have daily thrust themselves upon our attention in city streets, and insofar as we have given them a passing thought in our hurry to get by, we have placed upon them the stamp of our tacit approval—still under the spell of the old idea—upon the snap-judgment that they were all in the category of profit-seekers. We have regarded the little newsboy, bootblack and peddler as miniature captains of industry, taking the first step up the ladder of fortune in their embryo self-made career. As such, complete freedom of operation was their right, and God speed the future rulers of the land! If all these lads and lassies had been doing the same work but as wage-earners in the pay of employers, what a protest would have been made long ago against such an abuse of childhood!

This faulty construction of the body of our social law is the result of defective vision. The eyes of society suffer from hypermetropia. Its sight is adjusted to objects in the distance. The average citizen knows more about the national than about his local government; more about the policies of his state than of his county. And in reform, what would seem to be most obvious is frequently overlooked while efforts are bestowed upon the correction of evils more clearly seen because not so closely associated with the general life of the community. The one outstanding fact is made the object of attack regardless of correlated conditions. So has it been with child labor restriction. The public conscience was stirred at first by the wretched plight of children in mills and mines— their misery could be readily imagined and appreciated because they were conspicuous on the horizon, far removed from the daily life of the average man, and at length the protecting arm of the commonwealth was stretched forth to guard them against ill-usage. Through all this agitation, however, throngs of young children were being exploited for gain in the retail shops under the very eyes of multitudes of customers whose wants they supplied; and at every hour of the day and for half the night other hosts of little boys and girls were crying their wares in the public streets, jostled about by the crowds that took no heed.   Then in the course of time, the social vision readjusted itself, the focus shortened and the shop-workers loomed into view, and were granted the same measure of protection earlier afforded the factory children.   At a still later period, such legislation was made to apply to hotels, business offices, bowling alleys and other establishments.   But all these prohibitions affect the child only so far as his employment by others is concerned— he is still at liberty to exploit himself.

And now the community needs a new lens, one that will accommodate the social vision to all conditions, bringing into view the myriads of children at work in our city streets, at once the most familiar and the most neglected of the army of child laborers, for whom as yet there is no place in the protective economy of our labor laws.

MEDICAL INSPECTION IN SCHOOL A FACTOR IN IMPROVING THE HEALTH OF WORKING CHILDREN

BY

LEONARD P. AYRES

Thirteen years ago the school superintendents of America, assembled in convention in Chicago, discussed the problems then foremost in educational thought and action. Diligent search through the printed report of that meeting discloses no single mention of child health, no word about school hygiene, no address devoted to the conservation or development of the physical vigor of youth.

At that time eight cities in America had systems of medical inspection in their public schools. To-day the number of such systems is nearly 700. This development is without parallel in the history of education. No one there present had ever heard of a school nurse, for no city in the world employed one; but to-day over 100 American cities have corps of school nurses as permanent parts of their educational forces. Had anyone in that Chicago meeting dared prophesy that we should soon employ dentists to care for the teeth of our school children, his words would have been greeted with derision; but to-day nearly 100 cities employ staffs of school dentists.

Twelve years ago, those who discussed the problems of educating the mentally deficient, the blind, the crippled, and the deaf, thought and talked only from the standpoint of treatment in special institutions. But to-day New York City alone has in her public schools 150 classes for mentally deficient children, with ever-increasing provision for the other classes of unfortunates, and the work there is merely a sample of what is going on in the cities throughout our land.

These changes represent no passing fad or temporary whim. They are permanent, significant, and fundamental. They mean that a transformation has taken place in what we think as well as in what we do in education. They mean that the American common school has ceased to be merely a place where for a few brief years our children shall acquire useful information. Instead, it has entered upon a new rôle, in which it is destined to reach, and to reach profoundly, the whole of every child. These changes mean that in ever-increasing measure our schools are to reach the exceptional child as well as the normal, and are to make provision for his physical well-being as well as for his intellectual development.

This profound change in our educational practice did not come through the slow processes of philosophy, nor because we were awakened by the stirring words of voice or pen of any educational prophet. No schoolman can claim great credit for having hastened its advent. It was forced upon us, first by the natural results of compulsory education, and still more definitely and directly by three of the strangest allies that ever contributed to the work of social reform.

The First Reformer—The Child with Contagious Disease. The first of these three reformers was the child with contagious disease. When Boston began medical inspection in America in 1895, by dividing her schools into fifty districts and placing a doctor in charge of each district, she did so in the hope that the new measure would curb the waves of contagious disease that repeatedly swept through the ranks of the children, leaving behind a record of suffering and death. The experiment was successful, and when the other cities learned how Boston was solving the problem, they too began to employ school physicians and organize systems of medical inspection.

During the first years, the spread of the movement was slow, only one or two cities taking it up each year. Then these pioneers were followed by dozens of their sister cities, then by scores, and in the past few years by hundreds.

This sudden recognition of the imperative necessity for safeguarding the physical welfare of our children grew out of the discovery that compulsory education under modern city conditions meant compulsory disease.

The state, to provide for its own protection, has decreed that all children must attend school, and has put in motion the all-powerful but indiscriminating agency of compulsory education, which gathers in the rich and the poor, the bright and the dull, the healthy and the sick.

The object was to insure that these children should have sound minds. One of the unforeseen results was to insure that they should have unsound bodies. Medical inspection was the device created to remedy this condition. Its object was prevention and cure. But it was destined to have far greater influence than its early sponsors dreamed.

As school men watched the doctors discover and send home children suffering from contagious disease, they asked whence those diseases came. They examined their records of absences, and they discovered that in nearly every city the number of cases of contagion among children leaps up each year when the cold weather approaches, and the children return to school to sit quiet in close contact with their fellows, to drink with them from the same cup, and breathe dust-laden and artificially dried air. And when spring returns the windows are again opened and schools are closed for the summer, those who are left go forth to be comparatively free from disease until the return of the next school year.

Schoolmen pondered these facts well, and now in city after city schoolhouses are being constructed in which the paramount object is to have the rooms so clean, the drinking water so pure, the air so fresh, and the sunlight so plentiful that compulsory education shall no longer spell compulsory disease, but rather, compulsory health.

The sanitary drinking fountain and the individual cup are fast driving out the common and dangerous tin dipper. Sixty-nine cities already clean their schools with vacuum cleaners, and the days of the broom and the feather duster are numbered. We are nearing the day when our schools will be as clean as hospitals and for the same reasons.

Nor is it only within the four walls of the school building that provision is steadily being made for conserving health and developing vitality. The only educational movement that ever approached medical inspection in the rapidity of its development is the playground. Almost unknown ten years ago, it is now becoming as much a part of the modern school as the roof or the walls.

The movement for public school athletic leagues is spreading from city to city, and carrying with it the knowledge of how to give every boy and girl the physical advantages through exercise that were formerly reserved for those already so well endowed that they did not need them.

The child with contagious disease has done well and thoroughly his work of educational reform. The health movement in our public schools has been transformed during the past decade from a merely negative movement, having as an object the avoidance of disease, to a splendidly positive movement, having as its aim the development of vitality.

The Second Reformer—The Backward Child. The second of the strange allies that came to help us reshape our educational doctrines and practice was the mentally deficient child. We discovered that the dragnet of compulsory education was bringing into our schools hundreds of children who were unable to keep step with their companions, and because this interfered with the orderly administration of our school systems, we began to ask why these children were backward.

The school doctors helped us find the answer when they told us that hundreds of these children were backward purely and simply because of removable physical defects. And then we took the next great forward step, for we came to realize that children are not dullards through the will of an inscrutable Providence, but rather through the law of cause and effect.

This led to an extension of the scope of medical inspection to include the physical examination of school children with the aim of discovering whether or not they were suffering from such defects as would handicap their educational progress and prevent them from receiving the full benefit of the free education furnished by the state.

This work was in its infancy five years ago, but to-day more than 200 cities have systems of physical examination of their school children.

Nor was this the only contribution of the backward child. Along with the knowledge of the importance of physical defects came the realization that compulsory education lays a deep obligation on the state as well as on the parent. If it is to insist that every child shall attend school, it must provide schools fitted to the needs of every child. It is in response to this realization that throughout the land public schools are opening their doors and fitting their work to the peculiar needs of the blind, the deaf, the crippled, and the mentally defective. It is in response to this realization, too, that we are at last beginning to make special provision for that still more exceptional and vastly more important group made up of the children of special talent and even genius.

Just as the work begun with the object of excluding disease from the classroom has developed until it is now redounding to the benefit of all school children, so the special provisions devised for dealing with the backward child have developed and expanded until they now bid fair to benefit the children who are not backward.

Teachers, principals, and superintendents have watched the splendid work of the special classes in giving education to children who formerly were doomed to lives of uselessness to themselves and deep menace to the community. And as they have seen the seeming miracles these classes perform, they are asking why the same measure of small classes, skilled teachers, play, manual work, and abridged courses of study should not give even greater results among normal children.

The Third Reformer—The Tuberculous Child. The last of the three allies in the work of educational reform was no other than the great white plague—tuberculosis. In 1907, the city of Providence started an open air school for tuberculous children. During the following year two other cities followed her example. The third year five cities had open air schools. To-day the new work is being done in more than sixty.

In city after city across the country open air schools have demonstrated their ability to take pale, wasted, and sickly children and convert them into strong, vigorous, and healthy children. And, moreover, they have proven their ability to teach these ailing children faster and better than the regular schools in the same cities can teach the strong and normal children.

And school men, reading the lesson so clearly taught, are asking why all children should not be allowed to breathe pure air. In answer to their question school architects and heating and ventilating engineers are discarding their traditional ideas of ventilation, and are even now constructing school buildings with the avowed object of bringing to every boy and girl the advantages heretofore reserved for the tuberculous.

Keeping For the Strong the Benefits Developed for the Weak.   These three reformers—the child with contagious disease, the backward child, and the tuberculous child—have done their work well, and that work is not the mere provision for the needs of sick and exceptional children; it is the fundamental re-shaping of our educational aim.

For nineteen centuries the educational world has held, as the most perfect expression of its philosophy, that half line of Juvenal in which he pleads for the sound mind in the sound body.   It has remained for the first decade of the twentieth century to awake to a startled realization that Juvenal was wrong—wrong because he bade us think that mind and body are separate, and separately to be provided for.

Only now we have come to realize the error and to take steps to rectify it.   Only in the last few years have we begun to see that, educationally at least, mind and body are inseparable, and that the sound mind and the sound body are inextricably related—both causes and both effects.

All these things mean that it is our splendid privilege to see and to be a part of a movement which is profoundly transforming our traditional ideas of education.   They mean that our children and our children's children will be a better race of men and women than are we or were our fathers.

Public School True Instrument of Eugenics.   In recent years there has appeared a new science, calling itself eugenics, that seeks to discover the secrets of heredity and environment, and to develop methods that shall insure for future generations greater strength, more vitality, and enhanced intellect.   The aims of that new science are high and noble beyond those of almost any other form of human activity, but in their methods its advocates are wrong.

They are wrong when they seek to apply to the breeding of men the lore of the stock-breeder, because they overlook the deepest and most fundamental factors in man's nature.

What they are aiming at is the steady improvement of the human race, and that is coming.   But it is coming through the public school of the future; the school in which the physical, the mental, and the moral will be developed together and not separately; the school in which the child will not only live in healthy surroundings, but in which he will learn habits of health which will be lifelong.

child, and the tuberculous child.   Because of these lessons, th
the future will attend a school in which health will be contagi
of disease, in which the playground will be as important as
and where pure water, pure air, and abundant sunshine will
and not privileges.   He will attend a school in which he wil
to be either truant or tuberculous or delinquent or defective
best and fullest measure of education.

SESSION THIRTY-NINE

Room C.   Friday, August 29th, 2:00 P.M.

SYMPOSIUM BY SOCIETY OF DIRECTORS OF PHYSICAL EDUCATION IN COLLEGES,

PAUL PHILLIPS, M.D., *Secretary.*

PAUL PHILLIPS, M.D., *Chairman*

ARTHUR S. HURRELL, Buffalo, N. Y., *Vice-Chairman*

Program of Session Thirty-nine

DUDLEY A. SARGENT, M.D., Sc.D., Director of Heminway Gymnasium, Harvard University, Mass. "Indirect Training."

FREDERIC A. WOLL, B.S., M.A., Department of Hygiene, College of the City of New York. "The Value of an Objective Method in Testing the Vision of College Students."

ALBERT D. PINKHAM, M.A., B.Pd., Physical Director. "Outline of Hygiene Instruction in the Ethical Culture School, New York City."

FRANK W. WHITE, M.D., Professor of Physiology and Hygiene, Kansas State Normal College. "Student Housing and Sanitation; Methods of Inspection and Administration."

MAX GUTTMAN, M.D., Vienna, Austria. "On the Nearer Carrying Out of the Plan Decided Upon in 1910 for Taking Measurements of the Human Body." '(Manuscript not included.)

WALLACE A. MANHEIMER, B.S., Teacher of Physical Training, Commercial High School, New York City. "Sanitation of Indoor Swimming Pools." (Manuscript not included.)

ARTHUR M. BUSWELL, M.A., Assistant Sanitary Engineer, Colu
University, N. Y., and

W. W. HAVENS, Student Columbia University. "Liquid Chl
Versus Bleaching Powder as a Disinfectant for Swimming Po
(Joint paper.)

GEORGE L. MEYLAN, B.S., M.A., M.D., Associate Professor of Phy
Education and Medical Director Columbia University,
York. "A Study of the Physical Condition of Five Hun
College Students."

W. G. ANDERSON, M.D., D.P.H., Professor and Director Yale Unive
Gymnasium, New Haven, Conn. "The Teaching of Hyg
in Several of the Departments at Yale University." (M
script not included.)

INDIRECT TRAINING

BY

D. A. SARGENT

Dean Briggs in his annual report as chairman of Harvard's Athletic Committee makes the following quotation from the Yale *News*. "At West Point, where the daily practice lasts about forty-five minutes, Yale football teams have twice in succession been outplayed, outfought, and sent home—branded with defeat." The same might be said with equal truth of the athletic records of the Springfield Training School for Men and the Sargent Training School for Women. These institutions accomplish better results with less time devoted to direct practice of special sports than their foremost rivals. What are the reasons? You will naturally say that the schools at West Point, Springfield, and Cambridge are professional schools for which the students are carefully selected and put through a system of all-round physical training as part of their technical education, that fits them to excel in any kind of physical exercise or athletic sport.

If this is true the best way to prepare an athlete for excellence in a specialty would be to give him a broader and more extensive training instead of a narrower and more intensive training as is the tendency at the present time. This was the ideal of the ancient Greeks, and the system of classical education long carried on in many of our schools and colleges was founded on this theory of education.

The rapid advancement of science, the multiplication of trades and industries, and the general expansion of the whole field of knowledge, have made it absolutely necessary for a young man, who would educate himself for service, to concentrate his efforts while in school and college, and finally narrow himself down to some chosen specialty. Recent experience, however, has shown that unless the student was well grounded in certain well chosen, fundamental studies he soon reached his limitations in any specialty that he chose to adopt. The young man who ignores the classics, in order that he may devote more time to modern languages, soon finds that he must go back to his classics, if he would excel as a scholar in French, German or English. So the enthusiastic student of chemistry soon finds his advancement hampered unless he is well grounded in physics. The modern physicist cannot make much progress unless he is well up in mathematics. So the students in medicine, law, politics, or business must all hark back to certain primary

or basal studies in the field of general knowledge, if they would hope
to lift themselves much above the average in their chosen professions.

Studies in the languages, mathematics, physics, chemistry, biology,
history, political economy, etc., though fundamental in importance,
are generally looked upon by the student as of indirect value compared
to the specific work of a life calling. For this reason many a student
is inclined to loaf through school and college and reserve his enthusiasm
for his specialty be it business or a profession.

The evils of this method are now being quite generally recognized
in academic circles and the thoughtful students are entering with more
zeal into these indirect or preparatory courses.

The importance of indirect training as a preparation for excellence
in athletics has not received the attention it deserves until within a comparatively recent period. The young aspirant for athletic honors soon
chooses some specialty wherein he is likely to excel and devotes all his
zeal and energy to the practice of this one sport. Not infrequently
the selection of this specialty is determined by the young man's peculiar
build of physical qualifications. Thus it has been found by experience
that men of long thighs and slender arms make the best middle distance
runners, while those of shorter and more muscular arms and legs are
more likely to excel in short distance running. The star hurdlers and
jumpers usually have short bodies and long legs, while the oarsmen do
better with long bodies and relatively short legs. The weight throwers
must necessarily be large and heavy in trunk and limbs; the gymnast
strong in his arms, chest and shoulders; the wrestler in his neck, arms
and chest, shoulders and back; while the long distance or Marathon
runner has been found to be below the average athlete in size of trunk
and limbs. These are some of the natural physical characteristics
that distinguish different types of athletes, and render those having
these qualifications more likely to excel in special branches of sport.

But in the light of our present day knowledge of science and athletics
we now know that it is possible for a young man to excel in some forms
of sports without the natural qualifications that are possessed by the
expert, provided he has the good sense together with the energy, determination and persistency to bring all of his hitherto unused powers
into action.

In response to the keen competition now going on in athletics as in
all other human achievements, new methods are constantly being discovered, and old records are gradually yielding to the application of
science to sports as well as to business.

Let us trace the evolution of some of the events in modern athletics
and see how science and indirect training have contributed to their
perfection. Take for instance, the running high jump. The old style

was to run straight at the bar, curl the feet under the body while it was held in a perpendicular position, and land back to the bar. With this style of jumping, four feet six inches was a very good height to clear, and the ability to do so depended greatly upon the strength and spring in the legs and the swing of the arms upward. Another style was to run at the bar from the side and throw the legs straight forward and the arms upward so as to make what is termed the scissors jump. It was found that a tall man with long legs and a comparatively short body could usually jump higher by this method, than a tall man with a long body and comparatively short legs. The tall man soon learned that by straightening out his body and legs so as to make them more nearly parallel with the bar he could clear the bar at a much greater height, but that he usually landed on his back. This was the style in which the first 6-ft. high jump in modern times was made by M. J. Brooks of Oxford, England, in 1877. This style of jumping, although effective in clearing a greater height than had hitherto been cleared was neither pleasing to the spectator nor comforting to the performer.

The next style of six-foot high jumping was that worked out by W. B. Page and M. F. Sweeney. Page approached the bar like a panther and his take off from both feet was from a crouching position, so low that his knees and hands almost touched the ground. As he leaped into the air it was like the uncircling of a spring. He threw his feet over the bar, then turned adroitly on his side so as to avoid hitting the bar with his arm or shoulder, straightened out both trunk and limbs and landed on his feet facing the bar. Sweeney approaches the bar with a circular run and as he takes off from his left foot swings the right one violently into the air and turns just as he is above the bar, so as to land, facing the bar on the same foot from which he took off. Both Page and Sweeney use their arms, legs and body vigorously, not only in getting the elevation from the ground but in making the turn above the bar.

Now anyone who has carefully observed different contestants in high jumping must have noticed that the height attained did not depend so much upon the elevation of the head as upon that of the trunk and legs. As a matter of fact the height the head is raised varies little in different jumpers. The art of high jumping consists in getting the legs, hips and body as high as the head, and recovering one's equilibrium so as to land upon the feet. This is what Brooks of Oxford tried to do, but he, like most of the other "scissors" jumpers who attain great height invariably landed on his back. It remained for Horine, the young man from the Pacific slope, who beat the world's record in high jumping last year, with a jump of 6 feet 7 inches, to show us the desired method. Horine approaches the bar from the side in very much the same style that Brooks and Sweeney do, but just as he takes off from the ground, on the foot nearest the bar, he not only throws his legs, hips and trunk high in the air but swings his arms violently upward, sideward and backward in such a way as to carry his head and shoulders above the bar first, then as he straightens his body and legs, he fairly rolls over the top of the bar, so as to land on his feet—sometimes on hands and feet—but always face downward. Thus we see that in the evolution of the high jump, it is no longer a matter of developing only the legs and thighs, as was once thought, but that the muscles of the arms, chest, abdomen, shoulders and back are all necessarily involved in the final effort.

No one can doubt for a moment but that Page's training in long distance bicycle riding, Sweeney's training in general gymnastics, and Moffat's training in rowing were all contributing factors to the excellence which they later attained, as specialists in high jumping. Take another athletic event, for instance, the pole vault. Back in the seventies and eighties when the attainment of a height of 9 or 10 feet was considered a remarkable performance it was customary to train for pole vaulting by developing the muscles of the arms, chest and abdomen. Climbing the peg pole, going hand over hand up a rope, practicing "chinning" one's self with one arm, raising the feet while lying on the back, and all forms of gymnastics that would tend to strengthen the muscles of the upper part of the body, were thought to be the most desirable as a preparation for record performances in this event. Indeed, inasmuch as it was necessary to lift the feet, legs, and trunk over the bar by main strength it was deemed advisable to keep the lower extremities as light in weight as possible. Tom Ray, an Englishman, who was one of the first men to make a record of eleven feet, was accustomed to go hand over hand up the pole while it was poised perpendicularly. This method was prohibited at a later date. In 1887, when Ray's records were made, the full value of the run had not been considered. In fact the size and weight of the poles used made rapid running impossible. With the introduction of the lighter poles made of spruce or bamboo, the value of the run began to be more highly appreciated. Anyone can see how the speed with which one runs is a very important factor in the running broad jump but how running contributes to the attainment of greater height in the high jump or pole vault is not at first as apparent. It all depends upon the ability of the jumper to convert the speed and impetus of the run into an upward movement that will add to the height of the jump. This is why jumping from a block or inclined plane is more effective than jumping from a dead level. Moreover, the effect of the run upon the height of the jump depends very much upon the method or style assumed by the jumper. C. R. Fearing of Boston, who frequently used to jump over six feet from a level floor, ran only ten or twelve feet to his take off, which, however, was from a crouching position in which the muscles of the arms, chest, back and shoulders, were brought into powerful action. In pole vaulting the height of 12 and 13 feet now attained depends largely upon the speed and impetus of the run, supplemented by the spring at the take off, and the swing of the body forward and upward over the bar.

When it is considered that in vaulting a height of 13 feet a man who weighs 150 pounds does work enough to lift a weight of 2,000 pounds a foot high, in a few seconds, it will readily be seen that the force and energy necessary to accomplish this feat must be generated through the run and that the muscles of the entire body are involved in the final effort.

Thus it is evident that in the pole vault, as in the running high jump—two highly specialized athletic events—the ability to excel must ultimately depend upon the all-round development of the performer.

Did the time permit I think I could readily show that the same condition holds true of the shot putter, hammer and discus throwers, broad jumper, rowing man and football player. Even in as one sided an exercise as fencing I doubt if the winners in to-day's contests will be found one sided in their development.

If we look for good substantial reasons for this symmetry in development often possessed by experts who practice one sided or special sports and exercises, we will find them in the recent discoveries of anatomical and physiological sciences. Those of us who have made physical examinations have often noticed the inability of athletes to add to the girth of a particular group of muscles, like those of the forearm or calf, for instance, by localized exercises, after these muscles have attained a certain size. Why? Because here a balance of the coöperating formative forces has been reached. Larger muscles, or more muscle fibres, demand more connective tissue, arteries of larger calibre, and thus a heart of larger size.

Thus according to the observation made some time ago by Parks, the only way to develop the muscles of the calves, after they have reached their limit, is to exercise the muscles of the arms and trunk. In other words, when local groups of muscles have reached their highest point of efficiency, the only way to make them still more effective is to bring other groups into action which will improve the condition of the heart and lungs, and thus tend to reconstruct and improve the whole organism. Another way of accounting for this peculiar phenomenon of muscular activity is by what is termed the "all or none" theory.

In experimenting with the heart Bowditch discovered that the normal heart always contracted to its full limit at every beat, that is, always did its best. This is not true of other muscles as a *whole*, but Keith Lucas of the physiological laboratory of Cambridge, England, has found that it is true of the individual fibres of each muscle; when he makes an ordinary effort he uses only a few of these muscle fibres; when he makes a greater effort he brings still more fibres into action; but it is only when he makes extraordinary effort that he brings into play all the fibres of a single muscle and this very rarely occurs. The remarkable performance of a Sandow and other professional strong men and athletes may be accounted for by this "all or none" theory. By making tremendous muscular efforts day after day, they not only use more of the fibres of individual muscles but they gradually extend this action to a greater number of muscles. This was especially true, as I have shown, of Page, Sweeney and Horine in the high jump and would be equally true of many of the record pole vaulters, shot putters, discus throwers, etc.

Still another theory which is now being rapidly accepted would account in a measure for the remarkable performances of special athletes. This is Sherrington's theory of the "unification of the brain and nervous system."

The old theory used to be that special feats and exercises were executed not only by certain localized groups of muscles, but were presided over by certain localized brain centers.

Sherrington has shown conclusively that in making great physical efforts, as in making great mental efforts, the whole brain and nervous system may be involved.

Another theory, and perhaps the most important of all, is that advanced by Sherrington and supplemented by Dearborn of Tufts Medical School and Woodworth of Columbia University. This may be termed the Synergetic theory, or the theory that the body, as a whole, is involved in a universal nervous action continually.

It is well known that the contractile power of each individual muscle is always limited by the resistance of antagonists, which prevents the muscle being contracted, more than a third of its possible extent, that is possible when there are no resistances to be overcome. Sherrington maintains that there is a negative or inhibitory innervation in groups of muscles which are functional antagonists. Thus the highly specialized athlete learns from repeated practice not only to bring more muscles to his assistance but to get a greater amount of contractile force out of those muscles by inhibiting the contraction of those which are naturally antagonistic to them.

The synergetic theory also considers the expenditure of nerve force involved in maintaining an equilibrium in all the different postures and movements called forth in executing a difficult athletic feat, as well as the force involved in furnishing a fundamental base or purchase from which the different groups of muscles may act that are more immediately concerned in the special stunt or exercise.

Thus do the teachings of science gradually verify and confirm what so many of us have long accepted empirically. The Greeks, the Germans and the Swedes have shown their wisdom in adhering to their system of all-round physical training and even our highly specialized American athletes are beginning to realize the value of adopting a wider range of physical exercises as a preparation for their special events.

The important lesson to learn is that it matters little in what sport or exercise you engage if you enter into it with zeal, energy, vigor and enthusiasm. In so doing you will feel the effects in every fibre of your being, and in return will be able to throw yourself with greater power into whatever you undertake to do. With this comforting assurance you should enjoy all of the sports in their seasons, thus avoiding the drudgery and monotony of too close confinement to a single specialty and thus also making every sport in which you engage a means of indirect training for the one in which you would excel.

THE VALUE OF AN OBJECTIVE METHOD IN TESTING THE VISION OF COLLEGE STUDENTS

BY

FREDERIC A. WOLL

It has long been known to all eye specialists that to depend upon a subjective eye test such as is made with the test type for the determination of the amount and kind of refractive error present is not only misleading in the result obtained, but also wholly unsatisfactory in so much as the nature of the ametropia is not uncovered. That is to say, an individual may have defective vision, but the test for visual acuity will not at all determine whether the error of refraction is due to myopia, hyperopia, astigmia, or a combination of these errors of ocular refraction. To be sure it is not at all necessary in the course of medical inspection to know what the ametropia is. If the test shows that vision is impaired, the student should be sent promptly to an eye specialist, but the fact remains that it is part of our work to find the defects, and then advise the student to consult the specialist so that proper measures may be taken to relieve abnormal existing conditions. So far then as marked errors of ocular refraction are concerned, the test type is sufficient for us to find abnormalities. But, when small quantities of astigmia, hyperopia, or myopia are present, the test type is well nigh valueless because visual acuity is hardly effected. Nevertheless, it is these small quantities that cause the greatest annoyances to the student and are the direct cause of a large number of so-called eye reflexes.

Students in college or even in the high school or grades must necessarily use their eyes more during the school year than at other times. The days during the school year include the shortest days of the year. To work by artificial light is necessary. This artificial light is not always of sufficient power nor in a place where it will give the best illumination. Also there are many days that are dark and the light in the classrooms may be dim. On such days there is an additional tax put upon the students' eyes.

For the individual with perfect eyesight and good health, such conditions may not bring about more than just temporary inconvenience, but to the slightly hyperopic or hyperopic astigmatic eye, an additional strain on the eyes is added and this brings about the many reflexes that are so often found among those whose vision seems perfect when the test card is used. In fact, with the test card, a slightly hyperopic eye may register even better than perfect vision, thus throwing the examiner completely off his guard.

Why perfect visual acuity may be registered when using the test type card and still be done with an imperfect eye, can be easily understood if one knows the anatomy and physiology of the eye. It may be well to say here that when directed toward objects situated at infinity a perfect eye will focus the incident or parallel rays of light emanating from the object upon the retina with no physical effort nor strain. In other words, the normal eye adapted to view distant objects will be at perfect rest. Or, again there should be no other interocular activity than the physiological phenomenon necessary to register the incoming light which results finally in what we call sight.

When an object is situated within infinity, the emanating rays of light from that object are divergent and therefore take longer to come to a focus than do the parallel rays of light refracted through the same medium; hence such rays of light would come to a focus back of the eye if it were not for the accommodation being called into play; thus the power of accommodation comes into play only when near objects are viewed.

In the hyperopic eye, however, in order to get clear vision, this power of accommodation must also be used for distance, and when a near object is focused upon, the accommodation must be correspondingly increased. Thus the accommodation is active all the time. In the slightly myopic eye, clear vision is obtained by squinting. In either case the test type may not uncover the refractive error. Therefore, an objective method, one in which the examiner can for himself see what the conditions are, would seem to be a proper method to use in order to be able to give the student the best advice concerning his vision and the care of his eyes.

Skiascopy suggests itself as being the objective method to use. It is unnecessary for the examiner to do more than determine whether there is or whether there is not an error present. It is unnecessary for the examiner to know more than that the "shadow" moves "with" or "against" the mirror.

By following the methods of Cross of New York as explained in his book "Dynamic Skiascopy," one will be enabled to uncover a great many low errors of refraction and often anticipate the occurrence of eye reflexes. For instance: If a student is 18 years of age, is in the freshman class in college, and shows an error of refraction by the aid of the skiascope and the test cards give the vision as normal, the examiner will at once know that that acuity of vision is gotten at the expense of nerve energy. He may say to that student "so long as you have no headaches, no trouble reading, writing, or studying, you need not bother about your eyes, but there appears to be a small error present and as you get older and you advance in college and the demand on your eyes increases, you may begin to experience headaches, a dry sandy feeling in your eyes, a desire to avoid bright lights and sun light, it may be well for you then to consult an eye specialist and receive from him something in the way of so-called resting glasses."

Our experience at The College of the City of New-York has been that many of the students we have examined and advised in this way, will return to us later and say that they had gotten glasses within six months or a year after our advice had been given and that they are now working comfortably using their glasses only for their near work. Some of them begin by wearing their glasses for near work only, and as latent errors become manifest, wear their glasses all the time.

Hence, an objective method seems to be of great value, because:

1. You can determine whether normal vision is secured with or without intrinsic muscular effort.

2. It makes your examination worth more to the student because if there is an error you can give advice which will forewarn the student.

3. It makes your examination worth more to yourself because it brings about increased accuracy in your own work and increases the efficiency of your medical inspection.

4. It gives you definite information which you can record.

5. You can make a diagnosis independent of the student's intelligence or his evidence.

OUTLINE OF HYGIENE INSTRUCTION IN THE ETHICAL CULTURE SCHOOL, NEW YORK CITY

BY

ALBERT D. PINKHAM

So much has been said in this convention on what can and ought to. be done both for the normal and abnormal child that some may receive· the impression that but little is being done; that from a hygienic stand-point pupils of our schools are being sadly neglected. This may be true in some cases. But however much may remain undone, there are schools which are endeavoring to do what seems at present to be necessary for the welfare of their pupils, and I believe the Ethical Culture School of New York can be included in this classification. We may be groping in the darkness but we are seeking the light. Dr. Anderson has told you of what is being done at Yale University for the welfare of the student body. I am going to tell you as briefly as possible what is being done in 'the way of hygienic instruction and applied hygiene at the Ethical Culture School. A school composed of primary, grade, and high school pupils. We do not claim that we are doing more or better work than any other school, but we do feel that we are doing as much, and doing it just as well—perhaps, however, we may be doing it a little differently.

Our plan of giving instruction and working out the practical problems may not be as complex as some others, but we believe we are getting results, and results are what the school is seeking for in all directions. The working principle there has always been that when results do not appear changes and experimentation must be made until the expected does occur.

The educational and medical profession now pretty generally agree that our public school pupils should be adequately instructed in the methods and possibilities of preventive medicine, and in the principles and reasonableness of public hygiene.

A desirable course of instruction seems to consist in first studying the conditions and needs of the schools in which the subject is taught and then giving instruction to the pupils in each case along those lines in which they seem most deficient and most in need, rather than to overload them with subject matter, phases of which in some cases are unnecessary, until the whole assumes the nature of a burden, and its absorption be-comes a task rather than a pleasure and benefit. So far the Ethical Culture School has worked along this line of theory, realizing that its pupils come from homes in which hygienic conditions and instruction

are given careful attention. The presentation of the subject has therefore been in accordance with the following plan:

In the Primary School, instruction is given principally by the class
teachers, with helpful suggestions from the teachers of the physical
department as occasion may demand, limited to personal hygiene.

In the Elementary School instruction is given by the class teachers,
supplemented by suggestions from subject teachers, and frequent talks
on personal and school hygiene by teachers of the physical department
staff, in which, as occasion requires, charts and other forms of illustration are used.

Plans of presentation are modified somewhat to meet the needs in
the open air department of the school.

It is in the open air school that our special emphasis in hygiene work
was made last year. The field is so large and with us in an experimental
stage so that it will not be possible to go into detail concerning it. I
would like to refer in a very general way to its organization.

The selection of pupils was made from anaemic neurasthenic and
those somewhat backward mentally in their grade work. Children of
tuberculosis tendencies were not considered. Not to deplete the indoor
classes the following restriction was made in regard to selection. The
class teachers in each of the two divisions in the 4th, 5th and 6th grades
were allowed to name ten pupils from their classes who seemed to be most
in need of outdoor conditions. From these ten, six were selected by
school physician, and a psychologist employed for the purpose, who
gave careful physical and mental examinations. This allowed thirty-six
pupils, the remaining twenty-four were selected from application of
outside pupils upon the recommendation of their family physician.
These were, however, given the same physical examination as the others,
and if accepted by the school physician were placed in the outdoor
schools. This allowed us three grades of twenty in each grade. These
were under instruction of three class teachers and the principal. The
periods for school organization were divided about as follows:

Two-quarters of the time were devoted to study and class room work;
one-quarter for play and recreation periods, and one-quarter for rest
period.

Very careful attention was given to the dietary conditions, special
advice as regards home diet being given in each case, while at the school
hot lunches were served for all.

As I said in the beginning, the work is in an experimental stage with
us. While the results shown from other open air schools, especially
with tubercular children, has been most wonderful, we feel with the
Ethical School the results are so gratifying that an additional class will
be formed next year, that of the 7th grade. We have found a marked

increase in weight and general health conditions of the outdoor pupils. A marked increase in the ability for mental grasp. Practically the same ground has been covered as by the indoor pupils but in very much less time. We have been exceedingly gratified with the general health conditions of the school. There has been a freedom from coryza and other forms of infectious diseases much more marked than with the indoor classes. The clothing used has been similar to that used in all outdoor schools, the felt cases for the lower part of the body, with sweaters and Parker jackets for the upper part; woolen mittens or gloves were worn. During the latter part of the winter months the children showed a much less susceptibility to weather conditions than at the beginning, and were less observant of body protection. So well pleased were the children with the outdoor conditions that I fail to recall any case where preference was expressed for a change to indoor conditions.

We have placed the emphasis of the class work in the first year, for it seems here that the pupils are more susceptible to impressions, and better fitted for obtaining this formal work than in the lower grades; consequently it is in grade VIII that attention is first given to regular class instruction.

In the High School, careful foundation is laid in the Biology department during the first year for the work which is continued throughout the High School course.

Following is a general and brief synopsis of the subjects as taken up in this grade:

OUTLINE OF PHYSIOLOGY AND HYGIENE COURSE—GRADE VIII

OBJECT OF COURSE

Object of Course Stated: (1) To form correct hygienic habits and to fix these habits by constant repetition out of school as well as in school.

(2) To furnish such information concerning the structure and function of the organs of the body as will help the pupil to appreciate the reasons for the rules of hygiene laid down.

THE SKELETAL AND MUSCULAR SYSTEM

Postures: Show pupils who stand well—good postures in standing and sitting—importance of good postures and upright carriage—functions of bones and muscles.

Reading: The Body at Work, Chapters I and II.

The Skeletal System: Bones at different ages; show skeleton; name important parts; call attention particularly to double curve in vertebral column and arch of foot; the skull and ribs as protection; round shoulders; curvature of spine; get part of long bone from butcher, show blood supply and marrow (bones are living structures); get ball and sockets and hinge joints from butcher; show synovial fluid, cartilage, ligaments, tendons; dislocation, strain and sprains, how treated.

Reading: The Body at Work, Chapters V, VI and VII.

The Muscular System: The importance of muscular exercise, gymnasium and other means than gymnasium:

Determine by experiment, effect of exercise

(a)   On rate of pulse beat;

(b)   On rate of respiration;

(c)   On body temperature, tested under tongue and follow up; how a muscle acts—note contraction of biceps; kinds of exercise out-of-doors; rest; examine boiled piece of meat for structure of muscle.

Reading: The Body at Work, Chapters III and IV.

The Circulatory System: Function—Study model of heart; show diagram of circulation on chart; arteries, veins, capillaries—functions of each; the flow of blood; examine blood under microscope; function of corpuscles—clothing and circulation.

Reading: The Body at Work, Chapters IX to XIII inclusive.

The Respiratory System: The exchange of gases; show osmosis; measure lung capacity; try holding breath, note length of time; show model of lungs; refer to composition of air as given in Chemistry course; test air in room for C. O. 2; importance of fresh air at night; how the air is renewed; how to ventilate; show box with candle to illustrate ventilation; visit basement to study system of ventilation of school building; clothing and respiration; how to breath; temperature and moisture; dust and its dangers; the voice; suggest deep-breathing exercises; explain importance.

Reading: The Body at Work, Chapters XV and XVI.

The Digestive System: Food and its uses; the digestive system and process; show model or use chart; teeth; observe model; show teeth of cow or horse and some carnivor; care of teeth, sets, kinds; have pupils examine their own mouths and report on teeth present and missing; effect of tight clothing on digestion.

Reading: The Body at Work, Chapters XVIII to XXI inclusive; Chapter XXII.

The Skin and Its Functions: Show that skin excretes water by placing hand on cold glass plate; the skin as an organ of protection, an organ of absorption, and an organ of sensation (show different thickness in different places) and as a regulator of temperature; bathing, times, kinds; clothing—conductors and non-conductors of heat—illustrate by experiment; care of the nails.

Reading: The Body at Work, Chapters XXVI and XXVII.

The Nervous System and Senses: Functions of the nervous system; test reaction time of a number of pupils, both boys and girls; care of nervous system.

The *Special Senses*, sight, hearing, taste, smell, and touch briefly described. Rules of hygiene for the care of the eyes and ears—especially how and when to study.

Reading: Community Hygiene in part as given in "*Town and City*," particularly Chapters I, II, III, V, VII, VIII, XIII, XIV, XV, XVI, XVII, XVIII, XIX, XX, XXIV, XXV, XXVIII, XXIX, and XXX.

This class instruction is supplemented in the High School by the following work of the Physical department:

Bi-monthly talks are given to all high school pupils in the physical culture classes, on subjects of personal, school and community hygiene.

Monthly assemblies are held at which outside speakers are secured to give talks, frequently illustrated, on subject of Community, State and Federal hygiene.

So far the results strongly indicate that the subject of hygiene in the Ethical Culture School is presented in such a form as to be readily observed by the pupils and to prove a source of real and lasting benefit.

Practical hygiene in the school is conducted according to the following plan:

In conjunction with the school physician a thorough physical examination is made of each pupil in the Kindergarten, Elementary, and High School departments at the beginning and close of the school year, and at other times as special cases require. This includes test of vision, hearing, nervous control, and the muscular system, and an inspection of the teeth, throat, and nasal passages, and the condition of the lungs, heart, spine and feet. This examination, with the health sheet submitted by the parents or family physican, serves as a guide in arranging the school work to the best possible advantage. Any abnormal conditions which are observed are at once reported to the parents, and when possible, cases requiring special work or supervision are attended to in the school. But when the conditions seem to demand either more time than the schedule of the school will permit, or the services of a specialist, parents are so advised. Careful attention is given to the adjustment of all desks and chairs. For the purpose of a more thorough study of the children, and as a precautionary measure against contagious diseases, frequent inspection is made of the class rooms. This inspection is conducted in the Kindergarten and lower grades daily, since it is with the small children that the greatest care must be taken. All cases of a suspicious nature are at once referred to the school physician and the necessary action taken concerning them. A daily report of all absences is sent to the Physical Director, and those cases in which prompt information as to the cause of the absence has not been received are carefully investigated. Children who have been absent for a period of two days or longer are examined before being allowed to return to class, and when the absence has been due to contagious disease, are permitted to return to school only on presenting a certificate from the Board of Health. At regular intervals the lockers and classrooms, including closets, desks, books, etc., in the different departments, are thoroughly disinfected, and at other times when special occasion requires. Individual drinking-glasses, which are sterilized bi-weekly, are used in all the class-rooms, and all milk, used in the school for drinking purposes, is properly pasteurized. Adequate arrangements are made to provide for any emergency cases which may arise in the school.

The school has installed one of the finest systems of ventilation and in addition the building each day at the close of the school session is flooded for several hours with fresh air.

Valuable as we consider our ventilating system, which is a slight modification of the Plenum system, we are trying in several of the rooms experiments with the electric fans to improve the condition of the room by increased circulation of the air. The water for drinking purposes is filtered twice for the coolers, and ice is not allowed to come in contact with the water. Arrangements for individual soap and paper towel service are made throughout the school; in the lavatories deodorizing agents are not required for there are no foreign odors. The culinary department is under the supervision of the school physician, and next year there will be a trained nurse in constant attendance at the school. As there has been more or less discussion of athletic conditions at this Congress I feel that possibly the attitude of the school in this regard might not come amiss here, if treated hygienically.

In athletics, the policy of the school has always been conservative; the benefits of a healthy athletic spirit and of athletics in general when pursued in moderation are recognized; but when carried to excess are considered decidedly injurious and undesirable. The spirit is not to permit the boy to hazard his health in a struggle for medals, but to engage in his sport for sport's sake. Individuality is merged in the general good of the entire school. Physical exercise is compulsory, but pupils are exempt for satisfactory reasons furnished by the home or school physician. Girls are not allowed to exercise during the menstrual periods. I might say in general that the health, safety and comfort of the pupils is always the earnest concern of the school.

STUDENT HOUSING AND SANITATION, METHODS OF INSPECTION AND ADMINISTRATION

BY

FRANK WARREN WHITE

The problem of inspecting rooming and boarding houses and the supplying of a reliable list of rooms and boarding houses to a large number of people who may be entirely unfamiliar with local conditions has long been recognized as a very important one. Work along this line is often done in connection with large conventions, where great numbers of people need to be housed and have no time for a personal search for suitable accommodations.

Young Men's Christian and Young Women's Christian Associations have long been in the habit of keeping on file a list of desirable rooms, which, in many cases, have been visited by someone employed for this purpose and a record made. For this service it is quite common for them to make a small charge per year for keeping the rooming house on their list.

In the schools and colleges this work has been gradually coming to the front, although not with the rapidity that it should. Some of our largest colleges and universities have been very slow to appreciate their responsibility for the hygienic conditions, as well as the moral atmosphere, which surrounds the students, many of whom are away from home for the first time and thrown upon their own resources and likely to make mistakes in the hygiene of their college life which will extract a heavy toll in wrecked health in later years.

Magazine articles on this subject have not been numerous and I hope to see more along this line in our standard publications, so that the people at home may get a better conception of the work that our educational institutions are doing along the line of preserving the health and morals of the student of to-day.

The problem of the small college or school with modern and accessible dormitories is a small one beside of that of the large university with inadequate or no dormitories, where the students are scattered around through the community. The larger the community, it seems to me the more important does this knowledge and control of the housing situation become and incidentally the more need for an efficient and well organized committee to take charge of this work of inspection and listing.

Three years ago the President of the Kansas State Normal College, feeling that the list of the rooming houses which had always been kept was not adequate and that a school which this year registered something over twenty-nine hundred (2,900) students should have some more thorough basis for this list, appointed a Faculty Committee to look into the matter and report to the faculty. The old method was to allow any landlady to fill out a form setting forth accommodations and sign it. This list of rooming houses was open for students to consult and judge solely on the householder's statements, which in most cases were correct but in some others might give a more favorable impression than conditions would warrant. The committee recommended the establishment of systematic inspection, and devised several forms for procuring information, sent a letter to the householders informing them of the intention of the committee to collect some facts for use by the committee, and in general made a survey of the field and the information was gotten by student members of the college Y.M.C.A., who went from door to door and made a very useful canvass, giving them an idea of the number of rooming houses in the city and much useful information, but did not go far enough to warrant them in compiling an approved list of rooms.

On the coming of the writer of this article to the Kansas State Normal College, he was immediately appointed by the President as chairman of the committee, which had already done some valuable work and cleared the ground so to speak for further building.

It is the belief of the committee, some of whom served on the original committees, as well as the President, that the State represented by the school in this case stands in the relation of guardian to those coming from outside of the city of Emporia, and that it should try to see that the students are placed under the very best possible conditions and in so far as may be, stand *in loco parentis* to these students who are away from home. The personnel of the committee was not selected by the President without regard for fitness, and for that reason we find on the present committee, the Instructor of Bacteriology, who makes the analyses of water samples taken from suspected wells and cisterns, besides doing his share of the regular house inspection. And I might say here that two years ago we departed from the former procedure and asked the faculty members of the committee to make the inspections personally, and in this way it lends more weight to the inspection and the reliability of the report.

The resident nurse is also a member and is able to render valuable assistance on account of her training. The head of the Household Science would be particularly interested in the inspection of the boarding houses and student clubs and is therefore a member. The Dean of Women also is among the members and obviously is able to render good service because of her confidential relations with the women of the school. The remaining members were no doubt chosen for their scientific and personal aptitude for the work and sympathy with its aim, and numbered the Professor of Biology and Zoölogy, Instructor of Physiology and Physics, and the Professor of Manual Training.

Thinking to be prepared for any emergency, one of our first acts was to ask the State Board of Health for the power of Deputy Health Officers, which it was glad to grant, and the members of the committee were duly commissioned, as arms of the State Board of Health, so that should there be any reason to force an entrance to observe conditions in any house where entrance was refused, the entrance might be forced and the State Board would fight the case for us if it should be carried to court. The householder has everything to gain and nothing to lose by the committee's visit. As a matter of fact we have never forced an entrance and hope we won't have to. We can soon bring them to terms by ordering their students out of the house.

Before beginning the systematic inspection of rooming houses for permanent record, a campaign of education in the local press was begun; articles on the work of the committee explaining that it was undertaken not to violate the privacy of their house, but for the benefit of both householders and students were published, and the idea given time to be understood before the actual inspection was undertaken. A few asserted that they wouldn't allow anyone to inspect their houses, etc., but by the time their houses were reached they had decided that they were a little hasty and that they would only hurt themselves by such an attitude and possibly they realized later that the committee had no axe to grind and only had the good of everybody concerned at heart. The advantages of being on an approved list appeals to many and has the tendency to cause the landladies to keep better houses so as to be classified higher.

The visiting card of the committee, so that if the householder desires to know who the inspector is and what his credentials are, is shown below:

Kansas State Normal School
Committee on Student Health and Sanitation

FRANK W. WHITE, M.D., Chairman
LYMAN C. WOOSTER
HARRIET L BARBER
H. H. BRAUCHER
W A. VAN VORIS
BETH W. MULL
NELLE BURLINGAME
F U. G AGRELIUS

Commissioned as Deputy Health Officers under tne Seal of the State Board of Health, November 23, 1911

This gives them the assurance that the inspector is who he pretends to be and not someone trying to find out whether there is a piano in the house and then report the fact to a piano salesman, or the advance agent for a sneak thief.

The permanent record for filing by the chairman of the committee is shown below and is almost self-explanatory:

Inspection of Student Rooming and Boarding Houses
Kansas State Normal School

Name *Jones Mrs. W. R.*   No. and Street. *107 Walnut St.*

Front E W N S   Family *H Y W.*   Sons *2*   Daughters *3*

Number of rooms—Furnished *3*   Unfurnished *0*   Men or women roomers

Floor	Size	Windows	Floor Covering	Position	Rate	
2	8 x 10 x 8	2	Straw M.	N.W.	7	8
2	9 x 11 x 8	2	Nailed Carp	N.E.	8	9
3	8 x 10 x 7	1	Crex Rug	S.	5	6

Will cooking be allowed? *Yes*   Will laundering be allowed? *Yes.*

Do you give board? *No*   Rate per week ——   Rate board and room per week ——

Heating: Furnace?   Hot water?   Steam?   Gas? ✓   Oil?   Wood?   Coal? ✓

Light: Electric?   Gas? ✓   Oil?   Acetylene?

Water: City? ✓   Well? ✓   Condition? *60/100*   Cistern? —   Condition? ——

Sewer connections? ✓   Bath-room? *No*   Tub? *No*   Hot water? *No*   Toilet? *OK.*

Cellar? ✓   Drainage? ✓   Screens? *1/2*   Flies? *Fair*   Mosquitoes? *Few.*

Yard and alley *Medium*   House *Old*

Neighborhood *Good.*   Can you use student help? *No*

Will you report all cases of sickness with suspicious symptoms or known-to-be infectious or contagious diseases to the Chairman of this Committee, and observe quarantine and fumigating regulations when necessary? *Yes.*

References 1. *H. R. Smith*   2. *Prof. Van Voris.*

Remarks:

Rooms vacant now *2*

Classification *C.*

Date *4/17/13.*   Inspected by *L. C. Wooster*

If it is a west front a line is drawn through W in this manner W. Our rule calls for only one sex in a rooming house, not that it would in the majority of cases be any cause for alarm, but that there may be as little opportunity for laxness in relations of the men and women of the school as possible, in this phase of their student life which we can control. We are very proud of the morals of our school and want to bring to bear every agency which will tend to continue this condition in a teacher's college, where those who are to teach our children are being educated.

A check mark for instance after the word "furnace" would mean that the house has furnace heat. Under "screens," it is of interest whether they have half screens or full screens.

A winter inspection would not tell much about flies and mosquitoes, but the condition of the yard and alley might give some very strong indications. The house whether old or new, brick or wood, painted or unpainted, etc., would be important notes. The line "Can you use student help?" is inserted to help the Employment Bureau of the Young Women's and Young Men's Christian Associations and by the secretaries looking over these reports they often get information that helps many a needy student to get the work necessary to keep him or her in school. The importance of the sick report of the landlady is self-evident and aids the chairman of the committee to keep track of the communicable diseases and prevent their spread. If a house were inspected when school starts in September and there were six empty rooms, the "rooms vacant now" line would read 6, and then if two weeks later she would telephone back that she had filled four of her rooms (as she should to keep us informed) then the record would be amended to read as follows: "Rooms vacant now" 62 so that we plan to keep a continuous record of the number of rooms vacant in order that a student will not go looking for rooms which are already filled. And last but not least, the judgment of the member who inspected the house as to the classification which is marked A highest and B, C, D, progressing down. If classed as E the house is never listed where students can get access to it.

This form just described is filed in the office of the chairman, while a partial copy of it is placed for student reference in loose leaf form arranged by streets, the low numbers on top. This second form contains enough information so that the student can judge as to whether he would care to go and see the room, but does not give all the information at the committee's disposal. The form is shown on next page:

W.

List of Student Rooming and Boarding Houses

Name *Jones Mrs. W. R.*   No. and Street. *107 Walnut*

Number of rooms—Furnished *3*   Unfurnished *0*

Will cooking be allowed? *Yes*   Will laundering be allowed? *Yes.*

Do you give board? *No* Rate per week ——   Rate board and room per week ——

Heating: Furnace?   Hot water?   Steam?   Gas? *✓* Oil?   Wood?   Coal? *✓*

Light: Electric?   Gas? *✓* Oil? *✓* Acetylene?

Water: City? *✓* Well? *✓* Cistern? *Not recommended.*

Sewer connections? *✓*   Bath-room? *No* Tub? *No* Hot water? *No* Toilet? *OK.*

Can you use student help? *No.*

References 1. *H. R. Smith* 2. *Prof. Van Vorix.*

Remarks: *Closets in 2 rooms.*

Classification *C*   Date *4/17/13*

Rooms vacant now *2*

The listed rooms for men are obtainable in the general office where they are in charge of the general office secretary, while the list for women is in the office of the Dean of Women.

Exceptions to the ruling in regard to women and men rooming at the same house are very rarely made by the committee. I think only one this year, of which the form below might serve for an example, where, let us suppose, the landlady to have a son and daughter, and after getting all the facts, such as the necessity for working on the girl's part, and the good character of all concerned, an exception might be made, and a permit granted the landlady for a certain length of time.

We also have a form of permit for students which is not shown, but follows the same idea of official sanction. Neither form is used often, for precedents are not desirable, as it is important to treat everybody strictly alike.

The work of the Social Committee and that of the Housing Committee naturally touch at many points and often we ascertain whether the student is allowed the use of the parlor to receive company and whether the landlady proposes to enforce the ten o'clock rule for callers, etc.

Rooming Permit

Permission is hereby granted to Mrs. J. R. WILLIAMS,

at No. 1015 CATHERINE .... St. to furnish rooms to the following

students: MISS MARY EDWARDS

under the following conditions: THAT SHE IS TO ROOM WITH YOUR

DAUGHTER AND IS TO WORK FOR HER BOARD.

until JUNE 1, 1913.

Date MARCH 21, 1913. *Frank W. White, M.D.*

Chairman Rooming Committee.

The work of the committee works out in the following manner: Mrs. Smith calls up and says that she has rooms to rent to students, the telephone operator asks if the rooms have been listed by the committee; if she says yes, he makes a note for the chairman that Mrs. Smith has three rooms for rent. The chairman takes the permanent record and the record in the students' clip and changes the figures in the "Rooms vacant Now" line from 0, which was true last semester, when her house was full, to 3, which is correct for the present, since she now has three unoccupied. If she says the house has not been visited by the committee, the operator makes a note for the committee that Mrs. Smith, 805 Boylston Street, has rooms and wishes them listed. The chairman hands the address to the member responsible for the district in which Boylston Street is located, and he visits the house and if classified "D" or higher it is listed in due order and Mrs. Smith's name appears in the approved list to which the students have access when looking for a good room.

A few weeks after school opens each semester the student addresses are checked over to see if there are any new people keeping roomers, whose houses have not been inspected, and these are at once attended to.

What do we do when a student violates the rules, you will ask next. In the first place our authority is not directly over the householder, but over the student, and our attention is first directed to the student, who is sent a notice to change his or her room and the reason given if we have the entire facts, and the student is given a reasonable time to find a new room, the location of which he or she is required to file with the committee at once. We have had but one case in which the committee ruling was questioned, and in that case the President backed up the decision of the committee and the student moved as requested. Any further demurring in a similar case after the President had affirmed a ruling would, without doubt, result in the student being asked to get his education elsewhere since he or she did not care to abide by the rules of the institution.

In the matter of infectious diseases we send an "Exclusion Card" to each teacher in whose classes the student is enrolled, and the student

KANSAS STATE NORMAL SCHOOL.

EXCLUSION CARD.

M _Harry K. Tuttle_

is excluded from all classes until further notice.

Date _____ 3/17 ____ 1913

Frank W. C. White, M.D.

4-2134   Chairman Committee on Student Health and Sanitation.

and the student is not readmitted to classes until the Readmittance Card, signifying that the chairman of the Committee has received from the student the release from quarantine issued by the city Board of Health, is presented.

KANSAS STATE NORMAL SCHOOL.

RE-ADMITTANCE CARD.

M _Harry K. Tuttle_

is allowed to return to classes, beginning

3/17 ____ 1913

Frank W. C. White, M.D.

4-2133   Chairman Committee on Student Health and Sanitation.

As a result of this constant supervision of infectious diseases among the students we have been remarkably free from epidemics of any kind, and we are prone to believe that the inspection of student rooming and boarding houses, the resident nurse and small hospital equipment and the medical examinations, have been no mean factors in producing this happy result.

Before speaking of the boarding houses, I might take up a little more in detail the wells and cisterns seen while inspecting houses. These are carefully examined, the curbs for cracks in the cement and for proper size and height, while wooden flooring is marked "dangerous," unless very closely matched and properly sloped and particularly in the case of wells, is the distance from the nearest stable or privy noted and the slope of adjoining lots. In connection with the cisterns the date of the last cleaning and whether it has a filter are recorded.

The boarding houses and clubs are inspected by the committee and the refrigerator, cellar, water supply, filters, flies, screens, etc., receive special attention, and the reports of these are kept in a separate index. From time to time different members drop in at the different dining clubs and eat a sample meal, and in this way, we keep in touch with the conditions in the dining rooms and the quality of food served.

The work of this committee has not reached the stage where it takes no time or energy to keep it going smoothly, nor will it ever reach that stage, but it does show results that are well worth the efforts put forth, and each year it goes a little easier, as the students and householders realize that this is the established order which will be enforced without fear or favor. We have much left to accomplish. Our lists are not perfect and are constantly changing, necessitating repeated revision of both the office file and list for students.

As the work goes on, we hope for a gradually rising standard of excellence in the quality of the rooms offered, so that rooms that are now classified as "D" will be listed as "E" because of the increasing number of medium and high-grade rooms that will be available. New problems of administering the regulations arise every day. It takes much time of the members of such a committee rightly to discharge their duties, but the results are bound to be worth while in raising the standard of living and efficiency among the students of any school or university, where this work is carefully carried out.

LIQUID CHLORINE VS. BLEACHING POWDER AS A DISINFECTANT FOR SWIMMING POOLS

BY

A. M. Buswell and W. W. Havens

Early in April of this year, we began a series of tests on the Columbia University swimming pool with a view to working out a permanent plan of administration under which the pool could be continuously disinfected, and the possibility of the spread of disease from that source eliminated. At the time the tests were undertaken, a refiltration plant had been in operation nearly a year. The water is pumped from the pool into a sedimentation tank, a little coagulant added, and then the water is passed through sand filters back to the pool. This circulation is maintained for about twelve hours a day and the rate of pumpage such that the entire volume of the pool is filtered once every two days. The results of this system were all that could be desired from the standpoint of color and turbidity, but the bacteriological count was rather high (500-1000 bacteria per cc.), especially after days of large attendance.

"Bleaching Powder" was first tried, using the equivalent of .5 part per million of available chlorine twice a week. This was not enough to keep down the number of bacteria below 100 per cc. and the amount was increased to one part per million of available chlorine twice a week. With this treatment the pool could be kept practically sterile but there were occasional complaints of taste and irritation of the mucous by the bathers. There are two additional disadvantages to the use of "Bleaching Powder." First: The Bleaching Powder must be thoroughly stirred up with a considerable quantity of water in order to get the calculated efficiency, or else some special method of application, such as dragging it around in the pool in bags, must be used. Second: "Bleaching powder" is by no means a substance of constant composition. The available chlorine may range all the way from ten to thirty-five per cent., and the services of a chemist are continually required in order to obtain a uniform treatment, when "bleach" is used.

In view of these facts the use of liquid chlorine was attempted. Chlorine dissolves so slowly in water that it did not seem advisable to pass the gas directly into the pool. Five gallon bottles of water were connected in series to the cylinder of liquid chlorine and saturated by bubbling the gas through them. In this way there was no escape of the gas to cause nuisance and a saturate solution was readily obtained. The exact strength of the solution was at first determined by adding

KI to a 10 cc. portion and titrating against standard $Na_2 S_2 O_3$. The necessity of this analysis was obviated by constructing an hydrometer of such dimensions that the strength of the chlorine solution could be determined from its specific gravity.

The saturate chlorine solution was fed by a uniform feed device to the effluent from the filters at such a rate that .3 parts per million of chlorine, figured on the water filtered, were added. Since the volume of the pool is filtered every two days, the total treatment was 1.8 parts per million per week, as compared with two parts per million per week found necessary when "bleach" was used. The efficiency of this treatment was all that could be desired from the standpoint of bacteria count, the number of bacteria being kept below 100 per cc. up to the end of the term, and by adding the chlorine slowly and continuously the taste and odor were removed and there was no evidence that the bathers were aware of the use of chlorine.

The cost of treatment with the two different disinfectants is practically identical at the present state of the market. The slow uniform feeding of the chlorine solution insures thorough distribution of the disinfectant and removes the nuisance of taste and odor. And the simple device for determining the strength of the solution of chlorine by means of an hydrometer insures uniform treatment without the services of a chemist.

This system was approved by Mr. H. L. Norris, Superintendent of Buildings and Grounds, and is now in operation at the Columbia pool.

A STUDY OF THE PHYSICAL CONDITION OF 500 COLLEGE STUDENTS

BY

GEORGE L. MEYLAN

The responsibility of the college for the health of students was first recognized by President Stearns of Amherst College who wrote in his first annual report in 1855: "No one thing has demanded more of my anxious attention than the health of the students. The waning of the physical energies in the midway of the college course is almost the rule rather than the exception among us, and cases of complete breaking down are painfully numerous."

The direct result of President Stearn's efforts was the organization of a department of hygiene and physical education at Amherst College in 1860. Unfortunately, the general adoption of the Amherst plan by other American colleges did not begin until about 1890, but since that time nearly every institution of higher training in this country has organized a department of hygiene and physical education in charge of a medically trained director. These departments vary considerably in organization, activities, and methods of administration, and particularly in the emphasis placed on the various activities directed and supervised by such departments.

During the last ten years there has been a rapidly growing tendency to place more emphasis upon the medical supervision of the students' health. One of the prominent features of this work is a thorough medical examination prescribed to all students soon after admission to college. The examination includes data on family and personal history, measurements, tests of vision, hearing and muscular strength, and examination of the various organs. The data recorded serve as a basis for advice to the student in all matters of hygienic living such as exercise, diet, bathing, rest, program of studies, etc.

The great importance of making these examinations is shown by the large percentage of remediable physical defects found. The following tables show the results of the examination of 500 freshmen at Columbia University:

Age	Number	Percentage
Under 16 years................	1	.2%
16 to 17......................	21	4.2%
17 to 18......................	81	16.2%
18 to 19......................	158	31.6%
19 to 20......................	102	20.4%
20 to 21......................	69	13.8%
21 to 22......................	35	7. %
22 to 23......................	20	4. %
23 to 24......................	8	1.6%
Over 24......................	5	1. %

Average..............................19 years, 2 months
Youngest.............................15 years, 11 months
Oldest...............................24 years, 6 months

Weight

Average.........................60.962 kilos or 133.5 lbs.
Lightest.........................43.   kilos or 94.6 lbs.
Heaviest.........................90.   kilos or 198. lbs.

Height

Average.........................171.62 cm. or 68.6 inches.
Shortest.........................150 cm. or 60. inches.
Tallest.........................192 cm. or 76.8 inches.

Total Strength (According to Intercollegiate Strength Test)

Average.....................................542.34 kilos.
Lowest......................................205.   kilos.
Highest.....................................865.   kilos.

Eyesight

Right Eye. Emmetropic.................................219 or 43.8%
Myopic..................................... 81 or 16.2%
Hyperopic.................................. 26 or 5.2%
Astigmatic only............................ 96 or 19.2%
Astigmatic and myopic...................... 63 or 12.6%
Astigmatic and hyperopic................... 15 or 3. %
Left Eye. Emmetropic.................................240 or 48. %
Myopic..................................... 89 or 17.8%
Hyperopic.................................. 22 or 4.4%
Astigmatic only............................ 79 or 15.8%
Astigmatic and myopic...................... 54 or 10.8%
Astigmatic and hyperopic................... 16 or 3.2%

Hearing

Right Ear. Normal........:451 or 90.2%   Defective.......49 or 9.8%
Left Ear. Normal........452 or 90.4%   Defective......48 or 9.6%

HEART

Rate.   Average rate at rest, horizontal position.................... 77

Lowest   rate at rest, horizontal position.................... 38

Highest rate at rest, horizontal position.................... 120

Average rate at rest, vertical position.................... 87

Lowest   rate at rest vertical position.................... 46

Highest rate at rest, vertical position.................... 144

Average rate after exercise, vertical position.............. 138

Lowest   rate after exercise, vertical position.............. 72

Highest rate after exercise, vertical position.............. 184

Rhythm. Normal.................................... 477 or 95.4%

Intermittent................................ 3 or .6%

Irregular.................................... 13 or 2.6%

Irritable.................................... 7 or 1.4%

Size.   Normal.................................... 459 or 91.8%

Small.................................... 12 or 2.4%

Slight hypertrophy.......................... 27 or 5.4%

Marked hypertrophy.......................... 2 or .4%

Organic murmurs............................ 23 or 4.6%

GENERAL CONDITION OF THE HEART

Normal.................................... 375 or 75. %

Weak.................................... 15 or 3. %

Fair.................................... 90 or 18. %

Strong.................................... 20 or 4. %

LUNGS

Normal.................................... 409 or 81.8%

Various abnormalities........................ 91 or 18.2%

NASAL FOSSAE

Right.   Normal.................................... 405 or 81. %

Obstructions, etc.......................... 95 or 19. %

Left.   Normal.................................... 378 or 75.6%

Obstructions, etc.......................... 123 or 24.4%

TEETH

Excellent.................................... 24 or 4.8%

Good.................................... 152 or 30.4%

Fair.................................... 221 or 44.2%

Poor.................................... 78 or 15.6%

Very poor.................................... 25 or 5. %

PHARYNX

Normal.................................... 270 or 54. %

Catarrh.................................... 230 or 46. %

TONSILS

Normal.................................... 404 or 80.8%

Hypertrophied.......................... 96 or 19.2%

SKIN

Color.   Normal......................................470 or 94. %
        Pale.. 30 or 6. %
Condition. Normal....................................390 or 78. %
        Dry.. 5 or 1. %
        Eruptions..................................105 or 21. %
Fat.   Normal....................................443 or 88.6%
        Less than normal........................... 39 or 7.8%
        More than normal........................ 18 or 3.6%

HEAD

Normal......................................212 or 42.4%
Carried forward..............................288 or 57.6%

SPINE

Normal.................................. 38 or 7.6%
Kyphosis only............................. 54 or 10.8%
Lordosis only............................. 36 or 7.2%
Scoliosis only............................. 51 or 10.2%
Kyphosis and lordosis...................... 57 or 11.4%
Kyphosis and Scoliosis..................... 48 or 9.6%
Lordosis and scoliosis..................... 44 or 8.8%
Kyphosis, lordosis and scoliosis................172 or 34.4%

SHOULDERS

Normal...................................279 or 55.8%
Right lower...............................156 or 31.2%
Left lower................................. 65 or 13. %

CHEST

Normal...................................308 or 61.6%
Flat.......................................108 or 21.6%
Contracted................................ 26 or 5.2%
Small..................................... 50 or 10. %
Chicken breast............................. 5 or 1. %
Funnel shape.............................. 3 or   .6%

ABDOMEN

Normal...................................256 or 51.2%
Protruding................................119 or 23.8%
Relaxed................................... 97 or 19.4%
Fat....................................... 28 or 5.6%

HERNIA

Right inguinal.............................3 or   .6%
Left inguinal.................................7 or 1.4%
Umbilical...................................1 or 2. %

```
Normal..........................................377 or 75.4%
Right leg longer................................ 96 or 19.2%
Left leg longer................................. 27 or  5.4%
```

FEET

```
Good arches (both feet)........................256 or 51.2%
```

Weak Arch

```
Right.    1st degree....................................59 or 11.8%
          2d  degree....................................37 or  7.4%
          3rd degree....................................27 or  5.4%
Left.     1st degree....................................60 or 12. %
          2d  degree....................................33 or  6.6%
          3rd degree....................................28 or  5.6%
```

Flat Foot

```
Right.    1st degree....................................55 or 11. %
          2d  degree....................................39 or  7.8%
          3rd degree.................................... 8 or  1.6%
Left.     1st degree....................................56 or 11.2%
          2d  degree....................................42 or  8.4%
          3rd degree.................................... 9 or  1.8%
```

GENERAL CONDITION

(Based on development, strength and vitality as estimated by the examiner)

1—best condition; 5—poorest condition.

```
1.............................................. 4 or   .8%
2.............................................. 98 or 19.6%
3.............................................333 or 66.6%
4.............................................. 63 or 12.6%
5.............................................. 2 or   .4%
```

SESSION FORTY

Thursday, August 28th, 9:00 A.M.

MEETING OF THE AMERICAN PHYSICAL EDUCATION ASSOCIATION

·R. Tait McKenzie, M.D., *Chairman*

Miss Alta Wiggins, Buffalo, N. Y., *Vice-Chairman*

Program of Session Forty

R. Tait McKenzie, M.D., Professor Physical Education and Therapy; Director of the Department of Physical Education, University of Pennsylvania; President of the American Physical Education Association. "The Wisdom of Health as Taught in a Great University."

James M. Anders, M.D., LL.D., Professor of Medicine and Clinical Medicine, Medico-Chirurgical College, Philadelphia; Officier de l'Instruction Publique. "Physical Education in the Public Schools with Special Reference to United States."

Paul R. Radosavljevich, Ph.D., Pd.D., Assistant Professor Experimental Pedagogy, New York University. "Physical Measurements of Pupils in Mostar (Herzegovina, Austria)."

Gordon B. Trowbridge, Assistant Director Physical Training Public Schools, Boston, Mass. "Some Fundamentals in Physical Training in Public Schools."

C. Ward Crampton, M.D., Director of Physical Training, New York Public Schools. "Blood Ptosis—A Test of Vaso-Motor Efficiency."

William Stecher, B.S.G., Director of Physical Education, Public Schools, Philadelphia, Pa. "Has School Gymnastics an Appreciable Effect Upon Health?"

CLOUDESLEY BRERETON, M.D., London County Council, Ha
England. "Criteria of Physical Exercises in the Light
tion as a Whole."

PROF. MANUEL VELAZQUEZ ANDRADE, Mexico City. "La
fisica en las escuelas de Mexico. Resultados a que se ha

CHARLES A. RANLETT, Instructor in Military Drill, Bosto
"Military Drill in Public Schools." (Manuscript not i

LEONHARD F. FULD, Ph.D., New York. "Hygienic Costume
School Girls." (Manuscript not included.)

THE WISDOM OF HEALTH AS TAUGHT IN A GREAT UNIVERSITY

BY

R. TAIT MCKENZIE

When a university undertakes to occupy the last four years of a boy's growing life she must first take into account his physical condition as well as his mental acquirements and should safeguard his health and educate his physical powers with as much accuracy and intelligence as is exercised in the rest of his college work.

At the University of Pennsylvania every man when he registers at the bursar's office for the first time receives an appointment card for physical and medical examination. After filling in a blank referring to his past health and habits he takes a shower bath and reports at the physical director's office. When the tape line has recorded his length, breadth, and thickness and after he has pushed, pulled, grasped and lifted his best he is placed standing upright with feet together and his posture and figure are examined. By an arrangement of mirrors he can see his own back without moving. Flat chest, uneven shoulders, or lateral curvature are at once evident to him. The broken down arch that has given vague pains in the feet is easily demonstrated, and ambition for better things is awakened in his breast. He is then put under treatment which runs in concord with his college course. After this inspection he lies down on a couch for further examination of the heart and lungs and a test of the hearing of each ear. On leaving the room he gets a card which he takes to the swimming instructor. If he cannot swim the length of the 100 ft. pool he is put under instruction, for every man must learn during his first year to take care of himself in the water. Last year 340 men were taught this necessary art, the rest having passed the test on entering. In the last eight years nearly 3,000 have been taught to swim.

Men having physical defects are given cards on which are printed lists of exercises suitable for every case. These are taken to the instructor on the gymnasium floor who demonstrates the movements and repeats them until the student has mastered them. Like the horse of the story a man may drink or not after this according to his thirst for physical perfection, but he has at least been led to the water. The treatment of graver disabilities that are met with in the thousand or more young men is a different matter. A man who shows an involvement of the lungs has his whole future at stake and his relation to the college community must also be considered. If the trouble is slight he is put under observation and treated by a specially appointed college physician if he is in residence and away from home. If he lives at home his family is informed that he must be put under treatment at once. By this kind of care he usually gains rapidly in weight and often throws off the infection with little or no interference to his college work, whereas if he neglected it he would have to leave college a sick or dying man after a losing struggle of a year or more. Gains of from ten to fifteen pounds and disappearance of symptoms after a few weeks open-air sleeping and prescribed feeding are frequently reported.

About 40 men in 1,000 show some serious disturbance in the circulation from irregularity of pulse to structural damage of the heart. These men must be protected from physical overstrain. They must be taught to nurse their physical resources and to take only such exercise as will build up their resistance. The squandering of their future in the fierce competition of athletics is forbidden. Every candidate for an athletic team must show a certificate of physical soundness given after examination each year when he reports for an athletic team or squad.

It is on the basis of these examinations that the director regulates the physical life of the Pennsylvania student. He may prescribe very light individual exercise given personally by instructors, or he may forbid a student to take any. He may assign him to the regular progressive class work of the gymnasium in winter and the open field in spring where his exercise is designed accurately to fit the requirements of college life, or he may allow him to elect football, baseball, basketball, swimming, rowing, fencing, boxing, wrestling, soccer, tennis, cricket, or golf, credit for his attendance being given during the time he is actively engaged on each squad. Whatever form of sport he may choose or whatever form of exercise may be allotted to him he must account for to the University for two hours a week taken under the direction of the department unless excused by the director himself.

Two things a student frequently questions. First, his right to take part in any sport whether he injures himself or not. He must frequently be convinced that in case of injury his friends and relatives must be considered. The reputation of the University is at stake. Part of its duty is to bring him through college stronger and better than when he entered instead of preparing him to spend the rest of his days nursing his increasing ailments. The second question is why he should spend two hours a week of a crowded roster in what at first seems to be something quite apart from his college studies. Fresh from his summer holidays he feels able to work twenty-four hours a day. The necessity for a corrective for the comparatively sedentary life must be explained and the possibility of educating his rapidly maturing physical powers must be impressed upon him.

It has frequently been a pleasant experience to have students, who at first object, come in at the end of the term and thank the director for his insistence. The examination of the eyes, which is conducted under the Department of Physical Education by an expert ophthalmologist with a number of assistants, takes place early in the term. A brief history of the sight is taken and the student is examined for distant vision, close vision, and muscular balance. The appearance of the eye ground is seen through the ophthalmoscope. After the examination he. receives one of three letters stating that (1) his eyes are all right; (2) that they require attention that should be given at the first leisure time; (3) that they should have immediate attention to enable him properly to go on with his college course.

One is tempted to quote statistics of the sudden cure of headaches and relief of other disabilities as well as the discovery of unsuspected defects and leaks of efficiency that have been stopped by this means. It is not difficult to pick isolated cases of striking improvement under this system.

There is nothing dramatic about the raising of a general average. Yet this is the aim for which the department works. By taking the entire class of 1909 through their four years of college life and comparing their measurements on entering and on graduation, we can show an average increase in height of one inch, in weight of seven pounds, and in expanded chest of three inches. The raising of a whole student community so much means the application of a strong lever, for the normal increase of growth between the age of entering and graduation does not count for five per cent. of it; and the progressive physical training must be held accountable for most of the rest of it.

There is, moreover, that increased skill and education of the physical powers which can neither be measured nor weighed. When the student comes out in his gymnasium suit on the floor of the gymnasium for his first year's course, he finds himself confronted by a problem which is going to determine his place in groups 1, 2, or 3. He has to circle a bar, must jump 3 ft. 6 in. high, must climb a rope hand over hand 18 ft. high. About fifty per cent. fail in these tests. Exercises follow to educate this power and after ten lessons on each piece of gymnastic apparatus he comes out with at least a bowing acquaintance with the particular form of activity for which it was designed. In fact about 90 per cent. are able to pass the tests after their ten lessons. To most college men time is valuable and the brisk half-hour twice a week ending with a shower or plunge in the swimming pool is enough at least to keep them aware that they are physically alive. But the average youth soon reaches out for new fields of conquest in the world of achievement and he graduates into an athletic squad as a matter of course. While the risks of athletics to life. and future usefulness have been grossly exaggerated as proved by the statistics so carefully collected by Morgan, Meylan, Anderson, Hammett, and others, there are some men to whom violent competition should be closed and there are still others who should be under medical supervision throughout their entire course.

There are two college physicians at Pennsylvania with a corps of assistants, and the University Hospital forms the center round which the other buildings cluster like a crescent, while in the center of the hospital is a student's ward. Their fourteen beds are seldom empty. These cases receive the attention of the Professor of Medicine in his daily rounds, and most of the beds are endowed by friends and relatives of those who have found them a haven of refuge during their college days. In an institution so large as Pennsylvania with its 5,000 men the danger of an epidemic must always be present in the minds of the University Committee on Hygiene, the members of the medical staff, and the least suspicion as to a throat, rash, or temperature means isolation until the question of contagion is beyond doubt. Fortunately no bad epidemic has got headway, although many have been averted by quick action of the physicians in charge and the Department of Hygiene. The committee on hygiene consists of a chairman, Dr. J. William White, a trustee and emeritus professor of surgery, the provost ex-officio, the professor of physical education, the professor of hygiene, and the professor of medicine. It occupies itself with general questions of student life, sanitary condition of the dormitories, sterilization of water in the swimming pool, the isolation of contagious cases, etc., and another committee occupies itself with the inspection of boarding houses to be approved by the University.

In this way the University of Pennsylvania tries to provide for the physical education, sanitation, and general health of its student body.

PHYSICAL EDUCATION IN OUR PUBLIC SCHOOLS WITH SPECIAL REFERENCE TO THE UNITED STATES

BY

J. M. ANDERS

The importance of physical education, particularly in our public schools, is year by year becoming more evident and convincing. At the outset the question may pertinently be asked in all seriousness whether educators have lived up to their reasonable responsibilities in the past, admitting the supreme importance of keeping the body strong and healthy as a prime requisite in racial supremacy.

The conception entertained in Germany and other European countries of the duty of the community toward the child is a broader one than that which prevails in most of our American cities. German cities have also introduced much physical education into their school courses, thus making their educational system meet the needs of the future adult population. They fully realize that the commercial, industrial and political outlook of a nation must ever depend upon the universality of the best sort of elementary education—an education that pays due consideration to the adequate development of both body and mind.

The genius of certain men whose minds found lodgment in infirm and delicate bodies is often advanced to show that large accomplishments and an inferior, handicapped physique go hand in hand. For example, in this list of notables we are informed belong Chopin, Stevenson, St. Bernard, Heine, and many others. Most writers are inclined to lose sight of the physiologic principle that man's mental powers and resistance bear a definite and practically direct relation to his muscle power, and some at least of the men of large achievements mentioned above were possessed of great muscular strength, brought about principally through systematic physical exercise of one kind or another.

Granting that there are definite, isolated instances of the sort yet, either as a class or individually, they do not rank with those geniuses whose minds are housed in a tabernacle which supplies the largest amount and purest stores of energy-material. Says Dr. James Frederick Rogers* on the point at issue: "It stands to reason that the more well ordered the body, the more active and vigorous the mind, and that anything which depresses the proper functioning of the physio-

*Popular Science Monthly, July, 1913.

logical machinery must impair in so much the product of that organ, both in kind and amount."

In general, America is well in advance in sanitation, and the death rate can compare favorably with that of any other country, but if the foregoing statements be accepted, we are not bestowing sufficient attention upon the question of physical education of the child—the man and woman of tomorrow. There are about 20,000,000 pupils in the public schools of America, and to ensure their future usefulness as citizens nothing is more vitally important than a harmonious, unbroken balance between the growth and development of mind and body.

A regular system of school inspection, which is carried out in about two-fifths of the pupils at the present day in America is to be advised and encouraged until it shall have been extended to the whole number, as an aid to the attainment and preservation of sound health. Those in authority need to be urged to sanitate more thoroughly our public school buildings, since many of those in existence are unsuitable, being uncleanly and uncomfortable, as well as ill-lighted and ill-ventilated. Obviously so long as school rooms are a distinct menace to the health of the pupils, and school inspection is not universally adopted, full success from a course of physical education, however excellently conducted, is not to be expected.

At present writing it should easily be possible to establish a general acceptance of the principle well known to hygienists, that good muscular development is equivalent to good physical development. Educators must assume the heavy responsibility of carrying out a form of physical training that is not less important than mental training, as an urgent economic factor, or civilizing agency supposed to yield increased health, usefulness and happiness, but which proportionately receives insufficient attention in most cities, at least. It is to be hoped that this Congress will produce many pioneers in the advancement of regular and adequate physical education in our public schools.

Among the recognized agencies to keep the body in health and to prevent its germicidal powers from running low, an adequate quantity of muscular activity is of first rate importance—more than this its general and rational enforcement among growing children in our public schools, would have a vital effect upon the far-reaching future of the American race. A proper interest in the national physique can be shown only by concerted effort on the part of educators to bring about an evenly balanced condition of mind and body during childhood and adult life.

Whether the prime motive is economy or is humanitarian, improved bodily training is urgently needed and the outlay in energy and money required to accomplish this object is only a tithe of the amount now lost.

The well-nigh universal tendency to push the head at the expense of the muscles and sinews in our public schools, colleges and universities, is deplorable in the extreme. It might be argued that an awakening to the situation with respect to the question is now in progress among those charged with the duty of educating the youth of our land and that physical culture has become an integral part of the curricula in many quarters. Granting the correctness of this view, it may be nevertheless affirmed that, as compared with the time and energy allotted to mental training that given to physical culture is wholly inadequate in by far the majority of American cities at least.

The playground movement, to which reference is made hereafter, for the benefit more particularly of children in our public schools, is deserving of every encouragement, although its advantages are to be regarded as being merely supplementary to those of a systematic training under the charge of a competent physical instructor.

The consensus of opinion among those who have examined the question critically, is to the effect that the human race is slowly undergoing muscular deterioration, and writers have cast about them for causes which may be held responsible for such a lamentable state of affairs. Dr. Friedman in discussing the question in its relation to the American race, has emphasized two main considerations in endeavoring to account for our lack of physical stamina, namely, the ingestion of physically inferior races from abroad and our own mode of living, especially the undoubted trend away from occupations requiring the use of the voluntary muscles. He further argues that "this is poor economy because our bodies are unable to supply the divers needs of our overactive minds."*

Surely it is none too soon to agitate the question of giving due attention to methods intended to counteract the tendency toward increasing over-activity of the mind—in short toward the too strenuous life. The principal aim should be to maintain the harmonious balance betwixt mind and muscle by regular and rational muscular exercises, which should obviously be enforced *pari passu* with the mental training and development, and graded to suit the age and physical condition of the individual pupil. The infant and young child will under favorable conditions take sufficient physical exercise, but unfortunately education begins too early in life, and what is worse soon develops into a "high pressure" system, at the expense of bodily vigor, since sufficient time is not allowed for regular muscular training and supplementary exercises.

I am in entire accord with the view that instead of starting the child at the public schools at the age of six, as is the present custom, it were

*Journal American Medical Association, March 9, 1912.

better to imitate the ancient Greeks, whose children were sent first at the age of eight. As bearing on this question I quote again from the timely article by Friedman: "Were the two years from six to eight spent in preventing the development of any tendencies toward physical defects, or correcting those that have already developed, and in forming in the child the habit of physical exercise, the time would be more profitably spent."*

Good muscular development, prudently maintained, brings with it good chest expansion, a circulation normally carried on, normal vigor and activity of mind, and splendid digestion, as well as assimilation—in a word, sound health. This is the most valuable asset which the child can possess, furnishing an escape from pulmonary tuberculosis later on, from spinal curvature, chronic dyspepsia, neurasthenia, and doubtless many of the acute infections, owing to the increased resistance offered by the system.

Such a course would not entail loss of mind development, it being an established fact that both the intellect and understanding develop without instruction during early childhood, and that the child learns more easily and comprehends more quickly for having commenced later on. What could be more logical or more natural, in view of the foregoing facts, than for our educators and school boards to unite in a new and improved plan, having for its object the assigning to physical education its rightful place in the education of the juvenile mind.

The changes required in the present curricula of our public schools would be found to present no insurmountable difficulties, since sufficient definite instruction in physical culture could be given with but little expenditure of time—in a single hour per day. Perhaps the principal obstacle to such a course at present would be a lack of properly qualified instructors, which are indispensably necessary. The physical training should be flexible and adapted both to the class and individual, so as to insure the completest physical development without risk of harmful effects. In some of our cities, e. g., Philadelphia, a period of 15 minutes is given over to physical exercises daily, and these are carried out under the direction of the regular teachers, there being no specially or properly qualified teachers to supervise the work for the great majority of the classes. Hence in Philadelphia, and the same is true of other municipalities, as a consequence of lack of time, teachers and facilities, physical education may be in all fairness said to be wholly inadequate.

A clearer conception of the physical benefits of systematic and proper muscular exercises, and the manner of their production, should be more generally entertained, especially among those responsibly and directly

*Loc. cit.

connected with the education of mind and body of the rising generation. The primary effect of increased activity of the muscles is to stimulate the process of oxidation whereby the production of carbon dioxide is hastened, and the demand for oxygen is enlarged. It is the increased exchange of carbon. dioxide and oxygen taking place in the muscles themselves that promotes the normal metabolic processes (nutrition) and muscle power, as well as the general health of the human economy.

It may assist some of my hearers to an intelligent understanding of the principles and practical application of the scientific phase of the subject if I briefly present a few added physiological details. There is a constant process of decay going on in every tissue of the body, the waste products being eliminated by certain excretory organs, namely, the skin, lungs and kidneys. Now it is these disintegrating and eliminating processes that are facilitated by muscular activity, while at the same time, through its invigorating effect upon the circulation of the blood and the respiration, the same structures are properly repaired by the increased amount of renovating materials thus brought to them. Rest after muscular exercise is not only beneficial, but necessary in view of the fact that during the period of activity more energy is utilized than is produced, so that a call upon the energy stored during previous periods of repose, is made. Not only must rest follow exercise, but it must be in turn alternated with recreation.

Notable advances have been made in recent times in the majority of American cities in the matter of providing opportunity for supplementary recreation exercises in suitable playgrounds, and excursions on holidays and during the summer vacation to the country. The scheme pursued in Paris of appointing directors of sports who on holidays in the parks and playgrounds induct the young Parisians into the kinds of out-door games and exercises most suitable for adoption with a view to their proper physical development, has been profitably imitated elsewhere.

There is, however, a real danger in permitting the weak and delicate to participate in games for which they are totally unequal. On the other hand, in general, healthy boys may be left to their own inclinations as regards their recreative exercises. The tendency to specialization in athletic sports is to be deprecated everywhere and with respect to competition in games in elementary schools, or indeed before the age of 18 years, I do not hesitate to state that the physical damages sustained far outweight any advantages that may possibly accrue therefrom.

The educational advantages or habit-producing effects of systematic exercises in youth, are scarcely less important as a factor in physical development than an improved organic vigor and increased endurance as the result of muscular activity. It is a matter of common observation that if the habit of taking muscular exercise be formed thus early, it is more likely to be maintained during after life than if physical training be first taken up at a later period.   .

The pupil learns incidentally the true value of ventilation both at school and in the home.   More important is the ·training of the child for submissiveness to control, and for methodical arrangement.   Physical culture, as is well known, also strengthens the will power and makes for greater alertness and quicker perception.

If the foregoing arguments be accepted then the methods to be pursued would appear to call for consideration here.   The details of the subject, however, do not belong to my theme, although graded lessons, which have been ably advocated by William A. Stecher, G.G.,* in physical training and games, are to be strongly advised and encouraged.

At present writing, physical culture in the public schools in general is in a transition stage, a stage that can scarcely be said to be replete with promise of the dawn of that day when the body shall receive proper cultivation.   There is urgent need of safeguards against what has been aptly termed "the mechanical and perfunctory tendencies of routine officialism."   On the other hand those bodies which are in immediate control of our elementary educational system cannot much longer neglect the subject of physical education without inviting the just censure of public and professional opinion.

*Handbook of Graded Lessons in Physical Training and Games, Part I, II, III, published by John J. McVey, Philadelphia.

PHYSICAL MEASUREMENTS OF PUPILS IN MOSTAR, HERZEGOVINA (AUSTRIA)

BY

P. R. RADOSAVLJEVICH

The original purpose of this study was to investigate thoroughly the problem of the relation between bodily development and intellectual activity of school children by means of experimental psychological investigation and school anthropometry. The study was begun in 1904 at the suggestion of my two university teachers in Zurich—Dr. Ernst Meumann, director of the psychological laboratory and Dr. Rudolf Martin, director of the anthropological laboratory.

The individuals who furnished the basis of this study were both children and adults, males and females, educated and noneducated, European and American, including 4,634 persons, between the ages of the new born and 65 years. The bulk of these individuals are pupils from the elementary and secondary schools of two cities and one village in Austro-Hungary. I studied and measured pupils of five public elementary schools, one high gymnasium, one high school for girls, one mercantile school, one industrial school in Mostar, Herzegovina, two training schools for teachers in Zombor (Hungary), and two public schools in a Slavonian village. In addition to that I had a few school children from the public schools of Belgrade (Serbia), Agram (Kroatia) and Zurich (Switzerland). In America I studied and measured several hundred children in New York City (Public School No. 10, Bronx), Bayonne and Garfield, N. J., and one public elementary school and high school in Palo Alto, Cal. Many European and American teachers and university students, as well as a large number of European peasants and South-Slavic laborers of America are included here.

In this paper I will refer only to the pupils from the high gymnasium for boys, the elementary and secondary public schools of Mostar (a town in an Austrian province). All pupils are of the same nationality. They are Serbs or Kroatians but of three religious faiths— Greek Orthodox, Catholic and Mohammedan.

The measurements of these pupils include:

1. *Standing Height* (upright position without shoes), from the ground to the vertex, measured by Martin's anthropometer.

2. *Sitting Height*, taken between the vertex and the plane of the tuberosities of the ichia (bony prominences of the buttock) on which

the body rests when in a sitting position.   Measured by the same anthro-pometer.

3. *Total Horizontal Circumference of the Head*, measured by the anthropometric tape, over the frontal prominences and over the occipital prominences.

4. *Weight of the Body*, measured by Jaraso's *Personenwage*.

5. *Maximum Length of the Head* (from the glabella taken as the fixed point, to the most prominent part of the occiput of the head), measured by Martin's calipers.

6. *Maximum Width of the Head* (the distance above the level of the ears on a line with the frontal sinuses), measured by the same calipers.

7. *Maximum Height of the Head* (from the vertex to the tragus of the ear), measured by Martin's anthropometer.

8. *Maximum Length of the Right and Left Ear* (from the highest to the lowest point of the auriculara), measured by another Martin's calipers.

9. *Maximum Width of the Right and Left Ear* (maximum diameter at right angles to the length; line from the ear basis to the under border of the auricle), measured by the same caliper.

10. *Color of the Eyes*, measured by Martin's *Augenfarben-Tafel*.

11. *Color of the Hair*, measured by Fischer's *Haarfarben-Tafel*.

12. *Color of the Skin*, measured by von Luschan's *Hautfarben-Tafel*.

13. *Dynamic Power of the Right and Left Hand*, measured by Sternberg's *Dynamometer*.

By means of the three head diameters (*i. e.*, length, width and height) I studied the following cephalic indices and formulæ:

(14)   *Latitudinal or Cephalic Index =*

$$= \frac{\text{Max. Width} \times 100}{\text{Max. Length}}, \text{ with the following classification:}$$

1. Hyperdolichocephaly......................... $\times$—69.9
2. Dolichocephaly............................. 70—76
3. Mesocephaly................................76.5—80.9
4. Brachycephaly.............................81.0—85.9
5. Hyperbrachycephaly........................86.0—$\times$.

(15)   *Altitudinal or Verticax Cephalic Index =*

$$= \frac{\text{Max. Height} \times 100}{}, \text{ with the following classification:}$$

Max. Length
1. Hyperchamaecephaly..........................X—64.9
2. Chamaecephaly.......................,.........65—69.9
3. Orthocephaly................................70—74.9
4. Hypsicephaly...............................75—X

(16) *Cephalic Index of Height =*

$$= \frac{\text{Max. Height} \times 100}{\text{Max. Width}}.$$

(17) *Cephalic Module of Schmidt =*

$$= \frac{\text{Max. Length} \times \text{Max. Width} \times \text{Max. Height of Head}}{3}$$

(18) *Cephalic Capacity =*

(a) For males: 0.000337 (Length—7) $\times$ (Width—7) $\times$ (Height—7) $\times$ 406.01.
(b) For females: 0.000400 (L—7) $\times$ (W—7) $\times$ (H—7) $\times$ 206.60
with the following classification:

1. Physiological microcephaly................ X—1150 cm.[3]
2. Elatocephaly..........................1150—1300 cm.
3. Oligocephaly..........................1300—1400 cm.
4. Metricephaly....,...................1400—1500 cm.
5. Megalocephaly........:................1500—X   cm.

Besides the full name of each pupil, age (year and the day of the month), birth place, sex, grade, religion and social conditions, the intelligence of the pupil was also noted. In some cases I used single psycho-physical tests (almost all pupils have been tested in regard to their immediate memory or range of attention); in other cases a series of tests, involving the principal mental functions was applied, but finally I abandoned this method of judging school intelligence, and divided all the pupils into three main groups ("bright," "dull" and "average") on the basis of a synthesis of their schools' marks and teacher's personal judgment, with the condition that in both cases the marks in mathematics, physics and grammar are of the first rate in "bright" pupils.

The method of study was individual-collective, all the tests and measurements being made by myself. The *môdus operandi* was uniform, but the time does not allow me to enter into this subject. The mass of the material to be dealt with is too great, however, to be satisfactorily treated within the necessary limits of the present paper. I will restrict it to the most general conclusions in regard to the relation between the height and weight of body, cephalic indices, circumference, strength of the hand-grip and color of the eyes, hair and skin, on one hand, and the school brightness of the pupils on the other hand.

The following tables give the most general results with special reference to age, sex and school brightness (Tables I–III):

TABLE I

Age in Years	Number of Cases	Height (Cm.)		Weight (Kg.)	Circumference (Mm.)	Head Measurements (Mm.)					Dynamic Power (Kg.)	
		Standing	Sitting			Length	Cephalic Index	Vertical Index	Width	Height	Right Hand	Left Hand
6	88	111.85	62.35	19.498	509	176.8	81.58	64.02	144.06	113	8.67	8.15
7	248	116.84	64.67	20.719	512.9	177	82.11	64.87	144.5	114.5	9.97	9.65
8	306	121.76	66.15	23.726	519.5	178.3	82.03	64.88	146	115.5	11.33	11.00
9	360	126.67	68.76	26.077	924.1	179.3	82.43	64.52	148	115.5	13.24	12.44
10	212	131.52	70.13	28.248	522.4	180.1	82.73	65.18	148.5	117	14.89	13.79
11	179	135.45	72.36	31.048	527.0	181.4	82.03	64.64	148.5	117	16.50	15.71
12	151	140.73	75.12	34.264	527.8	181.9	82.64	65.01	150	118	19.29	17.14
13	125	147.96	78.02	38.543	529.0	183.8	81.74	64.03	150	117.5	22.50	20.02
14	89	153.62	80.57	44.025	531.7	184.8	82.11	64.23	151.5	118.5	25.69	23.20
15	76	160.11	83.09	48.148	535.1	186	82.75	64.10	153.5	119	31.73	25.82
16	43	164.15	86.50	53.984	537.8	188	82.45	64.89	155	122	40	35.30
17	22	167.05	88.38	57.847	536.4	189.4	82.54	65.61	156	124	44.50	39.93
18	7	172	90.40	62.040	540.9	193.8	81.35	64.77	157	125	50.56	43.40
19	6	173.40	90.85	62.855	539.7	19.2	82.11	65.26	156	124	50.40	44.90
20	4	173.95	90.95	62.945	539.8	192.1	81.77	64.58	157	124	50.10	45.24

TABLE II

Age in Years	Number of Cases		Height (Cm.)				Weight (Kg.)		Circumference (Mm.)		Head Measurements (Mm.)										Dynamic Power (Kg.)			
			Standing		Sitting						Length		Width		Height		Cephalic Index		Vertical Index		Males		Females	
	Males	Females	Males	Females	Males	Females	Males	Females	Males	Females	Males	Females	Males	Females	Males	Females	Males	Females	Males	Females	Right Hand	Left Hand	Right Hand	Left Hand
6	38	50	112.35	111.40	62.65	62.05	19.845	19.152	509.2	508.8	178	175	145	143	114	112	81.46	81.71	64.04	64	9.35	9.30	8.05	7.05
7	198	50	117.15	116.53	64.84	64.5	20.085	20.454	513.4	512.5	179	174	145	144	116	113	81.56	82.76	64.8	64.94	10.8	10.46	9.14	8.85
8	205	101	122.08	121.44	66.3	66	23.884	23.568	519.3	519.8	180	176	147	145	117	114	81.67	82.39	65	64.77	12.5	12	10.17	10.5
9	105	165	127.14	126.00	69.05	68.59	26.854	25.300	523.5	524.8	181	178	149	147	117	114	82.32	83.15	64.44	64.61	15	14.30	11.48	11.48
10	152	60	133.05	131.85	70.26	70	28.944	27.642	527.4	528.8	182	180	149	148	118	115	82.42	81.67	65.19	65.17	16.85	16.1	12.94	13
11	149	30	135.42	135.05	72.13	72.59	31.854	30.243	527.1	528.5	182	181	150	149	118	116	82.97	82.32	65.84	64.44	19	18.42	14	14.15
12	105	40	140.42	143.05	74.3	75.05	33.084	34.045	529.8	529	184	181	151	149	118	117	82.07	81.42	64.13	65.38	21.64	20.14	16.95	16.98
13	87	38	147.59	148.45	77	79.05	37.945	39.142	532.3	531.1	186	183	151	149	119	117	82.26	81.97	63.93	64.64	25	23.04	20	19.4
14	74	75	153.2	154.05	79.95	81.20	43.154	44.905	535.8	535.2	186	183	153	150	119	118	83.33	82.16	63.08	63.48	29.5	27	21.88	20.5
15	75		160.22	160	83.18	83	48.243	48.054	537.8		188	185	155	152	120	118	82.45		64.52	63.78	33.8	31.14	29.69	
16	43		164.15		86.50		53.984		536.4		189		155		122		82.54		64.89		40	35.3		
17	22		167.05		88.38		57.849		540.9		193		150		124		82.15		65.71		44.5	39.93		
18	7		172.0		90.40		62.940		539.7		190		157		125		81.77		65.26		56	43.4		
19	6		173.4		90.85		62.855		539.8		192		157		124				64.58		50.4	44.9		
20	4		173.95		90.95		62.945								124						50.1	45.24		

TABLE III

Age in Years	Number of Cases		Height (Cm.)		Weight (Kg.)		Circumference (Mm.)		Cephalic Index		Dynamic Power (Kg.)			
											Right Hand		Left Hand	
	Bright	Dull	Bright	Dull	Bright	Dull	Bright	Dull	Bright	Dull	Bright	Dull	Bright	Dull
6	25	10	111.80	111.25	20.120	19.347	511	510	83.2	81.8	8.69	8	8.24	8
7	76	38	116.88	116.04	20.618	20.700	512	512	86.0	84.3	10.05	9.90	9.98	9.45
8	87	41	120.98	121.68	23.870	23.542	518	519	84.2	82.2	11.45	11.50	11.20	10.98
9	79	36	126.73	126.57	26.420	26.104	523	522	86.2	84.2	13.80	13.04	13.00	12.00
10	79	30	131.64	131.55	27.469	28.300	522	522	86.4	83.9	14.56	15.02	13.04	13.14
11	68	27	136.04	135.94	31.268	31.015	526	527	86.1	83.2	16.89	16.04	16.90	15.04
12	43	26	140.98	140.44	34.940	34.108	527	526	86.3	84.9	19.80	19.10	17.70	17.00
13	23	14	148.40	147.68	37.543	38.486	528	529	86.4	82.8	22.20	22.80	20.05	19.84
14	20	9	153.98	153.49	44.000	44.000	532	530	86.7	83.4	26.04	25.40	24.00	23.50
15	22	10	161.48	160.47	48.563	48.200	534	534	84.6	83.3	32.10	31.54	25.05	25.68
16	11	7	164	163.80	54.756	53.845	538	537	85.4	84.2	39.42	39.10	35.45	34.98
17	14	7	166.82	167	57.90	57.147	536	536	86.1	83.3	45	44.10	40	38.95
18	13	7	172.32	172.05	62.450	62.980	540	539	85.6	85.3	50.08	50.45	43.54	43
19	9	5	172.85	173.15	62.142	62.052	539	539	85.2	85.1	50	49.85	45.80	44.45
20	4	3	172.45	174.25	62.734	63.125	539	540	84.8	83.8	48.70	50	45.05	46

From these three tables of average values it is seen:

First. There is a steady but irregular increase in the height and weight of body from 6 to 20 years of age—standing height shows an increase of 62.10 cm., weight, 42.447 kg.; sitting height, 28.60 cm. Similar increase is shown by circumference of the head (398 mm.), and dynamic power, 41.43 kg. for the right hand, and 37.09 kg. for the left hand. A slight increase is shown also by the length, width and height of the head— 163 mm., 12 mm., and 11 mm. respectively. In regard to the cephalic indices such an increase is not shown; both cephalic index and vertical index are more or less constant throughout the ages studied, *i. e.*, all ages are characterized by the same typical shape of the head—they are more or less brachycephalic and chamaecephalic.

Secondly. Sex difference is very slight and irregular in all measurements throughout the ages studied.

Thirdly. Differences due to the school brightness are also very slight and irregular in all measurements throughout the ages tested.

These three main results are based on average values only. The following tables (Tables IV–VI) show that even such too general conclusions change if we take in account individual distribution of cases.

Fourthly. In regard to the cephalic index, for example, they are almost all types of shape of head at every age, with a predominance of brachycephaly. These is also true with reference to the sex and brightness of pupils. Average values in school anthropometry must be studied and evaluated with reference to the distribution of cases, maxima and minima, variation, number of cases and so on.

Fifthly. Other measurements (including color of the eyes, hair and skin) also do not show relation with school brightness of pupils.

Sixthly. Social conditions, religious faith and birthplace (country or city) of pupils shows no relation with their sex and school brightness. Time does not permit me to compare even these most general results with the curious and sweeping conclusions derived from many school anthropometricians, anthropologists and the followers of experimental psychology and experimental pedagogy. School anthropology of to-day is trying to fight out its own independence in both theoretical and practical aspects.

TABLE IV—CEPHALIC INDEX AND AGE

Ages in Years	VI	VII	VIII	IX	X	XI	XII	XIII	XIV	XV	XVI	XVII	XVIII	XIX	XX	Totals	%
75–75.9	2	2	2			1	1									8	} 2.3% Dolichocephaly
76	1	2	2	3	1		1		1		1		1			12	
77	2	3	3		1	1	1						1			12	} 11.2% Mesocephaly
78	2	7	7	1	1	1	1	1	1			1		1		22	
79	4	7	4		2	3		1								22	
80	5	7	7	6	4	2	3	1	1	1	1		1	1		40	
81	4	14	12	11	8	6	4	7	1	2		1		1	2	72	} 57.5% Brachycephaly
82	4	18	19	15	13	5	5	9	4	4	3	1	1	4	1	104	
83	3	9	22	17	23	15	9	5	5	6	5	3	1	5	2	126	
84	2	4	10	13	6	16	9	2	7	8	6	2	5	7		91	
85	2	5	6	15	16	11	11	13	2	2	3	4	3	2	2	99	
86	1	4	7	9	8	5	8	3		3	4	5		4	3	66	} 29% Hyperbrachycephaly
87	1	7	5	4	10	3	2	1	1		1	1	1			34	
88		6	3	6	2	3	2		1	2		1	1			29	
89	1	5	5	4	5	3	5	1	1		1	1	1		1	31	
90	1	2	4	3	2	2	2			1	1		1			20	
91		4	1	2	1		1									14	} 249
92		3	1	1	1	2	2			1	1					11	
93		1	2	1	1	1	1		1		1	1		1		9	
94	1	2	3	2	2	1	1	1		1			1			14	
95				1					1							8	
96		2	2	2	2	1				1			1			9	
97—97.9			1	2					1							4	
	VI	VII	VIII	IX	X	XI	XII	XIII	XIV	XV	XVI		XVIII	XIX	XX		
Minimum	75.7	75.6	75.8	76.7	76.8	75.8	76.1	78.2	70.9	76.1	75.9		77.9	80.1	81.8		
Mean	82.5	84.9	83.2	85.2	85.1	84.6	85.4	84.6	85	84.4	84.8		85.4	85.1	84.4		
Maximum	95.1	96.5	97.2	97.8	96.9	96.8	95.8	97.2	96.3	96.3	93.7		97.2	94.9	90.7		
Variation	19.4	20.9	21.4	20.9	19.9	20.9	19.7	19	19.4	20.2	17.8		19.3	14.8	8.9		
Cases	35	114	128	115	109	95	69	37	29	32	18		20	14	7		

Totals: 8 } 20; 12 }; 96; 492; 249

TABLE V.—CEPHALIC INDEX, AGE AND SCHOOL BRIGHTNESS—VALUES FOR "BRIGHT" PUPILS

Age in Years	VI	VII	VIII	IX	X	XI	XII	XIII	XIV	XV	XVI	XVII	XVIII	XIX	XX	Totals	%	
78	—	1	1	—	—	—	—	—	—	—	1	—	—	—	—	2		Mesocephaly
79	1	1	1	—	—	1	—	—	1	—	—	—	—	—	—	4	16 6%	
80	2	2	2	1	—	—	—	—	—	—	—	—	—	—	—	10		
81	3	5	3	2	1	2	—	—	—	—	1	—	—	—	1	18		Brachycephaly
82	6	3	6	3	3	3	1	—	1	—	—	—	1	—	—	23		
83	5	5	6	3	3	2	1	—	3	1	2	1	3	1	2	37	137 50.7%	
84	4	2	4	5	—	4	2	—	3	3	—	3	—	3	—	35		
85	1	2	3	5	2	2	1	1	1	1	—	1	—	—	—	24		
86	1	2	5	2	2	3	2	5	—	1	1	—	—	1	1	32		Hyper-brachycephaly
87	1	3	1	3	1	1	1	—	—	1	—	—	—	—	—	14		
88	—	3	1	2	1	1	—	—	—	—	—	—	—	—	—	15		
89	—	2	1	2	1	1	—	—	—	—	—	—	—	—	—	11		
90	2	1	1	—	1	2	1	—	—	—	—	—	—	—	—	7		
91	1	2	1	1	—	1	—	—	—	—	—	—	—	—	—	7	117 43.3%	
92	—	2	—	1	—	—	—	—	—	—	1	—	—	—	—	7		
93	1	—	1	1	—	1	—	—	—	—	—	—	—	—	—	4		
94	3	1	1	—	1	1	—	—	1	—	—	—	—	—	—	8		
95	—	—	—	—	—	—	1	—	—	1	—	—	—	—	—	4		
96	2	1	—	—	—	—	—	—	—	—	—	—	—	—	—	5		
97	1	—	—	—	—	—	—	—	1	—	—	—	—	—	—	2		
Minimum	79.8	78.8	78.2	81.8	80.1	79.9	80.8	81.2	83.7	82.3	80.2	84.5	80.8	83.1	81.8			
Mean	83.2	86	84.2	86.2	86.4	86.1	86.3	86.4	86.7	84.6	85.4	86.1	85.6	85.2	84.8			
Maximum	87.8	96.5	96.9	97.9	96.9	95.8	94.8	95.9	96.3	95.2	92.2	91.3	97.2	90.8	90.7			
Variation	8	17.7	18.7	15.9	16.8	15.9	14	14.7	12.6	12.9	12.7	6.8	16.4	7.7	8.9			
Cases	25	76	87	79	79	68	43	23	20	22	11	14	13	9	4			

TABLE VI—CEPHALIC INDEX, AGE AND SCHOOL BRIGHTNESS—VALUES FOR "DULL" PUPILS

Ages in Years	VI	VII	VIII	IX	X	XI	XII	XIII	XIV	XV	XVI	XVII	XVIII	XIX	XX	Totals	%
75–75.9	2	2	3	3	1	1	1	—	—	—	1	—	—	—	—	9 } 22	3.9% } Dolicho-cephaly
76	1	2	3	3	1	1	1	1	1	1	—	—	—	—	—	13	
7	2	3	3	—	1	1	1	1	—	—	—	1	—	—	—	12	
78	2	6	6	1	1	1	—	1	1	—	—	—	1	—	—	20 } 81	13.7% } Meso-cephaly
79	3	6	3	—	1	2	2	1	1	1	—	—	—	—	—	18	
80	3	5	5	6	2	2	2	1	1	1	1	1	1	1	—	31	
81	3	9	9	9	7	4	2	3	1	2	2	1	1	—	1	51	
82	3	15	13	14	11	2	3	7	4	3	3	1	1	1	1	83 } 353	59.6% } Brachy-cephaly
83	2	4	16	12	19	11	4	5	4	4	4	2	2	1	—	89	
84	1	2	6	10	12	13	6	1	1	4	4	2	2	1	—	69	
85	1	3	5	10	12	9	10	1	1	3	3	1	—	1	1	61	
86	—	2	2	4	6	3	5	1	—	3	3	3	—	—	—	35	
87	—	4	4	2	7	2	1	1	—	1	1	—	1	—	—	22	
88	—	3	2	2	1	2	1	—	—	—	—	1	1	1	—	15	
89	1	2	3	2	3	2	3	—	—	—	—	—	1	1	—	19 } 136	} Hyper-brachy-cephaly
90	1	1	3	2	1	1	1	—	—	—	1	—	—	1	1	11	
91	—	2	1	2	1	—	—	1	—	—	—	—	—	—	—	7	
92	—	1	1	—	—	—	—	—	—	—	—	—	—	—	—	4	
93	—	1	1	—	—	—	1	1	—	—	—	—	—	1	—	5	
94	1	1	1	1	1	1	1	—	1	—	—	—	—	—	—	6	
95	—	1	—	—	—	—	—	1	—	—	—	—	—	—	—	5	
96	—	—	—	—	1	—	—	—	—	—	—	—	—	—	—	4	
97	—	—	—	—	—	—	—	—	1	—	—	—	—	—	—	3	

	VI	VII	VIII	IX	X	XI	XII	XIII	XIV	XV	XVI	XVII	XVIII	XIX	XX
Minimum	75.7	75.6	75.8	76.7	76.8	75.9	76.1	78.2	76.9	76.1	75.9	78.5	78.9	80.1	81.8
Mean	81.8	84.3	82.2	84.2	83.9	83.3	84.9	82.8	83.4	83.3	84.2	83.3	85.3	85.1	83.8
Maximum	95.1	96.4	97.2	97.4	96.8	96.8	95.8	97.	95.9	94.9	93.7	95.4	95.9	94.9	89.7
Variation	19.4	20.8	21.4	20.7	20	20.9	19.7	19.	19	18.8	17.8	16.9	18.8	14.8	7.9
Cases	10	38	41	36	30	27	26	14	9	10	7	7	7	5	3

SOME FUNDAMENTALS IN PHYSICAL TRAINING IN PUBLIC SCHOOLS

BY

GORDON B. TROWBRIDGE

Physical training should begin in the kindergarten and be continued through the high school if possible. It will then become a habit with a child so that he may continue with some form of physical recreation during the remainder of his life. However, this will depend to a large extent upon the kind of instruction and inspiration he receives from the teacher.

Place For Physical Training. The proper place for the teaching of physical training is in a free space, well lighted and well ventilated. It should be conducted by a special teacher, each class having its regular daily period in the gymnasium.

Unfortunately many cities find it necessary to have the physical work given in the regular classroom. Hence I shall discuss the subject from this standpoint.

Under these conditions, the work best suited to the child of the first three grades seems to be imitative plays and games. In the first and second grades, the child is at the age when he imitates. In fact, the greater part of a child's play is imitative. Hence I believe the imitative games and plays are the most natural form of physical activity for young children.

In the third grade we see the child changing from the imitative and showing an inclination to take the initiative. Here we may advantageously include some free standing gymnastic work. It is valuable for its educational and hygienic effect; it teaches a child to act promptly and to exert his full energy, one of the best lessons he can learn; it is the beginning of a healthy habit.

Hygienically it stimulates heart action; in fact, it stimulates all organs of the body; it breaks down tissue and hastens the removal of waste products; it replenishes all tissue through the medium of the blood. The result depends upon the presentation of the work by the teacher. If given in a slow, unattractive manner, the work becomes a farce and the child develops the deplorable habit of doing his work carelessly. If given with vigor and animation, he becomes enthusiastic and really enjoys doing those movements which are fundamental in the games and plays. Every exercise should be executed with a large, full, active muscular movement extending to the limit of motion.

The real game spirit does not develop much before the third grade, although this depends to some extent upon the child and the instruction.

Many teachers are antagonistic toward running games in the class-room, primarily owing to the danger, and secondarily to the fact that they do not understand the games and the physical side of the child. The solution of this I shall endeavor to show a little later. With due respect for the danger that enters into school-room play, it is a splendid training for the judgment of the child and for the control of the body.

In teaching a new game, it would be better to walk through the game rather than to run. Use a few children instead of the whole class, and the order in the room can then be maintained.

Many teachers now recognize the fact that to obtain the best results in mental work the periods should not be longer than twenty to twenty-five minutes; this should be followed by a short period of physical activity (three to ten minutes) with windows open.

Frequent exertions, to their full capacity, aid the healthy growth of the mental and physical powers. It is evident that as yet we have not come into a full realization of the physical side of the child's life, when we keep him inclosed in the vitiated atmosphere of a school-room for five hours a day. The modern ventilating systems are fine pieces of mechanism but frequently fail to do their work. At present there does not seem to be anything that is an improvement over the open window for admitting fresh air.

In Boston, the Board of Education has made it a rule that the windows on one side of the room shall be kept open at all times unless the temperature falls below 67 degrees. This I believe to be one of the best rules ever inaugurated.

Grammar Grades. In the upper grades, the work changes slightly but the principles remain the same. Free standing gymnastics, dancing, and games must here form the basis of the physical work. The dances should be carefully selected, tending toward individual effort instead of couple dances.

The free standing gymnastics should be few in number, vigorous in execution, prolonged in repetition and, above everything else, should be corrective.

About ninety per cent. of the school children have very bad posture. The protruding abdomens, round shoulders, flat or depressed chest are the ever present conditions among school children. Balancing the weight forward over the arch of the foot, back exercises for straightening the dorsal curve, breathing exercises for elevating and expanding the chest, and coöperation between child and teacher are the fundamentals for correcting bad posture.

Games. Games are important. Children are very fond of them when they are properly played. They are unexcelled as an instrument for obtaining control of a class of children. Mutual respect and fairness for the other fellow are the important lessons that they teach.

Supervision. Elementary school supervision by the special teacher should occur at frequent intervals (two to four weeks). The most helpful manner of carrying out supervision is through suggestion and demonstration for the teacher and the children.

Physical Training in High Schools. In high schools, the problem is a different one. The principles of application remain the same but we have a free space and a larger variety of apparatus, dancing, games, and drills to choose from.

The dancing is a comparatively new feature in the work but a valuable and an interesting one, if properly taught. If the aesthetic dancing the pupils should have sufficient drill upon the fundamental movements so that they will become mechanical.

The aesthetic dance develops a high degree of co-ordination, and well executed. The movements must be large, full, and well extended or the dancing will develop into a posing, instead of poising, with many pupils.

The apparatus and games develop a high degree of co-ordination, courage, skill, endurance, strength and control of the mental and physical powers of the child.

The gymnasium periods should be daily in order to obtain the greatest degree of efficiency, and anything less than two periods a week is very unsatisfactory.

During the periods of exercise in the gymnasium is an exceptional opportunity to teach the hygiene of dress, exercise, *correct posture* and deep breathing.

This, however, devolves and depends upon the teachers of physical training; they must be well trained to perform these duties.

Qualifications of Grade Teachers. The importance of a teacher being qualified physically, as well as mentally, to do the work of teaching in a grade school cannot be over-emphasized. In the past, very little attention has been given to the physical qualifications in selecting teachers. We are now approaching the time when it will be necessary for all persons, intending to become teachers, to pass a physical examination when entering the service.

It may become necessary for Boards of Education to encourage and, in fact, to make it obligatory for teachers to take part in some form of physical activity for the purpose of keeping themselves in good physical condition for the performance of their duties. They will then be prepared not only to understand but to sympathize with the physical activities of child life.

It might be advisable for Boards of Education to support some form of physical exercise adapted to the needs of teachers.

The selection of teachers who have strong bodies, good digestion, good mental capacity, well balanced minds, and who are in sympathy with their work will solve the problem of getting effective instruction in the public schools.

BLOOD PTOSIS—A TEST OF VASO-MOTOR EFFICIENCY

BY

C. WARD CRAMPTON

We have few if any accurate scientific tests of health. On this account school hygiene shares with other branches of medicine a relative inability quickly and certainly to test the failure or success of its methods.

We labor to improve the health of school children and to increase their prospects of life by physical training, athletics, instruction in hygiene, school lunches, open air classes, changes in ventilation and the like and invariably experience difficulty in clearly and honestly stating what gain has been made by our work.

It is true that such records as increase of haemoglobin and decrease in abseuse rates have their value, and certain strength and endurance tests have some merit, but they are all subject to error, incomplete or difficult to control.

The ideal test must state numerically the condition of an individual as a whole as regards his ability to live vigorously or it must state the efficiency of a fundamental necessity of living in terms which may serve as a basis for comparison.

During the course of an exhaustive study on blood pressure* [NOTE.— Olympic Congress Lectures Gold Medal Thesis, St. Louis Exposition 1904. "Blood Pressure in Its Relations to Physical Training Procedure."], I presented a test which fulfills the latter requirements.

It is a statement of the efficiency of the vaso-motor system in responding to the necessity of, raising the blood pressure upon rising from the recumbent to the standing position.

In the perfectly normal vigorous male the blood pressure will rise from 8 to 10 mm. of mercury upon assuming the standing position. In one damaged by disease, overwork or unhygienic living or weakened by inactivity, the blood pressure will fail to rise and may fall as much as 10 mm. of mercury. The heart rate acts in exactly the opposite fashion, rising in proportion to weakness as much as 45 beats a minute, but only in exceptional cases falling.

These two adjustments are independent, one often masking the failure of the other and both must be considered and balanced. If

*Physical Education Review, 1905-1906; Medical News, Sept. 16, 1905.

blood pressure were alone considered many cases showing a high heart rate would be given a good rating when it should be poor and vice versa.

This test has been put into regular routine practice by R. Tait Mc-Kenzie, M.D., of University of Pennsylvania, Geo. H. Meylan, M.D., Columbia University, Dr. Raycroft of Princeton, Dr. Storey of the College of the City of New York, Dr. Marks of Pittsburg and Dr. McCurdy of Springfield, and others, in examination of athletics for "permission to compete" and for other purposes.

It is based upon the following facts:

1. If the blood were contained in flaccid tubes without support it would, upon standing, drop to the lowest possible point and remain there. There would be none to reach the heart and none would be pumped to the head. A complete blood ptosis would occur and death would result at once. This does not occur because there is some mechanical support and the blood vessels are not flaccid but held to a narrow lumen by circular muscles in turn controlled by the sympathetic nervous system. The most capacious system of blood vessels in the body are the splanchnic veins; these can hold all the blood volume if released from the vaso-constrictor efforts of the nervous system.

In the perfectly normal there occurs upon rising from the recumbent position a vaso-constriction effort which squeezes these veins and raises blood pressure which more than overcomes the added hydrostatic load. In the subnormal this vaso-constriction effort is relatively weak and ineffective and does not raise the blood pressure in the upper body but allows it to fall under hydrostatic pressure. There is a blood ptosis due to the relative failure of vaso-motor tone. This may be mild, merely a failure to raise the pressure or a fall of the systolic pressure 5 or 10 mm. in which case we may still call our patient fairly normal. It may be a more complete failure allowing the systolic pressure to drop to 40 or 50 at which point the patient faints from cerebral anaemia. This is the familiar picture seen when a convalescent patient with vaso-tone damaged rises prematurely from a sick bed and, robbing the splanchnic veins of mechanical support by emptying the bladder, falls to the floor.

The most severe grade of vaso-tone paralysis occurs as a terminal phenomenon in poisoning from disease in which case the patient literally bleeds into his abdominal veins.

Vaso-tone is then a function essential to life; a delicate measurement of its efficiency such as is indicated in the foregoing is worthy of consideration as an important indication of the condition and vitality of the whole body which depends upon vaso-tone for its proper functioning.

It would then seem to be necessary merely to observe the amount of rise and fall of the systolic pressure at a convenient point in the upper body to determine the efficiency of the vaso-motor system and its reverse, the amount of blood ptosis.

Another fact presents itself in the increase in heart rate which accompanies vaso-tone failure. Hill states that the heart, as it were, comes to the rescue of the falling pressure by beating faster in a successful endeavor to re-establish it, its rate increasing in proportion to the necessity. In this case we would discover weakened vaso-tone by either increased heart rate or fall in blood pressure or both, but only by taking both into consideration, we may arrive at a correct estimation of the weakness.

Another explanation maintains that the increased heart rate does not raise the pressure but merely reveals it, for the heart furnished with a lessened charge of blood is able to send it into the arteries more quickly.

From my own observation it is clear that a single patient will show in successive readings a variation of blood pressure and heart rate which compensate each other while the consideration of both will reveal no change in vaso-tone efficiency.

The balancing of these two is a matter of some importance. The usual range of the systolic pressure is from + 10 to — 10 of the heart rate increase from 0 to 44 as observed from records of a large number of cases. Upon a statistical balancing of these two series of frequencies and assigning equal percentages to equal ranges the following scale is constructed.

PERCENTAGE SCALE

VASO-MOTOR TONE   C. Ward Crampton, M.D.

500 Park Ave., New York City

BLOOD PRESSURE

Heart Rate Inc.	Increase					0	Decrease				
	+10	+8	+6	+4	+2	0	—2	—4	—6	—8	—10
0– 4	100	95	90	85	80	75	70	65	60	55	50
5– 8	95	90	85	80	75	70	65	60	55	50	45
9–12	90	85	80	75	70	65	60	55	50	45	40
13–16	85	80	75	70	65	60	55	50	45	40	35
17–20	80	75	70	65	60	55	50	45	40	35	30
21–24	75	70	65	60	55	50	45	40	35	30	25
25–28	70	65	60	55	50	45	40	35	30	25	20
29–32	65	60	55	50	45	40	35	30	25	20	15
33–36	60	55	50	45	40	35	30	25	20	15	10
37–40	55	50	45	40	35	30	25	20	15	10	5
41–44	50	45	40	35	30	25	20	15	10	5	0

NOTE.—In case of increase in pressure higher than +10 add 5% to the +10 column for each 2 mm. in excess of 10.

This scale provides a convenient and intelligible method of recording and reporting cases and permits a numerical statement of the function in question. Its 100 mark indicates a perfectly efficient working of the vaso-motor system under test, the zero is approximately the point where the average person is unable to maintain the erect posture.

The technique of the test is as follows:

The sphygmoomanometer is adjusted over the brachial artery and the patient is placed on a comfortable couch with a low pillow. The heart state is counted by quarter minutes and a gradually decreasing rate is usually observed. Counting should continue until two successive quarter minutes are the same, this is multiplied by four, and recorded. The systolic pressure is then taken, preferably by auscultation. The patient stands, the heart rate is counted as before until it reaches the "standing normal" when it is recorded and the blood pressure is then taken. The differences are calculated and reference is made to the scale.

For example—Case XX: L. V. age 17 years claims to be in good condition at 11.20 A.M.

	Pulse Rate	Blood Pressure
Horizontal....................	68	100
Vertical.....................	104	94
Difference................:........	+36	− 6
Percentage record, 20.		

This is a very poor record taken from an apparently normal strong young football player of exceptional ability who had previously given records above 80.

I was at a loss to account for this for questioning failed to bring out any history of loss of sleep, dissipation or illness. He looked quite as "fit" as usual. He was absent next day and remained home for a week with a "cold and fever." It is evident that the test revealed a weakened vaso-tone, the beginning of actual illness before any other symptom could be noted. Others who have used this test have noted similar cases.

This test has been used to follow athletes through a course of training and as the basis for choice for the entry of one of several athletes of equal ability in an important race where only one might compete. It has been used to guide the daily exercise of athletes to guard against overwork and approaching staleness. It has been found useful in guiding treatment of the neurasthenic and overworked.

It has been used in school hygiene to determine the amount of physical cost of school procedures of various kinds. The following is a typical record.

Time	Increase Pulse Rate	Increase Blood Pressure	Percentage	Remarks
9:45 A.M.....	0	+10	100	Slept well, no exercise
10:45 A.M.....	0	+ 4	85	After lesson in physics, standing
11:50 A.M.....	8	+10	95	After lesson in algebra
12:24 A.M.....	5	+ 6	85	After lesson in French
1:10 P.M.....	6	+ 8	90	After lunch and rest
2:00 P.M.....	14	+ 8	80	After history lesson
2:35 P.M.....	16	+ 4	70	After slow one-mile run

This shows that one period of work in the physics laboratory (which required continued standing) was more expensive than a slow mile run. It also showed that this was partially regained in the next period, lost again during the French period and partially regained by rest at the lunch period. This record also shows the importance of considering both heart rate and blood pressure.

This test opened a wide field of investigation hitherto unworked. The effect of various modes of ventilation, of feeding, exercise and other hygienic procedure may be tested and recorded in terms which may be statistically stated and easily compared with a control series of records.

It has been used to test the amount of relaxation of vaso-tone resulting from various forms of physical exercise and shows clearly that exercise is expensive of nervous energy and should be followed by rest and recuperation.

This test will not reveal more than it assumes to test, i. e., the efficiency of the vaso-motor system. It will not show the presence of a mitral lesion any more than it will a decayed tooth. Nor will it test other factors of efficiency such as will power, inhibition or skill, it does provide a means of making a definite record of an all important bodily function. Those who work to mold schoolroom and other living conditions for the purpose of improving health and efficiency may be able by this means to measure the benefit resulting from their labors.

HAS SCHOOL GYMNASTICS AN APPRECIABLE EFFECT UPON HEALTH?

BY

WILLIAM A. STECHER

The chief aim of school gymnastics is to maintain and increase health, to develop and increase organic strength. Corrective work is a subdivision of this aim.

The second aim is to develop and increase skill, also courage, determination, quick reaction and other mental qualities. Have these results been accomplished by modern school gymnastics?

Gymnastics was introduced into some of the schools of Europe in the early part of the last century. It now is an essential part of the schooling of all boys, and of a yearly increasing number of girls. In the cities, as a rule, the work is done in well equipped gymnasiums and is in charge of specially trained teachers of gymnastics. In the rural districts the work is in the hands of the regular class teachers who, where there is no gymnasium, conduct the work out of doors. These class teachers receive special training for conducting gymnastics at the different training schools conducted by the various states. Teachers attending the special courses are paid for their attendance. It may be well to insert here that in Europe most class teachers are men. That this fact has a direct bearing upon the teaching of a subject like gymnastics is self-evident. In several European countries the work of both special and regular teachers in the cities as well as in the country districts is supervised by inspectors of gymnastics appointed by the government.

So far as the United States is concerned one may say that gymnastics, generally, has not been recognized as an integral part of school work. While most large cities have gymnastics it may be said that most small cities and practically all rural communities have no physical training at all.

The type of the work in most of our cities is instruction within the class room by the regular class teacher who, as a rule, is a woman. In several large cities the newer school buildings have either one or two gymnasiums. The work in these buildings is conducted in the gymnasium by the class teacher. A third type of work is conducted in several cities where new buildings have a gymnasium. This consists of having a specially trained teacher of gymnastics in such building who conducts the work of all classes in the gymnasium. Then, lastly, there is a type of work conducted by an increasing number of cities. This consists of work in the school yards. The corridors or class rooms are used only during inclement weather.

A handbook with complete, specially prepared lessons in physical training is generally used by the class teachers. The work in all cities is usually supervised by special teachers of physical training who, generally, are graduates of physical training normal schools. As there is no central authority in educational matters, the uniformity of aim and method found in European countries is entirely lacking in the United States. Each city, yes, at times, each district of a city, does as it pleases.

Coming now to the time devoted to physical training we find that in Europe two hours weekly, as a rule, are given over to gymnastics. In several German states three hours weekly is the rule. During the last few years the demand for an obligatory play afternoon in addition to the two, respectively three hours of regular gymnastics has arisen. This demand has been granted in a few cities. Where this play afternoon has been introduced the pupils and teachers report for several hours of play on one of the large playfields of the city. These playfields often are as far as one hour's walk from the home or school of some of the attending children. Where introduced this work is compulsory for all the children attending school.

In the United States the time set aside for physical training in the elementary schools varies from 10 to 15 minutes daily, that is from 50 to 75 minutes per week. In the high schools during the first year it usually consists of two weekly periods of 45 minutes each, from which the time for changing suits is to be deducted. In some cities the second high school year is like the first, in others it consists of only one period devoted to physical training. Very few high schools have more than one period per week during the last two years; many having no prescribed work at all. It appears, therefore, that the time devoted to regular gymnastics in the United States is about one-half to one-third of that used for the like purpose in Europe.

The next question would be to determine the health-value of the work done. Does the physical training found in our schools have an appreciable effect upon the health of the pupils, and does it give to the participants the motor training, the neuro-muscular education generally claimed for it?

So far as the United States is concerned there are no reliable statistics available which give satisfactory answers to these questions. The statistics gathered by European nations, especially of those where every male citizen must become a soldier do, however, shed impressive light upon our problem. Let us take Germany, for instance, whose economic conditions are sufficiently like those of the United States to allow one to use for comparison the results of the accurate inquiries undertaken there.   In Germany every able man must serve his country from one to three years, either in the army or navy.   Every recruit undergoes a rigid physical examination and no one is exempt from service unless he is totally unfit.

The following figures cover the physical condition of every 100 males who presented themselves for service during the years 1903 to 1911:

Year	Percentage acceptable	Improvable; will be acceptable later	Questionable as to future availability	Unfit; not available
1903.........	57.1	14.7	19.5	8.5
1904.........	56.4	15.6	20.9	6.9
1905.........	56.3	14.7	22.0	6.8
1906.........	55.9·	14.7	22.7	6.5
1907.........	54.9	15.1	23.1	6.6
1908.........	54.5	15.2	23.8	6.3
1909.........	53.6	14.9	25.0	6.3
1910.........	·53.0	14.8	25.9	6.1
1911.........	53.4	15.1	25.1	6.3

The men who in the above table are classed as not available are the totally unfit for military service, the cripples, the blind, the incurably sick, etc.   This division in 1911, thanks to the increased efficiency in combating the causes leading to such total disability shows a decrease of 2.3 per cent. as compared to 1903.   An increase, however, of 5.6 per cent. of those classed as questionable, that is of those classed as being so weak and under-nourished that it is questionable if they can ever be brought up to the required physical standard is an ominous feature. The percentage of acceptable men, also, has decreased 3.7 per cent.

The significant point of this investigation, the point that bears directly upon our problem is the fact that irrespective of all that Germany has done for the physical improvement of its future citizens there has been a gradual decrease in military fitness during the years in question. The physical deterioration in cities, and also in communities preëminently industrial is further emphasized by the fact that in 1911 such parts of Germany show a lower percentage of acceptable men than do the agricultural sections, vide with Brandenburg 42.3; Hessia with ·46.6; Saxony with 48.6 and Silesia with 48.9 per cent.

. The economic condition of the United States and of Germany (in fact of practically all nations of Europe) is very similar.   In all we

˙find an enormous increase of the urban population at the expense of the country districts. So far as the hygienic conditions in cities are concerned sanitary engineers seem to agree that these are better in Germany than in the United States. If, then, Germany with its two, respectively three hours of compulsory physical training work has not been able to stop physical deterioration and is trying to ward this off with increased time and better facilities devoted to rational body building, we readily can see that our 10 to 15 minutes per school day or our two periods of gymnasium work per week can have only a slight influence upon the health of the pupils, and can not prevent physical decay.

Practically all of the physical training work done in the schools of the United States is insufficient, first as to quantity and second as to quality. In the greater part of the schools it is mainly relief work. In the hands of properly trained teachers it somewhat mitigates the bad effects of poor and prolonged seating. Most schools in the United States, however, have no physical training work at all.

In order to make school gymnastics a real health factor we first of all must recognize the fact that a few minutes of arm-stretching or of trunk bending between the desks in a school room can not be called physical training. If well executed this may be relief work. If improperly taught it often is an additional mental strain upon the pupils.

It was a grave mistake when here in the United States well-meaning enthusiasts told Boards of Education that the introduction of gymnastics into the schools could be accomplished with little expenditure of time and money; that all that was needed was to allow a few special teachers to go into a schoolroom, and teach a few calisthenics, and then have the class teacher repeat these with the pupils. So long as Boards of Education and the general public believe that what now is called school gymnastics is sufficient to safeguard the health of children we will accomplish little. It must be understood that health can not be increased nor maintained by 10 to 15 minutes of regulated exercise in a class room, in a basement or even in a school yard. Neither can this be done by 60 to 90 minutes per week spent in a gymnasium. If we take European experiences as a guide we must demand at least one hour daily of muscular work adapted to age and sex as the minimum requirement for effective school gymnastics.

Is it possible to get this time? Before answering this question it might be well to speak of a tendency displayed among some teachers of physical training to recognize as gymnastics only the work done according to their preconceived notions of what shall be embraced under this head. Generally, this means exercises done under their direction during the official periods and upon the pieces of apparatus invented to allow the execution of certain specific movements. If,

however, we recognize all natural forms of exercise like swimming,
tramping, sledding, ice and roller skating, vigorous games, running,.
gardening, etc., if rationally conducted as valuable gymnastic material
a solution of the problem is not as difficult as may appear.

If we accept these forms of exercise our problem changes and becomes
one of administration, of selecting and arranging for different *types* of
work. . We then can say that school gymnastics should embrace the
following types of directed work:

1.   *The Relief Exercises, i. e.,* selected exercises lasting one or two minutes to be
given by the class teacher in the school room whenever the pupils have been sitting.
for a long period.

2.   *The Gymnastic Lesson* to be given in a vacant well-ventilated room, hall or
corridor, in the gymnasium or in the yard.   In the elementary schools this daily period
should last 20 minutes.   In the high school there should be three weekly periods of.
45 minutes each (dressing time not to be counted in).

3.   *The Supplementary Work.* In the elementary schools this work should.
consist of:

(*a*)   Of exercises upon apparatus erected in the school yards and of organized.
games.

(*b*)   Of skating, running, jumping, throwing and similar exercises that may be
done in a school yard.   This obligatory period should last 40 minutes following immediately the close of the afternoon session.   One or more of the regular class teachers.
should supervise this period.

(*c*)   For the 7th and 8th grades, and for all pupils of the high schools there should'
be a weekly obligatory play afternoon lasting at least two hours.   On this afternoon
pupils should report upon a designated playfield.   The pupils of the 7th and 8th grades.
play under direction of their class teachers (or some one designated by the principal
of the school).   The high school pupils play under direction of their regular teachers of
physical training.   The teachers are assisted by the regular employees of the playfield.
The pupils and teachers report upon the fields at 1.30.   The time spent on the fields.
should be credited as regular school work.   No home work is to be given to the pupils.
on days spent upon the playfields.   On inclement days the pupils report at the school.

The scheme outlined above has the following advantages over the
forms of school gymnastics at present in vogue:

1.   It would give to all pupils at least five hours of regulated directed physical.
activity per week.

2.   It would utilize the play spaces now rapidly multiplying in most cities and
rural communities.

3.   It would encourage Boards of Education to enlarge the present school yards,
and to buy large adequate grounds for new schools.

4.   It would get the major part of school gymnastics out of the buildings into
the open air.

5. It would give to the pupils the necessary amount of formal neuro-muscular training adapted to their age, as well as the proper amount of free play.

6. In many cities now having physical training it immediately could be adopted without a great increase in cost.

7. It would increase the health and vitality of the pupils and decrease the time lost by sickness. This would mean less backwardness, and a smaller number of repeaters.

While the money spent for physical training would be increased this increase would be offset by decreased expenditures in other depart. ments of school work. The final result should be increased efficiency with the same financial expenditures.

Resolutions

1. The time at present devoted to school gymnastics, *i. e.*, 10 to 15 minutes daily is insufficient to have an appreciable effect upon the health of the pupils.

2. (a) In the elementary schools the time devoted to school gymnastics should be at least 20 minutes daily. This time should be supplemented by at least 40 minutes of play daily in the school yard. The yard should be equipped with simple forms of apparatus and with simple facilities for jumping, throwing and for the playing of games.

(b) For the 7th and 8th grades in place of this yard-play one afternoon of two hours should be spent upon playfields located within one hour's walking distance of the homes of the pupils.

3. (a) In the high schools the time devoted to gymnastics should be at least three periods of 45 minutes each per week during the four years' course.

(b) One afternoon of at least two hours should be spent weekly upon playfields situated within one hour's walking distance of the school.

4. The teaching of swimming should form a part of every scheme of school gymnastics that all children may learn to swim.

5. All forms of sane bodily outdoor exercise like skating, tramping, rowing, sledding, etc., should steadily be encouraged by the school in order to increase the time spent out of doors. For the older children—field days, athletic meets and all sane competitive sports should be encouraged.

6. We heartily endorse the resolution passed at the July, 1912 meeting of the National Educational Association urging upon Boards of Education the importance of providing school grounds of not less than one square rod (272 square feet) for each child, such school park to provide a space for play, and instruction in gardening as well as a place for recreation for all living in the district.

CRITERIA OF PHYSICAL EXERCISES IN THE LIGHT
OF EDUCATION AS A WHOLE

BY

CLOUDESLEY BRERETON

The time appears to have come when Education should recognise certain *vérités* de M. de la Palisse. And first and foremost of these is the obvious truth that education exists for the Child and not the Child for education, and secondly that though the subjects be many, the child is one, and that therefore whatever education is given to it, that education must be a whole in itself, or in other words the subjects, arts, crafts, or accomplishments that are taught, whether they be physical geography, or physical exercises, must no longer be taught in water-tight compartments, but must take account of each other's presence in the curriculum and as far as possible be linked up together into an organic whole. In the child we have only a single entity to deal with, with a single brain and a single personality, whether you are trying to teach it the laws of health, the game of cricket, the multiplication table or the church catechism. Owing to the prevalence of mechanical terminology we talk of furnishing the child's mind—a detestable phrase—as if it were a system of elaborate pigeon-holes for the reception of different kinds of knowledge, each completely distinct from the other, and carefully labeled like the Kantian categories. We become in fact slaves to the mechanical metaphors we employ, whereas the Child is really an organism one and indivisible. You cannot abstract a limb and replace it, like you can abstract and replace the cylinder of an engine. Should you desire to make any mental analysis, all you can do in the case of the living child is to concentrate your attention on some part of its anatomy and mentality and banish from your mind all other parts that are none the less there all the time, and in consequence unceasingly influencing the child through his senses, his nervous system, his power to associate ideas, etc., in a word through the waves of sensation and emotion that traverse his whole being and modify it from moment to moment. The mere fact of his acquiring the Latin word "mensa" makes him a different individual from what he was the instant before, not merely mentally but physically. And yet for the most part, hitherto those concerned with his mental education have largely gone their own way and looked on the training of the body as little or none of their business and ignored its ceaseless reactions on the mentality and morality of the child, and those concerned with physical exercises have at most complained of the over-

pressure caused by bookish education, and ignored the æsthetic intellec.
tual and moral influence of their own subject on the literary curriculum.
But of the two, the intellectuals are probably the most to blame. Too
often have they considered games as a mere relaxation or a means of
renewing the exhausted energies of the child, while in respect to physical
exercises they have, at most, regarded them as remedial, often as dis.
ciplinary or even penal, as in the case of compulsory drill. It is only
quite recently that some of us have looked on them as hygienic and
preventative. But we have got to take a still further step and consider
them as absolutely essential, as one of the basal elements underlying our
mental education, whose influence permeates or should permeate the
whole curriculum of education, no matter what its ramifications.

Let us give you straightaway one instance out of·many to show how
organically literary education depends on the right organisation of
physical exercises.

Of recent years we in England have woken up to the fact that the
modern languages and the mother tongue were badly taught. We
are discovering that one of our chief faults lies in the fact that we have
paid too much attention to the written word and neglected the spoken.
Yet how can we liberate the concentrated emotion compressed within
some powerful poem, unless we can render in speech the sound and melody
in which the poet symbolised them. Hence we are realising more and
more the necessity for clear speech and enunciation in those teaching
these subjects, if they are to arouse the emotions of the children they
teach, and emotion, I would point out, is far more powerful than mere
intellect, and far more important to train; for as Goethe said, it is the
mother-stuff alike of intellect and morality. We have then been driven
into inquiring how correct speech or elocution is taught, and here we have
found that very often breathing and voice production are being taught
by one person, right pronunciation or phonetics by a second, reading
and recitation by a third, and all these were working apart from one
another, while those who were teaching singing were also working on
independent lines. Yet in both cases the principal aim at bottom was
one and the same—the production of a beautiful voice. Further investigation, however, revealed the fact that there are at least two systems
of teaching breathing, if not more, while in one quarter it was maintained
and I think with some show of reason, that all breathing exercises without actual physical exercises of the limbs were only moderately beneficial. Again, the physical exercises in different establishments differ
greatly among themselves. There are what one may call the orthodox.
Swedish, modified Swedish, eclectic, with a more or less strong admix-
ture of German, not to mention the rhythmic methods and exercises
which approximate the French.

Could you have a greater muddle? And it is in the hope of getting you to clear up some of this muddle that I am venturing to address you to-day. I am obliged by my profession to take a bird's-eye view of education, to look on it first and foremost as a whole, and then to consult the specialists on those points that appear to need strengthening or remedial treatment. You are an assembly of the world; specialists on health and physical exercises—a sort of Œcumenical Council, who can define principles without, I hope, giving them the rigidity of dogmas. In fact, I cannot help believing that your subject has reached such a stage of development that you can find at least a certain amount of common agreement of what is best in principle and practise even if the agreement is merely provisional.

It is for this reason I propose to devote the latter half of this address to laying down certain principles that seem to me common to other regions of the educational field and to ask you if you consider them applicable, to apply them as criteria to the various systems of physical exercise in vogue. But, while expressing the hope that the Congress may be able to show by actual discussion, if not by actual resolutions, its adhesion to certain general principles and practices, I desire none the less to state that I am in no way a believer of the possibility or the desirability of trying to lay down one rigidly uniform system. In fact I am convinced that each nation should work out its own educational salvation and that its system of education should comply with and be in sympathy with the national genius. It is theoretically possible that the Swedish system is in every point the best there is for the Swedes, the German for the German, and the French for the French, though, personally, I should think it highly improbable that such was the case for the simple reason that in every matter under the sun we have so much to learn from one another, in fact I do not know otherwise why we have gathered here in an International Congress. Every nation that deliberately shuts itself off from international intercourse, criticism and study is, I am sure, poorer in the long run, than the nation that takes for its motto, "Prove all things, hold fast to that which is good." If intercourse with one's neighbours makes a man, it also largely makes a nation. But the opposite fault is equally pernicious, that is for a nation to adopt blindly and uncritically any subject for teaching or training, be it Civics or Sloyd, without finding out how far it will fit into the existing system of education and how far it is really in sympathy and harmony with the genius of the nation.

But before putting before you certain specific criteria of the value of the various systems of physical exercises at present in vogue, I shall I think, make my attitude in the matter more clear, if I set forth what seems to me the historical origin and line of development of physical exercises in relation to the growth of the arts and crafts and sciences, to which they are most closely allied.

Physical exercises are obviously not primordial but derivative. First came the primitive occupations of man—fishing, hunting, agriculture and the like. The overflow of joy attending successful fishing, hunting, etc., revealed itself in dancing and rude dramatic representations. These no doubt crystallized into regular games and ceremonies, the competitive element was developed and formal training became an art. The physical training was first probably mainly for the sake of skill and endurance, then gradually broadened into an art and later a science of health. In the same way music and dancing became an art and then a science. From the primitive arts, arose other sciences which again in their turn made further arts and further sciences possible.

If this very summary sketch of the growth of art and knowledge be a sound one, then it is only one more proof of the intimate inter-relation of the various branches of knowledge, of its fundamental oneness in fact and of the need of a corresponding unification in whatever type of education we adopt; a unification which is not only to the advantage of the child but also of the efficiency of the subjects which form his particular course of education.

This idea of the underlying unity of knowledge is mainly a modern one and is due to the gradual invasion of biological conceptions, thanks to Patrick Geddes, William James, Bergson and others which are gradually ousting the machine-made mechanistic ideas which have dominated our philosophical, religious, educational, social and political ideals for the last hundred years. The epoch of l'homme-machine is at last passing away and we are beginning to admit that man is not merely a machine but an organism. The advent of these vitalising conceptions means the substitution of the dynamic for the purely static view of things, and of the living organism in place of the artificial skeleton or *mannequin* that has been substituted for it, of the idea of life in place of the idea of the machine, of spontaneity in place of mechanical determinism. It also marks the decline in the cult of pure intellectualism and a rise in the stress laid on the factors of activity and action, as manifested in the educational sphere by the increasing valuation laid on learning by doing instead of the old learning by heart.

1. And this brings me to my first criticism: With which theory are the physical exercises in vogue to-day most in sympathy? Are they under the old mechanistic and more or less water-tight compartment conception of education in which the subjects were merely juxtaposed and not organically connected, with the inevitable tendency that the pro-

fessors or specialists in any particular subject tend to consider it first as a thing apart and then as a thing *sui generis* and lastly as a thing particularly sacrosanct, divorced from any connection with other subjects, and therefore to a large extent unchangeable? Or are they filled with the new conceptions that all kinds of knowledge and craft are inter-related, not only from historical but logical reasons and that there can be no progress in one without some beneficial effect on the others? In a word do they consider their subject as a living and integral part of the child's education, and therefore capable of modification and improvement, or as a sort of changeless piece of mechanism in the midst of the living corpus of education?

Man being very largely a machine in the eyes of those imbued with mechanistic theories, they are apt to become the unconscious slaves of their doctrines. Thus, since there is no difference between the actual shape of a machine, whether in repose or movement, so they are apt to think there is no difference in shape worth noticing between the body during repose or in actual movement, and therefore think that a large amount of the seemingly static attitude should be maintained in a dynamic movement.

Let me explain: The parts of the machine do, indeed, alter their places but not their shape, the piston rod and the driving wheel remain practically the same size, not so the muscles of the human frame which vary according as they are extended or contracted and there are others points of difference which the statically minded seem to ignore. In fact, if I may indulge in a seeming paradox, I would say that there is nothing like complete repose except in a state of death, that resembles the repose of the machine. Even in bed and asleep there is more or less a strain on and therefore deformation of the muscles, as all discover when they have to sleep in a strange bed. The static conception therefore seems to me more or less misplaced when transferred from the machine to man. In fact I am sufficiently a Bergsonian to believe we live in a state of perpetual motion. If these ideas are correct I think that every system of physical exercises should give a precedence to the question of teaching movements as such, rather than to the study of attitudes as such. In other words physical exercises should be essentially the art and science of physical movements. And so I come to my second criterium: Are the systems of physical exercises in vogue dominated by static or dynamic ideals?

I pass to a third point. According to certain superannuated ideas on attention we used to be taught that conscious attention was the best way of acquiring either knowledge or technique. Now we know that if they can be acquired directly by imitation or interest, it is so much saving of human energy. We possess in fact only a limited capacity for conscious attention and the best way of spending it is to use it for the mastering of difficulties that otherwise seem insuperable. The ideal to be aimed at in the acquisition of all subjects is unconscious or automatic attention. We learn best what we like best, when a sort of zest or joy accompanies our act of learning.

A certain amount of conscious attention is generally necessary at the learning of any new fact, process or movement; but the sooner the pupil can pass into the stage of unconscious attention the better for his rapid acquisition. I do not deny that a thing mastered with conscious effort sticks, but our stock of voluntary attention is so limited, it so soon gives out, that if the conditions of learning involved its expenditure on a large scale we should learn in the time at our disposal only a tithe and fraction of what we actually do. And this brings me to my third criterium:

How far are the present systems in vogue dominated by the doctrine of conscious attention only? And as a corollary I would ask, are they graduated to suit all ages and seasons and if so, does the graduation take into account the amount of conscious interest that a child of eight can give, which is of course far less than that of a student of 18.

Closely connected with this question is the question of rhythm which is destined to play a much more important part in education than hitherto. Set up a rhythm of interest between teacher and taught and anyone who has listened to an inspiring teacher will know what I mean, and you will have found a way of imparting knowledge from the child's point of view, with the maximum of effect and the minimum of effort, provided that the knowledge thus gained is speedily recapitulated by the recipient and thereby made his own. In the domain of games and physical exercises, the importance of rhythm is every day being recognised of more and more importance. It is in fact the *economic regulator* of the expenditure of force, and this then brings me to my fourth criterium: To what extent do the existing systems take into account the importance of rhythm?

I now come to certain points more especially connected with educational principles.

Hitherto in education, partly owing to large classes, partly to having until recently only one form of education, the classical, we have been too much engaged in trying to train the phalanx, to bring as many children up as possible to a certain pitch of efficiency, while if we had looked after the leaders it has been chiefly to train them on certain orthodox lines. The problem, however, of the future will largely consist in finding opportunities for the development of self-expression and originality in the child, while not losing sight of the need of keeping

them together, and this brings me to my fifth criterum: Which system
or systems in vogue is or are most or least likely to effect this?

Again we are gradually seeing the necessity, when practicable, in all
subjects of starting from the concrete and deriving the theoretical and
abstract side from it, instead of beginning in the ancient Euclidean fashion with certain artificially simplified definitions like those of a point
or a circle. The same is true again of the latest development in the
teaching of applied science to-day, especially when applied to the teaching of domestic economy in our schools. Everyone knows what a difficult subject organic chemistry is, but the whole problem alters its appearance when you start from the actual operations of the kitchen and laundry and build upon these instead of embarking on certain highly artificial and delicate processes that can only be handled by the advanced
chemist.

And this brings me to my sixth criterium: Do the systems in vogue
start directly from the concrete, i. e. from certain definite immemorial
human activities such as running, jumping and the like or from certain
artificial simplified concepts, i. e. certain artificially detached movements, many of which occur comparatively infrequently in an isolated
form in real life? In that case do they not develop a sort of abstract
grammar of movement which tends to become as meaningless and
distasteful to the average child as the paradigms of Greek verbs when
learnt apart from the reading of any author?

One of the great defects of teaching, especially in England, until
recently, has been an abuse of the analytic methods and a disregard
of the synthetic. Now we are beginning to see that analysis is mainly
necessary as a form of explanation or correction, or for taking difficulties
one at a time and that it should be always followed by some synthetic
practice. In other words it is little good learning every rule in the Latin
grammar if we do not learn to apply them by writing correct Latin.
In fact to learn the whole grammar first is the worst possible way of
learning the subject.

And this brings me to my seventh criterium: If we apply this principle to physical exercises must we not ask, do they only practise detached parts of some synthetic movement separately in order to be able
to repeat more perfectly the synthetic movement of which these separate
movements are a part? Or in a desire to make an analytic catalogue
of all seemingly possible movements quite irrespective of their probable
use and employment in real life, do they elaborate a sort of grammar
not merely of practical but of possible exercises. In other words do they
mainly make a study of disconnected movements for the sake of the
study, without being sufficiently careful to make, on all occasions, a
reintegration of such movements, either in the shape of natural actions,

such as running, jumping and the like or of games and dancing, which alone can render them purposeful in the eyes of the pupil or of immate_ rial application? And as a corollary to this one would ask as the eighth criterium: Are preparations for such games and dancing the natural aim and crown of such exercises, or are they regarded merely as a useful but not indispensable outcome and complement?

Next I propose to consider the influence of physical exercises on the ordinary school education under the threefold heading of intellectual, æsthetic and moral·education.

In intellectual education we are seeing more and more the need not merely of teaching all subjects in such a fashion that they lend them_ selves to providing opportunities for the child to express himself, not only in the shape of repetitions but in the shape of creative variations of what he has learnt. There must be of course some discipline, there must be certain conventions and traditions he must acquire, but the point is he must acquire them, they must not acquire him. We want to train a producer not a mere consumer; one who is master of his subject, not its slave; a person of intellectual thew and muscle, not a fatted calf; in a word, an individual who will think for himself while respectful of the opinion of others. The teaching of any subject or exercise should be judged then, among other things, from the point of view of its poten- tialities for self-expression, whether it be the mother tongue or dancing. But to insure this desirable state of affairs, it is necessary that the teach- ing itself should be as little wooden and mechanical as possible. These should be obvious to the child, not merely the distant goal, but some daily gain in the sense of added power or knowledge immediately realis- able. In a word he should see what it is all driving at and also how he can at once apply what he has already acquired. Thus, if he is learning a modern language, he should be encouraged to converse in it as far as possible; if he is studying arithmetic, he should be shown *pari passu* as far as possible, its practical applications; if he has some apparently artificial physical exercise, he should be speedily introduced to the natural exercise to which it leads up. It is not enough to show that it will ulti- mately give him health and strength. If you have ever had to admin- ister medicine you will know the effectiveness or inefficacy of that argument. You must also show him the useful exercise it is meant to help him to master. In a word it means a recognition of making the pro- cesses of learning more intelligible throughout to the pupil. And so I come to my ninth criterium: To what extent do the existing systems lend themselves to this desirable treatment?

The æsthetic element in education has been sadly neglected in the past, especially in England, owing no doubt in part to Puritan influences. The growing importance, however, attached by experts to the spoken word in language teaching, to acting and dancing for children, and to the cultivation of the arts and crafts within the schools themselves as basal to the more abstract forms of learning is everywhere indicative of a change. It means, in fact, nothing more or less than the renaissance of the artistic and creative spirit in education. And so I come to my tenth criterium:

Do the existing systems favour or not the creative and artistic spirit? Do they cultivate not merely the sense of strength but the sense of grace?

Real grace is by no means, as some people think, a cloak for weakness. It means the expenditure of the least effort necessary to produce a requisite effect, and as such is not only a thing of beauty, but also at bottom utilitarian because it makes for the conservation and economy of energy. Again it implies the absence of any unnecessary stiffness or antagonising of muscles, as may be seen from the movements of the most graceful animals in nature, such as the cat and the tiger. This fact is well known to any person who plays games, be it cricket or golf. Anything like the absence of litheness or suppleness is fatal to good play. Every golf player knows his movements must be rhythmic and not jerky and the same is true even of the mechanical arts, whether one speaks of the blacksmith or the weaver. Each instinctively aims at the minimum of stiffness compatible with the firmness requisite to maintain the attitude he adopts and the need of rhythmical movements in order to expend his energies as economically as possible, and this brings me to my eleventh criterium: To what extent do the different systems teach lithesomeness and eliminate the tendency to jerky actions?

I have come across several people who confound precision with grace. At bottom the difference to my mind is radical, for though a graceful movement may suggest precision, a precise movement need not necessarily be graceful. In fact the more precise a movement is, the more it resembles that of a machine, while the more rhythmical it is, the more it suggests life. Of course the machine may sometimes suggest life, but it suggests it because it is a machine, and the proof is that if you were told it was alive, you would immediately declare it was a machine, as the lifelike impression is only a minor one, being less powerful than the impression that it is really a machine. Any insistence on precision without at least an equal insistence on grace seems to me harmful, and so I come to my twelfth criterium:

Do they insist on precision to the detriment of grace?

Coming to the moral side of education I am free to admit that there is a certain disciplinary value in studying any distasteful subject, provided that all interest is not extinguished in the process. Nay I would go further and assert that there is a certain amount of hard work, difficulty and drudgery inseparably connected with the acquisition of any subject by the average child, and one recognises its tempering and hardening value as regards the formation of character. But the point is that there is no fear that any subject properly taught will not contain the requisite modicum of drudgery. On the contrary, judging by the results, the danger is all the other way, and the chief care of the skillful teacher must be to reduce it as far as possible to a minimum. All kinds of formal exercises necessarily possess this quality, whether they be drill in French irregular verbs or Swedish exercises. And this brings me to my thirteenth criterium: Do the exercises in vogue possess an inordinate amount of this unpalatable element? It would be valuable to have some information of the numbers of voluntary classes in the different countries practising the different styles to learn which are the most popular when the choice lies with the students.

These disciplinary elements may be regarded as a negative element in physical exercises, one must also look for positive elements as far as moral education is concerned, and for boys at least I am confident that physical exercises should possess some feat-performing and possibly competitive element if the latter is kept within due bounds, for the simple reason that the love of mastering difficulties and of daring and adventure is or ought to be the bottom instinct or at least heritage of every normal boy. We do not want him to break his neck, but we do not want either to deprive him of the possibility of trying his hand at feats that are calculated to develop his pluck, self-reliance and endurance. All that is necessary is to see that such feats are properly graded and under proper control. And this brings me to my fourteenth criterium: In which system or systems is this feat-performing element an integral part of the course?

It would be possible to propose tests for the systems in vogue from the point of view of the modern teachers of anatomy, physiology, psychology, and hygiene, but on these subjects you are far more competent to put questions than myself. I will, however, suggest three points in connection with the latter, two of which were suggested to me by experts and the third is one which would readily occur to any layman like myself.

The first is, whether jerky movements without apparatus are not really an inferior form of exercise because they entail a maximum loss of power, as may be readily seen between the sensation experienced from a lunge forward into the void, and punching, say, a boxing ball. One doctor has assured me he considers they are actually bad for the health, as productive of undue heart strain and cause fatigue far sooner than curvilineal movements in which the force mobilized is more evenly dispersed. And so I come to my fifteenth criterium: Does any one system more than another contain more of these debatable movements than others?

The second point is somewhat similar. I have already alluded to it. It is whether deep healthy exercises without arm and leg movements are not really harmful or at least far less beneficial than is thought. The critic who suggested to me this question pointed out that if on going out on a cold day one took several long breaths, one experienced no particular sensation of cold in the lungs, while if, owing to running or quick walking one's breathing increased, one then had the sensation of cold in different parts of the lungs, and his conclusion was that in the first case the portions of the lungs in ordinary use were merely over-inflated, while in the second the air really penetrated to the unused portion of the lungs. I suggest the matter for your discussion but its bearing on the ordinary breathing practices seems to me highly important, though I fancy breathing exercises pure and simple, are part and parcel of all systems.

My third point is that we are increasingly realising that health is not merely a physical but a mental and moral question. Food eaten with pleasure, work done with zest, do a person far more good than food or work he does not relish. Pleasure and joy, if produced by healthy incentives are the best tonics. And so I come to my last criterium. Which system incidentally provokes the greatest pleasure or joy in the pupil? There are of course various sources of pleasure, which are common to all systems such as that of stretching one's limbs or of mastering a certain technique like the multiplication table, but the pleasure I mean arises principally from causes I have already enumerated, the sense of suppleness, the delight in graceful movement, the intelligibility of the exercise performed and its immediate utilization. To what extent do the various systems produce these effects?

To sum up, then, the criteria themselves in reference to the various systems.

1. Are they regarded as a sort of water-tight compartment subject, distinct and complete in itself or as a part of education as a whole in organic connection with the games and other subjects in the curriculum? And again are they regarded as something sacrosanct not subject to change or its influence from other subjects? Or are they regarded as a progressive element in a system of education which is necessarily evolutionary?

2. How far are the underlying conceptions static or dynamic?

3. Are they dominated by the theory of conscious attention only? And are these exercises graded so as not to unduly strain the conscious attention of the younger children?

4. To what extent do they regard the importance of rhythm, as the great economic regulation of energy?

5. Do they favour the cult of self-expression and originality?

6. Do they spring directly out of the concrete in the way of being directly derivative from and leading up to certain natural human activities such as dancing, jumping, etc., or built up from certain detached movements that occur comparatively infrequently in an isolated form in real life?

7. Is their analytic work in the shape of detached movements, generally followed by the execution of the natural synthetic actions of which they are the analysis?

8. Have they developed the analytical side of their teaching beyond the requirements of the natural synthetic movements to which these analytic movements should lead up?

9. Are they directly preparatory to games and dancing, *i. e.* are games and dancing the necessary and inevitable crown and outcome of these theories and practices? To what extent do they appeal to the the child's intelligence and sense of acquiring knowledge and power?

10. To what extent do they foster the artistic and creative spirit? To what extent do they promote gracefulness?

11. To what extent do they encourage suppleness and litheness? Do they insist on precision to the detriment of grace?

12. Do they tend unduly from the disciplinary point of view to become dull and distasteful to the pupils?

13. Do they recognise the supreme value of the feat-performing element from the point of view of encouraging the adventurous spirit in boys, or merely tolerate its addition to the course? Is the feat-performing element an integral part of the course?

14. Do they contain in some cases more jerky than curvilineal movements, and are they therefore productive of unnecessary heart-strain?

15. Do they, from the hygienic point of view, tend to foster pleasure and joy in the child who practices them?

All these premises are naturally open to criticism, but I am convinced they are being increasingly held by leading educationists in England, America and on the Continent. As far as I am concerned they are naturally personal and do not in any way pretend to represent the views of the great municipality I serve. Their strength, if they have any, is that which is possessed by all true ideas, which only need to be put forward to win their way in the end.

And in conclusion I could add that if they are considered by you to to be largely established, then I think it must be further admitted that the system they appear the most to support are the French and the rhythmical of the Dalcroze type, while the system that appears to conform the least to these canons is the Swedish in its orthodox form. No doubt in the various modified forms in which the latter is practised the more objectionable features are not so apparent, but such modified forms are unfortunately far from pleasing the more rigid upholders of the system.

In venturing into your midst I have been induced to do so by the fact that being obliged to take a bird's-eye view of education I felt confident that you would not be indisposed to apply to such a special article on physical exercises, ideals and conceptions which have established or are establishing themselves in other parts of the field of education. Moreover we in England have a proverb that lookers on see most of the game, and I hope I may add in this case of the physical exercises. Even if the statement is excessive as it undoubtedly is in the present instance, I shall none the less thank you for allowing me to insist in your presence on the intrinsic oneness of education in spite of its numerous branches and ramifications.

LA EDUCACIÓN FÍSICA EN LAS ESCUELAS DE MÉXICO
RESULTADOS A QUE SE HA LLEGADO

POR

Manuel Velázquez Andrade

En la historia evolutiva de la educación física en nuestro país se destacan con lineamientos propios tres periodos:

I.   *Antes de la Conquista.*

II. *Desde 1849 hasta 1894 y 1902 y*

III. *Desde esta última fecha hasta el presente* (1913).

I.

Antes de la Conquista. Lo que caracterizó esencialmente a la educación corpórea de los antiguos mexicanos fué su tendencia marcadamente *utilitaria,* es decir, su finalidad que no era otra que hacer del individuo un *guerrero vigoroso, resistente, apto en el manejo de las armas de combate* y sobre todo, *valeroso y temible.*

Esta tendencia manifiestamente utilitaria de la educación corpórea no es de sorprendernos ni extrañarnos. En cada periodo de la vida de los pueblos la educación general ha sido de acuerdo con el objeto y ocupaciones principales de los agregados sociales y el fin y objeto principales de los antiguos mexicanos fué: *"pelear por sus dioses y por su patria;"* de aquí la necesidad de hacer de cada unidad humana un factor bélico eficiente.

Para llegar a este resultado la educación física comenzaba desde temprana edad con el *endurecimiento corpóreo,* el que alcanzaban sujetando a los niños a prácticas casi torturantes como eran la de bañarlos en el agua fria en invierno, acostarlos en lugares duros, hacerlos caminar largas distancias cargados con objetos pesados, ayunar, &.

Venían después los ejercicios gimnásticos, juegos, deportes, bailes y ejercicios militares. Todos estos ejercicios se practicaban no con un fin *higiénico o correctivo* sino por sus resultados *recreativos, propiciatorios, combativos* y *utilitarios.*

Los juegos y deportes no eran otra cosa sino ensayos de futuras actividades guerreras; sus bailes constituían un medio de implorar, rendir culto o aplacar las cóleras de sus dioses y el lado combativo estimulábase otorgando premios, abriendo concursos y celebrando fiestas públicas.

De los resultados felices de este género de educación fisica dan testimonio las inumerables conquistas que realizó esta raza dominando pueblos enemigos hasta llegar a formar con ellos el vasto Imperio Mexicano, siendo el elemento *hombre* considerado en su *vigor, resistencia* y *valor* el más importante factor en la lucha y en la victoria. No debe pues sorprendernos la importancia que la educación del hogar y la del Estado concedieron en aquellos tiempos a la cultura corpórea.

La Conquista acabó con tal educación y el gobierno colonial jamás se preocupó por sustituirla o revivirla en nuestra raza, nos dió, si, lo único que poseía: sus corridas de toros y el juego de pelota Vasca!

II.

Segundo Periodo. Puede dividirse en dos etapas: de 1849 a 1894 y de 1894 a 1902. La primera fué una faz enteramente *empírica;* la segunda, una faz de *tanteos.*

Le escuela de gimnasia alemana introducida en Francia por el Coronel Amorós e importada a nuestro pais por Turin, discípulo de Amorós, fue en esa época (1849) la sola escuela que se conocia y que se practicó como buena, especialmente en el ejército y un poco en el campo pedagógico. Componían este sistema algunos *ejercicios de aplicación,* muy pocos *correctivos* y otros de carácter marcadamente *atlético.*

Los discípulos de Turín y continuadores idólatras más tarde de sus enseñanzas, mantuvieron largo tiempo en la opinión pública y muy particularmente en la pedagógica la falsa idea de la perfección científica de un sistema cuyo *empirismo* es evidente y que hoy nadie podrá negar.

El criterio científico y pedagógico que en 1894 empezó a esbozar en Francia una orientación más racional de la educación gimnástica, condenando al mismo tiempo el *método amorosiano* por acrobático y hasta entonces considerado como pedagógico e higiénico, repercutió en México con un débil eco, pero lo suficiente para despertar, en el ánimo de los verdaderos educadores, la duda acerca de su valor educativo e higiénico.

En el campo escolar se inició a titulo de ensayo (1894) el sistema que la misma Francia principiaba a propogar como sustituto del Amorosiano y cuyos principios fisiológicos y pedagógicos se habían calcado del sistema de Ling.

Los viejos maestros mexicanos, últimos pilares de una escuela gimnástica que se derrumbaba, recibieron esta reforma con indiferencia y no secundaron el movimiento evolucionista, antes bien, se opusieron con la rutina de sus enseñanzas e invocando la tradición.

Este esfuerzo inovador no se perdió ni fué estéril, hizo que la atención del entonces Ministerio de Justicia e Instrucción Pública se fijase en el nuevo rumbo que las teorias pedagógicas que sobre educación fisica tomaban y desde ese instante se dejó sentir un movimiento reformista favorable.

A raíz de creada la Sub-Secretaria de Instrucción Pública y Bellas Artes (1902) uno de sus primeros acuerdos fue reformar el caduco y deficiente sistema de gimnasia que hasta entonces habia estado vigente en los establecimientos de instrucción primaria y secundaria, reforma que una Comisión compuesta de reputados pedagogos hizo en vista de las doctrinas y experiencias fisiológicas conocidas en muchos centros ·científicos y que eran moneda corriente en algunos paises de Europa, principalmente en Francia de donde surgieron. Dicha Comisión aceptó como *sistema de gimnasia racional el sistema sueco.*

Este paso inovador fue decidido y se llevó a la práctica comenzando por las escuelas dependientes de la Dirección General de Instrucción Primaria, la Escuela Nacional Preparatoria y las Escuelas Normales; pero para su eficaz realización y ejecución se tropezó desde luego con dos serias dificultades: la *falta de un cuerpo docente*, regularmente preparado y la carencia de *elementos materiales.*

La primera dificultad fue subsanada con la instrucción en forma de "*Academias Teórico Prácticas*" dadas a los maestros y la segunda aún subsiste aunque en menor grado.

III.

Tercer Periodo. La faz anterior, que conceptuamos de iniciación reformista, de *tanteos* y de propaganda activa se cristalizó, asumió el aspecto de una *verdadera inovación* de gran trascendencia con el Dictamen que emitió en 1909 una Comisión nombrada del seno del Consejo Superior de Educación y,en cuyo trabajo se fijaron las *bases de un sistema racional de educación física desde la escuela elemental hasta la profesional de acuerdo con las leyes del crecimiento fisiológico y psicológico y los principios de una sana pedagogía.*

Esta Comisión colocándose en un terreno enteramente desapasionado, aceptó como criterio pedagógico en la elección del sistema de ejercicios gimnásticos el *eclecticismo*, cuya doctrina ha encontrado franca aceptación entre los educadores excentos de prejuicios y orgullos nacionales.

El *eclecticismo* de este sistema consiste en los siguientes ejercicios:

I.   Gimnasia correctiva (sistema sueco modificado).

II.   Juegos y deportes (nacionales y extranjeros).

III.   Gimnasia de aplicación (natación, carreras, · saltos, luchas, pugilato, bailes rítmicos y excursiones campestres).

En la gimnasia correctiva se señaló el sistema sueco modificado por su superioridad *higiénica* y *educativa* que hasta sus más vehementes detractores le reconocen.

Respecto a juegos indica aquellos de carácter nacional y los deportes americanos e ingleses como son: el basket-ball, foot-ball, lawn-tennis, &. y por último como ejercicios de aplicación figuran los que hemos indicado.

La aceptación y aprobación de las ideas contenidas en este Dictamen por el Ministerio de Instrucción Pública y Bellas Artes produjo los siguientes resultados:

I.   La unificación del criterio científico y pedagógico respecto á concepto general de la educación física y su valor educativo.

II.   La aceptación tácita de una gimnasia racional y

III.   La sanción oficial al conjunto de doctrinas que informan el principio del *eclecticismo* en la educación corpórea.

Elevadas a la categoría de Ley las resoluciones emitidas en dicho Dictamen y consignadas más tarde en las "Instrucciones Metodológicas de Educación Primaria" en la parte aplicable a las escuelas primarias desde ese momento la educación física entró por el amplio camino de una *faz positiva*.

Este sistema de educación física se puso en vigor desde luego no sólo en los establecimientos primarios sino también en las escuelas Normales, de Artes y Oficios para Hombres y Mujeres y en las Industriales y si dicha reforma no alcanzó a las escuelas profesionales se debió a la falta de la acción personal de las autoridades escolares reformistas.

Tal es en síntesis el proceso evolutivo y el estado actual que guarda la educación física en nuestras escuelas.

Resumen:

La historia evolutiva de la educación física en las escuelas de México, presenta tres periodos:

I.   Antes de la Conquista.

II.   Después de la Conquista y el Gobierno Colonial y

III.   De 1849 a 1894; de 1894 a 1902 y de esta última fecha hasta 1913.

En el periodo pre-Colombino la educación corpórea de los aborígenes mexicanos fué esencialmente *utilitaria*.

Después de la Conquista, en la época Colonial y hasta 1849 no se dió ninguna atención a la cultura física.

De esta última fecha hasta 1894 dicha educación tuvo un carácter *empírico*.

De 1894 a 1909 fué una faz de *tanteos* y de 1909 hasta hoy ha evolucionado en un sentido *positivo*, es decir, de acuerdo con los principios, doctrinas y experiencias fisiológicas, psícologicas, pedagógicas y necesidades sociales de la vida moderna y práctica.

Actualmente el sistema de educación gimnástica aceptado en nuestras escuelas es el *ecléctico* cuyos fundamentos son:

I. Gimnasia correctiva (sistema sueco modificado).

II. Juegos gimnásticos y deportes atléticos y

III. Gimnasia de aplicación (natación, luchas, saltos, bailes rítmicos, excursiones, &.

Summary:

In the history of Physical Education in the Public Schools of Mexico we can see three different periods of evolution:

I. Before the Conquest.

II. After the Conquest and the time of the Colonial Government.

III. From 1849 to 1894, 1894 to 1909, and from this last date up to the present time.

During the first period, that is, before America was discovered the Physical Culture of the primitive Mexicans was characterized by its *utilitarian* purpose and scope.

After the Conquest till 1849, embracing the Colonial period, was entirely neglected the care of the body.

From this time to 1849 Physical Education was *empirical* in its bases.

From 1894 up to 1909 we can say was the time of *experiments* and from this date up to the present time it has taken a *positive* trend based on the physiological, psychological, pedagogical laws and needs of social and practical life.

The system of gymnastics developed in our schools now is based on the principles of *eclecticism* and is composed of the following exercises:

I. Corrective gymnastics (modified Swedish system).

II. Games and Athletics.

III. Applied gymnastics (swimming, wrestling, jumping, boxing, rhythmic exercises, camping, etc.).

SESSION FORTY-ONE

SYMPOSIUM ON MENTAL HYGIENE AND HYGIENE OF THE MENTALLY ABNORMAL CHILD

Arranged by the National Committee for Mental Hygiene,

LEWELLYS F. BARKER, M.D., *President*

STEWART PATON, M.D., *Chairman*

DR. A. W. HURD, Buffalo, N. Y., *Vice-Chairman*

"Mental Hygiene"

STEWART PATON, M.D., Director Mental Hygiene Exhibit, National Committee for Mental Hygiene, Princeton, N. J. "Essentials of an Education." (Manuscript not supplied.)

J. E. RAYCROFT, M.D., Director of the Department of Hygiene, Princeton University. "The Relation Between Recreation and Mental Hygiene." (Manuscript not supplied.)

C. MACFIE CAMPBELL, M.D., Associate Professor of Psychiatry, Johns Hopkins University, Baltimore, Md. "A Psychiatric Contribution to Educational Problems."

WILLIAM H. BURNHAM, Ph.D., Professor of Pedagogy and School Hygiene, Clark University, Worcester, Mass. "Some Principles of Mental Hygiene."

WILLIAM HEALY, M.D., Director Chicago Juvenile Psychopathic Institute. "Mental Abnormality and Misconduct." (Manuscript not supplied.)

L. PIERCE CLARK, M.D., Chief Consulting Staff, New York. "The Value of Psychopathic Clinics in the Public Schools."

"The Defective Child"

GRACE BOHNE, Director of Child Study Laboratory, Public Schools, · Rochester, N. Y. "The Relation of the Special Class in the Public Schools to the Community."

WALTER S. CORNELL, M.D., Director of Medical Inspection, Public Schools; Chief Medical Staff, Philadelphia House of Detention; Instructor Anatomy and Lecturer Child Hygiene, University of Pennsylvania. "The Medical Inspector and Feeble-Mindedness."

ARNOLD L. GESELL, Ph.D., Assistant Professor of Education, Yale University, New Haven, Conn. "The University in Relation to the Problems of Mental Deficiency and Child Hygiene."

HENRY H. GODDARD, Ph.D., Director of Research Training School, Vineland, N. J. "Who Is Mentally Defective; How Many Are They; How Can They Be Detected?"

A PSYCHIATRIC CONTRIBUTION TO EDUCATIONAL PROBLEMS

BY

C. MACFIE CAMPBELL

The title of this paper is to be taken literally as a contribution to the *problems* of education, and it deals with a problem which thrusts itself upon the physician whose special subject is mental disease. Impressed with the importance of the issues at stake, he is anxious to put before those interested in education the important facts at his disposal. The clinical worker comes to those interested in education not to advance dogmatic views but to demand help. Those responsible for directing the lines of educational progress have already a great number of problems before them. They have to determine what studies are most fitted to develop the intellectual life of the individual. They have to select courses of study and discuss methods of imparting information. They have to supply the developing individual with a useful body of information and to train him in methods of observation and adaptation, and in this training due attention must be paid to the development of physical efficiency. In carrying out these tasks the coöperation of the physician may be required to determine how far the development of the individual is interfered with by defects such as adenoids or enlarged tonsils, defects of eyesight or of hearing, etc. The responsibility of the medical profession towards the developing child is not fulfilled by merely attending to physical defects such as those above referred to; much more vital matters demand the best thought of the physician. These problems are brought before the clinical worker in mental disease in the following way: The patients who come to him for help, whether the diagnosis is nervousness or insanity, are to a large extent men and women, whose tissues are not affected by any infection or poison, but whose adjustment to the environment has, from more subtle causes, become seriously impaired; in tracing the causes of this break of adjustment the physician often sees how at an early stage help might have been given that was not given; the individual may have been educated to deal with the most abstruse intellectual questions, to enjoy the most refined æsthetic products, to show perhaps a great deal of physical dexterity, but no attention had been given to the management of many vital matters in the individual's life. The clinician can retrospectively see how the patient's life at a much earlier stage showed characteristic danger signals, which were ignored by those who might have been of use. He can frequently point to definite incidents, to moods, utterances and activities of the individual, which the parents of friends remember, but which they passed by as simply rather odd and not requiring further explanation, but which were the outcropping above the surface of serious internal difficulties. Looking back on a case it seems that something might have been done to correct the type of adjustment of the boy or girl, encouragement and instruction might have been of the greatest use, and the beginning of evasions and compensations and substitutions of an unhealthy nature might have been avoided. The parents rarely have sufficient insight into such matters, and the responsibility for dealing with the situation has not appeared to belong definitely either to the family physician, the teacher, or the religious instructor. The physician as a rule is unfortunately only called in when the child is physically ill or has pronounced mental symptoms; he is seldom consulted with a view to general advice on the mental hygiene of a child who has simply shown minor anomalies of mood, or speech or action. The underlying difficulties of adjustment of the individual are closely related to instinctive forces which have carefully been ignored in the education of children. It is not, perhaps, too strong a term to refer to this as a "conspiracy of silence." These instinctive forces are of extremely personal nature and are of much more fundamental importance than the exact amount of utilitarian or ornamental information which the individual possesses, or even than the technical ability which the individual shows with regard to the general solution of impersonal problems. It is the balance of these instinctive forces which frequently determines the happiness or misery of the individual, his mental health or sickness, his social efficiency or inefficient individualism. Those who are interested in the mental hygiene of the community want to have the coöperation of the teaching profession not only in the prophylaxis of mental disorders, but in the effort to eliminate from everyday life a variety of minor disqualifications in a great number of people who consider themselves quite healthy, and who do not consult a physician. These people find their life handicapped or rendered less efficient through the presence of certain inhibitions, moods, day-dreaming tendencies, jealousies, over-compensations, exaggerated enthusiasms, interest in fads, religious or dietetic, political or humanitarian; they may be hampered by incompatibilities in their home life and in their married life, by headaches, and palpitations, and minor invalidism of all sorts. An education which would eliminate such handicaps from the life of the individual would certainly bring society an appreciable step nearer the millennium. The mechanisms which are responsible for the development of many of these handicaps can only be understood when we honestly face the underlying driving factors of human life, and this is no easy task. The individual requires courage in order to see himself as he actually is, to remove his own image from the pedestal upon which he usually has it placed, to revise the official autobiography which he usually carries around with him. The precept of self-knowledge is not simple of execution; it is one of the fundamental tasks of a healthy education. The importance of self-knowledge, of mental analysis has been felt by the poet when he wrote:

> "Few families were racked
> By torture self-supplied, did Nature grant but this—
> That women comprehend mental analysis."

Had the poet been a clinician he would not have limited his remarks to the one sex. The philosophical essayist, too, has made equally penetrating comment on the value of that self-knowledge which is the essence of wisdom: "As we become wiser we escape some of our instinctive destinies. There is in us all sufficient desire for wisdom to transform into consciousness most of the hazards of life and all that has thus been transformed can belong no more to the hostile powers. A sorrow your soul has changed into sweetness, to indulgence or patient smiles, is a sorrow that shall never return without spiritual ornament; and a fault or defect you have looked in the face can harm you no more, or even be harmful to others * * * whoever is able to curb the blind force of instinct within him, is able to curb the force of external destiny also." This self-knowledge, however, goes contrary to the habits of a lifetime; it goes contrary to much that has influenced the child during the developing period; it requires a certain honest humility. A thorough overhauling of the house from attic to cellar, and even to the sewer if necessary, is a much more strenuous task than a complacent voyage around the living rooms where we are always ready to receive company; it sometimes forces one to make the acquaintance of a somewhat savage denizen of the underworld, a turbulent fellow, whose presence in the house we had consistently ignored and whose noisy demonstrations had been explained away as due to a variety of other causes. A candid and courageous investigation of the nature of human activities, in other words a common-sense psychology, would show us that our daily reactions are not so completely determined by logical thought and by clear purpose as we are pleased to think. Most of us have a strong prejudice to the effect that we are essentially reasonable beings and that our thought and life consist of logical purposeful activity. Blinded by this prejudice we frequently do not see the sources of our emotional variations and the rôle which these play in our intellectual beliefs and daily activity. When the physician tries to understand the real driving forces in the reactions of the insane, of the neurotic, and of the respectable citizen, he finds that in all three very similar life forces are at work.   In the case of the insane we have learned to trace the delusions and hallucinations of the patient to the inner conflicts which to a large extent have their centre in the instinctive life of the patient, a phase of the individual life which has been dealt with in an unhealthy and evasive manner.   In the case of the neurotic we can trace their anomalous emotions, their tricks of behaviour, their morbid fears, their scrupulous exaggerations, their invalidism to the same conflict of forces.   In the case of the respectable citizen we find that an examination of the same fundamental forces throws a great deal of light on his reactions, on traits of character, on his success or failure, on his likes and dislikes, his emotional variations, his prejudices and jealousies, his casual impulses and on many peculiarities of his ethical and religious and intellectual ideals.   We thus learn that beneath the clearly conscious life there is a welter of less clearly conscious forces.   Here there are trends, desires, latent wishes and longings and antagonisms, the existence of which is almost unknown to the individual.   In all of us there lurk the memories of painful experiences and conflicts which the individual had fondly hoped were eliminated but which he finds have only been repressed and thrust out of sight. The forms and shades that haunt this underworld are now becoming familiar to us; they bear the traces of all the stages of individual development, traces of the individual's reaction to the demands of nutrition, of his early reaction to the primary needs of ordinary cleanliness, of his early reaction to the demands of the sexual instinct at all the stages of its development with all its aberrant possibilities.   Other shades bear traces of the early relation of the child to his mother and father with all the complexity and intensity of these relations.   In this underworld we meet figures with childhood masks, but other shades flit past of savage nature.   These are the figures that haunt the underworld of every one of us; at night, when our personality is asleep, they come out and run riot in our dreams, and even in our waking life they play us tricks, influence our emotions, alter our activity, and cause us to make mistakes, slips of speech, slips of writing, lapses of memory, etc. In cases of mental disorder these forces have broken through to the surface in a much more serious manner; and, too frequently, the patient is brought to the physician when the break in compensation is final. Where the situation is more hopeful, the task of the physician frequently consists in educating the individual to deal correctly with those disturbing elements that have been repressed, to bring them into clear consciousness, to realize that there are other ways of meeting difficulties than by pretending that they do not exist.   In the adult the earliest evidence of some incipient maladjustment is frequently treated very lightly, and in the developing child the minor signs of latent conflicts receive very scant attention from those responsible for the child's education. Little oddities are only smiled at, the moodiness of the child is looked upon as perhaps self-explanatory, unusual interests are regarded with mild amusement, strong antagonisms which suddenly develop are not taken seriously, slight physical expressions of these conflicts are explained on a purely somatic basis, and even when a more glaring utterance or absurd action attracts notice the usual tendency is to pass it over as lightly as possible. The real mentality of the child is an extremely complex and difficult subject, the psychology of childhood, as usually taught, gives a quite inadequate means of understanding the actual living child. The adult accustomed to ignore the submerged trends in himself is of course blind to these trends in the child. Close observation of the child and frank willingness to see facts as simple happenings without repressing them because they are improper, or because they touch upon certain topics is an absolutely essential condition of doing justice to the education of the child. The education of the child does not begin with the imparting of school information, it begins when the child is put to the mother's breast; it is being educated when it is being taught to regulate the simple demands of cleanliness; it is being educated when its curiosity with regard to its own body and the bodies of its comrades and seniors is dealt with in the right way. The foundation of the child's emotional life is being laid by the caresses of the mother, and the intimate relation of child to mother is a much more prominent determinant of adult character than is usually realized. This affection forms deep grooves along which the emotional life will later flow and may seriously interfere with the free adaptability of the mature adult, and be at the basis of many serious abnormalities of mood; the individual may remain unmarried owing to the early fixation of his affection on his mother, or in more trying circumstances he may develop neurotic or psychotic symptoms which have their root in these childhood experiences. The relations between the girl and the father are liable to the same complications. In other cases the life of the individual is largely dominated in a subtle manner by the childhood relation to the parent of the same sex. It is impossible here to elaborate this topic, but emphasis must be laid on the practical importance of factors too often neglected, such as the unwise caresses sometimes lavished on the child, the sleeping arrangements of the child, and the possibility of the child becoming directly aware of the marital relations of the parents.

The education of the child will certainly necessitate the pruning of many side-shoots which tend to interfere with the vigor of the plant; there must be pruning, and certain trends will have to be repressed; but the method by which the child attains to its adult culture is extremely important, and culture can be dearly bought at the price of a neurosis.

The situation is most acute in relation to those topics which culture has
at the present day subjected to such strong repression, and it is of very
great importance that the developing child, with its keen interests and
curiosity and obscure organic promptings, should learn to deal in a healthy
mental way with factors which it cannot but feel have a certain importance and which will assert themselves. The simple natural curiosity
of the child as to sexual matters, if not met in a frank way, may lay the
basis for a good deal of difficulty in the child's life. We may assume
that the child is easily deceived and that it accepts the official lies, but
that is because we wish the child to be so, not because the real child
is so easily deceived in this way. When the child learns by experience
that a certain subject is taboo, when a child has been punished, or met
with an expression of horror for asking a simple question, the topic of
that question is invested with a certain emotional value which does not
naturally belong to it. The desire for information which meets with
this check has to find other channels of outlet, and we frequently find
that a certain general curiosity or precocious intellectual development
is often related to just such experiences in the child's life. The child
is frequently aware that it has been more or less deceived, a certain
distrust of and antagonism to those in authority is often the unfortunate
result, a neurotic child may even develop symptoms such as morbid
fears or peculiar compulsive actions With regard to the important
sexual instinct, which later it will take all the enlightened culture of the
individual to deal with correctly, it is deplorable that the child is encouraged to deal with the matter in a blind and evasive and dishonest way,
and has the feeling that there is no simple honest solution of the situation; he thus comes to believe that certain things have simply to be
ignored, that a compromise of make-believe has to be established, and
that he has to repress from memory or clear consciousness factors which
are too intolerable to be faced. When the organic promptings become
more acute and either chance experience or evil comradeship has led the
child to derive crude bodily satisfaction from its sexual organs the difficulty
is increased, the conflict between the various forces is necessarily severe
and in the individual case is sometimes disastrous. What does most
harm to the individual is not the occasional self-abuse during the developing period, but the fact that the whole situation should not be frankly
faced, and that the boy endeavors in an evasive and dishonest way to
eliminate its painful memory instead of being encouraged to see the
whole matter in the light of all the knowledge which the adult can give
him. Efforts are made to be frank with boys but in an unfortunate
way; thus it seems unwise to try to help a child in this direction by telling
the child that self-abuse leads to insanity, or by using other threats.
The aim is to let the child realize that the special instinct associated

with special organs is going to be one of the important elements in life
and is one of the highest responsibilities. The child should be encouraged
to be careful of himself because he feels that later he, too, will have to
take up adult responsibilities and because he is proud to prepare himself
for these responsibilities. To describe the various modes in which
unwise and unhealthy management of the sexual factor influences the
life of the individual would require a treatise on the neuroses supplemented by a treatise on culture generally; it would have to take into
consideration many questions of interest in religion and art and literature and the history of philosophy, and would throw a flood of light on
many a biography. From our present point of view what is important
is that at the period of life when the individual is being educated, *i. e:*,
is being given a certain organized body of information, is being trained
in certain intellectual processes, is being disciplined in social adaptation,
is learning skill in mechanical pursuits and physical exercises, the instinctive life receives so little attention; but, although neglected, it also is
developing, it is moulding intellectual interests, coloring the emotional
life, modifying enthusiasms, and influencing the whole personality in
the most intimate way. It receives remarkably little attention in our
educational schemes; it is considered barely respectable to discuss this
instinct, although its mismanagement is pregnant with all sorts of dangers
to the individual, and although the whole brilliant superstructure of
the individual life may be shattered on account of the unsoundness of
the instinctive foundations. Unless these foundations are sound the
intellectual structure may be of no use, energetic natures may be fettered
with strange inhibitions, cheerful dispositions haunted by dreadful
phantoms. Such is the problem of education which the psychiatrist
puts before the teaching profession. In order to deal with it a wide
coöperation will be necessary. Where the parents are not thoroughly
enlightened it is upon the teacher that the responsibility will fall of
detecting the presence of personal difficulties in the child's life, and of
either giving the assistance that is necessary or calling the attention
of the school psychiatrist to the child. It is not too much to hope that
many a child will therefore get assistance at a period when help is so
useful, that in future slight indications of difficulty will be taken seriously,
that substitutive and evasive reactions will be recognized as such, that
honesty and openness in dealing with vital matters shall be encouraged.
In that case the teaching profession will be one of the most important
factors in promoting the mental hygiene of the community. It will
be largely through the teachers that the conflict between culture and
nature will be softened. Through their efforts certain types of maladjustment may be met at the very onset, and through them the difficulties
of the neurotic may be considerably reduced. Many individuals may

feel that frank dealing with these natur
and that it is not in the interests of high
of the culture which we have inherited,
is the neurotic who pay the death dues of
do all we can to lessen their burden.

SOME PRINCIPLES OF MENTAL HYGIENE

BY

WILLIAM H. BURNHAM

Although the special study of the hygiene of instruction is a recent movement, nevertheless the well-established principles of mental hygiene have here a distinctly practical application. Among these are the following: (1) Attention to the present situation, which Janet has shown to be a gauge of sanity, and which Dr. Osler has emphasized as of prime importance for the mental health; (2) the development of habits of orderly association; (3) the normal reaction to feeling, which Freud and his students have shown to be vitally important; (4) suitable alternation of periods of work and rest, which Dr. Erb long ago emphasized as the most important principle in the hygiene of the nervous system. There is not time to discuss these principles in detail, but recent investigations have emphasized the third principle mentioned: the need of normal reaction to feeling; and some illustrations of this may be given because of its practical importance for mental hygiene in the school and in the home.

Anything that interferes with the normal reaction to feeling is likely to cause serious disturbance of health. In most cases of mental disorder there is some disturbance of the affective life; and in the ordinary states of worry and mental fatigue, usually the most trying factor is some conflict or repression of feeling. In fact in all states of worry there seems to be an affective element, which is related more or less remotely to the emotion of fear.

Recent experimental studies of the higher mental processes have brought us to close quarters with some of the elements of these affective states.

The mental world, to use the ordinary figure, is divided into two great hemispheres: That of sensation, images, ideas, what is present before the mind—what the Germans call the *Vorstellung*—on the one hand; and, on the other hand, that of organic and affective tendencies, attitudes, what is inherent in the mind—what the Germans call the *Einstellung*.

The more general attitude, or *Einstellung*, is usually the residuum of a long series of conscious reactions, but sometimes it is set up by a shock, by a single initial reaction, where there is a strong emotional coloring, as shown in many pathological cases, especially, perhaps, in hysteria.

In the laboratory, concrete attitudes are aroused by the setting of an experiment, and especially by the instructions given to an observer. In the school every method, every situation, every word of instruction or discipline by the teacher, has its affective influence in determining an attitude.

In the school we have been so busy teaching the conventional scholastic subjects that we have not had time to consider the deeper things that make for health and character. There is abundant evidence to show how important for pedagogical efficiency are the attitudes developed by the methods, the manner, and instructions of the teacher, and the general situations of the schoolroom. All these are apparently equally important for the highest mental health and development.

The school as well as the home is a great factor in producing these attitudes. The general attitudes represented by the words: Trust, cheerfulness, coöperation, loyalty, interest, success, are distinctly in contrast hygienically with those represented by the words: Distrust, antagonism, a feeling of disgust, injustice, suppression, failure. The sum total of the attitudes produced by the home, the school, the playground, and the rest, represent one's character and disposition.

We are just beginning to see the significance of these generic affective states, these attitudes, for health. Both psychology and psychiatry furnish convincing evidence. This could be shown best by concrete illustration if there were time.

Our psycho-physic mechanism is a machine for converting stimuli into reactions inherited from generations of human and prehuman ancestors; the impulse to react has become imperative. But the conventions of society, the rules of the game, the teachings of morality, and the like, in modern society inhibit this tendency to react. Hence the various perversions, interference, repression, and so on.

These pathological cases are instructive, because they show in large letters what happens in a normal individual. Any idea may become a foreign body in consciousness and a source of worry unless there is a normal reaction to the affective state connected with it. This is illustrated in a hundred ways in our daily experience. If you think of a thing you actually begin to do it; and many persons are never satisfied unless they complete the act. Begin the repetition of a well known quotation or proverb and one always is a little unsatisfied if he does not finish it. With some persons this impulse is so strong that they insist upon telling their whole story in their own way and are never at ease until they have done so. If I repeat the words: "A rolling stone," a score of my hearers will mentally fill out the series with the words of the well known proverb, and many will not be quite satisfied until I add the words, "gathers no moss." Thus we feel the need of adequate reaction in all cases from simple motor tendencies to our most deep-rooted instincts and masterful passions. Whenever this tendency to react is inhibited, we experience dissatisfaction and an incipient form of worry.

Let us turn aside here for a moment to note one of the paradoxes, we may say, of culture. Mental hygiene demands that our thinking should be straightforward and natural, that our associations and recollections should be free and unrestrained, that the stream of thought should flow without artificial checks or interference, and that feeling should be expressed by free and natural reactions. But the whole course of training and of education is largely repression. Natural and free reactions as the expression of feeling must be inhibited or postponed. Even spontaneous and natural associations must often be checked. Impulses and desires, and the resulting associated memories, must be controlled or suppressed, and in a hundred ways the natural and spontaneous mental processes are supplanted by conventional rules and opinions. Thus it comes to pass that the educated person not only does not dare to act as he feels, but he does not even feel and think in a natural way, because such a large part of his association complexes are repressed by traditional and artificial conventions. The outcome of modern psychiatrical investigation points to all this repression and artificiality as one of the causes of modern nervousness and mental disorder.

Every professional group illustrates this repression. The words that Miss Abbott puts into the mouth of "The White Linen Nurse" express the revolt of many in other callings against the repression of feeling and individuality by professional conventions.

"My face is all worn out trying to 'look alike'," she exclaims; "my cheeks are almost sprung with artificial smiles. My eyes are fairly bulging with unshed tears. My nose aches like a toothache trying never to turn up at anything. I'm smothered with the discipline of it, I'm choked with the affectation. I tell you, I just can't breathe through a trained nurse's face any more. I tell you, sir, I'm sick to death of being nothing but a type, I want to look like myself. I want to see what life could do to a silly face like mine if it ever got a chance. When other women are crying, I want the fun of crying. When other women look scared to death, I want the fun of looking scared to death."

Freud and his school have given many illustrations of the unhygienic effect of the repression of feeling and of the various methods of protection and the like that both normal and pathological individuals are wont to resort to when repression of the normal reaction occurs. Here, in fact, this school of psychiatrists have made an important contribution, which should not be underestimated because of their sometimes unfortunate psychological vocabulary. What Freud means by a repressed idea and unadjusted affect, is, I take it, in normal life, what experimental psychology means by an attitude, an *Einstellung*.

One thing they have noted is that there are many ways of reacting to feeling. A reaction may signify any one of a whole series of reflexes, from knocking a man down to resent an insult to ignoring it by philosophic reflection. But, beyond certain limits, an adequate reaction to feeling is necessary for the mental health.

In the pressure of modern business, in the complexity of modern social life, and in the difficulties of group instruction in the school, it is inevitable that the natural reaction to feeling must be repressed. The health of the individual will depend largely on his ability to adapt himself to these conditions and to find suitable vicarious reactions to such repressed affective states.

The hygienic measures emphasized by all these studies are the following:

First, keeping up the general mental health, the health level in the psychic sphere, which enables one to resist a considerable amount of strain. When mind and nerves are rested by a good vacation one doesn't mind controlling one's feelings. "It is simply a question," as Freud has said, "of how many such affective strains an organization can endure. Even an hysterical person will be able to retain a certain amount in an unadjusted state, but if through a summation of similar motives it increases beyond the individual's endurance, the impetus for conversion is formed;" *i. e.*, it becomes pathological.

Second, the habit, which may be developed from early childhood, of absolving or removing the repressed feelings, the traumas, as soon as they are produced, a habit, as we may say, of squaring one's mental and moral accounts each day. The hygienic value of confession, of which we have innumerable cases, consists precisely in this. A repressed feeling should not be harbored. A child, for example, should be trained to hold no grievance against a companion, but should have it out in some natural reaction.

A third hygienic measure, which is at least suggested by these studies, is the transfer or conversion of the painful idea by association with some intense interest or enthusiasm. Just as pathological cases show the protective activity of the mind in dissociating the affect from the troublesome idea and associating with something which is perhaps painful but endurable, so it is a natural question why the affect may not be associated with some more vital and interesting and positively pleasurable idea, which may serve in certain instances at least as a complete protection, or in other words, as practically a cure of the mental lesion.

Fourth, in any case the repressed energy can be utilized in activity, and of this we have many illustrations in the higher irradiations in art and literature and philanthropy and the like. Goethe tells us that when depressed he would express his feelings in a poem or the like.

Fifth, every interest is a possible means by which there could be a reaction, and the more interests one has, the more means of associating the unbearable idea with something interesting and vital. The school should develop a rudimentary philosophy of life—attitudes and interests—which will serve as protection against unbearable ideas.

1. The practical applications of all this in the schoolroom are obvious. In the first place, teachers ought to know something about the psychology of feeling, and they should be trained to avoid those situations, those methods of instruction and discipline, which produce antagonistic and unfortunate attitudes in their pupils. They should learn to avoid wherever possible the artificial repression of normal reaction to feeling; and in any case their appeal to, feeling should be made intelligently, with the knowledge of the psychological and hygienic significance of their methods of instruction and training.

2. Peculiar and sensitive children should be shielded, and as much as possible, spared from the occasions that arouse unfortunate attitudes and that tend to produce the abnormal repression of feeling.

3. The whole subject of methods of instruction and discipline should be studied in the light of modern psychology and hygiene, with regard to the attitudes produced quite as much as with regard to the intellectual results of school instruction and discipline.

4. Opportunity should be given for the development of many interests, i. e., for many forms of healthful reaction in the school.

The best way to develop a permanent interest is to do something. By attending to things, by doing things, interest is inevitably developed; and among the strongest and most wholesome interests are those in our own work and our various occupations. And thus an occupation represents a vital complex of associations and attitudes. It comes to be one of the most important things in an individual's character. It is almost a part of one's personality.

Vocational training, so-called, has many dangers, but the great merit of it from an hygienic point of view is that by giving one an opportunity to do something which one has a capacity for, it does develop certain permanent interests of a wholesome character; and just so far as the school develops interests in an occupation, or interests in books, or art, or science, or society, however crude, so far it develops the alphabets of healthful mental activity.

A certain percentage of mental disorder, we do not yet kn
large a part, can be prevented by mental hygiene; but we shoul
in the school; and we can have no adequate mental hygiene u
school is reorganized and attention given to the hygiene of feeli
to those fundamental attitudes and habits which favor normal
development and mental health, and until the school instead o
a place where worry, confusion, mental strain and habits of nerv
are liable to be developed, shall become a refuge where paren
send their children when threatened with nervous breakdown or
disorder.

THE VALUE OF PSYCHOPATHIC CLINICS IN THE PUBLIC SCHOOLS

BY

L. PIERCE CLARK

To-day experts frankly admit that when such severe nervous disorders as epilepsy and adolescent insanity are firmly established, they are approximately incurable in eighty per cent. of all cases. Our best efforts in treating these disorders are largely concerned in ameliorating the lot of such diseases. When one recalls the fact that one-fifth of the insane suffer from dementia praecox and that chronic epilepsy is present in at least one out of every five hundred of the general population of this country, we should be seriously impressed with the necessity of attacking the problem of the prevention of epilepsy and insanity in the most energetic and effective manner. The majority of these nervous and mental disorders are recruited from children in the early period of adolescence and a most painstaking research should therefore be directed to the errors in the developmental period of childhood. In this manner we may avoid or stay the progress of these chronic deteriorating mental and nervous disorders that at present fill the asylums and colonies. If we follow out this plan there is no good reason why we may not attain results akin to the marvelous achievements of preventative medicine in the domain of the infectious and contagious diseases. We physicians who have dealt with the chronic nervous maladies, such as dementia praecox and epilepsy, in asylums and public clinics have long been impressed with the fact that such cases, when brought to us for diagnosis and treatment, have shown symptoms for months or even years which observing parents and teachers have seen and noted, and had they been brought to our attention at their inception would have enabled us to rescue many of these sufferers from a life of permanent invalidism, to have conserved the health of many more, and certainly would have enabled us to be of signal aid in reducing the economic and social burden on the part of all concerned. The crying need, then, has been for earlier apprehension and treatment of these nervous and mental disorders. We should no longer be obliged to look back through a retrospect of years to note the small but important beginnings of these nervous and mental diseases, but should be on hand at such early periods to administer first aid at first hand. A number of means for remedying this defect have been put in operation, but still the lack of earliest detection and care of these cases exists. The nerve clinics in connection with hospitals and medical schools are doing good work, but are still not in close enough touch with the material. We must have better team work between the home, the school, and the medical expert. To that end I urge the formation of psychologic clinics in connection with the public schools, such clinics to be an integral part of these schools. Obviously these clinics can best be established first in our largest cities where the work of classification of the various types of abnormal children is already far advanced. Special sense defects, crippled children and general sanitation of schools are being looked into most admirably. Even a perfected system of the ungraded classes for the subnormal child has been established in many large cities and many excellent papers dealing with the problem of this group of children are on your congressional program.

Why should we attempt now to burden the public school system with this new medical problem to-day? Simply because the school is naturally the clearing house of child life. It is the place where the child meets with its first great stress with its fellows and equals in social and industrial competition. In short, it is the first great tryout for a life of usefulness and service, or the reverse. All of us feel how important it is that children should be well grounded in fundamental good mental and physical habits. Often the public schools furnish just these factors in sound development and little else. Only too often actual facts and the matter called educational plays little rôle in after life and is greatly subject to change or discard. All the principles, therefore, that go to make up the proper mental and physical habits of the child during school age are eminently the functions of an education system. Obviously the misfits and the maladjustments of such a developmental education are the immediate concern of such a system. Hence the necessity for the formation of proper clinics for all the neurotic and defective types of childhood. To carry out this policy well, the expert neurologist and psychiatrist must be requisitioned. It is no longer sufficient that psychologic studies of abnormal mental childhood should be made. The work of the future demands more than this. We want trained neurologists and psychiatrists to contribute their knowledge right here at the foundation of developmental childhood, the public school. Then it may be possible to put a stop to the ever increasing number of chronic and incurable nervous breakdowns at their very inception in school childhood.

Having delivered several addresses upon the subject of neural and mental clinics in the schools and having been frequently misunderstood by many of my audience in that they thought my remarks applied chiefly or solely to defective or backward children, I wish to reiterate here that I am speaking of clinics for the *neurotic* child, not for the imbeciles and the feebleminded.

The neurotic children embrace those affected with serious depressions, violent and impetuous temper amounting to the epileptic constitution before epileptic seizures appear; those afflicted with the types of shyness, timidity and the shut-in personality of Hoch's designation, from which dementia praecox is so largely recruited, and those children who suffer from panics, fears and obsessions who so greatly swell the ranks of the chronic nervous invalidisms of later life. Careful expert studies upon such children painstakingly and sympathetically made will throw a flood of light upon the cause of mental and nervous breakdowns of later life. The groundwork of three-fourths of all nervous maladies is laid in child life. It may be said in the light of the newer mental studies that the possibility of detecting fully two-thirds of all adolescent insanities and nervousness could be made in children during the ages of from six to fourteen if all the facts of that period were accessible. The enormous importance of a detailed physical and mental history of earliest child life is the one great obvious lesson of modern mental medicine to-day. Until this field be carefully explored by team work of the parents, teachers and physicians we have no just cause to lay so great a burden upon heredity and much of its fatalistic hope of any method of betterment of the neurotic child. However, the psychologic clinic should not stop with the analysis of its immediate issues in the makeup of the neurotic child; it must go further and search out the defects in home and family life and the economic and industrial conditions which form a just part of the child's break in life competition in gaining an education. We shall then be able to properly apportion each factor in causation of the condition and apply the wisest remedy.

There can be no doubt that in the neurotic makeup of child life *per se* lies the antisocial traits of the delinquent and criminal type of childhood as well, such as lying, stealing, truancy, sex perversion, and a host of others. It must be recognized that at heart there is little difference between the vicious and delinquent child and the neurotic child. The delinquent boy has the courage of his convictions, for convictions may be bad as well as good, and he projects his habits on others in the family circle or society at large, while the so-called purely neurotic child is a coward at heart and regresses into infantile habits of depression, shyness, timidity, excitements, panics, fears and obsessions.

It has been thought that the neurotic child group is a negligible one in point of numbers. I have but to remind you that the same was once thought of the subnormal children, whereas the latest estimates show it to be conservatively two per cent. of all school children. I do not hesitate in saying that the numbers of the neurotics are not less and are probably more than the mentally defectives.

What is the sociologic and economic value of this phase of our subject when contrasted to the feeble-minded? A great number of the neurotic children grow up into healthy men and women im later life and become a valuable asset to society, economically and socially, whereas there is little or no productiveness ever to be expected by even the most friendly treatment of the subnormal child. So even from a utilitarian point of view the neurotic child should be given our best study and efforts at correction and prevention of a hopeless invalidism of later life. We must search out by genetic methods of study and classify these neurotic trends in the child personality to see which trends are *benign*, as it were, and which point to an after life of comparative health. We shall then be able to view aright the residual characteristics or trends that are *malignant* and that spell the incurable neurotics and precocious dements of later life. The foregoing are but a few of the problems requiring analysis in the neurotic child life. Time forbids an extensive considera- tion of the many trends of interest we might profitably follow and lay bare in our subject. Suffice it to say that we have no curative remedies to-day to offer. A sufficient and frank study of the nervous child in all his manifestations is not yet at hand in any country. No remedy should be brought forward and applied except as we study and adapt it to the individual case. If it has taken painstaking researches for years, since the time of Sequin and Itard, to make possible a compre- hensive training, care and treatment of the subnormal child, the feeble- minded and imbecile class, how much greater must be the time and work required for us to formulate the proper general rules of treatment of the neurotic child, where there is a disordered nervous and psychic life to be set right and not a constant and definite deficit, as in the mental defective. The subnormals may be treated and cared for in groups; they are essentially gregarious and develop best by imitative habits, while the problem of the neurotic child's difficulty is an individual soul problem and must be handled as such.

The formation of good psychobiologic clinics for children is not a new suggestion. Almost every large city has something of the sort. But I here make a special plea for such clinics, to be formed as an integral part of the school system. It is not sufficient that a few rooms and a few physicians or psychologists be set aside for this work. I submit the work has its special and distinct problems and it is one worthy of the best trained and experienced neurologists and psychiatrists. There should be plenty of able trained social workers, sociologists, pedagogues and physicians in every specialty of medicine to set free the delicate mechanism of the neurotic child in his first great competitive and developmental race in life. Just as we are now entering a new phase of psychiatry, going from the generic and the group study to the special and individual, so it is needful in neurotic child study, not that a lot of cases be loosely studied, but that the very few be exhaustively and exactly analyzed; not by external means exclusively, such as taking the height, the weight, and cranial measurements, but we want an intensive study of the inner life, habits and the personality, its makeup and defects in normal trends of mind development.

One of the main reasons why these psychologic clinics should be established in and a part of the schools is that the latter have the full confidence of the parents. The schools are fully equipped institutions and are ready for the incorporation of such clinics. Any line of treatment laid down for the neurotic child must largely be an educational and training one, and in the diverse multitudinous units of the school system it is easy to supply the special therapy of mind and habit training. Such a clinic should include in its records (1) a definite statement of the specific defects of the abnormal behavior of the pupils in the normal grades and a list of the false adaptations to the standards; (2) a careful research of the family life and environment which may have contributed its share in causation of the child's nervousness; (3) intelligence, judgment, will and ethical tests by trained experts, and (4) last, but more important still, a complete analysis of the inner life of the neurotic child. Then, and not until then, should a mental prescription be given. Provisions for a follow-up record should be provided and a re-examination and review of the cases at certain definite intervals should be made.

A plan such as I have here fragmentarily sketched ought to throw a flood of light upon the budding defects of the educational fruit on the tree of knowledge, alike valuable for normal child development as well as the neurotic child. It will contribute its quota of facts in the changes needed in normal education. This is the day of coöperation no less urgent in any field of endeavor than in our study of the neurotic child. In the psychologic clinic for school children we need team work of trained teachers, psychologists, neurologists, psychiatrists and sociologists. The work will reflect credit and honor upon any and all investigators entering upon it.

It is unnecessary for me to add that the running of psychologic clinics as an integral part of the public school system must be carried on with great tact, skill, and with the greatest sympathy for the children and parents concerned. Any efforts in this field which do not meet these requirements will seriously handicap the choice fruition of the project and materially retard that still greater issue, the prevention of nervous and mental disorders in general.

THE RELATION OF THE SPECIAL CLASS IN THE PUBLIC SCHOOLS TO THE COMMUNITY

BY

GRACE BÖHNE

It is my aim to present to you an interpretation of the special class in the public schools in its true relation to the community.

Let me cite, at the outset, the problem as it is met by the average superintendent and principal where a special class is about to be formed.

The principal realizes the need of individual help with many cases. He accordingly chooses from his school a heterogenous group of children, some of whom are undoubtedly feeble-minded to a marked degree; others that are constant laggards in the grade and others who have always given trouble in discipline. Of course since "there are no bad boys" they must necessarily be feeble-minded.

This group, not less than eighteen or twenty in number, is segregated usually in the most undesirable room in the building. And to cap the climax, the principal places in charge a teacher whose many years of experience and service have neither improved her disposition, her looks, nor her personality. One whom he gladly eliminates from his grades and whom he would like to dismiss from service altogether, but his hand is stayed by public opinion, for many have known and loved her in her more efficient years—and do not realize that teachers, too, pass their years of useful service.

She is then placed in charge of this group with little or no special training and less equipment and admonished to return them to the regular grades as soon as possible.

Here undoubtedly is one of the grossest errors, for no teacher, however skillful, can restore to normality the child with definite brain lesions.

Imagine her distress and discouragement when harassed and expected to prove her worth by restoring these children to normality!

The principal, the teachers and the public stand back and watch to see the outcome of this venture. Antagonism from parents and the teachers adds to the problem within the room and the teacher finds herself entirely unable to cope with the situation, and the school official finds his attempt to benefit the individual far more destructive than constructive.

Do not think I have overdrawn this situation. During my years in special work I have tried to help and comfort many, many teachers who have faced the problem here pictured.

Imagine by comparison a properly organized class containing a maximum number of fifteen well defined cases. Place in charge the right woman and the class will be the greatest possible help in a school. Where such classes have been formed with properly trained teachers, the results have amply justified the organization. The relief to the grades alone is sufficient to warrant its place in the school. The special class should be a laboratory where opportunity is given to study the individual, where his capabilities have a chance for expression and where a proper estimate is placed on his limitations.

Through this special class, as a medium, the teacher becomes a social worker, reaching beyond the confines of her room into the homes to study the eugenical problems which have made necessary the special class.

It seems to me that the right choice of teachers must even precede the choice of pupils for the class, for the normal child, if improperly segregated will, without doubt, prove his efficiency in this laboratory where the best methods are used and the right teacher can make the special class of such high standard that the child returns to the grade when he has proved his efficiency with no stigma of feeble-mindedness. But she must be of the highest type of woman, one who understands not only the child, but also the parents and no expense should be spared to secure the desirable woman when found.

The public school limits its scope of activity when it fails of its opportunity to continue the education of the citizens sent forth. The appreciation, as expressed by the large attendance at social centers and evening schools testifies to the place and value of the public schools in the after school life of the average citizen. The opportunity afforded the public school to reach out through these avenues to inform and instruct the people should be utilized.

Special teachers should consider it part of their duties to address social centers, mothers' clubs, church societies, etc., and they should, by information gained when visiting parents in their homes, be able to inform and enlighten the public regarding the eugenical problems they have found.

Educators might right about face and establish the work with a broader understanding of the function of the special class in its relation to the community.

Proper segregation of the older subnormal children should be promoted with an aim to assist in the proper placement of these children in the various industrial activities in the world at large and a suitable place provided for the care of the types unfit to mingle with the community.

The work should be closely allied with juvenile and police court

work and various charitable organizations in order to prevent the improper confinement of irresponsible cases.

Those of us who have had the opportunity of viewing these problems
from more than one standpoint find the community slow to awaken
to the importance of adequate provision for the various types of mental
and moral helplessness. The public must take their stand and demand
that institutions be built to care for the unfit who are corrupting many
by their licentiousness. The special teacher finds herself facing a much
larger situation than that of a mere pedagogical problem and the community should unite forces and utilize the information which she is able
to give after painstaking investigations.

Not until her position as a social worker as well as that of a special
teacher is recognized will the public derive from her valuable fund of
information and from her skill the real worth of her ability and the real
meaning and value of the special class in the community.

THE MEDICAL INSPECTOR AND FEEBLE-MINDEDNESS

BY

WALTER S. CORNELL

This paper is brief. The subject of feeble-mindedness in its other aspects is considered in numerous other papers at this Congress. The thought of the writer, moreover, is to confine himself to the administrative aspect of the medical inspector's work in this field.

Advanced medical inspection, such as is done in Philadelphia, includes numerous activities. Not only is attention given to the contagious diseases and the common physical defects, but there is also a study of sanitation, of tuberculosis, of poor nutrition and of mental deficiency. Janitors are physically examined, medico-legal advice is given to the Bureau of Compulsory Education and special studies are made of delinquent children. The knowledge required to do this work is quite different from the knowledge required of the physician who is in general practice or who pursues any of the conventionally recognized specialties. In the past there has been no instruction given by our medical colleges in public health work and the little demand upon the physician for information and help in this field has not been accompanied by any remuneration. This is the reason for poor or mediocre work by the average physician who takes up medical inspection, at the time of the assumption of his duties, in the field of mental deficiency which we are now discussing, and in the fields of contagious disease and sanitation.

Both personal and professional qualifications are necessary to the physician who works in neurology or pediatrics and the work of the medical inspector in the realm of mental deficiency requires proficiency in both these branches.

Let us consider first the necessary personal qualifications of the medical inspector examining deficient children.

Such a man must understand children. If he is able to make them come to him without fear or embarrassment, he has achieved the most important requisite to the work. Numerous medical inspectors are pursuing their work handicapped by ignorance of the nature of the child. Not long since a boy of about fourteen years was sent to the school principal's office to see the medical inspector and was soundly scolded by the latter because he did not answer promptly, although the nervous condition of the boy and the fact that he was a stutterer was evident by his facial expression, his hands and convulsive gulpings. There are men quite well known as neurologists who work in a restricted field which seldom includes the handling of children and these, too, may commit disastrous errors. At the Society for Organizing Charity a year ago, the writer was asked to look at a boy who had been pronounced feeble-minded by a neurologist who had happened to pass through the play room where this boy and a number of others had been. It appeared that the neurologist in question had taken the boy by the shoulder and abruptly demanded in rather loud tones, "What is your name?" The boy was so scared that he opened his mouth and could not say a word, whereupon the gentleman before mentioned remarked, "That boy is an idiot" and walked on. Examination showed that there was nothing whatever the matter with the boy. This same temperamental difference, accentuated possibly by training, was also recently brought up in a discussion over the appointment of a teacher of a special class. Two teachers had been warmly advocated and the choice was made of one because the other occasionally showed "an unsympathetic hard streak" according to a member of the committee.

Not only is a certain temperament and disposition necessary for the proper handling of deficient children but tact is also required in the handling of their parents. Not long ago at the writer's clinic at the Bureau of Compulsory Education the presence of two or three visitors while a child was being examined and the statement to the parents that the child would never be normal caused a violent communication from the mother two or three days later, together with the threat that further "interference" with her child by the Bureau of Compulsory Education would lead to trouble. As a matter of fact one of the visitors was a medical inspector receiving special instruction and the other a visiting superintendent of schools, the child—a boy of fifteen—had been sent out of the room into the waiting room, and the mother, at the beginning of the examination had volunteered the information that the principal of the Germantown school wished to send her boy to the special class in a school near by because he was "not right." It is just such parents, however, that the student of mental deficiency continually encounters and the slightest error is likely to be magnified and remembered.

Finally in regard to personal qualifications, it is noteworthy that out of fifteen medical inspectors (five supervisors and ten especially chosen assistants) given special training by the writer and by the psychologist at the House of Detention, four were evidently not fitted to do the work. These four were not inferior in any other respect to the remaining eleven.

The professional qualifications of the mental examiner, if such we·

may call the medical inspector doing this special work, include a knowledge of the factors which cause mental deficiency and a knowledge of the clinical evidence of mental deficiency. The mental examiner must know considerable. sociology and psychology as well as what is now generally defined as the practice of medicine. Children reared in different neighborhoods, under different social conditions, under different school training, and children of different race respond differently.

So, too, in the matter of psychology, the mind is so complex that no few simple rules learned over night will suffice for more than the roughest kind of judgment. The Binet-Simon tests, now quite well known, require quite a fair knowledge of elementary psychology for their proper interpretation, and these, it may be remarked, do not take into account volitional or emotional factors, both of which are emphasized by investigators of delinquent children.

It may be remarked, also, that a solid preliminary education producing a sound scientific trend of thought is requisite to good work. The mental examiner must be sure of his conclusions and stick to them. His judgments, like other judgments, are comparisons and he must bear in mind constantly the normal child in distinction to the child he is examining. The examiner working for a considerable time among a certain class is in danger of forgetting what an average normal child exhibits in its mental development. Moreover, there is no medical work in which the examiner is so besought by anxious parents and sympathetic or unsympathetic teachers to change his diagnosis, these persons clinging to the idea that a change in the pronouncement will effect a change in the actual condition.

Specifically it may be stated that the professional equipment of the mental examiner of a strictly medical nature should include neurology (insanity, and organic and functional nervous diseases not accompanied by insanity), the eye, the nose, throat and the ear, nutrition in its newer aspects, the ductless glands, the toxemias, and the infections.

The relation of the medical inspection system and the individual mental examiner to the school system and to the teacher is very important. How shall we discover, diagnose and dispose of the mentally deficient children in the school system? There is no doubt, with two or three per cent. of all school children deficient in some degree, that milder cases must, perforce, be discovered by the class teachers and handled with such advice as the ordinary medical inspectors are able to give. Attention to the promotion records, the use of the Binet tests, reasonable attention to the sight, hearing and nutrition, and social service work in the homes constitute such non-special work. As to the feeble-minded children and the border line cases of older years, these may also be discovered and brought forward by the school teacher, accompanied by promotion records and the mental age expressed in Binet units but the diagnosis in these cases should be made by a specially qualified mental examiner. In these cases the matter is more serious. A responsible statement is required as to the existence of feeble-mindedness, a neurotic constitution and removable physical defects. The diagnosis of feeble-mindedness should result in the placing of the child in a special class where feeble-minded children only are accommodated, if such a class be conveniently situated, and it is evident that a certificate of a physician is the only excuse for the placing of a child in such a class. So, too, a physician's certification is required by law in the commitment of individuals as insane or feeble-minded and no other certificate is recognized by the courts. In Philadelphia no child is committed by the court to an institution for the feeble-minded without the presence in court of the examining physician. Finally the diagnosis of feeble-mindedness entails a life-disposition of the child entirely different from that of the ordinary child. The teacher in possession of, and protected by a physician's diagnosis of feeble-mindedness, is able earnestly to advise the parents of the advantage of permanent custodial care of the feeble-minded child, to the child itself, the parents and the community.

In the city of Philadelphia much work has been done in the discovery, diagnosis, disposition and registration of the feeble-minded. In 1911 a school census was taken revealing, according to the teachers' reports, 442 feeble-minded children of institutional grade, 2,500 border line cases and 6,000 dull children. Out of this number some 350 children have been diagnosed by medical experts as undoubtedly feeble-minded. Between 80 and 90 special classes in the public schools are in existence. At the House of Detention a psychologist, two class teachers and two physicians making physical examinations, assist the mental examiner. A clinic is held weekly at the Bureau of Compulsory Education and here numerous children are brought whose parents desire to secure their exemption from school attendance on the ground of mental deficiency, or whose teachers desire information on this point. Two clinics per week are held at the House of Detention and here cases nominated by the Chief Probation Officer, the Superintendent of the House of Detention and the judges themselves are examined. The Children's Bureau and the Society for Organizing Charity avail themselves of these clinics and of other expert advice. With the opening of the schools September, 1913, there will be established five branch clinics (probably afterward increased to ten), so that the work will not be limited by the distance of the school from the clinic.

The social aspect of this work is as important as its educational aspect. The future life of the child may, to a large extent, be determined during its school life. The realization that every child between eight and fourteen years of age is under the eye of the authorities, through the compulsory education law, makes us focus our efforts to recognize these cases at this time. For this reason in Philadelphia there has been inaugurated a central registration of feeble-minded and border line cases. Everyone who is familiar with the criminal courts is painfully aware of the questionable responsibility of a large proportion of the persons arraigned. Among those tried for murder, the border line cases of feeble-mindedness, the neurotic and the alcoholic insane, are even more in evidence. With an official registration dating back to the years of childhood, the physician's certificate being accompanied by evidence consisting of mental tests, social investigations, including the heredity, our judges, prosecuting attorneys and juries will doubtless sleep better. The American people will not be treated to the spectacle of a murder trial in which the defendant pleads insanity and the symptoms of degeneracy and subsequently claims sanity with the approbation of apparently reputable physicians and lawyers, these gentlemen taking part in the entire legal proceeding. The work of registration in Philadelphia is still young but at the Bureau of Compulsory Education have been already registered 84 institutional feeble-minded cases, 29 high grade feeble-minded cases (not enough deficient to warrant commitment without proven social disability or social offenses), and 52 border line cases. The House of Detention, the Bureau of Compulsory Education and the special classes of the public schools have contributed during the last year a total registration of 215 feeble-minded cases and 262 border line cases. During the coming year, with the increase in facilities, this work of registration will be greatly facilitated and the Register largely increased in size and importance. It is planned to consolidate the Register at the Bureau of Compulsory Education, where such records are legally required.

THE UNIVERSITY IN RELATION TO THE PROBLEMS OF MENTAL DEFICIENCY AND CHILD HYGIENE

BY

ARNOLD GESELL

A university has two functions always: to discover truth, and to teach it while it is new and fresh. In this way the university serves society. What truth? It is hard to draw the line anywhere, and surely the line should not be drawn to exclude the great social problem of mental defect.

At a conservative estimate two or three in every 1,000 are feeble-minded. Our population is 100,000,000; the total therefore is appalling. As a problem of social prevention this mass of feeble-mindedness spells $705,000,000, according to the estimate of Mary Richmond. (She assumes that one-third of the total of 300,000 of both sexes do not need custodial care, and estimates school care, exclusive of buildings at $175.00 per year for seven years and adult care at $100.00 per year for 23 years.) With about 2% of our elementary school population feeble-minded, with some 25% of our criminal population feeble-minded, with vice, pauperism, inefficiency and degeneracy untold due to feeble-mindedness, we have in this burden a social problem toward which a university may indeed feel a responsibility.

In 1856 the Connecticut Commissioners found "a settled conviction of a large majority of the citizens of the Commonwealth that idiots were a class so utterly helpless that it was a waste of time even to collect statistics regarding them." The university can do a part in the further unsettlement of this conviction.

There are three ways in which a university may approach and deal with the problems of mental deficiency.

I. University Research and Extension Departments in connection with State Institutions for the Defective and Delinquent.

Research is the basis not only of scientific progress but of public enlightenment. "One of the most remarkable phases of the movement in regard to the feeble-minded," says Dr. W. S. Fernald, a leading authority, "is the marvelous ways in which feeble-mindedness has become talked about, and the interest which is shown in the subject to-day compared to the interest which was manifested twenty-five years ago. This is largely due to the intensive work which has been done in the past ten years by Dr. Goddard at Vineland, and the work of Dr. Davenport at Cold Spring Harbor." This research work has been of fundamental importance. It is the only safe basis for publicity. Further advances in the movement for the control of feeble-mindedness will depend upon similar research. There is much that remains unknown.

There are at least five phases to the problem of mental deficiency: 1, the medical (etiological, anthropometric, biochemical and demographical); 2, the eugenic; 3, the sociological; 4, the pedagogical; 5, the psychological. Each of these phases has received investigative attention at Vineland. It may be said, indeed, that an embryo university has sprung up within this institution for the feeble-minded. As a teaching agency this research department has depended upon its summer classes for teachers of defectives; a summer course for physicians; and various extension efforts which are now organized in a distinct extension division.

Departments of psychological research have been established in other institutions for the feeble-minded and the epileptic, including the institution at Lincoln, Ill., and that at Faribault, Minn., which was the first to adopt the idea. These departments in direct connection with a vast amount of material for study, can do much which would be impossible at an official seat of learning where feeble-mindedness is supposed to be conspicuously absent. But now-a-days a university is not geographically limited by the campus. Its base of operations, by expeditions or branch stations, may be as distant as the Andes. If it is worth while to climb the Andes to get nearer the sun, it is worth while for our great universities to go to the institutions of the feeble-minded to study that which is still human enough to be part of the highest study of mankind. One very concrete demonstrated possibility therefore, is that departments of research, of normal training and of public extension service, be developed by universities in connection with their state institutions for mental defectives.

II. Psycho-Educational Clinics and Normal Training Courses in connection with University departments of psychology and education.

But all of the feeble-minded are not in institutions. A large fraction are in our public schools or more or less at large in our communities. Even the university in a small town can find considerable material for investigation and assistance in its radius. One way in which these local feeble-minded can be reached is by the psychological clinic. While the first university psychological clinic began with a *backward* child in 1896, at the University of Pennsylvania, under the direction of Dr. Lightner Witmer, a large proportion of the children who are brought to these clinics are feeble-minded. We may regard the psycho-clinic as one of the most direct avenues by which the university may enter the problem of mental deficiency, and exert an educative influence upon parents, teachers and community.

At present there are about a dozen universities which have established courses in clinical child psychology and which conduct genuine psycho-educational clinics as a regular or essential feature of the work.* These are the universities of Pennsylvania, Cincinnati, Washington, Minnesota, Pittsburgh, Leland Stanford, Kansas, Tulane, Yale, Harvard, Johns Hopkins. The first four were established in the departments of psychology; the second five in the departments of education; the last four have more or less connection with the departments of medicine. This fact itself is significant. It shows an identity of interest in the three fields which hitherto have had little in common.

All of the psychological clinics above mentioned are operated in conjunction with universities or medical dispensaries. The Child Study Laboratory at Chicago, founded in 1899 by Dr. Christopher, represents the principle of the clinic in official service as part of a large public school system.

The pedagogy of subnormal children and the training of special teachers for the subnormal constitutes a double but indivisible problem. The normal schools have hardly touched this problem. With one exception (the Brooklyn Training School) there is no normal school which conducts even a model class of feeble-minded children. Here is another important field for university activity. Normal training courses for teachers of special classes, supervisors, social workers, etc., are now conducted in summer sessions by the University of Pennsylvania, the University of Washington, and New York University. Harvard University offers a summer course on the study and treatment of the mentally abnormal with special reference to juvenile delinquency. New York University this year conducted five special classes in public school buildings of lower Manhattan.

One important requisite in the social control of feeble-mindedness, is the recognition and special treatment of defective children in the public schools. When all of these children have been segregated in special classes, society will be more ready to grasp the situation and to provide the proper after care and custody. A university, as a public service corporation, can assist cities and counties in the establishment of special classes and industrial "schools" for feeble-minded youth. A model school and training department under its permanent control would help to make the university effective in this field of social service. If a precedent is needed to justify such a departure, it would be found in model schools, which are now conducted by the School of Education in several universities.

*See list in article by Dr. J. E. W. Wallin in the Journal of Educational Psychology, Jan. 1911. (Revision forthcoming.)

III. A Five-Year Medical Course specializing in Child Hygiene.

There is a third possibility and that lies with the medical school. Of 24 medical schools which responded to a questionnaire of four years ago, 20 schools stated that they gave either no attention or only incidental attention to the subject of mentally defective children. This scant consideration is usually given in connection with psychiatry, pediatrics and neurology, with the result that the medical graduate's comprehension of the problem is frequently covered by a few meagre facts about thyroid extract, cretinism and stigmata of degeneration. Is the subject of mental deficiency and are all the related problems of retarded and atypical children to remain but incidental topics in the medical curriculum?

A few medical schools, notably Harvard and Johns Hopkins, are now giving formal courses on the subject. Conditions are fast changing. The application of clinical methods to the study of psychology; the experimental studies of human behavior; the genetic investigations of child development; the analytic method of interpreting psychoses; the multiplication of child welfare agencies; the growth of hygiene and preventive medicine, and finally the phenomenal rise and spread of medical inspection of schools—all these things are bringing many of the medical profession into a new attitude toward the birth, the growth and the rearing of children. Alongside of the combative interest in disease and injury, there is developing a somewhat different, dynamic or biological interest in health and development.

The new interests and endeavors in the conservation of children we group under a new and pregnant phrase, Child Hygiene. The establishment of departments and bureaus of Child Hygiene by the City of Boston, by New York City, the Russell Sage Foundation, the National Educational Association, and recently by the State of New York, is giving this term official as well as academic significance. Child Hygiene has two possible interpretations—in a mass sense it is that phase of public hygiene which is concerned with the lives and the vitality of children; in a specific sense, it is the application of the principles of psychology, education and medicine to the diagnosis and the control of the development of individual children. Child Hygiene includes of course the problems of mental deficiency; but it also includes the problems of mental retardation and deviation, delinquency, juvenile neuroses, speech defects, etc., and always the relation of physical factors to developmental irregularities. Child Hygiene is destined to become a distinct specialty, both as a division of social medicine and as an enlargement of pediatrics which will embrace in a unified manner the mental and physical development of the whole period of childhood.

And what shall be the training of this new child hygienist, which will best fit him to serve in municipal and state departments of child hygiene, as a physician to child welfare institutions, as an examiner for juvenile courts, as a medical inspector or health officer of schools, and in a private capacity as expert adviser on the education and corrective treatment of exceptional children? He· will need a triple training in psychology, education and medicine.

There are three possibilities. 1. He may take a post-graduate course in psychology and pedagogy, electing some medical studies but specializing as a paedo-psychologist.   Dr. Terman has made some valuable suggestions in this direction.*

2. The student may take a straight medical course and supplement it with one year of post-graduate work in pediatrics, clinical psychology and educational pathology.

3. Or, we suggest, he may be given the opportunity of taking a special five-year medical course leading to the degree of Doctor of Child Hygiene (this course to be so arranged that he may with little inconvenience also obtain the regular degree of M.D.).

The second arrangement would be somewhat similar to that by which a student at Harvard University may now secure an analogous special degree, also in the field of preventive medicine, the degree of Doctor of Public Health (D. P.H.).   The special course is offered as a fifth graduate year supplementary to the regular medical course.

Although there would be many practical advantages in favor of such a supplementary one-year child hygiene course, especially for medical inspectors, there also are objections.   The point of view of developmental hygiene and of genetic and functional psychology are prejudices which can not be assumed in a few months, and which may also be somewhat antagonized by the habitual standpoint of four years of medicine, too anatomical and too pathological in spirit.   It has been claimed that too much microscope and scalpel unfit the medical man to think psychologically.   This will not be true if the medical student· for the first year is trained to think psychologically by diagnosing development and interpreting behavior.   The advantages of a five-year arrangement is that it permits the study of all the medical subjects from the point of view of child hygiene, and fosters from the beginning the desired attitude toward the mental and physical problems of child development.

One unquestionable advantage is that such a course will bring into integrated relation the overlapping and blended problems of the deficient, the backward and the nervously defective child.· And since it will

*Popular Science Monthly, May, 1912.

emphasize the potential, the incipient and the immature manifestations of mental defect it will lend its strength to the movements of preventive medicine in a field of enormous importance.

For brevity and concreteness I have hazarded an outline of an approximate curriculum for a five-year course of training, specializing in Child Hygiene. I have no desire to raise controversial questions with respect to Applied Psychology versus Medicine. It is too important that psychology, education and medicine be brought into a fruitful union. There should be no false distinctions. It must be admitted, however, that the historical position of the medical profession, its present legal position with respect to public health, sanitation, school inspection and probate commitment procedure; its traditional responsibility with respect to human life; and the basic importance of the medical sciences, would all seem to warrant a decisively medical training for this new profession of Child Hygiene, if it is to become a new profession.

This course is arranged on the basis of 1,000 hours per year; and presupposes two years of college work including general biology, modern language, anthropology and organic chemistry. The allotted hours for specific subjects correspond *roughly* to the requirements for the regular medical course. The hours in pediatrics, psychiatry and neurology have been increased.

A MEDICAL COURSE SPECIALIZING IN CHILD HYGIENE

First Year	Second Year	Third Year
Hours	Hours	Hours
Anatomy............ 450	Pathology and Bacteri-	Therapeutics and Phar-
Bio-Chemistry and Nu-	ology.............. 450	macology.......... 175
trition............. 200	Physiology........... 150	Principles of Medicine.. 75
Histology.......!.... 125	Anthropometry 50	Minor Surgery........ 50
Embryology.......... 75	Neurology (Anatomy) . 75	Physical Diagnosis..... 50
Genetic Psychology.... 100	Principles of Education. 50	Pediatrics............ 100
Experimental Psychol-	Evolution and Eugenics 50	Mental Deficiency and
ogy of Behavior..... 150	History of Education.... 50	Juvenile Delinquency
——	Speech Defects........ 25	(with Clinical Dem-
Total............1,000	Clinical Child Psychol-	onstration)......... 100
	ogy (Norms of Devel-	Oral Hygiene and Den-
	opment)........... 50	tal Clinic.......... 50
	Physical Diagnosis..... 50	
	——	(*Continued next page*)
	Total............1,000	

A Medical Course Specializing in Child Hygiene—*Continued*

Third Year		*Fourth Year*		*Fifth Year*	
	Hours		Hours		Hours
Physical Education and		General Surgery	125	Obstetrics	80
Games	35	Surgical Clinic	25	Orthopedics	80
Course of Study and		Nervous Diseases of		Public Hygiene and	
Hygiene of Instruc-		Children	25	Sanitary Architecture	90
tion	100	Child Welfare Agencies.	50	Medical Clinic	100
Clinical Neurology	50	Dermatology	25	Ophthalmology	50
Medical Clinics	75	Medical Clinics	150	Otology	50
Dispensary Service	65	Psychiatry	100	Juvenile Psychiatry and	
Clinical Microscopy	75	Clinical Child Psychol-		Educational Thera-	
		ogy with Dispensary		peutics	300
Total	1,000	Service	500	Medical Inspection of	
				Schools (with prac-	
		Total	1,000	tical service)	200
				Educational Adminis-	
				tration and Child	
				Jurisprudence	50
				Total	1,000

WHO IS MENTALLY DEFECTIVE—HOW MANY ARE THERE—AND HOW CAN THEY BE DETECTED?

BY

HENRY H. GODDARD

A prominent American is quoted as saying, "The trouble with this problem of the feeble-minded is that there are so many of us." This remark suggests at once the necessity for discussing the question— Who is feeble-minded?—and at the same time the difficulty of answering it.

The feeble-minded do not constitute a distinct species of the human family, nor is feeble-mindedness a disease characterized by definite symptoms which one can diagnose and declare are present or absent. It must be understood that the term is a relative one, and there is no doubt, as Binet has well said, that the man who is normal in the rural districts of France might well be feeble-minded if you put him in Paris. This further agrees with the common expression, "That we are all a little feeble-minded or feeble-minded along some lines." Such being the case it might be asked, why is it necessary to define the term at all since it seems to be indicative of a condition that is universally present? One can only reply that if you choose to apply the term in this way it becomes necessary to say the important question is, how feeble-minded is one? As a matter of fact, the term has been defined in a practical way for a practical purpose. The universally accepted definition is that formulated by The Royal College of Physicians of London. This definition was adopted by The Royal Commission appointed to study the problem of feeble-mindedness and is quoted by Tredgold. He says "amentia," which is what we mean by feeble-mindedness in the generic sense, may be defined as "a state of mental defect from birth or from an early age, due to incomplete cerebral development in consequence of which the person affected is unable to perform his duties as a member of society in the position of life to which he is born."

They define a "feeble-minded person" in the specific sense, or what we call a moron, as "one who is capable of earning a living under favorable circumstances, but is incapable, from mental defect existing from birth or from an early age, (a) of competing on equal terms with his normal fellows, or (b) of managing himself and his affairs with ordinary prudence." We see from this that while we all may be a little feeble-minded there is a degree of feeble-mindedness below which the condition becomes significant, and the line is drawn at the point where an individual ceases to be capable of competing with his fellows on equal terms, or of managing his own affairs with ordinary prudence. The importance of drawing the line at this point consists in the social consequences. Any person who is unable to compete with his fellows in the struggle for existence, or who cannot manage his own affairs with ordinary prudence, is bound to be sooner or later a burden to the community.

To the utterer of the witticism with which we began, we may then reply, "You need not worry unless you are so feeble-minded that you cannot manage your own affairs with ordinary prudence," for it is only those who fail in this who become a problem. It is important to note that the definition says, "Those who are incapable because of *mental defect existing from birth* or an early age," and in that connection it is important to realize that *most of such incapacity is due to a mental defect that has existed from birth or an early age.*

This is a proposition that at first glance will be questioned, and perhaps even permanently rejected by many, but the truth of it is coming more and more to be realized. Perhaps the matter may be made clearer by putting it in another form.

We may say that the human family is composed of individuals of all grades of intelligence, from the lowest to the highest, but the particular grade of intelligence is characteristic of the family possessing it, and is transmitted. If human matings always took place between persons of the same level of intelligence we should have generation after generation of children of the same intelligence as their parents. As a matter of fact this comes much nearer being the case than is easily believed by those who look at individual families of their acquaintance and discover how different from either parent are the children, in intelligence. But we have only to look back into history a little to discover families of superior intelligence where the level has been maintained through three, four, perhaps six generations. One thinks at once in America of the Adams family and the Edwards family and many others. These high levels of intelligence grade down to the average man, where again, we find very much the same thing occurring; the great majority of people are what we may call of average intelligence, and we may trace them, generation after generation, in any particular family, and find the level is fairly maintained. We are now learning that the same thing holds true when we go below the average to those of very low intelligence. Now if we follow this descending scale of intelligence from the Adams and Edwards families down to the imbecile level we come somewhere in the scale to a point or degree of intelligence that is just about sufficient to enable a person to compete with his fellows and manage his affairs with ordinary prudence. It is in this border zone that we find those people who would be considered normal in intelligence under simple conditions, such as the peasant life of France or the simple farmer's life of our own country, whereas if you put them into the city under the complex conditions that exist there, they would inevitably fail of success and be unable to manage their affairs under such complicated circumstances, and would therefore become a burden and a menace and be properly called feeble-minded.

We have said that some might object to admitting that those who are incapable of competing in the struggle for existence, or of managing their own affairs with ordinary prudence, show this incapacity by reason of a *mental defect*; in other words, it is a somewhat new thought to most people that these individuals who *do not* get along, are actually *incapable* of getting along. The popular idea is that they could if they would; that they are careless or lazy, or vicious, or have some other peculiarity of mind which they could easily change if they were so inclined. Still more frequent is the notion that education could have changed it. If these people had only been to school and had had good training they would have been capable of taking care of themselves. No one denies that this is true in a certain percentage of cases of these failures in life, but the important contention and thing to be borne in mind is, that of these people a vastly larger percentage than has ever been realized are *actually feeble-minded.* Indeed, so large is the percentage that the burden of proof has shifted, and we have come now to the position where the first thing we must think of all such cases is, *perhaps they are feeble-minded.* That is to say, perhaps they could not possibly help being as they are, because they were born with a mental defect, or acquired it at an early age. Our answer to the question, "Who is feeble-minded?" reduces itself to this: Every person who is incapable of competing on equal terms in the struggle for existence, or is incapable of managing his own affairs with ordinary prudence, is *possibly* a feeble-minded person, and it is probably safe to say that unless we can demonstrate that there is *some other adequate reason* for his incapacity, it is correct to regard him as a feeble-minded person and to treat him accordingly. The actual determination of this point will be discussed in the third part of our paper.

How Many Feeble-Minded People Are There? In the census of 1890 one of the questions that was asked was, "Are there any idiots or imbeciles in your family?" The result of that inquiry showed that one in five hundred of the population was feeble-minded—idiot or imbecile. It is difficult to guess what proportion of the true number of those who are incapable of managing their own affairs with ordinary prudence was obtained by such a question, but certainly it must have been small, both because people naturally object to designating members of their family as idiotic or imbecile, unless they are very marked cases and the fact cannot be concealed; and second, because the ordinary person does not recognize the people of whom we are speaking as being mentally defective. For some years it has been concluded by those who are familiar with the problem of feeble-mindedness, that at least one in three hundred was a safe estimate. Still more recently and based upon more careful studies, we have said one in two hundred and fifty, and sometimes some one has dared to say, one in two hundred of the population.

. The Royal Commission above referred to, found for England one to every two hundred and seventeen of the population, and for Ireland one to every one hundred and seventy-five, and for Scotland one to every three hundred and eighty-four, while a recent careful survey of one fairly average county of the State of Michigan has given one to every *one hundred and eighty-seven* of the population as feeble-minded.

Our study of the mentality of an entire school system of a thousand children resulted in finding 2% of these children feeble-minded. A number of smaller studies in different places have shown at least this number.

Dr. Terman of Leland Stanford University tested a small system of eight hundred children and found twenty-five feeble-minded; this would be a little over 3%. Since the school population is roughly one fifth of the general population, "2% of the school children," and "one in two hundred of the general population," mean the same thing, approximately, and there is every indication that this is a conservative estimate. There are some who question this high percentage, but no one has as yet demonstrated that it is incorrect, and those who have begun to investigate have quickly discovered that this estimate is not too high. For example, the writer himself questioned the percentage when applied to New York City. The seven hundred and fifty thousand public school children there would give on the basis of 2% fifteen thousand children in the public schools as feeble-minded. It was almost unbelievable. But a careful investigation (see the author's report on Ungraded Classes, in the New York School Inquiry) showed that the estimate was probably an under, rather than an over, statement of the fact. A prominent educator in a personal letter to the writer said, "I used to think your estimate that 2% of school children are feeble-minded was ridiculously high; I now, after an investigation of the school children, am convinced that it is conservative." Whether we may yet be compelled to place it somewhat higher than we do now, I believe we are perfectly safe in considering that one in two hundred of the population, or 2% of school children, are so mentally defective as to be incapable of competing with their normal fellows in the struggle for existence; incapable of managing their own affairs with ordinary prudence. The significance of this state of affairs, for society in general, the writer has pointed out elsewhere.

How Can the Feeble-Minded be Detected? Every one knows how to recognize the idiot and the low-grade imbecile. They show it in their faces; they show it in their talk if they talk at all, and in many other ways the condition is manifest. But the real problem comes when we consider the high grade imbecile and the moron; these people that, to the casual observer, are *like the rest of us* but who, if allowed to go on, and attempt to take their places in the world, soon show that they are incapable of competing on equal terms and are incapable of managing their own affairs with ordinary prudence. As yet we have done very little toward detecting these people, except by the cumbersome method of experiment, that is to say, we have allowed them to go on and try to take their places in the world and when they have failed we have of late been asking the question, "Are they feeble-minded?" and we are learning that it must many times be answered in the affirmative. But such a procedure is wasteful, unjust and cruel, and we must have something better.

It is of the utmost importance that these defectives be recognized early before they have made shipwreck of life, before they have become a menace to society and done the damage which they surely will do if they are not protected and cared for. As already stated, we have now learned that this condition does not manifest itself in the bodily condition, at least not to any degree that can be recognized easily. It remains, then, to discover some method of detecting the quality of the mentality in these cases, and of detecting it early. Thanks to the work of the child-study people and the child psychologists we now know fairly well what is the normal rate of development in childhood and what mental processes are ripe at the various years of life, and thanks to the great work of Professor Binet we now have a method of determining the condition of any particular child in relation to this standard, and the Binet-Simon Measuring Scale of Intelligence is eminently satisfactory in the hands of one who understands its use. In certain doubtful and borderline cases one's judgment of an individual may be confirmed by certain other tests, but in most cases the Binet Scale itself is ample for the purpose. While some people object to the scale the objections are theoretical and hundreds of users the country over are daily demonstrating its practical value in the solution of this problem, and so far as the writer knows there is no one who has used it enough to get expert with it, who is not enthusiastic in its support. The universal comment is, "The more I use it the more wonderful I find it."

In concluding this paper I may sum up the case and sho
cance at the same time:

1. *Vast numbers of people whom we have heretofore tho
or ignorant are actually mentally defective and cannot do better t*

2. *The proportion of these in the population is so large as
a most serious problem in our social life.*

3. *If we recognize the situation, and admit the facts, we ca
and easily detect these cases in early childhood, and then by a
ment reduce to a minimum the seriousness of the problem.*

SESSION FORTY-TWO

Room B.   Friday, August 29th, 9:00 A.M.

CONFERENCE ON "BINET-SIMON SCALE"

Arranged by LEWIS M. TERMAN, Associate Professor of Education, Stanford University, Cal.

LEWIS M. TERMAN, *Chairman*

DR. F. S. CREGO, Buffalo, N. Y., *Vice-Chairman*

Program of Session Forty-two

FRED KUHLMANN, Ph.D., Director of Research, Minnesota School for Feeble-Minded and Colony for Epileptics, Faribault, Minn. "The Degree of Mental Deficiency in Children as Expressed by the Relation of Age to Mental Age."

W. H. PYLE, Professor of University of Missouri, Columbus, Mo. "The Value to Be Derived From Giving Mental Tests to All School Children."

OTTO BOBERTAG, Assistant in Institute for Applied Psychology, Breslau, Germany. "Some Theses Regarding the Scientific Use of the Binet Scale for Measuring Intelligence." Read by G. M. Whipple.

DR. CARRIE R. SQUIRE, Chicago, Ill. "Some Requirements of Graded Mental Tests."

DR. CHARLES SCOTT BERRY, University of Michigan, Ann Arbor, Mich. "Some Limitations of the Binet-Simon Tests of Intelligence."

DR. JOSIAH MORSE, University of South Carolina, Columbia, S. C. "A Comparison of White and Colored Children, Measured by the Binet Scale of Intelligence."

E. A. DOLL, B.A., Training School, Vineland, N. J. "Suggestions on the Extension of the Binet-Simon Measuring Scale."

GRACE FERNALD, M.D., State Normal School, Los Angles, Cal.   "The Use of the Binet Scale With Delinquent Children."

J. E. WALLACE WALLIN, Ph.D., Director of Psychological Clinic, School of Education, University of Pittsburgh, Pa.   "Current Misconceptions in Regard to the Functions of the Binet-Simon Testing and of Amateur Psychological Testers."

A. J. SCHREUDER, M.D., Director of Medical Pedagogical Institute, Arnhem, Netherlands.   "Some Dutch Experiences with the Binet Scale."

HENRY H. GODDARD, Ph.D., Director of Research Training School, Vineland, N. J.   "The Reliability of the Binet-Simon Measuring Scale of Intelligence."

LEWIS M. TERMAN, Associate Professor of Education, Leland Stanford Junior University, Stanford, Cal.   "Suggestions for Revising, Extending and Supplementing the Binet Intelligence Tests." Read by G. M. Whipple.

THE DEGREE OF MENTAL DEFICIENCY IN CHILDREN AS EXPRESSED BY THE RELATION OF AGE TO MENTAL AGE

BY

F. KUHLMANN

The object of this paper is to offer a rough means of correcting in part an error that is being commonly made in judging the grade of intelligence of children by their mental ages or number of years of mental retardation, and to discuss some assumptions that are involved. The error referred to is that of regarding the difference between the chronological and the mental age as representing the true degree of mental deficiency, independently of what the chronological age is. Binet and Simon themselves seem not to have escaped this error, since they place the limit of normality at two years, regarding children with a mental age of more than two years less than their chronological age as defective children. The truth of the matter is that a year of difference between the mental and chronological ages represents a decreasing degree of mental deficiency with increasing chronological age.

There are two reasons for this. Bobertag* recently pointed out that the rate of normal mental development in children probably decreases with age. Mental progress is rapid for the first few years and becomes slower as maturity is approached. The year cannot therefore be taken to represent a unit of mental growth, or used in expressing the degree of mental deficiency. We have at present no means of really measuring the rate of mental development and its changes. But there is evidence of some change of rate. It is suggested by the decreasing rate of brain development from birth to maturity. But there is more direct evidence. We can readily recognize by general observation the difference in mental development between a normal two-year-old and a normal three-year-old child. Between the ages of six and seven this difference is already difficult to discover in this way; and from the ages of eleven to twelve the recognition of progress by ordinary observation is quite impossible. However, a further factor enters here, which will be discussed later.

Some results with mental tests also indicate a decreasing rate of mental development with increase in age. Bobertag notes that for eight tests the difference in performance for six and seven-year-old

*Uber die Intelligenzpruefungen—nach der Methode von Binet und Simon. Zeitschr. f. angew. Psychol., 1912.

normal children was 31%. For seven other tests with eleven and twelve-year-old normal children this difference was only 16%. The present writer has found a similar result with the Binet-Simon tests. From the examination of about 700 public school children from six to fifteen years old the younger made greater progress in a year in the ability to pass the tests than did the older children. This was computed in the following manner. The percentage of the number of cases of each chronological age that passed each test given was found. The differences in the percentages of six-year-old and seven-year-old children, for example, passing a given test or group of tests could then be compared with this difference between seven-year-old and eight-year-old children, and so on. In attempting this comparison, however, it was found that the progress in the ability to pass a given test from one age to the next depended in the first place on the degree of difficulty of the test in question, the greatest progress being made in the moderately difficult tests and the least in the easiest ones. Consequently the tests were first divided into three groups; those that were passed by 1 to 29% of the children of a given age; those that were passed by 30 to 64%; and those that were passed by 65 to 100%. With this grouping the results on the point in question are given in the following table:

Age	No. Tests	1–29%	No. Tests	30–64%	No. Tests	65–100%	Average
6– 7....	3	14.3	3	23.7	8	3.4	13.8
7– 8....	7	20.3	2	19.0	11	3.6	14.3
8– 9....	2	12.7	11	18.2	8	6.0	12.7
9–10....	2	18.0	6	12.3	12	5.4	11.9
10–11....	2	13.5	8	15.5	10	8.0	12.3
11–12....	5	–5.0	5	3.4	9	1.4	–.6
12–13....	5	13.6	3	10.0	8	5.1	9.6
13–14....	3	9.0	6	–1.7	2	6.0	4.9
14–15....	3	6.7	3	6.0	0	...	6.4
Average..		9.5		11.9		4.9 .	

In this table the chronological ages are given in the first vertical column on the left. The third vertical column shows the amount of progress made from the sixth to the seventh year to be 14.3% for the three tests indicated in the second vertical column, which were passed by from 1 to 29% of the children taking them. It matters not now in what age groups these tests happened to be. The low percentage of passes indicates that they were in a higher age-group than the six or seven. This 14.3% is the average difference for the three tests between the percentage of passes of six and seven-year-old children. The column giving the figures for tests that were passed by 30 to 64% of the children shows a marked decrease in the amount of progress made in a year in the percentage of passes as the children grow older. The same is indicated in a lesser degree for the more difficult tests, seen in the third vertical column. For the easiest tests this indication is no longer evident. As to the normal rate of progress in mental development these results cannot be taken to indicate more than that there is a decrease in rate with age. They are not adequate to show the amount of decrease. They, however, suggest a further conclusion. This is that the ability to perform a given task grows rapidly at first and comes gradually to a stop as perfection is approached, following a course similar to the typical practice curve. It is seen in the table that when 65 to 100% of the children pass a test the average gain from one year to the next is only 4.9%, as compared with 11.9% when only 30 to 64% pass. Perhaps a more correct view to take of mental progress would be that each mental function involved in intelligence or mental development develops rapidly at first and comes gradually to a stop. But these functions do not all appear at the same time. The sensory functions, for example, are quite fully developed before some of the higher functions appear at all. A cross section, so to speak, at any age would then show the different functions in different stages and at different rates of growth. This complicates the task of determining the relative amount of progress in mental development as a whole from one year to the next very much. It is not the same thing that is developing at the different ages, and since the later appearing functions grow rapidly at first as well as the earlier appearing ones do the difference in a year's progress between the younger and older children is correspondingly decreased.

We may now consider the second reason why the difference between the chronological and mental ages does not represent the degree of mental deficiency. This is that the younger the child is the less time he has had to fall behind the normal in development. The feeble-minded children seem to make progress, but they do not develop as rapidly as do normal children. We note this in general observation. Their mental ages, also, as measured by the Binet-Simon tests, increase with age. Hence we may regard feeble-mindedness as a retarded *rate* of development. It is this rate of development as compared with the normal rate that represents the true degree of deficiency. The number of years behind in mental age becomes merely incidental to the chronological age. The same degree of mental deficiency may show only a fraction of a year behind the normal at one age and accumulate to a difference of several years before maturity is reached. A rate of development not retarded enough to be determinable by our present methods during infancy might show two or three years of mental retardation at the age of fifteen. A little computation will show that this second factor is probably much the more important of the two.

This suggests a further consideration referred to above. Young normal children of any given age seem more alike than older normal children of a given age. Three-year-old children are more alike than ten-year-old children. The stage of mental development for a given year with younger children stands out clear and distinct from that of the preceding and following years, whereas it does not do so in the case of older children. This is largely because the slight variations from the average normal rate of development have not yet had time in the case of the former to accumulate appreciable variations from an average normal degree of development, while for the older children this variation has become considerable, making ten-year-old children quite unlike each other. Thus, a bright ten-year-old child may have the mental development of an average normal eleven-year-old, and a dull, but still normal, ten-year-old may have the development of no more than the average nine-year-old. How much over-lapping within the range of what we now call normal there is for the higher mental ages we cannot say at present. But it is obvious that this second factor contributes as well as the first to our relative inability to recognize mental progress from one year to the next for the older children as compared with younger children.

We are now prepared to discuss the ratio of the mental age to the chronological as representing the true degree of mental deficiency. Stern* in discussing the Binet-Simon test results of various authors points out that the "intelligence quotient" obtained by dividing the mental age by the chronological would represent the degree of mental deficiency much more closely than merely the difference between the chronological and mental ages. He concludes, however, that since in feeble-mindedness there is a complete arrest of mental development at an earlier age than that at which the normal mind matures, as well as a retarded rate of growth, the intelligence quotient can represent the true degree of mental deficiency only

*Die psychologischen Methoden der Intelligenzpruefungen und deren Anwendung an Schulkindern. Bericht ueber den V. Kongress fuer experimentelle Psychologie. Berlin, 1912.

while the final mental age has not yet been reached. Since this point varies with the grade of intelligence in the first place, idiots coming to a complete stop in mental development at an earlier age than morons, conditions are still further complicated. If the intelligence of normal children is mature at thirteen to fifteen, for example, that of imbeciles might reach its maximum mental age of seven perhaps at the chronological age of about ten. Likewise idiots would reach their maximum mental age of two at a still earlier chronological age. After a given case had passed the age of his complete mental arrest his intelligence quotient would go on decreasing while his grade of intelligence remained the same. No empirical evidence is yet at hand for this final assumption, the possible truth of which must be considered in attempting to find a true index of the grade of intelligence from the mental and chronological ages. In the absence of such evidence it may not be profitable to discuss its validity further. We are now concerned with three propositions, which we may briefly state as follows: 1. The normal rate of mental development decreases with age. 2. Feeble-minded children develop mentally at a retarded rate. 3. Mental development comes to a complete stop earlier in feeble-minded children than it does in normal children. The present writer accepts the first two, but is inclined to put less stress on the importance of the first than Stern and Bobertag seem to do. For the third we are awaiting evidence. We have seen how the first enters as a factor making the difference between the chronological and mental ages no longer represent the true degree of mental deficiency. We may note now that it also enters as a factor making the intelligence quotient no longer represent the true degree of mental deficiency. This may be made clear with an illustration arbitrarily chosen. Let us suppose that we could measure mental development in terms of some definite unit, similar to the centimeter in spatial measurements, and assume that the normal child develops at a uniform rate of 50 units a year. We would than have the following for the first four years:

Year	1	2	3	4
Units per year	50	50	50	50
Total Units	50	100	150	200
Units at ½ rate	25	50	75	100

If a child were mentally two years at the age of four he would have developed 100 units, and the intelligence quotient would be $2/4$, or the same ratio given by dividing the mental units of 100 at the age of two by the mental units of 200 at the age of four. In this case the intelligence quotient gives the true grade of intelligence or rate of development. But suppose that the rate of mental development is not uniform from year to year, and that it decreases with age in something like the following manner:

Year..........................	1	2	3	4
Units per year..................	100	50	30	20
Total units.....................	100	150	180	200
Units at ½ rate................	50	75	90	100

In this case a child who is mentally two years at the age of four would have developed 150 units. But $150/200$ does not give the ratio of the intelligence quotient in this case. Or in other words, the intelligence quotient no longer represents the true rate of development, or degree of mental deficiency. There seem, therefore, to be two objections to taking the intelligence quotient as the true index of the grade of intelligence, even when we grant that it is a better index than the difference between the chronological and mental ages. First, it assumes the mental development in both normals and defectives progresses at a uniform rate; and second, it assumes that mental development continues in the defectives as long as it does in normals. Both of these objections together, however, do not seem to the present writer to be fatal to the practical usefulness of the intelligence quotient. Let us, on the basis of the intelligence quotient compute the course of mental ages for each rate of mental development, or degree of deficiency, from birth to the age of fifteen, taking the latter age as the point where mental development ceases for both normals and defectives. This gives the following courses of mental ages for the different intelligence quotients:

1	2	3	4	5	6	7	8	9	10	11	12	13	14	15
.1	.1	.2	.3	.3	.4	.5	.5	.6	.7	.7	.8	.9	.9	1
.1	.3	.4	.5	.7	.8	.9	1.1	1.2	1.3	1.5	1.6	1.7	1.9	2
.2	.4	.6	.8	.1	1.2	1.4	1.6	1.8	2	2.2	2.4	2.6	2.8	3
.3	.5	.8	1.1	1.3	1.6	1.9	2.1	2.4	2.7	2.9	3.2	3.5	3.7	4
.3	.7	1	1.3	1.7	2	2.3	2.7	3	3.3	3.7	4	4.3	4.7	5
.4	.8	1.2	1.6	2	2.4	2.8	3.2	3.6	4	4.4	4.8	5.2	5.6	6
.5	.9	1.4	1.9	2.3	2.8	3.3	3.7	4.2	4.7	5.1	5.6	6.1	6.5	7
.5	1.1	1.6	2.1	2.7	3.2	3.7	4.3	4.8	5.3	.5.9	6.4	6.9	7.5	8
.6	1.2	1.8	2.4	3	3.6	4.2	4.8	5.4	6	6.6	7.2	7.8	8.4	9
.7	1.3	2	2.7	3.3	4	4.7	5.2	6	6.7	7.3	8	8.7	9.3	10
.7	1.5	2.2	2.9	3.7	4.4	5.1	5.9	6.6	7.3	8.1	8.8	9.5	10.3	11
.8	1.6	2.4	3.2	4	4.8	5.6	6.4	7.2	8	8.8	9.6	10.4	11.2	12
.9	1.8	2.7	3.6	4.5	5.4	6.3	7.2	8:1	9	9.9	10.8	11.7	12.6	13
.9	1.9	2.8	3.7	4.7	5.6	6.5	7.5	8.4	9.3	10.3	11.2	12.1	13.1	14
1	2	3	4	5	6	7	8	9	10	11	12	13	14	15

In this table the first horizontal column gives the chronological ages from one to fifteen. The last vertical column on the right gives the mental ages at fifteen. The other figures give the mental ages at the different chronological ages for the different intelligence quotients. Thus, if a child's mental age is five at fifteen his intelligence quotient is 5/15, and his mental age will be .3 at 1 year, .7 at 2 years, 1 at 3 years, etc. The final test of the accuracy of the intelligence quotient as an index of the rate of mental development is its agreement or disagreement with empirical facts. We may give some evidence of such a test in comparing the course of average mental ages of a large group of feeble-minded children, 1,006 cases, with the increase in chronological age. In the following table are given results on the mental ages of the inmates of the Minnesota School for Feeble-minded. The children are first grouped into chronological age groups, 6–8 years, 9–11 years, etc., as seen in the first horizontal column. In the second horizontal column are given the corresponding average mental ages as found by the Binet-Simon tests. In the third are given the average mental ages as theoretically determined on the basis of the intelligence quotient. The computed mental ages are found on the basis of a mental age of 5.5 years at the age of 15, or an intelligence quotient of 55/150.

Age	6–8	9–11	12–14	15–17	18–20	21–30	31+
Average Mental Age	2.8	4.1	4.9	5.5	5.8	5.0	5.5
Computed Mental Age	2.6	3.7	4.8	5.5			
Difference	.2	.4	.1	0			

This comparison of empirical results with the theoretical determinations shows a close agreement. The largest difference is only .4 year. It will also be noted that according to these results, increase in the mental age stops at about the age of fifteen. This seems to accord somewhat with our supposition about the intellectual development of normal children, and might perhaps be given as a contradiction of Stern's assumption that development in the feeble-minded stops completely at an earlier age than it does in normals.

THE VALUE TO BE DERIVED FROM GIVING MENTAL TESTS TO ALL SCHOOL CHILDREN

BY

W. H. PYLE

The Binet-Simon tests have aroused much interest in many countries. They have been of much use in the examination of subnormal children. But it is out of the question, I think, to hope to use these or any similar tests in the examination of all the children of a school. For the school as a whole, we must select the best group tests. The majority of the pupils will need no further mental examination. For the few subnormal and supernormal children, we should continue to use the best form of individual tests.

The purpose of this paper is to set forth the value to be derived from giving group tests to all the children of a school, and to enquire into the best forms of test for this purpose. And, permit me to remark in the beginning that what I shall say is not based upon theory alone, but upon several years study of these tests as given to my students in the university, and as given to thousands of school children in many parts of the country. The group tests which I have used with most success are tests of logical and rote memory, tests of imagination, association and linguistic invention, the cancellation test and the substitution test.

Now, one of the important functions of the school is concerned with the learning of the child. The child is supposed to get knowledge and form habits. A child's getting knowledge and forming habits are dependent upon many things. Among these things, I may mention the following: The acuity of vision and audition, the child's retentiveness, range of attention and the degree of attention. The quickness with which a certain co-ordination can be built up by the child is dependent upon the child's hereditary nervous mechanism. How quickly facts can be got and how well they can be retained are dependent upon this same mechanism, and upon habits built up since the birth of the child. These facts of attention, perception, retentiveness, etc., which condition the learning of a child, as well as direct measures of learning capacity as applied to various kinds of work, are matters that can be experimentally determined. It is self-evident that if a teacher knew the individual differences of all her pupils, their various differences as to attention, memory, perception, imagination, and quickness of learning directly measured, she could certainly deal with these children more economically. Different types of pupils should often have different kinds of work and this work should often be presented in different ways to the different types. A teacher trying to teach pupils while being ignorant of their specific abilities is in the position of a man trying to run a machine although ignorant of the machine's mechanism. It may be said that the only test of a child that a teacher needs is the actual work in the school studies. It is true that if a teacher really knew what a child could do in the several studies, that would be all the information concerning the pupil's ability that she would need. But she usually does not know. And besides, if she did know, it would be profitable to know on what specific abilities the child's standing depends. She should know whether the child's standing depends upon good memory, quick learning, quick perception or upon hard work coupled with rather mediocre ability. We wish to determine by independent and specific tests the various abilities of the child. We wish to determine what the child *can* do independently of what he actually *does*. Moreover, the most convincing proof of the usefulness of giving mental tests to all school children comes from the teachers and superintendents that have given them. One superintendent that has been in a certain position for several years, informs me that by giving the set of mental tests to his school he had learned more about their capacities than he had learned in all the years of his superintendency before. To give an illustration, children were found of good ability as shown by the tests, who had been standing low in school work. Special attempts were made to get these pupils to do the work of which they were capable. The attempts were successful. Many others have reported the same experience with the tests. Mental tests will enable one to determine more accurately the specific abilities of pupils and the nature of these specific abilities. In a word, the value to be derived from giving mental tests to all school children, is a knowledge, a better and more accurate knowledge, of the pupils' minds. The use to which this knowledge may be put is of several kinds.

The Right Kind of Work. A knowledge of the individual differences as determined by the group tests and more extended individual tests in certain cases, will enable a teacher to select the right kind of work for the various pupils. Not all children are capable of doing the same kind of work. There are great differences in the same family, and much greater ones in the children of a school grade or room. While the main instinctive equipment of children is the same, there are still differences in mental functioning that we must take account of. Particularly is this true when we come to consider the extremes of the curve of distribution, the subnormal and supernormal. There is a considerable

number of children who can never do much at book learning. It is a **waste of** time to try to give them the ordinary education given to most **children.** There are other children at the other end of the curve, who **differ as** much in the other direction. These latter children are capable of much more abstract work and symbolic work at an early age than are the average children. The subnormal children must be given a different kind of education and longer time must be taken for it than is the case with the normal children. The supernormal children are capable of work of much higher type and capable of doing much more of it than is the case with the normal children. The group tests should be the first step toward separating these different types of children. The extreme cases and doubtful cases, should have further examination also, of course.

The Right Method. Children should be taught how to study, how to learn. What is the most economical method of study for a given child depends upon the mind of the child, depends upon the kind of memory he has, the range and degree of attention of which he is capable, his imagination, his ideational type, etc. In order to be able to teach the children their best methods of study, the teacher must determine by careful test the type of mind possessed by the individual children. To illustrate, let us consider memory: A child that is very quick to learn and that has a good memory, is likely to form a habit of preparing a lesson by a few minutes of concentrated work immediately preceding the recitation.. Now, such a person should be taught to make more than one attack upon the lesson, one of these being some time before recitation period, thereby getting the advantage that comes from repetition and taking time. On the other hand, the person who learns slowly and has a poor memory, should know that to learn a thing equally well with the fast learner, he must put in much more time and can by no means afford not to take the advantage that comes from hard work and frequent repetition.

The learning of a child is a process as definitely under the control of specific causes as is any other process in nature. A mind is a great complex of processes, and it is absurd to attempt to manipulate these processes, to control and develop them while being in ignorance of the nature of these processes and of their qualitative and quantitative relationships. Then, both what a child should study and how he should study it ought to be determined in part by the kind and amount of mind the child has. Group tests given to all the children will help the teacher to get the desired knowledge of the child's mind.

Gradation and Promotion. Three things ought to be considered in determining the grade to which a child should be assigned: (1) The child's ability; (2) the child's habits of study, and (3) the child's actual attainments. The most important of these is the first, because if the habits and the attainments are not what they should be, in most cases the faults can be corrected. In general, a child should be where his ability indicates that he should be, and a way should be found to get him to do the work of which he is capable.

The Specially Gifted. The group tests of all children would be of great assistance in picking out the specially gifted children, and would to some extent reveal the basis of the special ability. I have found this to be true even in the case of university students. By giving a number of mental tests to the students in my classes, I have found in nearly every case in certain specific abilities, the basis of the superiority of the capable students. It turns out that the best students in the class have a very superior memory, and are very quick at learning as determined by the substitution test. In a large class it practically never happens that the tests do not reveal some plain superiority in the students who make the highest standing in the class. I feel, therefore, that carefully given group tests would be of very great value to the teacher in getting her first estimate of the superior students. I think, however, that the group tests should be followed by much more extensive tests for the variants, the children who show considerable difference from the average.

Following a Child's Development. If careful mental tests were given to all the children of the school annually, one of the greatest benefits to the school would be the history of the child's development. The group tests can begin with the child's second school year. The results of the tests should be carefully recorded and kept as the permanent record of the school. Along with the mental records, would be, of course, records of the child's physical development, and his actual school grades. These records would show how fast the child develops, as a whole and in respect to each individual or specific trait. Such a record would be of very great value many times in the child's career. It would explain many things in the child's progress that would otherwise be inexplicable. Often a child's promotion should depend more upon a consideration of this record as a whole than upon his attainments at the time. Moreover, the value to the science of education of having such records of every child kept, all over the country, can hardly be estimated. Our education will be wasteful and unscientific until our procedure is based at every step upon accurate information concerning the child's development.

Summary

Group tests of all children will help to get a knowledge of their mental capacities, which will be of value:

(1) In determining the right kind of work for each child.

(2) In determining the best method of study for each child.

(3) In determining the subnormal and supernormal.

(4) In promotions.

(5) In gradation.

(6) In following a child's development.

(7) In contributing valuable information to the science of education.

NOTE.—For full discussion of these tests and norms for different ages, see the author's *Examination of School Children*, Macmillans, New York.

SOME THESES REGARDING THE SCIENTIFIC USE OF THE BINET SCALE FOR MEASURING INTELLIGENCE

BY

OTTO BOBERTAG

Much time and labor have been spent on applying and correcting the Binet Scale for measuring intelligence. But the amount of really available results has been comparatively small. This may be attributed partly to the fact that the Binet Scale has chiefly been used by experimenters who do not fully realise the numerous difficulties of a truly scientific method of testing. Therefore I should like to lay down some theses regarding the application of the Binet Tests as well as the mathematical treatment of the data derived from them.

1. In trying to adapt any test to the Binet Scale one must not think there is only one mode of giving a test. There are always several modes differing essentially one from another, though, to the untrained observer, they may seem to be fairly the same. Therefore every careful experimenter ought to be aware of all modifications which a test may possibly undergo in his hands; and, when describing his experiments, he ought to give every detail about them—not merely a rough statement of having used such and such test.

2. Many authors make use of some experimental device without duly regarding one of the chief peculiarities of the Binet Tests, namely, that they are what we may call "alternative tests." By this concept I mean such stimuli as to permit easy classifying of the reactions occasioned by them, either as right or as wrong ones. They differ, so far, from those tests which are especially adapted for correlational data because of permitting easy graduating of results and arranging the measurements in order of their standing or rank. All tests of the Binet Scale should therefore be tried and corrected till they may be considered good "alternative tests" in the sense given above.

3. This latter aim can be reached only by thoroughly examining and analysing the results, i. e. the answers and reactions of the children, from the purely psychological point of view. Then it will be found in what manner the variations of the answers or reactions are related to and dependent upon the corresponding variations of the questions or stimuli. This analytic examination of the data, not the mere

collecting of figures and constructing of tables and curves, ought to be the chief concern of every test psychologist.

4. The whole system of the Binet Scale is built upon the supposition that all tests are of equal value as measures of intelligence. Every such formula as : "5 + signs = 1 year" can only be used on this ground. The Binet Scale, counting all tests as equal units, does not and can not take account of the fact that human intellect is a complex or compound of many different "faculties." Each test ought to have a high value as test of general intelligence, but not as a test of some special faculty or other. The Binet Scale, therefore, is not consistent with any attempt that has been made to base it upon some psychological system or scheme of "faculties."

5. It is not meant by this that in the testing of children, especially of abnormal ones, the different mental functions should not be studied and, if possible, measured. But that is a task of its own and is not to be mixed up with the task of gauging the state or level of general intellectual development. No intelligent psychologist will regard the Binet Scale as a method of clinical diagnosis superseding all further investigation. Even if the scale were by far more perfect than it is at present, it only would be a means for the general survey of an individual's mental status, not for discovering all his peculiarities and defects.

6. In order to standardise any test for its use within the Binet Scale it is important also to get reliable quantitative results. In this respect some authors have been as careless as regarding the quality or content and mode of administering the tests. The main problem being: "How may a given test be proved characteristic for a certain age?" the answer is: by showing that the majority of normal children of this age pass the test.

7. This general statement, however, contains some special problems which I should like to sum up only, without entering in full particulars about them. First it ought to be fixed what is understood by "majority," yet not merely on the basis of some apriori assumption, but of some empirical data. Secondly, if any experimenter wishes to establish *norms* for intellectual development, he ought to make use of groups of children whose normality is safely guaranteed in every respect; above all, he ought to lay great importance upon testing a sufficiently large number of children to reduce chance errors as much as possible. Thirdly, to make such norms true *age*-norms it is necessary to be cautious in picking out the subjects with regard to their age and fixing the limits between which the age of those subjects should lie. Wherever these pre-

cautions are not taken the quantitative data of the experimenter can claim but slight value.

8.   Also in treating the numerical results of testing a, large number of children and in representing these results in some curve of distribu. tion great care should be taken to prove the validity of the so-called normal curve of distribution, for the results of the mental examination of children is by no means so easy a task as several authors seem to believe.   There is no difficulty in drawing a curve that looks somewhat like a normal curve of distribution, but such a vague statement has. certainly no scientific value.   At present it seems to me hardly possible to say what is the best and simplest way of treating the results of the Binet Tests so as to prove exactly their conformity to the normal curve.

SOME REQUIREMENTS OF GRADED MENTAL TESTS

BY

Carrie R. Squire

The call to a special conference on the Binet-Simon Scale is itself proof of the fact that the utility of this scale for mental diagnosis has received widespread recognition.

While educators and psychologists are for the most part agreed that a mental scale is needed, and that the Binet series is the most serviceable scale yet devised, this series even as revised in 1911 has many imperfections and limitations.

Before attempting to revise the Binet scale or adopt a new one it is first necessary that we come to some agreement upon the fundamental requirements of such a scale. The time assigned is far too short to detail all the requirements. I shall mention only a few of the requisites that have either been ignored or given scant attention in the Binet series.

The most glaring defect of the Binet series, as it seems to me, lies in the fact that the tests are not comparable age with age although such comparableness is the first essential of a mental scale. We have in the Binet scale a series of heterogeneous tests, varying in kind and until the last revision in number as well for the different ages. The merchant could just as reasonably use a yard and meter stick interchangeably, as the diagnostician test one set of functions at one age, and another set at a succeeding age. In view of this radical defect, the success with which the Binet scale has been used as an instrument of precision appears paradoxical. But we must grant after all that it is rather a crude instrument when we find that it obscures a very important law of mental growth. One of the most interesting findings of the scale I used, in which the tests were kept comparable throughout the series was that ability to perform the tests developed by slow degrees through the sixth, seventh to the the eighth year when there was a rapid gain in power followed by another period of slower growth with rapid gain again at about the end of the eleventh year of the beginning of the twelfth. This fact was as unexpected as it was interesting to me when I discovered it. It was forced upon my attention as soon as I began to tabulate results and was present throughout the whole series of tests. Although these periods of more rapid gain in mental power do not appear when one uses the Binet scale, I feel confident that they would be disclosed by any truly serial arrangement of tests.

What we have in the Binet series is not a graded mental scale but a series of separate general intelligence tests for each age that correspond fairly accurately to the age for which they are intended.   It seems strange that it has not occurred to Prof. Binet when revising the series to arrange it in a graduated scale since a majority of the tests are very well adapted to such an arrangement.

To illustrate: In the 1908 series the memory test for sentences as arranged by Prof. Whipple and the memory test for digits are already arranged in graduated steps.   The weights in the test for supraliminally different weight can readily be arranged so that there will be a gradually ascending degree of difficulty in the comparison.   Starting with Test No. 11 (copying a square) following this with a diamond we could also arrange a series of more and more complex figures to be copied.   Test No. 12 (the divided rectangle) also lends itself very readily to a serial arrangement through subdivisions.   The unfinished pictures (Test No. 21) by adding others might also be arranged in an ascending scale of difficulty.   I would also suggest that this test be further modified by having children complete the picture in preference to naming the missing parts.   The tests just mentioned will serve to illustrate how the Binet series could be arranged in a finely graduated mental scale.   The series without such serial arrangement is a rough instrument which as I have already shown fails to reveal the rhythmic character of mental growth. . Another advantage to be derived from the serial arrangement would be the elimination of all the inferior tests since fewer kinds of tests would be needed.

A second vulnerable point in the Binet tests is the assumption that they test native ability not acquired knowledge.   This presupposition would necessitate the exclusion of all tests dependent upon school training or upon special social training or even upon facility in the use of language.   As we know the Binet tests fall short on all of these counts. Decroly and Degand would exclude 30 out of the 56 in the 1908 series largely because of their dependence upon training.   While we grant that it is exceedingly difficult to eliminate the training factor altogether since we are testing minds in process of growth and this very process of growth involves a certain kind and amount of training, yet this training deals with practically universal factors, which because of their universality can be tested on the same basis as native ability.

This is not true, however, of the majority of the Binet tests ruled out by Decroly and Degand on the ground that they involve training since they do not possess this universality.   This is especially the case with those tests which are dependent upon facility in the use of language. The opinion of Dr. Ayers is voiced by others who have used the Binet series throughout a whole school system, that language tests are unfair to the children who either because of foreign parentage or some other cause have not acquired the usual facility in language.   Mental tests to be altogether satisfactory must therefore be restricted to tests of native ability.

There is another reason for the elimination of all tests dependent upon facility in the use of language. in the fact that the true measure of intelligence is not one's ability to talk glibly but one's ability to perform his part, whatever it may be. This brings us to a third prime requisite of a mental scale. All tests should be couched in terms of performance, of success in meeting an actual emergency. Of the 56 tests in the series of 1908 there are only nine—or less than one-sixth whose successful solution does not depend to a very large extent upon facility in the use of language. I believe Drs. Healy and Fernald have given us the only series of tests in which the language factor has been entirely eliminated. This series has even been used with success in testing the deaf and dumb. Although this series is too limited in scope, both in years tested and variety of tests to be comparable with the Binet series, it is very suggestive as to method. Prof. Terman's test of practical judgment is another excellent illustration of a test measured by ability to accomplish results. 'If a ball were lost in a circular field, show (not tell) the surest method of finding it.' I consider this the best test of practical judgment I have yet found; first of all, because it measures intelligence by success in meeting an emergency and also because it presents a very real problem to any child and by virtue of this fact its solution would waken keen interest. No set of problem questions, or alternatives, or definitions such as others, including myself, have used as tests of judgment would seem to the child nearly as worth while as this problem. of Prof Terman's. Could not a series of actual problems such as this, involving more and more factors, be arranged to give a well graded serial test of practical judgment? Such a set of judgment tests would form the crux of a whole scale. Involving the ability to think synthetically as such problems do, they would form a test of what Prof. Meumann calls the "higher intelligence" in contradistinction to the much mooted "general intelligence."

It is a truism with educators, that children of the same age mentally and chronologically will show considerable divergence in kinds of ability. One will have much better motor control than his age mate, another will exercise better judgment, and still another will possess a better memory. More than this, the rate of development with the same individual is likely to be uneven for different functions. Growth is apt to be lop-sided. As Prof. Seashore has said, "A child may be six years of age in one capacity and twelve in another and the important thing to know is this difference and direction of unsymmetrical development." He therefore insists that any flat age test must be interpreted in terms of specific capacity. We need to establish age norms for all the various capacities. Then the diagnosis for each individual should be based upon determinations of ability at all these different points. By such a procedure we could have some hope of ascertaining mental age with a fair degree of certainty. A fourth requirement of a mental scale would, therefore, be that it include tests, as far as possible, for all the fundamental capacities in which the mind functions. It should include tests for rapidity and accuracy of perception, for comprehension, for sensory discrimination, attention, rapidity and success in adjustment to a situation, ability to use old associations and build up new ones, and practical judgment.

I must here take exception to certain statements of Prof. Thorndike in his Cleveland address which seem to throw upon the scrap heap of discarded method all attempts at diagnosis of intelligence by reference to known and well-defined mental functions. In this address he seems to prefer to test that convenient but somewhat vague quantity "general intelligence." The "team of tests" (eight in all) by which Prof. Thorndike proposes to diagnose general intellectual ability would be just as excellent a team (and we believe much better) if each member were assigned its own well-defined function. What possible chance of progress is there through hiding known quantities under vague generalizations? Psychological analysis may have been carried to an extreme and become a barren end in itself. Nevertheless we cannot expect to apply our tests more accurately or successfully through ignoring their basic elements. Accordingly in the revision of the Binet scale let us see that age norms are established for all the fundamental mental traits. These norms should, however, be expressed in the form of concrete problems after the manner of the Binet series, not in the form of the desiccated test of the psychological laboratory. Each problem should also be accompanied by a clear statement of the capacity it is especially designed to measure.

It is also essential that a revised scale be accompanied by a complete formulation of experimental conditions and method of procedure, especially since the procedure with such a series differs radically from that of the ordinary laboratory test. Perhaps we would have experienced greater success with the Binet series had their experimental conditions been more fully stated. As it was the tests appear so invitingly simple that the psychologically uninitiated were inclined to believe they needed no method until Dr. Wallin gave us his "Practical Guide for the Administration of the Binet-Simon Scale."

While acknowledging our great indebtedness to the Binet-Simon tests, I believe we would have a far more serviceable scale if the four requisites I have offered and a method of procedure might receive attention in the next revision.

SOME LIMITATIONS OF THE BINET-SIMON TESTS OF INTELLIGENCE

BY

CHARLES SCOTT BERRY

As a result of the extensive use of the Binet(1) tests of intelligence during the past three or four years, many criticisms of these tests have been made, and numerous suggestions have been offered as to their improvement. One cannot read these criticisms and suggestions without seeing that there seems to be considerable difference of opinion as to the aim or purpose of this measuring scale.

Some of the critics think that all the tests which depend on school training should be omitted; others think that it is very questionable as to whether the 1911 measuring scale has been improved by the omission of such tests. Some criticise the measuring scale because it does not tell us in what particular psychological traits the subject is weak or strong, but merely gives us an idea of his intellectual level; others consider that the chief purpose of the measuring scale is to give us just such a general idea of the subject's intelligence. Some think that the tests should be so modified as to detect deviations from the normal in the realms of will and feeling; others think that such a modification would in a measure defeat the original purpose of the scale. Some think that the tests for the upper years should be at least in part different for the two sexes; others think that such a differentiation is not essential.

In view of the contradictory nature of many of these criticisms it has seemed to the writer that it might be well to consider Binet's conception of the aim or purpose of this measuring scale before proceeding to discuss its limitations. For evidently if our criticisms of the Binet tests of intelligence are to be valid they must take into consideration the purpose or aim of these tests. Of course the function of these tests of intelligence is, as the name indicates, to test intelligence, but the important question is as to what Binet means by intelligence. Perhaps the simplest way of approaching the subject is first to point out some of the mental traits that Binet does not include under intelligence. In the article entitled "The Development of Intelligence in Children,"(2) Binet states that he has not attempted to test all the aspects of intelligence, but rather pure or native intelligence. He draws a line between

1. For the sake of brevity the writer uses Binet to stand for Binet and Simon.

2. Alfred Binet et Th. Simon: Le développement de l'intelligence chez les enfants, L'Année Psychologique, Vol. 14, p. 74 ff.

pure intelligence, or native intellectual ability, and ability to get on well at school. The latter is the more comprehensive term as progress at school depends not only on native intelligence but also on will, feeling, attention, perseverance and docility. These latter qualities he points out are tested only to a slight extent by means of the tests of intelligence. So it does not follow that because one subject tests higher than another of the same age that the former will make better progress at school, as success at school involves the exercise of psychological characters, that are not measured to any extent by these tests of intelligence.

It is unquestionably of great importance that we test will, feeling, attention and other psychological functions which Binet has not attempted to measure by means of his measuring scale. But is it wise to test these psychological traits at the same time we test the intelligence of the child? Binet thinks not, and, as it seems to the writer, not without reason. If the intellectual ability of the child is to be adequately tested Binet points out that the examination period should not exceed thirty minutes, that the tests should be short and varied, and that the experimenter should remain with the child and encourage him to put forth his best effort. In this way the intellectual ability of the child is tested and not his will power or perseverance, as under such conditions even the most inattentive child will usually make a maximum effort. But just as soon as the tests are made longer and the period of the examination is extended then the examination is no longer a test of pure intelligence alone but a test of will power, attention and perseverance as well. From the results obtained by such an examination we should not be able to determine the relative importance of these two factors in the mental life of the child. And this is a distinction that it is highly important that we should be able to make.

If, then, will and the emotional nature are not included under the head of intelligence, just what are we to understand that Binet means by this term? In his article entitled, "New Methods of Testing Abnormals,"(1) he states that it is necessary to know in what sense to take this word intelligence which is so comprehensive in meaning. He points out that there is one function which from the standpoint of life is of extreme importance. This function is judgment. To judge well, to comprehend well, to reason well, these are the essential springs of intelligence. A person may be a moron or an imbecile if he is lacking in judgment, with good judgment, never. The result is that Binet in his conception of intelligence gives first place to judgment. It may be objected that judgment is a complex process and depends on several

1. A. Binet et Th. Simon: Méthodes nouvelles pour le diagnostic du niveau intellectuel des anormaux, L'Année Psychologique, Vol. 11, p. 196 ff.

more elemental traits. This may be true, and it may be wise to test these elemental traits, but even after we have done so we are not in a position to make any positive statement about the judgment of the subject without directly testing it. For we have no assurance that because the subject has certain elemental psychological traits well developed that he possesses the power of using these elemental traits in such a way as to get the best results. This can only be ascertained by testing the complex. And on the other hand, it does not follow that because certain psychological traits which are involved in judgment are not well developed that the judgment of the subject will be weak or defective. Hence, it seems to the writer that Binet's point is well taken that we need certain tests which will directly test the judgment.

In the article on "The Development of Intelligence in Children,"(1) Binet points out that it is necessary to distinguish between two types of intelligence which have often been confused, viz, "la maturité" of intelligence et "la rectitude" of intelligence. By maturity of intelligence he means the increase of intelligence with age. By "la rectitude" of intelligence he apparently means sanity or soundness of judgment. For example, a child of a certain age is not able to put three given words in one sentence. He makes two or three sentences. This child lacks maturity of intelligence or judgment. Another child is able to put the three words in one sentence but the sentence does not make complete sense. This latter subject has maturity of judgment but lacks soundness or correctness of judgment.

. Then it seems to be evident from a study of Binet's writings that he looks upon judgment as the most important aspect of intelligence, and that intelligence or judgment may be tested, both as to its maturity and as to its correctness.

Binet admits that intelligence is not measured apart from a large number of concrete circumstances. And the results that accrue from testing a subject depend on pure intelligence, on knowledge acquired outside of the school in advance of the usual time, on school knowledge which is acquired at a fixed time, and on knowledge of language which is acquired partly in school and partly outside of school. Yet he thinks his measuring scale will do justice to the child who has never attended school, for in the latter case the experimenter will place the emphasis on those tests which do test natural ability, such as the interpretations of pictures, questions of comprehension, etc. But Binet does not tell us in such a case how to evaluate the results. Evidently here is one limitation of the measuring scale. For if the purpose of the scale is to test native intellectual ability, as Binet claims, and if all the tests

1. Ibid. p. 80 ff.

are not of equal value as a means to this end then his system of counting which considers all tests as of equal value is defective, and is contrary to the very principle he has laid down.

If intellectual ability cannot be measured apart from a large number of concrete circumstances then it is evident that the tests should deal only with those objects and materials with which all children have had an equal opportunity of becoming acquainted. For example, when a subject is asked to name certain coins we presuppose sufficient experience with money of his character to enable a subject of a certain degree of intelligence to name them. But if one subject has been specifically taught the names of the different pieces of money then the fact that he possesses this knowledge will have little significance as a test of intelligence. For it is quite evident that a child may be directly taught the names of the coins and consequently may have this knowledge years ahead of the child who gets this information unaided. A knowledge test is mainly significant as a test of intelligence when the subject does not have the knowledge, and yet has had the experience which serves as a basis for that knowledge. Evidently if tests of intelligence are to be of equal value the tests which depend so largely on knowledge will have to be omitted. It seems to the writer that in place of such tests we might substitute learning tests simple, yet varied in character.

Another limitation of this measuring scale which Binet himself recognized is that the tests for the upper ages are too difficult. That seems to be the experience of all the experimenters who have used the scale extensively. During the past year the writer tested sixty-eight seniors in the University of Michigan with the adult tests of Binet. The result was that only three students succeeded in passing all five tests, and that only fifty-three per cent. passed three or more of the tests. This fact seems to show very clearly that the adult tests of Binet are too difficult. Evidently much work will have to be done before we succeed in getting suitable well-graded tests for adults and for the years from ten to fifteen. It is especially desirable to have adequate tests for these higher ages so that we can accurately diagnose the borderline cases.

Another limitation of the revised scale is that since tests are lacking for years eleven, thirteen and fourteen, we are not able accurately to estimate the intelligence of subjects whose mental age ranges somewhere between ten and fifteen. If a subject correctly performs all the tests under age ten and three under age twelve his mental age will be ten and six-tenths. In such a case if we had additional tests for ages eleven, thirteen and fourteen the probability is that the subject would test much higher, as we find in testing the younger children that they generally test one or two years higher than the age taken as a base. Until tests for eleven, thirteen and fourteen have been provided we cannot be sure of our results for ages ten and twelve. The probability is that we shall find it necessary to take into consideration sex differences in providing tests for these higher ages, because after the child has reached a certain age his training has become in a measure specialized. For example, in testing the seniors mentioned above the writer found that the boys did better than the girls in the following tests: "Draws inverted triangle," and "Gives difference between president and king;" but the girls surpassed the boys in "Draws design of cut paper unfolded," and "Gives sense of selection read." These differences may be due to differences in native intelligence, but the probability is that environmental differences are the chief factor. In selecting tests for the higher ages we can either choose subject-matter for our tests with which both sexes are equally familiar (a difficult matter at best) or we can use different tests for each sex.

A final limitation of the measuring scale is that the mode of procedure has not been standardized. In the first place, there is no uniformity of practice as to the number of tests that should be given the subject above the age taken as the base. For example, if the subject has correctly performed all the tests under age six, and two under age seven shall the experimenter stop there or go on and give additional tests under the higher ages? If all the abilities tested developed in normal children at the same rate and if the scale were accurately graded then we might lay down some general rule to the effect that the subject is to be given the tests under the ages above the age taken as the base until an age is reached under which he can perform no test. If we should adopt such a method evidently we should do an injustice to the child who has an unusual development along some one line. Possibly this difficulty might be overcome if we had a test of the same psychological trait under each age or under alternate ages.

In the second place, the methods of giving the individual tests have not been sufficiently standardized. The variations in results obtained by different experimenters can in some cases be largely accounted for by the difference of method employed. In fact one experimenter cannot compare his results with those secured by another with any reasonable degree of accuracy unless the method of giving the tests has been fully described, which few experimenters have done.

In the third place, there is not sufficient uniformity in regard to the tests that are being used. Some are using the 1908 tests, others are using the 1911 tests, and still others are using parts of these scales with modifications of their own or of other experimenters.

It seems to the writer that after all the work that has been done it is now possible to work out a series of tests which shall be known as the standard scale. Why should not this or some other association appoint a committee whose function it will be to revise each year the tests of intelligence in the light of the researches of that year? Thus we may have a scale, sufficiently standardized so that we can compare results of different experimenters. Such a committee could also render a valuable service in showing just how the tests should be given; in other words, in standardizing the method of procedure. Only in some such way can the Binet measuring scale most quickly be brought up to its highest stage of efficiency. At the present time it is the standardization of individual tests that is needed. We have now many good tests, but they are not yet standardized. Why should not some of the new tests suggested by Goddard, Healy, Terman, Squires and others be worked out individually in different parts of the country on large numbers of children, and in this way become standardized.

The writer does not believe that we should attempt to change the aim of the Binet measuring scale. Let it remain a means of testing intelligence, testing the maturity and soundness of judgment not in special fields but in the situations common to the complex life of our civilization. For ability of an unusual character along any one line is not conclusive evidence of good judgment when it comes to the practical affairs of life. Cases like the Genius of Earlswood Asylum disprove that idea. But after the general level of the child's intelligence has been discovered then we should seek to determine along what specific lines he has the most ability. If we would understand the nature of the child's psychic life something more is needed than any Binet scale no matter how well perfected it may be. The child should be tested by means of other scales as well if we are to know the extent of his knowledge, the nature of his interests, the strength of his will and the character of his emotional nature. But we cannot stop here if we would make a prognosis. We must know his physiological age and his anatomical age, as well as his personal and family history before we can pronounce judgment as to his future.

A COMPARISON OF WHITE AND COLORED CHILDREN MEASURED BY THE BINET SCALE OF INTELLIGENCE

BY

, JOSIAH MORSE

Wherever the methods of science have been inapplicable, or for some reason been left unapplied, opinion has held sway, and, as the adage has it, the number of opinions has equalled that of the men holding them. This, it need hardly be pointed out, is seen clearly in the literatures of religion, philosophy, ethics, politics, and many branches of the newer social sciences. It is notoriously true of discussions of race problems, even when the opinions have been held by scientists eminent in their own special domains. Thus we have a Boaz, who can see no essential difference between the negro and white races, and a LeBon, who is equally certain that a "mental abyss" forever separates the two peoples, and that the negro is the much inferior of the two.

In the hope that the Binet tests would yield a few grains of fact which might leaven the lump of opinion, the writer directed Miss Alice C. Strong, a graduate student at the University of South Carolina, to measure with the Binet scale, as revised by Goddard, the white and colored school children of Columbia, S. C. In order to be able to compare results with those obtained by Binet and Goddard it was decided not to attempt to experiment with modifications of their methods or tests, but to follow them closely, notwithstanding their faults and imperfections. These latter, of course, do not affect materially the results of a comparative study such as this one.

The same tests were given to both the white and colored children, under practically uniform conditions, or as uniform as they could be made, with the exception that some of the colored children tested were older than twelve years. The course of study in the colored school, which is a part of the public school system, is practically the same as in the white schools, and the quality of teaching is quite good. The examiner states that the children seemed to be at their ease in her presence, and to do their best. She could note no marked variation from the white children in the manner of responding. In almost every case the dress, cleanliness and manners of the children indicated that they came from good homes. The replies were usually couched in fewer words than those of the white children. There was less tendency to enter into conversation, and it was soon found that they were more at ease when reacting to the tests than when an attempt was made to talk with them about other things.

Of course it is always possible that different results might have been obtained by an examiner of their own race. The teachers selected pupils of varying ability in order that those tested might be considered representative of the whole. Two of the children tested so irregularly that they could not be graded. One of them, an eleven-year-old boy passed all of the six-year tests, failed on all of the seven-year tests, and succeeded with four of the eight-year tests. These two records were not included in the tabulations which are given for the remaining 123.

The distribution curve of the white children is here reproduced side by side with that of the colored children for the sake of comparison. Since nearly twice as many white children were tested as colored, the curve for the whites is drawn to half the scale.

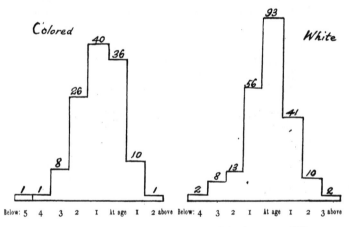

	Colored	White
Number testing 5 years below age..................	1	0
Number testing 4 years below age..................	1	2
Number testing 3 years below age..................	8	8
Number testing 2 years below age..................	26	13
Number testing 1 year below age...................	40 = 32.5%	56 = 24.9%
Number testing at age.............................	36 = 29.2%	93 = 41.3%
Number testing 1 year above age...................	10 = 8.1%	41 = 18.2%
Number testing 2 years above age..................	1	10
Number testing 3 years above age..................	0	2
Total..	123	225

The graph for the whites resembles closely that given by Dr. H. H. Goddard, based on two thousand measurements, but that for the colored is strikingly different. The number of white children testing at age is decidedly larger than any other group. The group of colored children testing one year below age is larger than that of those testing at age.

	Colored	White
More than one year backward	29.4%	10.2%
Satisfactory	69.8%	84.4%
More than one year advanced	0.8%	5.3%

There is a difference of nearly 15% in the satisfactory group, nearly three times as many are more than a year backward, and less than 1% are more than a year advanced.

How much this difference is due to racial inferiority and how much to home and environmental influences, differences in physiological age, or other subtle factors cannot be said. It is certainly not due to difference in school training. In order, however, to make the comparison as just as possible, the white children were divided into two groups— city children and mill children. The economic, educational and environmental conditions of the mill children are not greatly superior to those of the colored children. Here then we have groups that ought to show both the influence of environment and of heredity. There being only five grades in the mill school, only the corresponding grades of the other schools are considered in this comparison.

The graphs that follow show that the colored children make a better showing in the first five grades than they do in the first seven. They are still inferior to the whites, however. The proportion of colored children who are satisfactory is less than that of the mill children, which in turn is less than that of the city children. Less than 6% of the city children are more than a year backward, 18% of the mill children, and 26% of the colored children. None of either the mill or colored children test more than a year above age, while 10% of the city children do.

1. *City Schools*

                                        Number Testing
3 years below age...................... 1 = 1.1%
2 years below age...................... 4 = 4.2%
1 year below age......................13 = 13.7%
At age.............................42 = 44.2%
1 year above age....................25 = 26.3%
2 years above age.................. 8 = 8.4%
3 years above age.................. 2 = 2.0%

More than 1 year backward.............. 5.3%
Satisfactory...........................84.2%
More than 1 year advanced..............10.4%

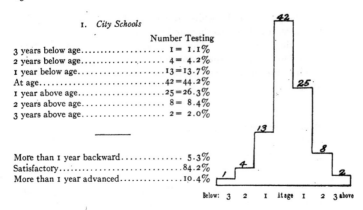

Below: 3   2   1   At age   1   2   3 above

2. *Colored School*

                                        Number Testing
3 years below age....................... 5 = 6.1%
2 years below age......................16 = 19.5%
1 year below age......................28 = 34.1%
At age..............................24 = 29.3%
1 year above age....................... 9 = 10.9%

More than 1 year backward..................25.6%
Satisfactory...........................74.4%
More than 1 year advanced.................. 0

Below: 3   2   1   At age   1 above

3. *Mill School*

                                        Number Testing
4 years below age....................... 2 = 3.3%
3 years below age....................... 3 = 5.0%
2 years below age....................... 6 = 10.0%
1 year below age......................18 = 30.0%
At age..............................22 = 36.6%
1 year above age....................... 9 = 15.6%

More than 1 year backward..................18.3%
Satisfactory...........................81.6%
More than 1 year advanced.................. 0

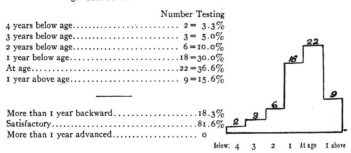

Below: 4   3   2   1   At age   1 above

In order to see whether this relative inferiority exists throughout, or whether the children of the colored race are as well endowed in the first school years as is generally believed, the following table was made. The children from six to twelve years old only are included; consequently the totals for the colored children differ from those of other tables.

TABLE I

	BELOW AGE		AT AGE		ABOVE AGE	
	White	Colored	White	Colored	White	Colored
6 years..........	19.4%	40.0%	30.6%	33.3%	50.0%	26.7%
7 years..........	13.9%	29.4%	61.1%	58.8%	25.0%	11.8%
8 years..........	18.5%	23.0%	55.5%	38.5%	26.0%	38.5%
9 years..........	32.2%	71.4%	41.9%	21.4%	25.9%	7.2%
10 years..........	55.1%	75.0%	27.6%	12.5%	17.3%	12.5%
11 years......,...	34.6%	43.7%	42.2%	50.0%	23.1%	6.3%
12 years..........	67.5%	77.0%	32.5%	23.0%		
Totals..........	34.5%	51.4%	41.2%	33.9%	24.3%	14.7%

TABLE II

Physical Age	IV	V	VI	VII	VIII	IX	X	XI	XII	Total
5 years....			1							1
6 years....	1	5	5	4						15
7 years....			5	10	2					17
8 years....			3	5	5					13
9 years....				2	8	3	1			14
10 years....				2	7	3	2	1	1	16
11 years....					1	4	2	8	1	16
12 years....						1		9	3	13
13 years....							1	6	3	10
14 years....							1	3	3	7
15 years....							1			1
Totals......	1	5	14	23	23	11	8	27	11	123

Table II shows how the colored children of the different ages tested. The Roman numbers represent the mental age. E. g., of the fifteen six-year-old children tested, one tested four, five five, five six, and four seven years, mentally.

The table differs from the corresponding table for the white children in several respects, the chief of which are:

There is greater irregularity; there are relatively more backward children; the number of those testing above age is conspicuously small; a large number test one year below age than at age.

Two who tested XII passed also some of the fifteen-year tests. It is quite possible that they might have made a better showing if there had been tests for the years XIII and XIV. The table shows however that more of the thirteen and fourteen-year-old children tested below XII than tested at XII. It is equally probable of course that some of the eleven and twelve-year-old white children might have been able to pass successfully XIII and XIV tests. Several of them passed some of the XV tests.

Table III shows how the Binet tests and the school standards compare for both races:

TABLE III

	Colored	White
In lower grade according to school standard.............	54 = 43.9%	44.4%
In lower grade according to Binet scale........!...........	19 = 15.4%	39.6%
In right grade according to school standard.............	59 = 48.0%	53.8%
In right grade according to Binet scale.................	55 = 44.7%	44.8%
In higher grade according to school standard.............	9 = 7.3%	2.2%
In higher grade according to Binet scale.................	43 = 35.0%	12.0%
Below school age according to school standard............	1 = 0.8%	
Below school age according to Binet scale................	6 = 4.9%	3.6%

According to the Binet scale, a larger number of white children are in a grade below their mental ability than above, whereas the reverse is true with the colored children; 19 are retarded and 49 (counting those who are below school age) are advanced beyond the level of their intelligence. The analysis of the data gives the following table:

TABLE IV

	Number Tested	Normal Grade	Number Retarded	Number Advanced	Below School Age
5 years backward	1			1	
4 years backward	1			1	
3 years backward	8		2	6	
2 years backward	26	10	2	13	1
1 year backward........	40	15	2	18	5
At age.................	36	26	6	4	
1 year advanced	10	4	6		
2 years advanced........	1		1		
Totals.................	123	55	19	43	6

In general it may be said that the colored children excel in rote memory, e. g., in counting, repeating digits (but not one was able to repeat twenty-six syllables) naming words, making rhymes, defining abstract terms and in terms of use, and in time orientations. They are inferior to the whites however in aesthetic judgment, observation, reasoning, motor control, logical memory, use of words, resistance to suggestion, and in orientation or adjustment to the institutions and complexities of civilized society. The following tabulation brings out clearly these differences:

Tests	White Better	Colored Better	About Equal
VI. Knowing morning and afternoon...........	......	2.2%	......
Definitions in terms of use................	......	9.6%	......
Execution of triple commission............	......	......	......
Right hand; left ear......................	6.5%	......	......
Aesthetic judgment.....................	31.8%	......	......
VII. Counting pennies........................	......	4.8%	......
Describing pictures.................	......	......	......
Omissions in pictures....................	8.0%	......	......
Copying diamond........................	31.3%	......	......
Naming four colors....................	15.5%	......	......
VIII. Comparing two remembered objects........	......	......	......
Counting backward.....................	......	20.9%	......
Naming days of week....................	......	......	......
Counting stamps........................	18.9%	......	......
Repeating five digits....................	......	11.0%	......
IX. Making change.........................	7.5%	......	......
Definitions superior to use................	6.2%	......	......
Knowing date..........................	......	5.6%	......
Naming months.........................	15.4%	......	......
Arranging weights......................	9.2%	......	......
X. Recognizing pieces of money..............	8.6%	......	......
Drawing two designs from memory.........	......	......	......
Repeating six digits......................	......	17.0%	......
Questions of comprehension..............	......	......	......
Using three words in a sentence...........	22.8%	......	......
XI. Seeing absurdities........................	5.5%	......	......
Using three given words in a sentence......	13.8%	......	......
Giving 60 words in three minutes..........	......	4.9%	......
Rhymes................................	......	5.7%	......
Dissected sentences.....................	16.5%	......	......
XII. Repeating seven digits....................	......	8.0%	......
Definitions of abstract terms.............	......	13.0%	......
Repeating 26 syllables...................	Impossible for colored		
Resisting suggestion......................	4.9%	......	......
Solution of problems.....................	......	10.7%	......

The children were roughly divided into three groups according to color. There were 34 dark children, 45 medium in color, and 43 light colored in this classification; 122 in all. Of the dark colored 14.4% tested below age, 76.7% tested at age, and 8.8% above age. Of the next group, some what lighter in color, 31.1% tested below age, 62.2% at age and 6.6% above age. Of the lightest group, 44.2% tested below age, 44.2% at age, and 11.6% above age. The darkest children are more nearly normal, the lightest show the greatest variation, both above and below normal.

The limitations of the study are evident. It is but a crude beginning of a subject that will doubtless soon be opened up and made to yield interesting and profitable data. No final conclusions are here offered, nor is any attempt made to settle the question of race superiority or inferiority. That requires investigation along many lines that are hardly begun as yet. But this much we are undoubtedly warranted in concluding from this study: that negro children from six to twelve, and possibly fifteen years, are mentally different, and also younger than American white children of corresponding ages, and that this condition is due, partly at least, to causes that are native or racial. That is, if MM. Binet and Simon had originally tested negro children, they would have worked out a scale from the results which would have been different from their present one in several respects, and which when applied to American white children would be found to be for the most part a year or more too young, though possibly there would be some tests which would yield the opposite results. Le Bon's contention that "each race possesses a mental constitution as unvarying as its anatomical constitution" seems to be borne out by the investigations.

Perhaps some day each branch of the human family will have a Binet scale of its own. Then, by a wholesale interchange of tests, as it were, it will be possible to determine wherein a given people are proficient and wherein deficient; and later perhaps, by adding coefficients and credits to settle mooted questions of racial rank. But this again belongs to the realm of speculation.

The point of greatest value brought out by this study is that possibly in the Binet scale a key has been found which will prove of the greatest service in the solution of problems in contemporary folk-psychology, and race and social adjustments.

SUGGESTIONS ON THE EXTENSION OF THE BINET-SIMON MEASURING SCALE

BY

E. A. DOLL

For thirty years psychologists have been attempting to arrive at satisfactory methods of measuring the intellectual abilities of individuals. In the last ten years heavy pressure has been brought to bear by the schools, the industries and manufactures, the custodial and corrective institutions, and the courts to arouse psychologists to an appreciation of the practical as well as the scientific value of such methods of intelligence-testing. In large measure the Binet-Simon Measuring Scale, devised to meet the needs of the schools for subnormal children in France, successfully meets these demands. But the present scale does not reliably measure intelligence beyond ten years of age. To be sure the present scale contains tests for twelve, fifteen, and adult years but Binet himself did not express much confidence in the tests beyond twelve, and recent investigation in this country and in Germany have demonstrated that they are not reliable. And if it be granted that these higher tests are not reliable, then it follows that the scale is not satisfactory beyond the tenth year, since there are then no tests in the advanced stages to permit of scoring additional points which might be passed beyond the twelfth year. It therefore becomes a matter of serious importance that the Binet-Simon scale, assuming it to be the best single method of determining intellectual levels, be extended beyond its present limits. Already several attempts have been made to extend the scale, and much has been done by way of tentative revisions. It is because most of these attempts have proved unsatisfactory that I aim to outline some of the fundamental principles which should guide us in methods of dealing with the problem.

But first let us note that there have been presented certain reasons why the measurement of the intelligence of adolescents and adults is impossible.

First, it is said that retardation in intellectual status need not of necessity carry with it social inefficiency, and that therefore we must measure something more than purely intellectual ability. This is undoubtedly quite true, but not to such an extent as to invalidate purely intellectual examination. Stern defines intelligence as "the general capacity of an individual consciously to adjust his thinking to new requirements; it is general adaptability to new problems and

conditions of life." Such a definition does not prevent clinical psychological examination from measuring characteristics which are supplementary to intelligence, such perhaps as emotional or sexual complexes,
temperament, acquired capacities and the like, but these are issues
which do not concern pure intelligence testing except for ·prognosis.
The purely intellectual examination is concerned with an individual's
present capacity for adaptation, and need measure only those mental
processes which contribute to or are elements of conscious adaptation
to environmental demands.

A second objection is, that during and after adolescence intellectual
development gives way to the development of emotion and will. As
one writer puts it: "With puberty comes the great upheaval of the
feelings and instincts, the new consciousness of a new self, and the
immense widening of social consciousness and social relationship."
But I do not know of any evidence that warrants us in assuming that
with an increased emotional and sexual development there is a complete
or even relative cessation of intellectual development. Indeed, the
evidence is quite to the contrary. It were a sorry comment on the
persons here present to say of them that since their twelfth birthdays
they developed only "will, self-assertion, self-criticism, social sense
and attitude, and emotional control." Judgment, reason, ideation,
and the rest receive but scant praise in this uncomplimentary catalogue.
We should all, I believe, resent the implication that we have no better
adaptability now than we had before leaving the grammar grades. How
much more reasonable, and at the same time how much more in accord
with the facts to assume, at least, for purposes of experimentation,
that intellectual capacity develops increasingly, tho perhaps in decreasing percentages of the total population, both quantitatively and qual-
itatively. It may be quite true that if we plot a curve of the total
population, using numbers of persons for abscissas and intellectual
capacity for ordinates, the curve might be logarithmic; that is to say,
as intellectual level is increased by slight amounts the numbers of persons having successively higher levels decreases by large amounts. Or,
we might say, that for a given arithmetical increase in intelligence
there is a corresponding geometrical decrease in the frequency of its
appearance. But this does not at all deny that intelligence does continue to develop indefinitely among a certain percentage of the population. Emotion and will play their parts in the formation of character
and temperament, and perhaps do determine the particular field of one's
life activity. They may even so affect the individual that he does not
use the inherent intellectuality that he has, but they do not necessarily
take the place of intellectual development. One's choice of vocation
or profession may be almost entirely influenced by many factors other

than intelligence, but one's success in that vocation or profession will depend upon the intelligence that he brings to bear in meeting the situations that arise in that environment.

A third objection is, that during adolescence intelligence is too fluid and indeterminate to be measurable. It is true that while intelligence certainly continues to develop during and after adolescence, it nevertheless develops with perhaps considerable variability during this period. The psychological changes of this period show extreme individual differences. Whether or not intellectual development is equally variable is by no means so sure, tho certainly possible. It is also true that the emotional and sexual developments of this period may be so considerable as seriously to interfere with the measurement of intellectual levels, however regularly these levels may have developed. These are, however, at best only possible hypotheses and not known facts. One reputable physician has gone so far as to say that "statistics for groups or individuals respecting height, weight, strength, scholarship, mental or physical endurance, medical or social condition, that are not referred to physiological age are inconsequential and misleading," and that "in future all our thought concerning the years nine to seventeen must be released from the idea of chronological age," and, by implication, be directed on the basis of physiological age. But I am pretty firmly convinced if the tests for this period are devised with proper ingenuity and care they will measure the intelligence of this period in their relation to chronological ages without being inconsequential or misleading. It is well to know that sex differences may be considerable, tho Burt claims that sex differences are least in the tests which are most truly tests of intelligence. It is also well to know that emotional complexes are frequent, that interests are fleeting and varied, that self-consciousness is at its height, but these and other characteristics of adolescence should serve merely to warn the intelligence-tester what difficulties he should be prepared to meet in his selection of tests, rather than to frighten him away from the problem. It is no wild generalization to say that the measurement of intelligence just before the adolescent period, from nine to twelve years inclusive, offered to Binet difficulties comparable to those of the later period, and yet to-day we are testing the intelligences of children of these years with a rather high degree of perfection. We need to know all the physiological and mental changes of the periods which we aim to measure, but this knowledge should be stimulative rather than deterrent, and while it is imperative to recognize the wide differences in the physiological development of adolescents, and indeed of all children, this need not necessarily be the basis of our study. Chronological age is, after all, the social and scholastic standard and measures of retardation are referred to it, and not to other ages.   Such difficulties as these are practical obstacles, issues which must be fairly met and overcome by the investigator instead of being made to serve as bases for his investigations.   And so he must evolve tests which are independent of sex differences, emotional complexes, fleeting and varied interests, self-consciousness, and the rest.

A fourth objection is that of qualitative divergences of intellectual abilities as against quantitative increases.   It is said that at and after adolescence the intelligence does not become greater but rather spreads out, fanlike, at the level which it has attained by this time.   It is undoubtedly true that when the final level of intellectual development is reached one's abilities still continue to spread out and to amplify at that level, even if one's capacities do not grow further.   But it does not logically follow that the intelligence of all individuals spreads out at the same level, nor that the level is reached at adolescence.   We ought rather to compare mental growth to the growth of a tree, which spreads its branches at a number of different levels.   And in intelligence testing we must be careful to test levels rather than diversifications. We must measure abilities not acquisitions.   And here again we must not be led away from the *facts* of low or of high degrees of ability by the causes for them.   Those causes may be of vital importance for certain purposes, but they must not obscure the truth of the facts.

Whether or not we admit upon theoretical grounds that the intelligence can be measured beyond twelve years, it is of the greatest importance that those who believe in the possiblity of extension keep clearly in mind in the experimental investigation of the problem the essential principles, both theoretical and practical, to which graded tests should conform.   I shall venture to review these principles in some detail. They are, in the main, those upon which the Binet Scale is founded and which have been developed in a number of tentative series of tests that have been proposed by various writers.

1.   There should be as complete and definite knowledge, or in the absence of knowledge, as clear hypotheses as can be obtained of the psychology of the age levels under consideration.

2.   . From these mental functions there should then be careful and accurate selection of those which are known to be, or for experimental purposes are assumed to be, essential or contributory to intelligence. In practice these functions may display themselves in the forms of comprehension, generalization, definition, logical comparison, interpretation, analysis, synthesis, language, invention, observation, report, and so on.   There needs to be made a careful analytical catalogue of these possible forms, after which they should be. subjected to considerable experimentation for empirical determination of which of them are truly

intellectual and which only apparently so. In this connection there should be a clear distinction drawn between intellectual and pedagogical functions. Binet and others clearly point out that scholastic success may be quite sharply independent of intelligence, and *vice versa*.

3. There should be painstaking selection of objective tests under definitely formulated considerations of the psychology involved, tests whose successful performance shall give reliable indications of the presence or absence or degree of development of the particular intellectual process under examination. Such tests should be:

(*a*) Relatively little affected by previous training or environment.

(*b*) They should be relatively little subject to errors of chance or of previous preparation.

(*c*) They should require only short times and not too much perseverance for their performance. They ought to permit of complete administration in less than an hour.

(*d*) They should preferably require little or no apparatus, or at any rate simple and inexpensive apparatus.

(*e*) They should be easy to administer and easy to credit and should permit of easy and rapid apprehension of the task to be performed. For purposes of crediting they should permit of simple plus or minus with perhaps some subjective appraisal between these.

(*f*) They need not necessarily test the same mental processes at each age level, nor need every test be applicable to each level. An intelligent adult may fail utterly at a child's test for reasons not ascribable to lack of intelligence.

(*g*) It is desirable that some single tests permit of quantitative measurement thru serial grading, like the Binet picture test.

(*h*) They must be intrinsically interesting in order to command and fix attention and effort. If the subject has no natural interest or motive for performing a given test his performance may not be representative of his best ability.

(*i*) They must permit of repetition which shall be void of practice effects, unless practice itself is being studied.

(*j*) They must give fairly constant results and be free from any considerable variation either individual or group. It is to be noted that a test with any appreciable mean variation is not valuable for diagnostic purposes. They should also for this purpose be free from personal equation of the examiner and from subjectivity of the examinee. The coefficient of reliability should be at least 60 or .70.

(*k*) They must be so constituted for purposes of final grading that they are of approximately equal value so that success in some tests may be substituted for failure in others. For this same purpose there should be an equal number of tests for each age-level in order to evaluate for final score the tests which are passed beyond the "basal" year at which all tests are passed. If it is found that intelligence does not develop in levels which are clearly differentiated by successive chronological years, there must be established a factor of evaluation for adding single tests of one level to those of another.

(*l*) Most important of all, the individual tests must truly measure the intellectual processes for which they are intended. If simple judgment is under examination, emotional preferences must be eliminated in the tests; if logical memory is examined it should not be thru a rote memory test.

Having carefully selected or devised tests for a tentative graded series the next step is that of scientifically accurate experimentation with these theoretically satisfactory tests, followed by a standardization in method and gradation of those tests which prove reliable. By scientifically accurate I mean experimentation under rigid control, such as sufficient number of subjects, non-selection of subjects, absence of all disturbing factors in examiner or subject, entire impersonality in administering the tests and in evaluating the results, statistical treatment of the objective results, and reduction of subjective impressions to a minimum. There must be no changes of method or of procedure except for definite reasons and under definite controls. Tests of this sort should always be administered individually for standardization, since it is upon individuals that subsequent diagnoses and examinations will be made. The results of group tests are too much affected by disturbing factors of various kinds to be entirely reliable as standards for individual performance. From the probably large number of tests tried out, only a few will yield satisfactory results. It is necessary for diagnostic purposes to know what proportion of individuals in unselected groups satisfactorily pass the test, and a single test may be graded at that age at which it is successfully passed by approximately 75% of the subjects of the same age. It may appear after experimental study that beyond a certain age limit the percentile system which Whipple recommends will have to supplant the statistical 75% correlation with chronological age. And from the tests which do prove reliable those should be selected which best conform to the requirements of intelligence-testing, *e. g.*, those which require little or no apparatus or material, or those which are least affected by such factors as personal equation, practice time, or the like. It is not necessary that there be intercorrelation between the various single tests except where tests are of the same qualitative order. A person of excellent judgment may not, for instance, have an equally good capacity for abstract definition (should each of these be indicative of intelligence) just as in the scale already in use children show marked deficiencies in some lines and perhaps precocity in others. Neither need there be strict correlation between the tests and school ability or social efficiency since these are too much affected by elements other than intellectual, such as persistence and ambition. In the light of our present knowledge it is a little difficult to conjecture what is the best basis for correlation, tho it is to be hoped that the correlation with chronological age that has proved so satisfactory thus far will continue to do so.

Regarding the selection of tentative tests it may or may not be necessary to construct new ones. There are already many excellent tests and series of tests in the literature of the subject. Most of them are not, however, satisfactory from the point of view of graded intelligence tests. Nevertheless, many of them can undoubtedly be used and can be made to adapt themselves to the requirements of graded intelligence-testing.

In conclusion I may say that practically all of the objections to an extension of the Binet Scale are but echoes of the earlier criticisms of this instrument which, in the hands of many, has been so much abused and misunderstood; objections which probably are no greater than those which Binet overcame in arriving at the completion of the scale now so widely accepted. But let us assume a more hopeful, tho carefully critical, attitude for creating and standardizing tests for the adolescent and adult end of the scale. In England much has already been accomplished. The task is difficult and is worthy of the best efforts of years of tireless and unified application. We are justified in a feeling of pessimism if we expect to complete at once the work which Binet so ably began. But his was a work to stimulate emulation in the best of us, and the results obtained will surely be proportional to the energy expended.

THE USE OF THE BINET SCALE WITH DELINQUENT CHILDREN

BY

GRACE M. FERNALD

A popular impression prevails throughout the United States that we have finally achieved an absolutely accurate standard for measuring mentality, quite irrespective of the conditions under which the individuals tested may have developed. The opinion has been strengthened by statements from certain social workers and psychologists until trained and untrained workers throughout the country are applying the tests to many diverse situations. The purpose of the present paper is to enquire whether such an opinion is justified by the facts. Have we really proved any such thing concerning the Binet tests?

First we have the question of the suitability of the tests to the type of cases which must be examined in court. After three years of work in testing public school children the writer is ready to admit that the Binet tests may be applied with reasonable accuracy to the children in the eight grades of the public school to determine in a brief time, the child's level of general intelligence. Special defects in the tests when used in this way have been, and still are the subject of investigation and will not be discussed here. Four years' experience with juvenile court children, first in Chicago and then in Los Angeles has convinced me that the Binet tests do not apply in the same way to the street child who, in many cases, has not even the leavening influence of over-much schooling.

Three years ago Dr. Huey made the following statement: "The Binet norms have been worked out with children of the working classes of Paris and vicinity. They may need some revision when applied to other social classes and other regions even in France. It needs to be tried out and extended if possible beyond the age of thirteen, and revised wherever revision is certainly indicated. Additional tests can be added for any given age, as we find that children of that age come to do certain mentally significant things with established degrees of perfection."*

Dr. Huey suggests two very important points here, one of which seems to have been pretty generally overlooked in work with the Binet tests and particularly in investigations of juvenile court children. So

*Edmund B. Huey: The Binet Scale for Measuring Intelligence and Retardation. Journ. of Educ. Psychol. Oct. 1910. p. 436.

far as I know, no attempt has been made to modify the Binet tests in such a way that they shall be particularly fitted to juvenile court cases.

Perhaps it will seem that no such an adjustment of material is needed, but we certainly have no evidence, at present, to show that the same tests which will fit the more regular, orderly, school-attending children are also adequate for those who live very different sorts of lives.

A large per cent. of the children in the courts of our principal cities come from parents of foreign birth. In many cases the children themselves have been in this country only a short time. This means that, in a certain per cent. of cases the language factor is important. If the child speaks some other language besides English at home and, as in Chicago, frequently goes to a school where some other language is spoken, then the tests must be given in that language. If we insist on the giving of the tests by a trained person, this means that the person who gives the tests must be really fluent in the language in question. I have seen three methods of procedure which seem to me to introduce an incalculable error. One is to bring in an outsider who speaks the language but who knows nothing of the technique of the tests, and have him translate the tests to the child; another is for the experimenter to attempt to use a language which he speaks with difficulty; finally, I have even seen the tests given and the results recorded when, in addition to the difficulty of the tests the child is struggling with the language.

Many of the children come from homes which have been disorganized from one cause or another. In an investigation of all the repeaters who came into the Juvenile Court of Chicago, in 1910, it was found that over eighty per cent. came from broken up homes and a still larger per cent. from homes where one or both of the parents drank to excess. This means that a considerable proportion of delinquents are typical street children. This life produces a type, sharp, active, original, but not given to verbal abstractions. Words are something to be used when necessity demands, but definitions, comparisons, etc., are unnatural. A child who has continuous schooling or comes from a good home gets a certain amount of training in verbal expression as such, but the street child without much school acts rather than talks unless the talking furthers some end or satisfies some personal curiosity. Consequently he responds awkwardly to those tests which are most verbally abstract or else regards them as foolish. I have heard the "bunch" discuss the "guy" and the tests in a way that would not be very highly edifying to the experimenter who thought he had the confidence and interests of the children throughout the tests. Dr. Ayres* has already mentioned the fact that the tests are verbal or depend on school training. Whether

*Leonard P. Ayres. The Binet-Simon Measuring Scale for Intelligence: Some Criticisms and Suggestions. Psychol. Clinic. 5; No. 6. Nov. 15, 1911. 187-196.

this criticism is serious when applied to certain classes of children or not, it certainly must be taken into account in the case of juvenile court children.

Moreover, many of the tests involve concepts which the environment of the average court child is particularly unsuited to give. I can think of no better illustration of this point than the cases described in a report of an investigation made by Dr. Goddard and Miss Hill.* In all fifty-six girls, who had been inmates of a reform school at some time were examined. According to the Binet tests all but four of these girls were classed as feeble-minded, although twenty-five of them did the eleven or the twelve year tests. The average age was 18½. The 1908 series was evidently used as the statement is made that the four who were not feeble-minded passed the 13-year tests.

The authors describe twelve of the cases, which they say are typical, more in detail. Of these twelve cases, eight had alcoholic fathers, four alcoholic mothers, seven mothers who were known to be immoral. Only one is reported as having one decent parent. Here is one of the cases as given in the report. Number 4 is fourteen years 11 months old; tests 10 years; mother died of tuberculosis, was opium fiend; father was confirmed drunkard, several times in jail. Brother George, 9 years old, in orphanage for feeble-minded; father and mother and two small children lived in one small room; there were often other inmates; child was nervous; poor in school—about second grade; fond of all kinds of children's play; very irresponsible; sent to store for two articles will come back with one, sure to forget the other. Sent down stairs for potatoes, will be gone for fifteen minutes and come back without them. When asked "why" will say she had forgotten; can pick out air on the piano; reads in the third reader with difficulty; very stubborn, excitable, sensitive, cries easily; fond of children but cannot be trusted with them; committed to the reformatory as a delinquent child—had been on streets for several months before commitment; *expelled from school* one year before commitment as her influence was considered bad for the other children; mother sent her into the streets to beg for money from men to be used to buy drink; the child was unchaste with them and took the money gotten in this way to her mother; she has no idea what *charity* is, says *"Board of Healthy;"* Justice, has nothing to say; goodness she defines; she could not give a word that rhymes with day without assistance. (This case is given here in full as described by the authors.)

Two facts seem to me to stand out as one reads this, unfortunately, not unusual history of the delinquent child. First that the environment is not conducive to physical or mental development, and secondly,

*Henry F. Goddard and Helen F. Hill. Delinquent Girls Tested by the Binet Scale. The Training School. 1911.

that the very tests cited by Goddard are particularly unsuited to the case. Why should she define charity as anything but the "board of health?" That seems to be about the nearest thing to it that experience ever gave her. Justice! Where has it ever touched her? The wonder is that she can define goodness or read in the third reader even if she does do the latter with difficulty, and as for rhymes without explanation—where would she have met them? Another case (No. 5 in Goddard's paper) with fully as pleasant a life history as the one just cited—father drinking man; mother probably immoral; brother just home from reform school, etc.; is graded as 12 years of age; can repeat seven digits, give rhymes, etc. "But she could not repeat a sentence of twenty-six syllables, though this comes in the twelve-year tests. She did not know the difference between pleasure and honor, poverty and misery, pride and pretention and the like." Again, what experience has she had to give her these distinctions of meaning. Yet she is classed as one of those "who could be made, or could have been made, had they been taken early enough, happy and useful in an institution for the feeble-minded."

We do not insist for a moment that the cases described above might not turn out to be feeble-minded. All we say is that, without further study of them we have not sufficient evidence to so classify them. The results of my study of Juvenile Court girls at the State Reform School and at the Detention Home show about the same percentage of defectives as that reported in the paper just mentioned if the Binet scale is used as the only standard. I should never so classify many of them, however, without further study. In a number of cases of boys which we have had a chance to follow up, the classification according to the Binet scale would have been very unfortunate. One small boy of eleven caught a fly as a definition of that insect and suggested that there were plenty of houses in the neighborhood when asked to define a house. He had already been graded as feeble-minded by another examiner. He had been the moving spirit in a burglary that required the utmost ingenuity. He did all the motor tests well and finally during eight months in a good environment made three grades in a Chicago public school. When we first took the case he was living in a lean-to at the rear of a saloon with a drunken father and stupid stepmother and three younger brothers. He was born in Poland and had never been to school.

During the last year six cases rejected by institutions and schools as mentally defective have shown a similar lack of accuracy in the diagnosis when allowed to develop under proper conditions. All one over-grown thirteen-year-old boy needed was a suit of clothes and a safety razor. Another boy was a victim of self-abuse and bad environment, still another had adenoids and tonsils sufficiently enlarged to be responsible for anything, especially when taken in conjunction with a drunken father.

A study of Dr. Goddard's and Miss Hill's paper will show that the cases cited are no more extreme than other cases described by them and that the two girls' cases described as normal were fully as erratic in behavior as any of the rest. To decide that eleven of the 56 who did the eleven but not the twelve-year-old test and the fourteen who did the eleven but not the ten-year-old test were all candidates for feeble-minded institutions seems an unwarranted conclusion. The statement made by the authors, "any person who has lived in any sort of an average environment for the requisite number of years is able to do these tests even though he has never been to school even for a day, and by failing to do these they manifest a mental defectiveness," cannot apply to the following ten and eleven year old tests: Uses three words in one sentence; defines charity, justice, goodness; repeats sentences of twenty-six syllables. Surely a child couldn't be expected to put the dissected sentences together if he had never learned to read. Whether the authors would call the environment of any one of the twelve cases described average, is perhaps another question.

Another difficulty with the Binet tests which becomes especially serious in connection with delinquent children is the inadequacy of the tests, after the twelve-year age. The majority of court cases are the very ages of the lacking tests, i. e., 12 to 20 years. As Dr. Goddard counts in the two papers he has published, the child who passes the twelve-year test but fails above that gets progressively a year more behind in mental age for every year he adds to his chronological age in spite of the fact that there are no intermediate tests. This does not seem logical. If the child grows mentally more capable year by year from twelve to eighteen, then we ought to have tests for these years. If he doesn't grow mentally, then the eighteen-year-old child who passes the twelve-year tests is one year retarded according to the old scale, or if he fails on the fifteen-year tests of the new series he is four instead of six years retarded at most. Perhaps, however, he might have passed the thirteen and fourteen year tests if we had them and so been only two years retarded. That Dr. Goddard has classified in this way is shown by a study of both of his papers. The average age of the girls in the paper just mentioned was 18½ years. All but four are classed as feeble-minded, though 25 of them came within 2 years of the thirteen year tests. In a second paper by Mrs. Gifford and Dr. Goddard* the results illustrate the point even more clearly. One hundred delinquent children selected at random were examined. Of these one was classed

*Mrs. E. Garfield-Gifford and Henry H. Goddard. Defective Children in the Juvenile Court. The Training School. Vol. VIII., 132-135. 1912.

as normal, 33 backward, and 66 feeble-minded. The exact statement is as follows: "This makes 34 that are less than four years backward. Beyond this four-year point, however, there is no possibility that these children can ever be made normal nor can they ever be considered entirely responsible." Now an examination of the tables given in the paper shows that all of those classified as merely backward were under 14 years of age, while the 66 classified as "distinctly feeble-minded" were all over 14 years of age.

The need of an extension of the Binet tests has already been pointed out by several investigators. What the writer wishes to emphasize here is that the lack of tests from 12 to 18 years is a much more serious matter in delinquent cases than in ordinary school cases because a larger per cent. of the court cases fall within these years.

The fact that all of the children over fourteen, and none of those under fourteen, grade as "distinctly feeble-minded" may signify that these children are high-grade defectives, and consequently that the feeble-mindedness is not manifest at an early age, or it may indicate the particular unsuitability of the Binet tests in the years above ten, (all but four of the children above fourteen years of age graded nine years or above), and of a need for the modification and extension of these tests. What it shows has certainly not been established. My experience with delinquents would make me very skeptical of any tests that gave only one normal out of one hundred or at best only thirty-four who were not "distinctly feeble-minded."

That the tests from ten years on are too difficult for the child who has what can be called an average environment has been suggested by several investigators. If this is finally granted it makes a most extensive change in the percentages already so positively stated and so generally accepted. A further point which seems to need investigation is whether these tests are not particularly unsuited to the requirements of the street child.

What is our standard after all? Don't we go in a circle? We start out with a given number of school children and examine them with the Binet tests. We say those who pass are normal, and those who fail are defective. By what final standard do we judge this? Some say by the school grade, while others would use the Binet test to check up the school and show its defects. All the while we are not agreeing on our definition of standard. One group of people seem to be using the school as a check on the Binet test and another group is using the tests as a check on the school, while still another group—and an increasingly large group—is applying them to the court type of child, with this poor, inadequate environment, as if the tests had been checked up in any way as a standard for such cases.

To the writer there seems to be only one way of standardizing any tests, and that is by checking them up, with the child's future success or failure in a reasonably good environment. In any graded series, we must adjust the tests we use to the child's environment, unless we believe in the doctrine of mental faculties. His native ability can only be shown by the result of his reaction to his environment. Given a certain environment, he will develop certain mental complexes in terms of that environment. The only method I can see of even approximately testing his native capacity is by starting with something with which he is quite unfamiliar, and determining his rate of learning, type of association, ability to analyze, in such a case. Several very good studies of this sort have been made, containing many valuable suggestions, but so far as I know, none of these tests have been standardized, and some of them are as yet unpublished.

We need both types of tests, a graded series on the plan of the Binet scale to give us the opportunity to estimate quickly, if roughly, the general ability of the child, and then a further series of standardized tests to determine his capacity in various directions. When we have determined this latter we must follow the case up as a physician does, changing the prescriptions when necessary.

The main suggestion for a modification of the Binet tests is, that more motor, game type of tests be introduced for children who obviously are unfamiliar with the more abstract school type of test. The writer has had an amusing illustration of this difference in connection with a rather difficult puzzle box and an intricate ear model. Term after term, and class after class I have sent down, at random, to the training school for a seventh or eighth grade boy to open the box or to take apart the ear model after some really bright prospective teacher (a high school graduate) has failed. The boys become at once so interested in the box or the ear that they forget to be embarrassed in the presence of from thirty to fifty young ladies. Their average time on the box is three and a half minutes and on the ear model about two minutes.

The same thing is illustrated more strikingly still in court cases. The boys, particularly, have an entirely different attitude toward the tests like the analytical form board, the puzzle box, a series of directions for opening a lock, from that which they show toward the definition of goodness and justice, or even the distinction between abstract terms! This does not mean that we should not make use of verbally abstract tests but that we should supplement them by the other type of tests. We might also adjust our verbal abstractions somewhat to the child's environment.

In conclusion it seems to me that the first need of the present time is the education of the general public so that a real scientific investigation of delinquent cases will be possible. If instead of starting every one on the Binet tests we could have court cases handled in such a way that our diagnosis would be verified and amplified by adequate follow-up work, that the child would actually be studied till we know something about him, we should gradually get data that would be of real value. This certainly ought to be perfectly feasible if our courts and reform schools work together with the physician and the psychologist. After a child once becomes a delinquent he becomes a ward of the state and must be followed up in some fashion or other. A beginning of such a program has been made under private auspices in the Chicago Psycho-Clinic and officially at Seattle, but it is exceedingly difficult in the average court to get such a program carried out. This seems to me, however, the only way of settling the problems under discussion.

Doubtless a considerable per cent. at least of the girls will be found to be defective. There seems to be every reason why the feeble-minded child should be a potential delinquent under bad conditions, but it seems to me that we must check this extreme confidence in the Binet test until we have made further investigations, and that we must create public sentiment that will give us the facilities to make this investigation.

CURRENT MISCONCEPTIONS IN REGARD TO THE FUNCTIONS OF BINET TESTING AND OF AMATEUR PSYCHOLOGICAL TESTERS

BY

J. E. WALLACE WALLIN

Brevity is said to be the soul of wit, but it often subjects one to the charge of dogmatism. Because of the time restrictions imposed upon this paper, I fear that I shall appear somewhat dogmatic in the theses which I shall lay down in a more or less categorical fashion. Should this be the case, I shall have to refer to other publications in which I have dilated upon the same topics.* The conclusions at which I have arrived have been formed as a result of the psycho-clinical study of a variety of mental types, including the epileptic, insane, feeble-minded, backward, normal, and supernormal.

1. The first popular misconception to which I invite your attention is the idea that *mere formal psychological testing* by any system of tests whatsoever is all there is to a psychological examination; that *testing* is the Alpha and Omega of mental examination. The fact is that formal testing is only *one* of the many phases of a mental examination. To be sure, it is a fundamentally important phase. The development of an objective controlled psychological testing technique has brought order out of chaos in the field of psycho-educational diagnosis, and has done more than anything else to render the work of psychological examination respectable and scientific. But, while this is so, it must not be forgotten that there are many important clinical and developmental aspects of mental deviations which cannot adequately be revealed by mechanical testing. Just as a skilled medical examination means more than simply taking the pulse, temperature, or respiration, or merely inspecting, palpating, or auscultating the patient, so a skilled psychological examination means more than merely giving a limited number of stereotyped psychological tests.

What I have said applies equally well to the Binet system of tests. This system furnishes us with a simple series of controlled tests for making

*E. g., Experimental Studies of Mental Defectives, 1912. Danger Signals in Clinical and Applied Psychology, Journal of Educational Psychology, 1912, p. 224. Clinical Psychology: What It Is and What It Is Not, Science, 1913, p. 895. Reaverments Respecting Psycho-Clinical Norms and Scales of Development, Psychological Clinic, 1913, p. 89. The Functions of the Psychological Clinic, Medical Record, 1913, September 20.

an interesting *preliminary* survey of the child's intellectual level. Assuming that the scale is accurate—and this I shall discuss presently—it affords us a means of *roughly* determining the child's mental development. Such an approximate means, however, we already have in the pedagogical tests and grading of the schools. It is entirely doubtful whether the Binet tests will afford to an *amateur* in clinical psychology or pathologic pedagogy any deeper insight into the mental operations of the child's mind than the pedagogical tests afford to the observant teacher. The Binet scale contributes something of considerable value to the examining technique of the skilled mental examiner, provided it is properly applied and provided the various sources of error are eliminated; but the Binet tests *do not give a differential diagnosis* of cases; they afford no means of determining, except in a limited degree, the specific nature of the child's mental variations, or of identifying types, or of locating causes or, except in certain obvious cases, of prognosticating the outcome. Of this, more anon. The Binet scale is not a substitute for erudition, technical skill, or a university course. It is simply *one* means of making technical skill function at its maximum.

2. Because psychological diagnosis involves more than the ability to administer a set of formal mental tests, it is preposterous to suppose that one may become a competent psycho-educational examiner by taking a short university course on mental tests or by taking a six weeks' summer course in a training school for teachers of mental deficients. There is no royal road either to psychological or physical diagnosis. There is no educational magic by which we can, in a five or ten weeks' course, transform an ordinary observer into a psychic wizard and confer upon him occult powers by which he will be able to divine or dissect the mental makeup of children.

Let me say here that the evils which have been creeping insidiously into clinical work in education and psychology may be partly attributed to the recent practice of psychologists, most of whom are in no sense clinical men, of offering courses on "mental and physical tests" to all "comers," with the implication that anyone who takes the courses will be qualified to diagnose children in the schools. Unfortunately those who take such courses usually make exactly this implication, and believe that somehow miraculously they have become competent examiners, even though the instructor has taken pains to emphasize the fact that no one can become a reliable educational diagnostician without spending several years in the technical *didactic* study of psychology and education, and in the first-hand *clinical* study of different mental types. I have deliberately limited eligibility to my psycho-clinical practicum to three classes of students: First, to those who desire to fit themselves to become expert *professional psycho-educational examiners* and who are willing to spend sufficient time to make themselves thoroughly competent; second, to those who seek to develop skill in the technique of administering certain mental tests, in order to qualify as *trained assistants* to the expert diagnostician, and third, to those who, seeking a practical course in child psychology, desire to observe and study children in the concrete by means of tests, for the sake of gaining insight into children's minds from a new viewpoint, and not for the sake of qualifying themselves as psycho-clinical examiners. I would no more regard the two latter classes of students as competent clinicists than I would regard students who had taken an introductory experimental course in psychology as competent university professors of psychology. My demonstration clinics are, of course, open to all who take the didactic courses. Unless the departments of education and psychology in universities adopt higher standards of what constitutes clinical work in psychology and education they must be held accountable for producing the type of amateur in education which is duplicated by the medical faker in the field of medicine. The medical schools since coming under university control have been very assiduous in raising their standards and in driving the potential quacks out of the profession. The duty of university departments of education and psychology is very plain.

To be sure, psycho-educational amateurs, whether teachers, nurses, or physicians without extensive psychological or educational training, may be competent to administer formal psychological tests, provided they have been sufficiently trained. My experience indicates that it requires two exercises per week during a ten weeks' summer course so to train teachers, principals, social workers, and college graduates that they will be able to administer merely the Binet tests with *accuracy* and *facility* and with *confidence* in themselves. But although it is possible to prepare measurably competent testers in short courses on mental tests and on the psychology and pedagogy of mentally exceptional children, we must not, therefore, deceive ourselves with the thought that we are thereby training competent psycho-educational *diagnosticians*. A person trained in short psychological and educational courses can no more be considered a skilled psychological and educational clinicist than a nurse who has had even three full years of training can be considered a skilled physician or surgeon. The skilled psycho-clinicist would no more think of intrusting his diagnoses to the "mental tester" than the skilled physician or surgeon would intrust his diagnoses to the nurse. The rôle of the Binet tester and the nurse is precisely similar— their function is that of the assistant to the trained specialist. The medical nurse may serve as a trained examining assistant, taking the pulse, temperature, and respiration, assisting in the examinations, and administering treatment. Likewise, the mental tester may serve as a trained examining assistant, gathering various data, administering certain tests, and supervising treatment, but neither the nurse nor the Binet nor any other psychological tester is a skilled diagnostician. The mental diagnostician must be able not merely to locate the mental *level* but also to form a comprehensive psycho-clinical picture of his case. In order to prognose with measurable accuracy, he must be able to trace symptoms to causes, and correctly to differentiate types. Mere psychological testing does not indicate whether we are dealing with cases of infantilism or simple imbecility, of cretinism or mongolism, of moronity or backwardness, of backwardness or dullness, of inherent or merely apparent mental deviation, of permanent or recoverable impairment, of progressive chorea or paralysis, of psychotics or neurotics, of epilepsy or hysteria. But a diagnosis involves the making of precisely such differentiations.

From what I have said it is evident that psycho-clinical diagnosis and prognosis must be based on the entire symptomatology of the cases and not merely on a few mechanical tests. Hence, let us disillusion ourselves of the smug belief that psychological and educational diagnoses are easy or trivial matters. In many cases they are considerably more complicated and baffling than physical diagnoses; and in any case a skilled psycho-educational diagnostician will require a preparatory course of training not one whit less technical or elaborate than the courses required by the skilled oculist, neurologist or psychiatrist. If the science and art of psycho-educational diagnosis could be mastered in a summer course or a couple of short university courses, it would be safe to set it down as humbug. Several teachers of more than average training, who have taken my courses and who have elsewhere observed or tested feeble-minded or backward cases almost daily during a six weeks' summer term, have remarked that they have been unable satisfactorily to diagnose all cases which they have studied even under these very favorable conditions, and that they regard it as entirely improbable that teachers, nurses, or physicians who have been trained to give a few formal psychological or educational tests have thereby acquired such a profound understanding of the children's mentality that they are qualified to educationally classify them correctly and to direct their educational development.

The above reasons, among others, have lead me to affirm repeatedly that the department of psycho-educational diagnosis in the schools belongs in the educational division and not in the department of medical inspection. No medical inspector could make a satisfactory *educational* diagnosis and offer sane advice regarding the child's educational development unless he is a technically trained educationist.

3. A third set of misconceptions relates to the accuracy of the Binet-Simon scale. On the one hand, there are the exploiters or enthusiasts who claim that the tests are *"infallible,"* and certain serious and perfectly sincere students who, somewhat more modestly, claim that the tests are *"astonishingly accurate."* On the other hand, there are able students who claim that the tests are *utterly worthless* or only of *secondary consequence.* During several years I have been making a study of the tests with a considerable variety of cases, and have gradually formed the conclusion that the tests are of considerable value to the trained examiner and that they enable us to classify institutional and school cases, *relatively* to one another with a fair degree of accuracy. On the other hand it is absurd to say that the tests are absolutely accurate. While in some cases they do locate the mental level surprisingly well, in other cases they fail utterly so to do. They are certainly not an infallible or even reliable short cut for differentiating many backward from feebleminded cases or normal from supernormal cases; and many dilettanti, who adhere naively and uncritically to the Binet system, are to-day making many diagnoses which are monstrous and pernicious. These conclusions, originally suggested in testing epileptics, have been confirmed in my work with noninstitutional and school children. The latter cases have embraced numerous types, ranging through all degrees of mental capacity—idiots, imbeciles, morons, and backward, normal, and supernormal children. With these cases I have employed three methods by which to test the accuracy of the scale.

First, I have *compared* the *Binet rating* or classification with the *pedagogical classification* of the consecutive Pittsburgh school cases which were thoroughly examined. Age 6–7 was considered as the normal age for grade I. Briefly, the Binet rating gave 80.5% as retarded, 2.7% as exactly at age, and 15.7% as accelerated (based on 184 cases), while the pedagogical rating gave 89.4% as retarded, 8.5% as on time, and only 2% as accelerated (based on 152 cases).

· Second, I have determined in units of years the *gross amount of mental and pedagogical retardation and acceleration* of all those children tested whose school records were such as to make it possible satisfactorily to determine the degree of pedagogical deviation (134 cases). The mental variations were recorded in years and fractional parts of years by the point system used in the Binet scale; and the pedagogical deviations were determined more or less according to the age-grade method. The difference between the point in the course where the child was at the time of the examination and where he should have been according to his age was determined in years and fractions of years. Graph I shows that the gross amount of Binet retardation amounted to 343 3

GRAPH I

TOTAL AMOUNT OF BINET-SIMON AND PEDAGOGICAL VARIATION SHOWN BY 134 PITTSBURGH SCHOOL CASES.

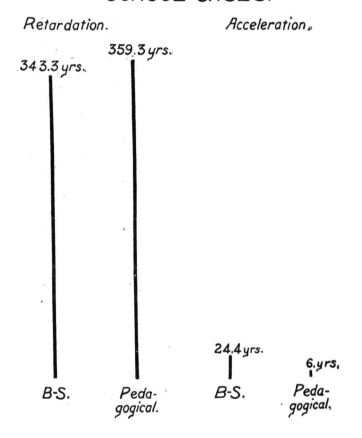

Retardation.   Acceleration.

343.3 yrs.   359.3 yrs.

B-S.   Peda-   B-S.   Peda-
            gogical.   gogical.

24.4 yrs.

6. yrs.

years as against 359.3 years of pedagogical retardation; and the corresponding figures for acceleration were 24.4 years, as against 6 years. By both of the above methods the retardation is seen to be less by the Binet than the pedagogical rating, while the amount of acceleration is decidedly more by the Binet than by the pedagogical rating.

These methods of comparison, however, are subject to criticism, and I shall, therefore, pass on to the third and more important method. According to this, all the consecutive cases which have been thoroughly examined (184 cases) were first classified strictly according to the Binet system, with the exception that only those who were retarded *more* than 3 years were classified as feeble-minded, while children less than 9 years chronologically, who were retarded 2 years or over or less than 3 years were not so classified. It is thus apparent that I have classified less cases by the Binet tests as feeble-minded than the Binet system permits. In the second place, I have gathered all available data on the cases by other psychological tests and by other inquiries, and have based my final diagnosis on all the facts which I was able to secure. The results appear in Graphs II and III. Here there is only time to point out that the Binet rating exaggerates the number of accelerated and feeble-minded cases and minimizes the number of backward cases. It gives 10% more feeble-minded cases and from 15% to 20% less backward cases.

My conclusion that mental testers who base their diagnoses on the Binet system will brand too many children as feeble-minded is abundantly confirmed by recent reports from Binet testers in the public schools. To cite only two instances: In one city 49.7% of 600 retarded children (unselected, so far as I can gather), and in another 80% of about 300 admissions to special classes, were classified as feeble-minded. In the latter city the astonishing statement is made that this number includes only 15% of the subnormals in the school system who should be in special classes. What a terrible focus of feeble-minded degeneracy this city must be. Apply this same ratio of feeble-mindedness to the 6,000,000 retarded children in the schools of the country, and we get a feeble-minded school population of from 3,000,000 to 4,800,000! Of course, this is ludicrously absurd. Certainly not more than 10% of these retardates are feeble-minded. Nay, I will venture the assertation that the oft-repeated statement, "that 2% of the general school population is feeble-minded" exaggerates the real situation. The actual number is probably about 1%.

It is entirely clear to my mind that there are scores of so-called psychological testers in the schools of the country, illy trained in the essentials of educational diagnosis, who are daily making pronouncements about children which are *worthless, unscientific, deceptive, or per-*

GRAPH II
CLASSIFICATION OF CONSECUTIVE CLINIC CASES.
Psychal. Clinic , Univ. of Pitt.
Based on the Binet Testing (1908 scale).

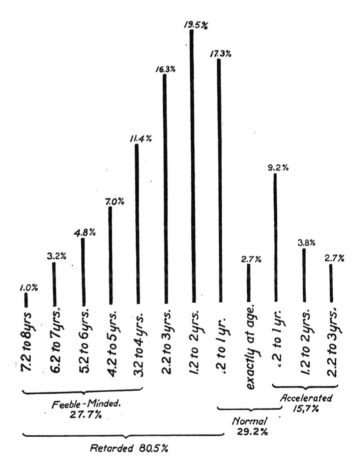

19.5%

17.3%

16.3%

11.4%

9.2%

7.0%

4.8%

3.8%

3.2%

2.7%   2.7%

1.0%

7.2 to 8 yrs

6.2 to 7 yrs.

5.2 to 6 yrs.

4.2 to 5 yrs.

3.2 to 4 yrs.

2.2 to 3 yrs.

1.2 to 2 yrs.

.2 to 1 yr.

exactly at age.

.2 to 1 yr.

1.2 to 2 yrs.

2.2 to 3 yrs.

Feeble - Minded.
27.7%

Normal
29.2%

Accelerated
15,7%

Retarded 80.5%

GRAPH III

CLASSIFICATION OF CONSECUTIVE CLINIC CASES.
Psychol. Clinic, Univ. of Pitt.
BASED ON ALL THE AVAILABLE FACTS.

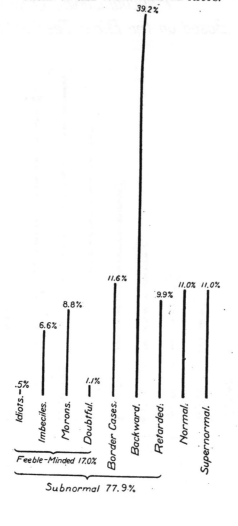

nicious. I have examined children whom I have been forced to classify · as idiots, because that was the prognosis, although they have tested absolutely normal by the Binet scale. On the other hand, I have refrained from classifying as feeble-minded, but have classified as psy-chasthenics, or Freudian neurotics with mental retardation, certain high school students and university men ranging in age from 17 to 28 years, who have only graded between 11 and 12 years in the Binet scale and would thus clearly be rated as feeble-minded by the dilettante using these tests. It needs to be re-emphasized that there are other clinical and developmental phases aside from intellectual arrest involved in feeble-mindedness, and that it is an entirely questionable, unscientific and dangerous procedure to permit amateurs to brand children as feeble-minded solely upon the basis of intelligence tests. Parents should have the right by statute to demand an examination of a child before he can be placed in a subnormal class, but such an examination, or at least the final diagnosis, should be made by a specialist whose verdict is authoritative. As I have emphasized in another paper at this Congress*, there is now only one type of specialist adequately trained for psychological and educational diagnosis and advice; namely, the psycho-educational clinicist, provided, however, that he is as thoroughly trained as any medical expert.

Fourth and finally: The impression prevails that adequate and reliable clinical norms can be established by *group* tests or by the *random testing* of *limited numbers of children*. But the group tests of the educational psychologist may be valueless because these are necessarily graphic tests, and the number and length of graphic tests must be limited in clinical work; and because children have been shown to do better when they work in groups than when they work singly. Accordingly it is not to the group results of the educational psychologist, but the individual results of the clinical psychologist, that we must go for our clinical norms.

To what a strange pass we may come if we permit ourselves to believe that reliable clinical norms can be established by testing at random limited numbers of children, is best seen by a critical examination of the numerous revisions of the Binet-Simon 1908 scale. The authors' own 1911 revision seems to be largely theoretical and concessive, made in deference to various criticisms, instead of being based on the actual retesting of large masses of normal children as, by all standards of scientific work, it should have been.

*The Distinctive Contribution of the Psycho-Educational Clinic to the School Hygiene Movement, Proceedings of the Fourth International Congress on School Hygiene, Buffalo, Session 14, Aug. 27, 1913.

Moreover, some of the changes introduced into the 1911 scale fly directly in the face of scientific warrant; *e. g.*, the *date* test is placed in Age VIII, although the authors say that "boys of nine are just able to retain dates." Eleven-year-old children are said to succeed in composing simple sentences containing three designated words, in giving sixty words in three minutes, and in giving abstract definitions; and yet these tests, in the interest of theoretical reconstruction, are placed in an age in which they do not belong, namely, Age XII, thus leaving an important age vacant. It would be interesting to know the evidence on which the 7-digit and rhyme tests are placed in Age XV. As a matter of fact, the XV-year norms, not to mention any others in this revision as well as in certain other revisions, are practically worthless.

Of the American revisions which have appeared in rapid succession, it may be said that in *one* case a revision has been made on the performances of feeble-minded persons; in *no* case has an *extensive number* of individuals been tested in *every* age that has been revised (with possibly one exception); in *some* cases revisions have been made in ages in which only from 15 to 20 children have been tested, while in *other* cases norms have been revised and supplied, although *not a single child* has been tested in the ages concerned; in *no* case have the revisions been made from the testing of children who have *just passed their birthdays*; and in *no* case has the *wide-range* method of testing been used which has been found essential* for purposes of testing the accuracy of the placing of the tests themselves, but the testing has usually been confined to two or three age-steps. Work of this sort must inevitably tend to foster disrespect and contempt for scientific work in this field. Norms established in this manner may have a certain theoretical interest, but for the purpose of the reliable diagnosis of the cases which daily come to the clinic they may be entirely valueless. Worst of all, these norms because of the claims made as to their reliability, are appropriated and used by large numbers of uncritical Binet testers who are neither psychologists nor scientists, and thereby pupils are judged or stigmatized on the basis of unproved assumptions.

Future progress in clinical psychology on the side of mental tests will consist in the elaboration and standardization of valid measuring scales of intellectual, motor, and socio-industrial development†. But such scales can only be established by the systematic and comprehensive testing of large masses of boys and girls of each age. In the younger years, semi-yearly norms should be established. The number of tests in each age should be increased rather than decreased. Norms should

*Experimental Studies of Mental Defectives, 1912, pp. 21, 28-31, 55, 142.
†See Human Efficiency, Pedagogical Seminary, 1911, p. 74. f.

be established for the same type of tests; that is, for the same mental functions throughout all the ages of childhood and adolescence. In addition to normal norms of performance, we also need normal norms of variation. No one man can hope to accomplish this program of work. The work needs to be systematically parcelled out piecemeal among specialists, or it must be undertaken in its entirety by well-endowed private or government bureaus.

SOME DUTCH EXPERIENCES WITH THE BINET SCALE

BY

A. J. SCHREUDER

In 1910 I introduced the Binet-Simon Scale into Holland by a paper, read in the general assembly of the Pedagogical Society, and printed in the Journal of this Society. My own experience was, that the scale was of astonishing accuracy, both for normal and for subnormal children, but I found the tests for the lower years somewhat too easy, and those for the last years too hard, particularly the tests for 13 years.

Some of the tests should be revised for Dutch children. This is especially the case with the repetition of sentences. I found that Dutch children repeat less syllables than the Parisian ones. A French syllable is a smaller unity than a Dutch one. I found it better to use sentences consisting of words of one syllable and I suppose that will also be the test in English.

The number of figures repeated at the different ages is in Holland the same as in France, but Dutch children show the tendency to define better than by use at an earlier age than the Parisian child did.

It is desirable that each test be studied by itself by testing the same child by the same test at intervals of about half a year. For that purpose an alternative set of questions is necessary for some tests. By doing this, one will make valuable observations concerning the successive stages of growth and concerning the manner in which a child proceeds from one stage into the other.

Another inquiry was made by Prof. Wiersma, University of Groningen, Holland. He tested 141 children of an elementary school; the results have been given in a paper read for the National Congress on Child Study, held this summer in Amsterdam.

Age	No.	—	=	+	% —	% =	% +
6	25	1	19	5	4.	76.	20.
7	21	3	14	7	14.3	52.4	33.3
8	26	3	14	9	11.5	53.8	34.6
9	17	6	8	3	35.	47.	18.
10	30	11	14	5	36.6	46.8	16.6
11–12	22	10	10	2	45.4	45.4	9.1
Total	141	34	76	31	24.1	53.9	22.

The above table shows 54% were normal, 24% subnormal, and 22% supernormal. But this table also shows that for the young children the tests are too easy, for the elder ones too hard.

Among the tested children were 21 in a school class lower than their age. In three cases the reason for retardation was not an intellectual one; two were often traveling with their parents, and one had a defect of speech. Now it was remarkable that of the other 18 cases not less than 15 by the Binet tests had been indicated as subnormal and only three as normal. Prof. Wiersma found the Binet results in accordance with the teachers' experiences.

Another point of interest for you may be the following concerning sex differences.

	NUMBER		PER CENT.	
	Boys	Girls	Boys	Girls
—	18	16	26.5	21.9
=	33	43	48.5	58.9
+	17	14	25.	19.2
Total	60	73	100%	100%

The above table shows the percentage of both subnormal and supernormal is higher for the boys than for the girls. This is in accordance with the fact that the highest and the lowest intellectual manifestations are more frequently found among men than among women.

In different manners Prof. Wiersma tested the correlation between the Binet results and other intellectual faculties, and in each case he found a clear and manifest correlation. I will give only one example. He tested the number of words children could make by the letters of the Dutch word droom (that means dream). The test was made by 62 children in the age of 9, 10, 11 and 12 years. Results, compared with the results of Binet measuring, are shown thus:

	—	=	+
Number of tested children	23	29	10
Average number of combined words..........	2.7	3.7	4.3

As you see, the aptitude in making new words corresponds to the mental levels of the Binet Scale.

Making words is suggested as a new test by Prof. Wiersma. The following table shows the number of tested children and the average number of words produced:

Age	Number of Tested Children		Average Number of Words
6	15		0
7	20		1
8	25	—	1.8
9	20		1.8
10	24		3.8
11	29		4.40
12	24		4.41

This table shows a regular increase; the first requirements for a graded mental test. Now comes the question, at what age children are making three, or four words. This problem is solved by the following table:

Age Years	Number of Children Making 3 Words	Per Cent. of Children Making 3 Words	Number of Children Making 4 Words	Per Cent. of Children Making 4 Words
6	0	0	0	0
7	2	10.	1	5.
8	7	28.	6	24.
9	6	30.	2	10.
10	20	83.3	14	58.3
11	28	96.5	22	75.1
12	23	96.	17	71.

These figures show, that making 3 words is particular for the age of 10 years; making 4 words for the age of 11 years.

I think this is a very good example of the methodical research for the standardization of new tests. For international purpose, however, such tests are useless. The new code test in the revised scale of Dr. Goddard is a fine example of a test for international use. The revised scale of Goddard must be revised again for international use. The repetition of sentences, the 60 words in 3 minutes' test and the differences of abstract words are not satisfactory for international use. But nearly all the other Binet tests are suitable for international application and this proves again the superiority of the work of Binet, the man of high and practical science.

THE RELIABILITY OF THE BINET-SIMON MEASURING SCALE OF INTELLIGENCE

BY

HENRY H. GODDARD

There are obviously two ways of arriving at a conclusion as to the reliability of a method. These might be called the philosophical or logical, and the practical. By the former, one considers the work to be done and the method proposed, and in view of facts supposed to be known, or laws supposed to be demonstrated, decides whether the method is adequate to the work to be accomplished. The other is empirical, and consists of trying the method out and observing the result and arriving at a conclusion as to whether the method adequately accomplishes what is desired. History is full of instances where these two do not agree. So common is this that it has become almost a proverb that "theory and practice seldom agree." So-called science has many times been humiliated by finding its predictions not borne out in practice. Sometimes it is that science has declared a certain method sure to yield satisfactory results, but when it comes to be applied it fails. Equally often the laugh has been given to the scientists who have declared that such a thing cannot work because of such and such principles which it violates, only to find later that it *does* work and becomes accepted as a universal practice. In all such cases, when we come to review the theory in the light of experience, we discover that there has been a failure to appreciate all the factors involved, or a mis-understanding of the real significance of some of the factors. So true is this that it hardly needs argument or illustration, but a couple of cases may make the matter a little more clear.

Until Wilbur Wright appeared there were plenty of people who declared that it would never be possible for man to fly, because of such and such laws and principles which could not be overcome, but to-day men are flying, and the theorists are busy explaining why their theory did not hold true.

Some years ago, no less a scientist than Professor Simon Newcomb declared in a published work on astronomy, speaking of refracting telescopes: "We must, therefore, consider that, in the great refractors of recent times, the limit of optical power for such instruments has been very nearly attained." The great refractors of the time to which he referred were the 26-inch glass of the Naval Observatory and others of about the same size. These could never be surpassed in size because

what would be gained in the greater light-gathering power of the larger
lens would be more than offset by the secondary aberration which "no
art can diminish," he declares. To-day we are successfully using
refracting telescopes of nearly double the size of those he referred to
as the limit.

The consequences of all this is, that to-day the practical man who
has a problem to solve, does not hesitate to try a proposed method
simply because the scientist assures him that it will not work.

The Binet-Simon Measuring Scale of Intelligence has passed through
the same experience as many another proposed method. The writer
confesses to having been thoroughly skeptical of its value the first time
it was presented, but the need for some measure of intelligence was
great; indeed it was imperative; and so it seemed necessary to try anything that was proposed as a solution of this problem, and with this
thought the measuring scale was tried.

There are still psychologists who assert that intelligence cannot be
measured, and others who have said that even if it can be measured,
the Binet scale cannot and does not measure it. *The fact is that intelligence is being measured*, and *is being measured by the Binet scale*, and
that *practical results of far-reaching importance and significance are continually being obtained from the use of this scale.* In more than one
institution for mental defectives the whole treatment of the children
is determined and conditioned on the basis of the mental level as determined by the Binet scale, and the results are uniformly satisfactory.
In the public schools, wherever it has been faithfully tried, it has not
been repudiated, and more and more school people are coming to rely
upon the results obtained with it.

We may conclude this portion of the paper by calling attention
to the fact that opinions in regard to the Binet-Simon Scale at present,
are divided into two groups; the opinions of the theorists who have not
used it, and who assert that it is not of much value, and the opinions
of those who have given it a fair and practical test, and who assert
that the more they use it the more satisfactory they find it.

I wish to devote the rest of this paper to a consideration of the degree
of reliability. This is of course a different matter. It is one thing to
say that the scale will measure intelligence, it is another thing to assert
that it will measure it to a fine degree and that the results may be relied
upon absolutely. We would point out in the beginning that there is
no necessary connection between the accuracy of the scale and the
question: "Who is feeble-minded?" The tests show how a child compares with a normal child down to a very slight difference. The question
of whether the child is feeble-minded or not is one which experience
alone can answer. Binet, it is true, has asserted his belief that for children

over nine years of age, those who are more than three years backward are mentally defective; for those under nine, they are mentally defective if they are more than two years backward by the scale. But he nowhere argues for the close accuracy of this estimate, and as that is not our problem at the present time we shall not discuss it further than to say that our experience strongly confirms Binet's estimate in so far as the extreme limits are concerned, that is to say, those who are as much backward as he says are practically always feeble-minded, and it is probable some who test a little less than two or three years, respectively, are also mentally defective.

. The problem before us now is: To what extent may we rely upon the results of any particular test? For example, if a child tests six years and two points may we say that he has the mentality of a normal child of six and a half years approximately, or must we always allow a margin of variation, and can we say only that he is six and a half plus or minus a half year or a whole year, or some constant quantity? I point out at this place also that we are at present using the scale in what I believe to be a much stricter way than Binet himself would attempt to defend. At least we do not find anywhere in his writings any statement that a child who tests six and four points is to be considered of higher grade than one who tests six and three or six and two points. He never speaks of anything except a child having a mental level of six, or of seven, or of eight, as the case may be. This is an important point to note, for many users and especially critics of the scale are inclined to think that it is a serious matter if at one time a child tests six and four points, at another time six and one, if two examiners make that much difference in the results the critic is inclined to think it is a serious fault. As a matter of fact there is no doubt that Binet would consider the matter unimportant. And we are in great danger of attaching too much importance to a variation of two or three points in the year. Nevertheless experience has demonstrated that the scale is wonderfully accurate even down to a variation of only one or two points, and as a rule the child that tests six and four points is better than the one who tests six and two, even though as said, Binet would simply say that they both test six and therefore are of the same mental level.

In considering this phase of our topic we may make mention of some of the things that are supposed to affect the result and consider to what extent or how serious is this influence.

First, we have the question of the training of the examiner. In regard to this we may say at the outset that for the most accurate results, a considerable degree of training is requisite. No one can give on the piano the rendering of a classic work without elaborate and long and careful training, yet many a person gets a great deal of satisfaction

for himself from a performance on the piano following little practice
and which is very distracting to the neighbors. The situation is similar
here. Almost anyone with reasonable intelligence and a slight amount
of study may use the Binet Scale and get results that are of interest
and value to himself, but they must not base *important action* upon the
results of their findings. The results may be as much as a year out
of the way, either too high or too low, according to the temperament
or peculiarity of the examiner.

We may next ask how do two different examiners agree in their results.
This is in reality a part of the previous question; that is to say, if two
examiners are untrained their errors may be in opposite directions,
and hence the results quite divergent. Just as, if one is highly trained
and the other untrained they will disagree. Well trained examiners,
however, agree to a surprising extent.

Here are a few illustrations of children tested a number of times
by different individuals: A boy twenty years old tested 8^4, 8^3, 8^4, 8^4, 8^4.
A low grade boy twenty years old tested six times as follows: 3^3, 3^3,
2^4, 3^1, 3^3, 3^3. The third testing 2^4 was by an inexperienced person.
Another one, a girl nineteen years old has been tested seven times, as
follows: 6^1, 6^1, 6^3, 6, 5^3, 6^1. In this case the 6^3 and the 5^3 records
were both by inexperienced persons. These are typical, so that we can
assert that well trained examiners agree to within one or two points in
their results.

The temperament of the examiner plays some part, and in rare
instances we find persons who find it very difficult to get accurate results.
There are two difficulties; one person is so strongly inclined to help that
unconsciously she gives help to the child and he tests always too high.
Then there is the opposite type of person whose whole attitude is discouraging and the child does not do his best, and such an examiner will
always get the child too low. But such persons are fortunately rare,
and as a rule the results as above stated come out remarkably uniformly.

I have often been asked if I would take the evidence of the Binet
examination in opposition to all other tests; I invariably reply, "certainly not." I have always expected to find cases where the Binet
test would give a result which acquaintance with the child and clinical
experience or school experience would contradict; in such case the situation would have to be studied very carefully and probably an immediate
diagnosis could not be given. It must be said, however, that such a
case has rarely, if ever, appeared among normal children. I have in
mind one case, where a child tested more than three years backward
and yet was a satisfactory pupil, and the result of the Binet test was a
surprise to everyone who knew her. I was unable to study this case

more closely, and up to the present time have not followed it up to see what the lapse of time has shown in regard to it.

What I consider one of the most severe tests that the Binet Scale has received, has been at the hands of the superintendents of institutions for the feeble-minded; these men know the feeble-minded child, in all grades and degrees. Their long experience has enable them, more or less unconsciously, to recognize the grade of the defective child with a high degree of accuracy. In the last two years many of these men have been using the Binet Scale. At the last annual meeting at Lapeer, Michigan, the only objection that anyone presented to the scale was that in a few rare instances children passed the scale who were considered by the superintendent actually feeble-minded. I cannot doubt the accuracy of the judgment of these men and so am inclined to conclude, and there are other facts that argue in the same direction, that either the scale is on the whole a little too easy, or else that there are some exceptional cases which the scale does not fit. If there is to be an error in the scale, and we could hardly expect to get one without, it certainly is better that it should err in the direction of being a little too easy rather than that of being too hard.

This testimony is the more interesting because it is contrary to the feeling of a good many people who either have not used the test extensively, or have used it only on school children, and not being familiar with defective children as they are known in institutions, cannot believe that the children are actually backward or defective, and consequently conclude that the tests are not too easy, but on the contrary are too hard.

Another matter concerning which there is a great deal of misconception, is the question of the effect of school education upon the child's ability to answer the questions. Many people think that the school child has an undue advantage, or the child that has not been to school, an undue disadvantage, when he comes to face the questions of the Binet Scale. That such is not the case rests upon the fact, which we must accept, although it is somewhat new, that the child's mind develops at a definite rate and that until the child has developed to the necessary level he is unable to answer the questions that belong to that level. A six year old child cannot answer the seven year old questions, not because he has not been to school but because he has not yet arrived at the mental development sufficient, and furthermore he cannot be taught to answer those questions because he has not sufficient mental development to understand the teaching. Conversely he will answer the questions if he is of the mental level whether he has been to school or not. This, in the main, is true of the Binet questions; there are, to be sure, some questions to which this does not apply. There are a few cases where a child may be taught in school a rote system or answer which will enable him to pass the test somewhat higher than his actual mental age, but these questions are few; they are scattered in different sections of the scale in such a way that no one child is likely to get and profit by more than one, or in extreme cases two of them, so that so far as this difficulty is concerned the child will never be more than one or two points above what he actually ought to be, even if he gets all the advantage of this special point.

Another point that should be brought out at this juncture is a matter which so far as the writer knows has been practically ignored by those who feel that the tests can not be as accurate as they are claimed to be. This is in reality the fallacy of division. We admit freely that any child is liable to miss any particular question of those set for his age, we therefore conclude that he is equally likely to miss them all. That is fallacious. The point may be illustrated if we take first a hypothetical case. The criterion for putting a question at a particular age, is that it is of such difficulty that it can be answered by at least 75% of the children of the age in which it is placed. We have therefore the following argument: Suppose a child misses the first question in, for example, age seven, there is still one chance in four that he is seven years old mentally, because one-fourth of the children do miss that question. The same statement may be made of question No. 2 in that age, but now if he misses both of those questions the chance that he is still seven is not one in four but only one in sixteen, according to the doctrine of probability. If he misses three questions the chance that he is seven years old is only one in sixty-four, and for four questions, one in two hundred and fifty-six, and for the five questions, one chance in one thousand and twenty-four. Certainly no one can ask for anything better than a scale concerning which we are able to say, if a child has missed all of the five questions set for any particular year there is only one chance in a thousand that he has the mentality of that year. As a matter of fact some of the questions are answered by a larger percentage than seventy-five, which of course correspondingly reduces his chances of being of that age when he has missed all the questions. Taking the results actually obtained, the percentage of children actually answering each question, as found from the testing of two thousand children, we have the following figures: there is one chance in fifteen hundred for the five year old child who misses the questions for five years, being five years old mentally; for the six year child it is one in two thousand six hundred and twelve; for the seven year child, one in two hundred and fifty thousand; for the eight year old child, one in one hundred and forty thousand; for the nine year old child, one in one thousand five hundred and fifty-two; for the ten year old child, one in one thousand seven hundred and forty-six;

for the eleven year old child, one in thirty thousand four hundred and eighty; for the twelve year old, one in nine hundred and twenty-six. On the basis of these figures it would seem that we need not be need-lessly worried for fear we are doing an injustice to a child when we say he cannot be normal at the particular age, when there is less than one chance in a thousand that we have erred.

There is one correction to be made to this argument, and that is, that the doctrine of probabilities applies in this way, that is, by multi-plying the ratios, only when the five questions of each age test five different processes, to what extent this condition is fulfilled by the Binet questions it is somewhat difficult to say since our psychology is not yet fully up to that determination, but a study of the questions will convince anyone that it is true to a high degree. In some cases there may be two questions that test to a certain extent the same mental process, but it will be found also that there are other processes involved, and so it is probable that we are not incorrect in multiplying the ratios.

I have not attempted in this article to present the evidence in proof of the statements that I have made, for it would be impossible in the time allotted to this paper to present even a fraction of it. I have been com-pelled to content myself with giving an explanation of certain points which are usually troublesome to those who look at the scale as one might say from the outside.

In conclusion I can only sum it all up by expressing my conviction born of experience, which certainly is not too limited, that while I do not deny that the scale could be improved, yet for practical purposes of giving us a remarkably accurate idea of the child's mental develop-ment at any age from three to twelve it hardly needs improvement but may be safely used as it is and the results obtained confidently relied upon.

The one thing that we need now is to agree upon the use of the scale and to establish a uniformity in some of the questions that are somewhat ambiguous and a uniform method or scoring the result in the case of some of the questions where there is some little likelihood of diverse judgments in what we consider a satisfactory answer.

SUGGESTIONS FOR REVISING, EXTENDING AND SUPPLEMENTING THE BINET INTELLIGENCE TESTS

BY

Lewis M. Terman

We will consider the following topics in order:

(a) Selection of children for standardizing the tests.

(b) The question of age grouping.

(c) The per cent. of correct responses necessary for placing a test.

(d) Needed shifting of tests.

(e) Criteria for the elimination and substitution of tests.

(f) Desirable number of tests per age group.

(g) Suggestions for extending and supplementing the scale.*

(a) *Selection of Children for Standardizing the Tests.* It has been suggested that for this purpose we should only make use of children whose normality is beyond dispute, carefully rejecting those who are known to be retarded or advanced. In my opinion, this is not only not necessary, but also incorrect in principle. We do not know, prior to use of standardized tests, which children are normal. We can, to be sure, identify without use of the tests the children who are greatly advanced or greatly retarded; but since we can not know the exact degree of such retardation or advancement it will ·be unsafe to make any eliminations at all.

It is evident that we can not use the age-grade distribution of children in school as a guide for the elimination of the exceptionally bright and exceptionally dull, for the reason that the average school system is productive of much more retardation than acceleration. Nor can we use the teacher's classification of children as bright, average, dull, etc., as a guide. The basis for any selection of "norms" for use in standardizing the tests can only be arbitrary, and nothing is left but to avoid as rigidly as possible every kind of selection.

*Questions relating to uniformity of procedure in giving the tests and in securing responses, while of cardinal importance, are purposely omitted from this discussion. Some of these problems I have touched upon in a paper presented at the Conference on the Education of Backward, Truant and Delinquent Children held in connection with this Congress.

Interesting and valuable suggestions as to the correct placing of the tests have been made by Dr. Kuhlmann on the basis of his tests of feeble-minded persons. It is possible in this way to arrive at a comparison of the relative difficulty of the tests for feeble-minded persons of different degree of defect. Taking, for example, those feeble-minded persons (of all ages) who test at five years mental age, we can compare the relative ease or difficulty *for them* of the tests in age groups IV, V, VI, VII, etc. However, as has been pointed out also by Dr. Kuhlmann, such a comparison offers no guarantee that the same differences in difficulty would hold for normal five-year children. There are two reasons why this might not be the case: (1) the feeble-minded individual may not be evenly retarded along all lines; and (2) even if the retardation were regular it is possible that the feeble-minded individuals (whose real age is necessarily much greater than their mental age) might all test too high or too low, most probably too high. To use the norms secured from normal children for determining the mental age of the feeble-minded, and then to use the results from the feeble-minded as a basis for arranging the tests in order of difficulty for normals is to reason in a circle. It is possible that an arrangement of the tests *might* hold for normal children; but this is an hypothesis to be tested rather than a legitimate assumption on which to base a revision of the scale.

(b) *The Question of Age Grouping.* Another question in the determination of age norms relates to the proper choice of subjects according to age. Shall we take children of all ages or only those whose birthday falls within a month or two of the date when the test is made? And if we take all ages, shall we group them around the full year or around the half year?

Ideally, perhaps, it would be preferable to use children of approximately even age only, as Bobertag and Kuhlmann have urged. Practically, however, there are two serious difficulties in this procedure. In the first place, many of the children under eight or nine years of age do not know the month of their birth; and secondly, it would not be easy by this plan to get access to representative six year old children since most children do not enter school until a little after reaching the age of six.

It appears to me that if we do not confine our tests to children of even age, but use the entire range of ages instead, it will be preferable to group together the children whose ages fall between six and seven, seven and eight, eight and nine. There are two weighty reasons for this. In the first place, it is not always possible with younger children to ascertain the birth month; and secondly, in common parlance the term "ten years old" is nearly always understood to include all children who have reached the tenth birthday but not yet the eleventh. It is the average intelligence of children so classified that determines for most of us the content of the expression "ten-year intelligence," etc. To break up the habit which all of us have formed of classifying children in this way is more than we can reasonably expect of the average teacher or physician, the two classes of persons who will most often be called upon to think intelligence in terms of mental age.

(c) *The Per Cent. of Correct Responses Necessary for Locating a Test.* This is a mooted question. Binet's standard, also that of Terman and Childs, was a shifting one, varying from 60 to 90 per cent. according to the character of the upward curve for the test in question. Goddard, Kuhlmann and Bobertag, on the other hand, recommend the 75 per cent. standard.

Bobertag considers at length the theoretical justification for this rule and comes to the conclusion that no definite proof of its correctness is available. The fact, however, that this standard gives us a distribution of mental ages for children of each age group closely approximating the so-called normal curve of distribution is, in the opinion of Bobertag, a weighty argument in its favor.

It is true that for the intermediate ages from about 7 to 11 this standard does cause approximately 50 per cent. to test "at age" and not far from 25 per cent. to fall on either side. This is not the case, however, in the upper years, where, as we ascend, fewer and fewer test at age. Bobertag notes this fact but does not seem to attach special significance to it as far as the present question is concerned.

Indeed there is no evident reason why we should expect 50 per cent. of the children of any physical age to test at age (that is, within six months either way, of exact age), 25 per cent. to test +1 or more and 25 per cent. −1 or more. If we go far enough up in the age group we soon come to a point where a range of two or three years of mental age will be necessary to include 50 per cent. of the children of a given chronological age group; and conversely if we move in the other direction we reach a point where a range of much less than a year in mental age will include 50 per cent. of a given chronological age group. In other words, the relation between the 75 per cent. standard and the 50 per cent. testing "normal" is purely an accidental one, due to the chance ratio holding for a certain period between chronological age and the rate of mental development. Mental development, as Bobertag points out and as all workers in child psychology have long recognized, does not proceed in such a way that a year's added age always brings the same relative amount of advancement. On the other hand, mental growth, like growth in weight, should be thought of in terms of percentile increment rather than of absolute increment.

Since the range that will include 50 per cent. as testing at the expected mental age is a regularly decreasing one as we ascend into the upper age groups, it follows that by the Binet method our standard as to what constitutes under-age or over-age intelligence shifts in the same way, being a coarse standard in the lower years and a finer one in the upper. For illustration, a three year old child in order to test just below age (−1) must be two or three times as defective as a twelve year old who tests −1, since the former will be excelled by 80 or 90 per cent. of the children of his year group and the latter by not more than about 60 per cent. of the children in his year group. Similarly, to test just above age (+1) the three year old child must be ever so much more intelligent (relatively to age) than the twelve year old who tests + 1. Accordingly, our search should not be for a standard which will cause 50 per cent. to test "at age," but rather for one which will reveal the true median *intelligence quotient* for non-selected children of each age. What we really want to know about a given child is how he tests with reference to the *median* child of his years rather than whether or not his intelligence is exceeded by that of 90 per cent., 75 per cent., or 60 per cent. of the children of his age group.

Seeing that as we ascend into the upper age groups where the scale is essentially a finer one than at the lower end (that is, capable of distinguishing more minute differences in intelligence) a lower and lower percentage standard of correct responses is necessary for placing the test in the year where it belongs (the limit approached apparently being 50 per cent.), it would seem that if the scale were refined all along the line so as to measure differences as small as those now measured at the upper end, the proportion of correct responses to be used as a criterion in placing the tests would have to be uniformly a little more than 50 per cent. Such, I believe, is the case.

However, considering that we do not yet have sufficient and suitable tests for dividing up the lower years into small fractions, our aim for the present should be merely to find such a standard as will cause the number testing at −1 to equal the number testing at +1, the number at −2 to equal the number at +2, etc. The search for a single per cent. standard which will cause 50 per cent. to test at age is beside the point.

(*d*) *Needed Shifting of Tests.* In passing it may be well to point out that the failure to take into account the fact that a higher per cent. of correct responses is necessary for placing a test in the correct age group in the lower end of the scale than in the upper gives an exaggerated impression of the too great ease of the lower and of the too great difficulty of the upper portions of the scale.

That the Binet scale of 1908 is subject to more or less error from the

incorrect placing of tests is, however, generally admitted.   Data which
I have secured during the last two years indicate that the shifting of
tests in the Terman and Childs revision of 1911 was probably somewhat too great, particularly if allowance be made for our procedure in
grouping the children according to age.   I believe it will be shown, however, that the revisions made by Binet (1911), Kuhlmann and Goddard
will have to undergo further correction in the directions suggested by
Terman and Childs.   Among the tests which, according to my data,
need shifting as much as one year from the age group assigned to them
by Dr. Kuhlmann are "aesthetic comparison," "definition according
to use," "three commissions," "distinguishing forenoon and afternoon,"
"drawing a diamond," "comparison from memory," "naming sixty
words in three minutes," and possibly a few others.

(e) *Criteria for the Elimination and Substitution of Tests.*   In the
elimination of unsatisfactory tests and the substitution of new ones
it is necessary to bear in mind the essential requirements of intelligence
tests in general.   Of these we may mention at least five:

1.   A reliable test must bring much the same factors into play
with all the subjects on whom it is used.   A test, for example, which
gives rise to embarrassment in timid subjects and thus balks the intellectual processes or renders them artificial is undesirable.   Such tests
as those of naming words, finding rhymes, etc., ought to be subjected
to critical experiment on this point.   A test may in subject A be a test
chiefly of attention or application, in subject B a test of rote memory,
and in subject C a test of ability to overcome embarrassment.   Or,
used several times successively upon the same individual a test may
bring now one kind of mental operation, now another into play.   To
avoid the latter error, "reliability coefficients" need to be worked out
for each test, after the method of Abelson; and to avoid the former
error it will be necessary to have for each test a controlled introspective
analysis of the factors determining the response.

2.   The tests must be such as will bring responses that can be graded
with certainty, giving little play to the personal equation of the grader.
It is perhaps not feasible to dispense with tests which permit only the
coarse grading as right of wrong, but when the test brings a fairly large
proportion of responses which are hard to classify even on this rough
basis its usefulness is seriously impaired.   The interpretation and
description of pictures, some of the "comprehension questions," reading
for memories, giving sense a selection, copying a square or a diamond,
drawing designs from memory, and a few others, involve this source
of error to a greater or less extent; although if sufficiently explicit rules

are laid down for their grading it may not be necessary to eliminate for this cause any of the tests above named.

3. On the other hand, accuracy, or exactness, is not the sole criterion of a good test. It must also be usable. Some of the tests which give the best results under ideal laboratory conditions and where rapidity is not a consideration are impossible of use under the limitations of time and equipment which usually prevail in the case of Binet testing.

4. The test must really be a test of intelligence, and not chiefly of school training, home influence or other accident of environment. Past experiments indicate fairly definitely the direction in which real tests of intelligence are likely to be found; namely, among the tests of complex rather than of elementary mental processes.

5. A test for a given year group should fit that age as exactly as possible. The fact that a test is too hard say for six and too easy for age eight does not necessarily mean that it fits age seven exactly. For some to fit exactly while others do not, as is true of the Binet series, means that the tests of a given age group are of unequal difficulty and thus productive of error.

(f) *Desirable Number of Tests per Age Group.* All admit that error is introduced by having an unequal number of tests in the different age groups when mental age is reckoned according to the Binet 1908 plan. Later, Binet (as well as Bobertag, Kuhlmann and others) recommends equalizing the number of tests to avoid this error. Terman and Childs propose to solve the difficulty by giving credit for a test in proportion to the number of tests in its group, thus doing away with the necessity of keeping the number in the different groups equal. Kuhlmann objects to this plan on the ground that it involves an assumption which he believes we had no right to make, namely, that "a test has the greater value for determining mental age the less the number of tests in its age group."

But is not this a self-evident fact, rather than an assumption? If there were only four tests for each age group in Binet's scale instead of five, we should of course have to assign to each only four-fifths as great a value as they now have. What is true in this respect for the scale as a whole is true for the individual age groups.

It may be objected that if the age groups are unequal in number of tests and this method of assigning value is adopted it would be necessary in some cases for a child to pass eight or ten tests beyond the last year where he fails in none in order to earn an extra year of credit, while in other cases four or five tests would suffice. This is true, but it does not in the long run introduce any error. This will be evident if it is remembered that the *chances* of passing four, five, six, seven, or more tests in a given age group depend upon the number of tests in that group.

It appears to me highly desirable to adopt a plan of reckoning test age which avoids the necessity of keeping the number of tests in the different age groups equal. It not infrequently happens that a test is omitted by mistake. Still more frequently an interruption occurs, or a misunderstanding, which affects the response and makes it necessary to omit such test from our reckoning. To do this always invalidates the Binet method of granting a fifth of a year credit for each test passed. By the plan proposed by Terman and Childs it is only necessary in such cases to change the "unit value" of the tests in the year group concerned.

In case we were to insist, however, upon an equal number of tests in each year, either four or six tests would be more convenient than five, inasmuch as our year is divided on a duo-decimal instead of on a decimal system. It is awkward for most people to interpret such expressions as 8.4 years, 8.8 years, etc.; 8 years 4 months, or 8 years 8 months, is much simpler.

(g) *Suggestions for Extending and Supplementing the Scale.* It is unnecessary to emphasize the need of extending the scale at both extremes, at the lower end along the lines suggested by Dr. Kuhlmann and at the upper end as far as to eighteen or twenty years. Also the scale needs to be enriched throughout its length by the addition or substitution of tests which would involve types of mental functioning little tested by the present scale, which probably tends somewhat to favor the abstract type of thinking as contrasted with practical judgment

Finally, several additional scales could no doubt be devised which would greatly extend the usefulness of intelligence tests. (1) There should be one or more new scales on the order of the Binet-Simon scale and resembling the latter sufficiently to be used interchangeably with it. (2) It might be possible to work out a set of tests for mass use which would give results very closely approximating those of individual testing.

3. For the purpose of better analyzing the character of mental growth step by step it would be desirable to have a scale made up of a small number of serial tests each of which would show the development of a type of mental functioning from childhood to the age of fifteen or above.

4. Finally, we need very much a rough scale of pedagogical tests which could be applied at a single sitting. These would not test intelligence directly but they would often aid us in interpreting the results of intelligence tests. It goes without saying that a rough test of this sort would not take the place of the extended and accurate scales which we stand greatly in need of for pedagogical research, and that its value would be strictly confined to the purposes just indicated.

SESSION FORTY-THREE

Room D.   Saturday, August 30th, 9:00 A.M.

CLUB WOMEN'S CONFERENCE

Mrs. Frank Shuler, *Chairman*

Mrs. Lafon Riker, *Vice-Chairman*

Mrs. Eli Hosmer, Buffalo, N. Y., *Vice-Chairman*

Program of "Woman's Work in School Hygiene"

Arranged by Mrs. S. S. Crockett, Chairman Public Health Department, General Federation of Women's Clubs

A SYMPOSIUM ON "WHAT CLUBS OF WOMEN CAN DO IN SCHOOL HYGIENE"

Mrs. Adelaide M. Coburn, California. "What Women's Clubs Can Do For Hygiene in Schools."

Mr. E. G. Routzahn, New York City. "What Clubs of Women Can Do In School Hygiene."

Mrs. Charles Ott, Pennsylvania. "The Story of an Effort to Teach Sex Hygiene to a Hundred Pennsylvania Mill Girls."

Miss Elsa Denison, New York. "What Shall We Do About It?"

WHAT WOMEN'S CLUBS CAN DO FOR HYGIENE IN SCHOOLS

BY

MRS. ADELAIDE M. COBURN

At this stage in the development of hygienic ideals, it is difficult to suggest much that is original; much that has not been thought out and developed into a working hypothesis by our increasingly efficient school boards. However, the millennium has not quite yet been reached, and there are one or two suggestions which may be made.

The first I have to offer is not altogether new, nor supremely startling, yet it to me apprehends a long standing and habitual negligence. I advise club women to *visit* the schools. I am acquainted with one school, which is, I think, fairly representative. It is located in a wealthy, cultured town—a town which affords every modern convenience for its children: automobile conveyances, domestic science, manual training, music, drawing, a swimming tank, and the latest hygienic toilet appliances and drinking fountains; but on the teacher's list of visitors for the year, I found *two*. Only two people—I need hardly say these were each mothers—had taken the trouble personally to inspect the working of these appliances of modern thought, for which they had freely voted their money. No business man would be so culpably neglectful of any other investment. Fortunately, owing to the high grade of teachers we are getting in these days, and the qualifications demanded of school trustees under the present zeal for civil service reform in public officials, the condition in most of our school rooms is satisfactory. That is, while the children are in the school rooms. But club women can, by personal inspection, make sure that this agreeable condition prevails in every school where a club is located.

This leads me to my second point, which is this: Women's clubs can educate the mothers regarding the dietary of their children. Not long since I heard a mother, who had lost her only child, say, "Now that it is too late, I can attend scientific lectures, and learn how to care for children; but when mine was little, I had no one with whom to leave him, so had to stay at home and care for him; but alas, my love, which was great, was not a sufficient equivalent for my colossal ignorance of babies' needs, and so I am alone in the world now." This is what the clubs can do. They can have expert lectures, illustrated by moving lantern slides, in the school house as a social center. To these the mothers may come, bringing with them their babies, and there learn something of the effect of oxygen on the human body; of the quality and quantity of foods, necessary for the nourishment and growth of children's bones and muscles, heart and lungs.

One teacher told me of a boy in her school, who, each day, ate a ten-pound lard pail full of lunch—a lunch consisting of bacon, pickles, dough-nuts, pie of varying degrees, and the inevitable beans, which forms the basis of our country dietary. Of course the lad was fat, happy, gorged, and stupid the rest of the day, resembling nothing so much as a snake sunning himself by a log. Another teacher told me of three boys in one family, who slept in one small room, together with their grandfather. The room held a stove heated to its capacity each evening. It was also the general smoking apartment of the men of the family, and the cigarette smoke was so dense that, as we used to say in New England, you "could cut it with a knife." The children—seven, nine, and ten years of age—slept there without the slightest ventilation, every crack hermetically sealed. The grandfather insisted it was too cold to open a window. Often, in the morning, the pillows were satu-rated with blood from the children's noses. Each handsome little brown eye was ringed with dark streaks, and it is easy to imagine the listless, yawning condition in school next day, of three naturally bright children. I, myself, in the West, have seen cabbage, raw onions and stewed brown beans fed to a six months' old baby. Surely there is some-thing for women's clubs to do when anywhere in our country such ignorance of hygienic conditions prevails.

A third point I wish to make is one in which I know I shall meet with strenuous opposition, but which has been borne in upon me for many years. I refer to compulsory vaccination in the schools. I believe more incurable diseases are inoculated into healthy children by this means than are transmitted in any other way. When Jenner invented the vaccine, its necessity was appallingly apparent. In an epoch when filth was associated with godliness; when the religious and hygienic standard was that of the pious nun who "thanked God water had not touched her body in sixty years;" diseases engendered by filth were appallingly frequent and deadly. But those conditions no longer prevail. The bath tub, even though on ordinary occasions it serves as a depository for the family washing, may be found in practically every house outside a few congested districts in our largest cities, and the conditions which demanded universal and compulsory vaccination no longer exist. But in our fervent zeal for *doing something* and respect for tradition, we still go on torturing and endangering the lives of our healthy children. In one period of vaccination in a town exceptionally up to date in its hygienic conditions, one child lost his life, another was saved by the amputation of his arm, while a third, inoculated with the "white plague" died after three years of slow torture and daily death. These three lives were sacrificed in a country town in which there had never been previously, nor has there been since, a single case of smallpox known. Women's clubs can see that in our enthusiasm for protection against one disease of which the danger is so slight as to be infinitesimal, we do not inoculate our children with the bacteria of skin diseases, malaria, typhoid, and that most terrible scourge of our modern life, tuberculosis.

Women's clubs can help to discourage our present frenzy for athletics carried to an extreme which threatens the heart and lungs of our boys; the short dashes calling suddenly on the heart for its utmost exertion, and the excessively long runs, the intense strain of which menaces both heart and lungs.

The last opportunity for the club women which I shall mention is perhaps the most important of all. She can bend her energies to the elimination of the eternal cigarette. Many California towns, urged by the clubs have passed ordinances against the sale of cigarettes to boys under twenty-one years of age. There seems to be something peculiar about the cigarette habit. Smokers occasionally indulge in a pipe, perhaps three or four times a day in a cigar; but no such abstemiousness is practiced by the cigarette maniac. Even in sleep the fingers involuntarily curl to the motion of rolling a cigarette, and no waking moment is allowed to be lost to the solace of this consolation to man's progress through life.

There are many other avenues open to the club woman's footsteps; open air schoolhouses, playgrounds, gymnasiums—but these have each been treated so fully in other papers, I do not need to take your time for further discussion.

In my home state, California, the women have in their hands a weapon which if wisely used, will give to the children, their rightful heritage of life, health, and the pursuit of happiness. The ballot may not do all that is hoped for it, for as Mrs. Poyser says, "I'm not denying the women are foolish. God Almighty made 'em to match the men." But we give our highest efforts toward clean, right living for our boys and girls.

WHAT CLUBS OF WOMEN CAN DO IN
.SCHOOL HYGIENE

BY

E. G. ROUTZAHN

Few men's clubs are like most women's clubs in their aims and methods and significance to the community at large. Most women's clubs are vastly different from all but the very few men's clubs in the extent of their interests outside of their own membership and in the variety of their services to their several communities.

Most men's clubs are first for the man and the men of the club, and but seldom is there thought or service for those outside of the pale.

Probably most women's clubs, *surely* a majority of them, share with non-members a considerable proportion of their time, their thought, their funds and their efforts. Again, the typical club woman is in no sense the counterpart of the typical club man. This indisputable, but frequently misunderstood fact, has been the basis of much misapprehension as to clubs, club women, and club work. A controlling proportion of club members and club leaders are home makers and housewives. They are mothers or wives or sisters or teachers or counsellors of children and young people. They practice much of what they preach. Much more of the practicing depends upon the extent to which others listen to the preaching—and agree to the practice.

Among other matters these club women are interested in school hygiene. They have many reasons for being interested. In a family with four children there are four *big, vital* reasons for being interested. They have a right to be interested. It is not presuming intrusion, but proprietory privilege for them to know conditions, to study ideals, and to press the adoption of what is good and timely. To a large extent the school is but a coöperative home. It is the home working out some of its important functions and solving some of its vital problems in' a coöperation which enables the general manager of the home to secure the use of equipment and of trained helpers utterly beyond the financial resources of the average home. Moreover, the home, or the single household, cannot possibly provide for the single child all alone in that household, or the family group of children of diverse ages the opportunities for "team play" or associated effort we now believe to have such significance in the work, the study and the recreation phases of the child's life. Since the school is but a phase of the home, an agency for doing in groups what the home cannot do so well singly, there surely are indisputable rights the home may claim in understanding and in shaping the policy of the school.

The women's club to-day offers one of the most hopeful mediums for the expression and direction of this share of the home in the experiences of the school. The single club in the smaller community, the federation or group of clubs in the larger community, is likely to include a pretty general representation of the many home and community-groups seeking to express an intelligent sympathetic interest in the school as an agency of the home.

And until we have a new type of men's clubs, the home-school interests of the fathers and big brothers must be represented largely by the women's clubs. Some day the men may raise the cry of "no taxation without participation," and participation presupposes attention and consideration.

Briefly, the clubs may do their biggest work in school hygiene along the following lines:

To provide a board of strategy for general direction of local efforts in school hygiene.

To guide the community in its school hygiene work so that emphasis will not be misplaced, effort be not misdirected, and funds be not misspent.

To enlist local authorities and specialists and leaders in giving their best thought to a consideration of school hygiene problems.

To organize committees and other groups for coöperative study and effort along strategic lines.

To assign or to secure the acceptance of special "jobs" or pieces of work by various interested and capable individuals or groups, with more or less recognition of their fitness for particular undertakings.

The human tendency in the more public phases of life is to place a conspicuous barrier about what we do and to hang high a banner bearing our trade-mark and our claim of personal ownership or personal production.

This morning we will hear a fascinating record of purposeful effort and achieved results, but it is hoped that through this school hygiene movement may be given the club women of America a new and larger vision of their peculiar opportunities. It is hoped that through you who are here to-day may be held up the lure of the less spectacular and the less proprietory, but the more far-reaching approach to the school hygiene needs of the community. It is hoped that there will be revealed to the club women who have already done so much, a deeper, broader, bigger, more fundamental, more significant, and more alluring possibility than mere "doing things," however important it may be to "do things."

The need in this field is more for generals than for privates; for architects than for draughtsmen; for builders than for carpenters; for leaders than for followers—for those who get things done by others more than for those who use all of their time and strength and resources in doing things.

The school people do not need someone to tell them that they should employ a school nurse so much as they need someone to convince the community that school funds should be expended in providing a school nurse.

There is less need of the clubs raising funds for a nurse's salary, than for the spending of money in well directed educational effort to induce the community to invest its own funds in a nurse.

There is less gain likely to result from club resolutions and a club deputation asking for a school nurse, than from a club invitation to various community leaders to "get together" in understanding the need and working out the necessary plan for securing a nurse.

There is greater gain in the general acceptance of the school nurse idea through having the "sample" nurse provided by a general committee, than if the "women's club nurse" is accepted by the community as a special enterprise of a group of women who seem to insist upon intro-ducing unusual ideas into the schools of the city.

Or, again, if the club has $5.00 to spend in health education printed matter, it will probably mean more in the end to invest this in educating the educators—the school people or the health people—than a few leaflets or pamphlets or posters for use by a few teachers or a limited number of pupils.

Or, the club may better spend that $5.00 in getting a number of clubs, parents, associations, the D. A. R., the U. D. C., and other or-ganized groups to each one provide some literature or unite in supporting the school or health officials in furnishing the desired matter for school use.

In other words, we may return to the original proposals already set before you.

The average American community is badly in need of a board of strategy—not leaders of forlorn hopes; not the skilled and brave com-batants in personal warfare; not a picturesque personality or commanding figure for winning followers. Not any of these, but instead the thought-ful, earnest, hard-working warrior—dreamers who outline the cam-paigns and prepare for the battles to come. More and more in every phase of social welfare we need the groups of well equipped people who step aside from the crowd and take time for the larger strategy of the community well being.

In exercising this board of strategy function a most important service will be in guiding and guarding the school hygiene movement, the general health movement, and all welfare movements.

In one direction, we need to know that the label is honest and true. On the other hand we need protection against the trivial or lesser things.

In one very excellent school system they have medical inspection which meets the requirements of the state law, but until the inspection nurse sees the same child a year later, there is no effort, no machinery, nothing to ensure using the results of the inspection save in acute cases. Medical inspection, to be true to the label, includes whatever may be needful to secure proper coöperation on the part of teacher, pupil, parent, and physician, so that the result of the inspection may be fully utilized.

However clean the meat shop, the meat supplies may become a disease carrier through unclean kitchen employees.

However clean the back yards, little has been done to guard against disease, because dirty back yards are not responsible for disease.

Guard the milk supply as we will, yet babies will continue to die because of bad feeding.

We may well fight the fly—there are sufficient aesthetic reasons for so doing; we may well seek to remove the breeding places of the fly— and yet if we wish to make the fly absolutely harmless and if we wish to tackle our present fly problem from another angle, we will seek to control and destroy the discharges from the bodies of sick people. The fly himself is not dangerous; the dirt he carries is not dangerous; it is the disease germs from human bodies in that dirt.

THE STORY OF AN EFFORT TO TEACH SEX HYGIENE TO A HUNDRED PENNSYLVANIA MILL GIRLS

BY

MRS. CHARLES H. OTT

In Bethlehem, Pa., a few responsible women became acutely conscious of the fact that their girls in the mills were not having their chance. A big sister club was organized and generous privileges were offered the hundred girls that responded 'to the call. College girls, mature women of opportunity and teachers all helped in the work. Once a month for four months it was my privilege to come to these girls and give them a series of talks on sex hygiene. The twenty-five years of experience as a physician's wife helped me to do the work that seemed mine to do. These girls ranged in age from twelve to twenty years and my work with them early convinced me of their need to know. In all my club work I never saw a more responsive or appreciative group of listeners—no sex consciousness on their part, but a serious and trusting attention. The effort to retain the emotions that our opening musical numbers always created, ever dominated the opening thoughts of my talks. It never seemed difficult to tell the girls what they needed to know concerning the physiology of sex, the need to be clean mentally and physically, and of the beauty that comes from persistent and prayerful effort. Some definite truths were told concerning the use of alcohol and lastly how breaking the laws of chastity will bring loathsome disease, insanity and too often death to the dear little baby that most girls love so well. Happily parents, preachers and teachers gave their sympathetic approval of this effort.

WHAT SHALL WE DO ABOUT IT?

BY

ELSA DENISON

We have three years before the next Congress.

That is plenty of time to do in the 1,000 cities of 48 states every one of the things described to-day as of benefit to children in a few cities and a few states.

The last three years have been devoted to proving over and over again the value of school medical inspection, of adequate heating, ventilation, etc.

The greatest service of women's clubs during the next three years will be to apply everywhere what we already know; to use all the machinery already available in every city and every county, and to carry out definite programs based on the proven experience of other communities.

The cities and towns where there is not adequate medical inspection, examination and treatment of physical defects, where all school buildings are not properly cleaned, ventilated, heated, lighted, outnumber 10 to 1 the cities and towns where even a beginning has been made.

There is no need for more organizations of women. There is no need for wasting precious time while communities "grow up" to health facts. There is no need for added experimentation about the more important phases of school hygiene, i. e., the physical condition of the children themselves and the environment they go to school in.

May I suggest, therefore, that our "prophesies and promises" for the next three years group themselves under the following four heads:

1. *Use Fact-Giving Machinery.* Women's clubs will use the machinery already in full swing to avoid being handicapped by lack of facts. Reference agencies like this Congress, the United States Bureau of Education, bureaus of municipal research, the Russell Sage Foundation, state and local boards of health, tuberculosis associations, etc., are spending thousands of dollars every year getting facts, making them available, answering questions. There are books like Allen's "Civics and Health" and Burk's "Health and the School" which cover all sides of school hygiene.

2. *Draw One Hundred Per Cent. Pictures.* Women's clubs will use the machinery of all organized women whether in their clubs or in other clubs to give to their city a 100% picture of school health needs in that

city. If an inspecting committee finds one school with unwashed windows and dirty floors, the club machinery will ask, "How many more?" If 90 out of every 100 children in our schools were found with decaying teeth, club women will ask, "How many more?" And "How can they *all* be fixed?" If a building is found with one open air room for 20 children and bad air for 980 children in all other rooms, club women will ask, "What's the use?"

3. *Enlist Professional Coöperation.* Women's clubs will use the machinery of their local medical and dental associations and their local groups of business men to secure:

> (a) Publicity about health needs not met.
>
> (b) Preliminary volunteer examinations.
>
> (c) Financial support by the city.

Women's clubs, when necessary, will overcome the inertia of these groups of men by getting newspapers to say they will be glad to print health facts; by securing the consent of the school board to preliminary examination, by arranging time and place and equipment, by enlisting hospital coöperation, by getting up meetings for parents, by presenting health needs for next year in the form of adequate budget appropriations for medical inspectors and nurses to be endorsed by business men and taxpayers.

4. *Solve Outside-the-School Health Problems.* Women's clubs will use the machinery of the whole city administration to correct conditions affecting the health of school children outside of school buildings. Constant watching, reporting to authorities specific bad conditions, following up promised improvements, will be given to the questions of clean streets around schools and for play; prompt garbage removal; where drinking water comes from; how milk is analyzed; what cake, candy, soda and ice cream in shops near schools is made of, etc. Recent exposures in New York have shown poisoned candy and unspeakable ice cream sold by reputable firms unquestioned by the health department. Somebody in the city government is responsible for all these things. Women's clubs as private agencies can never take the place of the city machinery and will register before their city budget is voted whether the city needs more inspectors, more money for some department or more work for the same money.

In our discussions may I suggest that each of us tell specifically what definite things can be done along one or more of these lines for the children in our cities?

SECTION FIVE

CLINICS, CONFERENCES AND CONSULTATIONS

SESSION FORTY-FOUR

Exhibit Hall. 4:00 to 6:00 P.M. Daily

(a) Monday, Tuesday and Thursday and Friday, 4:00 to 6:00 P.M. Psycho-Educational Clinics and Conferences (for demonstration and discussion). J. E. WALLACE WALLIN, Ph.D. *in charge.*

(b) Wednesday, 4:00 to 6:00 P.M. Demonstration of Serial Group Tests for the Measurement of the Rate of Mental Growth and Improvement. J. E. WALLACE WALLIN, Ph.D. *in charge.*

SESSION FORTY-FIVE

Exhibit Hall. Daily

CONSULTATION BUREAU

(a) Bureau open daily.

(b) It furnished information on the less technical problems of school hygiene to those desiring such service.

(c) It assisted applicants to personal and official sources of information on subjects covered in the program of the Congress.

(d) Representatives of national organizations and capable individuals were invited to announce "office hours" in which they met inquirers.

(e) Conferences were arranged when possible for those individuals who wished to secure information from specified individuals.

E. G. ROUTZAHN, Department of Surveys and Exhibits, Russell Sage Foundation, New York City, *in charge.*

SESSION FORTY-SIX

Iroquois Hotel, Committee Room No. 2

(a) Tuesday, August 26th, 8:00 P.M. "Round Table on Ventilation." C.-E. A. WINSLOW, Chairman New York State Commission on Ventilation, *in charge.*

SECTION SIX

GENERAL MEETINGS

(See pages 309 to 336 of Volume I)

SECTION SEVEN

Program of Associations meeting in Buffalo at the same time as, but not in conjunction with, this Congress.

I. PROBATION AND JUVENILE COURTS

Arranged by the National Probation Association

Morning Meetings at Hotel Lafayette; Afternoons at Hotel Statler

Tuesday, August 26th, at 9:30 A.M. Truancy.

Tuesday, August 26th, at 2:00 P.M. Defective Delinquents.

Wednesday, August 27th, at 9:30 A.M. Delinquent Girls.

Wednesday, August 27th, at 2:00 P.M. Juvenile Courts and the Feeble-Minded.

Thursday, August 28th, at 9:30 A.M. Probation for Felons and Drunkards.

II. NATIONAL CONFERENCE ON THE EDUCATION OF BACKWARD, TRUANT, DELINQUENT AND DEPENDENT CHILDREN

Hotel Statler, August 26-28.

COMMITTEE MEETINGS OF THE CONGRESS

Meetings of the following committees scheduled:

(a) Permanent Committee on International Congresses on School Hygiene.

(b) Committee on Resolutions.

(c) Committee on Recommendations to the Permanent International Committee.

Report in Summary, of John H. Lascelles, Treasurer-General, Fourth International Congress on School Hygiene

GROSS RECEIPTS:

Individual Subscriptions and Memberships from the Citizens of Buffalo	$21,425.65
Appropriation from the City of Buffalo	30,000.00
Exhibition Space	3,650.00
Advertisements in Manual	5,854.50
Subscriptions and Memberships from Outside the City of Buffalo, Received Through Dr. Storey	6,796.08
Subscription from John D. Rockefeller	2,500.00
Total Receipts	$70,226.23

DISBURSEMENTS:

Local Expenses of the Executive Committee of the Citizens Committee	$18,973.01
Appropriation for the Secretary-General	30,275.00
Returned to Subscribers	6,406.74
Publication of Manual	3,512.70
Publication and Distribution of the Transactions . . .	11,058.78
Total Disbursements	$70,226.23

INDEX

(* indicates illustration)